NATIONAL PLUMBING CODE HANDBOOK

McGRAW-HILL HANDBOOKS

ABBOTT AND SMITH · National Electrical Code Handbook, 8th ed.
AMERICAN INSTITUTE OF PHYSICS
    American Institute of Physics Handbook
AMERICAN SOCIETY OF MECHANICAL ENGINEERS
    ASME Handbook: Engineering Tables
    ASME Handbook: Metals Engineering—Design
    ASME Handbook: Metals Properties
AMERICAN SOCIETY OF TOOL ENGINEERS · Die Design Handbook
AMERICAN SOCIETY OF TOOL ENGINEERS · Tool Engineers Handbook
BEEMAN · Industrial Power Systems Handbook
BERRY, BOLLAY, AND BEERS · Handbook of Meteorology
BRADY · Materials Handbook, 8th ed.
COMPRESSED AIR AND GAS INSTITUTE · Compressed Air Handbook, 2d ed.
CROCKER · Piping Handbook, 4th ed.
CROFT · American Electricians' Handbook, 7th ed.
DAVIS · Handbook of Applied Hydraulics, 2d ed.
FINK · Television Engineering Handbook
HENNEY · Radio Engineering Handbook, 4th ed.
HUNTER · Handbook of Semiconductor Electronics
JOHNSON AND AUTH · Fuels and Combustion Handbook
JURAN · Quality-control Handbook
KETCHUM · Structural Engineers' Handbook, 3d ed.
KING · Handbook of Hydraulics, 4th ed.
KNOWLTON · Standard Handbook for Electrical Engineers, 8th ed.
KURTZ · The Lineman's Handbook, 3d ed.
LABBERTON AND MARKS · Marine Engineers' Handbook
LAUGHNER AND HARGAN · Handbook of Fastening and Joining of Metal Parts
LE GRAND · The New American Machinist's Handbook
LIDDELL · Handbook of Nonferrous Metallurgy, 2 vols. 2d ed.
MAGILL, HOLDEN, AND ACKLEY · Air Pollution Handbook
MANAS · National Plumbing Code Handbook
MARKS · Mechanical Engineers' Handbook, 5th ed.
MARKUS AND ZELUFF · Handbook of Industrial Control Circuits
MARKUS AND ZELUFF · Handbook of Industrial Electronic Control Circuits
MAYNARD · Industrial Engineering Handbook
MORROW · Maintenance Engineering Handbook
O'ROURKE · General Engineering Handbook, 2d ed.
PACIFIC COAST GAS ASSOCIATION · Gas Engineers' Handbook
PERRY · Chemical Business Handbook
PERRY · Chemical Engineers' Handbook, 3d ed.
STANIAR · Plant Engineering Handbook
TERMAN · Radio Engineers' Handbook
URQUHART · Civil Engineering Handbook, 3d ed.

NATIONAL PLUMBING CODE HANDBOOK

Standards and Design Information

Edited by

VINCENT T. MANAS, P.E.

Consulting Engineer

Chapters relating to research and special technical material by Herbert N. Eaton, formerly Chief, Hydraulics Laboratory, NBS

First Edition
Based on National Plumbing Code ASA A40.8

McGraw-Hill Book Company, Inc.

New York   **Toronto**   **London**

1957

NATIONAL PLUMBING CODE HANDBOOK

THE MAPLE PRESS COMPANY, YORK, PA.

This handbook interprets by illustration and explanatory remarks the American Standard National Plumbing Code, ASA A40.8-1955. It will enable the reader to grasp readily the general scope and intent of the Code covering the hydraulics and pneumatics involved. Printed in bold print underneath the Code regulations are explanatory comments in nontechnical language. Illustrations follow, identified by paragraph numbers.

Parts I and II cover the practical Code regulations which will be of interest to those engaged in plumbing design, plumbing-code preparation, and the study of plumbing in general. This will include engineers, architects, plumbing contractors, journeymen, apprentices, building contractors, public health officials, colleges of engineering, plumbing-trade schools, architectural and engineering students, technical libraries, and many others affiliated with the plumbing industry.

Part III covers those phases of the sciences of hydraulics and pneumatics which are inherent in plumbing systems; it will hence be of interest to engineers, researchers, and students.

A great deal of the scientific and research data produced at the National Bureau of Standards and other nationally recognized research centers and universities is published here for the first time.

A few examples of the usefulness of this handbook are:

For the design engineer—Where no mandatory ordinance is in effect, Parts I and II illustrate safe and sanitary minimum standards. The engineer's experience and his comprehension of the functions and life expectancy of the installation which he is designing will dictate the extent of upgrading desirable.

For the contractor—This handbook offers authoritative evidence of installation requirements affecting public health, sanitation, and safety.

For the student—Information is provided as to minimum requirements for a safe plumbing installation.

The American Standard ASA A40.8-1955, National Plumbing Code, is the successful culmination of a 30-year effort. The first plumbing code to achieve national prominence was the "Hoover Code," 1928, revised 1932. In 1949, under the auspices of the U.S. Department of Commerce and the Housing and Home Finance Agency, a committee was organized, named the Coordinating Committee for a National Plumbing Code, comprising representatives of the following organizations:

American Public Health Association
American Society of Mechanical Engineers
American Society of Sanitary Engineering
Building Officials Conference of America
Conference of State Sanitary Engineers
National Association of Plumbing Contractors
Western Plumbing Officials Association

In addition, there was an advisory committee consisting of representatives of the following government agencies:

Department of the Army
Department of the Navy
Department of Agriculture
Veterans Administration
General Services Administration
United States Public Health Service

The Coordinating Committee studied the existing plumbing codes; the plumbing research conducted at the National Bureau of Standards, at the University of Iowa, and at other testing laboratories; and the reactions to many field installations, in order to arrive at the most authoritative recommendations for suitable plumbing materials as well as for safe and efficient plumbing techniques.

The committee recorded its findings in 1951 in a pamphlet entitled "Report of the Coordinating Committee for a National Plumbing Code," published by the Government Printing Office. The report was favorably received by the plumbing world, and the American Society of Mechanical Engineers and American Public Health Association jointly undertook to sponsor it before the American Standards Association as a proposed American Standard. The American Standards Association investigated and verified the report's findings and in 1955 adopted it as an American Standard.

VINCENT T. MANAS

CONTENTS

History of The National Plumbing Code

The first plumbing code to achieve national prominence and regard was the Hoover Code, published in 1928 and revised in 1932. This was the popular name given to BH13, Recommended Minimum Requirements for Plumbing. It was the culmination of work started by the Subcommittee on Plumbing of the U.S. Department of Commerce, in 1921. A preliminary report known as BH2 had been prepared in 1922 and was followed by about five years of research at the National Bureau of Standards before BH13 was undertaken.

The late Dr. Roy B. Hunter of the National Bureau of Standards initiated studies of the hydraulics and pneumatics of plumbing systems which made it possible to provide the committee with technical information. Dr. Hunter was succeeded by Herbert N. Eaton, Chief of the Hydraulics Laboratory, assisted by John L. French and Robert S. Wyly. The research was considerably expanded and has contributed greatly to our present knowledge.

In 1928, the American Standards Association organized its Sectional Committee on Minimum Requirements for Plumbing and Standardization of Plumbing Equipment, A40. A preliminary Plumbing Code A40 was produced in 1942 and expanded in 1944.

In 1933, the National Association of Master Plumbers published its Standard Plumbing Code, and revised it in 1942.

In 1936, a major revision of the BH recommendations was accomplished by the Central Housing Committee for Plumbing, and in 1940, this revision was published by the government as BMS66, Plumbing Manual.

In 1938, the Western Plumbing Officials initiated the first draft of their Uniform Plumbing Code.

In 1941, when the United States became involved in World War II, the plumbing industry, like other industries, was called upon to conserve critical materials by recommending minimum requirements of materials and labor. The National Association of Plumbing Contractors, the United Association of Journeymen and Apprentices of the Plumbing and Pipe Fitting Industry (American Federation of Labor), and the government agencies readily collaborated and developed the Emergency Plumbing Standards. These standards were published by the government and remained effective

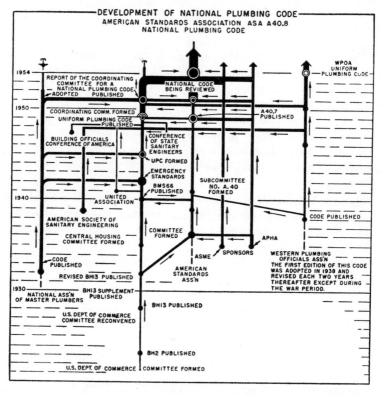

throughout the war years. These standards can be considered as the first plumbing code to function successfully on a nationwide basis.

After the war, the plumbing industry felt that the favorable experience with the Emergency Plumbing Standards had made that wartime standard a natural foundation on which to build a peacetime standard. Therefore in 1946, a Joint Committee, known as the Uniform Plumbing Code Committee, was formed by the National Association of Plumbing Contractors, the United Association of

Journeymen and Apprentices, and the interested government agencies, for the purpose of drafting a peacetime standard. To provide accurate and conclusive data on the pneumatics and hydraulics of plumbing systems, extensive research was performed at the National Bureau of Standards, Washington, D.C.; the University of Iowa; the University of Illinois; the U.S. Public Health Service Environmental Center, Cincinnati, Ohio; and at other nationally recognized laboratories. In order that at least some of this research could be observed by members of industry at large, a sound motion picture entitled "Toward a Uniform Plumbing Code" was produced, which enjoyed wide circulation.

In 1949, the Uniform Plumbing Code, applying to dwelling units, was produced by this committee and published by the government.

Then it was decided by the organizations comprising the Uniform Plumbing Code Committee to expand the Uniform Plumbing Code to apply to all types of structures, not only dwelling units. Organizations concerned with developing and administering codes were invited to participate in drafting an expanded code and to appoint delegates to serve on the committee. The committee called itself "The Coordinating Committee for a National Plumbing Code." The combined experience and qualifications of the membership was impressive and represented all major elements of the plumbing industry.

Two of the member organizations of the Coordinating Committee, the American Public Health Association and the American Society of Mechanical Engineers, then submitted a report to the American Standards Association with the recommendation that it be considered for designation as an American Standard. The industry councils and task committees of the American Standards Association spent three years in investigating the merits of the provisions in the report. A few changes were suggested, and the Coordinating Committee concurred.

The report was then approved by the American Standards Association for designation as American Standard National Plumbing Code, ASA A40.8-1955.

Part One

NATIONAL PLUMBING CODE

Basic Principles

The basic principles enumerated as a preamble to the National Plumbing Code are basic goals to environmental sanitation worthy of accomplishment through properly designed, acceptably installed, and adequately maintained plumbing systems. Some of the details of plumbing construction must vary, but the basic sanitary and safety principles are the same. The results desired and necessary to protect the health of the people are the same everywhere. The following principles merit serious study. Furthermore, as unforeseen situations arise which are not covered in the body of the Code, the principles may serve to define the intent.

Principle No. 1: All premises intended for human habitation, occupancy, or use shall be provided with a supply of pure and wholesome water, neither connected with unsafe water supplies nor subject to the hazards of backflow or back siphonage.

Principle No. 2: Plumbing fixtures, devices, and appurtenances shall be supplied with water in sufficient volume and at pressures adequate to enable them to function satisfactorily and without undue noise under all normal conditions of use.

Principle No. 3: Plumbing shall be designed and adjusted to use the minimum quantity of water consistent with proper performance and cleaning.

Principle No. 4: Devices for heating and storing water shall be so designed and installed as to prevent dangers from explosion through overheating.

Principle No. 5: Every building having plumbing fixtures installed and intended for human habitation, occupancy, or use on premises abutting on a street, alley, or easement in which there is a public sewer shall have a connection with the sewer.

Principle No. 6: Each family dwelling unit on premises abutting on a sewer or with a private sewage-disposal system shall have, at least, one water closet and one kitchen-type sink. It is further recommended that a lavatory and bathtub or shower shall be installed to meet the basic requirements of sanitation and personal hygiene.

All other structures for human occupancy or use on premises abutting on a sewer or with a private sewage-disposal system shall have adequate sanitary facilities but in no case less than one water closet and one other fixture for cleaning purposes.

Principle No. 7: Plumbing fixtures shall be made of smooth nonabsorbent material, shall be free from concealed fouling surfaces, and shall be located in ventilated enclosures.

Principle No. 8: The drainage system shall be designed, constructed, and maintained so as to guard against fouling, deposit of solids, and clogging, and with adequate cleanouts so arranged that the pipes may be readily cleaned.

Principle No. 9: The piping of the plumbing system shall be of durable material, free from defective workmanship, and so designed and constructed as to give satisfactory service for its reasonable expected life.

Principle No. 10: Each fixture directly connected to the drainage system shall be equipped with a water-seal trap.

Principle No. 11: The drainage system shall be designed to provide an adequate circulation of air in all pipes with no danger of siphonage, aspiration, or forcing of trap seals under conditions of ordinary use.

Principle No. 12: Each vent terminal shall extend to the outer air and be so installed as to minimize the possibilities of clogging and the return of foul air to the building.

Principle No. 13: The plumbing system shall be subjected to such tests as will effectively disclose all leaks and defects in the work.

Principle No. 14: No substance which will clog the pipes, produce explosive mixtures, destroy the pipes or their joints, or interfere unduly with the sewage-disposal process shall be allowed to enter the building drainage system.

Principle No. 15: Proper protection shall be provided to prevent contamination of food, water, sterile goods, and similar materials by backflow of sewage. When necessary, the fixture, device, or appliance shall be connected indirectly with the building drainage system.

Principle No. 16: No water closet shall be located in a room or compartment which is not properly lighted and ventilated.

Principle No. 17: If water closets or other plumbing fixtures are installed in buildings where there is no sewer within a reasonable distance, suitable provision shall be made for disposing of the building sewage by some accepted method of sewage treatment and disposal.

Principle No. 18: Where a plumbing drainage system may be subjected to backflow of sewage, suitable provision shall be made to prevent its overflow in the building.

Principle No. 19: Plumbing systems shall be maintained in a sanitary and serviceable condition. See definition "Plumbing."

Principle No. 20: All plumbing fixtures shall be so installed with regard to spacing as to be reasonably accessible for their intended use.

Principle No. 21: Plumbing shall be installed with due regard to preservation of the strength of structural members and prevention of damage to walls and other surfaces through fixture usage.

Principle No. 22: Sewage or other waste from a plumbing system which may be deleterious to surface or subsurface waters shall not be discharged into the ground or into any waterway unless it has first been rendered innocuous through subjection to some acceptable form of treatment.

CHAPTER 1

Definitions

Definitions provide a common language in plumbing, by means of which, irrespective of locality or custom, similar meaning can be given to the various portions of the plumbing system.

In order that these definitions may be more clearly understood, an illustration has been included where it is felt that it is needed.

Because the primary purpose is to define terms rather than words, the definitions are arranged alphabetically according to the first word of the term rather than the noun.

Definition of Terms

Administrative Authority. The administrative authority is the individual official, board, department, or agency established and authorized by a state, county, city, or other political subdivision created by law to administer and enforce the provisions of the plumbing code as adopted or amended.

▶   The administrative authority referred to here is generally the chief of the plumbing-inspection department of the municipality. Under certain rules it is a board or commission that is legally designated by law, but in most cases the authority of said board is delegated to the chief plumbing inspector, who has the responsibility to interpret the requirements of the code or grant special permission where it is justifiable.

Air Gap. An air gap in a water-supply system is the unobstructed vertical distance through the free atmosphere between the lowest opening from any pipe

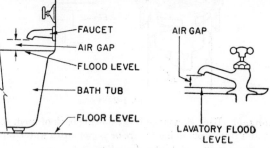

Fig. 1-1

or faucet supplying water to a tank, plumbing fixture, or other device and the flood-level rim of the receptacle.   See Fig. 1-1.

Anchors.   See *Supports.*

Approved.   Approved means accepted or acceptable under an applicable specification stated or cited in this Code, or accepted as suitable for the proposed use under procedures and powers of the administrative authority.

▶   Acceptable to the administrative authority enforcing the plumbing code.

Area Drain.   An area drain is a receptacle designed to collect surface or rain water from an open area.

▶   A receptacle provided with a strainer, which permits surface or rain water to flow through at the specified rate.

Backflow.   Backflow is the flow of water or other liquids, mixtures, or substances into the distributing pipes of a potable supply of water from any source or sources other than its intended source.   (See *Back Siphonage.*)

Backflow Connection.   Backflow connection or condition is any arrangement whereby backflow can occur.

▶   Any physical connection between a potable-water-supply system and any other source which is not potable irrespective of whether or not it is separated by a valve or check valve.

Backflow Preventer.   A backflow preventer is a device or means to prevent backflow into the potable-water system.

▶   A device which prevents contaminated water or liquids from being siphoned into the potable-water system.   Figure 1-2 illustrates one type of backflow preventer.

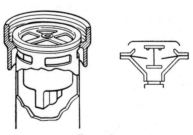

FIG. 1-2

Back Siphonage.   Back siphonage is the flowing back of used, contaminated, or polluted water from a plumbing fixture or vessel into a water-supply pipe due to a negative pressure in such pipe.   (See *Backflow.*)

Battery of Fixtures. A "battery of fixtures" is any group of two or more similar adjacent fixtures which discharge into a common horizontal waste or soil branch. See Fig. 1-3.

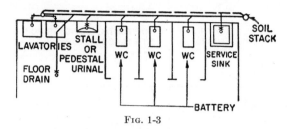

Fɪɢ. 1-3

▶   Fixtures need not be located in the same room, but must be under one occupancy or ownership.

Boiler Blowoff. A boiler blowoff is an outlet on a boiler to permit emptying or discharge of sediment.

▶   This also applies to the hot discharge from a water-storage tank or any other equipment which may discharge hot water over 140°F or steam.

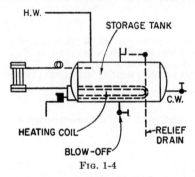

Fɪɢ. 1-4

Branch. A branch is any part of the piping system other than a main, riser, or stack.

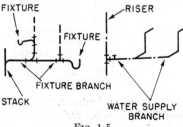

Fɪɢ. 1-5

Branch Interval. A branch interval is a length of soil or waste stack corresponding in general to a story height, but in no case less than 8 feet, within which the horizontal branches from one floor or story of a building are connected to the stack.

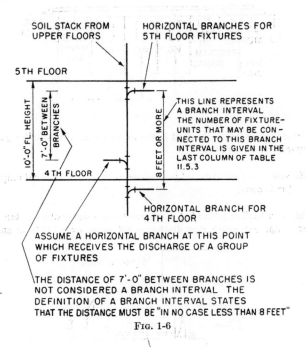

FIG. 1-6

Branch Vent. A branch vent is a vent connecting one or more individual vents with a vent stack or stack vent.

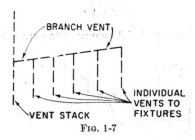

FIG. 1-7

Building. A building is a structure built, erected, and framed of component structural parts designed for the housing, shelter, enclosure, or support of persons, animals, or property of any kind.

Building Classification. Building classification is the arrangement adopted by the administrative authority for the designation of buildings in classes based upon their use or occupancy.

Building Drain. The building (house) drain is that part of the lowest piping of a drainage system which receives the discharge from soil, waste, and other drainage pipes inside the walls of the building and conveys it to the building (house) sewer, beginning 3 feet outside the building wall. See Fig. 1-8.

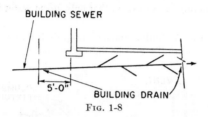

BUILDING SEWER

5'-0"

BUILDING DRAIN

FIG. 1-8

▶   Figure 1-8 illustrates a building drain extending **5** feet beyond the building wall to the house sewer. Most local codes require that the house drain extend at least **3** feet beyond the building wall, but some local requirements range from **2** to **10** feet.

Building Sewer. The building (house) sewer is that part of the horizontal piping of a drainage system which extends from the end of the building drain and which receives the discharge of the building drain and conveys it to a public sewer, private sewer, individual sewage-disposal system, or other point of disposal.

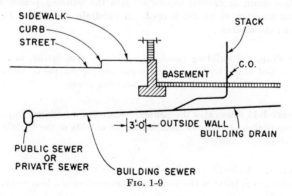

SIDEWALK
CURB
STREET

STACK

C.O.

BASEMENT

3'-0" OUTSIDE WALL
BUILDING DRAIN

PUBLIC SEWER
OR
PRIVATE SEWER

BUILDING SEWER

FIG. 1-9

Building Storm Drain. A building (house) storm drain is a building drain used for conveying rain water, surface water, ground water, subsurface water, condensate, cooling water, or other similar discharge to a building storm sewer or a combined building sewer, extending to a point not less than 3 feet outside the building wall.

▶   Same as a building drain, Fig. 1-8, except that only storm water is carried by pipe.

Building Storm Sewer. A building (house) storm sewer is the extension from the building storm drain to the public storm sewer, combined sewer, or other point of disposal.

▶   Same as building sewer except that only storm water is carried by pipe

Building Subdrain. A building (house) subdrain is that portion of a drainage system which cannot drain by gravity into the building sewer.

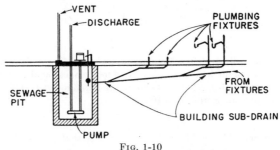

Fɪɢ. 1-10

▶   The wastes from a subdrain are collected by gravity into a drainage sump or ejector, and then these collected wastes are discharged into the building drain or carried separately into the building sewer, depending on the quantity to be discharged. A subdrain should not be confused with a subsoil drain.

Building Trap. A building (house) trap is a device, fitting, or assembly of fittings installed in the building drain to prevent circulation of air between the drainage system of the building and the building sewer.

▶   Figure 1-11 illustrates the general location of a building trap. A building trap is also sometimes installed on the outside of the building or at the inlet of a septic tank.

Circuit Vent. A circuit vent is a branch vent that serves two or more traps and extends from in front of the last fixture connection of a horizontal branch to the vent stack.

▶   The circuit vent illustrated in Fig. 1-12 is the vent from a horizontal branch taken between the first two fixtures and connecting into the main vent. A circuit vent is similar to a loop vent except that a loop vent connects into the stack vent, forming a loop.

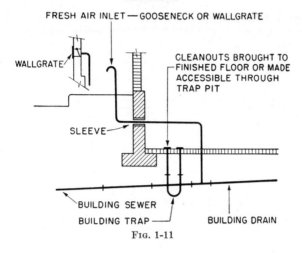

FIG. 1-11

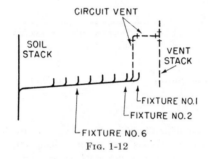

FIG. 1-12

Code. The word "code" when used alone shall mean these regulations, subsequent amendments thereto, or any emergency rule or regulation which the administrative authority having jurisdiction may lawfully adopt.

▶ Code does not necessarily mean that it is an ordinance, unless it has been officially passed and adopted by a municipality. The ASA A40.8 National Plumbing Code or the report of the Coordinating Committee for a National Plumbing Code are not mandatory. They represent a guide or standard similar to the National Electric Code or other standards produced by recognized groups or associations as standards of recommended practice.

Combination Fixture. A combination fixture is a fixture combining one sink and tray or a two- or three-compartment sink or tray in one unit.

►   Figure 1-13 illustrates a "combination" sink and tray. A two- or three-compartment sink likewise is a "combination fixture" when installed together.

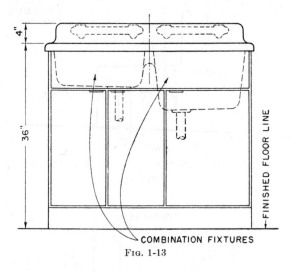

COMBINATION FIXTURES

Fig. 1-13

Combined Building Sewer. A combined building sewer receives storm water and sewage.

►   The use of a combined building sewer is gradually decreasing because of the increased populations and greater loads imposed upon present sewers and the fact that its use imposes an unnecessary load on the treatment plant. It is far more economical to provide separate sanitary and storm sewers.

Combination Waste and Vent System. A combination waste and vent system is a specially designed system of waste piping embodying the horizontal wet venting of one or more sinks or floor drains by means of a common waste and vent pipe adequately sized to provide free movement of air above the flow line of the drain.

►   A combination waste and vent system is a new design found expedient and economical and adopted by many modern codes in the past few years. It was first initiated by the Western Plumbing Officials' Association. It consists of providing a horizontal pipe of sufficient size to permit the flow of liquid and air at the same time and of relieving vents at the end and beginning of the run. See Fig. 1-14.

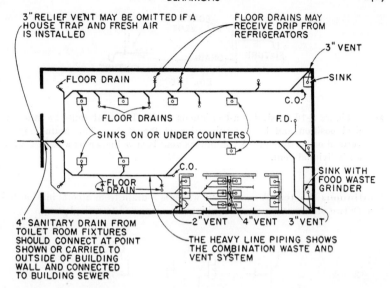

FIG. 1-14

Common Vent. A common vent is a vent connecting at the junction of two fixture drains and serving as a vent for both fixtures.

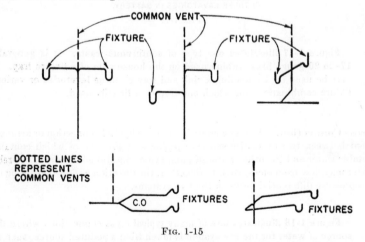

FIG. 1-15

▶ Figure 1-15 illustrates several types of common vents; actually a common vent is also called a back vent in some parts of the country.

Continuous Vent. A continuous vent is a vertical vent that is a continuation of the drain to which it connects.

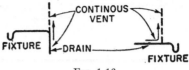

Fig. 1-16

▶ Figure 1-16 illustrates a continuous vent. The vent must be in a vertical position and be a continuation of the drain. The drain may be vertical or horizontal. A continuous vent is also known as a back vent or an individual vent.

Continuous Waste. A continuous waste is a drain from a combination fixture or two or three fixtures in combination connected to a single trap.

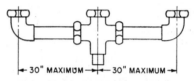

CONTINUOUS WASTE (DRAIN) FOR THREE-
COMPARTMENT SINK, OR THREE TRAYS
OR THREE LAVATORIES IN BATTERY

Fig. 1-17

▶ Figure 1-17 illustrates one type of continuous waste. It is generally 17- to 20-gauge brass tubing used on the house side of a fixture trap. It may be used for connecting a sink and tray or three lavatories or various fixture combinations for which one trap is ordinarily used.

Cross Connection. A cross connection is any physical connection or arrangement between two otherwise separate piping systems, one of which contains potable water and the other water of unknown or questionable safety, whereby water may flow from one system to the other, the direction of flow depending on the pressure differential between the two systems.

▶ Figure 1-18 illustrates one of many typical cross connections where the source of water for the fire system is taken from a polluted source, such as a river, and the potable-water supply is cross connected into the fire main as an emergency supply. A check or valves are not considered a safe separation between the potable- and nonpotable-water supplies; the cross connection is therefore considered positive.

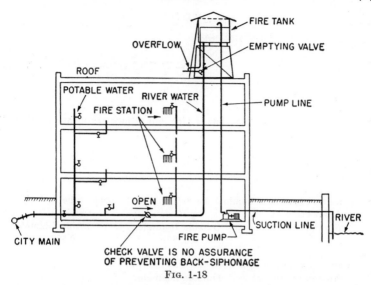

FIG. 1-18

Dead End. A dead end is a branch leading from a soil, waste, or vent pipe, building drain, or building sewer, which is terminated at a developed distance of 2 feet or more by means of a plug or other closed fitting.

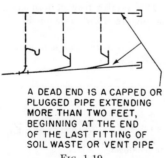

A DEAD END IS A CAPPED OR PLUGGED PIPE EXTENDING MORE THAN TWO FEET, BEGINNING AT THE END OF THE LAST FITTING OF SOIL WASTE OR VENT PIPE

FIG. 1-19

▶   Figure 1-19 illustrates a dead end. Any extension of a pipe longer than 2 feet to which no fixture wastes into is a dead end.

Developed Length. The developed length of a pipe is its length along the center line of the pipe and fittings.

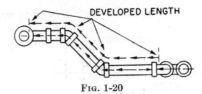

DEVELOPED LENGTH

Fig. 1-20

▶ Figure 1-20 illustrates how a pipe and fittings are measured along its developed length.

Diameter. Unless specifically stated, the term "diameter" is the nominal diameter as designated commercially.

▶ As an example of nominal diameters, type L copper tube is designated as follows:

Nominal Diameter	Outside Diameter	Inside Diameter
½ in.	0.625 in.	0.527 in.

Standard-weight pipe is designated as follows:

Nominal Diameter	Outside Diameter	Inside Diameter
½ in.	0.840 in.	0.622 in.

It can be noted that there is a difference in the diameter of the copper tube and iron pipe. They are, however, designated as ½ inch nominal diameter for both. It is also to be noted that the tubing outside diameter will be the same for type K, L, or M; the thickness of the metal is taken in the inside diameter. This is also true of iron pipe where standard, extra strong, or double strong are of the same outside diameter.

Double Offset. A double offset is two changes of direction installed in succession or series in continuous pipe.

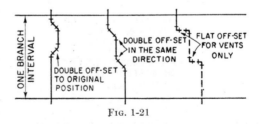

ONE BRANCH INTERVAL

DOUBLE OFF-SET TO ORIGINAL POSITION

DOUBLE OFF-SET IN THE SAME DIRECTION

FLAT OFF-SET FOR VENTS ONLY

Fig. 1-21

▶ Figure 1-21 illustrates a double offset where the pipe returns to its original position or where it offsets twice in the same direction but within one branch interval.

Drain. A drain is any pipe which carries waste water or water-borne wastes in a building drainage system.

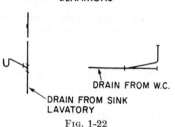

Fig. 1-22

Drainage System. A drainage system (drainage piping) includes all the piping within public or private premises, which conveys sewage, rain water, or other liquid wastes to a legal point of disposal, but does not include the mains of a public sewer system or a private or public sewage-treatment or disposal plant.

▶ **The drainage system includes all piping as described in the foregoing definition but does not include any part of the venting system. The venting system and the drainage system are part of the plumbing system.**

Durham System. Durham system is a term used to describe soil or waste systems where all piping is of threaded pipe, tubing, or other such rigid construction, using recessed drainage fittings to correspond to the types of piping.

The Durham system was first developed by the Durham Brothers about the year 1880 in New York City. They initiated the idea of using screwed pipe and fittings on the drainage system. Prior to that time, lead and cast iron were generally used for both underground and above the ground within the building.

Effective Opening. The effective opening is the minimum cross-sectional area at the point of water-supply discharge, measured or expressed in terms of (1) the diameter of a circle, (2) if the opening is not circular, the diameter of a circle of equivalent cross-sectional area.

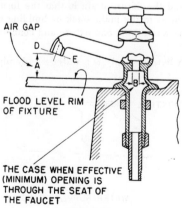

Fig. 1-23

▶ The effective opening is the opening within the supply fitting which forms the smallest waterway, whether this opening is round or square. (See Fig. **1-23.**)

Existing Work. Existing work is a plumbing system or any part thereof which was installed prior to the effective date of this Code.

▶ Existing work cannot be made to comply with the requirements of a new ordinance because a new law cannot be made retroactive, unless an alteration is made that would require compliance with the new ordinance. A building erected several years prior to the adopted plumbing code might contain many violations. If these violations affect the safety or health of the occupants, then it is necessary to set a time limit for their correction.

Fixture Branch. A fixture branch is a pipe connecting several fixtures.

▶ Figure **1-24** illustrates several fixture branches in the drainage system.

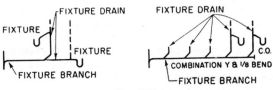

Fig. 1-24

Fixture Drain. A fixture drain is the drain from the trap of a fixture to the junction of that drain with any other drain pipe.

▶ Figure **1-24** illustrates a fixture drain. The difference between the fixture branch and the fixture drain is that the former carries the waste from several fixtures to the main stack or building drain, and the fixture drain handles the waste from one fixture and connects it with the branch.

Fixture Supply. A fixture supply is a water-supply pipe connecting the fixture branch.

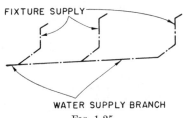

WATER SUPPLY BRANCH
Fig. 1-25

▶   Fixture supply is the individual pipe which supplies either hot or cold water to a fixture.   See Fig. 1-25.

Fixture Unit.   A fixture unit is a quantity in terms of which the load-producing effects on the plumbing system of different kinds of plumbing fixtures are expressed on some arbitrarily chosen scale.

▶   The data on which a fixture unit is based are expressed as a mathematical formula.   Explanatory data will be found in Part III.

Fixture-unit Flow Rate.   Fixture-unit flow rate is the total discharge flow in gallons per minute of a single fixture divided by 7.5 which provides the flow rate of that particular plumbing fixture as a unit of flow.   Fixtures are rated as multiples of this unit of flow.

▶   This definition should not be confused with the fixture-unit or load-factor definition, although they are related in the over-all problem.   The fixture-unit flow rate designates only the measured amount of water discharged through the waste plug of a fixture in gallons per minute.

Flood-level Rim.   The flood-level rim is the top edge of the receptacle from which water overflows.

▶   In a lavatory it is the top edge of the fixture over which water would flow.   The overflow opening in a lavatory or bathtub is not related to the flood-level rim.

Flooded.   A fixture is flooded when the liquid therein rises to the flood-level rim.

▶   This term applies to any fixture which is part of the plumbing system.

Flush Valves.   A flush valve is a device located at the bottom of the tank for the purpose of flushing water closets and similar fixtures.

▶   Figure 1-26 illustrates several component parts of a water-closet flush tank.   A flush valve is located within the tank, and it provides the discharge through which the fixture is flushed.

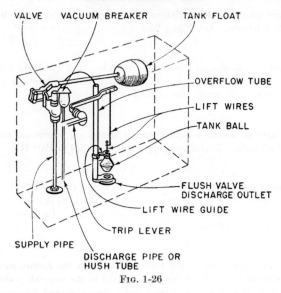

VALVE   VACUUM BREAKER   TANK FLOAT

OVERFLOW TUBE

LIFT WIRES

TANK BALL

FLUSH VALVE
DISCHARGE OUTLET

LIFT WIRE GUIDE

TRIP LEVER

SUPPLY PIPE

DISCHARGE PIPE OR
HUSH TUBE

Fig. 1-26

Flushometer Valve. A flushometer valve is a device which discharges a predetermined quantity of water to fixtures for flushing purposes and is actuated by direct water pressure.

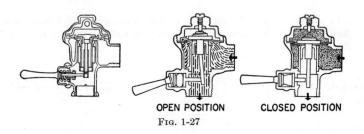

OPEN POSITION   CLOSED POSITION

Fig. 1-27

▶   Flushometer valves provide a predetermined amount of water for each cycle. The two most common types of flushometer valves are the piston, and the diaphragm illustrated in Fig. 1-27.

Frostproof Closet. A frostproof closet is a hopper that has no water in the bowl and has the trap and the control valve for its water supply installed below the frost line.

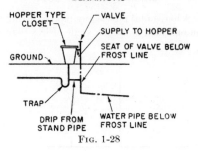

FIG. 1-28

▶ A frostproof closet has been outlawed by most codes in the country because of the possibility of contamination of the water supply. This is possible, as illustrated in Fig. 1-28.

Grade. Grade is the slope or fall of a line of pipe in reference to a horizontal plane. In drainage it is usually expressed as the fall in a fraction of an inch per foot length of pipe.

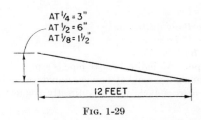

FIG. 1-29

▶ Figure 1-29 illustrates slope, fall, or grade as applying to a drainage pipe.

Horizontal Branch. A horizontal branch is a drain pipe extending laterally from a soil or waste stack or building drain, with or without vertical sections or branches, which receives the discharge from one or more fixture drains and conducts it to the soil or waste stack or to the building (house) drain.

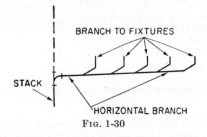

FIG. 1-30

▶ Figure 1-30 illustrates a horizontal branch of a drainage system.

Horizontal Pipe. A horizontal pipe is any pipe or fitting which is installed in a horizontal position or which makes an angle of less than 45 degrees with the vertical.

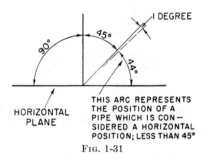

THIS ARC REPRESENTS
THE POSITION OF A
PIPE WHICH IS CON—
SIDERED A HORIZONTAL
POSITION; LESS THAN 45°

FIG. 1-31

▶   In the drainage and venting system, horizontal pipe refers to an installation in relation to a horizontal plane.   See Fig. 1-31.

House Drain. See *Building Drain.*
House Sewer. See *Building Sewer.*
House Trap. See *Building Trap.*
Indirect Waste Pipe. An indirect waste pipe is a pipe that does not connect directly with the drainage system but conveys liquid wastes by discharging into a plumbing fixture or receptacle which is directly connected to the drainage system.

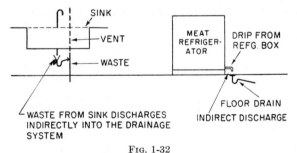

FIG. 1-32

▶   Figure 1-32 illustrates an indirect waste pipe.

Individual Vent. An individual vent is a pipe installed to vent a fixture trap and which connects with the vent system above the fixture served or terminates in the open air.

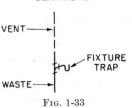

FIG. 1-33

► Figure 1-33 illustrates an individual vent.

Industrial Wastes. Industrial wastes are liquid wastes resulting from the processes employed in industrial establishments and are free of fecal matter.

► Industrial wastes containing acids that would damage drainage or vent piping or containing residues that would stop up the piping must be treated before being discharged.

Insanitary. Contrary to sanitary principles—injurious to health.
Interceptor. An interceptor is a device designed and installed so as to separate and retain deleterious, hazardous, or undesirable matter from normal wastes and permit normal sewage or liquid wastes to discharge into the disposal terminal by gravity.

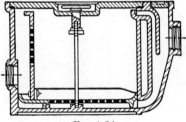

FIG. 1-34

► Figure 1-34 illustrates a standard-type grease interceptor.

Leaching Well or Pit. See *Individual Sewage-disposal System.*
Leader. A leader (downspout) is the water conductor from the roof to the building storm drain, combined building sewer, or other means of disposal.

► A leader is interpreted to be the pipe generally installed within the building to carry rain water only.

Liquid Waste. Liquid waste is the discharge from any fixture, appliance, or appurtenance in connection with a plumbing system which does not receive fecal matter.

► Discharges from processing vats, storage-water tanks, or similar equipment are liquid wastes.

Load Factor.   Load factor is the percentage of the total connected fixture-unit flow rate which is likely to occur at any point in the drainage system.   It varies with the type of occupancy, the total flow unit above this point being considered, and with the probability factor of simultaneous use.

▶   **Load factor represents the ratio of the probable load to the potential load.   It is a reconcilement of the average rates of flow of the various kinds of fixtures, the average frequency of use, the duration of flow during one use, and the number of fixtures installed.   See Part III.**

Local Ventilating Pipe.   A local ventilating pipe is a pipe on the fixture side of the trap through which vapor or foul air is removed from a room or fixture.

▶   **Plumbing fixtures requiring a local ventilating pipe are becoming obsolete.   Certain special devices such as sterilizers are sometimes provided with a local ventilating pipe in order to remove vapors.   A local ventilating pipe is not connected into the regular venting system of the drainage system.**

Loop Vent.   A loop vent is the same as a circuit vent except that it loops back and connects with a stack vent instead of a vent stack.

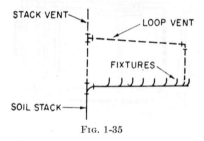

Fig. 1-35

▶   **A loop vent is the pipe which connects a horizontal branch upstream and is then looped back into the soil or waste stack.   See Fig. 1-35.**

Main.   The main of any system of continuous piping is the principal artery of the system, to which branches may be connected.

▶   **Main is applied to the drainage or water-supply system and is generally the lowest horizontal piping.   In the drainage system it is the house drain. In the water system it is the distributing main, whether located in the basement or on the top floor.**

Main Sewer.   See *Public Sewer.*
Main Vent.   The main vent is the principal artery of the venting system, to which vent branches may be connected.

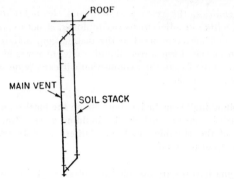
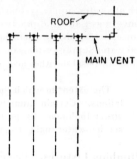

FIG. 1-36

▶ The main vent is either a vertical pipe which collects one or more branch vents or a horizontal pipe to which a number of vent stacks are connected before they go through the roof. See Fig. 1-36.

May. The word "may" is a permissive term.

Nuisance. The word "nuisance" embraces public nuisance as known at common law or in equity jurisprudence. Whatever is dangerous to human life or detrimental to health; whatever building, structure, or premises is not sufficiently ventilated, sewered, drained, cleaned, or lighted, in reference to its intended or actual use; and whatever renders the air or human food or drink or water-supply unwholesome are considered nuisances.

Offset. An offset in a line of piping is a combination of elbows or bends which brings one section of the pipe out of line but into a line parallel with the other section.

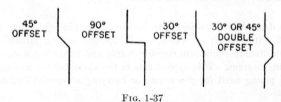

FIG. 1-37

▶ An offset may be made at an angle of 30 to 45 degrees or 90 degrees in any piping of the plumbing system. See Fig. 1-37.

Person. Person is a natural person, his heirs, executors, administrators, or assigns; and includes a firm, partnership, or corporation, its or their successors or assigns. Singular includes plural; male includes female.

Pitch. See *Grade*.

Plumbing. Plumbing includes the practice, materials, and fixtures used in the installation, maintenance, extension, and alteration of all piping, fixtures, appliances, and appurtenances in connection with any of the following: sanitary-drainage or storm-drainage facilities, the venting system and the public or private water-supply systems, within or adjacent to any building, structure, or conveyance; also the practice and materials used in the installation, maintenance, extension, or alteration of the storm-water, liquid-waste, or sewerage, and water-supply systems of any premises to their connection with any point of public disposal or other acceptable terminal.

▶ The extent to which "plumbing" is inclusive depends on the local regulations. Certain municipalities do not include the building sewer (from street to house) as part of the plumbing system. Others exclude the service-water main (from street to meter.)

Plumbing Fixtures. Plumbing fixtures are installed receptacles, devices, or appliances which are supplied with water or which receive or discharge liquids or liquid-borne wastes, with or without discharge into the drainage system with which they may be directly or indirectly connected.

▶ This definition is not so all-inclusive as it appears. A boiler may require a water-supply outlet; yet it is not a plumbing fixture. Some types of equipment require water supply, direct or indirect waste, yet are not themselves considered plumbing fixtures. A commercial refrigerator may have an indirect waste, but it is not a plumbing fixture.

Plumbing Inspector. See *Administrative Authority.*
Plumbing System. The plumbing system includes the water-supply and distribution pipes; plumbing fixtures and traps; soil, waste, and vent pipes; building drains and building sewers, including their respective connections, devices, and appurtenances within the property lines of the premises; and water-treating or water-using equipment.

▶ This definition is too inclusive because it covers equipment which may require water supply or waste, yet is not part of the plumbing system. Air-conditioning equipment requires water and waste but is not part of the plumbing system.   This applies also to the sprinkler fire systems and the special piping used for processing or carrying of special liquids or semiliquids.

Pool. A pool is a water receptacle used for swimming or as a plunge or other bath, designed to accommodate more than one bather at a time.

▶ Information on swimming pools will be found in Part III.

Potable Water. Potable water is water which is satisfactory for drinking, culinary, and domestic purposes and meets the requirements of the health authority having jurisdiction.
Private or Private Use. In the classification of plumbing fixtures, private applies to fixtures in residences and apartments and to fixtures in private bath-

rooms of hotels and similar installations where the fixtures are intended for the use of a family or an individual.

▶ In a commercial building a toilet accessible only to a specific office is considered a private toilet. This distinguishes between a toilet used by a few and one available to the general public where the frequency of use and the subsequent load on the system is much greater.

Private Sewer. A private sewer is a sewer privately owned and not directly controlled by public authority.

▶ A sewer owned by the owner of the property (not necessarily the person occupying the house or building) is a private sewer. The owner thereby has the responsibility of maintaining the sewer in good operating condition.

Public or Public Use. In the classification of plumbing fixtures, public applies to fixtures in general toilet rooms of schools, gymnasiums, hotels, railroad stations, public buildings, bars, public comfort stations, or places to which the public is invited or which are frequented by the public without special permission or special invitation, and other installations (whether pay or free) where a number of fixtures are installed so that their use is similarly unrestricted.

Public Official. See *Administrative Authority.*

Public Sewer. A public sewer is a common sewer directly controlled by public authority.

Relief Vent. A relief vent is a vent the primary function of which is to provide circulation of air between drainage and vent systems.

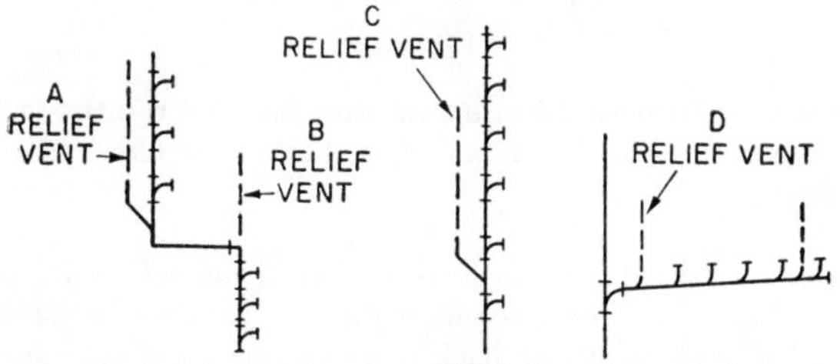

FIG. 1-38

▶ A relief vent is installed to prevent excessive pressures from developing in the drainage system that may cause siphonage or back pressures to the fixtures nearby, also to relieve pressure at congested points where the flow may tend to develop slugs, causing overloads on the drainage system because of the lack of proper circulation of air. Figure 1-38 illustrates a few of these conditions in a drainage system.

(a) When a stack offsets at an angle of 90 degrees, there is a tendency for the flow to slow down as it goes from the vertical to the horizontal. If air cannot escape freely, it could cause a back pressure against the fixtures near the offset; therefore a relief vent is installed to permit air to escape and permit atmospheric pressure to prevail.

(b) Where water flowing in a horizontal pipe is offset to a vertical, there is a tendency for the water to accelerate and produce a negative pressure which could siphon the fixtures installed close to the offset. A relief vent would dissipate this negative pressure by introducing air and would prevent siphonage of the fixture traps in its path.

(c) In a tall building, at every 10 or 12 stories, the soil stack could become filled from the flow from the upper stories. To avoid excessive negative pressures at these points, a relief vent is installed to provide the necessary air to balance the system to atmospheric conditions and prevent siphonage of fixtures on the lower floors.

(d) Should the stack become overloaded at peak times and the fixtures on the horizontal branch be discharged at the same time, there would be possibility of siphoning traps near the stack. A relief vent placed between the fixture and the stack will provide air for balancing the air pressures within the horizontal branch.

Return Offset. A return offset is a double offset installed so as to return the pipe to its original alignment.

RETURN OFFSET

Fig. 1-39

▶ This is similar to an offset except that the pipe returns to the same or nearly the same position it was first, before the offset took place. See Fig. 1-39.

Revent Pipe. A revent pipe (sometimes called an individual vent) is that part of a vent-pipe line which connects directly with an individual waste or group of wastes, underneath or back of the fixture, and extends either to the main or branch vent pipe.

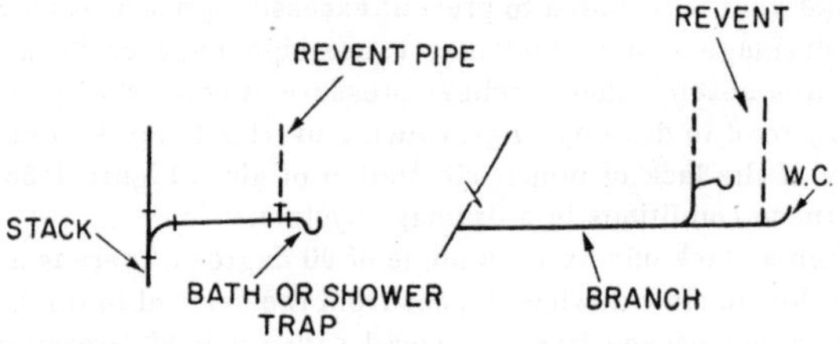

REVENT PIPE   REVENT
W.C.
STACK   BATH OR SHOWER TRAP   BRANCH
Fig. 1-40

▶ Figure 1-40 illustrates a revent pipe.

Rim.   A rim is an unobstructed open edge of a fixture.

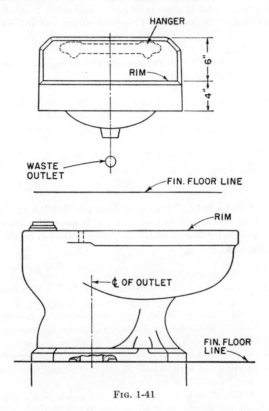

FIG. 1-41

▶   Figure 1-41 illustrates the rim of a wall-hung lavatory and a floor-mounted water closet.

Riser.   A riser is a water-supply pipe which extends vertically one full story or more to convey water to branches or fixtures.

Roof Drain.   A roof drain is a drain installed to receive water collecting on the surface of a roof and to discharge it into the leader (downspout).

▶   There are several types of roof drains, designed for specific purposes. See Part III for detailed information.

Roughing-in.   Roughing-in is the installation of all parts of the plumbing system which can be completed prior to the installation of fixtures. This includes drainage, water-supply and vent piping, and the necessary fixture supports.

▶ When the roughing-in is completed, the plumbing system is ready to receive a test.   This is done prior to concealing the roughing-in in order to ascertain that all threads and connections are gas and watertight.

Sand Interceptor. See *Interceptor.*
Sanitary Sewer. A sanitary sewer is a pipe which carries sewage and excludes storm, surface, and ground water.

▶ Sanitary sewer might also carry processing wastes, acid wastes, and clear-water wastes from special equipment, which because of their chemical components should not be discharged into a storm sewer.

Secondhand. Secondhand as applied to material or plumbing equipment is that which has been installed and has been used, removed, and passed to another ownership or possession.

▶ The fact that a fixture is removed from one location and reinstalled in another does not make it secondhand.   This refers, for instance, to large hotels or apartment houses where the owner may wish to relocate or renovate bathrooms.

Separator. See *Interceptor.*
Septic Tank. A septic tank is a watertight receptacle which receives the discharge of a drainage system or part thereof and is designed and constructed so as to separate solids from the liquid, digest organic matter through a period of detention, and allow the liquids to discharge into the soil outside of the tank through a system of open-joint or perforated piping or disposal pit.
Sewage. Sewage is any liquid waste containing animal or vegetable matter in suspension or solution and may include liquids containing chemicals in solution.
Shall. The word "shall" is a mandatory term.
Side Vent. A side vent is a vent connecting to the drain pipe through a fitting at an angle not greater than 45 degrees to the vertical.

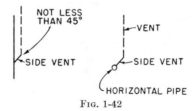

Fig. 1-42

▶ Figure 1-42 illustrates a side vent.

Size of Pipe and Tubing. See *Diameter.*
Slope. See *Grade.*
Soil Pipe. A soil pipe is any pipe which conveys the discharge of water closets, urinals, or fixtures having similar functions, with or without the discharge from other fixtures, to the building drain or building sewer.

Soil Vent. See *Stack Vent*.

Stack. A stack is the vertical main of a system of soil, waste, or vent piping.

Stack Group. Stack group is a term applied to the location of fixtures in relation to the stack so that by means of proper fittings vents may be reduced to a minimum.

▶   Stack grouping is similar to stack venting of a group of fixtures. The fixtures must be so located as to enable the soil stack or waste stack to act as a vent, without causing positive or negative pressures that would disturb the trap seals of the fixtures. (See *Stack Venting*.)

Stack Vent. A stack vent (sometimes called a waste vent or soil vent) is the extension of a soil or waste stack above the highest horizontal drain connected to the stack.

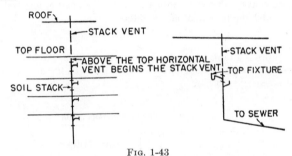

Fig. 1-43

▶   Figure **1-43** illustrates a stack vent.

Stack Venting. Stack venting is a method of venting a fixture or fixtures through the soil or waste stack.

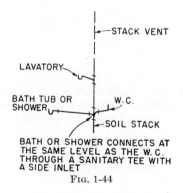

Fig. 1-44

▶   Fixtures must be grouped within a predetermined distance from the soil or waste stack so that individual venting will not be necessary. This applies only to a one-story building or the top floor of a multistory building. See Fig. 1-44.

Storm Drain. See *Building Storm Drain.*
Storm Sewer. A storm sewer is a sewer used for conveying rain water, surface water, condensate, cooling water, or similar liquid wastes, exclusive of sewage and industrial waste.
Subsoil Drain. A subsoil drain is a drain which receives only subsurface or seepage water and conveys it to a place of disposal.

▶   It is generally an open-joint or perforated drain which is installed around the exterior of the building to collect underground water. A subsoil drain conveys this water into a sump or to a point of disposal so that it will not enter the basement of a building.

Sump. A sump is a tank or pit which receives sewage or liquid waste, located below the normal grade of the gravity system, and which must be emptied by mechanical means.

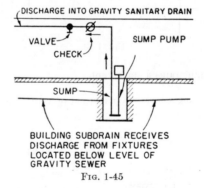

BUILDING SUBDRAIN RECEIVES
DISCHARGE FROM FIXTURES
LOCATED BELOW LEVEL OF
GRAVITY SEWER

Fig. 1-45

▶   A sump receiving clear liquid waste may be an open sump and may be discharged into the drainage system. A sump receiving the discharge from other than liquid waste must be a tight sump and must be vented to the atmosphere. See Fig. 1-45.

Supports. Supports, hangers, and anchors are devices for supporting and securing pipe and fixtures to walls, ceilings, floors, or structural members.
Trap. A trap is a fitting or device so designed and constructed as to provide, when properly vented, a liquid seal which will prevent the back passage of air without materially affecting the flow of sewage or waste water through it.

Trap Seal.   The trap seal is the maximum vertical depth of liquid that a trap will retain, measured between the crown weir and the top of the dip of the trap.

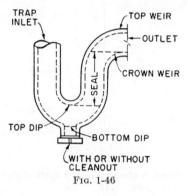

Fig. 1-46

▶   Figure 1-46 illustrates a trap and trap seal within the scope of these definitions.

Vacuum Breaker.   See *Backflow Preventer*.

Vent Pipe.   See *Vent System*.

Vent Stack.   A vent stack is a vertical vent pipe installed primarily for the purpose of providing circulation of air to and from any part of the drainage system.

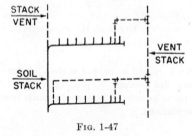

Fig. 1-47

▶   Figure 1-47 illustrates a vent stack.

Vent System.   A vent system is a pipe or pipes installed to provide a flow of air to or from a drainage system or to provide a circulation of air within such system to protect trap seals from siphonage and back pressure.

Vertical Pipe.   A vertical pipe is any pipe or fitting which is installed in a vertical position or which makes an angle of not more than 45 degrees with the vertical.

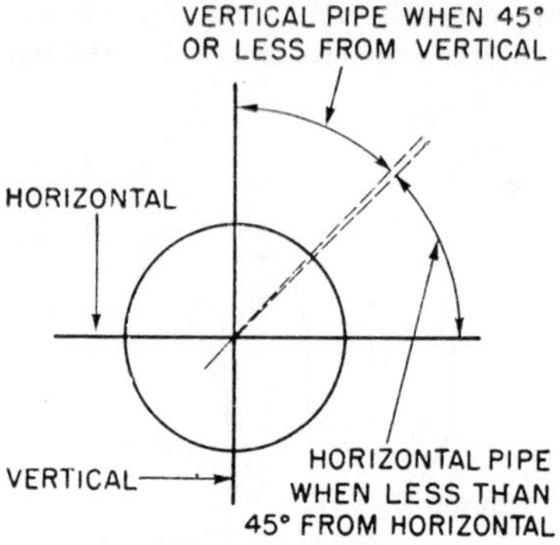

VERTICAL PIPE WHEN 45°
OR LESS FROM VERTICAL

HORIZONTAL

VERTICAL

HORIZONTAL PIPE
WHEN LESS THAN
45° FROM HORIZONTAL

FIG. 1-48

▶ In the drainage and venting system, a vertical pipe is the pipe installed within the arc shown in Fig. 1-48.

Waste. See *Liquid Waste* and *Industrial Wastes.*
Waste Pipe. A waste pipe is a pipe which conveys only liquid waste free of fecal matter.

▶ The pipes from a sink, lavatory, bathtub, shower, washing machine, or food-waste grinder are all waste pipes. Any liquid waste discharged from a fixture or appliance goes into a waste pipe. Discharge from water closets, urinals, and fixtures for human wastes go into soil pipes.

Water-distributing Pipe. A water-distributing pipe in a building or premises is a pipe which conveys water from the water-service pipe to the plumbing fixtures and other water outlets.

▶ Water outlets are valved or capped outlets left for extension to boilers, sprinkler systems, fire equipment, processing piping, and the like. It is mandatory that these outlets be protected against contamination as part of the plumbing regulations.

Water Main. The water (street) main is a water-supply pipe for public or community use.

▶ The water main may be installed in the public street or alley or within private property, but as long as it is under the jurisdiction of the municipality or water company it is not part of the plumbing system.

Water Outlet. A water outlet, as used in connection with the water-distributing system, is the discharge opening for the water (1) to a fixture; (2) to atmospheric pressure (except into an open tank which is part of the water-supply system); (3) to a boiler or heating system; (4) to any water-operated device or equipment requiring water to operate, but not a part of the plumbing system.

▶ Protection against possible backflow of contaminated water or toxic liquids into a water outlet is still the responsibility of the administrative authority in charge of plumbing in order to safeguard the potability of the water.

Water Riser Pipe.   See *Riser*.
Water-service Pipe.   The water-service pipe is the pipe from the water main or other source of water supply to the building served.

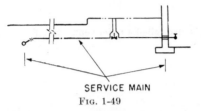

SERVICE MAIN
FIG. 1-49

▶ Figure 1-49 illustrates water-service pipe as generally classified in several communities.

Water-supply System.   The water-supply system of a building or premises consists of the water-service pipe, the water-distributing pipes, and the necessary connecting pipes, fittings, control valves, and all appurtenances in or adjacent to the building or premises.
Wet Vent.   A wet vent is a vent which receives the discharge from wastes other than water closets.

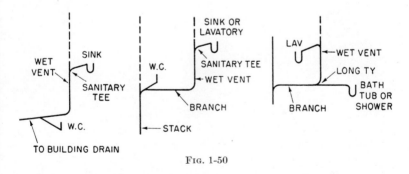

FIG. 1-50

▶ A wet vent also serves as a waste, but is limited to small-rated fixtures (not more than three fixture units each), and the wet vent is loaded to not more than half of its capacity.   See Fig. 1-50.

Yoke Vent. A yoke vent is a pipe connecting upward from a soil or waste stack to a vent stack for the purpose of preventing pressure changes in the stacks.

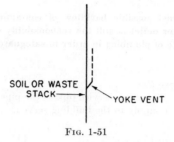

SOIL OR WASTE STACK

YOKE VENT

Fig. 1-51

► A yoke vent is also called a relief vent. See Fig. 1-51.

General Regulations

2.1   Conformance with Code

2.1.1   All plumbing systems hereafter installed shall conform at least with the provisions of this Code.

▶   The requirements prescribed within the National Plumbing Code may be considered the minimum deemed necessary adequately to safeguard the health and safety of any community from the potential hazards which are inherent in the installation of a plumbing system.

2.2   Grade of Horizontal Drainage Piping

2.2.1   Horizontal drainage piping shall be run in practical alignment at a uniform grade.

▶   See the table giving approximate flow velocity of sewage for given slopes and pipe diameters on page 11-5.
It is good practice to design for velocities of approximately 2 feet per second in order to scour the pipes, thus lessening the possibility of stoppages.
The generally recommended slopes are for pipes 3 inches in diameter and less at $\frac{1}{4}$-inch fall per foot and for pipes 4 inches in diameter and larger at $\frac{1}{8}$-inch fall per foot.

2.3   Change in Direction

2.3.1   Fittings.   Changes in direction in drainage piping shall be made by the appropriate use of 45 degree wyes, long- or-short-sweep quarter bends, sixth, eighth, or sixteenth bends, or by a combination of these or equivalent fittings. Single and double sanitary tees and quarter bends may be used in drainage lines only where the direction of flow is from the horizontal to the vertical.

2.3.2   Short Sweeps.   Short sweeps not less than 3 inches in diameter may be used in soil and waste lines where the change in direction of flow is either from the horizontal to the vertical or from the vertical to the horizontal and may be used for making necessary offsets between the ceiling and the next floor above.

NATIONAL PLUMBING CODE

CAST IRON SOIL FITTINGS

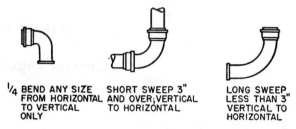

¼ BEND ANY SIZE   SHORT SWEEP 3"   LONG SWEEP
FROM HORIZONTAL   AND OVER; VERTICAL   LESS THAN 3"
TO VERTICAL   TO HORIZONTAL   VERTICAL TO
ONLY   HORIZONTAL

CAST IRON DRAINAGE FITTINGS

SHORT TURN   LONG TURN   EXTRA LONG
                                        TURN

FIG. 2-1

▶ Figure 2-1 illustrates paragraphs 2.3.1 and 2.3.2 as they concern change in direction.

From	To	Diameter of pipe (in.)	Install
Vertical......	Horizontal	3 and larger	A short sweep, or a 90-deg long-turn drainage elbow
Horizontal...	Vertical	3 and larger	A quarter bend, or a 90-deg short-turn fitting
Vertical......	Horizontal	Less than 3	A long sweep, or an extra-long-turn elbow
Horizontal...	Vertical	Less than 3	A quarter bend, or a 90-deg short-turn fitting
For venting in any direction...............			A quarter bend, or a 90-deg short-turn fitting

2.4 Fittings and Connections

2.4.1 Fittings Prohibited. No fitting having a hub in the direction opposite to flow or tee branch shall be used as a drainage fitting. No running threads, bands, or saddles shall be used in the drainage system. No drainage or vent piping shall be drilled or tapped.

▶ All fittings used for connecting drainage piping or for change in direction in the drainage system must be of a type and installed in a manner that under normal conditions of flow will prevent gorging and stoppage of piping, air binding, undue frictional losses, and unnecessary pipe noises. This paragraph does not prohibit special fittings and connections made for special purposes or specially designed for drainage and vent piping, such as fittings specially made for wall-hung fixtures (water-closet bowls, urinals, sinks); nor does it prohibit commercially known F & W, Stringer, or similar fittings.

2.4.2 Heel or Side-inlet Bend. A heel or side-inlet quarter bend shall not be used as a vent when the inlet is placed in a horizontal position.

R. H. SIDE   LOW HEEL   HIGH HEEL
INLET   INLET   INLET

QUARTER BENDS
Fig. 2-2

▶ When intended for service as a vent, but installed incorrectly, a heel or side inlet of a quarter bend soon becomes clogged. The correct positions for service as a vent are when using a side-inlet quarter bend, side-inlet upright, or full-size hub horizontal; when using a high-heel inlet, heel upright, or full-size hub upright; when using a low-heel inlet, heel upright.
All side inlets may be used as branch waste connections in any position.

2.4.3 Obstruction to Flow. No fitting, connection, device, or method of installation which obstructs or retards the flow of water, wastes, sewage, or air in the drainage or venting systems in an amount greater than the normal frictional resistance to flow shall be used unless it is indicated as acceptable in this Code or is approved by the administrative authority as having a desirable and acceptable function and as of ultimate benefit to the proper and continuing functioning of the plumbing system. The enlargement of a 3-inch closet bend or stub to 4 inches shall not be considered an obstruction. None of the methods described in paragraphs 2.28.1, 2.28.2, and 2.28.3 shall be considered as obstruction to flow.

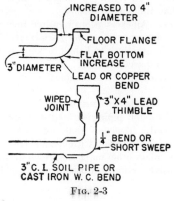

INCREASED TO 4"
DIAMETER

FLOOR FLANGE

FLAT BOTTOM
INCREASE

3" DIAMETER

LEAD OR COPPER
BEND

WIPED
JOINT

3" X 4" LEAD
THIMBLE

$\frac{1}{4}$" BEND OR
SHORT SWEEP

3" C. I. SOIL PIPE OR
CAST IRON W. C. BEND

Fig. 2-3

▶ Until water-closet outlets are so designed as to permit a 3-inch standard floor flange, it is necessary to increase the bend or stub at the floor line to 4 inches in diameter in order to accommodate the horn or closet outlet. See Fig. 2-3.

2.5   Repairs and Alterations

2.5.1   Existing Buildings. In existing buildings or premises in which plumbing installations are to be altered, repaired, or renovated, deviations from the provisions of this Code are permitted, provided such deviations are found to be necessary, conform to the intent of this Code, and are approved in writing by the administrative authority.

2.5.2   Health or Safety. Wherever compliance with all the provisions of this code fails to eliminate or alleviate a nuisance which may involve health or safety hazards, the owner or his agent shall install such additional plumbing or drainage equipment as may be found necessary by the administrative authority.

2.6   Sewer and Water Pipes

2.6.1 Water-service pipes, or any underground water pipes, shall not be run or laid in the same trench as the building sewer or drainage piping, except as provided for in Chaps. 10 and 11.

▶ See Part III for research and testing of various piping materials and their characteristics as to loads, joints, and root penetration.

2.7   Trenching, Excavation, and Backfill

2.7.1   Support of Piping. Buried piping shall be supported throughout its entire length.

2.7.2   Tunneling and Driving. Tunneling may be done in yards, courts, or driveways of any building site. When pipes are driven, the drive pipe shall be at least one size larger than the pipe to be laid.

2.7.3   Open Trenches. All excavations required to be made for the installation of a building-drainage system, or any part thereof within the walls of a building, shall be open trench work and shall be kept open until the piping has been inspected, tested, and accepted.

2.7.4   Mechanical Excavation. Mechanical means of excavation may be used.

2.7.5   Backfilling. Adequate precaution shall be taken to ensure proper compactness of backfill around piping without damage to such piping.

2.7.6   Backfill Material. Trenches shall be backfilled in thin layers to 12 inches above the top of the piping with clean earth which shall not contain stones, boulders, cinder fill, or other materials which would damage or break the piping or cause corrosive action. Mechanical devices such as bulldozers, graders, etc., may then be used to complete backfill to grade. Fill shall be properly compacted.

▶   **When excavating a trench, sufficient undisturbed earth should remain at the bottom so that the pipe, both joints and barrel, rests on and is fully supported by undisturbed earth.**

2.8 Structural Safety

2.8.1 In the process of installing or repairing any part of a plumbing and drainage installation, the finished floors, walls, ceilings, tilework, or any other part of the building or premises which must be changed or replaced shall be left in a safe structural condition as determined by the proper administrative authority.

▶   **In the case of the proper administrative authority, reference is made to the safety of the structure. Therefore, the building department is the proper authority.**

2.9 Workmanship

2.9.1 Workmanship shall conform to generally accepted good practice.

2.10 Protection of Pipes

2.10.1 Breakage and Corrosion. Pipes passing under or through walls shall be protected from breakage. Pipes passing through or under cinder or concrete or other corrosive material shall be protected against external corrosion by protective coating, wrapping, or other means which will prevent such corrosion.

2.10.2 Cutting or Notching. No structural member shall be weakened or impaired by cutting, notching, or otherwise, except to the extent permitted by the proper administrative authority.

2.10.3 Pipes through Footings or Foundation Walls. A soil or waste pipe or building drain passing under a footing or through a foundation wall shall be provided with a relieving arch; or there shall be built into the masonry wall an iron-pipe sleeve two pipe sizes greater than the pipe passing through, or equivalent protection shall be provided as may be approved in writing by the administrative authority.

2.10.4 Freezing. No water, soil, or waste pipe shall be installed or permitted outside of a building or in an exterior wall unless adequate provision is made to protect such pipe from freezing where necessary.

▶   **The entire plumbing system should be reasonably safe against leakage of water or gases due to defective materials, imperfect connections, chemical corrosion, settlement, vibrations of the ground or structure, temperature changes, freezing, or other causes due to installation or due to damages caused to the structure.**

2.11   Damage to Drainage System or Public Sewer

2.11.1   It shall be unlawful for any person to deposit by any means into the building drainage system or sewer any ashes; cinders; rags; inflammable, poisonous, or explosive liquids; gases; oils; grease; or any other material which would or could obstruct, damage, or overload such system or sewer.

▶   The discharge from the new type of plumbing appliances used for food-waste grinding and washing machines is not intended to be included as being unlawful.

2.12   Industrial Wastes

2.12.1   Wastes detrimental to the public sewer system or detrimental to the functioning of the sewage-treatment plant shall be treated and disposed of as found necessary and directed by the administrative authority or other authority having jurisdiction.

▶   It is further intended that for commercial or industrial installations the following information pertaining to characteristics of the wastes should be given to the administrative authority:
   (*a*) Nature of processing which yields the waste.
   (*b*) Composition and concentration of chemical mixtures in process.
   (*c*) Quantity of waste to be treated and to be wasted into the system.
   (*d*) Water demands of the industrial process.
   (*e*) Kind of waste treatment to be used, its capacities, methods of treatment, nature and disposition of products resulting from treatment.

2.13   Sleeves

2.13.1   Annular space between sleeves and pipes shall be filled or tightly calked with coal tar or asphaltum compound, lead, or other material found equally effective and approved as such by the administrative authority.

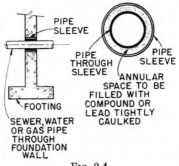

Fig. 2-4

▶ Figure 2-4 illustrates an annular space to be made watertight, where it is essential to prevent surface water from entering the building or where a pipe passing through a floor is to be made watertight.

2.14 Ratproofing

2.14.1 Exterior Openings. All exterior openings provided for the passage of piping shall be properly sealed with snugly fitting collars of metal or other approved ratproof material securely fastened into place.

2.14.2 Interior Openings. Interior openings through walls, floors, and ceilings shall be ratproofed as found necessary by the administrative authority.

2.15 Used or Secondhand Equipment

2.15.1 It shall be unlawful to purchase, sell, or install used equipment or material for plumbing installation unless it complies with the minimum standards set forth in this Code.

▶ Fixtures, piping, and other equipment to be installed in a plumbing system must conform to the minimum standards of the plumbing code. Used pipe of unknown source is dangerous to use in the potable-water system because of the serious health hazard involved.

2.16 Condemned Equipment

2.16.1 Any plumbing equipment condemned by the administrative authority because of wear, damage, defects, or sanitary hazards shall not be reused for plumbing purposes.

2.17 Depth of Building Sewer and Water Service (outside of Building)

2.17.1 Sewers and water-service piping shall be installed below the recorded frost penetration, but in no case less than _____ feet _____ inches for sewer and _____ feet _____ inches for water piping below grade.

▶ Spaces left open are to be filled, based on local conditions. In southern regions though there is no frost to contend with, heavy traffic requires a minimum depth, depending on the location and type of roadbed. In northern areas, the depth will depend on frost penetration plus an additional margin of safety.

2.18   Piping in Relation to Footings

2.18.1   Parallel.   No piping shall be laid parallel to footings or outside bearing walls closer than 3 feet, except as may be approved by the administrative authority upon a finding that a lesser distance is safe.

2.18.2   Depth.   Piping installed deeper than footings or bearing walls shall be 45 degrees therefrom, except as may be approved by the administrative authority upon a finding that a greater angle is safe.

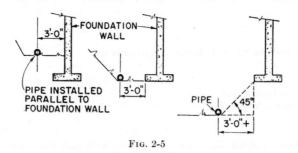

Fig. 2-5

▶   Figure 2-5 illustrates this requirement.

2.19   Drainage below Sewer Level

2.19.1   Drainage piping located below the level of the sewer shall be installed as provided for in Chaps. 10 and 11.

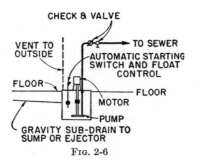

Fig. 2-6

▶   Fixtures or drainage piping located below the invert of the sewer in the street or place of disposal requires a separate system of piping.   The fixture discharge is to be made by gravity into a tight ejector pit and then pumped by mechanical means into the building drain or as a separate connection into the building sewer. See Fig. 2-6.

2.20 Connections to Plumbing System Required

2.20.1 All plumbing fixtures, drains, appurtenances, and appliances used to receive or discharge liquid wastes or sewage shall be connected properly to the drainage system of the building or premises, in accordance with the requirements of this Code.

2.21 Sewer Required

2.21.1 Every building in which plumbing fixtures are installed shall have a connection to a public or private sewer except as provided in paragraph 2.22.1.

2.22 Individual or Private Sewage-disposal System

2.22.1 When a public sewer is not available for use, sewage and drainage piping shall be connected to an individual sewage-disposal system found to be adequate and approved by the administrative authority.

▶   A private sewage-disposal system may be a community sewage-disposal plant or a septic tank for an individual home. See Chap. 16, Individual Sewage-disposal System.

2.23 Location of Fixtures

2.23.1 Light and Ventilation. Plumbing fixtures, except drinking fountains and single lavatories, shall be located in compartments or rooms provided with ventilation and illumination conforming to recognized published standards.

▶   Mechanical ventilation and electric lighting are being recognized as equal to ventilation and illumination through windows, skylights, or shafts. Modern equipment lends itself to automatic and reliable operation.

2.23.2 Improper Location. Piping, fixtures, or equipment shall not be located in such a manner as to interfere with the normal operation of windows, doors, or other exit openings.

▶   Figure 2-7 illustrates recommended minimum spacing about bathroom and toilet-room fixtures.

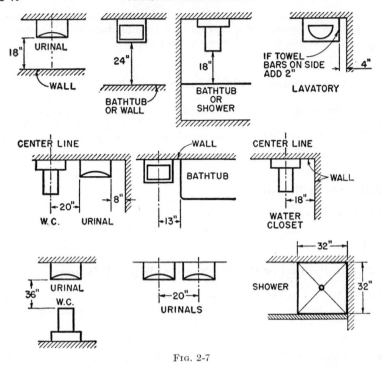

Fig. 2-7

2.24 Piping Measurements

2.24.1 Except where otherwise specified in this Code, all measurements between pipes or between pipes and walls, etc., shall be made to the center lines of the pipes.

2.25 Venting

2.25.1 The drainage system shall be provided with a system of vent piping which will permit the admission or emission of air so that under no circumstance of normal or intended use shall the seal of any fixture trap be subjected to a pressure differential of more than 1 inch of water.

▶   Schedules of pipe sizes and loading tables have been developed so that under normal conditions pressures of fixture traps within the plumbing system will not develop more than 1 inch of water-pressure differential.

2.26   Ventilation Ducts

2.26.1   Ventilation ducts from washrooms and toilet rooms shall exhaust to the outer air or form an independent system.

2.27   Water-closet Connections

2.27.1   Lead.   Three-inch lead bends and stubs may be used on water closets or similar connections, provided the inlet is dressed or expanded to receive a 4-inch floor flange.

2.27.2   Iron.   Three-inch bends may be used on water closets or similar connections, provided a 4- by 3-inch floor flange is used to receive the fixture horn.

2.27.3   Reducing.   Four- by three-inch reducing bends are acceptable.

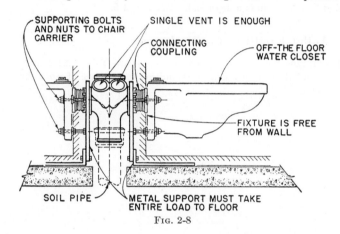

Fɪɢ. 2-8

▶   The present trend is to standardize the use of a **3**-inch water-closet bend with a **3**-inch floor flange. The new type water closets with a very short horn at the outlet permit the use of **3**-inch floor flanges. Wall-closet fittings for wall-hung fixtures are generally provided with straight thread couplings for adjustment when hanging fixtures. A permanent gas and watertight connection must be obtained by means of gaskets, or other satisfactory means. All metal parts coming in contact with fixture discharge should be corrosion resistant. Chairs supporting fixtures should not impose any of the fixture weight onto the interior wall of the structure. See Fig. **2-8**.

2.28   Dead Ends

2.28.1   In the installation or removal of any part of a drainage system, dead ends shall be avoided except where necessary to extend a cleanout so as to be accessible.

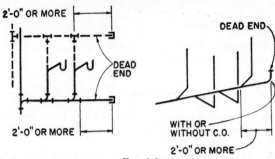

Fig. 2-9

▶   Any piping extended 2 feet or more for any purpose except as an extension to a cleanout is a dead end.   See Fig. 2-9.

2.29   Toilet Facilities for Workmen

2.29.1   Suitable toilet facilities in accordance with Table 7.21.2 shall be provided and maintained in a sanitary condition for the use of workmen during construction.

CHAPTER 3

Materials—Quality and Weight

3.1 Materials

3.1.1 Minimum Standards. The materials listed in this chapter shall conform at least to the standards cited when used in the construction, installation, alteration, or repair of any part of a plumbing and drainage system, except that the administrative authority shall allow the extension, addition, or relocation of existing soil, waste, or vent pipes with materials of like grade or quality.

▶ Substitutions found necessary should be permitted when in the considered judgment of the administrative authority such substitutions conform to the intent of the Code.

3.1.2 Use of Materials. Each material listed in Table 3.5 shall conform to at least one of the standards cited opposite it. Its use shall be further governed by the requirement imposed in other chapters of the Code. Materials not included in the table shall be used only as provided for in paragraph 3.1.1. Materials shall be free of manufacturing defects or damage, however occasioned, which would, or would tend to, render such materials defective, unsanitary, or otherwise improper to accomplish the purpose of this Code.

▶ Each chapter of the Code indicates the general requirements of material for specific systems. See Part III for a résumé of specifications applicable to materials included in Table 3.1.1.

3.1.3 Specifications for Materials. Standard specifications for materials for plumbing installations are listed in Table 3.5. Products conforming at least to any of the specifications listed for a given material shall be considered acceptable.

NOTE 1. Abbreviations used in Tables 3.5 refer to standards or specifications as identified below.

ASA   American Standards approved by the American Standards Association, 70 East 45th Street, New York 17, N.Y.

ASTM   Standards and Tentative Standards published by the American Society for Testing Materials, 1916 Race Street, Philadelphia 3, Pa.

FS   Federal Specifications published by the Federal Specifications Board and obtained from the Superintendent of Documents, Government Printing Office, Washington 25, D.C.

AWWA   Standards and Tentative Standards published by the American Water Works Association, 500 Fifth Avenue, New York 18, N.Y.

CS   Commercial Standards representing recorded voluntary recommendations of the trade, issued by the U.S. Department of Commerce and obtainable from the Superintendent of Documents, Government Printing Office, Washington 25, D.C.

MSS   Standards published by the Manufacturers Standardization Society of the Valve and Fittings Industry, 420 Lexington Avenue, New York 17, N.Y.

SPR   Simplified Practice Recommendations representing recorded recommendations of the trade and issued by the U.S. Department of Commerce, Washington 25, D.C.

NOTE 2. ASTM standards are issued under fixed designations; the final number indicates the year of original adoption, or in the case of revision, the year of last revision. T indicates Tentative. In the CS series of standards, also, the final number indicates the year of issue. For Federal Specifications, the year indicated in Table 3.5 is that of the date of issue or that of the latest revision or amendment.

NOTE 3. All standards and specifications for materials are subject to change. Designations carrying indication of the year of issue may thus become obsolete. Table 3.5 gives the full designations of standards current at the time this Code is printed. As provided in paragraph 3.4.1, the administrative authority is required to review this table and have it brought up to date at intervals not exceeding 2 years.

3.1.4 Identification of Materials. Each length of pipe and each pipe fitting, trap, fixture, and device used in a plumbing system shall have cast, stamped, or indelibly marked on it the maker's mark or name, the weight, type, and classes of the product, when such marking is required by the approved standard that applies.

▶   Most manufacturers desire to trade-mark their products, not only as an indication of quality but to be able to identify them after they have been installed.

3.2 Special Materials

3.2.1 Lead. See Table 3.5. Sheet lead shall be not less than the following:
For safe pans—not less than 4 pounds per square foot
For flashings of vent terminals—not less than 3 pounds per square foot
Lead bends and lead traps shall be not less than $\frac{1}{8}$ inch wall thickness.

3.2.2 Copper. Sheet copper shall be not less than the following:
Safe pans—12 ounces per square foot
Vent-terminal flashings—8 ounces per square foot

3.2.3 Calking ferrules shall be manufactured from red brass and shall be in accordance with the following:

Pipe sizes (in.)	Inside diameter (in.)	Length (in.)	Minimum weight each	
			Lb	Oz
2	$2\frac{1}{4}$	$4\frac{1}{2}$	1	0
3	$3\frac{1}{4}$	$4\frac{1}{2}$	1	12
4	$4\frac{1}{4}$	$4\frac{1}{2}$	2	8

3.2.4 Soldering bushings shall be of red brass in accordance with the following:

Pipe sizes (in.)	Minimum weight each		Pipe sizes (in.)	Minimum weight each	
	Lb	Oz		Lb	Oz
$1\frac{1}{4}$	0	6	$2\frac{1}{2}$	1	6
$1\frac{1}{2}$	0	8	3	2	0
2	0	14	4	3	8

3.2.5 Floor Flanges. Floor flanges for water closets or similar fixtures shall be not less than $\frac{1}{8}$ inch thick for brass, $\frac{1}{4}$ inch thick and not less than 2-inch calking depth for cast iron or galvanized malleable iron. If of hard lead, they shall weigh not less than 1 pound 9 ounces and be composed of lead alloy with not less than 7.75 per cent antimony by weight.

Flanges shall be soldered to lead bends or shall be calked, soldered, or screwed to other metal.

Closet screws and bolts shall be brass.

▶ **Bolts and nuts for wall hanging fixtures shall be of heavy-construction steel to fully carry the weight that will be placed on the carrier by the fixture and users.**

3.2.6 Cleanouts
  (a) Cleanout plugs shall be of brass and shall conform to Federal Specification WW-P-401.
  (b) Plugs may have raised square or countersunk heads.
  (c) Countersunk heads should be used where raised heads may cause a hazard.

Table 3.5   Materials for Plumbing Installations

Materials	See paragraphs 3.1.3 and 3.4.2			Other standards remarks
	ASA	ASTM	FS	
Nonmetallic piping:				
Clay sewer pipe	....	C13-50 / C200-50T	SS-P-361a (1942)	Standard strength / Extra strength
Concrete sewer pipe for sizes 4 to 24-in.	....	C75-52 / C14-52	SS-P-371 (1937)	Reinforced / Nonreinforced
Bituminized-fiber sewer pipe and fittings	....	....	....	Type I / CS 116-44[2]
Asbestos-cement sewer pipe	....	....	SS-P-351 (1953)	[1,2]
Ferrous pipe and fittings:				
Cast-iron soil pipe and fittings	A40.1-1935	A74-42	WW-P-401 (1935)[3]	Extra heavy and service weights[2] / AWWA 1908
Cast-iron water pipe	A21.2-1953	A44-41	WW-P-421 (1931)[4]	
Cast-iron (threaded) pipe	A40.5-1943	....	WW-P-356 (1936)	
Cast-iron (screwed) fittings	B16.4-1949	....	WW-P-501b (1945)	
Cast-iron drainage fittings	B16.12-1953	....	WW-P-491a (1945)[5]	
Wrought-iron pipe	B36.2-1950	A72-52T	WW-P-441b (1952)[6]	
Steel pipe	B36.23-1950	A120-47	WW-P-406 (1944)	Types I and II
Open-hearth iron pipe	B16.3-1951 (150 lb)	A253-51T	WW-P-406 (1944)[7]	Type III only
Malleable-iron fittings		A338-51T*		
Nonferrous pipe and fittings:				
Brass tubing	H27.1-1953	B135-52[8]	WW-T-791-1931	
Brass pipe	B16.24-1953 (150 and 300 lb.)	B43-52	WW-P-351 (1930)[9]	
Brass or bronze flanges and flanged fittings	B16.18-1950			
Cast-brass soldered joint fittings				For copper water tube
Cast-brass solder joint drainage fittings	B16.23-1953			
Bronze screwed fittings, 125 lb.	B16.15-1947	B42-52	WW-P-460-(1945)	MSS-SP-10
Copper pipe	H26.1-1949	B75-52	WW-P-377 (1932)	
Seamless copper tubing			WW-T-797 (1932)[10]	
Copper water tube (KLM)	H23.1-1953	B88-51	WW-T-799a(1943)[11]	SPR 217-49
Wrought-copper and wrought-bronze solder joint fittings	B16.22-1951			
Flared fittings for copper (water) tubes	A40.2-1936			
Lead pipe and traps			WW-P-325 (1944)	CS 95-41 CS 96-41

	ASA	ASTM	Federal	
Miscellaneous:				
Calking lead			QQ-L-156(1934)[12] Type I	CS 94-41
Sheet lead			QQ-L-201(1953)[13]	
Sheet brass		B36-52 B121-52	QQ-B-611a(1938)	Grade A
Sheet copper	G8.8-1937	B152-52	QQ-C-501a(1941)[14]	
Galvanized-iron and steel sheets		A163-39 A93-52T	QQ-I-716(1942)[15]	
Galvanized pipe and fittings		A120-47	WW-P-406(1944)	
Cement lining	A21.4-1939		WW-P-406(1944)	Sec. 18.6
Coal-tar enamel (protective coating)				Sec. 18.7 AWWA 7A.6-1940
Soft solder		B32-49	QQ-S-571b(1947)	
Fixture-setting compound			HH-C-536(1936)	
Air-gap standards	A40.4-1942			
Backflow preventors	A40.6-1943			
Valves:				
Bronze gate			WW-V-54(1946)[16]	
Cast-iron gate			WW-V-58(1945)	

* Intended only for use where ASA B16.3 (150 lb) and B16.19 (300 lb) are not adequate.

[1] Asbestos-cement sewer pipe shall meet Federal Specifications SS-P-351 (1940) including Amendment 2, dated Jan. 14, 1942, except for the following substitutions:

Sizes only 4, 5, and 6-inch
Class—nonpressure tests
Lengths: 10 feet—out of roundness, inside diameter; ±¼ inch
Hydrostatic strength: not applicable
Flexural strength—9-foot span
4-inch pipe—560 lb
5-inch pipe—900 lb
6-inch pipe—1,290 lb
Crushing strength
4-inch pipe—1,740 lb
5-inch pipe—1,680 lb
6-inch pipe—1,420 lb
Tests: one specimen from each 300 lengths of pipe.

[2] See Code chapters for limits of recommended usage.

[3] Amendment 4, dated July 18, 1951, subject: Pipe and Pipe Fittings, Soil, Cast Iron.

[4] Amendment 3, dated Apr. 26, 1940, included.
[5] Amendment 1, dated Feb. 7, 1946, included.
[6] Amendment 2, dated Feb. 8, 1943, included.
[7] Amendment 1, dated June 9, 1945, included.
[8] Mercurous nitrate test required.
[9] Errata 1, dated August, 1933, included.
[10] Amendment 1, June 27, 1946.
[11] Amendment 1, dated Nov. 18, 1946, included.
[12] Amendment 1, dated June 2, 1942, included.
[13] Amendment 1, dated May 27, 1942, included.
[14] Amendment 3, dated November 1948. included.
[15] Amendment 1, dated Apr. 19, 1946, included.
[16] Amendment 1, dated Sept. 30, 1946, included.

▶   See Part III for descriptive data on cleanouts.

3.3   Alternate Materials and Methods

3.3.1   Existing Premises.   In existing buildings or premises in which plumbing installations are to be altered, repaired, or renovated, the administrative authority has discretionary powers to permit deviation from the provisions of this Code, provided that such a proposal to deviate is first submitted for proper determination in order that health and safety requirements, as they pertain to plumbing, shall be observed.

▶   **If it is necessary to use certain materials or methods of design in order to match previous work, it may be done provided the previous work is not a health hazard.**

3.3.2   Approval.   Provisions of this Code are not intended to prevent the use of any material, device, method of assemblage or installation, fixture, or appurtenance not specifically authorized, provided such alternate has been approved by the administrative authority, in accordance with this section.

▶   **New material is acceptable provided the suitability of such material, device, or method has been proved by test or experience to the satisfaction of the administrative authority.**

3.3.3   Evidence of Compliance.   The administrative authority shall require sufficient evidence to enable him to judge whether proposed alternates meet the requirements of this Code for safety and health.

3.3.4   Tests.   When there is insufficient evidence to substantiate claims for alternates, the administrative authority may require tests of compliance as proof to be made by an approved agency at the expense of the applicant.

3.3.5   Test Procedure.   Tests shall be made in accordance with generally recognized standards; but in the absence of such standards, the administrative authority shall specify the test procedure.

3.3.6   Repeated Tests.   The administrative authority may require tests to be repeated if, at any time, there is reason to believe that an alternate no longer conforms to the requirements on which its approval was based.

3.4   Approved Materials

3.4.1   Periodic Review.   The administrative authority shall periodically, at least once every 2 years, review the approved list of specifications and standards for materials in Table 3.5 and in Chap. 7, Plumbing Fixtures, to check the designations, numbers, etc., which are used for identification, and if there are later issues shall submit them for their legal adoption.

NOTE.   All standards and specifications for materials are subject to change; therefore they need to be reviewed and brought up to date periodically.   It is particularly important to review those standards and specifications which show a year of approval. Often such standards become obsolete in later years.

▶ For example, the Cast Iron Soil Pipe Institute, in **1951**, established a new standard for service-weight pipe, prescribing that there be only two weights of pipe—extra heavy and service weight. This new standard rendered obsolete and possibly unavailable several weights that were previously available.

3.4.2 Specific Usage. Each chapter of this Code indicates specifically the type of material permitted for the various parts of the plumbing system. The standards for each of those materials are given in Table 3.5.

3.5 (See Table 3.5.)

CHAPTER 4

Joints and Connections

4.1 Tightness

4.1.1 Joints and connections in the plumbing system shall be gastight and watertight for the pressures required by test, with the exception of those portions of perforated or open-joint piping which are installed for the purpose of collecting and conveying ground or seepage water to the underground storm drains.

4.2 Types of Joints

4.2.1 Calked Joints. Calked joints for cast-iron bell-and-spigot soil pipe shall be firmly packed with oakum or hemp and filled with molten lead not less than 1 inch deep and not to extend more than $\frac{1}{8}$ inch below the rim of the hub. No paint, varnish, or other coatings shall be permitted on the jointing material until after the joint has been tested and approved.

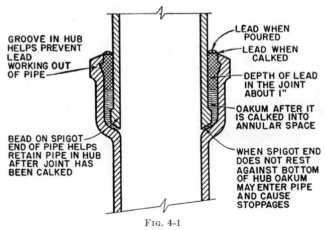

GROOVE IN HUB HELPS PREVENT LEAD WORKING OUT OF PIPE

LEAD WHEN POURED

LEAD WHEN CALKED

DEPTH OF LEAD IN THE JOINT ABOUT 1"

OAKUM AFTER IT IS CALKED INTO ANNULAR SPACE

BEAD ON SPIGOT END OF PIPE HELPS RETAIN PIPE IN HUB AFTER JOINT HAS BEEN CALKED

WHEN SPIGOT END DOES NOT REST AGAINST BOTTOM OF HUB OAKUM MAY ENTER PIPE AND CAUSE STOPPAGES

FIG. 4-1

▶ Figure 4-1 illustrates a hot-poured joint in a cast-iron soil pipe.

4.2.2 Threaded Joints—Screwed Joints. Threads shall conform to American National Taper Pipe Thread, ASA B2.1-1945 or FS GGG-P-351a.

All burrs shall be removed. Pipe ends shall be reamed or filled out to size of bore, and all chips shall be removed. Pipe-joint cement and paint shall be used only on male threads.

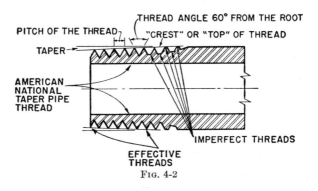

Fig. 4-2

▶   Figure 4-2 illustrates various portions of a threaded pipe end.

4.2.3 Wiped Joints.   Joints in lead pipe or fittings, or between lead pipe or fittings and brass or copper pipe, ferrules, solder nipples, or traps, shall be full-wiped joints. Wiped joints shall have an exposed surface on each side of a joint not less than ¾ inch and at least as thick as the material being jointed. Wall or floor flange lead-wiped joints shall be made by using a lead ring or flange placed behind the joint at wall or floor. Joints between lead pipe and cast iron, steel, or wrought iron shall be made by means of a calking ferrule, soldering nipple, or bushing.

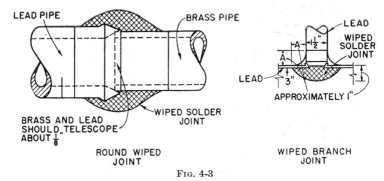

Fig. 4-3

▶   Figure 4-3 illustrates the appearance of a 3- by 1½-inch wiped branch joint. The dimensions of the joint at points *A* for 1½-inch lead pipe should be about 1 inch. Branch joints are generally narrower than round joints.

4.2.4 Soldered or Sweat Joints. Soldered or sweat joints for tubing shall be made with approved fittings. Surfaces to be soldered or seated shall be cleaned bright. The joints shall be properly fluxed and made with approved solder. Joints in copper water tubing shall be made by the appropriate use of approved brass water fittings, properly sweated or soldered together.

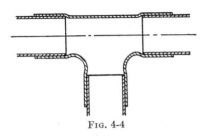

Fig. 4-4

▶   Copper tube and fittings are readily soldered because the oxides are easily reduced by ordinary fluxes, so that the surfaces to be soldered can be kept chemically clean while they are being jointed by solder.

Part III contains general data on solders and their application as well as information on annular space requirements.

4.2.5 Flared Joints. Flared joints for soft-copper water tubing shall be made with fittings meeting approved standards. The tubing shall be expanded with a proper flaring tool.

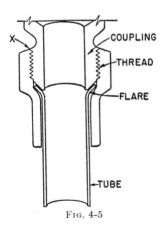

Fig. 4-5

▶   Figure 4-5 illustrates a flared fitting cut away, which shows the anchorage of the flared tube by the coupling shank. Where flared fittings are used under streets or other locations subject to vibrations from traffic or heavy equipment, it is safe to tack the fitting with a drop of solder on each side of the coupling at point X. This will prevent loosening of the coupling and possible leaks occurring at the joint of the anchorage of the tube.

4.2.6 Hot-poured Joints. Hot-poured compound for clay or concrete sewer pipe shall not be water absorbent and when poured against a dry surface shall have a bond of not less than 100 pounds per square inch. All surfaces of the joint shall be cleaned and dried before pouring. If wet surfaces are unavoidable, a suitable primer shall be applied. Compound shall not soften sufficiently to destroy the effectiveness of the joint when subjected to a temperature of 160°F nor be soluble in any of the waste carried by the drainage system. Approximately 25 per cent of the joint space at the base of the socket shall be filled with jute or hemp. A pouring collar, rope, or other device shall be used to hold the hot compound during pouring. Each joint shall be poured in one operation until the joint is filled. Joints shall not be tested until 1 hour after pouring.

4.2.7 Precast Joints. Precast collars shall be formed in both the spigot and bell of the pipe in advance of use. Collar surfaces shall be conical with side slopes of 3 degrees with the axis of the pipe, and the length shall be equal to the depth of the socket. Prior to making joint contact, surfaces shall be cleaned and coated with solvents and adhesives as recommended in the standard. When the spigot end is inserted in the collar, it shall bind before contacting the base of the socket. Material shall be inert and resistant to both acids and alkalies.

4.2.8 Brazed Joints. Brazed joints shall be made in accordance with the provisions of Section 6 of the Code for Pressure Piping, ASA B31.1-1951.

▶ Brazed joints where necessary would mostly be used for water piping rather than drainage piping. An example of necessary brazing or welding would be in a replacement job where it would be impossible to remove and reinstall a piece of pipe. Brazing or welding of vent piping is satisfactory except where there are labor restrictions.

4.2.9 Cement Mortar Joints. Cement joints shall be used only when specifically permitted in other chapters of this Code or when approved by the administrative authority, as sufficient to accomplish the purpose of this Code. A layer of jute or hemp shall be inserted into the base of the joint space and rammed to prevent mortar from entering the interior of the pipe. Jute or hemp shall be dipped into a slurry suspension of portland cement in water prior to insertion into bell. Not more than 25 per cent of the joint space shall be used for jute or hemp. The remaining space shall be filled in one continuous operation with a thoroughly mixed mortar composed of 1 part cement and 2 parts sand, with only sufficient water to make the mixture workable by hand. After ½ hour of setting, the joint shall be rammed around the entire periphery with a blunt tool to force the partially stiffened mortar into the joint and to repair any cracks formed during the initial setting period. Pipe interior shall be swabbed to remove any material that might have fallen into the interior. Additional mortar of the same composition shall then be troweled so as to form a 45-degree taper with the barrel of the pipe.

▶ Generally it is difficult to achieve a rootproof joint. The power of seemingly fragile roots to break through is one of nature's miracles.

4.2.10 Burned Lead Joints. Burned (welded) lead joints shall be lapped, and the lead shall be fused together to form a uniform weld at least as thick as the lead being joined.

▶ Lead burning in plumbing work is an art which is rapidly disappearing because of shortage of experienced mechanics. Lead burning and lead brazing are very satisfactory if done skillfully.

4.2.11 Asbestos-cement Sewer-pipe Joints. Joints in asbestos-cement pipe shall be made with sleeve couplings of the same composition as the pipe, sealed with rubber rings. Joints between asbestos-cement pipe and metal pipe shall be made by means of an adapter coupling calked as required in paragraph 4.2.1.

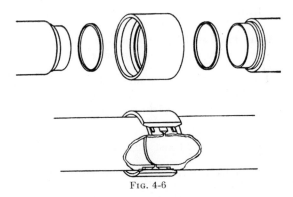

Fig. 4-6

▶ Figure 4-6 illustrates a joint between two lengths of asbestos-cement pipe. See Part III for data and performance of this type of piping.

4.2.12 Bituminized-fiber Pipe Joints. Joints in bituminized-fiber pipe shall be made with tapered-type couplings of the same material as the pipe. Joints between bituminized-fiber pipe and metal pipe shall be made by means of an adapter coupling calked as required in paragraph 4.2.1.

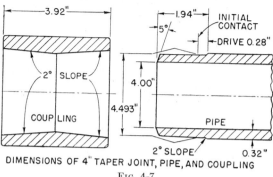

DIMENSIONS OF 4" TAPER JOINT, PIPE, AND COUPLING

Fig. 4-7

▶　　Bituminized-fiber pipe is used for house-to-street sewer connections. The pipe and fittings have mating tapers which when properly swaged together form a watertight root-resistant connection. This pipe can be cut with an ordinary hand saw. The pipe and couplings are joined by placing a wood block against the last coupling and hitting it with a few blows of a hammer to drive the lengths together inside the coupling. The same process is used for joining couplings. The pipe comes in 8-foot lengths and weighs 2.7 pounds per foot of 4-inch pipe.

4.3　Use of Joints

4.3.1　Clay Sewer Pipe. Joints in vitrified-clay pipe or between such pipe and metal pipe shall be made as provided in paragraphs 4.2.6 and 4.2.7.

4.3.2　Concrete Sewer Pipe. Joints in concrete sewer pipe or between such pipe and metal pipe shall be made as provided in paragraphs 4.2.6 and 4.2.7.

4.3.3　Cast-iron Pipe. Joints in cast-iron pipe shall be either calked or screwed, as provided in paragraphs 4.2.1 and 4.2.2.

4.3.4　Screw Pipe to Cast Iron. Joints between wrought-iron, steel, brass, or copper pipe and cast-iron pipe shall be either calked or threaded joints made as provided in paragraphs 4.2.1 and 4.2.2 or shall be made with approved adapter fittings.

4.3.5　Lead to Cast Iron, Wrought Iron, or Steel. Joints between lead and cast-iron, wrought-iron, or steel pipe shall be made by means of wiped joints to a calking ferrule, soldering nipple, or bushing as provided in paragraph 4.2.3.

4.3.6　Copper Water Tube. Joints in copper tubing shall be made either by the appropriate use of approved copper fittings, properly sweated or soldered together, or by means of approved compression fittings as provided in paragraphs 4.2.4 and 4.2.5.

▶　　See Part III for information on copper tube.

4.4   Special Joints

4.4.1   Copper Tubing to Screwed Pipe Joints.   Joints from copper tubing to threaded pipe shall be made by the use of brass converter fittings.   The joint between the copper pipe and the fitting shall be properly sweated or soldered, and the connection between the threaded pipe and the fitting shall be made with a standard pipe size screw joint.

4.4.2   Brazing or Welding.   Brazing or welding shall be performed in accordance with requirements of recognized published standards of practice and by licensed or otherwise qualified mechanics except when it is determined by the administrative authority to be equivalent procedure for the purpose of this Code.

4.4.3   Slip Joints.   In drainage and water piping, slip joints may be used only on the inlet side of the trap or in the trap seal and on the exposed fixture supply.

4.4.4   Expansion Joints.   Expansion joints must be accessible and may be used where necessary to provide for expansion and contraction of the pipes.

4.4.5   Ground-joint Brass Connections.   Ground-joint brass connections which allow adjustment of tubing but provide a rigid joint when made up shall not be considered as slip joints.

4.5   Unions (Screwed)

4.5.1   Drainage System.   Unions may be used in the trap seal and on the inlet side of the trap.   Unions shall have metal-to-metal seats.

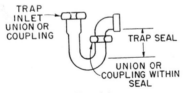

Fɪɢ. 4-8

▶   Figure 4-8 illustrates a fixture trap and the location of the unions or couplings.   They must be installed on the fixture side of the trap or within the trap seal, so that gas cannot escape into the room in the event of a loose connection.

4.5.2   Water-supply Systems.   Unions in the water-supply system shall be metal to metal with ground seats.

▶   Unions may be used anywhere in the water-supply system, except that it is poor design to install unions concealed in the building construction where a leak may occur and incur costly repair.   It is preferable to use right and left couplings in order to assure permanent leakproof joints.

4.6   Water-closet, Pedestal-urinal, and Trap-standard Service

4.6.1   Fixture connections between drainage pipes and water closets, floor-outlet service sinks, pedestal urinals, and earthenware trap standards shall be made by means of brass, hard-lead, or iron flanges, calked, soldered, or screwed to the drainage pipe.   The connection shall be bolted, with an approved gasket or washer or setting compound between the earthenware and the connection. The floor flange shall be set on an approved firm base.   The use of commercial putty or plaster is prohibited.

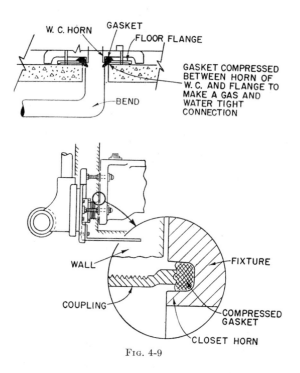

Fig. 4-9

The use of putty and plaster is still prevalent in some communities. When putty is used, there is no assurance that the connection will remain gastight.   When plaster is used, there is a possibility of breaking the fixture if it has to be removed at any time.   See Part III for data on off-the-floor fixtures.

Figure 4-9 shows the accepted method for installing wall-hung and floor-mounted fixtures.

4.7 Prohibited Joints and Connections

4.7.1 Drainage System. Any fitting or connection which has an enlargement, chamber, or recess with a ledge, shoulder, or reduction of pipe area that offers an obstruction to flow through the drain is prohibited.

4.7.2 No fitting or connection that offers abnormal obstruction to flow shall be used. The enlargement of a 3-inch closet bend or stub to 4 inches shall not be considered an obstruction.

4.8 Waterproofing of Openings

4.8.1 Joints at the roof, around vent pipes, shall be made watertight by the use of lead, copper, galvanized-iron, or other approved flashings or flashing material. Exterior-wall openings shall be made watertight.

4.9 Increasers and Reducers

4.9.1 Where different sizes of pipes, or pipes and fittings are to be connected, the proper size increasers or reducers or reducing fittings shall be used between the two sizes.

CHAPTER 5

Traps and Cleanouts

5.1 Traps

5.1.1 Fixture Traps. Plumbing fixtures, excepting those having integral traps, shall be separately trapped by a water-seal trap, placed as close to the fixture outlet as possible.

(a) Provided, that a combination plumbing fixture may be installed on one trap, if one compartment is not more than 6 inches deeper than the other and the waste outlets are not more than 30 inches apart.

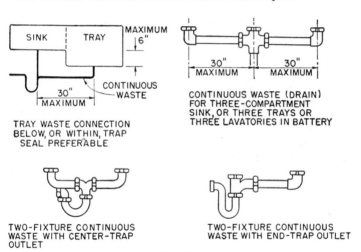

TRAY WASTE CONNECTION BELOW, OR WITHIN, TRAP SEAL PREFERABLE

CONTINUOUS WASTE (DRAIN) FOR THREE-COMPARTMENT SINK, OR THREE TRAYS OR THREE LAVATORIES IN BATTERY

TWO-FIXTURE CONTINUOUS WASTE WITH CENTER-TRAP OUTLET

TWO-FIXTURE CONTINUOUS WASTE WITH END-TRAP OUTLET

FIG. 5-1

▶ Figure 5-1 illustrates various types of continuous wastes that may be used when connecting a two- or three-compartment fixture. In the case of a two-compartment sink with a food-waste disposer under one compartment, it is best to use a directional fitting as shown on Fig. 5-2.

(b) Provided, that one trap may be installed for a set of not more than three single-compartment sinks or laundry trays or three lavatories immediately adjacent to each other in the same room, if the waste outlets are not more than

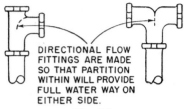

DIRECTIONAL FLOW
FITTINGS ARE MADE
SO THAT PARTITION
WITHIN WILL PROVIDE
FULL WATER WAY ON
EITHER SIDE.

Fig. 5-2

30 inches apart and the trap is centrally located when three compartments are installed.

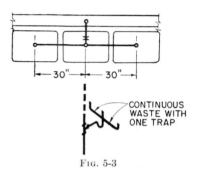

CONTINUOUS
WASTE WITH
ONE TRAP

Fig. 5-3

▶   A trap for each fixture eliminates odors which develop because of air circulation through a continuous waste.   Odors are caused by food particles, lint, soap, and other wastes which adhere to the sides of the pipe and putrefy.   Separate fixture traps also prevent backing up of waste into the lower compartment of a combination fixture when the compartments are of different depths, such as a sink and tray.

5.1.2   Distance of Trap to Fixture.   The vertical distance from the fixture outlet to the trap weir shall not exceed 24 inches.

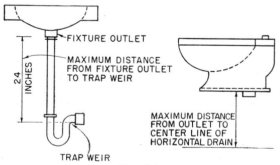

FIXTURE OUTLET

MAXIMUM DISTANCE
FROM FIXTURE OUTLET
TO TRAP WEIR

24 INCHES

TRAP WEIR

MAXIMUM DISTANCE
FROM OUTLET TO
CENTER LINE OF
HORIZONTAL DRAIN

Fig. 5-4

▶   The maximum length of 24 inches is advisable only to meet special conditions. The shorter the distance from the fixture outlet to the trap, the better the trap will function. A long tailpiece causes greater velocity, and excess velocity siphons the trap seal. When the distance from the fixture outlet to the trap weir needs to be more than 12 inches, increase the size of the fixture drain one pipe size in order to reduce the velocity through the trap and prevent siphonage of the trap seal.

The same principle applies to the distance from an integral fixture trap, as in a water closet, to the connection with a horizontal drain. A water closet, of course, is designed and constructed so that flushing will siphon its contents. This action also siphons its trap seal, but the trap seal is restored by the refill provided in the flush tank or in the flushometer. Actually there is no limitation of distance from the outlet of the water closet. The limitation applies to the distance from the trap to the vent. See Fig. 5–4.

5.2   Type and Size of Traps and Fixture Drains

5.2.1   Trap Size.   The size (nominal diameter) of trap for a given fixture shall be sufficient to drain the fixture rapidly but in no case less than given in Chap. 11, Table 11.4.2.

5.2.2   Relation to Fixture Drains.   No trap shall be larger than the fixture drain to which it is connected.

5.2.3   Type of Traps

(a) Fixture traps shall be self-cleaning other than integral traps without partitions or movable parts, except as specifically approved in other sections of this Code.

(b) Slip joints or couplings may be used on the trap inlet or within the trap seal of the trap if metal-to-metal ground joint is used.

(c) A trap integral with the fixture shall have a uniform interior and smooth waterway.

5.2.4   Drum Traps

(a) Drum traps shall be 3 or 4 inches in diameter and shall be provided with a water seal of not less than 2 inches.

(b) The trap screw shall be one size less than the trap diameter.

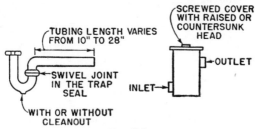

FIG. 5-5

▶ The National Plumbing Code as well as most modern local plumbing codes recommend the use of P traps and drum traps. See Fig. 5-5.

A number of other types of trap are on the market, but they are not used so commonly as the standard traps, either because they are more expensive or because they have some structural complications.

Properly designed antisiphon traps resist back pressure and self-siphonage more effectively than the standard P trap. But because they have interior partitions or movable parts, they are apt to clog sooner; or they become corroded and the partitions break down. As these accidents could happen without the knowledge of the owner, these traps are no assurance of safe operation.

The supposed advantage of the antisiphon trap is that its greater resistance to siphonage makes it possible to extend the drain line farther without venting than is advisable with a standard trap. Recent laboratory research has shown that correct design and correct balancing of the drainage system also make safe the installation of unvented drain lines, as recommended by the National Plumbing Code.

Other traps commonly used besides the standard P trap and drum trap are shown in Fig. 5-6.

SELDOM USED OR REQUIRED

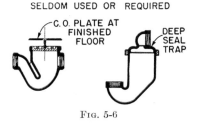

Fig. 5-6

5.3   General Requirements

5.3.1   Trap Seal.   Each fixture trap shall have a water seal of not less than 2 inches and not more than 4 inches, except where a deeper seal is found necessary by the administrative authority for special conditions.

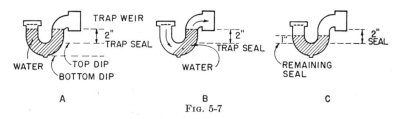

Fig. 5-7

▶ The plumbing system should be designed so that positive or negative pressures greater than 1 inch are not developed within the fixture drain.

Figure 5-7 illustrates what occurs when a trap is subjected to a negative pressure.

(*a*) The normal trap seal of the trap.

(*b*) A negative pressure siphons the trap seal.

(*c*) The pressure removed, the remaining trap seal returns to normal position less 1 inch which was siphoned.

When a 1-inch water seal remains in a 2-inch trap seal, a positive or negative pressure meets the same resistance offered by a 2-inch water seal. The remaining 1-inch water seal provides the same relative safeguard in preventing sewer gas or vermin passage as does a 2-inch water seal.

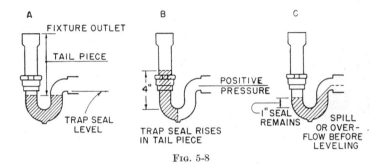

Fɪɢ. 5-8

Figure 5-8 illustrates what occurs when a trap is subjected to a positive pressure.

(*a*) The trap seal at normal level. When a positive pressure develops in the fixture drain, the seal is pushed upward toward the fixture outlet, creating a 4-inch water column as at *b*.

(*b*) When the pressure is removed suddenly, the column of water falls and some of the trap seal runs out through the drain as shown at *c*.

(*c*) If the pressure developed in the fixture drain is no greater than 1 inch, the seal loss will seldom be more than 1 inch. When a 1-inch seal remains in a trap, there is still sufficient water seal to protect the system against positive or negative pressure, not exceeding 2 inches.

5.3.2   Trap Cleanouts

(*a*) Each fixture trap, except those cast integral or in combination with fixtures in which the trap seal is readily accessible or except when a portion of the trap is readily removable for cleaning purposes, shall have an accessible brass trap screw of ample size protected by this water seal.

▶   Figure 5-9 illustrates a trap with a cleanout at the bottom and a trap which can readily be removed for cleaning.

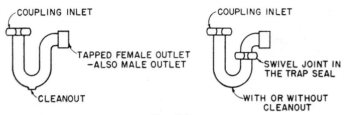

Fig. 5-9

    (b) Cleanouts on the seal of a trap shall be made tight with threaded cleanout plug and approved washer.

5.3.3   Trap Level and Protection.   Traps shall be set true with respect to their water seals and, where necessary, they shall be protected from freezing.

5.3.4   Traps Underground.   Underground traps, except P traps into which floor drains with removable strainers discharge, shall be provided with accessible and removable cleanouts.

5.3.5   Building (House) Traps

    (a) Each building trap, when installed, shall be provided with a cleanout and a relieving vent or fresh-air intake.

    (b) Relieving vents or fresh-air intakes need not be larger than half the diameter of the drain to which they connect.

    (c) Building (house) traps shall not be installed except where so required by the administrative authority, to accomplish the purpose of this Code.

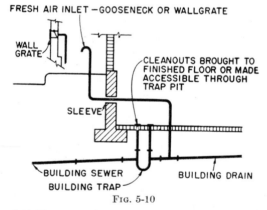

Fig. 5-10

▶   Figure 5-10 illustrates cleanouts brought up to grade unless they are located in an accessible pit.   A fresh-air inlet may be installed through the outside grate with a return bend such as a wall grate with a flap which prevents foul air from blowing out to the sidewalk or to the outside of the building.   The majority of local codes do not require a house trap.

5.3.6   Prohibited Traps

    (a) No trap which depends for its seal upon the action of movable parts shall be used.

(*b*) Full S traps are prohibited.

(*c*) Bell traps are prohibited.

(*d*) Crown-vented traps are prohibited.

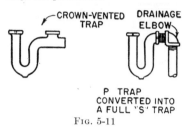

Fig. 5-11

▶ Figure 5-11 illustrates a crown-vented trap, also a P trap which is readily converted into an S trap.

5.3.7 Double Trapping. No fixture shall be double trapped

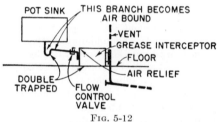

Fig. 5-12

▶ When a fixture is double trapped, it will become air bound and impair its operation. An example of double trapping often done is shown on Fig. 5-12.

5.4 Pipe Cleanouts

5.4.1 Location. Cleanouts shall be not more than 50 feet apart in horizontal drainage lines of 4-inch nominal diameter or less and not more than 100 feet apart for larger pipes.

5.4.2 Underground Drainage. Cleanouts, when installed on an underground drain, shall be extended to or above the finished grade level directly above the place where the cleanout is installed; or they may be extended to the outside of the building when found necessary by the administrative authority.

▶ In an underground drain the cleanout must be brought up to grade or to the finished floor. If a cleanout plug is located where there is traffic, the head should be countersunk to prevent accidents or breakage, or a recess in the floor must be provided.

Where it is impossible to extend the cleanout to grade or to the finished floor, the plumbing inspector may find it necessary to permit the extension

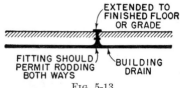

EXTENDED TO
FINISHED FLOOR
OR GRADE

FITTING SHOULD
PERMIT RODDING
BOTH WAYS

BUILDING
DRAIN

Fig. 5-13

of a dead-end pipe to the outside of the building wall, with a cleanout brought up to grade. This practice is permitted in some communities where a public sewer is very shallow. In a one-story building, it is more desirable to rod through the vent terminal at the roof than to install a long dead-end branch for a cleanout.

5.4.3 Change of Direction. Cleanouts shall be installed at each change of direction of the building drain greater than 45 degrees.

5.4.4 Concealed Piping. Cleanouts on concealed piping shall be extended through and terminate flush with the finished wall or floor; or pits or chases may be left in the wall or floor, provided they are of sufficient size to permit removal of the cleanout plug and effective cleaning of the system.

5.4.5 Base of Stacks. A cleanout shall be provided at or near the foot of each vertical waste or soil stack. For buildings with a floor slab on fill or ground or with less than 18-inch crawl space under the floor the following will be acceptable in lieu of a cleanout at the base of the stack: The building drain may be extended to the outside of the building and terminated in an accessible cleanout, or an accessible cleanout may be installed in the building drain downstream from the stack not more than 5 feet outside the building wall.

5.4.6 Building-drain Junction. There shall be a cleanout near the junction of the building drain and building sewer or a cleanout with wye branch inside the building wall.

5.4.7 Direction of Flow. Every cleanout shall be installed so that the cleanout opens in a direction opposite to the flow of the drainage line or at right angle thereto.

5.4.8 Cleanout plugs shall not be used for the installation of new fixtures or floor drains except where approved in writing by the administrative authority.

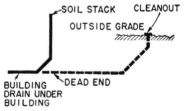

SOIL STACK   CLEANOUT

OUTSIDE GRADE

BUILDING
DRAIN UNDER
BUILDING

DEAD END

Fig. 5-14

▶   In an underground drain the cleanout must be brought up to grade or to the finished floor, as shown in Fig. 5-14. If a cleanout plug is located where there is traffic, the head should be countersunk to prevent accidents or breakage.

Where it is impossible to extend the cleanout to grade or to the finished floor, the plumbing inspector may find it necessary to permit the extension of a dead-end pipe to the outside of the building wall with a cleanout brought up to grade. This practice is permitted in some communities where a public sewer is very shallow. In a one-story building, it is more desirable to rod through the vent terminal at the roof than to install a long dead-end branch for a cleanout. See Fig. 5-14.

When the change of direction is 45 degrees or less, it is not necessary to provide a cleanout. When the change in direction is more than 45 degrees—for example, 90 degrees—a cleanout should be required. It is also necessary to make the change by means of 45-degree wyes and eighth bends. See Fig. 5-15.

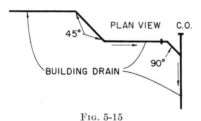

Fig. 5-15

If the cleanout cannot be extended, it can be made accessible by providing a plate as shown in Fig. 5-16. The plate *g* is held in place by a long screw *f*. The cleanout plug may be drilled and tapped to receive the long screw by using a raised-head plug *e*. Where it is necessary to conceal a cleanout plug, a covering plate or access door should be provided to permit ready access to the plug.

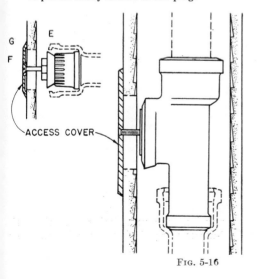
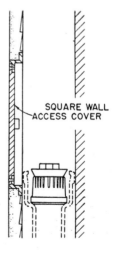

Fig. 5-16

Figure 5-17 illustrates two cleanouts: (*a*) raised hex-head cleanout and (*b*) flush slotted cleanout.

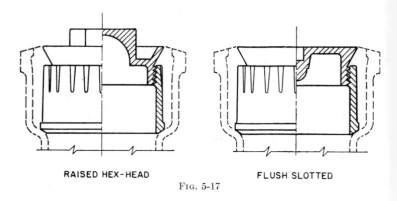

RAISED HEX-HEAD   FLUSH SLOTTED

Fig. 5-17

Figure 5-18 illustrates a cleanout with cutoff grooves and long lugs for adjustment to the plane of the floor and a round scoriated access cover.

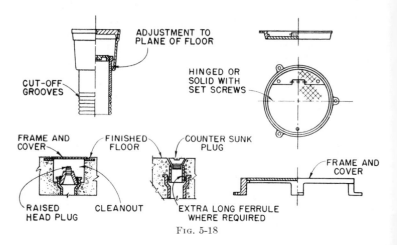

Fig. 5-18

5.5   Size of Cleanouts

5.5.1   Small Pipes. Cleanouts shall be of the same nominal size as the pipes up to 4 inches and not less than 4 inches for larger piping.

5.5.2   Large Pipes. For underground piping over 10 inches, manholes shall be provided and located at each 90-degree change in direction and at intervals of not more than 150 feet.

5.5.3   Covers. Metal covers shall be provided for manholes.

5.6 Cleanout Clearances

5.6.1 Large Pipes. Cleanouts on 3-inch or larger pipe shall be so installed that there is a clearance of not less than 18 inches for the purpose of rodding.

5.6.2 Small Pipes. Cleanouts smaller than 3 inches shall be so installed that there is a 12-inch clearance for rodding.

5.6.3 Calking. Cement, plaster, or any other permanent finishing material shall not be placed over a cleanout plug.

5.6.4 Concealment. Where it is necessary to conceal a cleanout plug, a covering plate or access door shall be provided which will permit ready access to the plug.

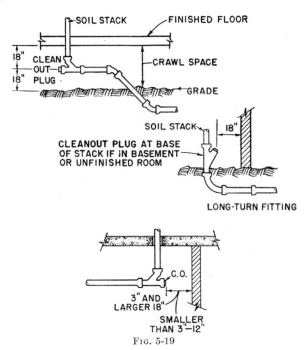

Fig. 5-19

▶   Figure 5-19 illustrates the clearance from the cleanout to the wall column or any other obstruction. There should be at least the same clearance vertically so that a mechanic may be able to work with the necessary tools.

5.7 Cleanout Equivalent

5.7.1 A fixture trap or a fixture with integral trap, readily removable without disturbing concealed roughing work, may be accepted as a cleanout equivalent, if there is no more than one 90-degree bend on the line to be rodded.

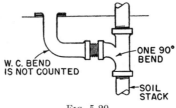

FIG. 5-20

▶   Figure 5-20 illustrates a cleanout equivalent.   In a one-story dwelling, a water-closet connection may be accepted as an accessible cleanout, also a sink or lavatory connection when the trap is readily removable.

5.8   Acidproof Traps

Where a vitrified-clay or other brittleware acidproof trap is installed underground, it shall be embedded in concrete to a thickness of 6 inches from the bottom and sides of the trap.

▶   This requirement does not apply to an acidproof metal trap or a trap made of material that will withstand shock or severe use.

CHAPTER 6

Interceptors—Separators and Backwater Valves

6.1 Interceptors and Separators

6.1.1 When Required. Interceptors (including grease, oil, and sand interceptors, etc.) shall be provided when, in the judgment of the administrative authority, they are necessary for the proper handling of liquid wastes containing grease, flammable wastes, sand, and other ingredients harmful to the building drainage system, the public sewer, or sewage-treatment plant or processes.

6.1.2 Approval. The size, type, and location of each interceptor or separator shall be approved by the administrative authority in accordance with generally accepted standards, and no wastes other than those requiring treatment or separation shall be discharged into any interceptor.

6.1.3 Separation. A mixture of light and heavy solids or liquids and solids having various specific gravities may be treated and then separated in an interceptor as approved by the administrative authority in accordance with paragraph 6.1.2.

▶ See Part III for data on the sizing of traps and on efficiency tests.

6.2 Grease Interceptors

6.2.1 Commercial Buildings. A grease interceptor shall be installed in the waste line leading from sinks, drains, or other fixtures in the following establishments when, in the judgment of the administrative authority, a hazard exists: restaurants, hotel kitchens or bars, factory cafeterias or restaurants, clubs, or other establishments where grease can be introduced into the drainage system in quantities that can effect line stoppage or hinder sewage disposal.

6.2.2 Residential Units. A grease interceptor is not required for individual dwelling units or any private living quarters.

▶ In a private home there would seldom be sufficient grease discharged to require mandatory installation of a grease interceptor.

The primary purpose of a grease interceptor is to assure free-flowing drainage through pipe lines at all times by intercepting, separating, accumulating, and recovering grease from the waste lines. The most positive and the simplest means of doing this in a grease interceptor is by employing the principle of flotation. The first essential in the operation of this principle is the elimination of excessive turbulence of the incoming waste. This is accomplished by correctly designed baffles which act to retard the flow, thus allowing the grease to separate from the liquid and rise to the surface, where it may be skimmed and removed.

A grease interceptor designed to separate grease globules from waste water does not, generally of itself, govern or regulate the flow of liquid through it at all times sufficiently to assure the separation, recovery, and retention of the maximum volume of grease. The flow-control fitting is utilized to distribute properly the discharge of waste liquid from one or more fixtures into the grease interceptor. (See official publication of the Plumbing and Drainage Institute describing testing and rating procedures for grease interceptors—Form PDI-G 101. Complimentary copies are available to architects, engineers, plumbing contractors, and plumbing inspectors.)

Figure 6-1 illustrates two widely used grease interceptors.

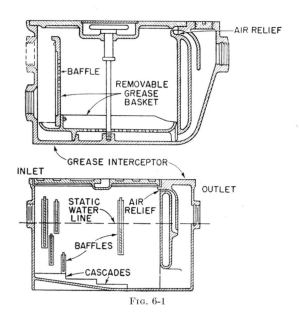

Fig. 6-1

6.3   Oil Separators

6.3.1   An oil separator shall be installed in the drainage system or section of the system where, in the judgment of the administrative authority, a hazard exists or where oils or other flammables can be introduced or admitted into the drainage system by accident or otherwise.

.4 Sand Interceptors

.4.1 Commercial Installations. Sand and similar interceptors for heavy
olids shall be so designed and located as to be readily accessible for cleaning and
hall have a water seal of not less than 6 inches.

.5 Venting Interceptors

.5.1 Relief Vent. Interceptors shall be so designed that they will not
become air bound if closed covers are used.   Each interceptor shall be properly
vented.

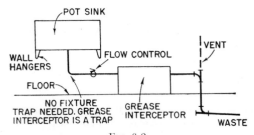

Fig. 6-2

Interceptors should have tight covers, readily removable for cleaning
and maintenance. The interceptor should be designed so as not to
become air bound; otherwise its contents might be siphoned.

Figure 6-2 illustrates a simple installation for a pot sink in a restaurant.

There is no advantage or need to provide a sink trap when the sink is
connected to a grease interceptor. The interceptor is a trap and will
prevent sewer gases from entering the house. A back vent is necessary
to prevent siphonage of its contents.

6.6 Accessibility of Interceptor

6.6.1   Each interceptor shall be so installed as to provide ready accessibility to
the cover and means for servicing and maintaining the interceptor in working
and operating condition.   The use of ladders or the removal of bulky equipment in order to service interceptors shall constitute a violation of accessibility.

6.7 Interceptor's Efficiency

6.7.1 Flow Rate. Interceptors shall be rated and approved for their efficiency as determined by the administrative authority and in accordance with
generally accepted practice.

6.7.2 Approval. No grease interceptor shall be approved until it has successfully passed the testing and rating procedure set up by the administrative
authority.

6.7.3 Water Connection. Water connection for cooling or operating an
interceptor shall be such that backflow cannot occur.

▶   Most interceptors are rated by their efficiency in separating and retaining grease discharged from a sink, dishwashing machine, or other equipment which discharges liquids and grease. The rating procedure used
by most manufacturers and required by most plumbing codes will be
found in Part III.

        Water-cooled or water-jacketed interceptors have been prohibited in
most codes because of the possibility of water contamination. A jacket
separating the waste water and the potable-water supply can readily be
fractured or corroded, permitting the waste water to contaminate the
building-supply water.

6.8 Laundries

6.8.1 Interceptors. Commercial laundries shall be equipped with an interceptor having a removable wire basket or similar device that will prevent strings,
rags, buttons, or other materials detrimental to the public sewerage system from
passing into the drainage system.

6.8.2 Intercepting Device. Basket or device shall prevent passage into the
drainage system of solids ½ inch or larger in size. The basket or device shall
be removable for cleaning purposes.

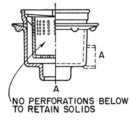
NO PERFORATIONS BELOW
TO RETAIN SOLIDS

A= SIZE—THREADED OR CAULK
BOTTOM OR SIDE OUTLET

DOME TOP TO PERMIT
FLOW WHEN DEBRIS
ACCUMULATES AT BASE
OF DRAIN

Fig. 6-3

▶   Figure **6-3** illustrates large laundry-basket drains which are installed
in a trough receiving the discharge from large laundry equipment and
which prevent clothing, rags, and other material from entering the plumbing
lines and causing stoppages. Some drains are equipped with a dome
strainer, offering less chance of debris stopping the openings and causing
floods.

6.9   Bottling Establishments

6.9.1   Bottling Plants.   Bottling plants shall discharge their process wastes into an interceptor which will provide for the separation of broken glass or other solids, before discharging liquid wastes into the drainage system.

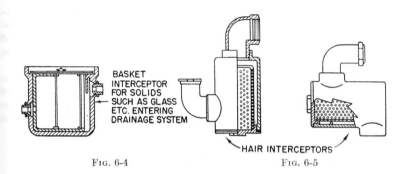

BASKET INTERCEPTOR FOR SOLIDS SUCH AS GLASS ETC. ENTERING DRAINAGE SYSTEM

HAIR INTERCEPTORS

FIG. 6-4   FIG. 6-5

▶   Basket drains similar to the type shown in Fig. 6-4 are often used to prevent broken glass from entering the sewage system.

In the case of plaster, as in a dental laboratory or doctor's office, plaster separators are recommended.

Typical hair interceptors are shown in Fig. 6-5.

6.10   Slaughterhouses

6.10.1   Separators.   Slaughtering-room drains shall be equipped with separators which shall prevent the discharge into the drainage system of feathers, entrails, and other materials likely to clog the drainage system.

6.10.2   Interceptors.   Slaughtering- and dressing-room drains shall be provided with interceptors approved by the administrative authority, in accordance with paragraph 6.1.2.

6.10.3   Food Grinder.   Wastes may discharge directly to the building drainage system.

6.11   Commercial Grinders

6.11.1   Discharge.   Where commercial food-waste grinders are installed, the waste from those units may discharge direct into the building drainage system and not through a grease interceptor.

6.11.2   Approval.   The administrative authority shall determine where and what type of interceptor is necessary, except that interceptors shall not be required for private living quarters or residential units.

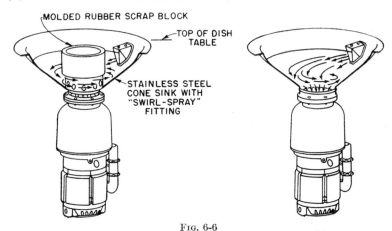

MOLDED RUBBER SCRAP BLOCK

TOP OF DISH TABLE

STAINLESS STEEL CONE SINK WITH "SWIRL-SPRAY" FITTING

Fig. 6-6

► Commercial grinders are commonly used for the disposal of slaughter-house wastes, such as waste meat, bones, entrails, eggshells, and similar wastes. These machines are placed at the points where the waste is produced, thereby eliminating the need of storing and carting it away. Commercial grinders are capable of disposing of 300 to 2,000 pounds of waste material per hour.

Figure 6-6 illustrates some commercial grinders.

6.12 Maintenance

6.12.1 Cleaning. Interceptors shall be maintained in efficient operating condition by periodic removal of accumulated grease.

6.13 Oil Interceptors

6.13.1 Where Required. Oil separators shall be installed when required by the administrative authority and shall conform to the requirements of paragraph 6.13.2.

6.13.2 Minimum Dimension. Oil separators shall have a depth of not less than 2 feet below the invert of the discharge drain.

6.13.3 Motor-vehicle Storage. Interceptors shall have a capacity of 6 cubic feet where not more than 3 vehicles are serviced, and 1 cubic foot in net capacity shall be added for each additional vehicle up to 10 vehicles. Where more than 10 vehicles are serviced, the administrative authority shall determine the size of separator required.

6.13.4 Motor-vehicle Servicing. Where storage facilities are not maintained, as in repair shops, the capacity of the separator shall be based on a net capacity of 1 cubic foot for each 100 square feet of surface to be drained into the interceptor, with a minimum capacity of 6 cubic feet.

6.13.5   Special-type Separators.   Before installing any special-type separator a drawing including all pertinent information shall be submitted for approval of the administrative authority, as being in accordance with this Code.

6.14   Backwater Valves

6.14.1   Fixtures Subject to Backflow.   The installation of backwater devices shall be in accordance with lawful requirements of the administrative authority having jurisdiction over the public sewer system.

6.14.2   Fixture Branches.   Backwater valves shall be installed in the branch of the building drain which receives only the discharge from fixtures located within such branch and below grade.

6.14.3   Material.   All bearing parts of backwater valves shall be of corrosion-resistant material.

6.14.4   Backwater valves shall be so constructed as to ensure a mechanical seal against backflow.

6.14.5   Diameter.   Backwater valves, when fully opened, shall have a capacity not less than that of the pipes in which they are installed.

6.14.6   Location.   Backwater valves shall be so installed as to provide ready accessibility to their working parts.

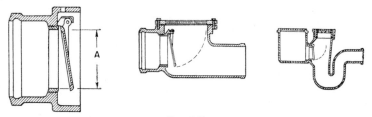

Fig. 6-7

▶   Figure 6-7 illustrates several types of backwater valves.   Opening *A* must be equal to the area of the pipe.   The trap seal must be at least **2** inches.

A backwater valve should be installed on the branch receiving the discharge of fixtures or other equipment located on the branch, as indicated in Fig. 6-8.

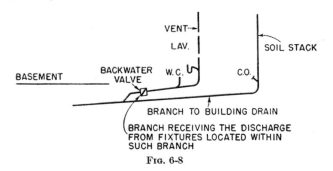

Fig. 6-8

CHAPTER 7

Plumbing Fixtures

7.1 General Requirements—Materials

7.1.1 Quality of Fixtures. Plumbing fixtures shall have smooth impervious surfaces, be free from defects and concealed fouling surfaces, and, except as permitted elsewhere in this Code, shall conform in quality and design to one of the following standards:

Staple Porcelain Plumbing Fixtures, NBS Commercial Standard CS 4-29.

Staple Vitreous China Plumbing Fixtures, NBS Commercial Standard CS 20-49.

Enameled Cast-iron Plumbing Fixtures, NBS Commercial Standard CS 77-48.

Earthenware (vitreous glazed) Plumbing Fixtures, NBS Commercial Standard CS 111-43.

Plumbing Fixtures (for) Land Use, F.S. WW-P-541b-1955.

Formed Steel Enameled Sanitary Ware, F.S. WW-P-542.

Formed Metal Porcelain Enameled Sanitary Ware, NBS Commercial Standard CS 144-47.

Hospital Plumbing Fixtures, NBS Simplified Practice Recommendation R 106-41.

Plumbing Fixtures, Fittings, Trim, R 227-47.

Lavatory and Sink Traps, R 21-46.

▶ **Manufacturers of plumbing fixtures voluntarily meet the foregoing commercial standards and specifications. Commercial standards are not mandatory upon any manufacturer, inasmuch as these standards are established voluntarily by a group of manufacturers producing similar commodities. However, the member organizations guarantee that their products conform with the requirements of the standard. The government in assisting manufacturers to develop commercial standards does so only as an unbiased coordinator of the various manufacturers, advises manufacturers as to method of procedure, provides a record of the meetings and maintains a record of acceptances of the standard, and publishes the completed standard for guidance of the buyers and sellers of the particular items. Standards and specifications are obtainable from the Superintendent of Documents, U.S. Government Printing Office, Washington 25, D.C.**

7.2   Alternate Materials

7.2.1   Materials. Sinks and special-use fixtures may be made of soapstone, chemical stoneware, or may be lined with lead, copper-base alloy, nickel-copper alloy, corrosion-resisting steel, or other materials especially suited to the use for which the fixture is intended.

▶   Special fixtures are those required for laboratory use, printing establishments, and other processing establishments where corrosion-resistant special fixtures are to be used. It is, however, essential that such fixtures be approved by the administrative authority in order to prevent unsanitary conditions.

7.3   Overflows

7.3.1   Design. When any fixture is provided with an overflow, the waste shall be so arranged that the standing water in the fixture cannot rise in the overflow when the stopper is closed or remain in the overflow when the fixture is empty.

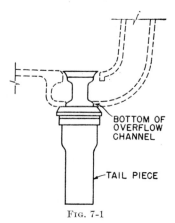

BOTTOM OF OVERFLOW CHANNEL

TAIL PIECE

Fig. 7-1

▶   Figure 7-1 illustrates the requirement of paragraph 7.3.1, showing that the bottom edge of the overflow opening in the plug is level below the bottom of the overflow channel, so that water cannot be trapped at the point shown by the arrow.

7.3.2   Connection. The overflow pipe from a fixture shall be connected on the house or inlet side of the fixture trap, except that overflows or flush tanks may discharge into the water closets or urinals served by them, but it shall be unlawful to connect such overflows with any other part of the drainage system.

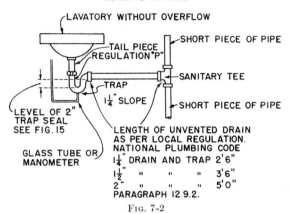

FIG. 7-2

▶ An overflow in a lavatory is a protection against self-siphonage of the trap seal. A current trend is toward lavatories without overflows. Eliminating the overflow eliminates the source of odors and lessens the cleaning chore. When lavatories without overflows are planned for installation, it is necessary to guard against siphonage of the trap seal by slowing down the discharge through the outlet. Loss of the trap seal permits sewer odors and vermin to enter the bathroom.

Flat-bottom lavatories are less likely to induce trap siphonage than round-bowl lavatories. Like a flat-bottom sink or bathtub, a flat-bottom lavatory, after draining, is left with a residue of water which drains slowly into the trap, restoring its water seal.

The following test for self-siphonage of lavatories may be used by anyone desirous of checking performance.

Install the lavatory in the normal position with a $1\frac{1}{4}$-inch drain-plug tailpiece and a P trap connected to a $1\frac{1}{4}$-inch drain line. The drain should slope $\frac{1}{4}$ inch per foot and connect into a sanitary tee. Install small sections of pipe at the top and bottom of the sanitary tee. The length of the drain from the trap weir to the vent should be in accordance with local requirements. (The National Plumbing Code permits a 2-foot 6-inch unvented drain pipe.) Fill the lavatory with water, then discharge by pulling the stopper or opening the pop-up fully. Repeat the test ten times. Observe the trap seal through a manometer or glass tube installed at the trap cleanout, as shown in Fig. 7-2. If any of the ten tests shows a trap-seal loss of more than 1 inch, the lavatory is considered as not meeting the test.

7.4 Installation

7.4.1 Cleaning. Plumbing fixtures shall be installed in a manner to afford easy access for cleaning. Where practical, all pipes from fixtures shall be run to the nearest wall.

▶   Floors and walls for toilets, bathrooms, kitchens, or wherever plumbing fixtures are installed should be of impervious materials that are easily washed. The space between the fixture and the wall should be closely fitted and pointed so that there is no chance for dirt or vermin to collect. In public toilet rooms, fixtures roughed and installed above the floor provide the most sanitary condition. Plumbing fixtures are generally constructed from impervious materials and have smooth surfaces so that soap and water would be all that are needed to produce a clean lustrous surface.

7.4.2   Joints. Where fixture comes in contact with wall and floors, the joint shall be watertight.

7.4.3   Securing Fixtures. Floor-outlet fixtures shall be rigidly secured to the floor by screws or bolts.

7.4.4   Wall-hung Bowls. Wall-hung water-closet bowls shall be rigidly supported by a concealed metal supporting member so that no strain is transmitted to the closet connection.

7.4.5   Setting. Fixtures shall be set level and in proper alignment with reference to adjacent walls. (See paragraph 4.6.1.)

▶   Figure **7-3** illustrates the surfaces in contact with walls or the floor to be pointed so that water cannot penetrate the edge. Likewise, floor or wall fixtures must be so bolted or attached as to make a gastight connection.

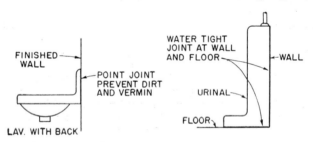

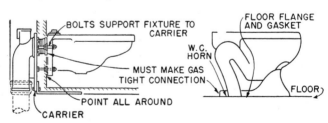

Fɪɢ. 7-3

7.5   Water-supply Protection

7.5.1   Supply Fittings. The supply lines or fittings for every plumbing fixture shall be so installed as to prevent backflow. (See paragraph 10.4.3.)

▶ Paragraph **10.4.3** refers to American Standards Association requirements for air gaps and vacuum breakers. Complete technical data are given and illustrations shown in Part III.

7.6 Prohibited Fixtures and Connections

7.6.1 Fixtures. Pan, valve, plunger, offset, washout, latrine, frostproof, and other water closets having an invisible seal or an unventilated space or having walls which are not thoroughly washed at each discharge are prohibited. Any water closet which might permit siphonage of the contents of the bowl back into the tank is prohibited.

7.6.2 Connections. Fixtures having concealed slip-joint connections shall be provided with an access panel or utility space so arranged as to make the slip connections accessible for inspection and repair.

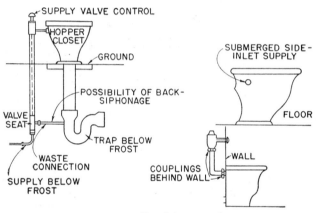

FIG. 7-4

▶ Figure 7-4 illustrates some of the prohibited fixtures and connections described in paragraphs **7.6.1** and **7.6.2**. Fixtures of this type are sometimes installed in rural areas where health authorities have no control. Most fixture manufacturers do not make these fixtures.

7.7 Water Closets

7.7.1 Public Use. Water-closet bowls for public use shall be of the elongated type.

7.7.2 Flushing Device. Water-closet tanks shall have a flushing capacity sufficient to properly flush the water-closet bowls with which they are connected.

7.7.3 Float Valves. Float valves in low-down tanks shall close tight and provide water to properly refill the trap seal in the bowl.

7.7.4 Close-coupled Tanks. The flush-valve seat in close-coupled water-closet combinations shall be 1 inch or more above the rim of the bowl, so that the flush valve will close even if the closet trapway is clogged; or any closets with flush-valve seats below the rim of the bowl shall be so constructed that, in case of trap stoppage, water will not flow continuously over the rim of the bowl.

7.7.5 Automatic Flush Valve. Flushometers shall be so installed that they will be readily accessible for repairing. When the valve is operated, it shall complete the cycle of operation automatically, opening fully and closing positively under the service pressure. At each operation the valve shall deliver water in sufficient volume and at a rate that will thoroughly flush the fixtures and refill the fixture trap. Means shall be provided for regulating the flush-valve flow. Not more than one fixture shall be served by a single flush valve. Protection against backflow shall be provided as specified in paragraph 10.4.3.

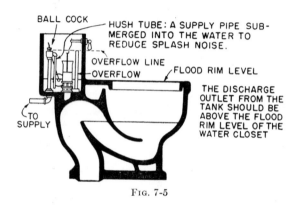

FIG. 7-5

▶   Figure 7-5 illustrates a close-coupled tank meeting the requirements of paragraph 7.7.4. Submerged ball caps in a water-closet tank must be provided with vacuum breakers or be so designed that a positive air gap exists between the contents of the tank and the water-supply inlet. It is further desirable that the supply pipe generally installed in a tank through the bottom be separated from the water contents of the tank so as to preclude any possibility of contaminating the potable-water system.

7.7.6 Seats. Water closets shall be equipped with seats of smooth non-absorbent material. All seats of water closets provided for public use shall be of the open-front type. Integral water-closet seats shall be of the same material as the fixture.

▶   Figure 7-6 illustrates a few of the seats generally acceptable for public and industrial use.

The main objectives are that the seats are open front, elongated, nonabsorbent, have a smooth surface, no sharp edges, no crevices or corners where dirt may accumulate on the hinges or seat, and are of a noncombustible material.

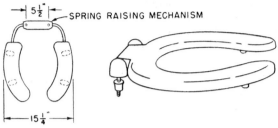

FIG. 7-6

7.8   Urinals

7.8.1   Automatic Flushing Tank.   Tanks flushing more than one urinal shall be automatic in operation and of sufficient capacity to provide the necessary volume to flush and properly cleanse all urinals simultaneously.

▶   **The objection to automatic flushing tanks is that the water usage is very high; therefore automatic flushing tanks should be considered only where they will be used temporarily.**

7.8.2   Urinals Equipped with Automatic Flush Valves.   Flushometers shall be as prescribed in paragraph 7.7.5, and no valve shall be used to flush more than one urinal.

▶   **The objection to using one flushometer for more than one urinal is the possibility that the urinals will not be flushed at all for a long time.   By providing individual flushometers, there is a good chance that they will be individually flushed during or after use.**

7.8.3   Trough Urinals.   Trough urinals shall be permitted only in places of temporary occupancy.   They shall be not less than 6 inches deep and shall be furnished with one-piece backs and have strainers with outlets at least 1½ inches in diameter.   The washdown pipe shall be perforated so as to flush with an even curtain of water against the back of the urinal.   This pipe shall be securely clamped as high as practicable to the back of the urinal.   Trough urinals shall have tanks with a flushing capacity of not less than 1½ gallons of water for each 2 feet of urinal length.

7.8.4   Equivalent Length.   Trough urinals shall be figured on the basis of one urinal for each 18 inches of length, provided that

24-inch trough equals 1 urinal
36-inch trough equals 2 urinals
48-inch trough equals 2 urinals
60-inch trough equals 3 urinals
72-inch trough equals 4 urinals

7.8.5   Floor-type Urinals.   Floor-type trough urinals are prohibited.

7.8.6   Surrounding Materials.   Wall and floor space to a point 1 foot in front of urinal lip and 4 feet above the floor and, at least, 1 foot to each side of the urinal shall be lined with nonabsorbent material.

▶   Trough urinals are recommended only for temporary use during construction. The equivalent lengths are indicated only to compute occupancy. The following is a generally accepted guide:

Temporary workingmen facilities—one water closet and urinal for each **30** workmen.

7.9   Strainers and Fixture Outlets

7.9.1   All plumbing fixtures, other than water closets and siphon-action washdown or blowout urinals, shall be provided with metal strainers having waterway area complying with paragraph **7.1.1.**

7.10   Lavatories

7.10.1   Waste Outlets.   Lavatories shall have waste outlets not less than $1\frac{1}{4}$ inches in diameter. Wastes may have open strainers or may be provided with stoppers.

7.11   Shower Receptors and Compartments

7.11.1   Shower.   All shower compartments, except those built directly on the ground or those having metal-enameled receptors, shall have a lead or copper shower pan or the equivalent thereof or as determined by the administrative authority. The pan shall turn up on all sides at least 2 inches above finished floor level. Traps shall be so constructed that the pan may be securely fastened to the trap at the seepage entrance, making a watertight joint between the pan and trap. Shower-receptacle waste outlets shall be not less than 2 inches in diameter and have removable strainers.

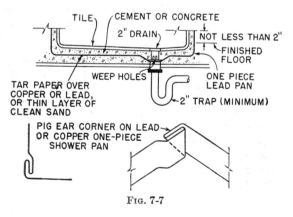

Fig. 7-7

The relationship of lavatory and sink outlets and the load imposed upon the plumbing system is worth considering in the design and the pipe sizing of a job. Information based on research will be found in Part III.

Figure 7-7 illustrates the method most commonly used when fabricating a shower pan from sheet lead. The lightest weight recommended for shower pans is 4 pounds per square foot; when sheet copper is used, it should not be less than 12 ounces per square foot.

Shower-stall floors should be completely lined with a 4-pound sheet-lead or 12-ounce sheet-copper pan and be turned up all around the walls at least 6 inches.

The corners of the lead pan should be folded tightly against the upstands and the tops soldered to prevent capillary action of water working itself onto the outside or into adjoining construction.

Where seams are necessary to joint large sheet-lead pans, the sheets should be lapped at least $\frac{1}{2}$ inch in the direction of flow to avoid pockets. Coat the lead on both sides with asphaltum compound. When there are wood floors under a lead pan, nailheads should be set and a layer of 15 pounds per square foot asphaltum-impregnated building paper placed between the wood and lead. A cement and clean sand mixture should be used inside the pan as a foundation for a tile floor.

Figure 7-8 illustrates a prefabricated shower compartment which is included within the scope of paragraph 7.11.1. It should have a leakproof receptor, and its finished surfaces and partitions should be impervious to water, soap, and body acids. The entire assembled shower compartment should be watertight, rigid, and easy to clean. The receptor should pitch sufficiently to drain completely, yet minimize slipping. It should be made of materials such as precast stone, cement aggregates, preformed metal, or other materials of similar qualities. The surfaces should be of smooth, nonabsorbent materials and without sharp corners. Vitreous porcelain may be considered a satisfactory finish. Paint or other finish that might peel is not considered sanitary.

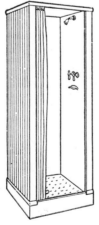

FIG. 7-8

7.11.2   On the Ground.   Shower receptors built on the ground shall be constructed from dense nonabsorbent and noncorrosive materials and shall have smooth impervious surfaces, or as provided in paragraph 7.11.1.

7.11.3   Dimensions.   Shower compartments shall have not less than 1,024 square inches in floor area and, if rectangular, square, or triangular in plan, shall be not less than 30 inches in shortest dimension.

▶   **The floor area recommended is the minimum for comfortable use by an adult bather.**

7.11.4   Construction.   Floors under shower compartments shall be laid on a smooth and structurally sound base and shall be lined and made watertight with sheet lead, copper, or other acceptable materials.   Shower compartments located in basements, cellars, or in other rooms in which the floor has been laid directly on the ground surface need not be lined.

7.11.5   Public or Institution Showers.   Floors of public shower rooms shall be drained in such a manner that no waste water from any head will pass over areas occupied by other bathers.

7.11.6   Walls.   Shower compartments shall have walls constructed of smooth, noncorrosive, and nonabsorbent waterproof materials to a height of not less than 6 feet above the floor.

7.11.7   Joints.   Built-in tubs with overhead showers shall have waterproof joints between the tub and walls, and the walls shall be waterproof.

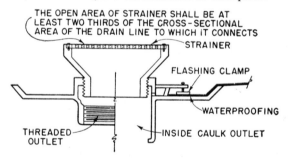

THE OPEN AREA OF STRAINER SHALL BE AT LEAST TWO THIRDS OF THE CROSS-SECTIONAL AREA OF THE DRAIN LINE TO WHICH IT CONNECTS

STRAINER

FLASHING CLAMP

WATERPROOFING

THREADED OUTLET

INSIDE CAULK OUTLET

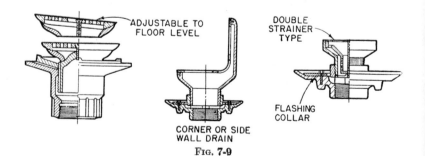

ADJUSTABLE TO FLOOR LEVEL

DOUBLE STRAINER TYPE

FLASHING COLLAR

CORNER OR SIDE WALL DRAIN

Fig. 7-9

▶ Figure 7-9 illustrates several types of shower drains for different conditions.

7.12 Sinks

7.12.1 Waste Outlets. Sinks shall be provided with waste outlets not less than 1½ inches in diameter. Waste outlets may have open strainers or may be provided with stoppers.

7.12.2 Food Grinders. Sinks on which a food-waste grinder is installed shall have a waste opening not less than 3½ inches in diameter.

▶ Most sinks today are manufactured to receive a basket strainer or a food-waste grinder; therefore a 3½-inch waste opening is commonly furnished. Figure 7-10 illustrates a basket strainer.

Fɪɢ. 7-10

7.13 Food-waste-grinder Units

7.13.1 Separate Connections. Domestic food-waste-disposal units may be connected and trapped separately from any other fixture or compartment.

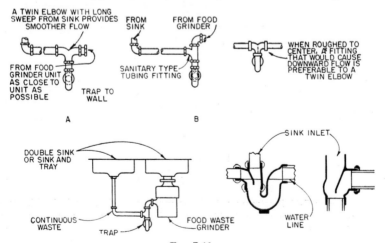

Fɪɢ. 7-11

Units may have either automatic or hand-operated water-supply control. (See Sec. 10.4.)

▶   Domestic food-waste-disposal units have been found to operate satisfactorily with a single trap receiving the discharge from both the sink compartment and food-waste-grinder compartment, provided a directional fitting is installed.   Figure 7-11 illustrates the installation.

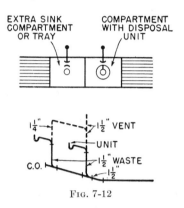

Fig. 7-12

Figure 7-12 illustrates the installation of a food-waste grinder when it is placed in a two-compartment sink.   Each compartment is separately trapped and vented.   This arrangement is believed to provide the most efficient method of installation.   A cleanout is desirable at the change of direction, and it may be placed either on the horizontal or on the vertical branch.

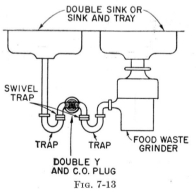

Fig. 7-13

Figure 7-13 illustrates a double-compartment sink roughed with separate traps into a center double wye.   This arrangement is not uncommon in alteration work as a means of avoiding costly reroughing.   Old piping should be carefully rodded and cleaned.

In multistory buildings, waste lines receiving the discharge of sinks equipped with food-waste grinders should be independent of any bathroom-fixture connection.

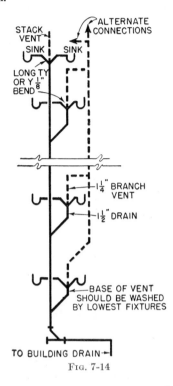

Fɪɢ. 7-14

Figure 7-14 illustrates a multistory-building installation of two sinks back to back, each sink provided with a food-waste grinder. Assuming that this is a six-story building with a total of 36 fixture units at the base of the stack, Table 11.5.3 prescribes a 2½-inch waste stack and a 2-inch vent stack. When two grinders are thus installed, use a long-turn tee-wye or a combination wye fitting and an eighth bend. This minimizes the possibility of pumping the discharge from one grinder into the adjoining grinder. It also permits more effective rodding of the branch and vertical waste lines.

When a single grinder is installed, a sanitary tee is satisfactory. Connect the lowest-floor unit or sink into the base of the vent stack, so that the lowest unit will keep the vent line clear.

Installations of food grinders into existing roughing usually are more troublesome than new installations. Old piping must be either thoroughly cleaned or replaced. The piping *must* be in good, clean condition. Otherwise it will cause unnecessary stoppages and additional expense.

Dishwashing machines are often installed alongside a kitchen sink which contains a food-waste-disposal unit. Most manufacturers of food-waste grinders provide a connection on the side of the grinder for connecting to a dishwashing machine. See Fig. 7-15.

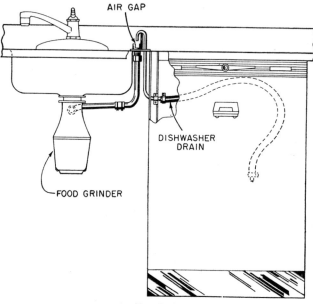

Fig. 7-15

When a pump-discharge-type dishwashing machine is connected to the side of the waste grinder or to the house side of a trap from a sink, the discharge from the dishwashing machine must flow through an air gap into the drain as shown.

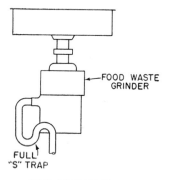

VIEW FROM REAR

Fig. 7-16

Figure 7-16 illustrates an installation of a grinder discharging into a full S trap. This would cause a siphonic action and siphon the trap seal at the end of the grinder's operation. The trap seal is sometimes partly replaced by the remaining water within the unit but not always sufficiently to make a tight seal within the trap.

7.13.2 Grease Interceptors. No food-waste grinder shall be connected through a grease interceptor.

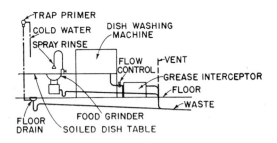

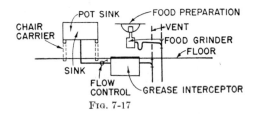

Fig. 7-17

► Figure 7-17 illustrates a method of connecting a food grinder when a grease interceptor is also required for a large dishwasher or kitchen-pot sink.

7.13.3 Commercial-type Grinders. Commercial-type food grinders shall be provided with not less than a 2-inch waste line. Each waste line shall be trapped and vented as provided in other sections of this Code.

► Commercial grinders are extensively used in restaurants and hotel kitchens, hospitals, drugstores, bars, food markets, processing plants, sculleries aboard ships, railroad dining cars, and many other places where food is prepared or processed. These grinders dispose of food waste at its source, thereby doing away with the need of storage cans, transporting containers to disposal points, or keeping the food waste in refrigerators until collected for disposal. Commercial size food-waste grinders can handle as much as 2,000 pounds of ground food per hour. These machines, when placed at the point where the waste is to be disposed of directly into the sewer, eliminate possible unsanitary conditions.

Referring to Fig. 7-18, unit *a* is generally installed ahead of a dishwashing machine for the purpose of prerinsing soiled dishes.

Unit *b* shows the water discharging into the cone for washing down all leftover food.

Unit *c* shows a rubber block used for scraping dishes, the rubber surface protecting dishes from breakage.

Unit *d* shows a large industrial machine to grind large quantities of waste food quickly and efficiently.   This type unit is used in large produce markets and institutions where 1,500 or 2,000 pounds of waste is disposed of per hour, eliminating the need of storage and labor for handling the disposal of the garbage.

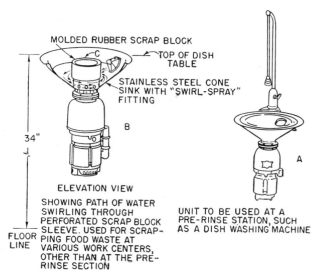

MOLDED RUBBER SCRAP BLOCK

C — TOP OF DISH TABLE

STAINLESS STEEL CONE SINK WITH "SWIRL-SPRAY" FITTING

B

34"

ELEVATION VIEW

SHOWING PATH OF WATER SWIRLING THROUGH PERFORATED SCRAP BLOCK SLEEVE. USED FOR SCRAPING FOOD WASTE AT VARIOUS WORK CENTERS, OTHER THAN AT THE PRERINSE SECTION

FLOOR LINE

A

UNIT TO BE USED AT A PRE-RINSE STATION, SUCH AS A DISH WASHING MACHINE

FIG. 7-18

7.14   Drinking Fountains

7.14.1   Design and Construction.   Drinking fountains shall conform to American Standard Specifications for Drinking Fountains (ASA Z4.2-1942).

7.14.2   Protection of Water Supply.   Stream projectors shall be so assembled as to provide an orifice elevation as specified by American Standard Air Gaps in Plumbing Systems (ASA A40.4-1942) and American Standard Backflow Preventers in Plumbing Systems (ASA A40.6-1943).

▶   A drinking fountain should have a stream projector that cannot be flooded or submerged in the event of stoppage and should be so directed and protected that it cannot be contaminated by the user.   See Fig. 7-19.

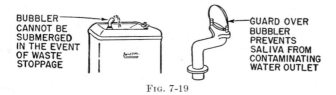

BUBBLER CANNOT BE SUBMERGED IN THE EVENT OF WASTE STOPPAGE

GUARD OVER BUBBLER PREVENTS SALIVA FROM CONTAMINATING WATER OUTLET

FIG. 7-19

7.15   Floor Drains

7.15.1   Trap and Strainers.   Floor drains shall have metal traps and a minimum water seal of 3 inches and shall be provided with removable strainers. The open area of strainer shall be at least two-thirds of the cross-section area of the drain line to which it connects.

7.15.2   Size.   Floor drains shall be of a size to serve efficiently the purpose for which they are intended.

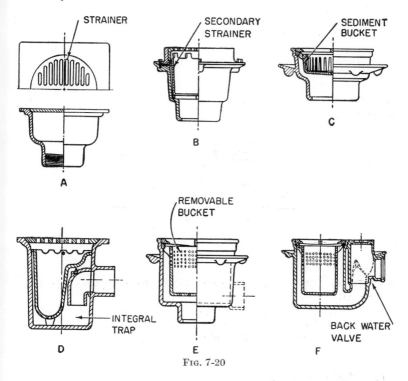

FIG. 7-20

▶   Whether or not drains have separate or integral traps, the requirements are the same.   Figure 7-20 illustrates various types of floor drains produced by most manufacturers.

(a) Strainers for all types of drains should be at least two-thirds of the area of the pipe to which the strainer is connected.

(b) A heavy type drain with secondary strainer.

(c) Drain with a sediment bucket where solids accumulate without impeding the flow.

(d) Drain with a sediment bucket and integral trap combined.

(e) Large removable buckets, such as are needed in a laundry or boiler room. After the buckets are removed, waste solids go through the strainer openings.

(f) Combination of a sediment bucket, trap, and backwater valve, used where backflow might occur.

7.16   Dishwashing Machines

7.16.1   Protection.   Domestic dishwashing machines shall meet requirements in paragraph 10.4.3.

7.16.2   Separate Trap.   Each unit shall be separately trapped or discharged indirectly into a properly trapped and vented fixture.

7.16.3   Air Gap.   Commercial dishwashing machines shall be connected through an air gap or as provided in Chap. 9, Indirect Waste Piping and Special Wastes.

7.16.4   Hot Water.   Dishwashing machines or similar dishwashing equipment not in private living quarters or dwelling units shall be provided with water at 160 to 180°F for sterilization.

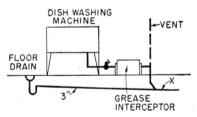

FIG. 7-21

▶   Figure 7-21 illustrates recommended methods for connecting commercial dishwashing machines.

Should stoppage occur downstream at point X, sewage cannot back up into the dishwasher as it would first show at the floor-drain level and therefore be quickly detected and a remedy applied.

7.17   Multiple Wash Sinks

7.17.1   Circular Type.   Each 18 inches of wash-sink circumference (circular type) shall be equivalent to one lavatory.

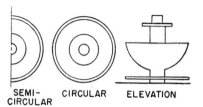

SEMI-   CIRCULAR   ELEVATION
CIRCULAR

Fig. 7-22

▶ Figure 7-22 illustrates circular and semicircular types. The circular sink is free standing so that washing may be done all around the wash sink. The semicircular is placed against a wall. These types of washing sinks are used where a large number of people must wash quickly. The sink is generally controlled by a foot pedal which is tripped by anyone around the wash sink. Where a large number of people wash continuously, continuous flow can be provided. The water is usually tempered in the tank.

7.17.2 Straight-line Type. Multiple wash sinks of the straight-line type shall have hot and cold combination spouts not closer than 18 inches from adjacent similar spouts, and each spout shall be considered the equivalent of one lavatory.

7.18 Garbage-can Washers

7.18.1 Discharge. Garbage-can washers shall not discharge through a trap serving any other device of fixture.

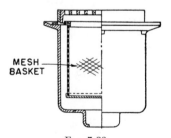

MESH
BASKET

Fig. 7-23

▶ Because of the solids usually washed off the walls and bottom of a garbage can, the discharge drain should be provided with a removable basket. The basket should be constructed so as to retain solids but permit liquids to flow out. See Fig. 7-23 for a typical installation.

7.18.2 Grease Interceptor. The discharge from a garbage-can washer shall be connected through a grease interceptor.

▶   Large quantities of grease are generally washed off the walls and bottom of garbage cans after they have been emptied. This grease can readily cause stoppages in the drainage system. A grease interceptor collects and separates the grease while the liquid continues into the sewer.

7.18.3 Baskets. The receptacle receiving the waste from garbage cans shall be provided with a basket or similar device to prevent the discharge of large particles into the building drainage system.

7.18.4 Connections. Water-supply connections shall conform to paragraph 10.4.3.

▶   There must be no possible cross connection or backflow connection between the water supply to the can-washing equipment and the sewer.

7.19 Laundry Trays

7.19.1 Waste Outlets. Each compartment of a laundry tray shall be provided with a waste outlet not less than $1\frac{1}{2}$ inches in diameter and with a stopper.

7.19.2 Overflow. Laundry-tray overflow shall conform to the requirements of paragraph 7.3.1.

▶   These requirements are applicable to residential laundry trays. See technical standards for information on commercial laundries.

7.20 Special Fixtures and Specialties

7.20.1 Water and Drain Connections. Baptistries, ornamental and lily pools, aquaria, ornamental fountain basins, and similar constructions, when provided with water supplies, shall be protected from back siphonage as required in paragraph 10.4.3.

7.20.2 Approval. Specialties requiring water and waste connections shall be submitted for approval of the administrative authority.

▶   In the installation of certain religious equipment or devices, it is necessary to provide for special functions required by the church. An example of this is a baptismal fountain where the waste must discharge into a small dry well in the earth, no other method being acceptable to the church.

7.21 Minimum Facilities

7.21.1 Wherever plumbing fixtures are installed, the minimum number installed of each type of fixture shall be in accordance with Table 7.21.2 unless otherwise specifically provided.

Table 7.21.2 Minimum Facilities[1]

Type of building or occupancy[2]	Water closets	Urinals	Lavatories	Bathtubs or showers	Drinking fountains[3]
Dwelling or apartment houses[4]	1 for each dwelling or apartment unit	....	1 for each apt. of dwelling unit	1 for each apt. or dwelling unit	
Schools[5]: Elementary..........	Male: 1 per 100; Female: 1 per 35	1 per 30 male	1 per 60 persons		1 per 75 persons
Secondary..........	Male: 1 per 100; Female: 1 per 45	1 per 30 male	1 per 100 persons		1 per 75 persons
Office or public buildings	No. of persons / No. of fixtures (Male): 1–15 : 1; 16–35 : 2; 36–55 : 3; 56–80 : 4; 81–110 : 5; 111–150 : 6; 1 fixture for each 40 additional persons. No. of persons / No. of fixtures (Female): 1–15 : 1; 16–35 : 2; 36–55 : 3; 56–80 : 4; 81–110 : 5; 111–150 : 6; 1 fixture for each 40 additional persons	Wherever urinals are provided for men, one water closet less than the number specified[2] may be provided for each urinal installed except that the number of water closets in such cases shall not be reduced to less than ⅔ of the minimum specified	No. of persons / No. of fixtures: 1–15 : 1; 16–35 : 2; 36–60 : 3; 61–90 : 4; 91–125 : 5; 1 fixture for each 45 additional persons		1 for each 75 persons
Manufacturing, warehouses, workshops, loft buildings, foundries and similar etablishments[6]	Number of persons / Number of fixtures: 1–9 : 1; 10–24 : 2; 25–49 : 3; 50–74 : 4; 75–100 : 5; 1 fixture for each additional 30 employees	Same substitution as above	1 to 100 persons, 1 fixture for each 10 persons over 100, 1 for each 15 persons[7,8]	1 shower for each 15 persons exposed to excessive heat or to skin contamination with poisonous, infectious, or irritating material	1 for each 75 persons
Dormitories[9]..........	Male: 1 for each 10 persons. Female: 1 for each 8 persons. Over 10 persons, add 1 fixture for each 25 additional males and 1 for each 20 additional females	1 for each 25 men. Over 150 persons add 1 fixture for each additional 50 men	1 for each 12 persons (separate dental lavatories should be provided in community toilet rooms. Ratio of dental lavatories for each 50 persons is recommended), add 1 lavatory for each 20 males, 1 for each 15 females	1 for each 8 persons in the case of women's dormitories, additional bathtubs should be installed at the ratio of 1 for each 30 females. Over 150 persons, add 1 fixture for each 20 persons	1 for each 75 persons

Table 7.21.2 Minimum Facilities (*Continued*)

Type of building or occupancy[2]	Water closets			Urinals		Lavatories		Bathtubs or showers	Drinking fountains[3]
	Number of persons	Number of fixtures		Number of persons (male)	Number of fixtures	Number of persons	Number of fixtures		
		Male	Female						
Theaters, auditoriums...	1–100	1	1	1–200	1	1–200	1	....	1 for each 100 persons
	101–200	2	2	201–400	2	201–400	2		
	201–400	3	3	401–600	3	401–750	3		
	Over 400, add 1 fixture for each additional 500 males and 1 for each 300 females			Over 600; 1 for each additional 300 males		Over 750, 1 for each additional 500 persons			

[1] The figures shown are based upon one fixture being the minimum required for the number of persons indicated or any fraction thereof.

[2] Building category not shown on this table. Will be considered separately by the administrative authority.

[3] Drinking fountains shall not be installed in toilet rooms.

[4] Laundry trays—one single compartment tray for each dwelling unit or two compartment trays for each 10 apartments. Kitchen sinks—one for each dwelling or apartment unit.

[5] This schedule has been adopted (1945) by the National Council on Schoolhouse Construction.

[6] As required by the American Standard Safety Code for Industrial Sanitation in Manufacturing Establishments (ASA Z4.1-1935).

[7] Where there is exposure to skin contamination with poisonous, infectious, or irritating materials, provide one lavatory for each five persons.

[8] 24 lineal inches of wash sink or 18 inches of a circular basin, when provided with water outlets for such space, shall be considered equivalent to one lavatory.

[9] Laundry trays, one for each 50 persons. Slop sinks, one for each 100 persons.

General. In applying this schedule of facilities, consideration must be given to the accessibility of the fixtures. Conformity purely on a numerical basis may not result in an installation suited to the need of the individual establishment. For example, schools should be provided with toilet facilities on each floor having classrooms.

Temporary workingmen facilities:
1 water closet and 1 urinal for each 30 workmen

24-in. urinal trough = 1 urinal.   48-in. urinal trough = 2 urinals.   72-in. urinal trough = 4 urinals.
36-in. urinal trough = 2 urinals.   60-in. urinal trough = 3 urinals.

Table 7.21.2 was compiled as a result of a great deal of research and many conferences with boards of education, public health officials, and administrators of commercial institutions.

"Specifically provided" means that where there is a local board or special authority which regulates requirements for the community these boards or authorities take precedence over the requirements set forth in Table 7.21.2.

7.21.2 (See Table 7.21.2.)

CHAPTER 8

Hangers and Supports

8.1 Strain and Stresses

8.1.1 General. Piping in a plumbing system shall be installed without undue strains and stresses, and provision shall be made for expansion, contraction, and structural settlement.

▶   Piping must be installed with proper pipe hangers or supports to provide leeway for pipe movements caused by contractions, expansions, and vibrations. Without proper supports there is the possibility of strain and fracture of the piping. Some pipe vibrations can be stopped or lessened by installing a layer of felt between the supports and the piping.

8.2 Vertical Piping

8.2.1 Attachment. Vertical piping shall be secured at sufficiently close intervals to keep the pipe in alignment and carry the weight of the pipe and contents.

8.2.2 Cast-iron Soil Pipe. Cast-iron soil pipe shall be supported at not less than at every story height and at its base.

8.2.3 Screwed Pipe. Screwed pipe (SPS) shall be supported at not less than every other story height.

8.2.4 Copper Tubing. Copper tubing shall be supported at each story for piping 1½ inches and over and at not more than 4-foot intervals for 1½ inches and smaller.

8.2.5 Lead Pipe. Lead pipe shall be supported at intervals not exceeding 4 feet.

Fig. 8-1

▶   Figure 8-1 illustrates the types of supports most commonly used for vertical piping. The thickness of the metal may vary from ³⁄₁₆ inch for lightweight water pipes to ⅜ inch and heavier for large-size pipe. The clamp around the pipe carries the load to the structure by means of the legs or extensions provided on one or both sides of the clamp.

The clamps rest on the floor, the clamp legs free from the structure. When the pipe expands, the clamp legs rise to accommodate the expansion, thus preventing strain and fracture. There are several types of clamps for specific requirements and structural weights. For instance, in buildings of one or two stories when the stack is supported on a pier at its base, there is no need for further support.

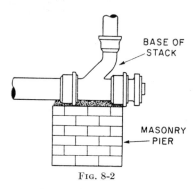

BASE OF
STACK

MASONRY
PIER

Fig. 8-2

In buildings higher than one or two stories, cast-iron soil pipe should be supported at every story height, in order to prevent the leaded joints from pulling out. Vertical screwed pipe needs support only at every other story. Copper water tubing, because of its flexibility, requires support not only at each story but at shorter intervals in order to prevent noises and vibration. Lead pipe is easily bent or thrown out of shape; therefore when used it should be supported closely.

8.3 Horizontal Piping

8.3.1 Supports. Horizontal piping shall be supported at sufficiently close intervals to keep it in alignment and prevent sagging.

8.3.2 Cast-iron Soil Pipe. Cast-iron soil pipe shall be supported at not more than 5-foot intervals.

8.3.3 Screwed Pipe. Screwed pipe (SPS) shall be supported at approximately 12-foot intervals.

8.3.4 Copper Tubing. Copper tubing shall be supported at approximately 6-foot intervals for piping $1\frac{1}{2}$ inches and smaller and 10-foot intervals for piping 2 inches and larger.

8.3.5 Lead Pipe. Lead pipe shall be supported by strips or otherwise for its entire length.

8.3.6 In Ground. Piping in the ground shall be laid on a firm bed for its entire length, except where support is otherwise provided which is adequate in the judgment of the administrative authority.

▶ Piping in a horizontal position requires hangers and supports similar to those illustrated in Fig. 8-3.

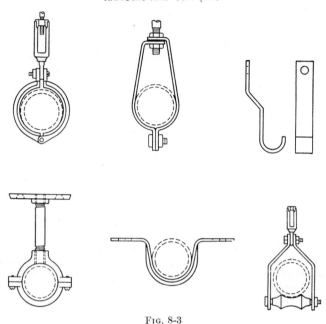

Fig. 8-3

8.4   Hangers and Anchors

8.4.1   Material.   Hangers and anchors shall be of metal of sufficient strength to maintain their proportional share of the pipe alignments and prevent rattling.

▶   Buildings, whether small or large, will settle, move, vibrate, and sway. These movements could result in serious damage to the plumbing piping unless the piping is permitted to move and expand with the building. Measurements of the movements are in most cases impossible to determine, but that movements do occur is proved by cracks on walls, floor board drawing away from baseboard, and similar deviations.   Some soils have a tendency to move during changing seasons.

8.4.2   Attachment.   Hangers and anchors shall be securely attached to the building construction.

8.5   Strains and Stresses

8.5.1   Installation of Pipe.   Piping in a plumbing system shall be so installed as to prevent undue strains and stresses.

8.5.2 Expansion and Contraction. Provision shall be made for expansion and contraction of piping and for structural settlement that may affect the piping.

8.5.3 Piping in Concrete. Piping in concrete or masonry walls or footings shall be placed or installed in chases or recesses which will permit access to the piping for repair or replacement.

8.6 Base of Stacks

8.6.1 Supports. Bases of cast-iron soil stacks shall be supported on concrete, brick laid in cement mortar, metal brackets attached to the building construction, or by other methods approved by the administrative authority.

8.6.2 Piping Material. Other piping material shall be so anchored as to take the load off the stack at the base.

▶ Water piping, particularly hot-water-supply and circulation piping, expands and contracts rapidly owing to changes in temperature. To avoid damage to the piping and to the building, it is necessary to install hangers that will support a long horizontal run. Because of expansion and contraction of the piping material when temperatures change, hangers should be chosen which permit the pipe to expand free of the building structure.

CHAPTER 9

Indirect Waste Piping and Special Wastes

9.1 Indirect Waste Piping

9.1.1 General. Wastes from the following shall discharge to the building drainage system through an air gap serving the individual fixtures, devices, appliances, or apparatus.

9.1.2 Food Handling. Establishments engaged in the storage, preparation, selling, serving, processing, or otherwise handling of food shall have the waste piping from all refrigerators, iceboxes, rinse sinks, cooling or refrigerating coils, laundry washers, extractors, steam tables, egg boilers, coffee urns, or similar equipment discharge indirectly into a water-supplied sink or receptor, and the waste outlet shall terminate at least 2 inches above the flood rim of such sink or receptor.

▶ An indirect waste, or an air gap on the waste of any device used for the purpose of handling or preparing food, is intended to prevent the possibility of waste backing up to where the food is placed and contaminating it. Hospital equipment such as sterilizers and laboratory sinks must be installed with a positive separation between the equipment outlet and the drainage inlet in order to prevent contamination.

Many kinds of appliances and equipment, such as commercial refrigerators, though not generally acknowledged by manufacturers to be part of the plumbing system, are part of it in so far as they are related to the safety of the potable-water-supply system. Improperly installed equipment would be a hazard to the water system of a building. Because this equipment is connected to the plumbing system, it must be installed in such a manner as to preclude any possibility of either causing contamination of the potable-water supply or being contaminated through backflow of drainage into this equipment.

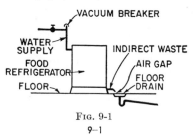

Fig. 9-1

Figure **9-1** illustrates a refrigerator, which requires a water-supply line to cooling coils and a discharge line for condensation.

In commercial refrigerators, food-storage cabinets, or water coolers, which require cold-water supply, the supply line must be provided with a vacuum breaker. When water under pressure is required, a pressure-type vacuum breaker must be installed so as to prevent possible backflow of either chemicals or contaminated water into the potable-water-supply system. Wastes from such equipment are discharged either by gravity or under pressure, depending on the equipment, and an air gap is required to prevent sewage from backing into the equipment.

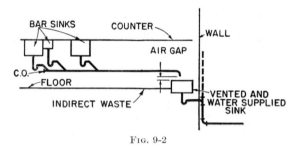

Fig. 9-2

Figure **9-2** shows a bar or soda-fountain sink counter. An indirect waste from such equipment will prevent sewage backing up into the sink. An indirect waste would also eliminate the need for exposed vents.

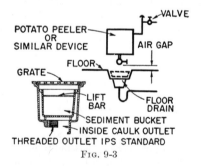

Fig. 9-3

Figure **9-3** shows a potato peeler, one of the devices installed in a commercial kitchen. This peeler should be provided with an indirect waste connection. An indirect waste also is necessary for a *bain-marie,* vegetable washers, and similar kitchen devices.

9.1.3 Commercial Dishwashing Machines. Dishwashing machines, except those in private living quarters or dwelling units, shall be indirectly connected, except that when a dishwashing machine is located adjacent to a floor drain the waste from the dishwashing machine may be connected direct on the sewer side of the floor-drain trap.

9.1.4   Interceptor.   An interceptor may be placed on the outlet side of the dishwashing machine, or on the discharge side of the indirect waste receptor.

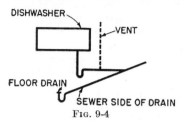

Fig. 9-4

► Figures 9-4 and 9-5 show two safe methods of connecting a commercial dishwashing machine.   Figure 9-4 shows the waste from the dishwasher connected directly into the drainage system.   A floor drain is connected to the horizontal waste to which the dishwasher waste connects.   Should there be a sewage backup in the line, it would overflow only onto the floor, but could not back up into the dishwashing machine, which is at least 2 feet higher.

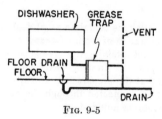

Fig. 9-5

Most codes require the installation of a grease interceptor where large quantities of grease are discharged through kitchen equipment.   Figure 9-5 illustrates a dishwashing machine discharging through a grease interceptor.

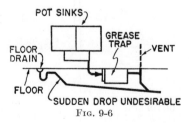

Fig. 9-6

Figure 9-6 shows a pot sink in a commercial kitchen discharging through a grease interceptor.

Where a commercial food-waste grinder is installed adjoining a dishwasher which discharges through a grease interceptor, the discharge of the food-waste grinder should connect upstream to the interceptor.

Research and experience have proved that a food-waste grinder shall not discharge into a grease interceptor. Figure 9-7 shows this condition.

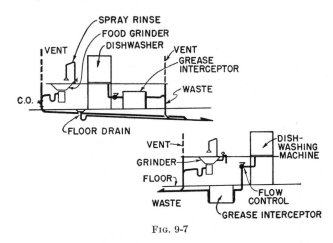

Fɪɢ. 9-7

Pot sinks in large kitchens contain a great deal of grease from pots and pans used in the preparation of food. Grease interceptors should be provided for separating and retaining the grease so as to keep the plumbing system free from stoppages. In many of the modern kitchens, food-waste grinders are installed at the preparation tables; the discharge from these grinders should not be connected through the grease interceptor, as the functions of both would be nullified.

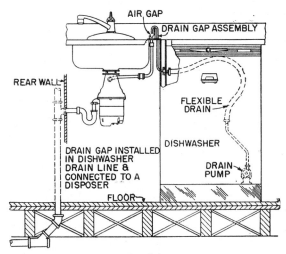

Fɪɢ. 9-8

When a pot sink or any other sink is connected through a grease interceptor, the fixture itself is not required to be trapped. The interceptor acts as a trap, and therefore another trap for the sewer would be double trapping and would cause air binding. A cleanout located above the level of the flood rim of the sink would permit rodding the line above the spill point in case of stoppage in the line.

A residential dishwasher should discharge into the drainage system through an air gap in order to prevent sewage backing up into the dish compartment in the event of a stoppage in the waste piping. Figure 9-8 illustrates the recommended method.

9.1.5 Connection.   Indirect waste connections shall be provided for drains, overflows, or relief vents from the water-supply system.

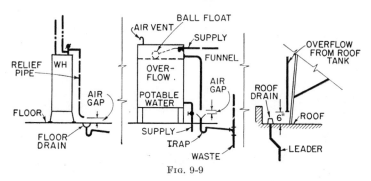

Fɪɢ. 9-9

▶   Figure 9-9 illustrates a relief pipe installed as an indirect connection over a floor drain. The overflow from a roof tank should spill close to a roof drain on the roof of the building. The discharge from the overflow should terminate at least 6 inches above the roof level. The overflow from a suction tank may be emptied through an indirect waste connection or into a sump or into a pit.

9.1.6 Sterile Materials.   Appliances, devices, or apparatus such as stills, sterilizers, and similar equipment requiring water and waste and used for sterile material shall be indirectly connected or provided with an air gap between the trap and the appliance.

9.1.7 Drips.   Appliances, devices, or apparatus not regularly classed as plumbing fixtures but which have drips or drainage outlets may be drained by indirect waste pipes discharging into an open receptacle as provided in paragraph 9.1.2.

▶   Sterilizers, water-treatment devices, water stills, and fixtures or devices containing food or drink should be connected to the sewer through an indirect connection. Otherwise, should the fixture trap seal be broken, there would be danger of contamination by backflow and by the sewer. See Fig. 9-10.

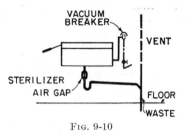

Fɪɢ. 9-10

9.2 Material and Size

9.2.1 The material and size of indirect waste pipes shall be in accordance with the provisions of the other sections of this Code applicable to sanitary-drainage piping.

▶ Pipe sizes must conform to the table of pipe sizes in relation to fixture units. Piping material may be similar to other sections of the plumbing system. Fittings should be of the recessed-drainage type for waste.

9.3 Length

9.3.1 Waste Pipe. Any indirect waste pipe exceeding 2 feet in length shall be trapped.
9.3.2. Maximum Length. The maximum length of the indirect waste to vent shall not exceed 15 feet.
9.3.3 Cleaning. Indirect waste piping shall be so installed as to permit ready access for flushing and cleansing.

▶ The purpose of the trap on long indirect waste lines is to prevent foul odors from entering the room. The odors are caused by air passing through putrefied matter which might be inside the pipe. The trap would prevent air circulation from the pipe into the room.

The length of an indirect waste pipe may vary slightly, depending on its diameter. A long indirect waste pipe that carries liquids that might cause odors should be provided with a hot-water connection for flushing at intervals. Any such flushing connections should be provided with means to prevent backflow.

An automatic primer may be installed for keeping an indirect waste pipe clean. Figure 9-11 illustrates a method of connecting.

An automatic primer provides the only means of maintaining proper and constant seal in basement-floor drain traps and other traps used infrequently. Seldom-used traps tend to lose their seals by evaporation. The primer is installed in a frequently used water-supply line and connected to the trap.

An automatic primer should be installed with a vacuum breaker to prevent back siphonage.

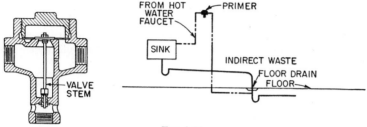

Fig. 9-11

9.4   Air-gap or Backflow Preventer

9.4.1   Provision of Air Gap.   The air gap between the indirect waste and the building drainage system shall be at least twice the effective diameter of the drain served and shall be as provided in paragraph 9.4.2 or 9.4.3.

9.4.2   By extending the indirect waste pipe to an open, accessible slop sink, floor drain, or other suitable fixture which is properly trapped or vented.   The indirect waste shall terminate a sufficient distance above the flood-level rim of the receiving fixture to provide the required air gap and shall be installed in accordance with other applicable sections of this Code.

9.4.3   By providing a break (air gap) in the drain connection on the inlet side of the trap serving the fixture, device, appliance, or apparatus.

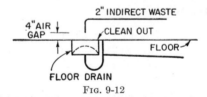

Fig. 9-12

▶   The length of an air gap in the drainage system is computed from the diameter of the waste line below the discharge.   For a 2-inch waste, the air gap should be 4 inches long.   See Fig. 9-12.

9.5   Receptors

9.5.1   Installation.   Waste receptors serving indirect pipes shall not be installed in any toilet room nor in any inaccessible or unventilated space such as a closet or storeroom.

9.5.2   Cleanout Location.   If the indirect waste receptor is set below floor level, it shall be equipped with a running trap set adjacent to the sink with cleanout brought level with the floor.

9.5.3 Strainers and Baskets. Every indirect waste receptor shall be equipped either with a readily removable metal basket over which all indirect waste pipe shall discharge, or the indirect waste-receptor outlet shall be equipped with a beehive strainer not less than 4 inches in height.

9.5.4 Splashing. All plumbing receptors receiving the discharge of indirect waste pipes shall be of such shape and capacity as to prevent splashing or flooding. No plumbing fixture which is used for domestic or culinary purposes shall be used to receive the discharge of an indirect waste pipe.

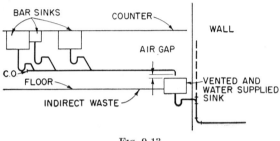

Fɪɢ. 9-13

► Figure **9-13** shows a bar or soda-fountain sink counter. An indirect waste from such equipment will prevent sewage backing up into the sink. An indirect waste would also eliminate the need for exposed vents.

9.6 Clear-water Wastes

9.6.1 Waste lifts, expansion tanks, cooling jackets, sprinkler systems, drip or overflow pans, or similar devices which waste clear water only shall discharge into a roof or into the building drainage system through an indirect waste.

► This regulation is for the purpose of avoiding sudden heavy loads in the drainage system. Where a large volume of water is discharged in a very short time, it is good practice to permit the liquid to spread over an area, then be drained at a rate that will not fill pipes to capacity. An exception to this caution is where a waste pipe has been provided specifically large enough to take care of the full load.

9.7 Condensers and Sumps

9.7.1 No steam pipe shall connect to any part of a drainage or plumbing system, nor shall any water above 140°F be discharged into any part of a drainage system. Such pipes may be indirectly connected by discharging into an interceptor or into the drainage system.

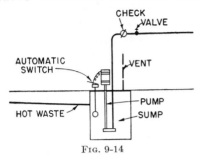

Fig. 9-14

▶ Condensate waste or discharges from hot-water tanks or a processing tank containing hot liquids should be discharged first into a sump or receptor. Where large quantities of hot water must be discharged, a cold-water supply may be provided to reduce the temperature below 140°F. See Fig. 9-14.

9.8 Drinking Fountains

9.8.1 Drinking fountains may be installed with indirect wastes.

9.9 Special Wastes

9.9.1 Acid Waste. Acid and chemical indirect waste pipes shall be of materials unaffected by the discharge of such wastes.

9.9.2 Neutralizing Device. In no case shall corrosive liquids, spent acids, or other harmful chemicals which might destroy or injure a drain, sewer, soil, or waste pipe, or which might create noxious or toxic fumes, discharge into the plumbing system without being thoroughly diluted or neutralized by passing through a properly constructed and acceptable dilution or neutralizing device. Such device shall be automatically provided with a sufficient intake of diluting water or neutralizing medium so as to make its contents noninjurious before being discharged into the soil or sewage system.

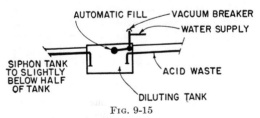

Fig. 9-15

▶ See Part III for specific use of acid- and corrosion-resisting materials and their application. A common method for neutralizing acid wastes is shown in Fig. 9-15.

Figure 9-16 shows an arrangement which connects the waste from several cup sinks in a laboratory into one continuous waste and then as an indirect waste into a funnel. (See paragraph 9.9.2.) Piping should be of a kind that will not be affected by acids and other corrosive liquid wastes. Duriron, lead, chemical clay, hard rubber, and similar materials are considered within the requirements of paragraph **9.9.1.**

When a separate system of acid wastes is installed whereby the wastes are run into a diluting tank as an indirect waste, then the air gap may be omitted.

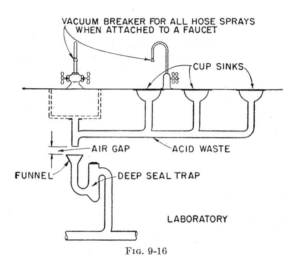

Fɪɢ. 9-16

Gooseneck faucets over laboratory sinks are equipped to receive a hose spray. Each faucet should be provided, as shown, with a vacuum breaker to prevent possible backflow of hazardous liquids as a result of leaving the spray and hose in the sink.

Figure 9-17 represents a laboratory with sinks located at the center of the room and a dwarf partition between sinks. Generally, it is not desirable to run vent piping through the center of the room; yet the trap seal of the sinks must be protected against self-siphonage. This can be accomplished by the arrangement shown, which is permitted by the National Plumbing Code. See Sec. **12.22,** Combination Waste-and-Vent System.

If floor drains are needed, they may connect directly into the horizontal line, each individually trapped. Only one stack vent need be full size, in order to take care of the total connected load in the branch waste. See the sink on the right-hand side of the drawing. Other sink vents may be the regulation size. The waste branch from an unvented sink must be two pipe sizes larger than the individual sink connection required.

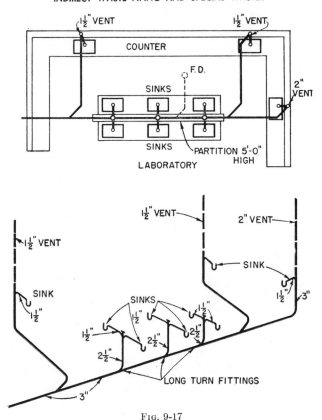

Fig. 9-17

9.10 Swimming Pools

9.10.1 Piping carrying waste water from swimming or wading pools, including pool drainage, backwash from filters, or water from scum butter drains or floor drains which serve walks around pools, shall be installed as an indirect waste pipe, utilizing any existing circulation pump, if necessary, when indirect waste pipe is below the sewer grade.

▶   See Part III for swimming-pool data.

CHAPTER 10

Water Supply and Distribution

10.1 Quality of Water Supply

10.1.1 Potable Water. Potable water is water which is satisfactory for drinking, culinary, and domestic purposes and meets the requirements of the health authority having jurisdiction.

10.1.2 Acceptable Sources. Where a public supply of potable water is not available, requirements satisfactory to the administrative authority shall be observed. (See Chap. 15.)

10.1.3 Nonpotable Water. Nonpotable water may be used for flushing water closets and urinals and other fixtures not requiring potable water, provided such water shall not be accessible for drinking or culinary purposes.

▶ Minimum standards have been established by the Public Health Service. In some states the requirements are higher than in others. The potability of water is judged by chemical and physical characteristics. A chemical analysis will determine the amount of soluble mineral substance. The following minerals in excess of the amounts shown would constitute grounds for rejection of a potable-water supply:

Mineral	*Ppm by Weight*
Arsenic	0.05
Selenium	0.05
Lead	0.1
Fluoride	1.5
Hexavalent chromium	0.05
Zinc	15.0
Copper	3.0
Iron and manganese	0.3
Magnesium	12.5
Chloride	2.5
Sulfate	2.5

Physical characteristics include the following:

Turbidity (silica scale) not to exceed 10 parts per million.

Color (platinum cobalt scale) not to exceed 20.

Water shall have no objectionable taste or odor. The bacteriological and microscopic analysis is important, as it indicates the sanitary quality of the water.

In many cases, analysis of the water is not sufficient; a sanitary survey also is necessary. This includes study of the source, area of supply from which the water is collected, or channels through which the water runs.

Municipal supplies are generally carefully guarded, analyzed, and treated.

Nonpotable water for nonpotable use is acceptable provided that it has no physical connection with the potable-water supply. (See Cross Connections.)

Industrial processing plants using large amounts of water for manufacturing purposes require at times a secondary supply of water whether potable or not; in such cases a private source or private wells are used.

At seashores, it is sometimes customary to use sea water for flushing of water closets and for other purposes of cleansing. This type of system must be separate from the others.

10.2   Color Code

10.2.1   Identification of Piping. All piping conveying nonpotable water shall be adequately and durably identified by a distinctive yellow-colored paint so that it is readily distinguished from piping carrying potable water. (See ASA Z53.1-1945 Safety Color Code for Marking Physical Hazards.)

▶   This color code has been in effect since 1945 to standardize the colors to be used to mark a physical hazard and to identify certain equipment. Yellow was the color selected to be painted on piping carrying nonpotable water.

10.3   Water Supply Mandatory

10.3.1 Every building in which plumbing fixtures are installed and which are for human occupancy or habitation shall be provided with an ample supply of pure and wholesome water.

10.4   Protection of Potable-water Supply

10.4.1   Cross Connections. Potable-water-supply piping, water-discharge outlets, backflow-prevention devices, or similar equipment shall not be so located as to make possible their submergence in any contaminated or polluted liquid or substance.

10.4.2   Approval of Devices. Before any device for the prevention of backflow or back siphonage is installed, it shall have first been certified as meeting the requirements of ASA A40.6-1943 by a testing laboratory determined by the administrative authority to be reputable. Devices installed in a potable-water-supply system for protection against backflow shall be maintained in good working condition by the person or persons having control of such devices. The administrative authority having jurisdiction may inspect such devices and, if found to be ineffective or inoperative, shall require the repair or replacement thereof.

▶   Figures 10-1 to 10-12 show examples of cross connections found in buildings today which should be avoided in a plumbing system.   Epidemics of typhoid, gastroenteritis, and other water-borne diseases have occurred from contamination of the potable water through such cross connections. Any condition which permits any piping or device carrying potable water to become submerged in contaminated liquids is a potential hazard.   This is equally true of a connection installed close to the surface of contaminated liquid whereby the negative pressure could be sufficient to siphon the liquid into the potable-water system.

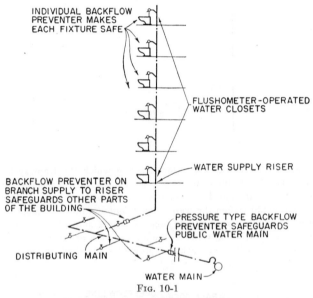

Fig. 10-1

Figure 10-1 shows cold-water riser in a multistory building which has connected to it on each floor a water closet without a backflow preventer. A break in the street main or in the water-distributing main of the building would cause the water in the riser to flow back into the service main or street main.   If a water closet in the building happened to be stopped up and its contents flooded to the rim of the fixture, the negative pressure in the riser, caused by water flowing down, would unseat the flushometer valve.   This would create a vacuum in the tailpiece which connects on top of the water closet.   The contents of the water closet would then rise in the tailpiece and flow down the cold-water riser, contaminating the water in the street main.   The extent to which the potable water could become contaminated depends on the length of time that such a condition is permitted to exist.   It would be hard to say how many buildings in the area would be drawing contaminated water after the street main was returned to normal operation.

A vacuum breaker on the outlet of each flushometer connection would prevent such an occurrence. A pressure-type backflow preventer at the point of entrance of the service main into the building would safeguard other buildings in the area.

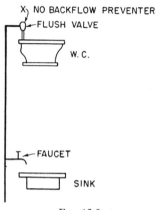

Fig. 10-2

Figure 10-2 illustrates a water closet in which the trapway has been clogged, permitting the contents to rise in the bowl. A negative pressure taking place in the supply line or the shutting off of the water riser in the basement could siphon the water-closet contents into the supply line. A return to normal operation could cause the contaminated water to be drawn into a glass of drinking water at the kitchen sink or lavatory.

A vacuum breaker or backflow preventer installed at point X would eliminate the hazard.

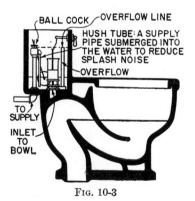

Fig. 10-3

Figure 10-3 shows a water closet with an integral tank. Where the bottom of the tank is below the rim of the bowl and where the ball cock is not protected by a vacuum breaker, backflow can occur when there is a negative pressure in the water system. (See paragraph 7.7.4.)

A stoppage in the water-closet trap would cause the liquid in the bowl to rise to the flood rim, then flow back into the lower section of the tank. This contaminated water can readily be siphoned into the potable-water system through the hush tube unless a vacuum breaker is provided above the water line of the tank ball cock.

The contents of the lavatory with integral supply connections below the flood-level rim can be siphoned into the water-supply system. The faucet outlet should be above the flood level of the lavatory, thus providing a 1-inch air gap. (See Fig. 10-4.)

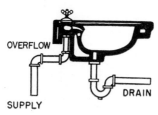

Fig. 10-4

Fixture	Minimum air gap (in.)	
	When not affected by near wall[1]	When affected by near wall[2]
Lavatories with effective openings not greater than ½-in. diameter..................................	1.0	1.50
Sink, laundry trays, and gooseneck bath faucets with effective openings not greater than ¾-in. diameter....	1.5	2.25
Overrim bath fillers with effective openings not greater than 1-inch diameter.............................	2.0	3.00
Effective openings greater than 1 in.................	[3]	[4]

[1] Side walls, ribs, or similar obstructions do not affect the air gaps when spaced from inside edge of spout opening a distance greater than 3 times the diameter of the effective opening for a single wall, or a distance greater that 4 times the diameter of the effective opening for 2 intersecting walls. (See chart 2.)

[2] Vertical walls, ribs, or similar obstructions extending from the water surface to or above the horizontal plane of the spout opening require a greater air gap when spaced closer to the nearest inside edge of spout opening than specified in note 1 above. The effect of 3 or more such vertical walls or ribs has been determined. In such cases, the air gap should be measured from the top of the wall.

[3] 2x effective opening.

[4] 3x effective opening.

FIG. 10-5

In Fig. 10-5 a bathtub with a faucet installed below the rim of the bathtub permits water from the tub to be siphoned into the water-supply system. All supply faucets should be at least 2 inches above the rim of the tub.

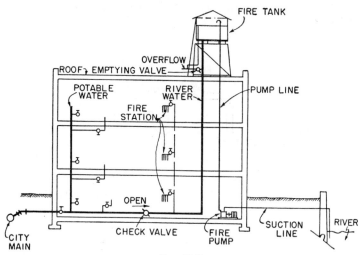

FIG. 10-6

Figure 10-6 shows that if the pressure in the fire-line supply tank is greater than in the city main, and if the check-valve flap is not tight, impure river water from the fire line can enter the drinking-water-supply system. A fire in the neighborhood could cause the condition, and it could result in the contamination of a large area. The two water supplies should have no direct contact unless a pressure-type backflow control is installed between them.

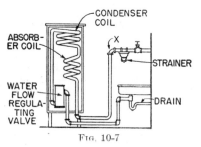

FIG. 10-7

Figure 10-7 shows that a break in the water-submerged condenser coil could cause a cross connection. A pressure-type vacuum breaker, installed at X, would be a safeguard against such a hazard.

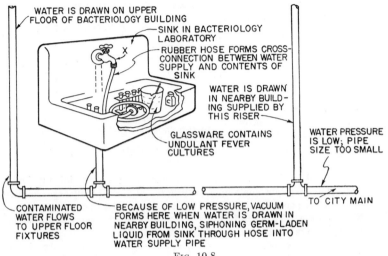

FIG. 10-8

A cross connection such as shown in Fig. 10-8 has actually occurred, causing an epidemic of undulant fever. Such a type of hose connection represents a direct cross connection. A vacuum breaker or backflow preventer placed at point X would prevent back siphonage.

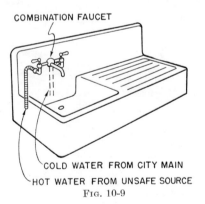

FIG. 10-9

The supply fixture shown in Fig. 10-9 is a cross connection. Any lowering of the pressure of the city main would permit unsafe water to enter the potable-water supply through the combination faucet. It is safer to install separate faucets for hot and cold water.

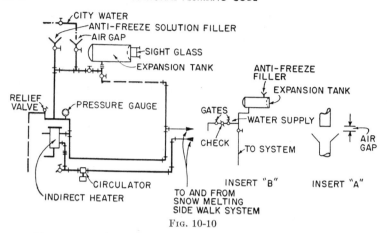

Fig. 10-10

Figure 10-10 illustrates one of the various methods of providing make-up water for a system containing antifreeze solution. Antifreeze solution generally is poisonous and must not be permitted to enter the potable-water system. To depend on valves is never a positive safeguard. Maintenance operators or owners might forget to shut off a valve, and check valves are never positive protection against back pressures. An air gap between the potable-water system and the piping containing the antifreeze solution is the only safe method of protection. A direct cross connection is dangerous and must be avoided.

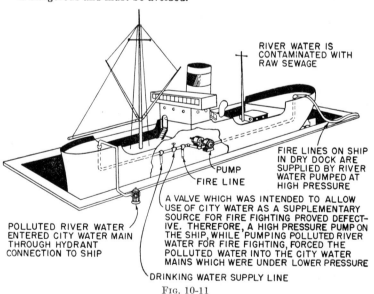

Fig. 10-11

Figure 10-11 shows how river water, supplemented by city water, was used for fire lines. A defective valve separated the waters. The pump on the fire line created a higher pressure in the fire line than existed in the city-water line. This condition existed for 2 weeks, causing the city water to become polluted over a large area.

The installation of a pressure-type backflow valve will safeguard the potable-water system against the river water being accidentally pumped into the potable city-water supply system.

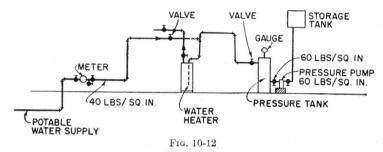

Fɪɢ. 10-12

Figure 10-12 illustrates a direct cross connection often found where potable water is supplemented by nonpotable water for the hot-water system. There is a higher pressure on the supplemental water supply of unknown origin. Slight opening of the valve could cause contamination not only to the potable water within the building, but the nonpotable water could flow into the street main and cause contamination of a large area of a community.

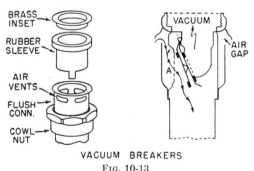

VACUUM BREAKERS
Fɪɢ. 10-13

Figure 10-13 illustrates several types of vacuum breakers commonly used on the flushing connection to a water closet. There is a lack of uniformity on the matter of testing vacuum breakers. A testing standard should be established by an unbiased laboratory.

10.4.3 Backflow. The water-distributing system shall be protected against backflow. Every water outlet shall be protected from backflow, preferably by having the outlet end from which the water flows spaced a distance above the flood-level rim of the receptacle into which the water flows sufficient to provide a "minimum required air gap" as defined in ASA A40.4-1942. Where it is not possible to provide a minimum air gap, the water outlet shall be equipped with an accessibly located backflow preventer complying with ASA A.40.6-1943, installed on the discharge side of the manual control valve. (See Chap. 17.)

10.4.4 Special Devices. Where it is not possible to provide either a minimum air gap or a backflow preventer, as may be the case in connection with cooling jackets, condensers, or other industrial or special appliances, the administrative authority shall require other approved means of protection.

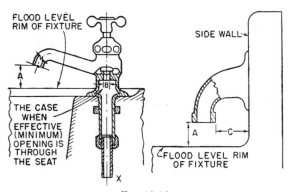

Fig. 10-14

▶   An air gap provides a more positive protection against backflow than a vacuum breaker because an air gap has positive effectiveness. A vacuum breaker depends on mechanical action, which might not function 100 per cent all the time. An air gap could fail only if someone deliberately blocks the opening.

Figure 10-14 illustrates an air break as required by ASA A40.4-1942.

Figures 10-15 and 10-16 illustrate an air gap in a house or suction tank.

10.5   Vacuum Breakers and Air Gaps

10.5.1 Flushometer. Flushometer shall be equipped with an approved vacuum breaker. The vacuum breaker shall be installed on the discharge side of the flushing valve with the critical level at least 4 inches above the overflow rim of the bowl.

10.5.2 Flushing Tanks. Flushing tanks shall be equipped with an approved ball cock. The ball cock shall be installed with the critical level of the vacuum breaker at least 1 inch above the full opening of the overflow pipe. In cases where the ball cock has no hush tube, the bottom of the water-supply inlet shall be installed 1 inch above the full opening of the overflow pipe.

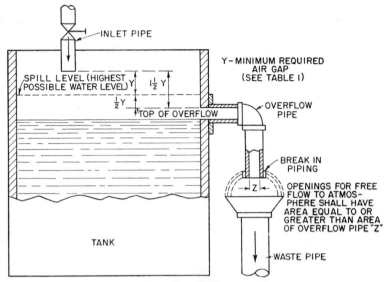

FIG. 10-15

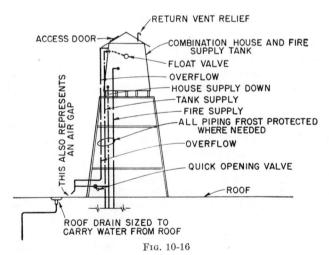

FIG. 10-16

10.5.3 Trough Urinals. Trough urinals shall be equipped with a vacuum breaker installed on the discharge side of the last valve and not less than 30 inches above the spray pipe.

10.5.4 Lawn Sprinklers. Lawn-sprinkler systems shall be equipped with a backflow preventer on the discharge side of each of the last valves. The back-flow preventer shall be at least 6 inches above the highest head, and at no time less than 6 inches above the surrounding ground. Where combination control valves and backflow preventers are installed, the bottom of the valve shall constitute the bottom of the backflow preventer.

10.5.5 Valve Outlet. Fixtures with hose attachments shall be protected by a backflow preventer installed 6 inches above the highest point of usage and on the discharge side of the valve.

10.6 Water-service Pipe

10.6.1 Except as permitted in paragraph 10.6.2, the underground water-service pipe and the building drain or building sewer shall be not less than 10 feet apart horizontally and shall be separated by undisturbed or compacted earth.

10.6.2 The water-service pipe may be placed in the same trench with the building drain and building sewer provided the following conditions are met:

The bottom of the water-service pipe, at all points, shall be at least 12 inches above the top of the sewer line at its highest point.

The water-service pipe shall be placed on a solid shelf excavated at one side of the common trench.

The number of joints in the service pipe shall be kept to a minimum.

The materials and joints of sewer and water-service pipe shall be installed in such manner and shall possess the necessary strength and durability to prevent the escape of solids, liquids, and gases therefrom, under all known adverse conditions such as corrosion, strains due to temperature changes, settlement, vibrations, and superimposed loads.

10.6.3 Stop-and-Waste Valve Combination. Combination stop-and-waste valves and cocks shall not be installed in an underground service pipe.

10.6.4 Private Water Supply. No private water supply shall be interconnected with any public water supply without the specific approval of the department of health.

▶   In selecting the kind of pipe to be used for the service main, the water characteristics or mineral contents of the water as well as the ground conditions should be given careful study. The kind of piping that has been used for many years locally and which is known to be satisfactory is a safe choice. The degree of exterior corrosion will vary with the ground composition, such as whether it is filled-in or solid undisturbed ground or rock. If filled-in ground, it is well to provide new clean earth at the bottom, sides, and top of the pipe to slow down the corrosive action which generally takes place in filled-in ground. Ground which has been filled with cinders, waste food, peelings, and the like is probably the least desirable into which to install any piping. See Part III.

Piping installed in one piece from the main to the house will safeguard the water supply it carries, even if installed in the same trench with the sewer. (See Sec. 11.2.)

Before the service-main trench is backfilled, the main should be tested by keeping up the full pressure available in the main at least 30 minutes without showing any leaks.

10.7   Water-pumping and Storage Equipment

10.7.1   Pumps and Other Appliances.   Water pumps, tanks, filters, softeners, and all other appliances and devices shall be protected against contamination.

10.7.2   Water-supply Tanks.   Potable-water-supply tanks shall be properly covered to prevent the entrance of foreign material or insects into the water supply.   Soil or waste lines shall not pass directly over such tanks.

10.7.3   Pressure Tanks, Boilers, and Relief Valves.   The drains from pressure tanks, boilers, relief valves, and similar equipment shall be connected to the drainage system through an indirect waste.

10.7.4   Cleaning, Painting, Repairing Water Tanks.   A potable-water-supply tank used for domestic purposes shall not be lined, painted, or repaired with any material which will affect either the taste or the potability of the water supply when the tank is returned to service.   Tanks shall be disconnected from the system during such operations, to prevent any foreign fluid or substance from entering the distribution piping.

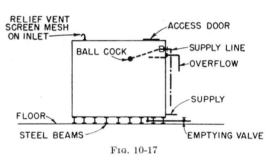

FIG. 10-17

▶   Pumps, tank, filters, softeners, and other equipment in the water-supply system can be safeguarded against contamination by providing a safe supply to such equipment.   Figures 10-15 and 10-17 illustrate methods used in safeguarding a suction-tank supply and screened air inlet.

10.8   Water-supply Tanks (House-suction Booster)

10.8.1   When Required.   When the water pressure from the city mains during flow is insufficient to supply all fixtures freely and continuously, the rate of supply shall be supplemented by a gravity house tank or booster system.

▶   The general practice is to provide one of the following methods for increasing the water pressure to the desired height:
   (a) Pumping the water to a roof tank and distributing it at the upper floor level.
   (b) Installing automatic pressure-pumping equipment directly into the water-supply system.

10.8.2   Support.   All water-supply tanks shall be supported in accordance with the building code or other regulations which apply.

10.8.3   Overflow Pipes for Water-supply Tanks.   Overflow pipes for gravity tanks shall discharge above and within 6 inches of a roof or catch basin, or they shall discharge over an open water-supplied sink.   Adequate overflow pipes properly screened against the entrance of insects and vermin shall be provided.

▶   Roof tanks are generally supported by high structures or installed in a penthouse.   The structural work is a function of the designing engineer. Suction tanks and intermediate tanks are supported on foundations or on structural members designed for the purpose.

Water-supply tanks require an overflow in order to prevent damage to the surrounding area in the event of failure of the automatic supply equipment.   The overflow pipe should be sized so as to permit equal amount of discharge in relation to the inlet or supply pipe.

The table in paragraph **10.8.6** provides approximate overflow sizes for various size storage tanks.   It is essential that the overflow pipe be computed on the basis of the incoming supply.

Roof or penthouse storage tanks should be equipped with quick-opening valves so that the contents may be released quickly in case of emergency. Should a fire occur in a building, it is essential that the weight of the water be removed before roof trusses or beams are weakened by the fire, causing the water tank to collapse.

Figure 10-16 illustrates a house tank over a roof provided with overflow and quick-emptying valves.

10.8.4   Tank Supply.   The water-supply inlet within the tank shall be at an elevation not less than is required for an air gap in an open tank with overflow, but in no case shall the elevation be less than 4 inches above the overflow.

▶   See Fig. 10-15.

10.8.5   Drains.   Water-supply tanks shall be provided with valved drain lines located at their lowest point and discharged as an indirect waste or as required for overflow pipes in paragraph 10.4.3.

10.8.6   Size of Overflow.   Overflow drains for water-supply tanks shall not be less than the following:

Drain pipe (in.)	Tank capacity (gal)	Drain pipe (in.)	Tank capacity (gal)
1	Up to 750	2½	3,001 to 5,000
1½	751 to 1,500	3	5,001 to 7,500
2	1,501 to 3,000	4	Over 7,500

Each drain line shall be equipped with a quick-opening valve of the same diameter as the pipe.

10.8.7 Gravity and Suction Tanks. Tanks used for domestic water supply, combined supply to fire standpipes and domestic water system, or to supply standpipes for fire-fighting equipment only shall be equipped with tight covers which are vermin and rodent proof. Such tanks shall be vented with a return-bend vent pipe having an area not less than one-half the area of the downfeed riser, and the vent opening shall be covered with a metallic screen of not less than 100 mesh.

Figure 10-17 illustrates a closed tank, suction or penthouse.

10.8.8 Pressure Tanks. Pressure tanks used for supplying water to the domestic water-distribution system, combined supply to fire standpipes and domestic water system, or to supply standpipes for fire equipment only shall be equipped with a vacuum-breaking device located on the top of the tank. The air inlet of this device shall be covered with a metallic screen of not less than 100 mesh.

Figure 10-18 illustrates one method for supplying water to a building when the street pressure is not sufficient to supply the needs of the building. The pump and compressor are automatically controlled through an electric control panel which provides air to the tank as needed, and the pumps supply water as needed.

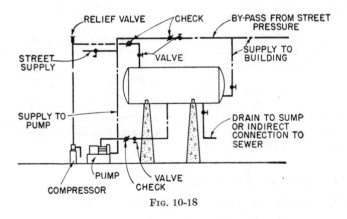

Fig. 10-18

10.9 Disinfection of Potable-water-system Piping

10.9.1 The administrative authority having jurisdiction shall require when necessary that the potable-water system or any part installed or repaired be disinfected in accordance with one of the following methods before it is placed in operation.

10.9.2　The system, or part thereof, shall be filled with a solution containing 50 parts per million of available chlorine and allowed to stand 6 hours before flushing and returning to service.

10.9.3　The system, or part thereof, shall be filled with a solution containing 100 parts per million of available chlorine and allowed to stand 2 hours before flushing and returning to service.

10.9.4　In the case of potable-water storage tank where it is not possible to disinfect as provided in paragraphs 10.9.2 and 10.9.3, the entire interior of the tank shall be swabbed with a solution containing 200 parts per million of available chlorine and the solution allowed to stand 2 hours before flushing and returning to service.

10.9.5　In the case of potable-water filters or similar devices, the dosage shall be determined by the administrative authority.

▶　　　Most codes do not require the disinfection of the water-supply piping or water-storage tanks.

10.10　Water-distribution Pipe, Tubing, and Fittings

10.10.1　Materials for water-distributing pipes and tubing shall be brass, copper, lead, cast iron, wrought iron, open-hearth iron, or steel, with appropriate approved fittings.　All threaded ferrous pipe and fittings shall be galvanized (zinc coated) or cement lined.　When used underground in corrosive soil, all ferrous pipe and fittings shall be coal-tar enamel coated and the threaded joints shall be coated and wrapped after installation.　(See Chap. 3 for Standards.)

▶　　　The selection of water piping is based on the expected life of the building, the water characteristics of the locality, and the general practice within the area of the building.　If a building is of a temporary nature, the less costly types might serve the temporary purpose.　For a permanent structure, care should be exercised to select the type that would stand up best and be least costly to maintain over the life of the structure.　Piping that will need to be replaced once or twice during the life of the structure will prove much more costly over the years than the installation of more durable pipes during the original erection.

10.11　Allowance for Character of Water

10.11.1　Selection of Materials.　When selecting the material and size for water-supply pipe, tubing, or fittings, due consideration shall be given to the action of the water on the interior and of the soil, fill, or other material on the exterior of the pipe.　No material that would produce toxic conditions in a potable-water-supply system shall be used for piping, tubing, or fittings.

10.11.2　Used Piping.　No piping material that has been used for other than a potable-water-supply system shall be reused in the potable-water-supply system.

See Sec. 10.1 for toxic conditions in the potable-water-supply system. See Part III for information on sizing the water-supply distributing system of a building. Undersized piping tends to cause pipe noises and water hammer.

Used pipe of an unknown origin should not be installed in a potable-water-supply system.

10.12 Water-supply Control

0.12.1 Water-supply Control. A main shutoff valve on the water-service pipe shall be provided near the curb and, also, an accessible shutoff valve with a drip valve shall be provided inside near the entrance of the water-service pipe into the building.

0.12.2 Tank Controls. Supply lines taken from pressure or gravity tanks shall be valved at or near their source.

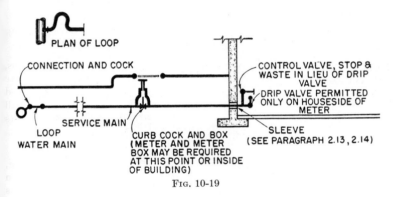

Fig. 10-19

Figures 10-19 and 10-20 illustrate a service main and controls.

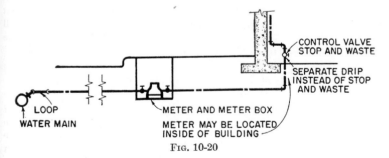

Fig. 10-20

10.12.3 Separate Controls for Each Family Unit. In two-family or multiple dwellings, each family unit shall be controlled by an arrangement of shutoff valves which permit each group of fixtures or the individual fixtures to be shut off without interference with the water supply to any other family unit or other portion of the building.

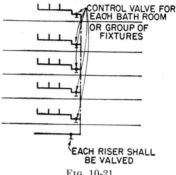

Fig. 10-21

▶   Figure 10-21 illustrates paragraph **10.12.3.**   The minimum control provides a valve for each bathroom in apartments or hotels or a valve per group of fixtures for other types of buildings.

10.12.4   Group Fixtures.   A group of fixtures means two or more fixtures adjacent or near each other.   In a one-family house one or two bathrooms adjacent or one over the other may be considered a group.

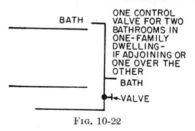

Fig. 10-22

▶   Figure 10-22 illustrates paragraph **10.12.4.**

10.12.5   Buildings Other Than Dwellings.   In all buildings other than dwellings, shutoff valves shall be installed, which permit the water supply to all equipment in each separate room to be shut off without interference with the water supply to any other room or portion of the building.

10.12.6   Water-heating Equipment.   A shutoff valve shall be provided in the cold-water branch line to each water-storage tank or each water heater.

10.12.7   Shutoff Valve at Meter.   The shutoff valve at the discharge side of the water meter shall be not less in size than the size of the building water service and shall be of the gate type or ground key stop.

▶   Where a curb valve is not mandatory, the installation of a control valve should be made at an accessible point.

In multistory buildings, a separate control valve for hot and cold water should be provided for each apartment. The valve must be located within the tenant's apartment. When two bathrooms are adjacent in a one-family house, one control valve for hot-water supply to both bathrooms and one for cold water to both bathrooms may be used. Individual fixture stops are desirable as a convenience when making minor repairs. See Fig. 10-23.

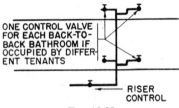

ONE CONTROL VALVE
FOR EACH BACK-TO-
BACK BATHROOM IF
OCCUPIED BY DIFFER-
ENT TENANTS

RISER
CONTROL

Fig. 10-23

10.13   Water-supply Distribution

10.13.1   Water-service Pipe. The water-service pipe from the street main to the water-distribution system for the building shall be of sufficient size to furnish an adequate flow of water to meet the requirements of the building at peak demand and in no case shall be less than ¾ inch nominal diameter.

If flushometers or other devices requiring a high rate of water flow are used, the water-service pipe shall be designed to supply this flow.

10.13.2   Demand Load. The demand load in the building water-supply system shall be based on the number and kind of fixtures installed and the probable simultaneous use of these fixtures.

10.14   Procedure in Sizing the Water-distribution System of a Building

10.14.1 The sizing of the water-distribution system shall conform to good engineering practice. Designed factors used to determine pipe sizes shall be adequate in the judgment of the administrative authority. (See Chap. 18 for guidance in the design of water-supply systems.)

▶   One method of sizing the water-supply pipe is explained in the example given below. It is not so accurate as that based on the detailed data contained in Part III, but for small buildings it should provide a satisfactory basis. The data are based on results of research at the National Bureau of Standards, as reported in BMS 79. (See Bibliography.) The example is the one-story ranch house shown in Figs. 10-24 and 10-25.

Figure 10-24 illustrates the plan of water distribution. Dotted figures represent the first-floor fixtures. Solid lines represent the basement fixtures.

Figure 10-25 is a diagram of the water distribution.

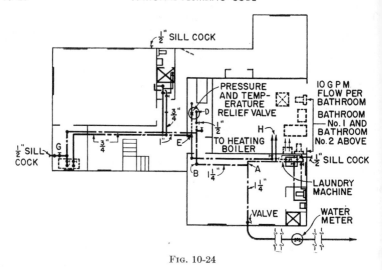

Fig. 10-24

Fig. 10-25

Table A. Conversion of Plumbing Fixtures to Fixture-unit Ratings

(Applicable to small homes)

Fixture	Fixture Units
1 water closet, flush tank	3
1 lavatory	1
1 bathtub with or without shower head	2
1 shower compartment	2
1 kitchen sink	2
1 disposal unit	1
1 laundry trap (1 to 3 compartment)	3
1 sill cock	4
1 laundry machine	3

Table B. Water-pipe Sizing

(For small buildings)

Sizes are computed to maintain a maximum velocity of 10 feet per second, based on water-pressure drop of 5 pounds per square inch per 100 feet.

Line	Service main diam (in.)	Inside piping diam (in.)	Developed length of piping (max ft)	Fixture-unit requirements (max quantity)
1	$\frac{3}{4}$	$\frac{3}{4}$	50	25
2	$\frac{3}{4}$	$\frac{3}{4}$	100	16
3	$\frac{3}{4}$	$\frac{3}{4}$	150	15
4	$\frac{3}{4}$	1	50	40
5	$\frac{3}{4}$	1	100	33
6	$\frac{3}{4}$	1	150	28
7	1	1	50	50
8	1	1	100	40
9	1	1	150	30
10	1	$1\frac{1}{4}$	50	96
11	1	$1\frac{1}{4}$	100	65
12	1	$1\frac{1}{4}$	150	55
13	$1\frac{1}{4}$	$1\frac{1}{4}$	50	150
14	$1\frac{1}{4}$	$1\frac{1}{4}$	100	100
15	$1\frac{1}{4}$	$1\frac{1}{4}$	150	65
16	$1\frac{1}{4}$	$1\frac{1}{2}$	50	250
17	$1\frac{1}{4}$	$1\frac{1}{2}$	100	160
18	$1\frac{1}{4}$	$1\frac{1}{2}$	150	130

Sizing is computed as follows:

Step 1: Determine the water pressure at the main. The water company or the city water department has this information. Note that Table B is computed to maintain a maximum velocity of 10 feet per second, based on a water-pressure drop of 5 pounds per square inch per 100 feet.

Step 2: Compute the number of fixture units to be supplied, including plumbing-connected appliances and sill cocks, using Table A. In this case, there are 45 fixture units.

Step 3: For 45 fixture units supplied by a main of 63 feet developed length, line 11 of table (Table B) is applicable. It indicates a 1-inch diameter for the service main, and $1\frac{1}{4}$-inch for the inside piping to point *A* (Fig. 10-25).

Step 4: Bathrooms 1, 2, and 3, plus laundry equipment and hose bib rate 28 fixture units. The developed length of supply piping (point *A*) i less than 50 feet; therefore line 4 is applicable, and it recommends 1-inch diameter.

Step 5: At point *B* (Fig. 10-25) the fixture-unit rating is 17, and the developed length of supply piping is 45 feet. Line 1 (Table C) is applicable, and it recommends ¾-inch diameter.

Step 6: Each section of piping is figured in similar manner.

Table C shows pipe sizes for multistory apartment buildings. It is a simplified basis for figuring mains, risers, or branches for combined ho and cold-water supply as well as for separate hot- or cold-water-supply piping.

Pipe sizes are computed for average distances and average water pressures in a large building.

10.14.2 Size of Fixture Supply. The minimum size of a fixture-supply pipe shall be as follows:

Fixture or Device	Pipe Size (in.)
Bathtubs	½
Combination sink and tray	½
Drinking fountain	⅜
Dishwasher (domestic)	½
Kitchen sink, residential	½
Kitchen sink, commercial	¾
Lavatory	⅜
Laundry tray, 1, 2, or 3 compartments	½
Shower (single head)	½
Sinks (service, slop)	½
Sinks, flushing rim	¾
Urinal (flush tank)	½
Urinal (direct flush valve)	¾
Water closet (tank type)	⅜
Water closet (flush valve type)	1
Hose bibs	½
Wall hydrant	½

For fixtures not listed, the minimum supply branch may be made the same as for a comparable fixture.

10.14.3 Minimum Pressure. Minimum, fairly constant service pressure at the point of outlet discharge shall be not less than 8 pounds per square inch for all fixtures except for direct flush valves, for which it shall be not less than 15 pounds per square inch, and except where special equipment is used requiring higher pressures. In determining the minimum pressure, allowance shall be made for the pressure drop due to friction loss in the piping system during maximum demand periods as well as head, meter, and other losses in the system.

10.14.4 Auxiliary Pressure—Supplementary Tank. If the residual pressure in the system is below the allowable minimum at the highest water outlet when the flow in the system is at peak demand, an automatically controlled pressure tank or gravity tank shall be installed of sufficient capacity to supply sections of the building installation which are too high to be supplied directly from the public water main.

Table C. Water-pipe Sizes
(Based on flush tanks)

No. of apts	Cold and hot water combined				Cold water				Hot water			
	Fixture units	Gpm	Copper	Galv	Fixture units	Gpm	Copper	Galv	Fixture units	Gpm	Copper	Galv
1	8	7	¾	¾	6	5	¾	¾	4.5	...	½	¾
2	16	12	¾	1	12	8	¾	¾	9	7	¾	¾
3	24	17	1	1¼	18	13	1	1	13.5	10	¾	1
4	32	21	1	1¼	24	17	1	1¼	18	13	1	1
5	40	24	1¼	1¼	30	20	1	1¼	22.5	16	1	1¼
6	48	28	1¼	1½	36	23	1¼	1¼	27	18	1	1¼
7	56	32	1¼	1½	42	25	1¼	1¼	31.5	21	1	1¼
8	64	34	1½	1½	48	28	1¼	1½	36	23	1¼	1¼
9	72	36	1½	1½	54	30	1¼	1½	40.5	25	1¼	1¼
10	80	38	1½	1½	60	32	1¼	1½	45	27	1¼	1½
11	88	41	1½	2	66	35	1½	1½	49.5	28	1¼	1½
12	96	43	1½	2	72	37	1½	1½	54	30	1¼	1½
13	104	45	1½	2	78	38	1½	1½	58.5	32	1¼	1½
14	112	47	1½	2	84	40	1½	1½	63	33	1¼	1½
15	120	48	1½	2	90	41	1½	2	67.5	35	1½	1½
16	128	50	1½	2	96	43	1½	2	72	36	1½	1½
17	136	52	1½	2	102	44	1½	2	76.5	38	1½	1½
18	144	54	2	2	108	46	1½	2	81	40	1½	1½
19	152	55	2	2	114	47	1½	2	85.5	41	1½	1½
20	160	57	2	2	120	48	1½	2	90	42	1½	2
21	168	59	2	2	126	50	1½	2	94.5	43	1½	2
22	176	60	2	2	132	51	1½	2	99	44	1½	2
23	184	62	2	2	138	52	1½	2	103.5	45	1½	2
24	192	63	2	2	144	53	2	2	108	46	1½	2
25	200	65	2	2	150	55	2	2	112.5	47	1½	2
26	208	67	2	2	156	56	2	2	117	48	1½	2
27	216	68	2	2	162	57	2	2	121.5	49	1½	2
28	224	70	2	2	168	58	2	2	126	50	1½	2
29	232	72	2	2	174	60	2	2	130.5	51	1½	2
30	240	73	2	2	180	61	2	2	135	52	1½	2
31	248	74	2	2	186	63	2	2	139.5	53	2	2
32	256	76	2	2	192	64	2	2	144	54	2	2
33	264	78	2	2	198	65	2	2	148.5	55	2	2
34	272	80	2	2	204	66	2	2	153	56	2	2
35	280	82	2	2	210	67	2	2	157.5	57	2	2
36	288	83	2	2	216	68	2	2	162	58	2	2
50	400	106	2	2	300	85	2	2	225	70	2	2
100	800	179	2½	2½	600	144	2½	2½	450	115	2	2
150	1,200	234	3	3	900	194	2½	2½	675	157	2½	2½
200	1,600	283	3	3	1,200	234	3	3	900	194	2½	2½
250	2,000	327	3	3	1,500	270	3	3	1,125	224	3	3

10.14.5   Low-pressure Cutoff.   When a booster pump is used on an auxiliary pressure system and the possibility exists that a pressure of 5 pounds per square inch or less may occur on the suction side of the pump, there shall be installed a low-pressure cutoff on the booster pump to prevent the creation of negative pressures on the suction side of the water system.   Other arrangements may be used if found adequate and if approved as such by the administrative authority.
10.14.6   Variable Street Pressures.   When the street main has a wide fluctuation in pressure during the day, the water-distribution system shall be designed for minimum pressure available.

▶   See Part III for data on water-pipe sizing and recommendations on specific requirements for special equipment.

10.14.7   Hazard and Noise.   Where water pressures are excessive, air changers or other approved mechanical devices shall be provided to reduce water hammer or line noises to such an extent that no pressure hazard to the piping system will exist.

▶   Excessive water pressure in pipe of inadequate size can cause breaks in the piping and serious damage in a building.   Excess pressure not only is hazardous to the piping system but causes undesirable noises and annoyance to the occupants of the building, due to water hammer.   See Part III for recommended design data to avoid high pressures and noises.

10.15   Hot-water Distribution

10.15.1   Hot-water Distribution Piping.   The sizing of the hot-water distribution piping shall conform to good engineering practice.   (See Sec. 10.14.)

▶   The procedure for sizing the hot-water distribution system is the same as for the cold-water distribution system.

10.16   Safety Devices

10.16.1   Pressure-relief Valve.   Pressure-relief valves shall be installed for all equipment used for heating or storage of hot water.   The rate of discharge of such a valve shall limit the pressure rise for any given heat input to 10 per cent of the pressure at which the valve is set to open.

▶   For example, a valve set to relieve at 90 pounds per square inch might override to 99 pounds per square inch.   The relief valve should be set so that, during the time thermal expansion is taking place, the pressure will not rise above the predetermined maximum.

10.16.2   Temperature-relief Valves or Energy-shutoff Devices.   Temperature-relief valves or energy shutoff devices shall be installed for equipment used for the heating or storage of hot water.   Each temperature-relief valve shall be rated as to its Btu capacity. At 210°F, it shall be capable of discharging sufficient hot water to prevent any further rise in temperature. As an alternative to the temperature-relief valve, and in lieu thereof, an energy-shutoff device may be used, which will cut off the supply of heat energy to the water tank before the temperature of the water in the tank exceeds 210°F.

▶ This type of relief valve must prevent a rise in temperature above 212°F. It should therefore be large enough to take care of the heat input of the heater. Furthermore, the relieving capacity of a temperature-relief valve should not be less than 1 gallon of water per hour for each 1250 Btu of heater capacity per hour.

Many explosions have been due not to lack of a relief valve on a hot-water tank, but to failures of the relief valve, such as faulty operation, improper location, insufficient size, or poor construction. Both the pressure-relief valve and the temperature-relief valve must be provided with a drain connection equal in diameter to the valve-discharge outlet. The end of the drain off should be located so that there is no danger of scalding a person near the appliance. Also the drain off should be located where it would not damage the plumbing fixture.

10.16.3 Approvals. Combination pressure- and temperature-relief valves or separate pressure- and temperature-relief valves which have been tested and approved by, or meet the specification requirements of, the American Gas Association or the National Board of Casualty and Surety Underwriters shall be considered acceptable.

10.16.4 Relief-valve Location. Temperature-relief valves shall be placed directly above tanks served and in no case more than 3 inches away from such tanks. Pressure-relief valves may be located adjacent to the equipment they serve. There shall be no check valve or shutoff valve between a relief valve and the heater or tank for which it is installed.

10.16.5 Relief Outlet Wastes. The outlet of a pressure, temperature, or other relief valve shall not be connected to the drainage system as a direct waste.

10.16.6 Pressure Marking of Storage Tank. Any storage tank hereafter installed for domestic hot water shall have clearly and indelibly stamped in the metal, or so marked upon a plate welded thereto or otherwise permanently attached, the maximum allowable working pressure. Such markings shall be placed in an accessible position on the outside of the tank so as to make inspection or reinspection readily possible. All storage tanks for domestic hot water shall meet the applicable ASME standards.

▶ See Figs. 10-26 to 10-31 for suggested locations of pressure-relief valves and temperature-relief valves.

Wherever a temperature-relief valve or combination temperature-and-pressure relief valve is installed, it is preferable that the valve stem or thermal element extend into the tank. In no case should it be more than 6 inches from the top of the tank. The element of the valve should be in direct contact with the hot-water flow.

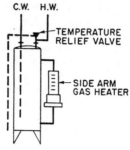

FIG. 10-26

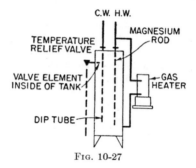

FIG. 10-27

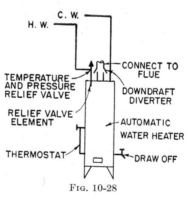

FIG. 10-28

If pressure-relief valves are used separately from temperature-relief valves, the pressure-relief valve should be placed either on the hot- or cold-water piping, as near to the tank as possible.

See Part III for technical information on control devices for hot-water equipment.

Figure 10-26 shows an old-style method of heating water. Because of the possibility of overheating this type of arrangement, it is most important

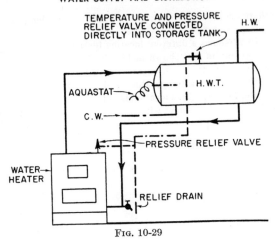

TEMPERATURE AND PRESSURE RELIEF VALVE CONNECTED DIRECTLY INTO STORAGE TANK

H.W.

H.W.T.

AQUASTAT

C.W.

PRESSURE RELIEF VALVE

WATER HEATER

RELIEF DRAIN

FIG. 10-29

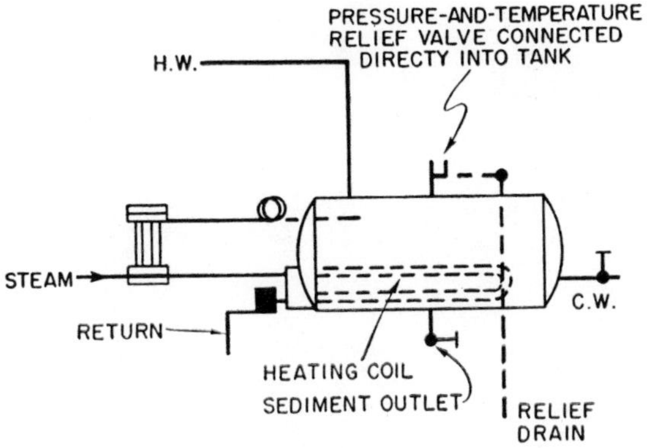

H.W.

PRESSURE-AND-TEMPERATURE RELIEF VALVE CONNECTED DIRECTY INTO TANK

STEAM

RETURN

C.W.

HEATING COIL

SEDIMENT OUTLET

RELIEF DRAIN

FIG. 10-30

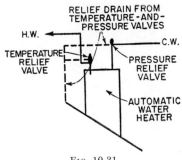

RELIEF DRAIN FROM TEMPERATURE-AND-PRESSURE VALVES

H.W.

C.W.

TEMPERATURE RELIEF VALVE

PRESSURE RELIEF VALVE

AUTOMATIC WATER HEATER

FIG. 10-31

that both temperature- and pressure-relief valves be provided for the equipment.

Figure 10-27 shows a different location for a relief valve.   This location is not so efficient as that shown in Fig. 10-26 because it is slightly below the hottest water in the tank.

Figure 10-28 shows a temperature-and-pressure relief valve above the storage-water heater.   This location is not so effective as when the thermal element is directly in contact with the upper section of the storage tank.

10.17   Miscellaneous

10.17.1   Drain Cock.   All storage tanks shall be equipped with adequate drain cocks.

Drainage System

11.1 Materials

11.1.1 General. Pipe, tubing, and fittings for drainage systems shall comply with the provisions in Chap. 3.

▶ The provisions are those in established standards. Table **3.5** in Chap. **3** provides reference to Federal Specifications or ASA Standards as well as ASTM or Commercial Standards. Each of those standards is applicable to a specific portion of the plumbing system.

11.1.2 Aboveground Piping within Buildings. Soil and waste piping for a drainage system within a building shall be of cast iron, galvanized wrought iron, galvanized open-hearth iron, galvanized steel, lead, brass, or copper pipe, or copper tubing.

11.1.3 Underground Piping within Buildings. Drains within buildings, when underground, shall be of cast-iron soil pipe. For buildings under two stories in height, the pipe may be of service weight. For buildings two stories or more in height, the pipe shall be of extra-heavy weight.

The following materials may be used underground when approved as safe by the administrative authority: galvanized steel or galvanized ferrous alloy, lead, or copper pipe, or copper tubing. Where threaded joints are approved for use underground, they shall be coated and wrapped after installation.

11.1.4 Fittings. Fittings on the drainage system shall conform to the type of piping used. Fittings on screwed pipe shall be of the recessed drainage type. (See Sec. 2.4.)

▶ The piping materials listed in paragraphs **11.1.2** and **11.1.3** are given as guides. Other kinds can be satisfactory, depending on local conditions, such as local soil characteristics, atmospheric conditions, and specific application to the work involved. See Part III.

11.2 Building Sewer

11.2.1 Separate Trenches. The building sewer, when installed in a separate trench from the water-service pipe, shall be cast-iron sewer pipe, vitrified-clay sewer pipe, concrete sewer pipe, bituminized-fiber sewer pipe, or asbestos-cement sewer pipe. Joints shall be watertight and rootproof.

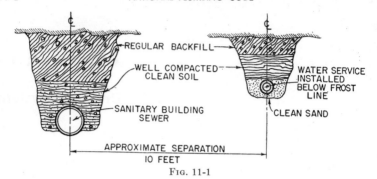

FIG. 11-1

▶ Figure 11-1 illustrates the installation of sanitary sewer and water-service pipe in separate trenches. Thus, should a break occur in the sewer or water line or a leak develop in poorly made joints, there is small possibility of the potable water being contaminated.

The building sewer, when installed in a trench *separate* from the water-service pipe, as in Fig. 11-1, may be constructed of any of the following kinds of pipe:

(*a*) Asbestos-cement pipe (rubber rings joints)
(*b*) Bituminized-fiber pipe (taper joints)
(*c*) Cast-iron soil pipe (either extra heavy or service weight)
(*d*) Concrete sewer pipe (cement mortar, hot-poured or precast joints)
(*e*) Vitrified-clay pipe (cement mortar, hot-poured or precast joints)

The use of either extra-heavy or service-weight cast-iron soil pipe is satisfactory, but standard-weight pipe may not be installed in buildings over two stories in height. Cast-iron soil pipe has recently been standardized to two weights, extra heavy and service weight.

11.2.2 One Trench. The building sewer, when installed in the same trench with the water-service pipe, shall be constructed of durable materials which are corrosion-resistant and shall be so installed as to remain watertight and be root-proof. The building sewer shall be tested with a 10-foot head of water or equivalent and found to be tight.

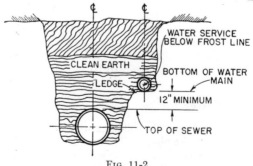

FIG. 11-2

Figure 11-2 shows sewer and water-service pipe in one trench. Because of the additional cost of providing separate trenches for the sewer and water-service pipe, some installations combine both services in the same trench. In order to provide a safeguard for the potable-water main, the water-service main should be placed at least 12 inches above the sewer main and on a side ledge.

The building sewer, when installed in the *same* trench with the water-service pipe, as in Fig. 11-2, shall be constructed of durable materials which are corrosion-resistant and shall be installed so as to remain watertight and root resistant. The following conditions must be met:

(a) The water-service pipe must be installed at least 12 inches above the top level of the building sewer pipe.

(b) The water-service pipe must be placed on a solid shelf at the side of the trench.

(c) The water-service pipe should be in one piece, between the building and the water main.

(d) The building sewer may be of any of the following kinds of pipe: extra-heavy cast-iron soil pipe with hot-poured lead joints, hot-poured or precast joints as per paragraph 4.2.6, joints as prescribed in paragraph 4.2.11 for asbestos-cement sewer pipe and as per paragraph 4.2.12 for bituminized-fiber pipe.

(e) The building sewer shall be tested after installation with not less than a 10-foot head of water or by means of an equivalent test.

Figure 11-3 shows the excavation necessary under a pipe hub and pipe barrel in firm contact with solid ground.

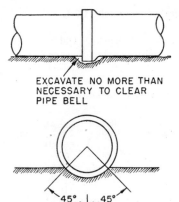

EXCAVATE NO MORE THAN
NECESSARY TO CLEAR
PIPE BELL

45°　45°

BOTTOM OF PIPE BARREL, INCLUDING
45° ARC FROM CENTER, SHOULD BE
IN FIRM CONTACT WITH SOLID GROUND.

FIG. 11-3

11.2.3 Sewer in Filled Ground. A building sewer or building drain installed in filled or unstable ground shall be of cast-iron pipe, except that nonmetallic drains may be laid upon an approved concrete pad if installed in accordance with paragraph 11.2.1.

▶　　The objective is that piping material which does not have the strength to bridge across unstable ground must be provided with a level support upon which the piping can rest without undue stress.

Regarding the provision "that nonmetallic drains may be laid upon an approved concrete pad," the necessity for a concrete pad under the piping arises only when the nonmetallic drains are to be installed in filled-in unstable ground under the building.

11.2.4　Sanitary and Storm Sewers.　Where separate systems of sanitary drainage and storm drainage are installed in the same property, the sanitary and storm building sewers or drains may be laid side by side in one trench.

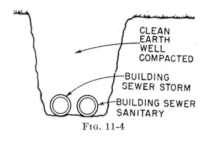

FIG. 11-4

▶　　Figure 11-4 illustrates paragraph 11.2.4.

11.2.5　Old House Sewers and Drains.　Old house sewers and house drains may be used in connection with new buildings or new plumbing and drainage work only when they are found, on examination and test, to conform in all respects to the requirements governing new house sewers, and the administrative authority shall notify the owner to make the changes necessary to conform to this Code.

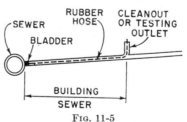

FIG. 11-5

▶　　Before reusing an old sewer it should be tested for flow and tightness. It is possible to test the sewer without excavating.　One of the methods is to use a partly filled bladder to which is attached a long rubber hose through which the bladder may be inflated.　The bladder is floated to the end of the building sewer.　It is then inflated and the sewer pipe filled with water.

If the pipe and joints are broken, it will not hold a proper level of water. See Fig. 11-5.

11.3 Drainage-piping Installation

11.3.1 Horizontal Drainage Piping. Horizontal drainage piping shall be installed at a uniform slope but at slopes not less than permitted in paragraphs 11.3.2, 11.3.3, and 11.3.4.

11.3.2 Small Piping. Horizontal drainage piping of 3-inch diameter and less shall be installed with a fall of not less than ¼ inch per foot.

11.3.3 Large Piping. Horizontal drainage piping larger than 3-inch diameter shall be installed with a fall of not less than ⅛ inch per foot.

11.3.4 Minimum Velocity. Where conditions do not permit building drains and sewers to be laid with a fall as great as that specified, then a lesser slope may be permitted provided the computed velocity will be not less than 2 feet per second.

▶ Generally the slope at which a horizontal drain is installed controls the velocity of the liquid waste flowing in the pipe. A 2-foot-per-second velocity is accepted practice for horizontal waste lines. This velocity will provide the scouring action necessary to maintain a pipe free from fouling.

Higher velocities, or greater fall per foot, increase the carrying capacity of the building drain. It is a good policy to design for the highest possible velocity, as it will tend to keep the drain pipe clean. When designing fixture branches, however, it should be borne in mind that high velocities in pipes with slopes greater than ¼ inch per foot can cause self-siphonage of the trap seal.

Table A provides a chart of approximate velocities for given slopes and diameters. This table was first computed for BMS 66. (See Bibliography.)

Table A. Approximate Flow Velocity of Sewage for Given Slopes and Pipe Diameters

Diam of pipe (in.)	Flow velocity (fps)			
	¹⁄₁₆-in. fall/ft	⅛-in. fall/ft	¼-in. fall/ft	½-in. fall/ft
1¼	....	....	1.61	2.28
1½	....	1.24	1.76	2.45
2	1.02	1.44	*2.03*	2.88
2½	1.14	1.61	2.28	3.23
3	1.24	1.76	2.49	3.53
4	1.44	*2.03*	2.88	4.07
5	1.61	2.28	4.23	4.56
6	1.76	2.49	3.53	5.00
8	*2.03*	2.88	4.07	5.75
10	2.28	3.23	4.56	6.44

House Trap and Fresh-air Inlet. The ASA A40.8 National Plumbing Code and the Report of the Coordinating Committee do not require the installation of a house trap and fresh-air inlet. However, in those cities where house traps are required and a new building is being constructed among old buildings that have house traps, it is not desirable to leave out the house trap and fresh-air inlet in the new building. But where a new community is being planned, the house trap and fresh-air inlet may be omitted.

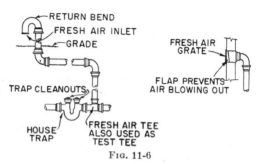

Fig. 11-6

Figure 11-6 illustrates the installation of a house trap and fresh-air inlet. The house trap may be installed in a concrete pit with cover, or the cleanouts may be brought up to the finished floor. The fresh-air inlet may be terminated with a return bend, or if located inside, it may be terminated at the outside front wall with a grate. When a grate is used, install a check or flap which will open readily as an air intake but will not permit a downdraft to blow foul odor into the street.

There are two schools of thought regarding the installation of a building trap in the building drain before connecting it with the building sewer. When a building trap is installed, it is claimed that it will prevent the flow of sewer gases into the plumbing system of the building and thereby avoid using the building system as a means of ventilating the public sewer. It is further claimed that by preventing these sewer gases from entering the building, corrosion of the piping system is reduced.

The fact that a fresh-air inlet is installed when a building trap is provided has proved to be insufficient under certain conditions in relieving the back pressure in the stacks and the building drain. It has been determined by tests that by not installing a building trap the flow and capacity of the building drain are improved.

It is further believed that by permitting the sewer gases to flow freely through the building system the possible concentration of hazardous gases in the street sewer is avoided, thereby preventing possible explosions.

11.4   Fixture Units

11.4.1   Values for Fixtures. Fixture-unit values as given in Table 11.4.2 designate the relative load weight of different kinds of fixtures which shall be

Table 11.4.2   Fixture Units per Fixture or Group

Fixture type	Fixture-unit value as load factors	Minimum size of trap (in.)
1 bathroom group consisting of water closet, lavatory, and bathtub or shower stall....	{ Tank water closet 6 / Flush-valve water closet 8	
Bathtub[1] (with or without overhead shower)	2	1½
Bathtub[1].	3	2
Bidet.	3	Nominal 1½
Combination sink and tray.	3	1½
Combination sink and tray with food-disposal unit.	4	Separate traps 1½
Dental unit or cuspidor.	1	1¼
Dental lavatory.	1	1¼
Drinking fountain.	½	1
Dishwasher,[2] domestic.	2	1½
Floor drains[3].	1	2
Kitchen sink, domestic.	2	1½
Kitchen sink, domestic, with food-disposal unit.	3	1½
Lavatory[4].	1	Small P.O. 1¼
Lavatory[4].	2	Large P.O. 1½
Lavatory, barber, beauty parlor.	2	1½
Lavatory, surgeon's.	2	1½
Laundry tray (1 or 2 compartments).	2	1½
Shower stall, domestic.	2	2
Showers (group) per head[2].	3	
Sinks:		
Surgeon's.	3	1½
Flushing rim (with valve).	8	3
Service (trap standard).	3	3
Service (P trap).	2	2
Pot, scullery, etc.[2].	4	1½
Urinal, pedestal, siphon jet, blowout.	8	Nominal 3
Urinal, wall lip.	4	1½
Urinal stall, washout.	4	2
Urinal trough[2] (each 2-ft section).	2	1½
Wash sink[2] (circular or multiple), each set of faucets.	2	Nominal 1½
Water closet:		
Tank-operated.	4	Nominal 3
Valve-operated.	8	3

[1] A shower head over a bathtub does not increase the fixture value.

[2] See paragraphs 11.4.3 and 11.4.4 for method of computing unit values of fixtures not listed in Table 11.4.2 or for rating of devices with intermittent flows.

[3] Size of floor drain shall be determined by the area of surface water to be drained.

[4] Lavatories with 1¼- or 1½-inch trap have the same load value; larger P.O. plugs have greater flow rate.

employed in estimating the total load carried by a soil or waste pipe and shall be used in connection with the tables of sizes for soil, waste, and drain pipes for which the permissible load is given in terms of fixture units.

▶ Those who are interested in tracing the mathematical origin of Tables 11.4.2 and 11.4.3, and verifying the conclusions will find complete data in Part III.

11.4.2 (See Table 11.4.2.)

11.4.3 Fixtures not listed in Table 11.4.2 shall be estimated in accordance with Table 11.4.3.

Table 11.4.3

Fixture drain or trap size (in.)	Fixture-unit value	Fixture drain or trap size (in.)	Fixture-unit value
1¼ and smaller.............	1	2½....................	4
1½......................	2	3.....................	5
2.......................	3	4.....................	6

▶ It is difficult to provide a rating for all plumbing fixtures as shown on Table 11.4.2 because of the larger number of fixtures made for special purposes, such as printers' sinks, laboratory sinks, and special hospital fixtures.   Special-purpose fixtures may be rated by the size of the trap recommended by the manufacturer.   It is hoped that eventually all manufacturers of fixtures and appliances will indicate the fixture-unit value on their products.   Such values for each fixture would greatly assist in accurately designing a plumbing system, especially for large buildings.   In the meantime, Table 11.4.3 provides an approximate rating of those fixtures not rated in Table 11.4.2.

11.4.4 Values for Continuous Flow.   For a continuous or semicontinuous flow into a drainage system, such as from a pump, pump ejector, air-conditioning equipment, or similar device, two fixture units shall be allowed for each gallon per minute of flow.

▶ Figure 11-7 illustrates sizing for an intermittent flow from a sump pump. The building has five soil stacks.   Stacks 1, 2, and 5 contain public-type fixtures.   Stacks 3 and 4 contain private-type fixtures.   The total fixture units for each stack are given.

Each stack is sized according to Table 11.5.3.   Horizontal branches from the base of a stack to the building drain are the same size as the building drain (Table 11.5.2), and the building drain is then sized according to its fall per foot.

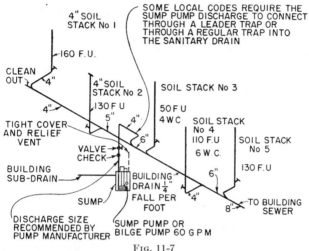

Fig. 11-7

The discharge from the sump is converted into fixture-unit values by multiplying the number of gallons flow by 2. It is recommended, however, where the discharge from the sump is connected to the building drain, that there be no connections from the gravity system for at least 10 feet downflow from the sump connection. If this is impractical, the building drain should be increased one pipe size. This prevents a heavy load concentration which could affect the fixtures on the lower floor where the stack is connected close to the sump discharge.

It would be preferable to connect large flows from the sump close to the point where the building drain leaves the building. Where the discharge is from pneumatic ejectors, or where heavy and abrupt discharges are to be expected, the discharge should be carried separately to the building sewer just outside the building wall.

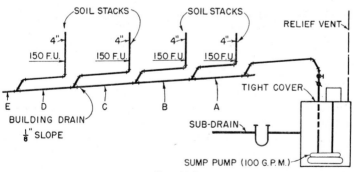

Fig. 11-8

Figure 11-8 illustrates another example of continuous-flow rate. The number of fixture units equivalent to a sump pump discharging 100 gallons per minute is 200 fixture units. According to Table 11.5.2, the drain may be sized as follows:

Sizing of Drain
Example: Fig. 11-8

Slope: ⅛ in./ft			Slope: ¼ in./ft		
Location	Number of fixture units	Diameter of drain (in.)	Location	Number of fixture units	Diameter of drain (in.)
Point A	200	5	Point A	200	4
Point B	350	5	Point B	350	5
Point C	500	6	Point C	500	6
Point D	650	6	Point D	650	6
Point E	800	8	Point E	800	6

It is desirable that the slope of the building drain be maintained uniformly throughout its length. If this is impractical, select a pipe size which provides for velocities of not less than 2 feet per second. (See Table A.)

Horizontal piping from a branch to a group of fixtures on the same level as the building drain should be the same as for the building drain. (See paragraph 11.5.2.)

A 3-inch building drain is large enough to serve two water closets, plus whatever additional small fixtures are desired, provided the total number of fixture units does not exceed the maximum permitted in Table 11.5.2. Blowout-type urinals are classified as water closets in computing the size of the building drain. The reason for this is that a blowout urinal will discharge as much water as a regular water closet in the same time.

11.5   Determination of Sizes for the Drainage System

11.5.1   Maximum Fixture-unit Load.   The maximum number of fixture units that may be connected to a given size of building sewer, building drain, horizontal branch, or vertical soil or waste stack is given in Tables 11.5.2 and 11.5.3.

11.5.2   (See Table 11.5.2.)

11.5.3   (See Table 11.5.3.)

▶   The following is an explanation of the theory which resulted in the establishment of Tables 11.5.2 and 11.5.3:

Developments inside a drainage and venting system are complicated. Individual fixtures have different rates of discharge due either (1) to the average rate of flow each time the fixture is used or (2) to the length of time of each discharge.

Table 11.5.2   Building Drains and Sewers

Diameter of pipe (in.)	Maximum number of fixture units that may be connected to any portion of the building drain or the building sewer			
	Fall per foot			
	$\frac{1}{16}$ in.	$\frac{1}{8}$ in.	$\frac{1}{4}$ in.	$\frac{1}{2}$ in.
2	. . . . .	. . . . .	21	26
2½	. . . . .	. . . . .	24	31
3	. . . . .	20[2]	27[2]	36[2]
4	. . . . .	180	216	250
5	. . . . .	390	480	575
6	. . . . .	700	840	1,000
8	1,400	1,600	1,920	2,300
10	2,500	2,900	3,500	4,200
12	3,900	4,600	5,600	6,700
15	7,000	8,300	10,000	12,000

[1] Includes branches of the building drain.
[2] Not over two water closets.

Table 11.5.3   Horizontal Fixture Branches and Stacks

Diameter of pipe (in.)	Maximum number of fixture units that may be connected to:			
	Any horizontal[1] fixture branch	One stack of 3 stories in height or 3 intervals	More than 3 stories in height	
			Total for stack	Total at one story or branch interval
1¼	1	2	2	1
1½	3	4	8	2
2	6	10	24	6
2½	12	20	42	9
3	20[2]	30[3]	60[3]	16[2]
4	160	240	500	90
5	360	540	1,100	200
6	620	960	1,900	350
8	1,400	2,200	3,600	600
10	2,500	3,800	5,600	1,000
12	3,900	6,000	8,400	1,500
15	7,000			

[1] Does not include branches of the building drain.
[2] Not over two water closets.
[3] Not over six water closets.

If it were normal practice to operate all fixtures at exactly the same moment, it would be simple to estimate what the total discharge flow would be at a given moment, but in a large building with many plumbing fixtures, all the fixtures never would be started and stopped exactly at the same moment under ordinary working conditions.

The theory that the fall of liquids within a stack continues to accelerate like a free-falling object is erroneous. As soon as the water from a horizontal drain enters the vertical stack, the force of gravity accelerates it downward; but within a short distance, usually within a one- or two-story drop, the friction against the interior walls of the pipe becomes equal to the force of gravity, thereby equalizing the rate of fall. From that point of equilibrium, the rate of fall down the stack continues unchanged until it reaches the base of the stack, provided, of course, that no lower horizontal branches also commence discharging, colliding, and interfering with the fall.

Therefore, the pipe sizes in Tables **11.5.2** and **11.5.3** are a reconcilement of the following considerations:

(a) Experience and good practice have established that the "normal fullness" of piping in first-class condition is one-quarter full.

(b) The remaining capacity is the margin of safety for unusual peak demand.

(c) Use the smallest size pipe that would carry away waste water from individual fixtures as rapidly as is consistent with good practice to avoid clogging.

(d) Avoid causing excessive pressures at points where the fixture drains connect to the stack. Pressures either negative or positive could reduce the trap seal to a dangerous level or blow sewer gas into the room.   (See Part III.)

11.5.4   Minimum Size of Soil and Waste Stacks.   No soil or waste stack shall be smaller than the largest horizontal branch connected thereto, except that a 4 by 3 water-closet connection shall not be considered as a reduction in pipe size.

▶   Figure 11-9 illustrates a one-story row house containing four dwelling units with the building drain underground.

In section *a* the water closet is stack-vented; the bathtub is wet-vented through the lavatory; the sink and dishwasher have a common vent.   See paragraph 12.10.2 for sizing when one plumbing fixture connects below the other.   If both plumbing fixtures connect at the same level, the vertical waste is sized according to Table 11.4.2 for the total number of fixture units; in this case, there are four fixture units, which require a 1½-inch waste.

In section *b* the water closet is stack-vented; the bathtub is wet-vented through the lavatory waste; the sink and food-waste grinder have a common vent.   The vertical waste below the sink connection is sized 2 inches, according to paragraph 12.10.2.   If both fixtures are connected at the same level, the vertical waste is 2 inches, because the total number of fixture units is five.

All fixtures in *c* are stack-vented except the sink, which is individually vented or back-vented. The back vent is 1¼ inches because the sink represents only two fixture units. The stack here must be 3 inches up to the highest fixture connection.

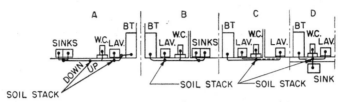

FIGURE IN CIRCLE GIVES NUMBER OF FIXTURE UNITS

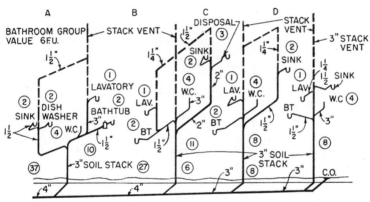

Fig. 11-9

In section *d* all fixtures are stack-vented, and regardless of climate the soil stack *must* be extended full size 3 inches in diameter through the roof as a stack vent.

The building drain is sized according to Table 11.5.2, and cleanouts are provided according to paragraph 5.4.1. Branches for connecting plumbing fixtures are vented at the distances provided in Table 12.9.3. The slope at which a branch is roughed should not exceed one pipe diameter (see paragraph 12.9.4).

There are other ways of wet venting a fixture which cannot be provided with a continuous or back vent. The principle of wet venting may be applied to a floor drain, a dental unit, or any other fixture which must be installed in the middle of a room and cannot be individually vented.

The advantage of wet venting is that it ensures a clear vent. There is no assurance that a back vent installed horizontally will remain open and effective, nor is there any way of knowing when it becomes clogged.

11.5.5   Minimum Size of Stack Vent or Vent Stack.   Any structure on which a building drain is installed shall have at least one stack vent or vent stack carried full size through the roof not less than 3 inches in diameter or the size of the building drain, whichever is the lesser.

▶   By reference to Fig. 11-9 it will be noted that stack *d* is shown full size through the roof but other stack vents may be reduced.

11.5.6   Future Fixtures.   When provision is made for the future installation of fixtures, those provided for shall be considered in determining the required sizes of drain pipes.   Construction to provide for such future installation shall be terminated with a plugged fitting or fittings at the stack so as to form no dead end.

11.5.7   Underground-drainage Piping.   No portion of the drainage system installed underground or below a basement or cellar shall be less than 2 inches in diameter.

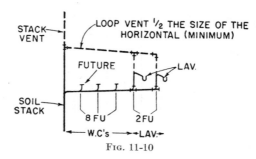

FIG. 11-10

▶   Figure 11-10 illustrates a toilet room with two water closets and two lavatories to be installed and roughing for a third water closet to be installed at some future time.   The branch must therefore be sized as though all three water closets were to be installed initially.

The total number of fixtures now installed are two public water closets and two public lavatories with a fixture rating of 8 + 8 + 2 + 2 = 20 fixture units.   Table 11.5.3, column 2, any horizontal fixture branch, shows that a 3-inch diameter pipe is satisfactory.   However, by roughing a future closet on this branch, the total number of fixture units that must be figured are 8 + 8 + 8 + 2 + 2 = 28 fixture units; therefore the diameter of the branch must be 4 inches.

There is also a difference in sizing the loop vent.   With a 3-inch horizontal branch a 1½-inch loop vent is adequate.   With a 4-inch horizontal waste, a 2-inch-diameter loop would be the minimum permitted.

11.6   Offsets on Drainage Piping

11.6.1   Offsets of 45 Degrees or Less.   An offset in a vertical stack, with a change of direction of 45 degrees or less from the vertical, may be sized as a straight vertical stack. In case a horizontal branch connects to the stack within 2 feet above or below the offset, a relief vent shall be installed in accordance with paragraph 12.18.3.

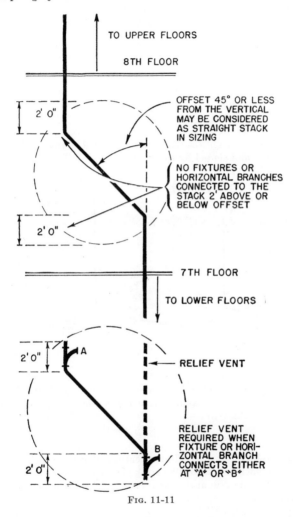

TO UPPER FLOORS

8TH FLOOR

2' 0"

OFFSET 45° OR LESS
FROM THE VERTICAL
MAY BE CONSIDERED
AS STRAIGHT STACK
IN SIZING

NO FIXTURES OR
HORIZONTAL BRANCHES
CONNECTED TO THE
STACK 2' ABOVE OR
BELOW OFFSET

2' 0"

7TH FLOOR

TO LOWER FLOORS

2' 0"   A

RELIEF VENT

RELIEF VENT
REQUIRED WHEN
FIXTURE OR HORI-
ZONTAL BRANCH
CONNECTS EITHER
AT "A" OR "B"

B

2' 0"

Fig. 11-11

Figure 11-11 shows that the relief vent may be installed either **as a ver**tical continuation of the lower section of the stack or as a side vent connected to the lower section between the offset and the next lower fixture or horizontal branch. The diameter of the relief vent must be no less than the diameter of the main vent or the soil or waste stack, whichever is the smaller.

Offsets of 45 degrees or less do not seriously affect the flow in the stack. Table 11.5.3 provides for loading of stacks not more than ½-full at any point. This partial loading is a safety factor. When a horizontal load is imposed at this point, the relief vent is necessary in order to prevent excess pressures from affecting the operation of the fixtures connected to the branch.

11.6.2 Waste Stacks Serving Kitchen Sinks. In a one- or two-family dwelling only in which the waste stack or vent receives the discharge of a kitchen-type sink and also serves as a vent for fixtures connected to the horizontal portion of the branch served by the waste stack, the minimum size of the waste stack up to the highest sink branch connection shall be 2 inches in diameter. Above that point the size of the stack shall be governed by the total number of fixture units vented by the stack.

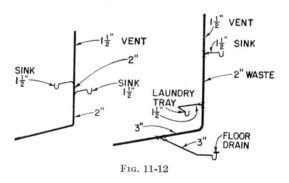

Fig. 11-12

11.6.3 Above Highest Branch. An offset above the highest horizontal branch is an offset in the stack vent and shall be considered only as it affects the developed length of the vent.

▶   Figure 11-13 shows that offsets occurring above the highest fixture or horizontal branch are part of the stack vent and do not affect the capacity of the stack. The vent at this point is of sufficient diameter to provide for air circulation.

11.6.4 Below Lowest Branch. In the case of an offset in a soil or waste stack below the lowest horizontal branch, no change in diameter of the stack because of the offset shall be required if it is made at an angle not greater than 45 degrees. If such an offset is made at an angle greater than 45 degrees, the required diameter of the offset and the stack below it shall be determined as for a building drain. (See Table 11.5.2.)

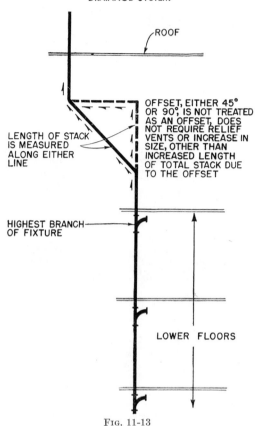

ROOF

OFFSET, EITHER 45°
OR 90°, IS NOT TREATED
AS AN OFFSET, DOES
NOT REQUIRE RELIEF
VENTS OR INCREASE IN
SIZE, OTHER THAN
INCREASED LENGTH
OF TOTAL STACK DUE
TO THE OFFSET

LENGTH OF STACK
IS MEASURED
ALONG EITHER
LINE

HIGHEST BRANCH
OF FIXTURE

LOWER FLOORS

Fig. 11-13

▶ Figure 11-14 illustrates an offset below the lowest horizontal branch. A 45-degree offset will not affect the size of the pipe, regardless of where such an offset occurs in the soil or waste stack. But if the offset is in a horizontal position (see definition of horizontal pipe), it is necessary to increase the diameter of the offset pipe.

This is done to avoid developing pressure or vacuum which will disturb the trap seal of the lower fixture. The threat of such a condition becomes more serious as the load in the stack is increased. The most critical area is at the base of the stack or at the lowest floor in a building, especially when an offset or change of direction occurs immediately below a plumbing fixture. A plumbing fixture should not be installed nearer than 2 feet from the offset.

11.6.5 Offsets of More Than 45 Degrees. A stack with an offset of more than 45 degrees from the vertical shall be sized as follows:

The portion of the stack above the offset shall be sized as for a regular stack based on the total number of fixture units above the offset.

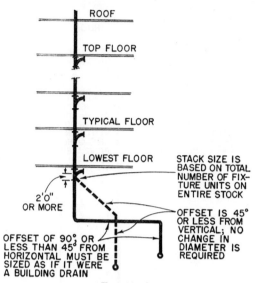

ROOF

TOP FLOOR

TYPICAL FLOOR

LOWEST FLOOR

STACK SIZE IS BASED ON TOTAL NUMBER OF FIXTURE UNITS ON ENTIRE STOCK

2'0" OR MORE

OFFSET IS 45° OR LESS FROM VERTICAL; NO CHANGE IN DIAMETER IS REQUIRED

OFFSET OF 90° OR LESS THAN 45° FROM HORIZONTAL MUST BE SIZED AS IF IT WERE A BUILDING DRAIN

Fig. 11-14

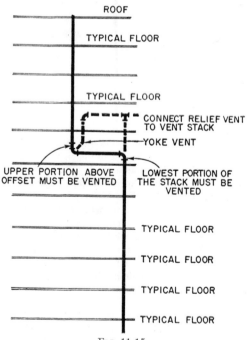

ROOF

TYPICAL FLOOR

TYPICAL FLOOR

CONNECT RELIEF VENT TO VENT STACK

YOKE VENT

UPPER PORTION ABOVE OFFSET MUST BE VENTED

LOWEST PORTION OF THE STACK MUST BE VENTED

TYPICAL FLOOR

TYPICAL FLOOR

TYPICAL FLOOR

TYPICAL FLOOR

Fig. 11-15

The upper portion of the stack above the offset shall be sized as for building drain. (See Table 11.5.2, column 5.)

The portion of the stack below the offset shall be sized as for the offset or based on the total number of fixture units on the entire stack, whichever is the larger. (See Table 11.5.3, column 4.)

A relief vent for the offset shall be installed as provided in Chap. 12, and in no case shall the horizontal branch connect to the stack within 2 feet above or below the offset.

▶   Figure 11-15 illustrates an offset of more than 45 degrees; in this case the offset is 90 degrees.

The upper portion of the offset must be provided with a relief vent in order to avoid back pressure affecting the fixtures located near the offset. The lower portion of the stack must be provided with a relief vent in order to safeguard the fixtures on the downstream portion of the stack.

In order clearly to illustrate the requirements of paragraph 11.6.5, Fig. 11-16 shows the sizing of a stack in a 12-story building where there is one offset between the fifth and sixth floors and another offset below the street floor.

Sizing is computed as follows:

Step 1: Compute the fixture units connected to the entire stack.   In this case, assume there are 1,200 fixture units connected to the stack from the street floor through the top floor.

Step 2: Size the portion of the stack above the fifth-floor offset.   There are 400 fixture units from the top floor down through the sixth floor. According to Table 11.5.3, column 4, 400 fixture units require a 4-inch stack.

Step 3: Size the offset on the fifth floor.   An offset is sized like a building drain.   According to Table 11.5.2, column 4, 400 fixture units require a 5-inch offset.

Step 4: Size the lower portion of the stack from the fifth floor down through the street floor.   The lower portion of the stack must be large enough to serve all the fixture units connected to it, from the top floor down, in this case, 1,200 fixture units.   According to Table 11.5.3, 1,200 fixture units require a 6-inch stack.

Step 5: Size the offset below the street floor the same as for a building drain.   The lower offset also has to be large enough to serve all fixture units from the top floor down, in this case, 1,200 fixture units.   According to Table 11.5.2, 1,200 fixture units require an 8-inch offset.   This 8-inch line is run full size to the building drain.

The fixtures on the sixth floor should be connected to the stack at least 2 feet above the offset.   If this is not possible, then connect them separately to the stack at least 2 feet below the offset, and if this is not possible either, run the fixture drain down to the fifth or fourth floor and connect to the stack there.

The offset on the fifth floor should be provided with a relief vent.   Sizing the offset larger than the stack and providing a relief vent will prevent pressures from building up at the point of offset and possibly siphoning or blowing nearby trap seals.

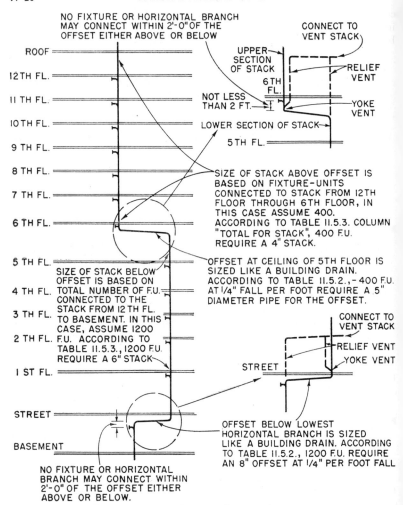

NO FIXTURE OR HORIZONTAL BRANCH MAY CONNECT WITHIN 2'-0" OF THE OFFSET EITHER ABOVE OR BELOW

CONNECT TO VENT STACK

ROOF

12TH FL.

11TH FL.

10TH FL.

9TH FL.

8TH FL.

7TH FL.

6TH FL.

5TH FL.

4TH FL.

3RD FL.

2TH FL.

1ST FL.

STREET

BASEMENT

UPPER SECTION OF STACK

6TH FL.

RELIEF VENT

NOT LESS THAN 2 FT.

YOKE VENT

LOWER SECTION OF STACK

5TH FL.

SIZE OF STACK ABOVE OFFSET IS BASED ON FIXTURE-UNITS CONNECTED TO STACK FROM 12TH FLOOR THROUGH 6TH FLOOR, IN THIS CASE ASSUME 400. ACCORDING TO TABLE 11.5.3. COLUMN "TOTAL FOR STACK", 400 F.U. REQUIRE A 4" STACK.

SIZE OF STACK BELOW OFFSET IS BASED ON TOTAL NUMBER OF F.U. CONNECTED TO THE STACK FROM 12TH FL. TO BASEMENT. IN THIS CASE, ASSUME 1200 F.U. ACCORDING TO TABLE 11.5.3., 1200 F.U. REQUIRE A 6" STACK

OFFSET AT CEILING OF 5TH FLOOR IS SIZED LIKE A BUILDING DRAIN. ACCORDING TO TABLE 11.5.2., – 400 F.U. AT 1/4" FALL PER FOOT REQUIRE A 5" DIAMETER PIPE FOR THE OFFSET.

CONNECT TO VENT STACK

RELIEF VENT

YOKE VENT

STREET

OFFSET BELOW LOWEST HORIZONTAL BRANCH IS SIZED LIKE A BUILDING DRAIN. ACCORDING TO TABLE 11.5.2., 1200 F.U. REQUIRE AN 8" OFFSET AT 1/4" PER FOOT FALL

NO FIXTURE OR HORIZONTAL BRANCH MAY CONNECT WITHIN 2'-0" OF THE OFFSET EITHER ABOVE OR BELOW.

Fig. 11-16

The critical points of a soil stack are at the base and where an offset occurs. Provide ample relieving vents at these points. Each branch should be properly sized and vented to prevent an unbalanced condition within the branch.

11.7 Sumps and Ejectors

11.7.1 Building Drains below Sewer. Building drains which cannot be discharged to the sewer by gravity flow shall be discharged into a tightly covered and vented sump, from which the liquid shall be lifted and discharged into the building gravity drainage system by automatic pumping equipment or by any equally efficient method approved by the administrative authority.

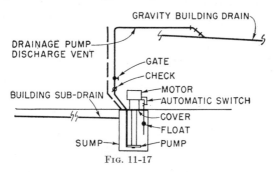

Fig. 11-17

▶ Sewage below the level of the sewer is generally handled through automatically controlled sewage pumps or air ejectors.

Figure 11-17 illustrates a simple installation for handling drainage which cannot be discharged by gravity into the public sewer.

When a limited number of fixtures are installed below sewer level, a single pump will be sufficient to handle the work; but when a large number of fixtures are involved, a duplex system should be used, so that in the event of a breakdown of one pump another would remain in operation. When a duplex unit is used, it is good practice to alternate the operation of the pumps automatically.

11.7.2 Storage Period. The storage of drainage in a sump or ejector shall not exceed a period of 12 hours.

▶ The storage period depends upon the number of fixtures installed in the sump or ejector system. There are times, for instance over a week end, when in industrial or commercial buildings the system need not operate regularly.

11.7.3 Design. Sump and pumping equipment shall be so designed as to discharge all contents accumulated in the sump during the cycle of emptying operation.

▶ If an automatic system is designed, it is generally arranged so that it will be in continuous operation until the contents of the tank are pumped out.

11.7.4 Venting. The system of drainage piping below the sewer level shall be installed and vented in a manner similar to that of the gravity system.

▶ The tables applying to the gravity system also apply to a subsoil system.

11.7.5 Duplex Equipment. Sumps receiving the discharge of more than six water closets shall be provided with duplex pumping equipment.

▶   Six water closets have been determined as the minimum to be installed with a single pump. There are exceptions to this rule, which must be judged by occupancy and availability of other facilities.

11.7.6 Vent Sizes. Building sump vents shall be sized in accordance with Table 12.21.5 but shall in no case be sized less than 1½ inches.

11.7.7 Separate Vents. Vents from pneumatic ejectors or similar equipment shall be carried separately to the open air as a vent terminal.

11.7.8 Connections. No direct connection of a steam exhaust, blowoff, or drip pipe shall be made with the building drainage system. Waste water, when discharged into the building drainage system, shall be at a temperature not higher than 140°F. When higher temperature exists, proper cooling methods shall be provided.

▶   Pneumatic ejectors have a tendency to discharge quickly, differing from the even flow of the centrifugal pumping equipment. It is therefore recommended that, where compressed-air ejectors are used, the venting system be separate from the gravity system.

Paragraph 11.7.8 protects the building piping as well as the building and public sewer. Extremely hot water or steam discharges may damage the piping. Hot-water discharge at more than 140°F or steam-discharge should first be collected into a sump pump, where it may cool off before flowing into the sewer.

11.8   Floor Drains

11.8.1 Accessibility. Floor drains shall connect into a trap so constructed that it can be readily cleaned and of a size to serve efficiently the purpose for which it is intended. The drain inlet shall be so located that it is, at all times, in full view.

11.8.2 Connection. Floor drains subject to backflow shall not be directly connected to the drainage system.

11.8.3 Provision for Evaporation. Floor-drain trap seals subject to evaporation shall be of the deep-seal type or shall be fed from an approved plumbing fixture or by means of an approved automatic priming device designed and approved for that purpose.

▶   The trap shall be either accessible from the floor-drain inlet or by a separate cleanout within the drain. Figure 11-18 illustrates several types of drains which meet these conditions.
   (*a*) Typical drain with integral trap, that may be cleaned through removable strainer at floor level.
   (*b*) Floor drain with combination cleanout and backwater valve, where there is a possibility of backflow.
   (*c*) Drain with combined cleanout, backwater valve and secondary bucket.

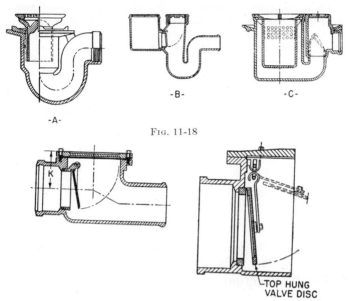

Fig. 11-18

Fig. 11-19

Figure **11-19** illustrates various types of backwater valves that may be installed where the level of the sewer is low and backflow may occur.

Where a floor drain is installed in a seldom-used location, the trap seal might evaporate and permit sewer gas to enter the building.   In such case it is well to provide means for refilling the trap seal.   Figure **11-20** illustrates one manner whereby a trap seal of a floor drain may be kept full at all times.

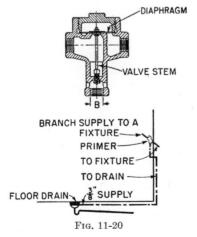

Fig. 11-20

Figure 11-20 shows the means of maintaining a proper seal in basement-floor drain traps and other traps used infrequently. Seldom-used traps tend to lose their seals by evaporation. A primer is installed in a frequently used water-supply line and connected to the trap. Water enters the primer, forces the diaphragm upward, and opens the valve, allowing water to replenish the trap seal. This method prevents foul and unsanitary sewer odors from entering the building.

11.8.4 Size. Floor-drain traps and drains, installed below a basement floor or underground, shall be not less than 2 inches in diameter.

11.8.5 Bell Traps. Bell traps are prohibited.

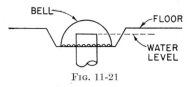

FIG. 11-21

▶   Figure 11-21 shows a bell-trap drain.

11.9   Frost Protection

11.9.1   No soil or waste pipes shall be installed or permitted outside of a building or concealed in outside walls or in any place where they may be subjected to freezing temperatures, unless adequate provision is made to protect them from frost.

▶   Protection may be by means of frost insulation in cold climates. In climates where the temperature will not be below freezing, there is no mechanical objection to outside installation.

CHAPTER 12

Vents and Venting

12.1 Materials

12.1.1 Vents. Pipe, tubing, and fittings for the vent-piping system shall comply with the provisions in Chap. 3.

12.1.2 Specific Type. Standards given in Table 3.5 apply to the specific materials approved for use and as indicated in the various paragraphs in this chapter as they apply to the venting system.

▶ The standard is a guide from which to select pipe and fitting best suited for the locality.

12.1.3 Piping. Vent piping shall be of cast iron, galvanized wrought iron, galvanized steel, and ferrous alloys, lead, brass, or copper pipe, or copper tubing.

▶ Materials listed in paragraph **12.1.3** are satisfactory for the work intended. Local experience should decide which materials are best for the locality.

12.1.4 Underground. Vent piping placed underground shall be cast-iron soil pipe, provided that other materials may be used for underground vents when found adequate and installed as directed by the administrative authority. Where threaded joints are permitted for use underground, they shall be coated and wrapped after installation and test.

▶ Tests have shown that other kinds of piping materials will stand up equally as well as cast iron under specific conditions. The local official can determine performance and suitability.

12.1.5 Fittings. Fittings shall conform to the type of pipe used in the vent system as required by paragraphs 12.1.2 and 12.1.3.

▶ For vents, experience has shown that the following are satisfactory: cast-iron soil fittings, copper fittings, cast-iron screw fittings, and malleable fittings. Therefore local judgment should determine the type best suited.

12.1.6 Acid System. Vent piping of acid-waste systems shall conform to that required for acid-waste pipe, except as may be found adequate by the administrative authority.

▶   Technical analysis of the performance requirement will affect the choice of pipe and fitting. Under certain conditions regular materials are satisfactory; under severe conditions the engineer who laid out the job and knows the performance requirement should be consulted.

12.1.7 Other Materials. Nothing in this section shall be deemed to preclude the use of other materials of equal or better quality when approved as such by the administrative authority.

▶   This paragraph permits the acceptance of new materials that through research and practice have proved satisfactory for specific usage. An example of this is asbestos-cement pipe for dry vents or copper tube for drainage installations. Numerous trial installations have been made during the past 8 or 10 years and have proved satisfactory; therefore such piping is now permitted by several local codes or for specific usage.

12.2 Protection of Trap Seals

12.2.1 Traps Protected. The protection of trap seals from siphonage or back pressure shall be accomplished by the appropriate use of soil or waste stacks, vents, revents, back vents, loop vents, circuit or continuous vents, or combinations thereof installed in accordance with the requirements of this chapter.

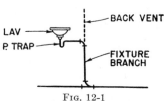

Fig. 12-1

▶   The objective is to provide a balance of air within the drainage system so that at no time will positive or negative pressures be greater than 1 inch at the trap seal of a fixture.

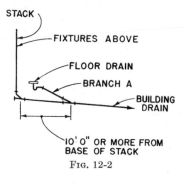

Fig. 12-2

Figure 12-1 illustrates a lavatory installed without a vent. The flow of the liquid in the pipe when the fixture is discharged creates a siphonic action which might pull the trap seal, but a back vent as shown by the dotted line would prevent it.

Figure 12-2 illustrates a floor drain placed near the base of a soil stack. When a heavy flow occurs in the stack, an abnormal positive pressure develops at the turn into the horizontal. The nearer a floor drain is placed to the stack, the greater the disturbance, and the trap seal might be siphoned.

Branch *A*, if 3 or 4 inches in diameter and longer than 5 feet, would be less apt to cause trap-seal disturbance.

12.3 Vent Stacks

12.3.1 Installation. A vent stack or a main vent shall be installed with a soil or waste stack whenever back vents, relief vents, or other branch vents are required in two or more branch intervals.

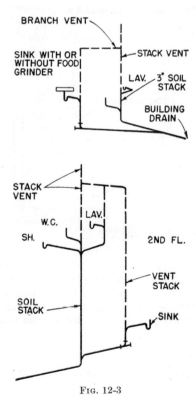

FIG. 12-3

►   Figure **12-3** illustrates this condition.   In a one-story building, branch vents may connect at the stack vent.   In a two- or more story building, a separate vent is required.

12.3.2 Terminal. The vent stack shall terminate independently above the roof of the building or shall be connected with the extension of the soil or waste stack (stack vent) at least 6 inches above the flood-level rim of the highest fixture.

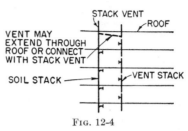

Fig. 12-4

►   **Figure 12-4 illustrates paragraph 12.3.2.**

12.3.3 Main Stack. Every building in which plumbing is installed shall have at least one main stack, which shall run undiminished in size and as directly as possible from the building drain through to the open air above the roof.

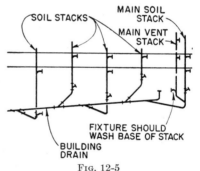

Fig. 12-5

►   This requirement is particularly for buildings where a large number of fixtures are installed and where long runs of pipe are necessary.   The main vent should be located so as to provide a complete loop for circulation of air through the system.   Figure **12-5** illustrates this point.

12.4 Vent Terminals

12.4.1 Roof Extension. Extensions of vent pipes through a roof shall be terminated at least 6 inches above it.

▶   Since the issuance of the National Plumbing Code, additional research has been made on frost closure, again bearing out the fact that the shorter the extension above the roof, the less chance for frost closure. See Part III.

12.4.2 Roof Garden. Where a roof is to be used for any purpose other than weather protection, the vent extensions shall be run at least 5 feet above the roof.

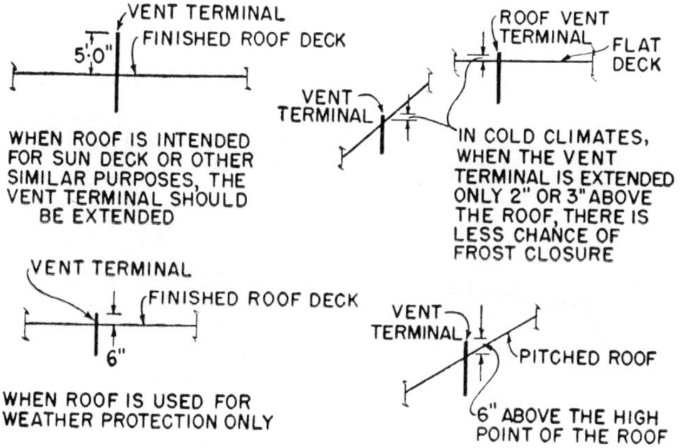

VENT TERMINAL
FINISHED ROOF DECK
5'·0"

WHEN ROOF IS INTENDED FOR SUN DECK OR OTHER SIMILAR PURPOSES, THE VENT TERMINAL SHOULD BE EXTENDED

ROOF VENT TERMINAL FLAT DECK

VENT TERMINAL

IN COLD CLIMATES, WHEN THE VENT TERMINAL IS EXTENDED ONLY 2" OR 3" ABOVE THE ROOF, THERE IS LESS CHANCE OF FROST CLOSURE

VENT TERMINAL
FINISHED ROOF DECK
6"

WHEN ROOF IS USED FOR WEATHER PROTECTION ONLY

VENT TERMINAL

PITCHED ROOF

6" ABOVE THE HIGH POINT OF THE ROOF

Fig. 12-6

▶   Figure 12-6 illustrates a vent-terminal extension where the roof is to be used as a sun deck, roof garden, or laundry drying area. The top of the vent terminal should be extended 6½ feet so that it is above the height of a person. Flooring or decks placed over the roof should be considered in measuring height. However, when the roof is not intended to serve other than structural purposes, there is no need of extending a vent terminal higher than 6 inches. Numerous experiments have proved that a vent terminal which extends only 2 or 3 inches above the roof is less apt to develop frost closure than a higher vent terminal.

12.4.3 Flashings. Each vent terminal shall be made watertight with the roof by proper flashing.

▶   Figure 12-7 illustrates some of the various types of flashings for stack-vent terminals, as follows:

Sketch *a* shows a flashing on a pitched roof. If the flashing is so constructed that air circulation from the attic space reaches it, frost closure will be lessened during severe cold weather. A piece of mesh screen under the roof prevents vermin from entering the house from the roof during warm weather.

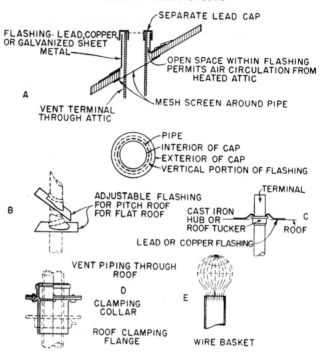

VENT STACK FLASHING SLEEVE
FIG. 12-7

Sketch *b* shows a commonly used flashing adjustable from horizontal to 45 degrees. It usually is made from 24-gauge galvanized iron, or 14-ounce cold-rolled copper, or 3-pound sheet lead.

Sketch *c* illustrates another method of flashing which brings the hub of cast-iron soil pipe in line with the roof. A copper or lead flashing is calked between the hub and the terminal extension. Prefabricated roof flashings using the same principle are available.

Sketch *d*. This flashing sleeve is available for various vent-pipe diameters and is easily installed. Lead or copper flashing is placed between the clamping collar and pipe, which assures a leakproof joint.

Sketch *e*. In a wooded area it is sometimes desirable to provide a wire basket at the top of the vent terminal to prevent leaves from falling into and clogging the vent pipe. The basket will also prevent birds from nesting inside a vent terminal.

12.4.4 Flag Poling. Vent terminals shall not be used for the purpose of flag poling, TV aerials, or similar purposes, except when the piping has been anchored to the construction and approved as safe by the administrative authority.

▶   In the case of a TV or radio aerial, the installation should be checked with the electrical safety departments to make sure that no hazards of fire or structural weakness exist.

12.4.5   Location of Vent Terminal.   No vent terminal from a drainage system shall be directly beneath any door, window, or other ventilating opening of the building or of an adjacent building, nor shall any such vent terminal be within 10 feet horizontally of such an opening unless it is at least 2 feet above the top of such opening.

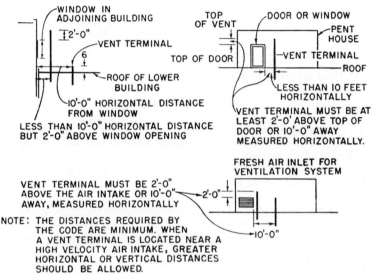

Fig. 12-8

▶   Figure 12-8 illustrates the location of a vent terminal when placed near a door or window.   The terminal should be extended at least 2 feet above the top of the door or window so as to prevent odors from entering the building.

Other sketches show examples of a vent terminal located near an adjoining building.   Where there is a window or door within 10 feet, the vent terminal should be extended at least 2 feet above the opening.   Where there is an air inlet, the vent terminal should be extended at least 2 feet above the air inlet to prevent the foul odor from the vent from being drawn into the building.

12.4.6   Extensions through Wall.   Vent terminals extending through a wall, when permitted by the administrative authority, shall be at least 10 feet horizontally from any lot line.   They shall be turned to provide an opening downward.   They shall be effectively screened and shall meet the requirements of paragraph 12.4.5.   Vent terminals shall not terminate under the overhang of the building.

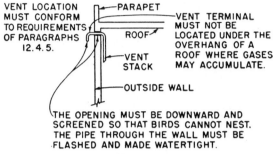

FIG. 12-9

▶   There are cases, such as roof gardens, where it is not desirable to extend a vent through the roof.   Under such conditions the vent terminal may be extended through the side as shown on Fig. 12-9.

12.4.7   Extensions outside Building.   No soil-, waste-, or vent-pipe extension shall be run or placed on the outside of a wall of any new building, but shall be carried up inside the building except that, in those localities where the temperature does not drop below 32°F, the administrative authority shall permit the installation outside the building.

▶   Except for appearance, there is no technical objection to the installation of soil and vent piping on the outside of the building, especially in climates where temperatures do not drop below 32°F for more than a few hours at a time.

12.5   Frost Closure

12.5.1   Vent Terminal.   Where there is a possibility of frost closure, the vent extension through a roof shall be at least 3 inches in diameter.   When it is found necessary to increase the size of the vent terminal, the change in diameter shall be made inside the building.

12.5.2   Increasers.   Change in diameter of vent terminals shall be made by use of a long increaser at least 1 foot below the roof.

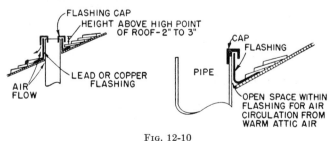

FIG. 12-10

▶ Figure 12-10 illustrates a method which might preclude the possibility of frost closure without the need of increasing the size of the vent.

12.6 Vent Grades and Connections

12.6.1 Grade. All vent and branch-vent pipes shall be so graded and connected as to drip back to the soil or waste pipe by gravity.

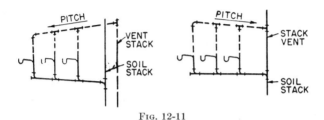

Fig. 12-11

▶ Figure 12-11 illustrates several methods recommended to permit the draining of vents from moisture due to condensation.

12.6.2 Vertical Rise. Where vent pipes connect to a horizontal soil or waste pipe, the vent shall be taken off above the center line of the soil pipe, and the vent pipe shall rise vertically, or at an angle not more than 45 degrees from the vertical, to a point at least 6 inches above the flood-level rim of the fixture it is venting before offsetting horizontally or before connecting to the branch vent.

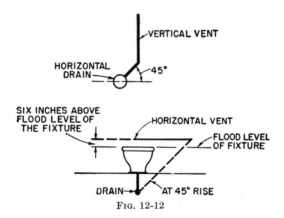

Fig. 12-12

▶ Figure 12-12 illustrates the requirements of paragraph 12.6.2.

12.6.3 Height above Fixture. A connection between a vent pipe and a vent stack or stack vent shall be made at least 6 inches above the flood-level rim of the highest fixtures served by the vent. Horizontal vent pipes forming branch vents, relief vents, or loop vents shall be at least 6 inches above the flood-level rim of the highest fixture served.

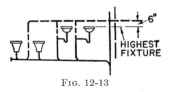

Fig. 12-13

▶   Figure 12-13 shows how a vent pipe is connected 6 inches above the flood-level rim of the highest fixture.

12.6.4   Side Inlet.   Side-inlet closet bends are permitted only in cases where the fixture connecting thereto is vented, and in no case shall the inlet be used to vent a bathroom group without being washed by a fixture.

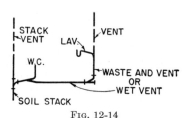

Fig. 12-14

▶   Figure 12-14 illustrates this requirement.   The main purpose of it is that a side-inlet vent generally becomes useless in a short time unless it is washed by the discharge from another fixture.

12.7   Bars and Soda-fountain Sinks

12.7.1   Bar and Fountain-sink Traps.   Traps serving sinks which are part of the equipment of bars, soda fountains, and counters need not be vented when the location and construction of such bars, soda fountains, and counters are such as to make it impossible so to do.   When such conditions exist, such sinks shall discharge into a floor sink or hopper which is properly trapped and vented.

▶   Figure 12-15 illustrates a soda-fountain counter with several compartment sinks.   The waste is carried to an open sump, with an air gap between the floor sump and the waste pipe.
      The sump is sometimes provided with a primer in order to keep the inside clean of scum and also to be certain that the trap seal is unbroken. The automatic primer should be provided with a vacuum breaker to prevent any possibility of back siphonage.   The sump waste should be trapped and properly vented.

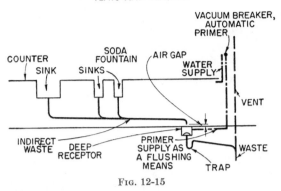

FIG. 12-15

12.7.2 Sumps. Sinks or sumps, receiving indirect waste, shall be located in a properly lighted and ventilated space.

▶   The important point here is to install the sink or sump at a location where it can be seen and maintained in clean condition.

12.8 Fixtures Back to Back

12.8.1 Distance. Two fixtures set back to back, within the distance allowed between a trap and its vent, may be served with one continuous soil or waste-vent pipe, provided that each fixture wastes separately into an approved double fitting having inlet openings at the same level.   (See paragraph 12.10.2.)

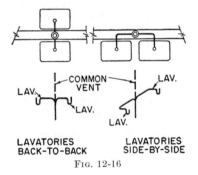

FIG. 12-16

▶   Figure 12-16 illustrates a fixture back to back.   Paragraph **12.8.1** also applies to fixtures side by side.

12.9 Fixture Vents

12.9.1 Distance of Trap from Vent. Each fixture trap shall have a protecting vent so located that the slope and the developed length in the fixture drain from the trap weir to the vent fitting are within the requirements set forth in Table 12.9.3.

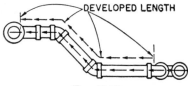

F̲ɪɢ. 12-17

▶   Figure **12-17** illustrates how to measure the developed length of a drain from the weir of a fixture trap to a vent opening, including an offset. The developed length is measured along the length of the pipe and fittings, following the turns. This developed length should conform to the developed lengths prescribed by Table **12.9.3**, column **2**.

12.9.2   Trap-seal Protection. The plumbing system shall be provided with a system of vent piping which will permit the admission or emission of air so that under normal and intended use the seal of any fixture trap shall not be subjected to a pressure differential of more than 1 inch of water.

12.9.3   (See Table 12.9.3.)

▶   Table **12.9.3** shows the distances from trap to vent for various size drains.

Table 12.9.3   Distance of Fixture Trap from Vent

Size of Fixture Drain (in.)	Distance Trap to Vent	
	Ft	In.
$1\frac{1}{4}$	2	6
$1\frac{1}{2}$	3	6
2	5	0
3	6	0
4	10	0

12.9.4   Trap Dip. The vent pipe opening from a soil or waste pipe, except for water closets and similar fixtures, shall not be below the weir of the trap.

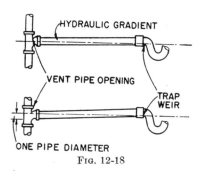

F̲ɪɢ. 12-18

Figure 12-18 illustrates the requirements of paragraph **12.9.4.** A fixture drain which slopes more than one pipe diameter between the vent opening and the trap weir has a greater tendency to self-siphon the trap seal than a fixture drain installed at a slope of not more than one pipe diameter.

A fixture trap installed on a 1¼-inch-diameter drain and within 12 inches of a vent opening but sloping more than one pipe diameter is apt to self-siphon the trap seal quicker than a fixture trap installed 4 feet away from a vent opening, but sloping ¼ inch per foot or slightly less than a pipe diameter.

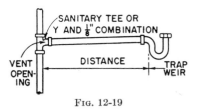

FIG. 12-19

Figure 12-19 illustrates the permitted distance from trap to vent according to measurements given in Table **12.9.3.** It is good practice to limit the slope to ¼ or ⅛ inch per foot. This will give a lower flow rate and reduce the possibility of self-siphoning of the trap.

The distances given in Table **12.9.3** will provide a safe installation. The extent to which the foregoing unvented drains are safe may be compared with the findings of tests conducted by the National Bureau of Standards.

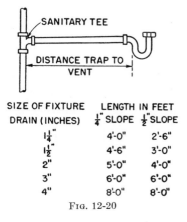

SIZE OF FIXTURE	LENGTH IN FEET	
DRAIN (INCHES)	¼" SLOPE	½" SLOPE
1¼"	4'-0"	2'-6"
1½"	4'-6"	3'-0"
2"	5'-0"	4'-0"
3"	6'-0"	6'-0"
4"	8'-0"	8'-0"

FIG. 12-20

Figure 12-20 illustrates the safe distance from trap center to vent opening when a sanitary tee is used at both ¼- and ⅛-inch slopes. The distance shown in Figs. 12-20 were recommended in the Uniform Plumbing Code (see Bibliography) and are shown here for comparison.

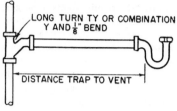

FIG. 12-21

SIZE OF FIXTURE DRAIN (INCHES)	LENGTH IN FEET	
	$\frac{1}{4}$" SLOPE	$\frac{1}{2}$" SLOPE
$1\frac{1}{4}$	1'-6"	1'-0"
$1\frac{1}{2}$	4'-0"	2'-0"
2	4'-6"	4'-0"
3	6'-0"	6'-0"
4	8'-0"	8'-0"

Figure **12-21** illustrates the safe distance from the trap-weir vent opening when using a long-turn tee-wye or combination wye and one-eighth bend at ¼- and ½-inch slopes.

It should be noted from the study of Figs. **12-21** and **12-22** that, when a long-turn fitting is used, the distance from trap to vent is reduced. This is due to the fact that a long-turn fitting increases the flow velocity in the fixture drain and therefore is more apt to produce self-siphonage.

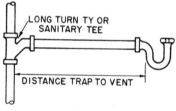

SIZE OF FIXTURE DRAIN (INCHES)	LENGTH IN FEET			
	LONG TY		SAN. TEE	
	$\frac{1}{4}$"	$\frac{1}{2}$"	$\frac{1}{4}$"	$\frac{1}{2}$"
$1\frac{1}{4}$	4'-0"	3'-0"	5'-6"	3'-0"
$1\frac{1}{2}$	6'-0"	3'-0"	7'-0"	3'-6"
2	8'-0"	4'-0"	11'-0"	5'-6"
3	12'-0"	6'-0"	12'-0"	6'-0"
4	16'-0"	8'-0"	16'-0"	8'-0"

FIG. 12-22

Figure **12-22** illustrates the results of tests conducted at the National Bureau of Standards. Note that a requirement for all tests is that a 1-inch trap seal remain in the trap at the completion of each test. During the tests, the total flow of water through the various drains was greater than under ordinary conditions.

When additional research has been completed, providing more data both on siphonage and on self-siphonage due to the effects of corrosion within the fixture drain, it may be possible to recommend distances from traps to vents which were found safe during the tests. The incidence of trap siphonage is considerably lessened when the following are used:

(a) A refill in a direct flush valve and a refill tube in a water-closet tank. A refill restores the trap seal after it has been siphoned during the flushing operation.

(b) Flat-bottom fixtures of at least 120-square-inch area. After flat-bottom fixtures have drained, enough water is left on the bottom to restore the trap seal.

Self-siphonage of a fixture trap is caused by many conditions, some of which are:

(a) Improper length of unvented fixture branch.

(b) Type of trap and amount of water in the seal, particularly depth.

(c) Excessive rate of discharge through the trap.

(d) Inadequate radius of trap; a cast trap, containing a shorter radius than a tube-drawn trap, will not siphon as readily because it offers greater resistance to pressure.

(e) Drain of too small diameter from trap outlet to vent connection.

(f) Incorrect diameter of P.O. (patent overflow) plug and tailpiece.

(g) Improper slope of drain pipe from trap to vent. (See Part III.)

12.9.5 Crown Vent. No back vent shall be installed within two pipe diameters of the trap weir.

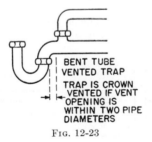

BENT TUBE
VENTED TRAP
TRAP IS CROWN
VENTED IF VENT
OPENING IS
WITHIN TWO PIPE
DIAMETERS

Fig. 12-23

▶ Figure 12-23 illustrates a crown-vented trap.

12.10 Common Vent

12.10.1 Individual Vent. An individual vent, installed vertically, may be used as a common vent for two fixture traps when both fixture drains connect with a vertical drain at the same level.

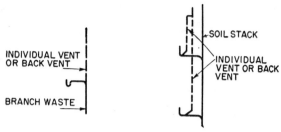

Fig. 12-24

▶   Figure 12-24 illustrates an individual vent.   Other names are "back vent" and "continuous vent."

12.10.2   Common Vent.   A common vent may be used for two fixtures set on the same floor level but connecting at different levels in the stack, provided the vertical drain is one pipe diameter larger than the upper fixture drain but in no case smaller than the lower fixture drain, whichever is the larger, and that both drains conform to Table 12.9.3.

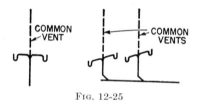

Fig. 12-25

▶   Figure 12-25 illustrates a common vent for a plumbing fixture.   It is a vent serving more than one fixture trap.

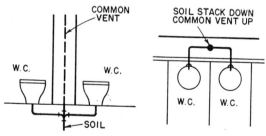

Fig. 12-26

Figure 12-26 illustrates other methods of installing a common vent. Two fixtures may be installed back to back with a common vent or side by side with a common vent.

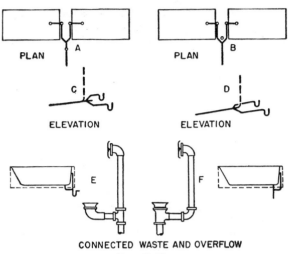

PLAN A   PLAN B

C   D

ELEVATION   ELEVATION

E   F

CONNECTED WASTE AND OVERFLOW

FIG. 12-27

Figure 12-27 illustrates another method of installing a common vent for two bathtubs, back to back. Sketch *a* shows the common vent taken on the downflow of the twin connections for the two bathtubs. Sketch *b* shows the common vent at the end of the run. Note that in sketch *c* the common vent installed on the downflow will remain clear, but that in sketch *d* it will eventually become clogged up by the backwash from the bathtub discharges.

Sketch *e* shows the most common method of installing a bath trap on a connected waste and overflow. Sketch *f* requires a special type of connected waste and overflow which is used when it is necessary to clear some structural interference.

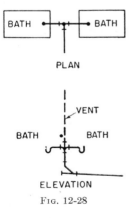

BATH   BATH

PLAN

VENT

BATH   BATH

ELEVATION

FIG. 12-28

The common vent for two fixtures will be more effective if it is installed as a vertical continuation of the vent as shown on Fig. 12-28.

Figure 12-29 illustrates the requirement of paragraph 12.10.2, where the fixtures are connected at two different levels and where the upper fixture drain is of the same diameter as the lower fixture drain. Under these conditions the waste pipe connecting both branches must be increased one pipe size. If the upper drain is a lavatory with a 1¼-inch waste, the vertical waste pipe may be 1½ inches in diameter. The fixture which has the lesser flow should be connected at the top to prevent the discharge from the upper fixture siphoning the trap seal of the lower fixture as the discharge passes the lower opening.

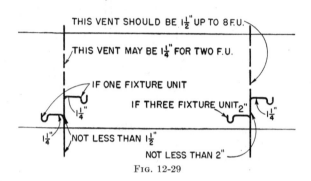

FIG. 12-29

12.11 Vents for Fixture Trap below Trap Dip

12.11.1 Hydraulic Gradient. Fixture drains shall be vented within the hydraulic gradient between the trap outlet and vent connection, but in no case shall the unvented drain exceed the distance provided for in Table 12.9.3.

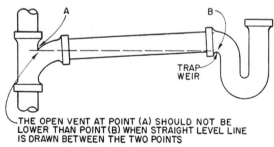

THE OPEN VENT AT POINT (A) SHOULD NOT BE LOWER THAN POINT (B) WHEN STRAIGHT LEVEL LINE IS DRAWN BETWEEN THE TWO POINTS

FIG. 12-30

▶   The hydraulic gradient as applied to a gravity drain and its vent connection is interpreted as shown on Fig. 12-30 as against the hydraulic gradient or grade line in Fig. 12-32. The grade line or hydraulic gradient in a water-supply system is always downward in the direction of flow. See Fig. 12-31.

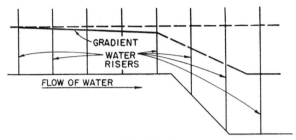

Fig. 12-31

12.11.2 Different Levels. If any stack has fixtures entering at different levels, the fixtures other than the fixture entering at the highest level shall be vented, except as may be permitted in other sections of this chapter.

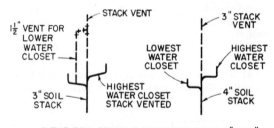

IF THE SOIL STACK IS INCREASED FROM 3" TO 4" THE LOWEST WATER CLOSET NEED NOT BE INDIVIDUALLY VENTED

Fig. 12-32

► Figure 12-32 illustrates the requirements for paragraph 12.11.2.

12.12 Wet Venting

12.12.1 Single-bathroom Groups. A single-bathroom group of fixtures may be installed with the drain from a back-vented lavatory, kitchen sink, or combination fixture serving as a wet vent for a bathtub or shower stall and for the water closet, provided that:

(a) Not more than one fixture unit is drained into a 1½-inch-diameter wet vent or not more than four fixture units drain into a 2-inch-diameter wet vent.

(b) The horizontal branch connects to the stack at the same level as the water-closet drain or below the water-closet drain when installed on the top floor. It may also connect to the water-closet bend.

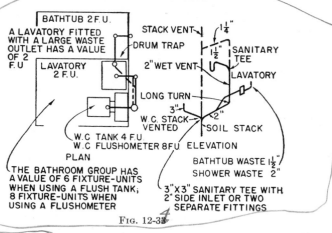

Fig. 12-33

Figure 12-33 shows an arrangement of wet venting a group of fixtures which has been found to be safe as a result of many years of practice and has been proved safe by tests conducted at various laboratories.

A bathroom group, total of seven fixture units, as follows: a flush-tank water closet rated four fixture units; a lavatory, one fixture unit, and a bathtub, two fixture units. However, as a group, the rating is computed only as six fixture units because of the improbability of all the fixtures being used at the same time. The lavatory waste may be used as a vent for the bathtub. The wet vent for the fixtures may be 1½ inches in diameter.

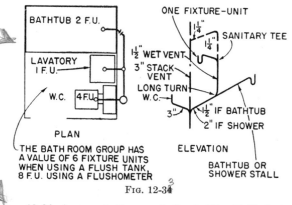

Fig. 12-34

Figure 12-34 shows a bathroom similar to Fig. 12-33, but with slight variations to meet other generally accepted methods of installation. The bathtub is provided with a drum trap and cleanout at floor, and the lavatory has a higher rating valued at two fixture units. This group of fixtures is still rated six fixture units on the basis of the over-all load that is computed for the stack.   However, the lavatory branch is now computed as two fixture units.   As paragraph **12.12.1**(*a*) permits only one fixture unit on a 1½-inch-diameter wet vent, this wet vent must now be increased to 2 inches as shown.

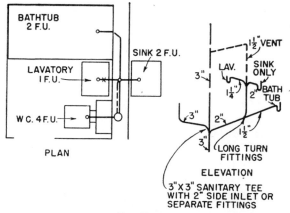

Fig. 12-35

Figure **12-35** illustrates a bathroom similar to the one shown in Figs. **12-33** and **12-34**, plus a kitchen sink back to back of the bathroom.

Figure **12-36** shows a grouping of bathroom fixtures and kitchen sink similar to that shown in Fig. **12-35**, except that the sink is connected separately into the horizontal drain.   Should a dishwasher or food-waste grinder be added at a later date, the separate sink waste would prove more satisfactory.

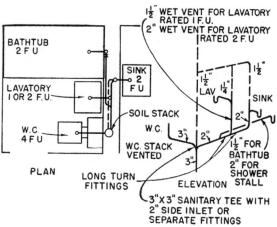

Fig. 12-36

Figure 12-37 illustrates an efficient roughing for the bathroom fixtures and for a kitchen sink adjoining the bathroom. The kitchen sink is fitted with a food-waste grinder. The maximum number of fixture units permitted by paragraph 12.12.1(a) is four. When a two-fixture-unit lavatory and a three-fixture-unit sink with food-waste grinder are installed, the 2-inch wet vent is too small. Therefore, the sink should be roughed separately onto the 3-inch stack. Being separately back-vented and connected below the water-closet inlet, the sink vent would also act as a relief vent for all the fixtures.

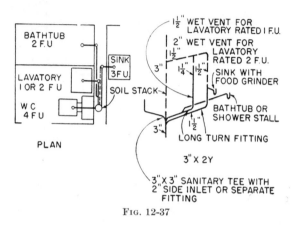

Fig. 12-37

Variations in fixture arrangements on a wet-vent system within the requirements of Sec. 12.12 are illustrated as follows:

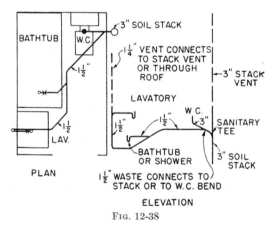

Fig. 12-38

Figure 12-38 shows an arrangement commonly used. The wet vent may connect at the soil stack through a side-inlet fitting or to a separate fitting below the water-closet connection, or it may connect into the water-closet bend as shown.

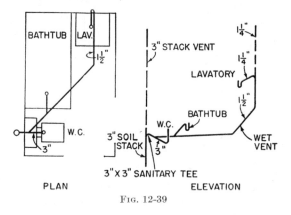

Fig. 12-39

Figure 12-39 shows an arrangement similar to the one in Fig. **12-38** except for the location of the fixtures.

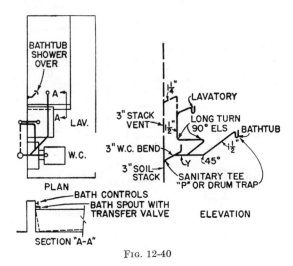

Fig. 12-40

Figure **12-40** illustrates another piping arrangement for a group of bathroom fixtures. It permits installation of the bathtub away from a window. The bathtub is a 5-foot left-hand recess type. The free end of the bathtub can be built up as shown in section *AA*. The shower over the bathtub is readily controlled through a transfer valve.

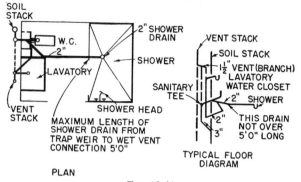

Fig. 12-41

Figure 12-41 illustrates a minimum-space toilet and shower room. This arrangement lends itself to many variations in design.

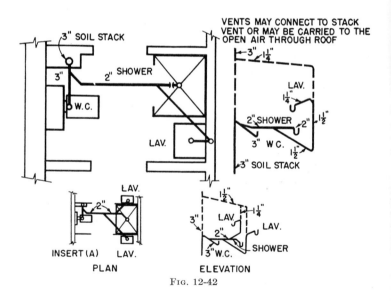

Fig. 12-42

Figure 12-42 is a modification of the fixture arrangement shown in Fig. 12-41. It is suitable in a hotel, for instance, or wherever a shower bathroom is installed between two bedrooms. A lavatory could be installed in each bedroom, in which case the size of the shower bathroom could be reduced, as shown in insert *a*.

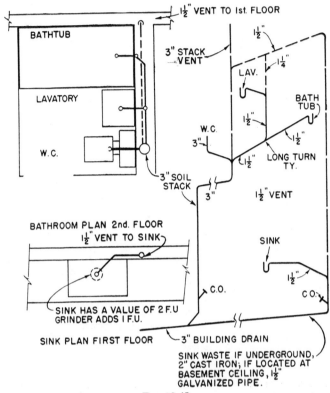

$1\frac{1}{2}"$ VENT TO 1st. FLOOR

BATHTUB

$1\frac{1}{2}"$

3" STACK
VENT

$1\frac{1}{4}"$

LAV.

BATH
TUB

LAVATORY

W.C.

$1\frac{1}{2}"$

W.C.

3"

$1\frac{1}{2}"$

$1\frac{1}{2}"$

LONG TURN
TY.

3" SOIL
STACK

3" $1\frac{1}{2}"$ VENT

BATHROOM PLAN 2nd. FLOOR
$1\frac{1}{2}"$ VENT TO SINK

SINK

C.O.

$1\frac{1}{2}"$

C.O.

SINK HAS A VALUE OF 2 F.U
GRINDER ADDS 1 F.U.

SINK PLAN FIRST FLOOR   3" BUILDING DRAIN

SINK WASTE IF UNDERGROUND,
2" CAST IRON; IF LOCATED AT
BASEMENT CEILING, $1\frac{1}{2}"$
GALVANIZED PIPE.

FIG. 12-43

Figure 12-43 illustrates wet venting of fixtures in a two-story one-family dwelling. A kitchen sink is on the first floor, located almost directly below the bathroom.

In Fig. 12-44 the bathroom is on the second floor. A two-compartment sink with food-waste grinder and a powder room near the kitchen are on the first floor.

To size the building drain, refer to Table 11.5.2; to size the fixture branches and stack, refer to Table 11.5.3, columns 2 and 3; and to size the venting system, refer to Table 12.21.5.

Figure 12-45 is an arrangement of fixtures similar to those shown in Fig. 12-43, plus a laundry tray and a water closet in the basement. The water closet, if properly located, may be wet-vented through the laundry-tray roughing. When connecting basement fixtures to the building drain, the connection should be made at least 10 feet downflow from the base of the stack. This distance is sufficient to permit the pressures generally developed at the base of a stack to become balanced, thereby causing less

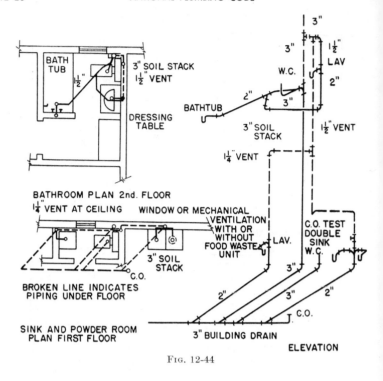

BATH TUB

3" SOIL STACK
1½" VENT

DRESSING TABLE

BATHROOM PLAN 2nd. FLOOR
1¼" VENT AT CEILING

3" SOIL STACK

BROKEN LINE INDICATES
PIPING UNDER FLOOR

SINK AND POWDER ROOM
PLAN FIRST FLOOR

3"

3"   1½"
          LAV
W.C.
             2"

2"   3"
BATHTUB

3" SOIL
STACK

1¼" VENT   1½" VENT

WINDOW OR MECHANICAL
VENTILATION
WITH OR
WITHOUT
FOOD WASTE   LAV.
UNIT

C.O. TEST
DOUBLE
SINK
W.C.

3"

2"   3"   2"

C.O.

3" BUILDING DRAIN

ELEVATION

C.O.

Fig. 12-44

disturbance to the trap seals of the fixtures located near the base of
the stack.

Figure 12-46, sketch *a*, shows piping underground when a crawl space
or basement is available. Sketch *b* shows the piping underground when
the elevation of the sewer is such as to require the building drain to be
installed as high as possible. Sketch *a* is also suitable for a top-floor
installation.

12.12.2 Double Bath. Bathroom groups back to back on a top floor consisting of two lavatories and two bathtubs or shower stalls may be installed on
the same horizontal branch with a common vent for the lavatories and with no
back vent for the bathtubs or shower stalls and for the water closets, provided
the wet vent is 2 inches in diameter and the length of the fixture drain conforms
to Table 12.9.3.

▶   Figure 12-47 illustrates a wet-vented double bathroom with the bathtubs
located at opposite sides of the bathroom wall. Sketch *a* is a diagram of
the piping when a crawl space or basement is included. Sketch *b* shows
when a shallow sewer must be installed. Placing the vent between the
two water-closet connections will serve the double purpose of keeping

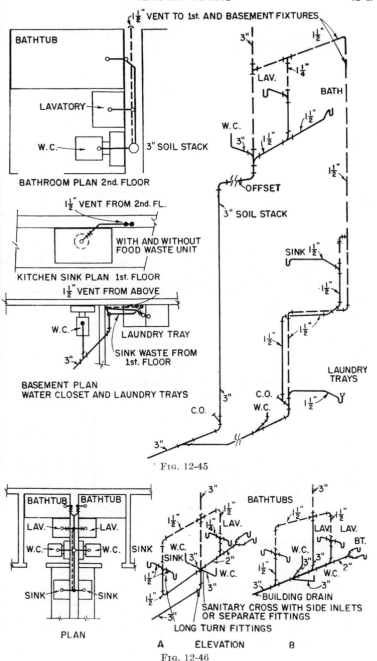

FIG. 12-45

FIG. 12-46

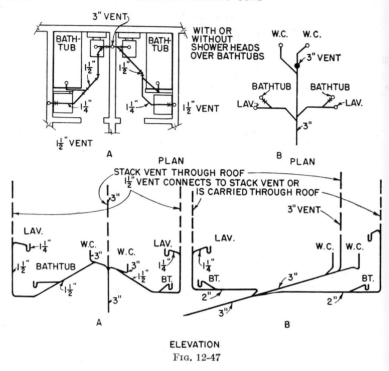

ELEVATION
FIG. 12-47

the base of the vent clear of stoppages and of providing balanced air pressure between the two water-closet connections.

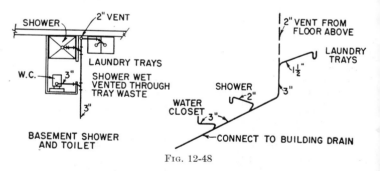

FIG. 12-48

Figure 12-48 illustrates a condition which should be watched carefully when roughing a set of fixtures, particularly where wet-vented fixtures are installed. The smaller flow-rated fixture should not be connected on the downflow of a large flow-rated fixture. A shower or bathtub should be connected ahead of the water closet in order to safeguard the smaller flow-rated fixture. This arrangement is suitable for a bathroom in the basement.

2.12.3 Multistory Bathroom Groups. On the lower floors of a multistory building, the waste pipe from one or two lavatories may be used as a wet vent for one or two bathtubs or showers provided that:

(a) The wet vent and its extension to the vent stack is 2 inches in diameter.

(b) Each water closet below the top floor is individually back-vented.

(c) The vent stack is sized as given in Table 12.12.3c.

Table 12.12.3c Size of Vent Stacks

Number of Wet-vented Fixtures	Diameter of Vent Stacks (in.)
1 or 2 bathtubs or showers	2
3 to 5 bathtubs or showers	$2\frac{1}{2}$
6 to 9 bathtubs or showers	3
10 to 16 bathtubs or showers	4

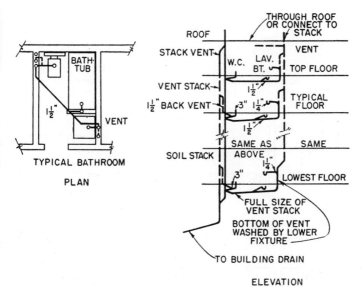

Fig. 12-49

Figure 12-49 illustrates wet venting of a fixture or a bathroom group in a multistory building. Installations of this type have been made in principal cities for many years and have proved safe.

The illustration shows a typical bathroom arrangement of a single bathroom on each floor with the bathtub wet-vented through the lavatory. The water closet on the top floor need not be vented, since it already is stack-vented. The base of the vent stack should be washed by the lowest lavatory, in which case the vent should connect full size into the soil stack.

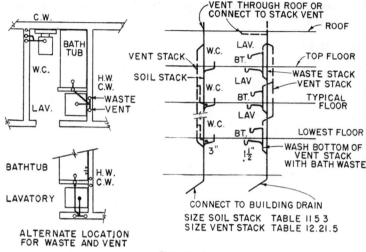

FIG. 12-50

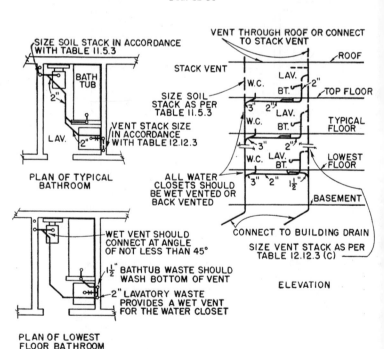

FIG. 12-51

Figure 12-50 shows the same bathroom arrangement as in Fig. 12-49, with an installation which probably is more economical and just as efficient. Soil, waste, and vent stacks are sized according to Tables 11.5.3 and 12.21.5. This arrangement will eliminate expensive framing of the floor construction which the piping arrangement in Fig. 12-49 will require. The bathtub is wet-vented through the lavatory.

2.12.4 Exception. In multistory bathroom groups, wet-vented in accordance with paragraph 12.12.3, the water closets below the top floor need not be individually vented if the 2-inch waste connects directly into the water-closet end at a 45-degree angle to the horizontal portion of the bend in the direction of flow.

Figure 12-51 illustrates an alternate method of wet-venting a single bathroom in which the bathtub and water closet are wet-vented through the lavatory by using pipe one size larger. Installations similar to those shown here have been used in many cities for more than 20 years.

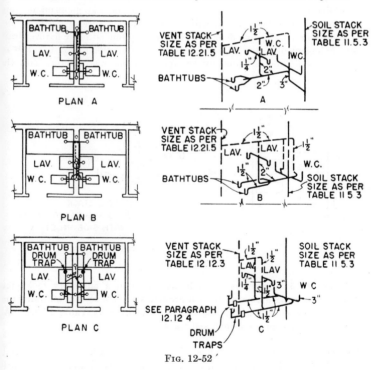

Fig. 12-52

Figure 12-52 illustrates various ways of roughing double bathrooms in a multistory building. Construction conditions often cause problems which require special roughing layouts.

Sketch *a* shows a conventional arrangement of fixtures, and the tw
bathrooms back to back are wet-vented. Some cities require an acces
door for the bathtub waste. This is not necessary when the joints for th
bath waste are sweated together, eliminating slip-joint connections a
possible leaks.

Sketch *b* shows a piping arrangement for two bathrooms back to back
The bathtubs are wet-vented through the lavatory waste. The wate
closets, except for those on the top floor, are individually vented.

Sketch *c* shows a piping design which in some cases might be not onl
more economical than *a* and *b* but more trouble-free, inasmuch as eac
bathroom waste pipe is independent. In this case the bathtub and wate
closet are wet-vented through the lavatory. The fixtures from eac
bathroom connect separately to the water-closet bend.

12.13   Stack Venting

12.13.1   One-bathroom Group. Except as indicated in paragraph 12.13.2
a group of fixtures, consisting of one bathroom group and a kitchen sink or com
bination fixture, may be installed without individual fixture vents, in a one
story building or on the top floor of a building, provided each fixture drai
connects independently to the stack and the water closet and bathtub c
shower-stall drain enters the stack at the same level and in accordance with th
requirements in Table 12.9.3.

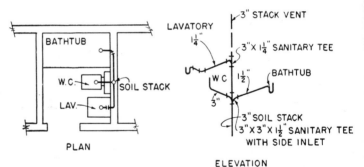

Fig. 12-53

▶   Figure **12-53** illustrates a single bathroom in a one-story residence
The bathroom fixtures are grouped around the stack so that all individua
fixture branches are within the lengths permitted by Table **12.9.3.** A
are vented through the **3-inch** soil stack.

12.13.2   Overtaxed Sewers. When a sink or combination fixture connect
to the stack-vented bathroom group and when the street sewer is sufficientl
overloaded to cause frequent submersion of the building sewer, a relief vent o
back-vented fixture shall be connected to the stack below the stack-vente
water closet or bathtub.

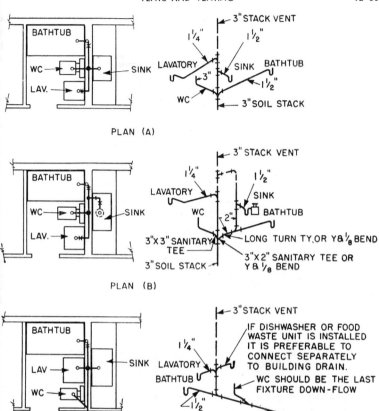

PLAN (A)

PLAN (B)

PLAN (C)

Fig. 12-54

Figure 12-54 illustrates a relief vent below a stack-vented water closet when a kitchen sink is installed as part of the group, as follows:

(a) This is the conventional arrangement in which the discharge from the bathtub or shower stall connects at the same level as the water closet through a side-inlet sanitary tee.

(b) By back-venting the sink and carrying waste below the water-closet connection, a relief is provided in the event that the building-drain elevation is close to the public sewer and the public sewer is already overtaxed. Back-venting the sink is also desirable when food-waste grinders or dishwashers are part of the kitchen sink.

(c) Certain localities require that a building drain be installed as high as possible in order to connect with either the sewer or place of disposal, in which case the water closet and bathtub or shower connect to the horizontal or building drain.

12.14 Individual Fixture Reventing

12.14.1 Horizontal Branches. One sink and one lavatory or three lavatories within 8 feet developed length of a main-vented line may be installed on a 2-inch horizontal waste branch without reventing, provided the branch is not less than 2 inches in diameter throughout its length, and provided that the wastes are connected into the side of the branch and the branch leads to its stack connection with a slope of not more than ¼ inch per foot.

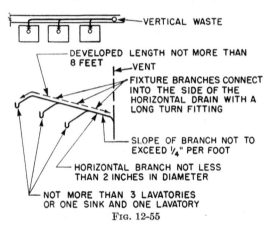

FIG. 12-55

▶ Figure 12-55 illustrates the provision of paragraph 12.14.1. The installation is limited to three lavatories or to one lavatory and one sink.

12.14.2 Where Required. When fixtures other than water closets discharge downstream from a water closet, each fixture connecting downstream shall be individually vented.

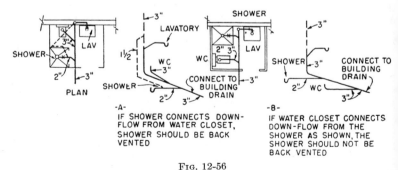

FIG. 12-56

► Figure 12-56 illustrates several such conditions.

(a) The shower must be separately back-vented in order to protect its trap seal.

(b) When the shower connects upstream from the water-closet connection, the shower trap may be considered to be wet-vented. See paragraph **12.4.3**.

12.14.3   Limits of Fixture Units above Bathtubs and Water Closets.   A fixture or combination of fixtures whose total discharge rating is not more than three fixture units may discharge into a stack not less than 3 inches in diameter without reventing, provided such fixture connections are made above the connection to the highest water closet, or bathtub tee-wye, the fixture-unit rating of the stack is not otherwise exceeded, and their waste piping is installed as otherwise required in paragraph 12.14.1.

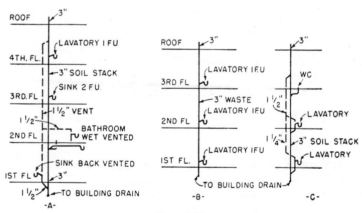

Fig. 12-57

► Figure 12-57 illustrates the requirements described in paragraph **12.14.3**.

(a) A bathroom on the second floor connects to the 3-inch soil stack. If the fixtures above the bathroom on the third and fourth floors do not total more than three fixture units, and if they also connect directly into the 3-inch soil stack, they need not be back-vented. The sink on the first floor must be back-vented.

(b) Three lavatories, one on each of three floors, may be connected directly into a 3-inch waste stack without a back vent.

(c) If a water closet is on the third floor and the lavatories are below it, each lavatory must be individually vented.

The developed length of each fixture branch must be within the limits prescribed by Table 12.9.3.

12.15   Circuit and Loop Venting

12.15.1   Battery Venting. A branch soil or waste pipe to which two but not more than eight water closets (except blowout type), pedestal urinals, trap standard to floor, shower stalls, or floor drains are connected in battery shall be vented by a circuit or loop vent which shall take off in front of the last fixture connection. In addition, lower-floor branches serving more than three water closets shall be provided with a relief vent taken off in front of the first fixture connection. When lavatories or similar fixtures discharge above such branches, each vertical branch shall be provided with a continuous vent.

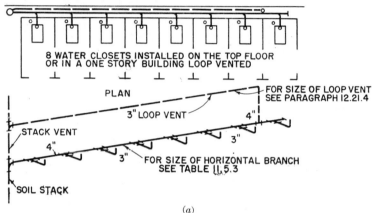

(a)

Fig. 12-58

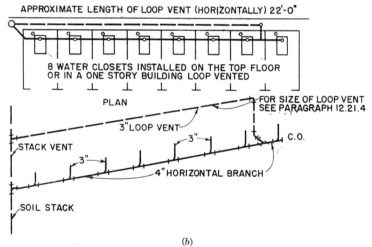

(b)

Fig. 12-59

Figures **12-58** and **12-59** represent a typical loop-vented water-closet row installed on the top floor of a building or in a one-story building.

(*a*) The horizontal branch is installed at the back below the water closet. The connections, therefore, are made with long-turn tee-wyes **or a** combination wye and eighth bend set flat.

(*b*) This is the same toilet room, except that the horizontal branch is directly under the water closets; therefore, the long-turn tee-wye or wye and eighth bend are installed with the inlet looking up.

The arrangement shown in *a* provides more satisfactory operation because it permits each closet to discharge into the side of the horizontal branch. This generally does not affect air circulation as much as when the water closet discharges through the top of the branch.

Blowout-type water closets or urinals should be individually vented.

Figure **12-60** illustrates a toilet arrangement similar to that shown in Fig. **12-59**, except that the installation applies to a multistory building.

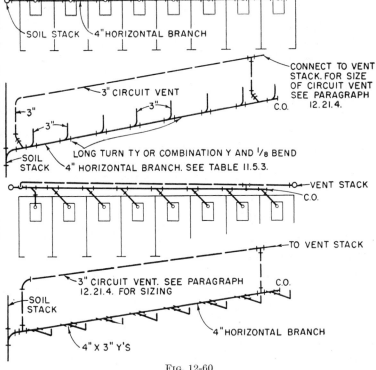

FIG. 12-60

12.15.2 Dual Branches. When parallel horizontal branches serve a total of eight water closets (four on each branch), each branch shall be provided with a relief vent at a point between the two most distant water closets. When other fixtures (than water closets) discharge above the horizontal branch, each such fixture shall be vented.

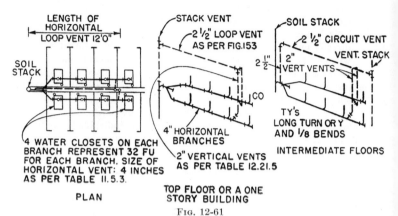

Fig. 12-61

▶ Figure 12-61 shows that the vent should be connected above the center line of the soil pipe, and the vent pipe should rise vertically, or at an angle of 45 degrees from the horizontal, to a point at least 6 inches above the flood-level rim of the fixture it is venting before offsetting horizontally or before connecting to the branch vent.

The size of the loop or circuit vent is computed from Table A in paragraph 12.21.4.

12.15.3 Vent Connections. When the circuit, loop, or relief vent connections are taken off the horizontal branch, the vent branch connection shall be taken off at a vertical angle or from the top of the horizontal branch.

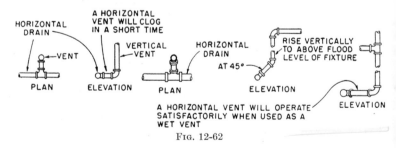

Fig. 12-62

▶ Figure 12-62 illustrates this general requirement. When a branch vent is run horizontally, the backwash or ordinary flow through the waste or soil pipe will have a tendency to clog the horizontal portion of the vent unless there is a fixture connected above it in the form of a wet vent. The branch vent should be taken at a 45-degree angle from the horizontal.

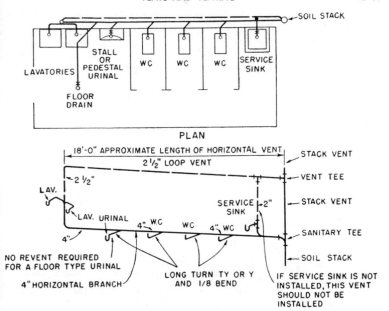

-A- ONE STORY OR TOP FLOOR INSTALLATION

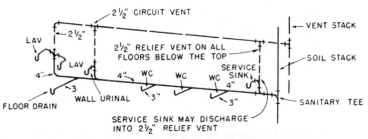

-B- OTHER THAN TOP FLOOR OF A MULTI-STORY BUILDING

Fig. 12-63

Figure 12-63 illustrates a loop and circuit-vented group of fixtures. Sketch *a* consists of water closets, urinals, and lavatories in a row in an installation on the top floor of a building or in a one-story building. Where a service sink is not needed, the relief vent is not needed.

Sketch *b* shows a group of fixtures with the addition of a floor drain in a multistory building. The length of unvented floor-drain branch depends on its diameter. Table 12.9.3 shows the length and diameter of pipe allowed.

When circuit and loop-vented fixtures are installed in a multistory building, a relief vent should be provided at the base connection into the horizontal. This is done by connecting the vent stack, full size, into or near the base of the soil stack, or by connecting the vent stack directly into the horizontal branch near the soil stack. The vent should be carried full size. (See Fig. 12-64.)

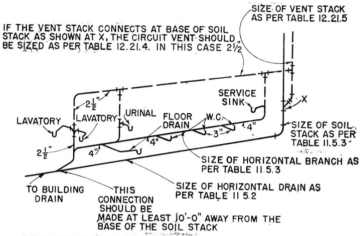

IF THE VENT STACK IS NOT CONNECTED AT THE BASE OF THE STACK AS SHOWN AT X, THEN THE CIRCUIT VENT IS INCREASED TO THE SAME SIZE AS THE VENT STACK

SIZE OF VENT STACK AS PER TABLE 12.21.5

IF THE VENT STACK CONNECTS AT BASE OF SOIL STACK AS SHOWN AT X, THE CIRCUIT VENT SHOULD BE SIZED AS PER TABLE 12.21.4. IN THIS CASE 2½

SERVICE SINK

LAVATORY   LAVATORY   URINAL   FLOOR DRAIN   W.C.

2½"   4"

SIZE OF SOIL STACK AS PER TABLE 11.5.3

SIZE OF HORIZONTAL BRANCH AS PER TABLE 11.5.3

TO BUILDING DRAIN   THIS CONNECTION SHOULD BE MADE AT LEAST 10'-0" AWAY FROM THE BASE OF THE SOIL STACK

SIZE OF HORIZONTAL DRAIN AS PER TABLE 11 5.2

PIPING FOR LOWEST TOILET ROOM IN A MULTI-STORY BUILDING
FIXTURE ARRANGEMENT SAME AS SHOWN ON PLAN FIG.12-63

*IF A LARGE LOAD, AT LEAST 50% OF THE MAXIMUM LOAD ALLOWED UNDER TABLE 11.5.3, IS CARRIED BY THE SOIL STACK, CONNECT THE VENT STACK AT BASE OF SOIL STACK AS SHOWN AT X, SO AS TO RELIEVE THE PRESSURE CREATED AT THIS POINT BY THE HEAVY FLOW.

Fig. 12-64

If the soil stack is carrying a load greater than 50 per cent of the total allowed by Table **11.5.3**, it is desirable to connect the vent stack near the base of the soil stack and to carry the discharge from the toilet on the lowest floor at least 10 feet downstream from the point at which the soil stack becomes a horizontal drain. This will relieve some of the pressures which generally develop at the base of a soil stack.

12.15.4 Fixtures Back to Back in Battery. When fixtures are connected to one horizontal branch through a double wye or a sanitary tee in a vertical position, a common vent for each two fixtures back to back or double connection shall be provided. The common vent shall be installed in a vertical position as a continuation of the double connection.

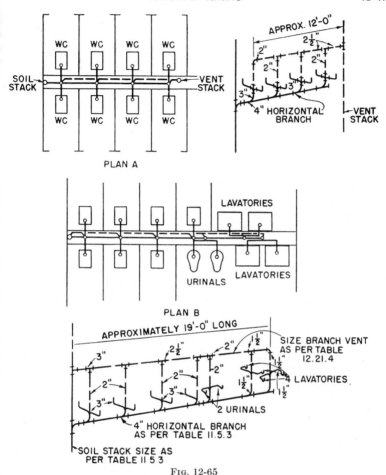

PLAN A

PLAN B

Fig. 12-65

▶ Figure **12-65** illustrates fixtures back to back in battery: (*a*) when water closets are installed on the top floor or on any floor in a multistory building, (*b*) when mixed fixtures are installed on the same horizontal branch.

Blowout-type water closets or blowout-type urinals may be vented by a common vent when back to back.

12.16 Pneumatic Ejector

12.16.1 Relief vents from a pneumatic ejector shall not be connected to a fixture branch vent but shall be carried separately to a main vent or stack vent or to the open air.

► A pneumatic ejector operates under high pressure or compressed air. If the relief vent or any part of the discharge system is connected to the gravity system, there is the possibility of blowing the trap seals of fixtures nearby which may be affected by its discharge.

Relief vents of other vents should be separately extended to the open air.

12.17   Relief Vents

12.17.1   Stacks of More Than 10 Branch Intervals.   Soil and waste stacks in buildings having more than 10 branch intervals shall be provided with a relief

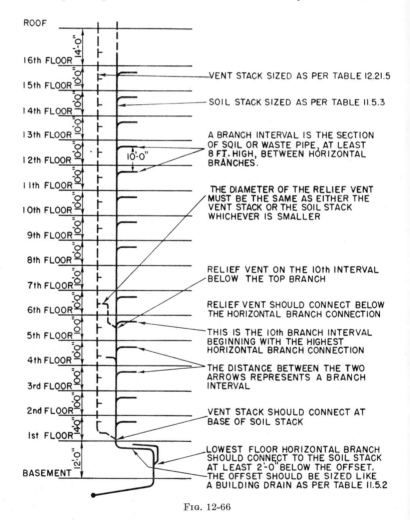

Fig. 12-66

vent at each tenth interval installed, beginning with the top floor. The size of the relief vent shall be equal to the size of the vent stack to which it connects. The lower end of each relief vent shall connect to the soil or waste stack through a wye below the horizontal branch serving the floor, and the upper end shall connect to the vent stack through a wye not less than 3 feet above the floor level.

▶ Figure 12-66 illustrates an important requirement which is often overlooked. In order to balance the pressures which are constantly changing within the plumbing system, it is necessary to provide a relief vent at various intervals, particularly in multistory buildings.

The illustration shows a building of 16 stories and basement.

A horizontal branch connection is shown at each floor except at the eighth-floor level where there is no horizontal branch. This means that, between the ninth-floor horizontal branch and the seventh-floor horizontal branch, there is only one branch interval. Between the fifth and fourth floors, the illustration shows two horizontal branches within one branch interval. The purpose in differentiating between horizontal lines and branch intervals is to prevent overloading of a stack within a short space.

Table 11.5.3 indicates, in the first column, the total load permitted in a horizontal branch and, in the last column, the total load that can be placed in a branch interval.

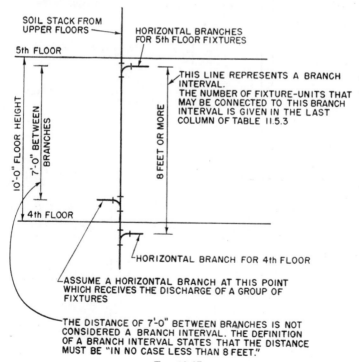

Fɪɢ. 12-67

Example: Assuming that the soil stack is 4 inches in diameter, the total number of fixture units allowed on a horizontal branch according to Table 11.5.3 is 160, but only 90 fixture units are permitted on the branch interval. It is necessary to increase the size of the soil stack or reduce the number of fixture units on the horizontal branch so that the system is not overloaded at any one point.

Assume that there are two horizontal branches to be connected within one branch interval of the soil stack. One branch serves 50 fixture units and the other 40 fixture units, totaling 90 fixture units. This is the maximum that may be connected within one branch interval. (See Table 11.5.3.) If the total fixture units were more than permitted within one branch interval, the soil stack would have to be increased in order to prevent overloading. See Fig. 12-67.

12.18   Offsets at an Angle Less Than 45 Degrees from the Horizontal in Buildings of Five or More Stories

12.18.1   Offset Vents.   Offsets less than 45 degrees from the horizontal, in a soil or waste stack, except as permitted in Chap. 11, Sec. 11.6, shall comply with paragraphs 12.18.2 and 12.18.3.

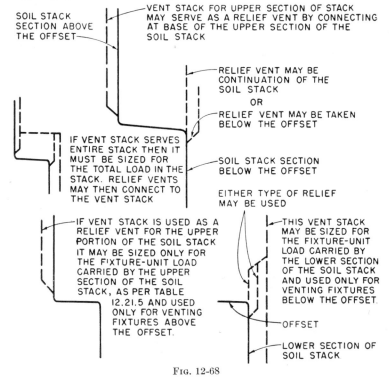

Fig. 12-68

12.18.2 Separate Venting. Such offsets may be vented as two separate soil or waste stacks, namely, the stack section below the offset and the stack section above the offset.

12.18.3 Offset Reliefs. Such offsets may be vented by installing a relief vent as a vertical continuation of the lower section of the stack or as a side vent connected to the lower section between the offset and the next lower fixture or horizontal branch. The upper section of the offset shall be provided with a yoke vent. The diameter of the vents shall be not less than the diameter of the main vent or of the soil and waste stack, whichever is the smaller.

▶   Figure 12-68 illustrates the requirements of paragraphs **12.18.1, 12.18.2,** and **12.18.3.**

     See Figs. 11-11 to 11-16 for offset reliefs.

12.19 Main Vents to Connect at Base

12.19.1 All main vents or vent stacks shall connect full size at their base to the building drain or to the main soil or waste pipe, at or below the lowest fixture branch. All vent pipes shall extend undiminished in size above the roof, or shall be reconnected with the main soil or waste vent.

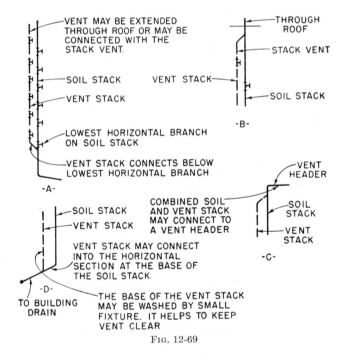

Fig. 12-69

▶   Figure 12-69 illustrates the requirements of this paragraph, as follows:

(*a*) The vent stack is connected at the base of the soil stack and extended through the roof.

(*b*) The vent stack may be combined with the stack vent and then extended through the roof as one pipe.

(*c*) The vent stack may be combined with the soil stack and connect into a vent header.

(*d*) The vent stack may connect into the horizontal portion at the base of the stack. In all cases, if possible, the discharge of a fixture or fixtures should be connected at the base of the vent stack before offsetting. In this manner the base of the vent stack is kept clear by the flow from these fixtures.

12.20   Vent Headers

12.20.1   Connections of Vents. Stack vents and vent stacks may be connected into a common vent header at the top of the stacks and then extended to the open air at one point. This header shall be sized in accordance with the requirements of Table 12.21.5, the number of units being the sum of all units on all stacks connected thereto, and the developed length being the longest vent length from the intersection at the base of the most distant stack to the vent terminal in the open air as a direct extension of one stack.

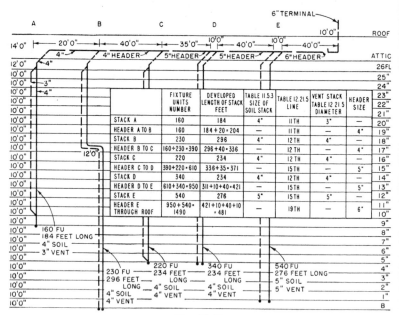

Fɪɢ. 12-70

▶   Figure 12-70 illustrates the method of computing vent-stack size and grouping into a vent header. The example shows how each stack is computed as part of the entire header.

12.21   Size and Length of Vents

12.21.1   Length of Vent Stacks.   The length of the vent stack or main vent shall be its developed length from the lowest connection of the vent system with the soil stack, waste stack, or building drain to the vent-stack terminal, if it terminates separately in the open air, or to the connection of the vent stack with the stack vent, plus the developed length of the stack vent from the connection to the terminal in the open air, if the two vents are connected together with a single extension to the open air.

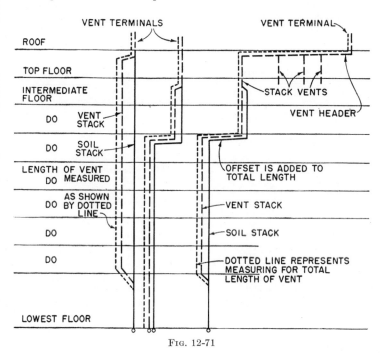

Fɪɢ. 12-71

▶   Figure 12-71 illustrates the manner in which the length of the vent or soil stack is computed. The total vertical distance is added to any horizontal runs or offsets.

12.21.2   Size of Individual Vents.   The diameter of an individual vent shall be not less than 1¼ inches nor less than one-half of the diameter of the drain to which it is connected.

▶   The smallest vent permitted is $1\frac{1}{4}$-inch-diameter pipe. Note that Table 12.21.5 permits only two fixture units on a $1\frac{1}{4}$-inch-diameter vent. However, when a vent is used as a relief on a horizontal waste or vertical soil, the vent may be reduced to half of the drain diameter, provided the number of fixture units connected or the length of the vent does not exceed the limit provided in Table 12.21.5.

12.21.3 Size of Relief Vent. The diameter of a relief vent shall be not less than one-half the diameter of the soil or waste branch to which it is connected.

▶   The vent must be computed from Table 12.21.5.

12.21.4 Size of Circuit or Loop Vent. The diameter of a circuit or loop vent shall be not less than one-half the size of the diameter of the horizontal soil or waste branch or the diameter of the vent stack, whichever is smaller.

▶   See Figs. 12-51 to 12-58.

Table A. Horizontal Circuit and Loop Vent Sizing Table

| Line | Soil or waste pipe diam (in.) | Fixture units (max number) | Diameter of circuit or loop vent (in.) | | | | | |
| | | | $1\frac{1}{2}$ | 2 | $2\frac{1}{2}$ | 3 | 4 | 5 |
			Max horizontal length (ft)					
1	$1\frac{1}{2}$	10	20					
2	2	12	15	40				
3	2	20	10	30				
4	3	10	. . .	20	40	100		
5	3	30	. . .	. . .	40	100		
6	3	60	. . .	. . .	16	80		
7	4	100	. . .	7	20	52	200	
8	4	200	. . .	6	18	50	180	
9	4	500	. . .	. . .	14	36	140	
10	5	200	. . .	. . .	. . .	16	70	200
11	5	1,100	. . .	. . .	. . .	10	40	140

Table A may be used in the following manner:
(a) Refer to Fig. 12-60 which shows that there are eight flush-valve water closets to be installed.
(b) Table 11.4.2 indicates that a valve-operated water closet has a fixture-unit value of eight.
(c) Figure 12-60 shows that there are eight water closets to be installed, each with a value of eight, or a total of 64 fixture units.
(d) These 64 fixture units require a 4-inch horizontal branch according to Table 11.5.3.‡

(e) By referring to Fig. 12-60, the length of the horizontal vent is seen to be approximately 24 feet.

(f) By referring to Table A, a 4-inch-diameter soil or waste pipe, to which there are not more than 100 fixture units connected and in which the vent length is not more than 52 feet, requires a 3-inch-diameter circuit or loop vent.

12.21.5 Size of Vent Piping. The size of vent piping shall be determined from its length and the total of fixture units connected thereto, as provided in Table 12.21.5. Twenty per cent of the total length may be installed in a horizontal position.

Table 12.21.5 Size and Length of Vents

Size of soil or waste stack (in.)	Fixture units connected	Diameter of vent required (in.)								
		1¼	1½	2	2½	3	4	5	6	8
		Maximum length of vent (ft)								
1¼	2	30								
1½	8	50	150							
2½	10	30	100							
2	12	30	75	200						
2	20	26	50	150						
1½	42	...	30	100	300					
3	10	...	30	100	200	600				
3	30	...	...	60	200	500				
3	60	...	...	50	80	400				
4	100	...	...	35	100	260	1,000			
4	200	...	...	30	90	250	900			
4	500	...	...	20	70	180	700			
5	200	...	...	...	35	80	350	1,000		
5	500	...	...	...	30	70	300	900		
5	1,100	...	...	...	20	50	200	700		
6	350	...	...	...	25	50	200	400	1,300	
6	620	...	...	...	15	30	125	300	1,100	
6	960	...	...	...	...	24	100	250	1,000	
6	1,900	...	...	...	...	20	70	200	700	
8	600	...	...	...	...	...	50	150	500	1,300
8	1,400	...	...	...	...	...	40	100	400	1,200
8	2,200	...	...	...	...	...	30	80	350	1,100
8	3,600	...	...	...	...	...	25	60	250	800
10	1,000	...	...	...	...	...	...	75	125	1,000
10	2,500	...	...	...	...	...	...	50	100	500
10	3,800	...	...	...	...	...	...	30	80	350
10	5,600	...	...	...	...	...	...	25	60	250

► See Part III for information on the capacity of soil and vent stacks.

12.22   Combination Waste-and-Vent System

12.22.1   Where Permitted.   A combination waste-and-vent system shall be permitted only where structural conditions preclude the installation of a conventional system as otherwise provided in this code.

12.22.2   Limits.   A combination waste-and-vent system is limited to floor drains and sinks.   It consists of an installation of waste piping in which the trap of the fixture is not individually vented.   Every waste pipe and trap in the system shall be at least two pipe sizes larger than the size required in paragraphs 11.5.2 and 11.5.3.

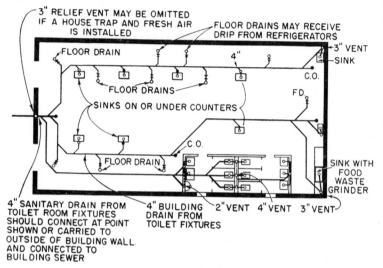

Fig. 12-72

▶   Figure 12-72 illustrates a system of waste piping which also serves as horizontal wet venting of one or more sinks or floor drains.   The dual function is accomplished by installing a common waste and vent pipe of sufficient size to provide free movement of air above the flow line of the drain.   This system is relatively new, having been developed during the past few years.

The Code permits a combination waste-and-vent system as a means of avoiding complicated design.   The designer, however, must plan the sizing and runouts of piping necessary to maintain a balance within the system and prevent trap siphonage.

It should be noted that this combination waste-and-vent system is for floor drains and sinks only.   It is not for water closets or urinals or other fixtures having high fixture-unit ratings.   Toilet-room fixtures are roughed in the conventional manner.   Their discharge is carried separately to the building sewer or may be connected to the building drain on the sewer side of the combination waste and vent.

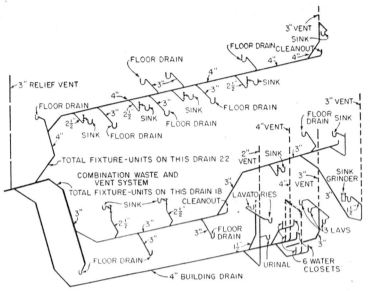

Fig. 12-73

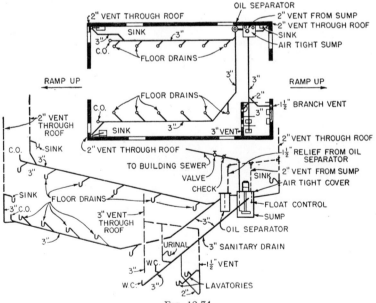

Fig. 12-74

Using Fig. 12-73 as an example, the piping is sized as follows:

(a) The branch carrying a load of 22 fixture units, according to Table 11.5.2 at ¼-inch fall per foot, requires a 2½-inch-diameter pipe and for 18 fixture units on the other branch, a 2-inch-diameter pipe. Paragraph 12.22.2 states that the waste pipe shall be at least two pipe sizes larger. For 22 fixture units it would be 4 inches, and for 18 fixture units it would be 3 inches.

(b) The individual fixture drain for a sink, as per Table 11.4.2, is 1½ inches. By increasing this drain two pipe sizes, the required size would be 2½ inches for each sink waste.

(c) Table 11.4.2 requires 2 inches for individual floor drains as a minimum. Two pipe sizes would be 3 inches. If there is difficulty in procuring 2½-inch drainage fittings, 3-inch drainage fittings may be used.

Figure 12-74 is another adaptation of a combination waste-and-vent system. This is applicable where the street sewer is above the system being installed and where it is necessary to install a receiving sump and discharge it by mechanical means.

CHAPTER 13

Storm Drains

13.1 General

13.1.1 Drainage Required. Roofs, paved areas, yards, courts, and court-yards shall be drained into a storm-sewer system or a combined sewer system where such systems are available.

▶ To comply with this paragraph it is important to compute the total amount of rainfall that might possibly fall over the area to be drained.

It is essential that the rain water be removed as rapidly as possible. Roof areas should be drained as quickly as the rain falls in order that undue stresses are not placed on the structure.

13.1.2 Prohibited Drainage. Storm water shall not be drained into sewers intended for sanitary sewage only.

▶ Most modern sewer installations in a city have separate systems: one for the sanitary sewer, which is discharged into the sewage plant, and one for the storm sewer, which is generally disposed of as clear water into a waterway.

13.1.3 Traps. Leaders and storm drains, when connected to a combined sewer, shall be trapped.

▶ Traps are required to prevent sewer odors and gases from discharging where they may be offensive.

If the leader box were located on the roof like the vent terminal so that offensive odors cannot enter the building, there would be no need for trapping. Actually the leaders would help to maintain circulation.

13.1.4 Expansion Joints. Expansion joints or sleeves shall be provided where warranted by temperature variations or physical conditions.

▶ This requirement is applicable to tall buildings where the movement of the pipe could be sufficient to damage the roof.

Expansion and improper anchoring of vertical pipes have caused roof drains to be pushed clear above the level of the roof and cause a break on the waterproofing and flashing.

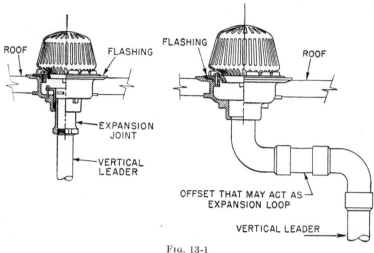

Fig. 13-1

Expansion may be taken care of by a properly designed roof expansion joint or horizontal branch which can take up the movement of the vertical pipe without affecting the roof box. See Fig. 13-1.

13.1.5 Subsoil Drain. Where subsoil drains are placed under the cellar or basement floor or are used to surround the outer walls of a building, they shall be made of open-jointed or horizontally split or perforated clay tile, or perforated bituminized-fiber pipe, or asbestos-cement pipe, not less than 4 inches in diameter. When the building is subject to backwater, the subsoil drain shall be protected by an accessibly located backwater valve. Subsoil drains may discharge into a properly trapped area drain or sump. Such sumps do not require vents.

▶   Subsoil drains serving outside seepage water or underground soils should be run into a clear-water sump.

Sumps should be mechanically operated. For a larger building or where it is not possible to watch the sumps, they should be of the automatic type.

In rural areas and for small buildings, subsoil drains may be connected to dry wells or discharged where the discharge will not harm adjacent property.

13.1.6 Building Subdrains. Building subdrains located below the public sewer level shall discharge into a sump or receiving tank, the contents of which shall be automatically lifted and discharged into the drainage system as required for building sumps.

► At times these subdrains might receive waste containing oil or gasoline or other inflammable liquids. In such cases, the discharge must go through an oil interceptor before it is collected into a sump or before discharging into any other disposal system.

13.2 Materials

13.2.1 Inside Conductors. Conductors placed within a building or run in a vent or pipe shaft shall be of cast iron, galvanized steel, galvanized wrought iron, galvanized ferrous alloys, brass, copper, or lead.

► Any dependable piping materials would be satisfactory. It is in this system of piping that new kinds of piping could be tested before being accepted for the drainage system, especially if the piping is exposed so that it can be watched.

13.2.2 Outside Leaders. When outside leaders are of sheet metal and connected with a building storm drain or storm sewer, they shall be connected to a cast-iron drain extending above the finish grade, or the sheet-metal leader shall be protected against injury.

13.2.3 Underground Storm Drains. Building storm drains underground, inside the building, shall be of cast-iron soil pipe.

► Outside leaders may be either metallic or nonmetallic. The lower section should be protected from damage by a heavy metal cover or a cast-iron boot.

Underground storm drains may be the same kind of piping as the building drain.

13.2.4 Building Storm Drains. Building storm drains underground, beneath the building, when not connected with a sanitary or combined sewer, shall be of cast-iron soil pipe or ferrous-alloy piping except that, when found to be adequate by the administrative authority, vitrified-clay pipe, concrete pipe, bituminized-fiber pipe, and asbestos-cement pipe may be used.

► In the preparation of a plumbing code, the local plumbing-code committee decides which kinds of piping are suitable for their area, and only the approved kinds need be spelled out as part of the local code.

13.2.5 Building Storm Sewers. The building storm sewer shall be of cast-iron soil pipe, vitrified-clay pipe, concrete pipe, bituminized-fiber pipe, or asbestos-cement pipe.

13.3 Traps

13.3.1 Main Trap. Individual storm-water traps shall be installed on the storm-water drain branch serving each conductor, or a single trap shall be installed in the main storm drain just before its connection with the combined building sewer, main drain, or public sewer.

▶   **When the storm leaders are connected into one storm building drain and then connected into the sanitary building drain or storm sewer, a building trap should be installed in order to prevent sewer gases entering the storm leaders.**

    If, however, the roof-drain boxes are so located as to preclude any possibility of sewer-gas odors, there is no technical reason to install the building storm trap.

13.3.2 Material. Storm-water traps, when required, shall be of cast iron.

▶   **Traps for the storm drains may be of cast iron or of other composites that have proved safe for the drainage system.**

13.3.3 No traps shall be required for storm-water drains which are connected to a sewer draining storm water exclusively.

13.3.4 Traps for individual conductors shall be the same size as the horizontal drain to which they are connected.

13.3.5 Conductor traps shall be so located that an accessible cleanout may be installed on the building side of the trap.

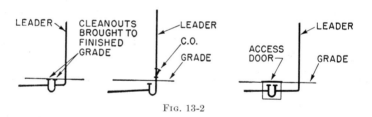

Fɪɢ. 13-2

▶   Figure **13-2** illustrates cleanouts for storm leaders.

13.4 Conductors and Connections

13.4.1 Conductor pipes shall not be used as soil, waste, or vent pipes, nor shall soil, waste, or vent pipes be used as conductors.

13.4.2 Rain-water conductors installed along alleyways, driveways, or other locations where they may be exposed to damage shall be protected by metal guards, recessed into the wall or constructed from ferrous-alloy pipe.

13.4.3 Combining Storm with Sanitary Drainage. The sanitary and storm-drainage system of a building shall be entirely separate, except that where a combined sewer is available the building storm drain may be connected in the same horizontal plane through a single wye fitting to the combined drain or sewer at least 10 feet downstream from any branch to the building drain or from any soil stack.

In certain cities it is permissible to connect both a sanitary and storm sewer into a combined street sewer. As populations increase and cities become more congested, this arrangement is becoming less desirable.

Figure **13-3** indicates how storm drains may be connected in locations which permit this combined use of the sewer. Some cities require that the storm drains discharge at the curb through a trench or pipe under the sidewalk. Separation of storm and sanitary drains is preferable.

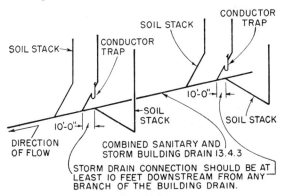

FIG. 13-3

13.4.4 Double Connections of Storm Drains. Where the sanitary and storm drains are connected on both sides of the combined sewer, single wyes shall be used and the requirements of paragraph 13.4.3 relative to the location of connections shall also apply.

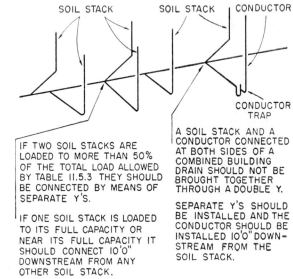

FIG. 13-4

▶ During a heavy rainstorm the conductor pipe will run almost to its full capacity and may cause pressures to develop on the soil-stack branch unless separated at least 10 feet. This is equally true of a soil stack carrying a relatively heavy load; see Fig. 13-4. If a 4-inch soil stack is loaded to 300 fixture units or more, it represents a relatively heavy load. If the same stack is loaded to 400 fixture units or more, it represents a full load.

13.4.5 Floor drains connected to a storm drain shall be trapped.

▶ When floor drains are connected to storm drains, putrefaction of waste matter entering and lodging in the storm drains causes odors, unless floor drains are trapped.

13.5 Roof Drains

13.5.1 Material. Roof drains shall be of cast iron, copper, lead, or other acceptable corrosion-resisting material.

13.5.2 Strainers. All roof areas, except those draining to hanging gutters, shall be equipped with roof drains having strainers extending not less than 4 inches above the surface of the roof immediately adjacent to the roof drains. Strainers shall have an available inlet area, above roof level, of not less than $1\frac{1}{2}$ times the area of the conductor or leader to which the drain is connected.

13.5.3 Flat Decks. Roof-drain strainers for use on sun decks, parking decks, and similar areas, normally serviced and maintained, may be of the flat-surface type, level with the deck, and shall have an available inlet area not less than two times the area of the conductor or leader to which the drain is connected.

13.5.4 Roof-drain Flashings. The connection between roofs and roof drains which pass through the roof and into the interior of the building shall be made watertight by the use of proper flashing material.

▶ Figure 13-5 illustrates various types of roof drains. Selection of design should be based on the type of roof.

Mushroom strainers provide a large elevated area for flat roofs where leaves and other debris may accumulate.

Flat strainers are necessary on a roof that is to be utilized as a sun deck or roof garden.

Sloped strainers and corner strainers are necessary when the drain is located in a patched roof or where the drain is placed at the corner of a roof and parapet.

In high structures, roof drains should be provided with expansion joints in order to compensate for structural or temperature variation, unless other means are provided for expansion.

The diameter or size of the drain outlet should be based on the rate of rainfall in the area to be drained.

The open area of the strainer should be $1\frac{1}{2}$ to 2 times the area of the pipe to which it connects.

STRAINER TO HAVE AN AVAILABLE
INLET AREA ABOVE THE ROOF OF
NOT LESS THAN 1 1/2 TIMES THE
AREA OF THE CONDUCTOR.

STRAINERS ON FLAT DECK
ROOF DRAINS SHALL HAVE
AN AVAILABLE INLET AREA
NOT LESS THAN TWO TIMES
THE AREA OF THE CONDUCTOR

STRAINER
TO BE
REMOVABLE

STRAINER TO
EXTEND AT LEAST
4" ABOVE THE
SURFACE OF THE
ROOF.

THREADED OR
INSIDE CAULK
OUTLET

FLASHING TO BE MADE
WATER TIGHT WITH DRAIN

THREADED OR
INSIDE CAULK
OUTLET.

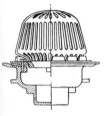
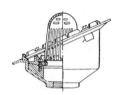
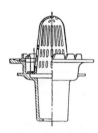

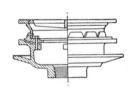

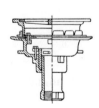

Fig. 13-5

13.6 Size of Leaders and Storm Drains

13.6.1 Vertical leaders shall be sized on the maximum projected roof area, according to Table 13.6.1.

Table 13.6.1 Size of Vertical Leaders

Diam of leader or conductor[1] (in.)	Max projected roof area (sq ft)	Diam of leader or conductor[1] (in.)	Max projected roof area (sq ft)
2	720	5	8,650
2½	1,300	6	13,500
3	2,200	8	29,000
4	4,600		

[1] The equivalent diameter of a square or rectangular leader may be taken as the diameter of that circle which may be inscribed within the cross-sectional area of the leader.

▶   Table A is an expansion of Table 13.6.1, showing the sizes of vertical leaders for rainfalls of 2 to 8 inches.

Table A. Expansion of Table 13.6.1 Vertical Leaders

Diam of leader (in.)	Normal rate of rainfall (in.)					
	2	3	4	5	6	8
	Square feet of roof area					
2	1,440	960	720	576	480	360
2½	2,600	1,733	1,300	1,040	865	650
3	4,400	2,933	2,200	1,760	1,470	1,100
4	9,200	6,133	4,600	3,680	3,070	2,300
5	. . . .	. . . .	8,650	6,920	5,765	4,325
6	. . . .	. . . .	. . . .	. . . .	9,000	6,750

13.6.2 Building Storm Drain. The size of the building storm drain or any of its horizontal branches having a slope of ½ inch or less per foot shall be based upon the maximum projected roof area to be handled according to Table 13.6.2.

▶   Tables 13.6.1 and 13.6.2 are based upon a maximum rate of rainfall of 4 inches per hour. If in any state, city, or other political subdivision, the maximum rate of rainfall is more or less than 4 inches per hour, then the figures for roof area must be adjusted proportionately by multiplying the figure by 4 and dividing the maximum rate of rainfall in inches per hour.

Table 13.6.2   Size of Horizontal Storm Drains

Diam of drain (in.)	Maximum projected roof area for drains for various slopes (sq ft)		
	$\frac{1}{8}$ in.	$\frac{1}{4}$ in.	$\frac{1}{2}$ in.
3	822	1,160	1,644
4	1,880	2,650	3,760
5	3,340	4,720	6,680
6	5,350	7,550	10,700
8	11,500	16,300	23,000
10	20,700	29,200	41,400
12	33,300	47,000	66,600
15	59,500	84,000	119,000

The U.S. Weather Bureau maintains statistics on the normal rate of rainfall in various localities and will furnish the information on request.

Table B, an expansion of Table 13.6.2, shows the sizes of horizontal storm drains for rainfalls of 2 to 6 inches.

Table B. Expansion of Table 13.6.2   Horizontal Storm Drains

Drain size (in.)	$\frac{1}{8}$-in. slope, inches rainfall					$\frac{1}{4}$-in. slope, inches rainfall				
	2	3	4	5	6	2	3	4	5	6
	Square feet of roof area									
3	1,644	1,096	822	657	548	2,320	1,546	1,160	928	773
4	3,760	2,506	1,880	1,504	1,253	5,300	3,533	2,650	2,120	1,766
5	6,680	4,453	3,340	2,672	2,227	9,440	6,293	4,720	3,776	3,146
6	10,700	7,133	5,350	4,280	3,566	15,100	10,066	7,550	6,040	5,033
8	23,000	15,333	11,500	9,200	7,600	32,600	21,733	16,300	13,040	10,866

Figure 13-6 shows approximately equivalent sizes of round and rectangular leaders. In computing the carrying capacity of leaders, there are three factors to consider: (1) dimensions, (2) cross-sectional area, and (3) inside perimeter (area of water contact).

A rectangular leader, because of its four walls and corners, offers greater friction loss, thereby diminishing its carrying capacity. To compensate for this loss, a rectangular leader needs to be about 10 per cent larger than a round leader to carry the same load.

In Fig. 13-6 the sizes for rectangular leaders which are shown as equivalents of the sizes of round leaders include the 10 per cent adjustment. In some cases, the rectangular sizes are more than 10 per cent larger.   **Where the computation of the equivalent size has resulted in an unavailable size, the next larger stock size has been given.**

ROUND LEADER			RECTANGULAR LEADER		
DIAMETER INCHES	CROSS SECTIONAL AREA, SQ. IN.	WATER CONTACT AREA, INCHES	DIMENSION INCHES	CROSS SECTIONAL AREA, SQ. IN.	WATER CONTACT AREA, INCHES
2	3.14	6.28	2 X 2 $1\frac{1}{2}$ X $2\frac{1}{2}$	4 3.75	8 8
3	7.07	9.42	2 X 4 $2\frac{1}{2}$ X 3	8 7.50	12 11
4	12.57	12.57	3 X $4\frac{1}{4}$ $3\frac{1}{2}$ X 4	12.75 14.0	14.5 14
5	19.06	15.07	4 X 5 $4\frac{1}{2}$ X $4\frac{1}{2}$	20.0 20.25	18 18
6	28.27	18.85	5 X 6 $5\frac{1}{2}$ X $5\frac{1}{2}$	30.0 30.25	22 22

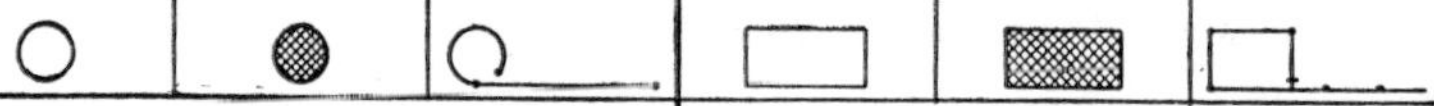

CIRCUMFERENCE AS STRAIGHT LINE   RECTANGLE AS STRAIGHT LINE

Fig. 13-6

13.6.3   Roof Gutters.   The size of semicircular gutters shall be based on the maximum projected roof area, according to Table 13.6.3.

Table 13.6.3   Size of Gutters

Diam of gutter[1] (in.)	Maximum projected roof area for gutters of various slopes (sq ft)			
	$\frac{1}{16}$ in.	$\frac{1}{8}$ in.	$\frac{1}{4}$ in.	$\frac{1}{2}$ in.
3	170	240	340	480
4	360	510	720	1,020
5	625	880	1,250	1,770
6	960	1,360	1,920	2,770
7	1,380	1,950	2,760	3,900
8	1,990	2,800	3,980	5,600
10	3,600	5,100	7,200	10,000

[1] Gutters other than semicircular may be used provided they have an equivalent cross-sectional area.

▶   Figure 13-7 illustrates comparative sizing for semicircular and rectangular gutters which aid in computing sizes.   The method of selecting sizes is similar to that used for circular and rectangular leaders.

SEMI-CIRCULAR GUTTERS			RECTANGULAR GUTTERS		
DIAMETER INCHES	CROSS SECTIONAL AREA, SQ. IN.	WATER CONTACT AREA, INCHES	DIMENSION INCHES	CROSS SECTIONAL AREA, SQ. IN.	WATER CONTACT AREA, INCHES
3	3.53	4.70	$1\frac{1}{2}$ X $2\frac{1}{2}$	3.75	5.5
4	6.28	6.28	$2\frac{1}{4}$ X 3	6.75	7.5
5	9.82	7.85	4 X $2\frac{1}{2}$ 3 X $3\frac{1}{2}$	10 10	9 $9\frac{1}{2}$
6	14.14	9.43	3 X 5	15	11
8	25.27	12.57	$4\frac{1}{2}$ X 6	27	15
10	39.77	15.7	5 X 8 4 X 10	40 40	18 18
∪	∪	∪ SEMI-CIRCLE AS STRAIGHT LINE	4"⌐ 10" ⌐4"	⌐_⌐	⌐__⌐ RECTANGLE AS STRAIGHT LINE

Fig. 13-7

13.7 Size of Combined Drains and Sewers

13.7.1 Conversion of roof area to fixture units of storm drainage system that may be connected to a combined sewer. The drainage area may be converted to equivalent fixture-unit loads.

13.7.2 When the total fixture-unit load on the combined drain is less than 256 fixture units, the equivalent drainage area in horizontal projection shall be taken as 1,000 square feet.

13.7.3 When the total fixture-unit load exceeds 256 fixture units, each fixture unit shall be considered the equivalent of 3.9 square feet of drainage area.

13.7.4 If the rainfall to be provided for is more or less than 4 inches per hour, the 1,000-square-foot equivalent in paragraph 13.7.2 and the 3.9 in paragraph 13.7.3 shall be adjusted by multiplying by 4 and dividing by the rainfall in inches per hour to be provided for.

▶ When a combined storm and sanitary sewer is to be computed, the area of the roof (in square feet) should be converted to fixture units in order to get the total load in fixture units. Then, the size of the drain may be computed from Table 11.5.2.

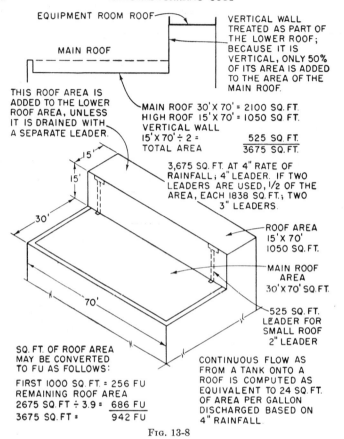

EQUIPMENT ROOM ROOF

VERTICAL WALL
TREATED AS PART OF
THE LOWER ROOF;
BECAUSE IT IS
VERTICAL, ONLY 50%
OF ITS AREA IS ADDED
TO THE AREA OF THE
MAIN ROOF.

MAIN ROOF

THIS ROOF AREA IS
ADDED TO THE LOWER
ROOF AREA, UNLESS
IT IS DRAINED WITH
A SEPARATE LEADER.

MAIN ROOF 30' X 70' = 2100 SQ. FT.
HIGH ROOF 15' X 70' = 1050 SQ. FT.
VERTICAL WALL
15' X 70' ÷ 2 =   525 SQ. FT.
TOTAL AREA   3675 SQ. FT.

3,675 SQ. FT. AT 4" RATE OF
RAINFALL; 4" LEADER. IF TWO
LEADERS ARE USED, 1/2 OF THE
AREA, EACH 1838 SQ. FT.; TWO
3" LEADERS.

ROOF AREA
15' X 70'
1050 SQ. FT.

MAIN ROOF
AREA
30' X 70' SQ. FT.

525 SQ. FT.
LEADER FOR
SMALL ROOF
2" LEADER

SQ. FT. OF ROOF AREA
MAY BE CONVERTED
TO FU AS FOLLOWS:

FIRST 1000 SQ. FT. = 256 FU
REMAINING ROOF AREA
2675 SQ. FT. ÷ 3.9 =   686 FU
3675 SQ. FT. =   942 FU

CONTINUOUS FLOW AS
FROM A TANK ONTO A
ROOF IS COMPUTED AS
EQUIVALENT TO 24 SQ. FT.
OF AREA PER GALLON
DISCHARGED BASED ON
4" RAINFALL.

Fɪɢ. 13-8

Example: (**Fig. 13-8.**) Assume that 4,600 square feet of roof area on the storm-drainage system is to be connected into a sanitary drain carrying 700 fixture units.

	Fixture Units
The first 1,000 sq ft	**256**
Remaining 3,600 sq ft divided by 3.9	**923**
Subtotal 4,600 sq ft	**1,179**
Add sanitary drainage system	**700**
Grand total	**1,879**

According to Table **11.5.2,** 1,879 fixture units require a 10-inch diameter drain.

The conversion of roof area to fixture units is based on a 4-inch rate of rainfall. If a different rate of rainfall is used, the computation changes proportionately.

13.8   Values for Continuous Flow

13.8.1   Where there is a continuous or semicontinuous discharge into the building storm drain or building storm sewer, as from a pump, ejector, air-conditioning plant, or similar device, each gallon per minute of such discharge shall be computed as being equivalent to 24 square feet of roof area, based upon a 4-inch rainfall.   (See Figs. 11-7 and 11-8.)

▶   Allow for the extension of walls above the building and the amount of rain that should be considered for runoff of the roof area itself.   Figure 13-8 illustrates this condition for a flat roof.   The roof area would then be 70 by 30 feet, or 2,100 square feet.   The wall area is 15 by 70 feet, or 1,050 square feet.   However, the wall area would not represent 100 per cent of the required drainage area.   One-half of the wall area is sufficient in calculating the proper drainage.   Add 2,100 square feet of roof area plus half of the wall area (525 square feet), or a total of 2,625 square feet.   According to Table 13.6.1, 2,625 square feet require a 4-inch-diameter conductor based on a normal rainfall of 4 inches per hour.

In the National Plumbing Code, after Tables 13.6.1 and 13.6.2, is given a formula for adjusting the roof area in square feet to rates of rainfall other than 4 inches.

The following is a formula for proportioning the sizes of leaders or drains to rates of rainfall other than 4 inches:

Example a for 5-inch Rainfall: Table 13.6.1 prescribes a 3-inch leader for a 2,200-square-foot roof area in a locality of 4-inch rainfall.   For 5-inch rainfall, this leader would be too small, as it could handle only $\frac{4}{5}$ of the rainfall.   To figure the correct size, invert $\frac{4}{5}$ to $\frac{5}{4}$ and multiply by 3: $5 \times 3/4 = 3.75$-inch leader.   As this is not a standard size, use the next standard size, 4-inch.

Example b for 3-inch Rainfall: Table 13.6.2 prescribes a 6-inch storm drain for a 7,500-square-foot roof area at $\frac{1}{4}$-inch slope in a locality of 4-inch rainfall.   For 3-inch rainfall, this drain would be too large, as it could handle $\frac{4}{3}$ of the load.   To figure the correct size, invert $\frac{4}{3}$ to $\frac{3}{4}$ and multiply by 6: $3 \times 6/4 = 4.5$-inch drain.   Use the next standard size, 5 inch.

CHAPTER 14

Inspection, Tests, and Maintenance

14.1 Inspections

14.1.1 New Work. All new plumbing work, and such portions of existing systems as may be affected by new work or any changes, shall be inspected to ensure compliance with all the requirements of this Code and to assure that the installation and construction of the plumbing system is in accordance with approved plans.

▶ Most cross connections and dangerous connections are made during changes and extensions of the original work. This is partially due to the fact that usually no inspection of the work is made and those installing the work are not aware of the danger.

14.2 Notification

14.2.1 Advance Notice. It shall be the duty of the holder of a permit to give notice to the administrative authority when plumbing work is ready for test or inspection.

14.2.2 Responsibility. It shall be the duty of the holder of a permit to make sure that the work will stand the test prescribed before giving the notification.

14.2.3 Retesting. If the administrative authority finds that the work will not pass the test, necessary corrections shall be made and the work shall then be resubmitted for test or inspection.

14.2.4 Test. Tests shall be conducted in the presence of the administrative authority or of his duly appointed representative.

▶ "Holder of a permit" does not always mean the licensed plumber to whom the permit is issued. The owner who installs his own work also is entitled by law to receive a permit.

While the responsibility as to the safety and correctness of the installed work is up to the holder of a permit, the inspector must see to it that no hazardous or improperly installed work is permitted to remain uncorrected.

14.3 Plumbing Plans

14.3.1 Examination of Plans. All plans and specifications required to be submitted shall be examined by the administrative authority for acceptability under the provisions of this Code.

▶   In a large or complicated plumbing installation, a complete set of plans
should be submitted and reviewed before a permit is given to proceed
with the installation.

Where the work is to be done by other than an experienced licensed
plumber, drawings showing the entire installation should be required so
as to avoid any question of interpretation of the plumbing requirements.

14.4 Violations

14.4.1 Notices of violations shall be written and mailed or delivered by the
administrative authority to the person responsible at the time inspection was
made.

▶   When an installation has been erroneously installed, the written
violation should clearly state what is wrong and what should be done to
correct the installation.

14.5 Reinspection

14.5.1 Reinspections. Reinspections of plumbing installations or any part
thereof shall be made when deemed necessary by the Administrative Authority.

14.6 Covering of Work

14.6.1 Requirements. No drainage or plumbing system or part thereof
shall be covered until it has been inspected, tested, and accepted as prescribed
in this Code.

14.6.2 Uncovering. If any building drainage or plumbing system or part
thereof which is installed, altered, or repaired is covered before being inspected,
tested, and approved, as prescribed in this Code, it shall be uncovered for inspection after notice to uncover the work has been issued to the responsible person
by the administrative authority.

▶   This requirement is in reference to possible tightness of the piping
underground or built into the wall. It is far less costly to test the work
properly when first installed than later to have to remove a brick or
plastered wall or cut out a concrete floor.

14.7 Material and Labor for Tests

14.7.1 The equipment, material, and labor necessary for inspection or tests
shall be furnished by the person to whom the permit is issued or by whom
inspection is requested.

▶   The cost involved in providing necessary test plugs, nipples, pumps,
and labor to prepare for the test is up to the licensed plumber or to the
owner when he is doing his own job. The tests should be conducted as
required by the Code.

14.8   Tests of Drainage and Vent Systems

14.8.1   The piping of the plumbing, drainage, and venting systems shall be tested with water or air.   After the plumbing fixtures have been set and their traps filled with water, the entire drainage system shall be submitted to a final test.   The administrative authority may require the removal of any cleanouts, to ascertain if the pressure has reached all parts of the system.

▶   A water test is simpler to make for a drainage and venting system and is effective in determining if the system is tight against leaks.   Care should be exercised as to the type of piping material, inasmuch as some joints will not withstand as much pressure as others.

Cast-iron soil pipe with hot-poured joints should not be tested for more than 10 stories.   Screwed pipe or Durham system may be tested for 15 to 20 stories at one time.   Copper tubing with sweat joints may be tested up to 20 stories.

14.9   Methods of Testing Drainage and Vent Systems

14.9.1   Water Test.   The water test shall be applied to the drainage system either in its entirety or in sections.   If applied to the entire system, all openings in the piping shall be tightly closed, except the highest opening, and the system filled with water to the point of overflow.   If the system is tested in sections, each opening shall be tightly plugged except the highest opening of the section under test, and each section shall be filled with water, but no section shall be tested with less than a 10-foot head of water.   In testing successive sections, at least the upper 10 feet of the next preceding section shall be tested, so that no joint or pipe in the building (except the uppermost 10 feet of the system) shall have been submitted to a test of less than a 10-foot head of water.   The water shall be kept in the system, or in the portion under test, for at least 15 minutes before inspection starts; the system shall then be tight at all points.

▶   In those parts of the country where temperatures normally drop below 32°F, no water tests should be made during the months of freezing weather. Even if the tests are completed before the temperature goes below freezing and then the temperature drops, there is a possibility of the oakum being saturated with water and the cast-iron soil pipe cracking at the hub.

14.9.2   Air Test.   The air test shall be made by attaching an air-compressor testing apparatus to any suitable opening and, after closing all other inlets and outlets to the system, forcing air into the system until there is a uniform gauge pressure of 5 pounds per square inch or sufficient to balance a column of mercury 10 inches in height.   This pressure shall be held without introduction of additional air for a period of at least 15 minutes.

▶ An air test is somewhat more rigid than a water test, as it is more difficult to find the leaks unless soap and water are used at the joints, or some odor is injected into the pumped air.

14.9.3   Final Test.   The final test of the completed drainage and vent system may be either a smoke test or a peppermint test.   Where the smoke test is preferred, it shall be made by filling all traps with water and then introducing into the entire system a pungent, thick smoke produced by one or more smoke machines.   When the smoke appears at stack openings on the roof, they shall be closed and a pressure equivalent to a 1-inch water column shall be built and maintained for 15 minutes before inspection starts.   Where the peppermint test is preferred, 2 ounces of oil of peppermint shall be introduced for each line or stack.

▶ The final test after all fixtures have been installed and the fixture traps filled with water is important.   The smoke test or peppermint test provides assurance that connections for water closets are absolutely gas and watertight and fixture traps sound.

14.10   Building Sewer

14.10.1   Test Required.   Building sewers shall be tested.

14.10.2   Method.   Test shall consist of plugging end of building sewer at point of connection with the public sewer and filling the building sewer with water and testing with not less than a 10-foot head of water, or a flow test as provided by the administrative authority may be substituted.

▶ A flow test for a building sewer will not always show that it is tight.
When the water-service main is installed in the same trench with the sewer, the piping should be of such type as to provide assurance that all joints are water and gastight.
When testing an existing sewer, it is not practical to dig up the ground to ascertain its condition.   Some areas provide that an existing sewer may be tested by inserting a partly filled bladder with a small rubber hose. The bladder is floated to the end of the sewer and then blown up so as to make a tight stoppage.   The sewer is then filled with water, with a 10-foot head, and watched for leaks.

14.11   Inspection and Test not Required

14.11.1   No test or inspection shall be required where a plumbing system, or part thereof, is set up for exhibition purposes and has no connection with a water or drainage system.

▶ This applies to exhibits which are of a temporary nature and which do not connect with the drainage system.

If chemicals or other injurious liquids are used, backflow preventors or airgaps must be provided in order to safeguard the water system of the building where the exhibits are being shown.

14.12   Test of Water-supply System

14.12.1   Upon completion of a section or of the entire water-supply system, it shall be tested and proved tight under a water pressure not less than the working pressure under which it is to be used.   The water used for tests shall be obtained from a potable source of supply.

▶   It is safer to test the system with a pressure at least 50 per cent higher than the pressure under which the system will be used.

14.13   Test of Interior Leaders or Downspouts

14.13.1   Leaders or downspouts and branches within a building shall be tested by water or air in accordance with paragraph 14.8.1 or 14.8.2.

▶   If the leaders are exposed to view and make no connection with the drainage system, there is no need to test the system.

14.14   Certificate of Approval

14.14.1   Upon the satisfactory completion and final test of the plumbing system a certificate of approval shall be issued by the administrative authority to the plumber to be delivered to the owner.

▶   A certificate of satisfactory and safe installation is essential for the owner to assure him the work has met all standards of good work.   This certificate will provide a warrant to the owner that the contractor and the inspection of the work have met all standards of good installation and that the building is safe to be occupied.

14.15   Defective Plumbing

14.15.1   Wherever there is reason to believe that the plumbing system of any building has become defective, it shall be subjected to test or inspection and any defects found shall be corrected as required in writing by the administrative authority.

▶   This is a difficult problem unless the ordinance provides for reinspection at frequent intervals.   Most cities do not have sufficient personnel to provide for this important service.

14.16 Maintenance

14.16.1 The plumbing and drainage system of any premises under the jurisdiction of the administrative authority shall be maintained in a sanitary and safe operating condition by the owner or his agent.

▶ This requirement is difficult to regulate unless reinspection is made part of the regulation, so that buildings are inspected at frequent intervals and violations discovered by proper inspection.

Part Two

SUPPLEMENT TO CODE

CHAPTER 15

Individual Water Supply

Introduction

Where connection to a municipal water supply or public water system is not possible, it is essential that certain precautions be taken in the development of individual supplies. Consideration must be given to the hydrological, geological, and bacteriological factors affecting the quantity and quality of available water. In many cases specific information on these matters may be obtained from the state or local health authorities. In any event, such authorities should be consulted prior to the development of any individual water supply.

Many residential areas not served by public water supply or sewerage system have been developed in which the lot sizes are inadequate to permit the proper location of individual water and sewerage systems. In such instances it would be well to give serious consideration to the development of a community water system to serve the entire area. The following requirements conform to those set forth in detail in Public Health Service, Supplement No. 185, "Individual Water Supply System" recommendation of the Joint Committee on Rural Sanitation.

15.1 General

15.1.1 Ground-water Supply. A ground-water supply should be properly located, constructed, and operated so as to be safeguarded against contamination.

▶ Private supplies are necessary in rural areas, where a city or public supply is not available. In such cases the developing and maintaining of this supply is entirely up to the property owner.

A few simple precautions are necessary in planning the system:

The source of supply must be potable and free from contamination.

Waste produced on the premises should not be permitted to gain access to the potable-water supply.

The construction of the system must be so effective as to prevent any chance of contamination.

15.1.2 Well Location. The well site shall be chosen to permit the well to be situated an adequate distance from existing and potential sources of contamination as specified in Table 15.3.2. In order to determine the separation necessary, it is essential to consider the character and location of the source of contamination, type of well construction, natural hydraulic gradient of water table, permeability of the water-bearing formation, extent of cone depression formed in the water table due to pumping the well, and the type of rock structure. In residential areas, the possible effect of new construction on the safety of the water supply should also be considered.

▶ **Actually there is no clearly defined distance a well should be from a cesspool or disposal field to be considered safe.**

The distance which the contaminated discharges from a disposal field or cesspool will travel before they may be considered safe depends on many variables: the slope of the ground, the porosity of the soil, the depth of the ground water, the direction of flow in relation to the cesspool.

If the soil is of sandy nature, a well may be considered properly located if it is 100 feet from the source of contamination, provided that the ground-water flow is in the opposite direction.

15.1.3   Classification.   Wells are hereby classified into four groups on the basis of construction, as follows: dug, bored, driven, and drilled. The type of well to be constructed will depend on the geology of the area and the depth of the water-bearing strata. Drilled wells, because of their greater depth, usually have greater yields and are less affected by drought. They are usually more desirable from a public viewpoint since they may be better protected against contamination than dug or bored wells.

•▶ **The source of water supply is rainfall. Part of the rainfall is absorbed by vegetation, part flows over the surface of the ground, part goes into lakes and rivers, and part percolates into the ground, where it is stored in large quantities.**

Rainfall as it reaches the ground is free from impurities, although as it falls through the atmosphere it picks up dust and other harmless impurities in the air. Science may change this condition in the future.

Rain water on striking the ground can come in contact with dangerous pollution.

Time is nature's way of purifying water. The water that percolates through the soil undergoes a filtering action; it can be clear and safe within a few hundred feet, unless the water which percolates through the ground flows through rock crevices or channels.

It is because of this filtering action of nature that it is possible to develop safe underground supplies.

15.2   Quantity and Quality of Water

15.2.1   Minimum Quantity.   The minimum quantity of water to provide for ordinary domestic use should be not less than 50 gallons per person per day. The well and pumping equipment shall be adequate to provide the required quantity of water at the rate of 5 gallons per minute.

15.2.2 Safe Water. The water shall contain no chemical or mineral substances capable of causing unfavorable physiological effects on those consuming the water.

▶ Developed wells of any kind should be checked by the local health department to be certain that the water meets all standards for potable water.

15.2.3 Chlorination. The water shall be free from pathogenic bacteria and other disease-producing organisms. The well should be chlorinated after construction or repair to remove any contamination which may have gained access to the supply. (The state or local health department should be contacted relative to possible bacteriological testing.)

▶ Because of the differences between one type of water and the extent to which it may be contaminated, it is essential that the local or state health department be contacted for advice.

It is essential that a well be sterilized after it has been completed or repaired.

This is accomplished by the use of a number of commercial disinfectants. Chloride of lime or commercial high-test hypochlorite, which can be procured at most drugstores, may be used.

If chloride of lime is selected, it may be used in the following manner: A thin paste is made by mixing a quantity of chloride of lime from a newly opened can with a small quantity of lukewarm water. Mix the paste in a gallon of water and then pour into the well.

Enough chloride of lime should be used so that a strong odor is noted. Allow the well to stand without disturbance for about 24 hours, and then pump out the well until the water is free from chlorine odor. The piping and pumping equipment should be sterilized in the same manner.

All sources of contamination should be removed before sterilization is attempted.

15.3 Location

15.3.1 Minimum Distance. The minimum distance between any groundwater point of origin and suction lines and any source of contamination shall be not less than that given in Table 15.3.2.

15.3.2 (See Table 15.3.2.)

15.3.3 Elevation. The well site should have good surface drainage and should be at a higher elevation than possible sources of contamination. The top of the well should be at least 2 feet above the highest known water mark and at least 50 feet measured horizontally from surface bodies of water.

▶ Water which has its source in limestone strata should be tested at regular intervals in order to ascertain its sanitary qualities.

Properly built wells, which have their source of supply in sand or gravel formations, are generally safe.

Table 15.3.2   Distances from Source of Contamination

	Distance (ft)[1]		Distance (ft)[1]
Sewer	50	Subsurface disposal fields	100
Septic tanks	50	Seepage pits	100
Subsurface pits	50	Cesspools	150

[1] These distances constitute minimum separation and should be increased in areas of creviced rock or limestone, or where the direction of movement of the ground water is from sources of contamination toward the well.

15.4   Construction

15.4.1   Depth. In no case shall an individual water supply be developed from a water-bearing stratum located less than 10 feet below grade.

Preferably, the water-bearing stratum should be located at least 20 feet from the natural ground surface.

▶   **Experience in the locality where the well is to be located is the best assurance of finding water. Knowledge and observation of the topography and the geology of the region will be of help.**

There is no infallible rule; the divining rod is no more than a guess.

15.4.2   Outside Casing. The well shall be provided with an outside water-tight casing extending at least 10 feet below and 6 inches above the ground surface. In the case of drilled or driven wells, the casing should be of steel or wrought iron. For dug or bored wells the casing should be of concrete 6 inches thick, except that in the case of the buried-slab type of dug or bored well the upper 10-foot section of casing should be of steel or wrought iron as provided for drilled wells. The annular space between the casing and the earth formation shall be grouted to a depth of at least 10 feet. The casing shall be large enough to permit the installation of an independent drop pipe. The casing should preferably be sealed in an impermeable stratum or extended several feet into the water-bearing stratum.

15.4.3   Cover. Every well shall be provided with a watertight cover overlapping the top of the casing or pipe sleeve. The annular opening between the casing or pipe sleeve and drop pipe shall be sealed either by extending the casing or pipe sleeve into the base of the pump or by some suitable type of "well seal."

15.4.4   Drainage. The well platform or pump-room floor shall be sloped to drain away from the well. The platform or floor shall be constructed of concrete at least 4 inches thick, or other material found equivalent thereto and approved by the administrative authority.

15.4.5   Dug or Bored Well. In the case of a dug or bored well, the cover shall overlap and extend downward at least 2 inches outside the wall or curbing of the well.

15.4.6 Pipe Sleeve. A pipe sleeve of sufficient diameter to permit removal of the drop pipe and cylinder or jet body shall be provided in the cover. The pipe sleeve should extend at least 1 inch above the cover.

15.5 Pumping Equipment

15.5.1 Pumps. Pumps shall be so constructed and installed as to prevent the entrance of any contaminating substances into the water supply.

15.5.2 Pump Head. The pump head shall be so designed as to prevent any contaminating substances from reaching the water chamber of the pump.

15.5.3 Well Cover. The pump shall be so designed as to effect a waterproof seal with the well cover or casing.

15.5.4 Priming. The pump shall be so designed and installed that priming will not be necessary.

15.5.5 Maintenance. The installation shall be so designed as to facilitate necessary maintenance and repair.

15.5.6 Protection. The well shall be protected against freezing by means of heating or by means of properly designed and installed underground discharge.

15.5.7 Pump Room. Where the pump room is situated in an offset from the basement, the pump-room floor shall be located not less than 18 inches above the basement floor.

15.5.8 Well Pits. The installation of well pits is not recommended.

15.5.9 Pressure Tank. A pressure tank with a minimum storage capacity of 42 gallons per dwelling unit should be installed.

CHAPTER 16

Individual Sewage-disposal System

Introduction

The most satisfactory method of disposing of sewage is by connection to a public sewerage system. Every effort should be made to secure public sewer extensions. When connection to a public sewer is not feasible and when a considerable number of residences are to be served, consideration should be given to the construction of a community sewer system and treatment plant. Specific information on this matter may be obtained from the local authorities having jurisdiction. In any event, such authority should be consulted prior to the installation of an individual sewage-disposal system. Sewage-disposal installations serving commercial establishments for multiple-dwelling units shall be designed in accordance with requirements of the administrative authority.

In those instances where the installation of a private residential sewage-disposal system cannot be avoided, the following requirements should be followed. These requirements are based on Public Health Service Reprint No. 2461, "Individual Sewage-disposal Systems," recommendations of the Joint Committee on Rural Sanitation. As a result of research studies conducted by the U.S. Public Health Service and sponsored by the Housing and Home Finance Agency, the Joint Committee is of the opinion that the report may be modified in the following respects:

1. Variations in shape of the septic tank within reasonable limits are permissible, provided that the total liquid capacity is not reduced below 500 gallons.

2. In so far as suspended-solids reduction is concerned, multicompartment tanks also appear to be satisfactory; however, when such tanks are used, the total liquid capacity should be not less than that set forth in the existing recommendations; no single compartment should contain less than 125 gallons; and the inlet and outlet connections and baffles for each compartment should follow the principles set forth for inlet and outlet connections and baffles in single-compartment tanks, provided such connections or baffles do not extend below the mid-depth of the liquid.

3. Consideration should be given to location of individual compartments and their location relative to each other to permit convenient access to all compartments, thus assuring complete servicing of the entire tank installation.

4. Only durable materials should be used in the tank construction if the costs of maintenance and replacement are to be considered in the economic evaluation of the individual sewage-disposal system to the property owner.

The research work referred to above was confined to the septic tank and therefore is not applicable to the complete disposal system. As additional information becomes available, it is expected that the joint committee will make such further revision of the recommendations as may be indicated.

16.1 General

16.1.1 Design. The design of the individual sewage-disposal system must take into consideration location with respect to wells or other sources of water supply, topography, water table, soil characteristics, area available, and maximum occupancy of the building.

16.1.2 Type of System. The type of system to be installed shall be determined on the basis of location, soil permeability, and ground-water elevation.

16.1.3 Sanitary Sewage. The system shall be designed to receive all sanitary sewage, including laundry waste, from the building. Drainage from basement floor, footings, or roofs shall not enter the system.

16.1.4 Discharge. The system shall consist of a septic tank discharging into either a subsurface disposal field or one or more seepage pits or into a combina-

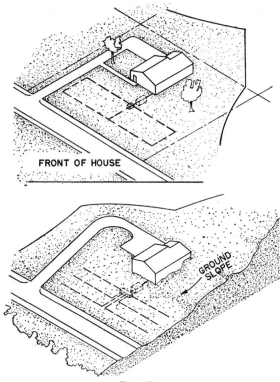

FRONT OF HOUSE

GROUND SLOPE

Fig. 16-1

tion of both, if found adequate as such and approved by the administrative authority.

16.1.5   Alternate Design.   Where soil conditions are such that neither of the systems mentioned in 16.1.4 can be expected to operate satisfactorily, approval of an alternate design shall be secured from the administrative authority with concurrence of the proper health authorities having jurisdiction.

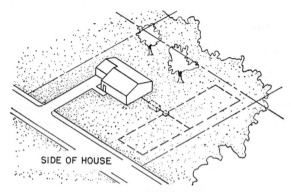

SIDE OF HOUSE

Fig. 16-2

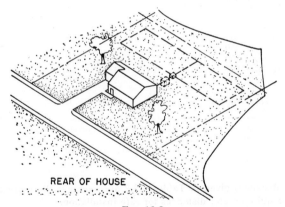

REAR OF HOUSE

Fig. 16-3

▶   Most local or state health departments will provide assistance in the design of a satisfactory private disposal system.

Local contractors in the business of installing individual disposal systems can provide valuable assistance in respect to local soil conditions and the over-all construction of a satisfactory system.

In swampy or flooded areas an absorption system is not satisfactory.

The size of the property must be considered, inasmuch as an individual disposal system for a large number of homes will require a larger lot than is ordinarily required when connection is made to a sewer.

In locating the septic tank, consider future extension of a public sewer so that a minimum rerouting of the building sewer will be necessary.

When the ground slopes to the front of the house, the tank and field should be located as shown on Fig. 16-1.

Figure 16-2 illustrates the location when ground slopes to the side.

Figure 16-3 illustrates the location when ground slopes to the rear.

16.2   Location

16.2.1   Distances. Table 16.2.2 provides for the minimum distances that shall be observed in locating the various components of the disposal system.

16.2.2   (See Table 16.2.2.)

Table 16.2.2   Location of Components of Sewage-disposal System

Type of system	Distance (ft)						
	Well or suction line	Water-supply line (pressure)	Stream	Dwelling	Property line	Disposal field	Seepage pits
Building sewer...	50	10					
Septic tank......	50						
Distribution box.	50						
Disposal field[1] ...	100	...	25	10	10		
Seepage pit......	100	...	50	20	10	20	20
Dry well........	50	...	...	10			
Cesspool[2]........	150	...	50	20	15	15	15

[1] This separation may be reduced to 50 ft when the well is provided with an outside watertight casing to a depth of 50 ft or more.

[2] Not recommended as a substitute for a septic tank. To be used only when approved by the administrative authority.

▶   **The distances given in Table 16.2.2 are average; there are conditions which require greater distances for safe installation.**

16.2.3   Septic Tanks. Septic tanks or other private means of disposal shall not be approved where a public sewer is available. Such means of disposal shall be discontinued when public sewers are made available, if directed by the legal authorities.

16.3   Building Sewer

16.3.1   Size. The sewer shall be of a minimum size to serve the connected fixtures as determined from Chap. 11 of the Code.

16.3.2 Slope. The sewer shall have a minimum slope as determined in Table 11.5.2 of the Code, except that the slope of the sewer 10 feet preceding the tank connection shall not exceed ¼ inch per foot.

The waste from all plumbing in the house, including kitchen sinks, food-waste disposal units, laundry trays, and washing machines, should discharge into the drainage system and then to the septic tank.

Grease interceptors for residences are not necessary. When kitchens or sculleries are built in camps or restaurants or where large quantities of grease may be discharged, a grease interceptor should be provided, in order to prevent large amounts of grease entering the septic tank and the distribution field.

In order to prevent high velocities at the entrance to the septic tank, 5 to 10 feet of the sewer ahead of the septic tank should not slope more than ¼ inch per foot.

Where rain-water downspouts are discharged onto the ground, the flow should be directed away from the distribution field and in no case connected to the septic tank.

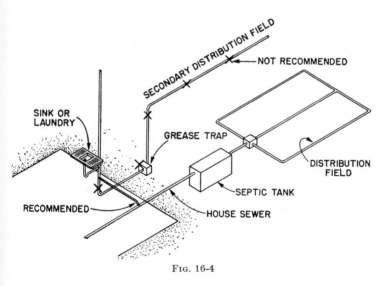

Fig. 16-4

Figure 16-4 illustrates how a sink waste should be connected to the drainage system.

16.4 Septic Tank

16.4.1 Capacity. The septic tank shall have a minimum capacity in accordance with the provisions of Table 16.4.2.

16.4.2 (See Table 16.4.2.)

Table 16.4.2   Minimum Capacities for Septic Tanks Serving an Individual Dwelling

Number of bedrooms	Maximum number of persons served	Nominal liquid capacity of tank (gal)	Recommended inside dimensions							
			Length		Width		Liquid depth		Total depth	
			Ft	In.	Ft	In.	Ft	In.	Ft	In.
2 or less..........	4	500	6	0	3	0	4	0	5	0
3.................	6	600	7	0	3	0	4	0	5	0
4.................	8	750	7	6	3	6	4	0	5	0
5.................	10	900	8	6	3	6	4	6	5	6
6.................	12	1,100	8	6	4	0	4	6	5	6
7.................	14	1,300	10	0	4	0	4	6	5	6
8.................	16	1,500	10	0	4	6	4	6	5	6

Liquid capacity is based on number of bedrooms in dwelling. Total volume in cubic feet includes air space above liquid level.

16.4.3   Multiple Compartments. In a tank of more than one compartment, the inlet compartment shall have a capacity of not less than two-thirds of the total tank capacity.

▶   In computing septic-tank capacity, the factor most often used is the number of bedrooms. When a food-waste disposal unit is installed, slight increase in tank capacity should be used, in order to take care of the additional solids and extend the period of pumping a septic tank.

Table A. Septic Tank Size

No. of bedrooms	Tank size (gal)	
	Without disposal units	With disposal units
2	500	750
3	600	900
4	750	1,125
For each additional bedroom, add...	180	270

If in the future it is expected to increase the number of bedrooms in a house, it is recommended that allowance be made for the increased size of the septic tank in the original construction.

Contrary to some opinions, an increase in liquid capacity going to the septic tank does not require an increase in the septic tank size. This applies to automatic dishwashers or clothes washers or any device using clear water.

The normal use of detergents for dishwashing, clothes washing, or as toilet-bowl cleaners will not interfere with the operation of the septic tank. Likewise the normal amount of salt water discharged into the septic tank from regeneration of water softeners does not affect its operation.

In large residential buildings, regeneration waste should be disposed of by other means than the septic tank.

16.4.4   Garbage Disposal.   Where domestic garbage-disposal units are installed or contemplated, the capacity of the septic tank shall be at least 50 per cent greater than the requirements given in Table 16.4.2.

▶   The 50 per cent greater capacity of the septic tank is based on the fact that food-waste grinders will add a certain amount of solids, and therefore to prevent too frequent cleansing of the septic tank this allowance is made. Additional research is being conducted for a clearer determination of this factor.

16.4.5   Length.   Septic tanks shall be at least twice as long as they are wide.

16.4.6   Construction.   Septic tanks shall be constructed of corrosion-resistant materials and be of permanent construction.   The cover of the tank shall be designed for a dead load of not less than 150 pounds per square foot and, if of concrete, should be reinforced and not less than 4 inches thick.

16.4.7   Manholes.   The inlet compartment must be provided with one manhole.   Other compartments may be provided with a manhole.   Manholes shall be at least 20 inches square or 24 inches in diameter and provided with covers which can be sealed watertight.   Manholes should be extended to grade. Where removable slab covers are provided, manholes are not required.

16.4.8   Baffles.   If inlet and outlet baffles are used, they shall extend the full width of the tank and be located 12 inches from the end walls.   Such baffles shall extend at least 6 inches above the flow line.   Inlet baffles shall extend 12 inches and outlet baffles 15 to 18 inches below the flow line.

16.4.9   Pipe Inlet and Outlet.   In lieu of baffles, submerged pipe inlets and outlets may be installed consisting of a cast-iron sanitary tee with a short section of pipe to the required depth as indicated in paragraph 16.4.8.

16.4.10   Invert.   The invert of the inlet pipe shall be located at least 3 inches above the invert of the outlet.

16.4.11   Dosing Chambers.   Dosing chambers are not required in the case of individual disposal systems.

▶   The principal points in the construction of a septic tank are:
Proper size for the intended liquid capacity.
Hermetically sealed construction.
The material selected to be able to resist the corrosive effects of the soil surrounding the tank and of the liquid contents of the tank.
Sufficiently strong to withstand earth loads on sides, top, and bottom.

Tank contents to be accessible through properly located manholes for periodic cleaning.

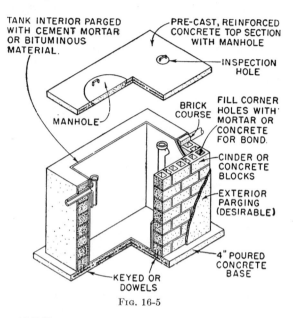

FIG. 16-5

Figure 16-5 illustrates some of the important points in the construction of a septic tank.

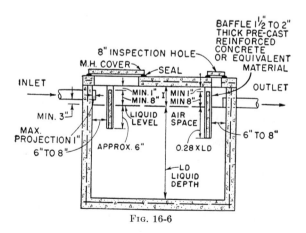

FIG. 16-6

Figure 16-6 illustrates the general dimensions and requirements of a concrete septic tank.

Instead of concrete baffles, sanitary-tee branches may be used, but the dimensions given for the baffles should be approximately the same.

Bituminous-coated steel tanks are extensively used, but while less costly will not give the length of service life of a concrete tank.

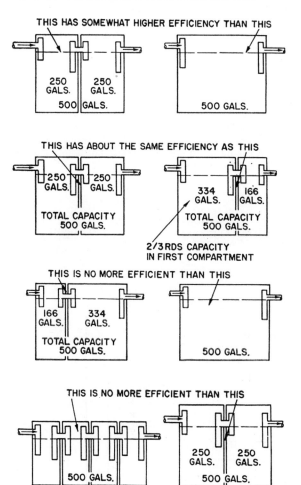

Fig. 16-7

The shape of the tank will have very little effect on its operation.

When wood forms are used for shaping a concrete tank, these forms should be removed from the interior of the tank.

When locating manholes on top of the tank, care should be taken that they clear baffles or tees so that access to the interior is assured.

A septic tank may be installed in one or several compartments; their efficiency is practically alike.

When installing several compartments, the total capacity must be the same or more than that required for a single compartment.

Figure 16-7 illustrates various methods of installing a septic tank with two or more compartments.

When installing several compartments, no compartment should have less than 25 per cent of the total capacity required.

Connections between compartments should be made by means of tees not elbows.

When it is found necessary to have increased septic tank capacity because of additional bedrooms or the installation of more bathroom fixtures or new plumbing-connected appliances, a new tank may be added to the existing installation. The new tank or compartment may be placed on either side of the present tank. The liquid capacity of the new tank or compartment should be 50 per cent greater but in no case less than one third of the existing capacity.

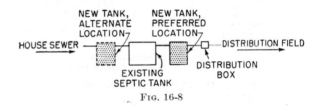

Fig. 16-8

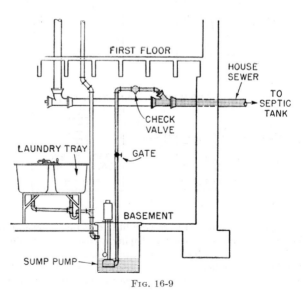

Fig. 16-9

Figure 16-8 shows the location of a new compartment.

Another problem which sometimes arises after a job is completed is the installation of plumbing fixtures in a basement and below the level of the septic tank. In such case, a sump pump may be installed to raise the sewage into the building drain.

Figure 16-9 illustrates a sump pump in the basement of a house receiving the waste from laundry trays or a laundry washing machine and pumping the sump pit contents into the building drain.

6.5 Distribution Box

6.5.1 Required. A distribution box shall be provided to receive the effluent from the septic tank to assure equal distribution to each individual line of the disposal field.

6.5.2 Connection. The distribution box shall be connected to the septic tank by a tight sewer line and be located at the upper end of the disposal field.

6.5.3 Invert Level. The invert of the inlet pipe shall be located 2 inches above the bottom of the box. The invert of the outlets to each distribution line shall be level with the bottom of the box and set at the same elevation.

6.5.4 Inspection. The sides of the box should extend to within a short distance of the ground surface to permit inspection. The box should be kept to the minimum size necessary to accommodate the inlet and outlets.

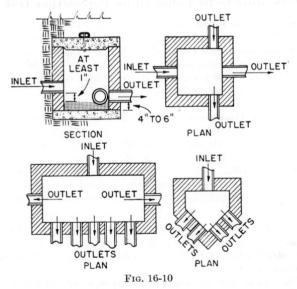

Fig. 16-10

Figure 16-10 illustrates the method generally used for locating the outlets from the box, when several laterals are used for the distributing field. The invert of all the outlets should be leveled so as to be sure that distribution to each field lateral is balanced.

16.6   Absorption Areas

16.6.1   Individual Residences. The absorption areas for individual residences shall be determined from Table 16.6.2.
16.6.2 (See Table 16.6.2.)

Table 16.6.2   Absorption Areas for Individual Residences

Time Required for Water to Fall 1 In. (min)	Effective Absorption Area Required in Bottom of Disposal Trenches (sq ft per Bedroom)
2 or less	50
3	60
4	70
5	80
10	100
15	130
30	180
60	240
Over 60	[1]

[1] Special design.

A minimum of 150 square feet should be provided for each dwelling unit.

16.7   Procedure to Be Followed for Percolation Test

16.7.1   Size of Test Holes. Not less than three holes shall be tested, each
to be 1 foot square and as deep as the proposed disposal trenches.
16.7.2   Variations in Soil Condition. Fill each hole to a depth of at least
6 inches and allow the water to seep away. Allowance shall be made for variation in soil conditions at the time of the test from year-round average conditions. Where exceptional conditions are encountered, greater depths of water
may be used or the test repeated.
16.7.3   Effective Absorption. Observe the time in minutes for the water to
seep away completely. Calculate the time in minutes for the water to fall 1 inch.
Average the results from the holes tested. The effective absorption area required
shall then be determined from Table 16.6.2.
16.7.4   Special Soils. Tests shall not be made on filled or frozen ground.
Where fissure-soil formation is encountered, tests shall be made under the direction of the administrative authority or the health department having jurisdiction.

▶   Test holes should be distributed over the entire area where the distribution field is going to be located, so as to get a good average condition.
The holes should be 6 to 12 inches wide and vertical to the bottom of the
proposed trench.

Holes can be square, or round holes may be bored with a post-type auger.

Placing about 2 inches of coarse sand or gravel at the bottom of the hole
will prevent scouring.

It is desirable first to saturate the soil of the hole thoroughly and then
proceed with the test.

Rate of percolation is obtained by the time in minutes for the water to fall 1 inch divided by the number of minutes used to percolate all the water in the hole.

To obtain the average rate for all the test holes, add the percolation rates for each hole and divide by the number of holes.

Not less than 150 square feet of absorption area should be provided for any residence.

Table B provides a schedule showing the number of square feet of trench under varying conditions.

Table B. Trench Size under Various Conditions

Time in which water falls 1 in. (min)	Square feet of trench required for each bedroom			
	Without food-waste unit or automatic washing machine	With food-waste unit	With automatic washing machine	With both food-waste unit and automatic washing machine
or less........	50	65	75	85
2–3............	60	75	85	100
3–4............	70	85	95	115
4–5............	75	90	105	125
5–10..........	100	120	135	165
0–15..........	115	140	160	190
5–30..........	150	180	205	250
0–45..........	180	215	245	300
5–60..........	200	240	275	330

When it takes longer than 1 hour for the water to fall 1 inch, other methods of percolation hould be developed.

6.8   Minimum Standards for Disposal-field Construction

6.8.1   Disposal-field Construction.   The minimum standards for disposal-field construction shall be as given in Table 16.8.2.

6.8.2   (See Table 16.8.2.)

Table 16.8.2   Design Features of a Disposal Field

Number of lateral branches.................... 2
Length of branch............................ 100 ft
Width of trench............................. 18 to 36 in.
Distance between laterals (parallel)............. 6 ft
Depth of trench............................. 18 to 36 in.
Slope of distributing pipe for each 100 ft.......... 2 to 6 in.
Depth of coarse material:
    Under pipe................................. 6 in.
    Over pipe.................................. 2 in.
Size of coarse material........................ $\frac{1}{2}$ to $2\frac{1}{2}$ in.

16.9   Disposal Trenches

16.9.1   Disposal Trenches. Disposal trenches shall be designed and constructed on the basis of the required effective percolation area.

16.9.2   Filter Material. The filter material shall cover the tile and extend the full width of the trench and shall be not less than 6 inches deep beneath the bottom of the tile.   The filter material may be washed gravel, crushed stone, slag, or clean bank-run gravel ranging in size from $\frac{1}{2}$ to $2\frac{1}{2}$ inches.   The filter material shall be covered by untreated paper or by a 2-inch layer of straw as the laying of the pipe drain proceeds.

16.9.3   Disposal Field. The size and minimum spacing requirements for disposal fields shall conform to those given in Table 16.9.4.

16.9.4   (See Table 16.9.4.)

Table 16.9.4   Size and Spacing for Disposal Fields

Width of trench at bottom (in.)	Recommended depth of trench (in.)	Spacing tile lines[1] (ft)	Effective absorption area per lineal foot of trench (sq ft)
18	18–30	6.0	1.5
24	18–30	6.0	2.0
30	18–36	7.6	2.5
36	24–36	9.0	3.0

[1] A greater spacing is desirable where available area permits.

16.9.5   Absorption Lines. Absorption lines shall be constructed of tile laid with open joints.   In the case of bell-and-spigot tile, it should be laid with $\frac{1}{2}$-inch open joints, at 2-foot intervals, with sufficient cement mortar at the bottom of the joint to ensure an even flow line.   In the case of agricultural tile the sections shall be spaced not more than $\frac{1}{4}$ inch, and the upper half of the joint shall be protected by asphalt-treated paper while the tile is being covered unless the pipe is covered by at least 2 inches of gravel.   Perforated clay tile or perforated bituminized-fiber pipe or asbestos-cement pipe may be used, provided that sufficient openings are available for distribution of the effluent into the trench area.

16.10   Seepage Pit

16.10.1   Seepage Pit. Seepage pits may be used either to supplement the subsurface disposal field or in lieu of such field where conditions favor the operation of seepage pits, as may be found necessary and approved by the administrative authority.

16.10.2   Water Table. Care shall be taken to avoid extending the seepage pit into the ground-water table.   Where the pit is used to receive the septic-tank effluent, the same limitations shall be placed on the location of the pit as on the cesspool.   (See paragraph 16.12.3.)

6.10.3 Pit Lining. Except as provided in paragraph 16.10.6 the pit shall be lined with stone, brick, or concrete blocks laid up dry with open joints that are backed up with at least 3 inches of coarse gravel. The joints above the inlet shall be sealed with cement mortar. It is customary to draw in the upper section of the lining.

6.10.4 Pit Covers. A reinforced-concrete cover shall be provided, preferably to finished grade. If the cover is over 30 inches square, it shall have an access manhole.

6.10.5 Bottom of Pit. The bottom of the pit shall be filled with coarse gravel to a depth of 1 foot.

6.10.6 Trees. When the seepage pit is located in close proximity to trees, need not be lined as indicated in paragraph 16.10.3; instead, it may be filled with loose rock.

6.10.7 Size of Pit. The seepage pit shall be sized in accordance with provisions in Table 16.10.8.

6.10.8 (See Table 16.10.8.)

Table 16.10.8 Requirements for Seepage-pit Design

Soil Structure	Effective Absorption Area Required per Bedroom[1] (sq ft)
Coarse sand and gravel	20
Fine sand	30
Sandy loam or sand clay	50
Clay with considerable sand and gravel	80
Clay with small amount of sand and gravel	160

[1] In calculating absorption wall area of pit, gross diameter of pit excavation shall be used.

6.10.9 Soil Structure. Heavy tight clay, hardpan, rock, or other impervious soil formations are not suitable for seepage-pit construction.

Seepage pits might be used to supplement or as an alternate to distribution fields. Some areas do not permit their use because of possible contamination of the water supply.

Where shallow wells are installed, seepage pits are not recommended. If installed, the following distances are recommended:

From any source of domestic water supply	100 feet
From any structure	20 feet
From any lot line	10 feet
From any septic tank	10 feet
From other seepage pits at least three times the diameter of the larger pit	

The effective area of a seepage pit is the entire wall area below the inlet and the bottom of the pit.

In constructing a seepage pit it is necessary first to ascertain that the absorption of the soil is satisfactory. Table C may serve as a guide for absorption requirements.

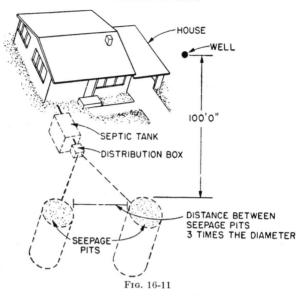

Fig. 16-11

The following example may serve to illustrate the method:
Assume:

> Three-bedroom home, with automatic washer
> Seepage pit to be 6 feet in diameter
> Inlet to be 3 feet below ground surface
> Excavation and percolation tests reveal:

Feet	*Soil Structure*
0 to 4.......	Soil with percolation rate slower than 60 minutes per inch
4 to 5.......	Hardpan formation
5 to 8.......	Stratum having percolation rate of 15 minutes per inch
8 to 20......	Stratum having percolation rate of 5 minutes per inch

Calculations:

(1) A 6-foot diameter pit (excavation) will provide **3.14** (π) $\times$ **6 feet** (diameter) = **18.8** square feet of wall area per foot of depth.

(2) No absorption area can be provided by the 0- to 4-foot or the 4- to 5-foot stratum.

(3) Effective absorption area that would be required in the 5- to 8-foot stratum having a percolation rate of **15** minutes per inch would be **90** (from Table C) $\times$ **3** (bedrooms) = **270** square feet.

(4) The 5- to 8-foot stratum will provide **18.8** $\times$ **3** (thickness of stratum) = **56.4** square feet of absorption area.

(5) Additional area that must be provided by lower lying stratum is **270** − **56.4** = **213.6** square feet.

Table C. Absorption Requirements

Time for water to drop 1 in. (min)	Absorption area below the inlet—for walls and bottom (sq ft)		
	Without food-waste unit or washer	With food-waste unit or washer	With food-waste unit and washer
2	30	40	50
3	35	50	60
4	40	55	70
5	45	60	80
10	55	75	95
15	65	90	110
30	110	150	190
60	210	280	360

Above 60 minutes, seepage pit should not be used.

(6) The 8- to 20-foot stratum with a percolation rate of 5 minutes per inch will require 60/90 (Table C) or two-thirds as much area as the 4- to 7-foot stratum having a percolation rate of 15 minutes per inch. Therefore, the additional area to be supplied must be 0.66 × 213.6 = 142.4 square feet.

(7) The 142.4 square feet of absorption area in the 8- to 20-foot stratum will be supplied by a depth of 142.4/18.8 = 7.6 feet, i.e., the seepage pit should extend 7.6 feet into the 8- to 20-foot stratum.

Table D. Wall Area of Cylindrical Pits

Diam of pit		Area of wall for each foot depth (sq ft)	Earth removed per foot depth (cu ft)
Ft	In.		
3	0	9.43	7.07
3	6	10.99	9.62
4	0	12.57	12.57
4	6	14.14	15.90
5	0	15.71	19.64
5	6	17.28	23.68
6	0	18.85	28.28
6	6	20.42	33.18
7	0	21.99	38.49
7	6	23.57	44.18
8	0	25.14	50.27
8	6	26.70	56.75
9	0	28.28	63.63

(8) Therefore, the total depth of the seepage pit should be:

Feet
0 to 4 . . . . . . 4 feet of impermeable soil
4 to 5 . . . . . . 1 foot of hardpan
5 to 8 . . . . . . 3 feet of absorptive soil
8 to 15.6 . . . 7.6 feet of absorptive soil
            15.6 feet = total depth of pit

Where two or more seepage pits are used, a distribution box should be installed to provide equitable distribution of effluent.

There are cases where a seepage pit or pits may be necessary to supplement the distribution field; in such cases the seepage pits are placed at the end of the field.

The wall area for various diameter cylindrical pits and the amount of excavation required are shown in Table D.

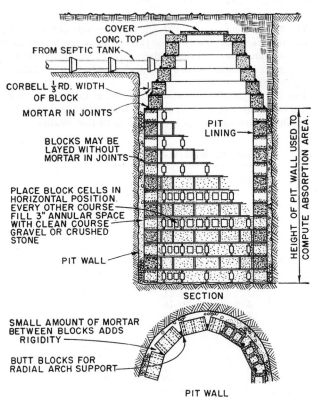

COVER
CONC. TOP
FROM SEPTIC TANK
CORBELL ⅓ RD. WIDTH OF BLOCK
MORTAR IN JOINTS
PIT LINING
BLOCKS MAY BE LAYED WITHOUT MORTAR IN JOINTS
HEIGHT OF PIT WALL USED TO COMPUTE ABSORPTION AREA.
PLACE BLOCK CELLS IN HORIZONTAL POSITION. EVERY OTHER COURSE FILL 3" ANNULAR SPACE WITH CLEAN COURSE GRAVEL OR CRUSHED STONE
PIT WALL

SECTION

SMALL AMOUNT OF MORTAR BETWEEN BLOCKS ADDS RIGIDITY
BUTT BLOCKS FOR RADIAL ARCH SUPPORT

PIT WALL

Fig. 16-12

The bottom of the pit is not computed for absorption. It should be noted therefore that a 4-foot-diameter pit has 12.57 square feet of absorption area and requires the removal of only 12.57 cubic feet of earth, while an 8-foot pit has 25.14 square feet of wall area, but requires that 50.27 cubic feet of earth be removed.

Figure 16-12 shows the construction of a seepage pit.

16.11 Dry Well

16.11.1 Dry Well Required. When necessary, a dry well shall be provided to receive the drainage from roofs, basements, or areaways.

16.11.2 Size of Dry Well. Large dry wells shall be constructed in general accordance with the requirements given for seepage pits, Sec. 16.10.

16.11.3 Small Dry Wells. For small dry wells handling limited quantities of water, the pit may consist of a 3-foot length of 18-inch-diameter vitrified-clay or cement pipe, filled with crushed rock or stone.

16.12 Cesspool

16.12.1 Use. The use of cesspools for disposal of sewage and their installation will be accepted only if no health hazard will result from such installation or use and if approval is obtained before work is begun from the administrative authority or the health department having jurisdiction.

16.12.2 Installations. Cesspool installations shall be considered only as a temporary expedient in those instances where connections to a public sewer system will be possible within a reasonable period of time.

16.12.3 Health Hazard. Because of the public health hazard involved, extreme care should be exercised in locating a cesspool. Under no circumstances shall the cesspool penetrate the ground-water stratum.

16.12.4 Construction. The construction of the cesspool shall comply with the requirements for seepage pits as given in Sec. 16.10.

▶ **References** used in the preparation of the recommendations made for septic tanks and seepage pits are U.S. Public Health Service, "Studies in Household Sewage Disposal," Public Health Service Environmental Health Center, Cincinnati 26, Ohio.

CHAPTER 17

Air Gaps, Backflow Preventers, and Drinking-fountain Standards

17.1 General

17.1.1 Backflow connections shall not be permitted between the piping system carrying a potable-water supply and any piping system or plumbing equipment carrying nonpotable water or water-borne waste.

▶ It is only within the past twenty or thirty years that the hazards related to the problem of cross connections have been recognized by sanitarians and engineers and studies undertaken for prevention and control.

It used to be common practice at processing plants, where both potable- and nonpotable-water supply were used, to install a check valve and line valve between the two supply lines, thus enabling the processor to draw potable water whenever the nonpotable water ran short. See Fig. **17-1.**

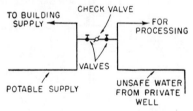

FIG. 17-1

Such arrangements proved to be dangerous cross connections. Inadvertently, the valves were left open, and where a check flap was improperly seated it permitted contaminated water to flow into the potable-water system of the building.

Legislation was passed in many states to prohibit cross connections, but inasmuch as this type of legislation is under local jurisdiction, enforcement varies considerably and in certain areas for all practical purposes can be called nonexistent.

17.2 Air Gaps

17.2.1 The air gap in a water-supply system is the unobstructed vertical distance through the free atmosphere between the lowest opening from any pipe or

faucet supplying water to a tank or plumbing fixture and the flood-level rim of
the receptacle.   (See Figs. 17-2 and 17-3.)

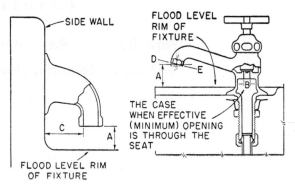

Fig. 17-2

▶   **An air gap is the most positive means of preventing backflow.**

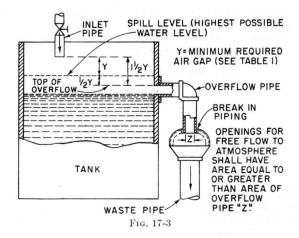

Fig. 17-3

17.2.2   The minimum required air gap shall be measured vertically from the
end of the faucet spout or supply pipe to the flood-level rim of the fixture or
vessel.

17.2.3   The water inlet to certain fixtures, such as water-closet flush tanks and
tanks or vats, may be difficult to protect with air gaps and therefore requires
special consideration.   (See paragraphs 17.2.5 to 17.2.9.)

17.2.4   The minimum required air gap shall be twice the diameter of the effective opening, but in no case less than given in Table 17.2.4.

Table 17.2.4   Minimum Air Gaps for Generally Used Plumbing Fixtures

Fixture	Minimum air gap	
	When not affected by near wall[1]	When affected by near wall[2]
Lavatories with effective openings not greater than $\frac{1}{2}$-in. diameter...............	1.0	1.50
Sink, laundry trays, and gooseneck bath faucets with effective openings not greater than $\frac{3}{4}$ in. diameter.....................	1.5	2.25
Overrim bath fillers with effective openings not greater than 1 in. diameter.............	2.0	3.00
Effective openings greater than 1 in.........	[3]	[4]

[1] Side walls, ribs, or similar obstructions do not affect the air gaps when spaced from inside edge of spout opening a distance greater than three times the diameter of the effective opening for a single wall, or a distance greater than four times the diameter of the effective opening for two intersecting walls. (See Fig. 17-2.)

[2] Vertical walls, ribs, or similar obstructions extending from the water surface to or above the horizontal plane of the spout opening require a greater air gap when spaced closer to the nearest inside edge of spout opening than specified in note 1 above. The effect of three or more such vertical walls or ribs has not been determined. In such cases, the air gap shall be measured from the top of the wall.

[3] Two times effective opening.

[4] Three times effective opening.

▶   Openings other than circular may be computed by using the cross-sectional area of the opening or by using the following equation:

$$\text{Air gap} - G = 2\frac{1}{4} \sqrt{A}$$

which represents $2\frac{1}{4}$ times the square root of the area of the opening.

17.2.5   Where it is not practical to provide a minimum required air gap above the flood-level rim of a tank or vat, an arrangement similar to that shown in Fig. 17-4 may be provided.

17.2.6   The overflow pipe or channel shall be so arranged as to allow overflow water a free discharge to atmosphere under all conditions, overflow piping to be provided with an adequate break in the piping as close to the tank as possible, and the area of the free opening shall be at least equal to that of the overflow pipe.   (See Fig. 17-3.)   Tank and overflow piping must be protected against freezing.

17.2.7   When water enters the tank at the maximum rate with all inlets open and all outlets closed, the size and capacity of overflow pipe or channel shall be sufficient to keep the water level from rising to more than half of the minimum required air gap as shown in Table 17.2.4, said distance to be measured above the top of the overflow.

17.2.8   The minimum air gap, as measured from the lowest point of any supply outlet to the top of the overflow opening, shall be one and one-half times the minimum air gap as required by Table 17.2.4. (See Fig. 17-4.)

17.2.9 If a tank or vat cannot be provided with an adequate air **gap** as required, a backflow (back-siphonage) preventer is required.

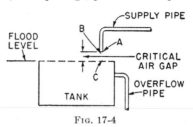

F<small>IG</small>. 17-4

►   **The** minimum air gap to be provided between a water-supply outlet and the highest point at which water will rise in a receptor or tank is called the critical air gap. Tests have shown that a vacuum of approximately one-half an atmosphere or 15 inches of mercury will protect any system from backflow. Figure 17-4 illustrates this point.

If instead of water flowing at point *A*, a back pressure occurs, air will be drawn into the pipe, causing a reduction in pressure below atmosphere at *B*. This backflow of air will have a tendency to make the surface of the water below it rise as shown in *C*. This flow of air over this surface tends to pile up the water toward the pipe opening.

If the velocity of the air is great enough and the surface of the water close enough to the pipe opening, some of this water will be carried vertically upward into the pipe opening and a backflow will occur.

The greater the velocity of air flow in the pipe, the greater the height through which the water can be lifted. This height represents the critical air gap.

The various factors which affect the critical air gap are:

(*a*) Maximum vacuum prevailing in the pipe opening or faucet outlet.

(*b*) Capacity of the air flow of the pipe opening or faucet.

(*c*) Total area of the opening and the shape of the opening.

(*d*) Location of the faucet or pipe opening in relation to nearby walls.

(*e*) Temperature of the surface water.

(*f*) Atmospheric conditions.

(*g*) Characteristics of the surface liquid if other than water.

17.3   Drinking-fountain Nozzles

17.3.1 Minimum Elevation. All drinking-fountain nozzles including those which may at times extend through a water surface with orifice not greater than $\frac{7}{16}$ (0.440) inch diameter or 0.150 square inch area shall be placed so that the lower edge of the nozzle orifice is at an elevation not less than $\frac{3}{4}$ inch above the flood-level rim of the receptacle.

17.3.2 The $\frac{3}{4}$-inch elevation shall also apply to nozzles with more than one orifice, provided that the sum of the area of all orifices shall not exceed the area of a circle $\frac{7}{16}$ inch in diameter.

17.3.3   Special conditions and certain other materials related to drinking fountains shall meet requirements as set forth in American Standard ASA A40.4-1942 and ASA Z4.2-1942, respectively.

17.4   Vacuum Breakers or Backflow Preventers

17.4.1   Required.   Backflow preventers shall be installed with any supply fixture, the outlet end of which may at times be submerged, such as hose and spray, direct flushing valves, aspirators and underrim water-supply connections to a plumbing fixture or receptacle in which the surface of the water in the fixture or receptacle is exposed at all times to atmospheric pressure.   The type of preventer referred to will not protect against flow when water is discharged through it into a space which is higher than atmospheric pressures.

17.4.2   Where.   Backflow preventers shall be installed between the control valve and the fixture and in such a manner that it will not be subjected to water pressure, except the back pressure incidental to water flowing to the fixture.

17.4.3   Backflow preventers shall not be installed on inlet side of control valve.

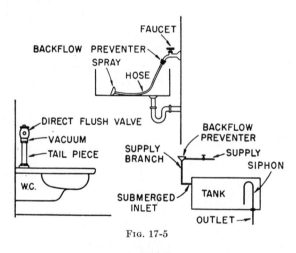

Fig. 17-5

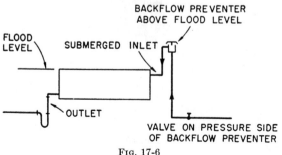

Fig. 17-6

▶ Figures 17-5 and 17-6 illustrate the requirements of the foregoing paragraphs.

17.5 Effective Opening

17.5.1 The effective opening is the minimum cross-sectional area at the point of water-supply discharge and is measured or expressed in terms of the diameter of a circle or, if the opening is not circular, the diameter of a circle of equivalent cross-sectional area. (See Fig. 17-2 point *B*.)

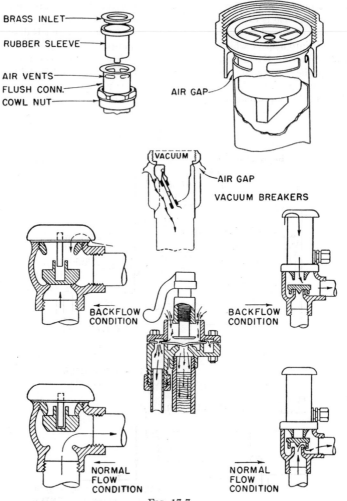

Fɪɢ. 17-7

17.6 Materials

17.6.1 Backflow preventers shall be made of corrosion-resistant material and shall be so designed and proportioned as to prevent deterioration or deformation under reasonable service conditions.

▶   Figure 17-7 illustrates several types of backflow preventers commonly used on the discharge side of a plumbing fixture or device.

There are, in addition, pressure-type vacuum breakers.   This type is designed to be installed under pressure.

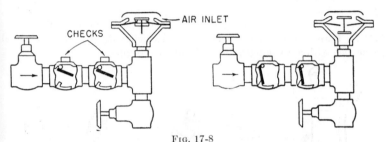

Fᴵɢ. 17-8

Figure 17-8 illustrates a pressure-type vacuum breaker.   However, it must be installed above the flood level of the fixture, device, or locality in order to be protected.   This applies to lawn sprinklers, also, as a lawn sprinkler is a water line that needs separation from a potable-water supply which is constantly under pressure.

17.7 Tests and Performance

17.7.1 Backflow preventers shall have been tested and approved to meet tests and performances as required for Backflow Preventers, ASA A40.6-1943.

▶   Because of the serious hazards that backflow may cause, vacuum breakers or backflow preventers should be tested and found satisfactory for the conditions under which they must operate.

17.8 Drinking-fountain Standards (ASA Z4.2-1942)

17.8.1 Material. The fountain should be constructed of impervious material, such as vitreous china, porcelain, enameled cast iron, other metals, or stoneware.

17.8.2 Installation. The jet of the fountain should issue from a nozzle of nonoxidizing, impervious material set at an angle from the vertical such as to prevent the return of water in the jet to the orifice or orifices from whence the jet issues.   The nozzle and every other opening in the water pipe or conductor leading to the nozzle should be above the edge of the bowl, so that such nozzle or opening cannot be flooded in case a drain from the bowl of the fountain becomes clogged.

17.8.3 Protection. The end of the nozzle should be protected by nonoxidizing guards to prevent the mouth and nose of the user from coming into contact with the nozzle. Guards should be so designed that the possibility of transmission of infection by touching the guards is reduced to a minimum.

17.8.4 Spattering. The inclined jet of water issuing from the nozzle should not touch the guard, and thereby cause spattering.

17.8.5 Cleansing. The bowl of the fountain should be so designed and proportioned as to be free from corners which would be difficult to clean or which would collect dirt.

17.8.6 Splashing. The bowl of the fountain should be so proportioned as to prevent unnecessary splashing at a point where the jet falls into the bowl.

17.8.7 Traps. One drain from the fountain should not have a direct physical connection with a waste pipe, unless the drain is trapped.

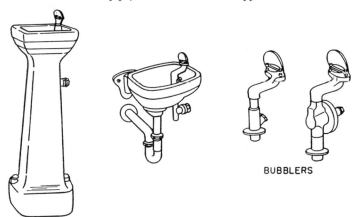

BUBBLERS

Fig. 17-9

▶   Figure 17-9 illustrates the various requirements.

17.8.8 Flow Regulator. The water-supply pipe should be provided with an adjustable valve fitted with a loose key or an automatic valve permitting the regulation of the rate of flow of water to the fountain so that the valve manipulated by the users of the fountain will merely turn the water on or off.

17.8.9 Height. The height of the fountain at the drinking level should be such as to be most convenient to persons using the fountain. The provision of several steplike elevations to the floor at fountains will permit children of various ages to utilize the fountain.

17.8.10 Flow. The waste opening and pipe should be of sufficient size to carry off the water promptly. The opening should be provided with a strainer.

▶   Most manufacturers comply with standards for drinking fountains in respect to materials and to fabrication which prevent back siphonage.

CHAPTER 18

Sizing the Water-supply System

General

Proper design of the water-distributing system in a building is necessary in order that the various fixtures may function properly. The amount of either hot or cold water used in any building is variable, depending on the type of structure, usage, occupancy, and time of day. It is necessary to provide piping, water heating, and storage facilities of sufficient capacity to meet the peak demand without wasteful excess in either piping or equivalent cost.

▶   This chapter gives the suggested procedure for sizing the water-supply system as contained in the National Plumbing Code. Flow charts show the capacities of commercial sizes of pipe in terms of "friction loss in head" for various degrees of interior roughness of pipe. An interesting study of this subject was performed by Dr. Roy B. Hunter at the National Bureau of Standards.

18.1 Preliminary Information

18.1.1 Available Pressure. Obtain the necessary information regarding the minimum daily service pressure in the area where the building is to be located.

▶   The local water department generally keeps records of the pressures in the mains at different hours of the day and night. It is essential to know the water pressures before sizing the water piping for a building.

18.1.2 Piping Material. Obtain all available local information regarding the use of different kinds of pipe with respect both to durability and to decrease in capacity with length of service in the particular water supply.

▶   The kinds of piping most commonly used in the water-supply system of a building include galvanized steel, galvanized wrought iron, copper pipe, and copper tube. The selection is based on local experience gained over the years and the type of structure to be erected. Local experience provides a guide for the selection of the type of piping that will give the longest service; in addition research on new materials will add to this.

18.2   Estimate of Demand Load and Pipe Capacity

18.2.1   Rate of Flow.   One of the important items that must be determined before any part of the water-piping system can be sized is the probable rate of flow in any particular branch of piping.   The rate of flow in the service line, risers, and main branches, however, will rarely be equal to the sum of the rates of flow of all connected fixtures.   In fact, the probability of every fixture in a large group being used at the same time is so remote that it would be very poor engineering to design the piping large enough to take care of such simultaneous flow.

18.2.2   Simultaneous Use.   The demand load in building water-supply systems cannot be determined exactly and is not readily standardized.   The two main problems to be considered are (1) the satisfactory supply of water for a given fixture and (2) the number of fixtures which may be assumed to be in use at the same time.

▶   The water demand for a group of fixtures and the requirements for carrying out wasted water have a relationship.   Both are based on a probable use of the fixture, depending on type, location, and how often each is to be used.   The need for water only for drinking purposes is small when compared to all other uses, such as bathing, washing, cleaning, and even cooking, that are related to residential use.

18.2.3   Daily Demand.   The minimum flow that will be satisfactory to the consumer depends greatly upon the consumer, his standard of living, his professional needs, size of family, garden requirements, and similar factors. Depending upon those factors, per capita water consumption for domestic use usually varies between 20 and 80 gallons per day.

18.2.4   Type of Building.   Experience indicates that the type of dwelling has considerable influence upon the water consumption.

18.2.5   Apartment Buildings.   In apartment houses the per capita daily water consumption is generally higher than in single-family houses.   This is due to the central metering system, which is not conducive to the saving of water and to the long hot-water lines, which result in high heat losses, thus in the wasting of the cooled water.   In designing water-supply systems for apartment houses, a daily per capita water consumption of 50 gallons may be considered a safe design figure.

18.2.6   Dwelling.   Although a considerable number of housing projects have been developed across the nation, conclusive water-consumption data have not been gathered as yet.   Nevertheless, it seems that the daily per capita water, consumption in housing projects falls in between the consumption in apartment houses and single dwellings at the same geographical location.   In general, a daily per capita water consumption of 40 gallons can be used as a safe design figure for housing projects.

▶   There is little recorded information on actual consumption of water by types of buildings and industries.   Daily consumption of water per person varies greatly throughout the country and is influenced by the following factors: metering or nonmetering of the water supply into the building; type of building, such as residential, hotel, commercial; nature of employment; climate; personal habits and hygiene; type of industrial or manufacturing processes.

When the water requirements are to be computed for manufacturing and processing purposes, specific needs must be considered, plus a margin of safety for expansion.

The water requirements for fixtures can be more readily computed from data made available by manufacturers and by reference to Table **18.3.2**, which indicates the approximate rate of flow to fixtures in gallons per minute.

Table **18.3.2** also assists in computing the flow to a group of fixtures such as a battery of water closets, lavatories, or urinals.

18.3   Flow and Pressure Required

18.3.1   Table 18.3.2 gives the rate of flow desirable for many common types of fixtures and the average pressure necessary to give this rate of flow.   The pressure necessarily varies with fixture design; with some, a much greater pressure is necessary to give the same rate of flow than with others.

18.3.2   (See Table 18.3.2.)

Table 18.3.2   Rate of Flow and Required Pressure during Flow for Different Fixtures

Fixture	Flow pressure[1] (psi)	Flow rate (gpm)
Ordinary basin faucet...............	8	3.0
Self-closing basin faucet.............	12	2.5
Sink faucet, $\frac{3}{8}$ in....................	10	4.5
Sink faucet, $\frac{1}{2}$ in....................	5	4.5
Bathtub faucet......................	5	6.0
Laundry tub cock, $\frac{1}{2}$ in.............	5	5.0
Shower............................	12	5.0
Ball cock for closet..................	15	3.0
Flush valve for closet...............	10–20	15–40[2]
Flush valve for urinal...............	15	15.0
Garden hose, 50 ft, and sill cock......	30	5.0

[1] Flow pressure is the pressure in the pipe at the entrance to the particular fixture considered.
[2] Wide range due to variation in design and type of flush-valve closets.

18.3.3   In estimating the load, the rate of flow is frequently computed in fixture units.

18.3.4   Table 18.3.5 gives the demand weight in terms of fixture units for different plumbing fixtures under several conditions of service.

Table 18.3.5   Demand Weight of Fixtures in Fixture Units[1]

Fixture or group[2]	Occupancy	Type of supply control	Weight in fixture units[3]
Water closet............	Public	Flush valve	10
Water closet............	Public	Flush tank	5
Pedestal urinal..........	Public	Flush valve	10
Stall or wall urinal.......	Public	Flush valve	5
Stall or wall urinal.......	Public	Flush tank	3
Lavatory...............	Public	Faucet	2
Bathtub.................	Public	Faucet	4
Shower head............	Public	Mixing valve	4
Service sink........... ..	Office, etc	Faucet	3
Kitchen sink.............	Hotel or restaurant	Faucet	4
Water closet............	Private	Flush valve	6
Water closet............	Private	Flush tank	3
Lavatory...............	Private	Faucet	1
Bathtub.................	Private	Faucet	2
Shower head............	Private	Mixing valve	2
Bathroom group.........	Private	Flush valve for closet	8
Bathroom group.........	Private	Flush tank for closet	6
Separate shower.........	Private	Mixing valve	2
Kitchen sink.............	Private	Faucet	2
Laundry trays (1 to 3)....	Private	Faucet	3
Combination fixture......	Private	Faucet	3

[1] For supply outlets likely to impose continuous demands, estimate continuous supply separately and add to total demand for fixtures.

[2] For fixtures not listed, weights may be assumed by comparing the fixture to a listed one using water in similar quantities and at similar rates.

[3] The given weights are for total demand. For fixtures with both hot- and cold-water supplies, the weights for maximum separate demands may be taken as three-fourths the listed demand for supply.

18.3.5   (See Table 18.3.5.)

18.3.6   Chart 18.1 gives the estimated demand in gallons per minutes corresponding to any total number of fixture units.   Chart 18.2 shows an enlargement of Chart 18.1 for a range up to 250 fixture units.

18.3.7   The estimated demand load for fixtures used intermittently on any supply pipe will be obtained by multiplying the number of each kind of fixture supplied through that pipe by its weight from Table 18.3.5, adding the products, and then referring to the appropriate curve of Chart 18.1 or 18.2 to find the demand corresponding to the total fixture units.   In using this method it should be noted that the demand for fixture or supply outlets other than those listed in the table of fixture units is not yet included in the estimate.   The demands for outlets (such as hose connections, air-conditioning apparatus, etc.) which are likely to impose continuous demand during times of heavy use of the weighted fixtures should be estimated separately and added to the demand for fixtures used intermittently, in order to estimate the total demand.

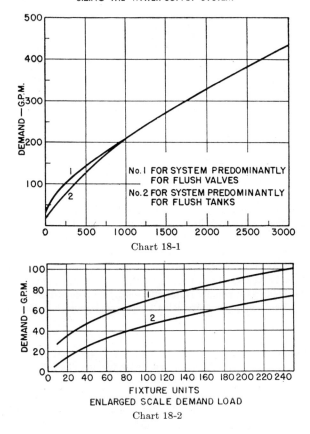

Chart 18-1

Chart 18-2

18.4   Sizing Cold-water-supply Piping

18.4.1   Pressure Loss.   As water flows through a pipe, the pressure continually decreases along the pipe, because of loss of energy from friction.   The problem is then one of ascertaining the minimum pressure in the street main and the minimum pressure required for the operation of the topmost fixture.   (A pressure of 15 pounds per square inch is ample for flush valves, but reference should be made to the manufacturers' requirements.   A minimum of 8 pounds per square inch should be allowed for other fixtures.)   The pressure differential thus obtained will be available for overcoming pressure losses in the distributing system and in overcoming the difference in elevation between the water main and the highest fixture.

18.4.2   Pressure Loss by Elevation.   The pressure loss, in pounds per square inch, caused by the difference in elevation between the street main and the highest fixture may be obtained by multiplying the difference in elevation in feet by the conversion factor 0.43.

18.4.3   Water Flow.   When water flows through a pipe, friction occurs as the result of the sliding of water particles past one another.   If the pipe wall is rough, the roughness projections cause additional friction, owing to the development of increased turbulence in the flowing water.   As the water flows along a smooth pipe, the pressure decreases as a result of a dissipation of energy arising from the internal friction set up by viscosity of the water.   This loss in energy is shown by the loss of pressure.   The pressure loss is proportioned to the length of straight uniform pipes and varies greatly with flow velocity, pipe diameter, and roughness of pipe.

18.5   Pipe Classification

18.5.1   On the basis of inside surface conditions, pipes may be classified as smooth, fairly rough, and rough, as follows:

18.5.2   Smooth Pipe.   The inside pipe surface shows no perceptible roughness.   Pipes made of copper, brass, or lead usually may be classified as smooth.

▶   In computing pipe sizes, factors for smooth piping should be applied only to the kinds of piping whose interiors will not become rough over a period of 15 to 20 years.   Long-lived smooth interiors are generally found in copper piping as it usually is not affected by lime deposits.

New kinds of piping promising long-lived smooth interiors are in the developmental stage.

18.5.3   Fairly Rough.   All ordinary pipes, such as wrought iron, galvanized iron, steel, and cast iron, after a few years of usage, may be called fairly rough.

▶   Steel and wrought-iron pipe sizes are computed largely on the basis of "fairly rough," in order to be assured that after a period of 15 to 20 years the flow capacity has not been seriously affected.

18.5.4   Rough.   Pipes that have deteriorated fairly rapidly for some 10 or 15 years after being laid are classified as rough.

▶   Computations on the basis of "rough" are usually made for buildings where new piping is to be added to old, especially if the piping will be steel or wrought iron, as most waters will have a tendency to reduce the piping diameter.

18.6   Flow Charts

18.6.1   Charts 18.3 to 18.5 give the pipe-fraction losses corresponding to these three types of pipes for various nominal diameters.

Example 1: A 2½-inch fairly rough pipe supplies 100 gallons per minute of water.   Find the friction loss in head if the pipe length is 200 feet.

Solution: Enter Chart 18.4 at 100 gallons per minute, and move along this line until it intersects the 2½-inch diameter line.   From this intersection point, move vertically down and read 4.5 pounds per square inch friction loss per 100 feet of pipe length.   Then the total friction loss will be 2 × 4.5 = 9 pounds per square inch.

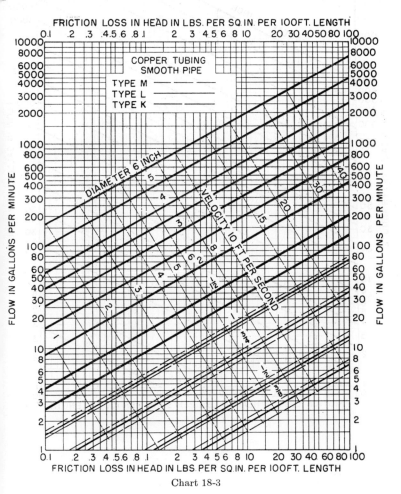

Chart 18-3

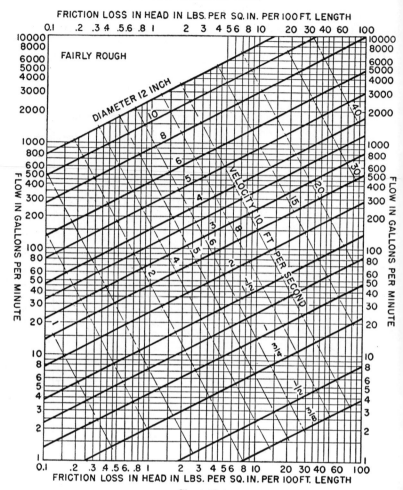

Chart 18-4

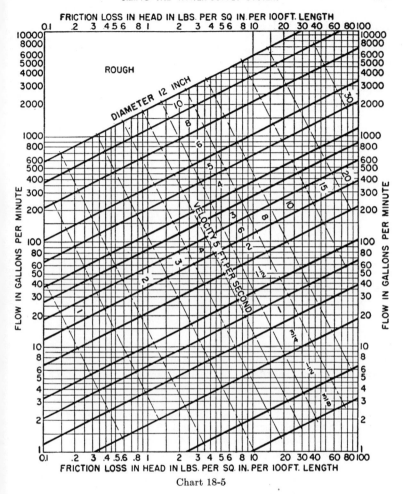

Chart 18-5

18.7   Fittings, Valves, and Meters

18.7.1   The pressure losses in the distributing system will consist of the pressure losses in the piping itself, plus the pressure losses in the pipe fittings, valves, and the water meter.   Estimated pressure losses for disk-type meters for various rates of flow are given in Chart. 18.6.

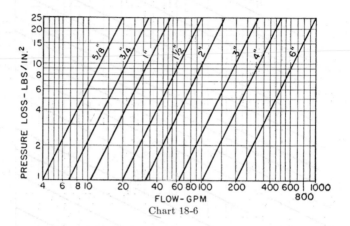

Chart 18-6

▶   The friction losses shown for copper tube, Chart **18.3**, may also be used for lead pipe.   They may also be used for plastic piping which carries water; this piping is often used in industrial plants.

Friction losses for new galvanized-steel or wrought-iron pipe may be figured from Chart **18.4**; where local water characteristics will lime the pipe in a relatively short time, use Chart **18.5**.

Chart **18.5** should be used when extending new piping in an old building when the old piping is badly limed, and when the piping will not remain full bored for a long time.

18.7.2   Flow limits for disk-type meters, which may be regarded as the limits of recommended ranges in capacities, are given in Table 18.7.3.   For information on other types of meters, the manufacturer should be consulted.
18.7.3   (See Table 18.7.3.)
18.7.4   Registration.   The registration on the meter dial shall indicate the quantity recorded to be not less than 98 per cent nor more than 102 per cent of the water actually passed through the meter while it is being tested at rates of flow within the specified limits (see Table 18.7.3) under normal test-flow limits.   There shall be not less than 90 per cent of the actual flow recorded when a test is made at the rate of flow set forth under minimum test flow.
18.7.5   Chart 18.7 (on page 18–23) shows the variation of pressure loss with

Table 18.7.3   Performance Requirements of Water Meters[1]

Pipe size (in.)	Normal test-flow limits (gpm)	Minimum test flow (hr)
$\frac{5}{8}$	1– 20	$\frac{1}{4}$
$\frac{3}{4}$	2– 34	$\frac{1}{2}$
1	3– 53	$\frac{3}{4}$
$1\frac{1}{2}$	5– 100	$1\frac{1}{2}$
2	8– 160	2
3	16– 315	4
4	28– 500	7
6	48–1,000	12

[1] American Water Works Association Standards.

rate of flow for various types of faucets and cocks, based on experimental data obtained at the State University of Iowa.

A $\frac{1}{2}$-in. laundry bib (old style)
B Laundry compression faucet
C_1 $\frac{1}{2}$-in. compression sink faucet (manufacturer 1)
C_2 $\frac{1}{2}$-in. compression sink faucet (manufacturer 2)
D Comb. comp. bathtub faucet (both open)
E Comb. compression sink faucet
F Basin faucet
G Spring self-closing faucet
H Slow self-closing basin faucet

18.7.6   The loss pressure through any fitting or valve can be expressed in pounds per square inch for any given rate of flow.   Experience has shown, how-

Table 18.7.8   Allowance in Equivalent Length of Pipe for Friction Loss in Valves and Threaded Fittings

Diameter of fitting (in.)	90-deg standard ell (ft)	45-deg standard ell (ft)	90-deg side tee (ft)	Coupling or straight run of tee (ft)	Gate valve (ft)	Globe valve (ft)	Angle valve (ft)
$\frac{3}{8}$	1	0.6	1.5	0.3	0.2	8	4
$\frac{1}{2}$	2	1.2	3	0.6	0.4	15	8
$\frac{3}{4}$	2.5	1.5	4	0.8	0.5	20	12
1	3	1.8	5	0.9	0.6	25	15
$1\frac{1}{4}$	4	2.4	6	1.2	0.8	35	18
$1\frac{1}{2}$	5	3	7	1.5	1.0	45	22
2	7	4	10	2	1.3	55	28
$2\frac{1}{2}$	8	5	12	2.5	1.6	65	34
3	10	6	15	3	2	80	40
$3\frac{1}{2}$	12	7	18	3.6	2.4	100	50
4	14	8	21	4.0	2.7	125	55
5	17	10	25	5	3.3	140	70
6	20	12	30	6	4	165	80

ever, that the simplest method of expressing losses in fittings and valves is to use the concept of an equivalent length of straight pipe. It has been found, for example, that a 1-inch, 90-degree elbow, introduces a loss which is equivalent to 2.2 feet of straight 1-inch pipe. Therefore, for each 1-inch, 90-degree elbow, 2.2 feet of 1-inch pipe are added to the total length of 1-inch pipe.

18.7.7 Estimated pressure losses for pipe fittings and valves in terms of equivalent pipe lengths are shown on Table 18.7.8.

18.7.8 (See Table 18.7.8.)

18.7.9 Table 18.7.9 lists the equivalent lengths for various special types of apparatus and fittings. The friction loss in water meters varies considerably with the design even in meters of the same nominal size. The values given in Table 18.7.9 are ample for the well-known meters now on the market.

Table 18.7.9 Equivalent Lengths of Iron Pipe to Give Same Loss as Special Fittings or Apparatus

Fitting apparatus	Nominal diameter of pipe (ft)			
	½ in.	¾ in.	1 in.	1¼ in.
30-gal vertical hot-water tank, ¾-in. pipe..	4	17	56	
30-gal horizontal hot-water tank, ¾-in. pipe	1.2	5	16	
Water meters (no valves included):				
⅝-in. with ½-in. connections...........	6.7	28	90	
⅝-in. with ¾-in. connections...........	4.8	20	64	
¾-in. with ¾-in. connections...........	3.4	14	45	
1-in. with 1-in. connections............	...	9	30	115
1¼-in. with 1-in. connections..........	...	4.4	14	54
Water softener.........................	...	50–200		

▶ The following example shows a step-by-step method of sizing water-supply piping for a two-story and basement house. Figure 18-1 illustrates a piping diagram for a residence.

Step 1: Compute the total number of fixture units from Table **18.3.5**, Demand Weight of Fixtures in Fixture Units. Answer: **21** fixture units.

Fixture	*Fixture Units*
Bathroom group A..............	6
Bathroom group B..............	6
Water closet, first floor..........	3
Lavatory, first floor.............	1
Kitchen sink...................	2
Laundry tray, basement.........	3
	21

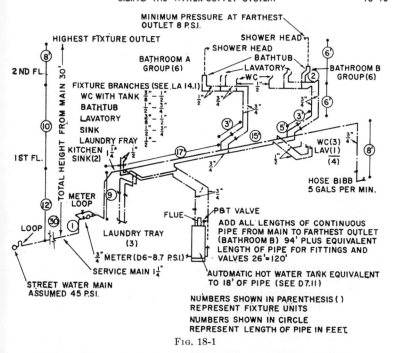

Fig. 18-1

Step 2: Compute the total water demand. Answer: 20 gallons per minute. This represents the probable normal peak demand of all fixtures installed. This does not mean that *all* fixtures are flowing at the same time, as that would be a very rare occurrence. To convince yourself, observe the practices in your home and business establishment.

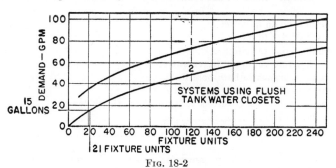

Fig. 18-2

Figure 18-2 illustrates an enlarged chart for assistance in figuring a small number of fixture units, such as is the case in this example. A line drawn horizontally from 21 fixture units meets curve 2 at 15 gallons per minute, which represents the possible demand.

Curve 2 is for a system using a flush tank. Curve 1 is for flush valves for which the demand is higher per fixture.

Step 3: Compute the loss in pressure because of an elevation of 30 feet from the street main to the highest fixture outlet. Answer: **13.02 pounds per square inch.**

Use the constant 0.434, which is the pressure per square inch in a column of water 1 foot high, multiplied by 30 feet: 30 + 0.434 = **13.02 pounds per square inch.**

Step 4: Compute the size of meter necessary for a demand of 20 gallons per minute. Answer: ¾ inch.

See Table 18.7.3, Performance Requirements of Water Meters. If no meter is installed, omit steps 4 and 5.

Step 5: Compute the pressure loss through the meter. Answer: **8.7 pounds per square inch.**

Compute this loss from Chart 18.6, Pressure Losses in Disk-type Water Meters.

Step 6: Compute the available pressure after deducting pressure losses. Answer: **15.28 pounds per square inch.**

Pressure at the main, in this example...................... **45.00 psi**
Less losses:
    At the fixture outlet........................... 8.00 psi
    From main to highest outlet.................... 13.02 psi
    Through meter............................... 8.70 psi
    Total losses.. **29.72 psi**
    Available pressure for overcoming friction resistance within
    piping... **15.28 psi**

Step 7: Compute the developed length of piping from the main in the street to the farthest outlet, which in this example is the shower head to bathroom *B*. Answer: **120 feet.**

Length of main in street.................................. **30 feet**
Length of rise to meter................................... 1
Length of rise to ceiling.................................. 9
Length across ceiling of basement......................... 40
Length of branch to bathroom *B*.......................... 8
Length to shower head, bathroom *B*....................... 6
Length of fittings coverted to equivalent piping lengths (see
    Table 18.7.9)... 26
Developed length....................................... **120 feet**

Step 8: Compute the pressure factor per 100 feet of developed length. Answer: **12.73 pounds per square inch.**

$$15.28 \text{ psi for } 120 \text{ ft} = 12.73 \text{ psi for } 100 \text{ ft}$$
$$\frac{15.28 \times 100}{120} = 12.73$$

Step 9: Compute diameter of the service main to produce 20 gallons per minute at a pressure of 15.28 pounds per square inch, using galvanized ferrous piping.   Answer: 1¼ inches.

The velocity through the piping should be not more than 10 feet per second in order to avoid water hammer and pipe noises.

Chart 18.4 illustrates how to compute the diameter of the service main, Friction Loss during Flow.   When the computation results in a diameter which would be difficult to obtain, select the nearest larger size that would be readily obtainable.

Where a water meter is not installed, compute the diameter of the service main.   Answer: 1 inch.

Pressure at the main (street) . . . . 45.00 psi
Less losses:
   At the fixture outlet . . . . 8.00 psi
   From main to highest outlet . . . . 13.02 psi
     Total losses . . . . 21.02 psi
  Available pressure overcoming friction resistance within
  piping . . . . 23.98 psi

$$\frac{23.98 \times 100}{120} = 18.31 \text{ psi}$$

To produce 20 gallons per minute at a pressure of 18.31 pounds per square inch would require a 1-inch diameter.

Step 10: Having determined the size of the meter, if one is installed, and the size of the service main, the pressure available for friction resistance within the piping, 12.73 pounds per square inch, is then applied to sizing the principal branches of the water-distributing systems.   In this example, the three principal branches and the computations for sizing them are as follows:

(*a*) The branch through which all cold water is supplied to the two bathrooms and to the powder room:

Cold-water fixture branch only	Fixture units Table 18.3.5 and note 3	Demand; Chart 18.2 (gpm)	Pipe size Chart 18.4 (in.)
3 water closets with flush tanks. . . .	3 × 3 = 9.00		
2 bathtubs.	¾ (2 × 2) = 3.00		
3 lavatories.	¾ (3 × 1) = 2.25	11	
1 hose bib.		5	
Total.	14.25	16	1

(*b*) **The branch supplying the water heater, laundry tray, and sink:**

Cold-water branch to heater	Fixture units Table 18.3.5 and note 3	Demand; Chart 18.2 (gpm)	Pipe size Chart 18.4 (in.)
1 kitchen sink, hot and cold.......	1×2 = 2.00		
1 set laundry trays, hot and cold...	1×3 = 3.00		
2 bathtubs, cold water only........	$\frac{3}{4}$ (2×2) = 3.00		
3 lavatories, cold water...........	$\frac{3}{4}$ (3×1) = 2.25		
Total.......................	10.25	8	$\frac{3}{4}$

(*c*) **The main hot-water branch from the water heater:**

Main hot-water branch	Fixture units Table 18.3.5 and note 3	Demand; Chart 18.2 (gpm)	Pipe size Chart 18.4 (in.)
2 bathtubs, hot water only........	$\frac{3}{4}$ (2×2) = 3.00		
3 lavatories, hot water only........	$\frac{3}{4}$ (3×1) = 2.25		
1 kitchen sink, hot water only.....	$\frac{3}{4}$ (1×2) = 1.50		
1 set laundry trays, hot water.....	$\frac{3}{4}$ (1×3) = 2.25		
Total.......................	9.00	7	$\frac{3}{4}$

Step 11: Compute the size of the branches for bathroom groups *A* and *B* in the same manner as the branches in Step 9 *a, b,* and *c* were computed:

Bathroom group *A*	Fixture units Table 18.3.5 and note 3	Demand; Chart 18.2 (gpm)	Pipe size Chart 18.4 (in.)
1 water-closet flush tank, cold water only.........................	$\frac{3}{4}$ (1×3) = 2.25		
1 lavatory, cold water only........	$\frac{3}{4}$ (1×1) = 0.75		
1 bathtub, cold water only.........	$\frac{3}{4}$ (1×2) = 1.50		
Total.......................	4.50	5	$\frac{3}{4}$

Bathroom group *B* is the same.

Step 12: Size the individual fixture branches in accordance with Table 18.3.5.

Table A shows the pipe diameters corresponding to nominal pipe sizes of different kinds of pipe.

Note that the interior diameters vary among the different kinds of pipe shown on Table A.

Copper tube I, L, and M has the same outside diameter in order that the same fittings may be used with any of the types.

Note also that the varying capacity of type M is greater than for type K of the same nominal diameter.

Another example of sizing the water-supply system follows:

Example 2: Assume a minimum street-main pressure of 55 pounds per square inch, a height of the topmost fixture above the street main of 50 feet, a developed pipe length from the water main to the highest fixture of 100 feet, a total load on the system of 50 fixture units, and that the water closets are flush-valve operated.   Find the required size of supply main.

Solution: From Chart 18.2 the estimated peak demand is found to be 51 gallons per minute.   From Table 18.7.3 it is evident that several sizes of meters

Table A. Pipe Diameters

| Diameter (in.) | Inside diameter (in.) | | | | | | |
| | Types of copper tube | | | Steel I.P.S. | | Brass I.P.S. | |
	K	L	M	Standard	Extra strong	Standard	Extra strong
⅜	0.40	0.43	0.45	0.49	0.42	0.49	0.42
½	0.53	0.55	0.57	0.62	0.55	0.63	0.54
¾	0.75	0.79	0.81	0.82	0.74	0.82	0.74
1	1.00	1.03	1.06	1.05	0.96	1.06	0.95
1¼	1.25	1.27	1.29	1.38	1.28	1.37	1.27
1½	1.48	1.51	1.53	1.61	1.50	1.60	1.49
2	1.96	1.99	2.01	2.07	1.94	2.06	1.93
2½	2.44	2.47	2.50	2.47	2.32	2.50	2.32
3	2.91	2.95	2.98	3.07	2.90	3.06	2.89
4	3.86	3.91	3.94	4.03	3.83	4.00	3.82
5	4.81	4.88	4.91	5.05	5.81	5.06	4.81
6	5.74	5.85	5.88	6.07	5.76	6.13	5.75

would adequately measure this flow.   For a trial computation, choose the 1½-inch meter.   From Chart 18.6 the pressure drop through a 1½-inch disk-type meter for a flow of 51 gallons per minute is found to be 6.5 pounds per square inch.

Then the pressure drop available for overcoming friction in pipes and fittings is $55 - (15 + 50 \times 0.43 + 6.5) = 12$ pounds per square inch.

At this point it is necessary to make some estimate of the equivalent pipe length of the fittings on the direct line from the street main to the highest fixture.   The exact equivalent length of the various fittings cannot now be determined since the pipe sizes of the building main, riser, and branch leading to the highest fixture are not known as yet, but a first approximation is necessary in order to make a tentative selection of pipe sizes.   If the computed pipe sizes differ from those used in determining the equivalent length of pipe fittings, a recalculation will be necessary, using the computed pipe sizes for the fittings.

For the purposes of this example assume that the total equivalent length of the pipe fitting is 50 feet. Then the permissible pressure loss per 100 feet of equivalent pipe is $12 \times 100/(100 + 50) = 8$ pounds per square inch.

Assuming that the corrosive and caking properties of the water are such that Chart 18.4 for fairly rough pipe is applicable, a 2-inch building main will be adequate.

The sizing of the branches of the building main, the risers, and fixture branches follow the principles outlined. For example, assume that one of the branches of the building main carries the cold-water supply for three water closets, two bathtubs, and three lavatories. Using the permissible pressure loss of 8 pounds per square inch per 100 feet, the size of branch determined from Table 18.3.5 and Charts 18.1 and 18.4 is found to be 1½ inches. Items entering the computation of pipe size are given in Table 18.7.10.

Table 18.7.10   Computation of Branch Size in Example 2

Number and kind of fixtures	Fixture units (from Table 18.3.5 and note 3)	Demand (from Chart 18.2)	Pipe size (from Chart 18.4) (in.)
3 flush valves...............	$3 \times 6 = 18$		
2 bathtubs..................	¾ $(2 \times 2) = 3$		
3 lavatories................	¾ $(3 \times 1) = 2.25$		
Total....................	23.25	38	1½

18.8   Upfeed and Downfeed Systems

18.8.1 The principles involved in sizing either upfeed or downfeed systems are the same. The principal difference in procedure is that in the downfeed system the difference in elevation between the house tank and the fixtures provides the pressure required to overcome pipe friction.

18.8.2 The water demand for hose bibs or other large-demand fixtures taken off the building main is frequently the cause of inadequate water supply to the upper floor of a building. This condition may be prevented by sizing the distribution system so that the pressure drops from the street-main to all fixtures are the same. It is good practice to maintain the building main of ample size (not less than 1 inch where possible) until all branches to hose bibs have been connected. Where the street-main pressure is excessive and a pressure-reducing valve is used to prevent water hammer or excessive pressure at the fixtures, it is frequently desirable to connect hose bibs ahead of the reducing valve.

18.8.3 The recommended procedure in sizing piping systems may be outlined as follows:

(1) Draw a sketch of the main lines, risers, and branches, indicating the fixtures served. Indicate the rate of flow of each fixture.

(2) Using Table 18.3.5, compute the demand weights of the fixtures in fixture units.

(3) Determine the total demand in fixture units and, using Chart 18.1 or Chart 18.2, find the expected demand in gallons per minute.

(4) Determine the equivalent length of pipe in the main lines, risers, and branches. Since the sizes of the pipes are not known, the exact equivalent length for various fittings, etc., cannot be made. Add up the equivalent lengths, starting at the street main and proceeding along the service line, main line in the building, and up the riser to the top fixture of the group served.

(5) Ascertain the average minimum pressure in the street main and the minimum pressure required for the operation of the topmost fixture. This latter pressure should be 8 to 15 pounds per square inch.

(6) Calculate the approximate value of the average pressure drop per 100 feet of pipe in the equivalent length determined in item 4. Do this according to the following rule:

$$p = (P - 0.43H - 10)\frac{100}{L}$$

where p = average pressure loss per 100 ft of equivalent length of pipe, psi

P = pressure in street main, psi

H = height of highest fixture above street main, ft

L = equivalent length determined in item 4

If the system is of the downfeed supply from a gravity tank, the height of water in the tank converted to pounds per square inch by multiplying by 0.43 replaces the street-main pressure and the term $0.43H$ in the equation in item 6 is added instead of subtracted in calculating the term p. In this case H will be the vertical distance of the fixture below the bottom of the tank.

(7) From the expected rate of flow determined in item 3 and the value of P calculated in item 6, choose the sizes of pipe from chart 18.3, 18.4, or 18.5.

▶ An illustrated example of sizing a building with several rises and a distributing main is shown in Fig. 18-3.

The first schedule or chart should show the basement piping, by size, as follows:

Assume a building as shown in Fig. 18-3. The minimum street pressure at the entrance of the main is 70 pounds per square inch. The pressure loss due to the elevation of the highest fixture above the street main is 0.434 × 72 ft total height = 31 psi.

The pressure required to operate the highest fixture at the outlet is 15 psi.

The total pressure required for the elevation and operation of fixture is 46 psi.

Pressure available for friction loss is 24 psi.

Allowable friction loss per 100 feet of pipe is 10.4 psi.

Building-service main 678 fixture units need 170 gpm.

See Chart 18.1, 678 fixture units indicate that 170 gpm will be the demand required.

The 230 hot-water-service fixture units need 70 gpm.

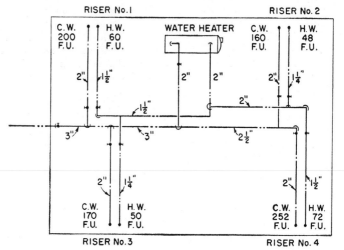

Fig. 18-3

The total requirements for hot and cold water should be figured on the basis of ¾ fixture unit for hot water and ¾ fixture unit for cold water.

Table B. Pipe Size for a Hot- and Cold-water System

Cold-water or hot-water pipe	Riser	Fixture units for each branch	Gpm for each branch	Branch size (in.)	Main fixture units	Main gpm	Main size (in.)
Cold water	4	252	100	2			
	2	160	82	2			
					412	105	2½
	Hot water	230	70	2	642	160	3
	3	170	85	2	812	195	3
	1	200	90	2	1,012	215	3
Hot water	4	72	37	1½			
	2	48	25	1¼			
					120	50	20
	1	60	32	1½			
	3	50	25	1¼			
					57	30	1½
	Main 1,012 × 0.67				678	170	3

Therefore, multiply the total fixture units for hot and cold water by 0.67 for the water service main.

A chart may be prepared for computing pipe sizes for a hot- and cold-water system as shown in Table B.

Figure 18-4 shows a diagram for riser 4. A similar diagram may be made for other risers.

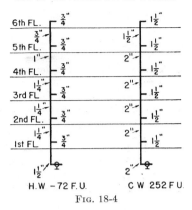

H.W – 72 F.U.   C W 252 F.U.

Fig. 18-4

A chart may be prepared as shown in Table C.

Table C. Riser Size for Hot- and Cold-water System

Hot- or cold-water riser	Riser	Floor	Fixture units installed	Gpm required	Branch size (in.)	Riser gpm	Riser fixture units	Riser size (in.)
Cold water	4	6	42	47	1½	42	47	1½
	4	5	42	47	1½	84	62	2
	4	4	42	47	1½	126	75	2
	4	3	42	47	1½	168	85	2
	4	2	42	47	1½	210	92	2
	4	1	42	47	1½	252	100	2
Hot water	4	6	12	10	¾	12	10	¾
	4	5	12	10	¾	24	18	1
	4	4	1	10	¾	36	22	1¼
	4	3	12	10	¾	48	28	1¼
	4	2	12	10	¾	60	32	1¼
	4	1	12	10	¾	72	37	1½

Fixtures using hot water take ¾ fixture unit for hot water and ¾ fixture unit for cold water.

When designing a water-piping system, consideration should be given to delivery of water to the water-supply system and the hot-water system; avoidance of all cross connections; allowance for lawn-sprinkling system, hydrants, and special appliances such as laundering machines, dishwashers, food-waste disposals, and every type of special equipment.

Piping should be designed so that in case of negative pressures in the water-supply pipe or stopped-up waste, drain, or waste piping there would be no possibility of siphoning waste water into the water-supply piping. Check valves are not considered adequate protection against backflow.

Hot-water return circulation should be provided for buildings of more than two stories or where the main extends more than 100 feet. The hot-water-supply piping should be sized in the same manner as the cold-water-supply system.

Water hammer in a piping system is caused by lack of air so that the liquid cannot be compressed; therefore a sudden stop in flow causes an impact. The reverberation of the water in the pipe continues with diminishing noise until it is finally clamped by friction within the piping.

Intense water-hammer pressures may be created without actually hearing the noise. An example of the force that can be created in a pipe due to water hammer is as follows:

When water is flowing at a rate of 10 feet per second and the flow is stopped very suddenly, the pressure is increased approximately 60 pounds per square inch above the flow pressure for each foot per second. This means that the 10 feet per second velocity is increased 60 times, a pressure of 600 pounds per square inch. To this, add the normal static pressure in the main.

Dangerous water hammer may be relieved by the installation of air chambers or shock absorbers placed as near as possible to the valve producing the water hammer. The greater the amount of air in an air chamber, the more effective it is.

Air chambers require constant maintenance. They must be designed for easy maintenance and located so as to be readily accessible so that air may be replenished at regular intervals.

More effective control of water hammer can be accomplished by the installation of custom-designed suppressors or shock absorbers. Properly designed shock absorbers operate satisfactorily for years.

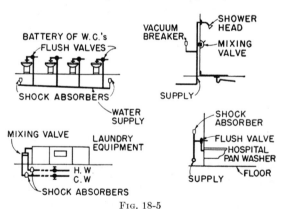

Fig. 18-5

Figure 18-5 illustrates the suggested location for installing shock absorbers.

Water pressures generally maintained by water companies range between 40 and 80 pounds per square inch except where the topography of the city is very hilly, in which cases certain portions of a water main carry as much as 150 or 200 pounds.

Where excessive pressures are found, it is necessary to provide pressure-reducing valves so as to eliminate excessive wear of fixture washers, leaky line noises, and pipe breaks.

A conservative pressure in a home, hotel, or similar type of building should not exceed 60 pounds per square inch. Pressure reduction may be affected by master-balanced pressure-reducing valves that will provide satisfactory flow for a project comprising many homes.

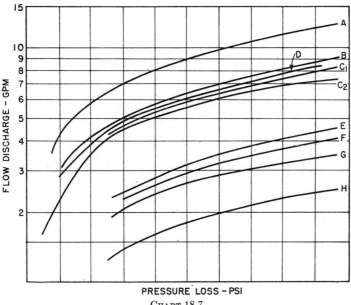

PRESSURE LOSS – PSI

CHART 18.7

CHAPTER 19

Guide on Administration

▶ Plumbing codes in the form of ordinances are an accepted fact by the people and their representatives.

There are, however, two trends, one in which relaxation of existing codes and controls is demanded, and the other in which plumbing codes are accepted which have unnecessary requirements.

In the preparation of a plumbing code we should not think of it as an isolated document of just local concern but as part of an over-all network of requirements that apply throughout the country, except as they may be affected by climate.

A plumbing code derives its justification for police power because it is mandatory only in so far as it protects the people against harmful conditions concerning health and safety, not for the personal benefit of any group or individual.

In the preparation of a plumbing code there are two points to be considered:

1. Rules which apply and govern the actual writing of a plumbing code should be made by a person or persons technically trained in the science of plumbing.

2. Questions and subject matter which are of a legal nature generally fall within the jurisdiction of an attorney.

A plumbing code is a manual of design and installation practices.

19.1 Title and Scope

19.1.1 Title: National Plumbing Code. This ordinance shall be known as the National Plumbing Code, may be so cited, and will be referred to in this ordinance as this Code.

The administration and enforcement of this ordinance shall be the duty of _____ who is hereby authorized to take such action as may be reasonably necessary to enforce the purpose of this ordinance. Such person or persons may be appointed and authorized as assistants or agents of such administrative authority as may be necessary to carry out the provisions of this Code.

▶ By constitutional provisions the various states either authorize the state legislature, city councils, or other governmental bodies or boards of health to enact plumbing codes or prohibit them from doing so.

It should first be ascertained that the legislative body to whom the proposed code will be submitted for enactment is empowered to pass upon it. There have been cases where a committee has spent a great deal of time in preparing such a code, the city council passed the law and then found out that the state law prohibited a city from passing a plumbing code.

19.1.2 Scope. The provisions of this Code shall apply to and govern plumbing as defined in this Code, including the practice, materials, and fixtures used in the installation, maintenance, extension, and alteration of all piping, fixtures, appliances, and appurtenances in connection with any of the following: sanitary drainage or storm-drainage facilities, the venting system, and the public or private water-supply systems, within or adjacent to any building or other structure, or conveyance; also the practice and materials used in the installation, maintenance, extension, or alteration of the storm-water or sewerage system of any premises to their connection with any point of public disposal or other terminal.

▶ **It is essential to state the scope of the Code.**
If the purpose includes regulating the installation and maintenance of plumbing, providing for examinations and licensing the persons engaged in the plumbing business, all accruing to the benefit of public health and the prevention of hazards, the code would carry considerable weight if ever brought to court.

19.1.3 Facilities. It is recognized that certain facilities in or adjacent to public streets are referred to in this Code, only a portion of which is under the ownership or the control of the owner or occupant of the building or premises to which this Code applies.

▶ **A plumbing code must give equal protection as the law.**
The Code must not deprive persons of their property without due process of law, such as arbitrarily imposing penalties or preventing a person from using his own property.
A code must not favor any particular class of persons. It must not prohibit others from entering the business on reasonably equivalent terms.
The principal reasons why courts hold laws invalid are that the laws are arbitrary, unreasonably restrictive. A study of court decisions would help determine what may or may not be done in the way of imposing restrictions.

19.2 License Required

19.2.1 Master Plumber's License. No person shall engage in the business of plumbing in the city of _____ unless licensed as a master plumber under the provisions of this Code.

19.2.2 Supervision of Work. No individual, firm, partnership, or corporation shall engage in the business of installing, repairing, or altering plumbing unless the plumbing work performed in the course of such business is under the direct supervision of a licensed master plumber.

▶ There should be no discrimination in requirements as to license, for example, requiring every individual master plumber in a partnership to have a license, but allowing a large corporation to practice with one licensed master in the organization.

Reasonable amount of credit should be given applicants for a master's license for their formal engineering training. It has been held proper to require plumbing installation to be under a licensed master's single supervision but improper to require the work to be done only by employees of a licensed master.

Both masters and journeymen are not licensed in all areas; this creates an inconsistency. For example, if only the masters are required to be skilled and to prove themselves by holding a license, courts have taken the view that it is inconsistent to allow journeymen to be untrained, as far as the law is concerned. Of course, the reverse situation would also be true.

One court held that prohibiting the Durham system in buildings more than three stories high but permitting them in buildings less than three stories was invalid.

19.3 Plumbers' Examining Board

19.3.1 Board Personnel. There is hereby established a plumbers' examining board (hereinafter referred to as the Board) to consist of not fewer than four members. One member shall represent the board of health, one member shall be a master plumber, one member shall represent the public, and one member shall be a journeyman plumber. Each member of the Board shall have had at least 5 years experience in his respective field. The members of the Board shall be appointed by the _____.

19.3.2 Meeting of the Board. The Board shall hold its first meeting not less than 30 days following the adoption of this ordinance. Thereafter, the Board shall meet at such intervals as may be necessary for the proper performance of its duties, but in any case not less than twice a year.

19.3.3 Examination and Certification. The Board shall establish standards and procedures for the qualification, examination, and licensing of master plumbers and journeyman plumbers and shall issue an appropriate license to each person who meets the qualifications therefor and successfully passes the examination given by the Board. The Board shall keep an official record of all its transactions.

19.3.4 Reexamination. Any person who fails to pass an examination as prescribed by the Board may apply for reexamination after the expiration of 30 days upon payment of the regular examination fee.

19.3.5 Temporary Permit. The Board may issue a temporary license pending examinations, provided the applicant holds a similar license from an equivalent board. Such permit shall not be valid for more than _____ days.

▶ The members of the Board, who are appointed or elected, should reside within the legal jurisdiction of the community.

It is most important that there should be at least four members on the

Board in addition to the plumbing inspector, who should vote only in the event of a tie.

One member of the Board should be a master plumber or certified plumbing contractor with at least 5 years experience as such.

One member should be a journeymen plumber with at least five years experience as a journeyman.

One member should be a registered mechanical engineer with at least 5 years experience in the field of plumbing design.

One member should be a public health engineer with at least 5 years experience in this field of public health.

The plumbing inspector shall act as a secretary of the Board and keep all records of the actions of the Board, issuance of licenses, revocations, examination results, violations, etc.

Each member of the Board shall be appointed for a term of at least 3 years at the initial formation of the Board when appointments should be made for 1, 2, 3, and 4 years, respectively, so that only one member is appointed in each year, except in case of resignation or death of one member.

The members shall prescribe powers and duties of the Board.

It is customary to compensate the members of the Board by payment of a fee for each attendance or meeting held in connection with official business.   Generally, this fee will be $5.00 to $20.00, depending on the time necessary to conduct the business.

19.4   Examination Fee

19.4.1   Any person desiring to be licensed as a master plumber or as a journeyman plumber shall make written application to the Board.   Examination fees for master and journeyman licenses shall be $_____ and $_____, respectively, payment of such fee to accompany the application.   Examination fees are not returnable.

▶   Fees should be established whereby the income from fees would take care of the cost of handling licensing, examination, and other expenses relative to this subject.   If the fees appear to be too high after 6 months or 1 year of operation, they should be proportionately reduced, or vice versa. Suggested fees:

Master Plumber or Plumbing Contractor License	$30.00
Renewal of above each year	30.00
Journeyman Plumbing Certificate	3.00
Renewal of above each year	3.00
Plumbing Inspectors License	1.00
Renewal of above each year	1.00
Examination fee for Plumbing Contractor	50.00
Examination fee for Journeyman	5.00
Examination fee for Plumbing Inspector	1.00

After a board of examiners has been put into effect, it is customary to provide a lead time before making it mandatory that a plumbing contractor, a journeyman, and an inspector must have a license to operate.

From **4** to **6** months is the generally accepted period allowed to give all those already operating time to procure a license.

Those already operating as plumbing contractor, journeyman, or plumbing inspector as defined by the administrative provision should be entitled to receive a certificate without the necessity of taking an examination.

19.5   Master Plumber's Bond

19.5.1   A person who has been issued a master plumber's license shall execute and deposit with the _____ a bond in the sum of $_____ , such bond to be so conditioned that all plumbing work performed by the licensee or under his supervision shall be performed in accordance with the provisions of this Code and that he will pay all fines and penalties properly imposed upon him for violation of the provisions of this Code.   A master plumber's license shall not be valid unless a bond is executed and deposited as herein provided.

▶   If it is desired to require master plumbers to give a bond either to the city to ensure compliance with the laws or for the benefit of customers, or for both purposes, the amount of the bond, the name of a surety, the provisions of the bond, the designation of the official who is to approve the bond, and where the bond shall be filed and kept are matters which should be included.

19.6   Expiration and Revocation of License

19.6.1   Annual Fee.   All licenses issued by the Board shall expire on December 31 of the year in which issued but may be renewed upon payment of fees in the amount provided in Sec. 19.4 and 19.5.   Expired licenses may be renewed at any time upon payment of the penalty of $_____ for journeyman plumber and $_____ for master plumber.

19.6.2   Revocation.   The Board may revoke any license if obtained through nondisclosure, misstatement, or misrepresentation of a material fact, or if a penalty has been imposed upon the licensee under section _____ of this ordinance.   Before a license may be revoked, the licensee shall have notice in writing, enumerating the charges against him, and be entitled to a hearing by the Board not sooner than 5 days from receipt of the notice.   The licensee shall be given an opportunity to present testimony, oral or written, and shall have the right of cross-examination.   All testimony shall be given under oath.   The Board shall have the power to administer oaths, issue subpoenas, and compel the attendance of witnesses.   The decision of the Board shall be based upon the evidence produced at the hearing and made part of the record thereof.   A person whose license has been revoked shall not be permitted to apply within 1 year from date of revocation.

19.7   Use of Licensee's Name by Another

19.7.1   No person who has obtained a plumber's license shall allow his name to be used by another person either for the purpose of obtaining permits or for doing business or work under the license. Every person licensed shall notify the Board of the address of his place of business, if any, and the name under which such business is carried on and shall give immediate notice to the Board of any change in either.

▶   The following are some of the items that should be spelled out in relation to licenses:

(a) Specific requirements for the issuance of a license or certificate of competency to those persons of good moral character or who have shown themselves fit after proper examination.

(b) Provision for the revocation of any license issued by the board and the necessary procedure.

(c) Provision for the issuance of a license without examination for master, journeymen, and plumbing inspectors who at the time of passing the law were actually engaged in the business.

(d) Board to set examination requirements for journeymen, master, and plumbing inspector.

(e) Term of license issued and conditions for renewal.

(f) License fees and renewal fees.

(g) Regulations prohibiting a person to do plumbing work or act as a plumbing inspector without a license.

(h) Penalties for violations of the licensing law.

The extent to which all the foregoing requirements are set up is dependent upon the size of the city or community.

The conditions upon which a master plumber or journeyman may receive, keep, and renew his license must be spelled out in detail. Usually there will be an examination, and the type and subjects of the examination, who shall give it, who shall grade the applicants, and what standards they shall use in determining whether an applicant is qualified should all be specified.

Revocation or reinstatement of license should be clearly defined. Revocation would result from

(a) License obtained through error or fraud or the recipient proved incompetent.

(b) Arbitrary violation of any of the rules or regulations of the local ordinance.

(c) Failure to pay lawful fee.

In all cases a written notice enumerating the charges against the person must be given and a hearing provided by the Board so that proper testimony be presented.

Any person whose license may have been revoked may be given the opportunity of applying and procuring a new license.

If desired, provisions for fine and imprisonment, revocation of licenses, or revocation of a permit, as punishment for violation of the plumbing code, may be specified, but each penalty must be given. It is not reasonable to revoke a license as punishment when a code mentions only a fine or imprisonment.

19.8   Plumbing Standards

19.8.1   Code Adopted.   The National Plumbing Code is hereby adopted and all installations, repairs, and alterations of plumbing shall, from the effective date of this ordinance, be performed in accordance with its provisions.   In the case of discretionary actions and determinations of the plumbers' examining board, relevant facts shall be considered and determinations made in the exercise of reasonable discretion, and all such determinations shall be final in the absence of abuse of discretion.

19.8.2   Official Copy.   Three copies of the National Plumbing Code shall be kept on file by the Board for inspection by and use of the public and shall be marked with the words "City of _____, official copy."

▶   **The National Plumbing Code is a guide.   It can readily be converted into an ordinance by due process of law.   As a guide it will be found necessary to make adjustments for climatic conditions; otherwise it is a very complete document.**

19.9   Permit for Plumbing Work

19.9.1   Issuance of Permit.   No plumbing work, unless excepted in this section, shall be undertaken prior to the issuance of a permit therefor by the _____.   A permit shall be issued to a licensed master plumber, except as provided in 19.9.2.

19.9.2   Exception.   Any permit required by this Code may be issued to any person to do any work regulated by this Code in a single-family dwelling used exclusively for living purposes, including the usual accessory buildings and quarters in connection with such building, provided the person is the bona fide owner of such dwelling and that the same will be occupied by said owner and that said owner shall personally purchase all material and perform all labor in connection therewith, and complying with the requirements of this Code.

19.9.3   Application for Permit.   Application for a permit for plumbing work shall be made on suitable forms provided by _____.   The application shall be accompanied by fees in accordance with schedule of fees.

19.9.4   Schedule of Fees

For	Fee
Each plumbing fixture and waste-discharging device...........	_____
New or reconstructed sewer connection......................	_____
Construction or reconstruction of cesspool...................	_____
Each septic tank...	_____
Each water heater..	_____
Each water-distribution system or service connection..........	_____
Repair or alteration of any plumbing system.................	_____
Any permit requiring inspection, minimum fee...............	_____

▶   **It has been found that in most states it is legally provided that any individual desiring to install the plumbing in his own home must as such be given the necessary permits.   The work as installed must comply with all** the rules and regulations of design and installation, including tests and inspection.

Many codes have been made invalid because they prohibit the legal owner of a proposed home from installing his own plumbing or making alterations and additions to his own home.

Provided the owner will abide by the plumbing code in every respect, this should be allowed.

19.10   Requirements for Plumbing Permits

19.10.1   Plans and Specifications.   No permit shall be issued until plans and specifications showing the proposed work in necessary detail have been submitted to the _____ and the Board has determined from examination of such plans and specifications that they give assurance that the work will conform to the provisions of this Code.   If a permit is denied, the applicant may submit revised plans and specifications without payment of additional fee. If, in the course of the work, it is found necessary to make any change from the plans and specifications on which a permit has been issued, amended plans and specifications shall be submitted and a supplementary permit, subject to the same conditions applicable to original application for permit, shall be issued to cover the change.

19.10.2   Repairs.   Repairs involving only the working parts of a faucet or valve, the clearance of stoppages, repairing of leaks, or replacement of defective faucets or valves may be made without a permit provided no changes are made in the piping to the fixtures.

► A substantial source of legal difficulty has been the failure to specify what constitutes, or to define, "repairs" which are permitted without a license.   This subject furnishes an occasion for producing illogical and, therefore, unreasonable provisions.   The question will be raised: "Why is it necessary to regulate installations receiving all sorts of inspections by public and private representatives and at the same time permit unauthorized, uninspected tampering with the water-supply system where the danger of infecting the water supply is just as great and more likely to occur?"   This question also arises in connection with allowing homeowners to do their own plumbing.

Every provision of the Code should be tested and also the code itself for indefiniteness, uncertainty and ambiguity, unreasonableness, illogicalness and discrimination.

19.10.3   Protection of Water-supply System.   The _____ shall make such rules and regulations in furtherance of the purposes of this Code, and not inconsistent with the specific provisions of this Code, for the installation, repair, or alteration of air-conditioning systems, water-treatment equipment, and water-evaporated devices as may be deemed necessary to properly protect the water-supply system.

▶ In the preparation of every provision of a plumbing code it should be remembered that the person attacking the code will be represented by a lawyer, the person defending the code will be a lawyer, and the judge who will decide the case will be a lawyer. Therefore, it is important to make the provisions clear and reasonable and to check the law whenever a doubt arises.

Generally, from the legal point of view, the public health is sufficiently protected if there are provisions specifying materials and ways of installation, a permit procedure, requirement of inspection and certification of compliance by a plumbing inspection, and installation by licensed personnel. Imposing requirements beyond these, such as sticker ordinances, would ordinarily be held superfluous and therefore unreasonable.

19.11   Enforcement

19.11.1   Inspections and Tests. It shall be the duty of the _____ _____ to enforce the provisions of this Code and to make the inspections and tests required thereunder.

19.11.2   Right of Entry. The administrative authority shall prepare, and it and its authorized representatives shall carry, sufficient identification and shall exhibit same before entering any premises for the purpose of inspecting any plumbing system at such times as may be reasonably necessary to protect the public health.

19.12   Penalty

19.12.1 Any person violating any provision of this ordinance shall be punishable by fine of not less than _____ dollars ($_____) nor more than _____ dollars ($_____) or imprisonment for not less than _____ days nor more than _____ days.

▶ In the usual case where the plumbing inspector handles the permits, it is important to specify what he can and cannot do, what he should do about violations, for example, and that he prepare a written report and submit it to the city or county prosecutor for action.

Detailed provisions setting forth the scope of authority of the plumbing inspector should be included, and in any case where he is to be given discretion whether to do or not to do something or whether he shall or shall not allow something, his actions in this respect should be governed by a provision requiring him, in all such cases, to hold a hearing with or without sworn witnesses and affidavits, or otherwise to investigate the facts, and to base his decision upon the relevant facts.

The definition of "plumbing" is an important one. Also a "master plumber" and a "journeyman" should be carefully and completely defined and the position and status of apprentices made clear. The distinction between master and journeyman and what they may lawfully do should be set out in detail.

Master Plumber of Certified Plumbing Contractor. An individual having a regular place of business who, by himself or through a person or persons in his employ, performs plumbing work and who has successfully fulfilled the examination and requirements prescribed by the Board.

Journeyman Plumber or Certified Journeyman. Any person other than a certified plumbing contractor who engages in or works at the actual installation, alteration, repair, and renovating of plumbing and who has successfully fulfilled the examination and requirements prescribed by the Board.

Plumbing Inspector. Any person employed by a city, town, or village for the purpose of inspecting plumbing work and installations in connection with health and safety requirements and ordinances and who has successfully fulfilled the examination and requirements prescribed by the Board.

Such work as outlined below should be permitted without a license.

(*a*) Plumbing work done by a property owner in a home owned and occupied by himself.

(*b*) Plumbing work done by a regularly employed individual acting as a maintenance man, incidental to and in connection with the business in which he is employed, and who is not engaged in the occupation of plumbing for the general public.

CHAPTER 20

Mobile-home Standards

Introduction

The primary objective of these standards is to provide a sanitary installation within a trailer coach or mobile home. It is also of importance that a method or standard be established, agreeable to manufacturers of trailer coaches, that would coordinate the location of the sewer and water outlets which must be connected at a trailer park.

The interest of the manufacturers of mobile homes as well as of the operators of trailer parks has been considered together with the welfare and safety of the public.

▶ The standards developed and published as part of the Report of the Coordinating Committee for a National Plumbing Code and the American Standard ASA A40.8 National Plumbing Code are but a guide toward final development.

For this reason this chapter, dealing with mobile homes and trailer parks, should be considered as tentative as further study is being given to this work.

These standards were initiated by the American Society of Sanitary Engineering and prepared by the Trailer Home and Trailer Parks Committee.

20.1 Definitions

20.1.1 Definitions of terms as defined in Chap. 1 shall apply except as otherwise specifically provided in this chapter.

20.1.2 Trailer coach shall mean a self-contained unit designed for the shelter of one or more persons as a residence or for other use as permitted by the administrative authority for the serving of drinks, food, or as a comfort station and which can readily be moved or transported from one locality to another on its wheels and which is provided with plumbing facilities.

20.1.3 Sewer connection is that portion of the drainage piping which extends as a single terminal under the trailer for connecting with the trailer-park drainage system.

▶ The title "trailer coach" has been changed to "mobile home" because of the large number of modern coaches which today serve as year-round homes.

It is because of the acceptance by the public of this type of residence that regulations to establish satisfactory and sanitary installations were developed.

It is as important to maintain a mobile home in proper sanitary condition as a private residence.

20.1.4   Water-service connection is that portion of the water-supply piping which extends as a single terminal under the trailer for connection with the trailer-park water-supply system.

▶   This is well regulated by most health departments. See Chap. 21 for additional information.

20.1.5   Administrative Authority.   The administrative authority is the individual, official, department, or agency established and authorized by a state, county, city, or other political subdivision to administer and enforce the provisions of the plumbing code as adopted or amended.

▶   The regulations for mobile homes are not so simply enforced as regulations for a residence.

Unless standards are developed and accepted by the Mobile Homes Manufacturers Association and by the nonassociation manufacturers, enforcement is left to local authorities.

This becomes a burden on the buyer, as in most cases he is ignorant of local plumbing-code laws and only becomes acquainted when he is informed that he is not permitted to park his trailer coach in the county or must undergo a plumbing change to meet local ordinances.

A national standard governing the plumbing requirements will benefit the public at large.

20.1.6   Drainage system means and includes all the piping within or attached to the trailer which conveys sewage or other liquid wastes to and including the sewer connection.

20.1.7   Plumbing.   Plumbing is the practice, materials, and fixtures used in the installation, maintenance, extension, and alteration of all piping, fixtures, appliances, and appurtenances in connection with any of the following: sanitary-drainage or storm-drainage facilities, the venting system and the public or private water-supply systems, within or adjacent to any building, structure, or conveyance; also, the practice and materials used in the installation, maintenance, extension, or alteration of the storm-water, liquid-waste, or sewage and water-supply systems of any premises to their connection with any point of public disposal or other acceptable terminal.

20.1.8   Potable Water.   Potable water is water which is satisfactory for drinking, culinary, and domestic purposes and meets the requirements of the health authority having jurisdiction.

20.1.9   Left side of trailer is defined as the side farthest from the curb when the trailer is being towed or is in transit.

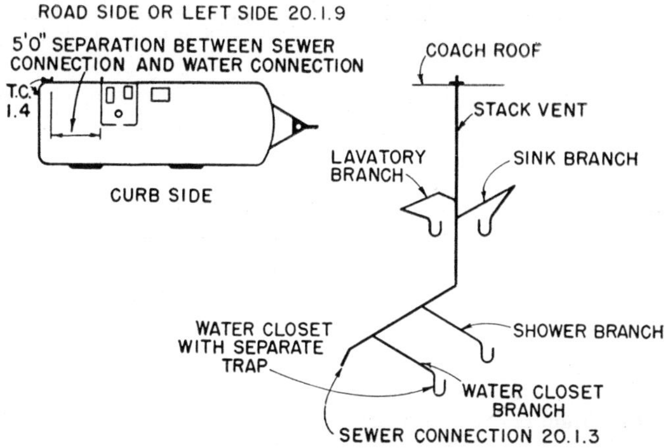

ROAD SIDE OR LEFT SIDE 20.1.9

5'0" SEPARATION BETWEEN SEWER CONNECTION AND WATER CONNECTION

COACH ROOF

T.C. 1.4

STACK VENT

CURB SIDE

LAVATORY BRANCH

SINK BRANCH

WATER CLOSET WITH SEPARATE TRAP

SHOWER BRANCH

WATER CLOSET BRANCH

SEWER CONNECTION 20.1.3

Fig. 20-1

▶ Figure 20-1 shows the location of the sewer connection and water-service connection on a trailer coach as required in paragraphs 20.1.3 and 20.1.4. The sewer connection must be on the left side of the trailer, which is the road side. The water connection must be at least 5 feet from the sewer connection, toward or at the rear of the trailer.

20.2   General Regulations

20.2.1   Plumbing Systems.   Plumbing systems, including repairs and additions, hereafter installed shall conform with the provisions of this chapter.

▶ For definition of horizontal or vertical pipe see Fig. 1-48.

20.2.2   Horizontal Drainage Piping.   Horizontal drainage piping shall be run in practical alignment at a uniform grade.

▶ A grade of $\frac{1}{8}$ to $\frac{1}{4}$ inch per foot will provide a scouring effect and keep the piping clear and be less apt to have stoppages.

20.2.3   Obstruction to Flow.   Any fitting, or connection which has an enlargement, chamber, or recess with a ledge, shoulder, or reduction of the pipe area, that offers an obstruction to flow through the drain or any fitting, trap, or connection that offers abnormal obstruction to flow is prohibited.

▶ Many coaches have had specially made fixtures and fittings installed, only to find later that stoppages are frequent, because the system was improperly designed.

20.2.4 Supports. Piping shall be securely supported to keep it in alignment without undue strains or stresses, and provisions shall be made for expansion and contraction during travel.

20.2.5 Freezing. All piping and fixtures which would be subject to freezing temperatures when traveling through cold climates shall be insulated to preclude the possibility of freezing.

▶ **Electric tape or proper insulation will protect the plumbing system when traveling or while located in climates where temperatures might damage the system.**

20.2.6 Workmanship shall be of such character as to accomplish the results sought to be obtained in this chapter.

20.2.7 Light and Ventilation. Water-closet compartments shall be provided with adequate light and ventilation.

20.2.8 Ratproofing. All openings through which piping or other conduits pass through floors or walls shall be properly sealed with permanently attached collars of metal or other material that will prevent the passage of rats or other vermin.

20.2.9 Equipment Condemned. Plumbing equipment condemned by the proper administrative authority because of wear, damage, or defects as a sanitary or safety hazard shall not be reused.

20.2.10 Connections to Plumbing System. All plumbing fixtures, drains, appurtenances, and appliances used to receive or discharge liquid or water-borne wastes shall be properly and individually connected by means of metal pipe or tubing to the common outlet of the trailer-drainage system.

20.2.11 Sewer Connection. A watertight connection between the trailer-drainage system and the trailer-park sewer connection shall be made by means of a readily removable semirigid or flexible connector acceptable to the administrative authority.

20.2.12 Location of Piping or Fixtures. Piping, fixtures, or equipment shall be so located as not to interfere with the normal operation of windows, doors, or other exit openings. Operating devices shall be accessible for repair or servicing.

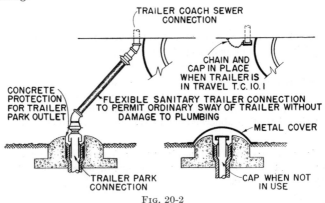

Fig. 20-2

▶ Figure 20-2 illustrates a connection at the trailer which should be either at a 45-degree angle or looking downward, so that there will be no kink or sag in the connection. A flexible connection is needed so that it can be adjusted to the desired distance. A suggested trailer-park outlet is shown.

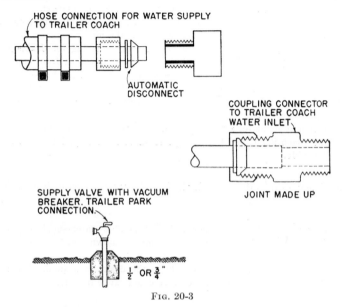

FIG. 20-3

Figure 20-3 shows a water connection.

20.3 Materials

20.3.1 Drainage and Vent Systems. Pipe and fittings for the drainage and vent systems shall be as provided in Chap. 3 of the Code and as follows:
- (a) Copper tube with sweated joints, drainage type.
- (b) Galvanized steel, galvanized wrought iron, or galvanized ferrous alloy.
- (c) Lead pipe not less than $\frac{1}{8}$ inch wall thickness.
- (d) Fittings for the drainage system shall be American National Taper Threads, recessed type. Vent fittings may be galvanized, malleable, or cast iron. If lead is used, all joints shall be wiped. Wiped joints shall have an exposed surface on each side of the joint not less than $\frac{3}{8}$ inch and at least as thick as the material being jointed.

20.3.2 Water Piping. Water piping shall be brass, copper, wrought iron, open-hearth iron, steel or copper tubing, type L, with appropriate approved fittings. All ferrous pipe and fittings shall be galvanized.

▶ The difference between a residence and a mobile home, in respect to kinds of piping and fixtures used, is the stresses to which these materials are subjected in a mobile home versus a stationary home.

In the case of drainage and venting, weight must be considered. Copper-tube pipe and fittings, type M, is of the least weight.

Plastic tube might shortly provide an excellent piping for a mobile home; it is flexible and sufficiently strong to withstand a great deal of shock.

Plastic fixtures also are beginning to appear on the market.

Water piping for a trailer must withstand all types of water characteristics, some of which might adversely affect the piping.

The basis of selection of the proper type of piping for drainage and water supply for a trailer coach is somewhat different from that for a house. The location of the house is permanent, and the selection of piping should be based on local conditions and practices. A trailer coach may be moved from one part of the country to another and be subjected to aggressive waters as well as nonaggressive waters. Therefore, the selection of piping for a trailer should be on the basis of the life expectancy of the coach itself, and the piping should be so arranged as to be readily replaceable.

20.3.3 Used materials are prohibited in the construction or installation of the water-supply system.

▶ This paragraph refers specifically to potable-water-supply piping for mobile homes. Used piping from an unknown source might bring contamination.

Used pipe is equally undesirable in the drainage system. Used pipe might be partly clogged and therefore could cause trouble.

20.4 Fixtures

20.4.1 Quality of Fixtures. All plumbing fixtures shall be made of approved materials with smooth, impervious surface.

20.4.2 Trailer-coach Fixtures. Plumbing fixtures installed in the trailer shall be of materials that will withstand road shock and be so attached to the structure of the trailer as to be resistant to vibration or settling.

20.4.3 Resistance to Shock. Resistance to shock shall be determined by tests over a period of actual use of 1 year or by equivalent simulated laboratory tests.

20.4.4 Fixture Traps. Each plumbing fixture shall be provided with a trap containing not less than a 2-inch water seal.

20.4.5 Location of Traps. Traps shall be so located as to preclude the possibility of trap-seal loss during transportation or ordinary use.

▶ The objectives in selecting fixtures for a mobile home are the same as for a stationary home: easy cleaning, smooth surface that will not absorb moisture nor cause odors, material that will resist discoloration.

The trap should be so located and vented as to provide a trap seal at all times.

When a trap seal is lost, air currents might occur within the piping which would permit foul odors to enter the living space of the mobile home.

20.4.6 Water Closets for Trailers

(a) Water closets shall be constructed of such durable materials as to be transported in trailers over the highways without injury or impairing their capacity to operate.

(b) Water closets shall not permit the spillage of trap-seal contents during transit and shall perform in a sanitary manner.

(c) It should not be possible to flush a water closet except when the trailer is connected at a trailer camp to a water-supply and sewage-disposal system.

(d) Each water closet shall be provided with approved backflow or vacuum-breaker device to prevent contamination of the potable-water system.

(e) Water closets shall be provided with a water supply adequate to thoroughly cleanse the interior of the water closet when the valve is operated.

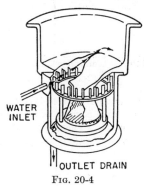

WATER INLET

OUTLET DRAIN

Fig. 20-4

▶ Some special types of water closets for a mobile home are the grinder, water-operated, the marine, and the hopper type.

Figure 20-4 illustrates a water-operated grinder closet.

Fig. 20-5

Figure 20-5 illustrates an electrically operated grinder closet which combines the features of a regular wash-down bowl with an electric motor to operate the grinder.

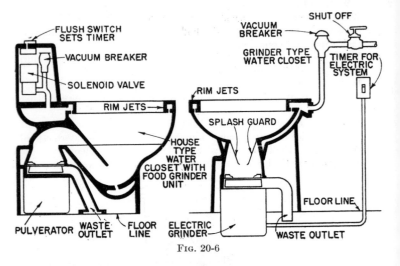

FIG. 20-6

Figure 20-6 illustrates another grinder-type closet.

These closets have the dual purpose of utility and the disposal of food waste within the mobile home. These types have had limited acceptance for residences, as food-waste grinders are preferred in kitchens near the source of waste.

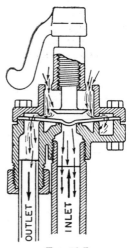

FIG. 20-7

Manufacturers of mobile homes recognize the possibility of backflow; therefore above-the-rim faucets are usually provided for lavatories, sinks, and bathtubs and vacuum breakers for water closets with tanks or with flush valves.

Figure 20-7 illustrates a valve for flushing trailer-coach water closets. This valve incorporates antibackflow features. This valve can be used safely on other supply piping to prevent backflow of polluted water into the potable-water supply system.

20.5 Drainage Piping

20.5.1 Installation. Horizontal piping shall be installed at a uniform slope and in no case less than $\frac{1}{8}$ inch per foot slope.

20.5.2 The size of soil and waste piping shall be in accordance with Tables 20.5.3 using Table 20.5.4 when necessary to determine fixture unit ratings.

▶   Based on the values so established in Table **20.5.4**, pipe sizes have been established for trailer coaches as given in Table **20.5.3**.

20.5.3 (See Tables 20.5.3*A* and *B*.)

Table 20.5.3A   Size of Main Soil Stack

Fixture Connection	Minimum Size (in.)
More than 6 fixture units connected to stack	3
6 fixture units or less connected to stack	2
Lavatory branch waste and trap	$1\frac{1}{4}$
Sink branch waste and trap	$1\frac{1}{2}$
Shower branch waste and trap	$1\frac{1}{2}$
Bath branch waste and trap	$1\frac{1}{2}$
Water-closet branch waste:	
Four-unit type	3
Two-unit type	$1\frac{1}{2}$

Table 20.5.3B   Trailer Fixture-unit Ratings

Fixtures	Fixture Units
Water closet with 3-in. integral traps	4
Water closet with separate traps	3
Water closet, grinder type, with $1\frac{1}{2}$-in. trap	2
Lavatory with less than $1\frac{1}{8}$-in. outlet	1
Sink with less than $1\frac{1}{8}$-in. outlet	1
Sink with larger outlets	2
Shower with less than 2-in. outlet	2
Shower with 2-in. outlet	3
Bathtub with less than 2-in. outlet	2

▶   Fixture-unit ratings for trailer coaches differ from standard-type fixtures because of the smaller-size fixture and the lower rates of flow. Standard-type water closets have been rated the same as for a house; however, trailer coaches are most often fitted with special-type water closets which prevent trap-seal spillage during transportation. The most frequent types are the grinder type, the hopper type, and the marine type.

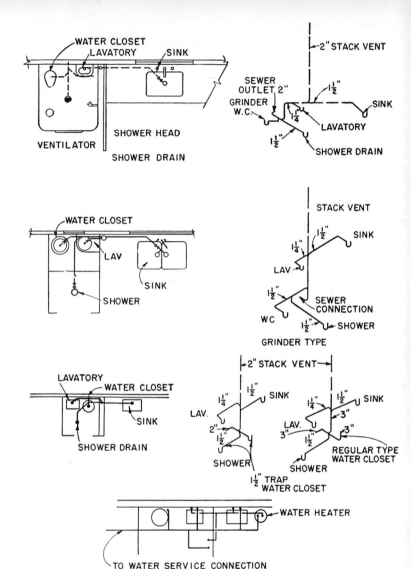

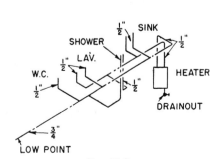

Fig. 20-8

20-10

The rating of the various types has been established by preliminary flow test, and Table 20.5.4 establishes these values.

20.5.4 Trailer-drain Outlet. Trailer-drain outlet shall terminate on the road side of the trailer at rear of wheel housing and be visible from the side of the trailer when in transit. Each outlet shall be provided with a tight cap or plug for closure when not connected to a sewer. The lap or plug shall be permanently affixed to the trailer body.

20.5.5 Group Venting. A group of fixtures consisting of one water closet, or shower or bathtub, one lavatory, and a kitchen sink may be installed without individual fixture vents and as a stack-vented group. Each fixture branch shall be installed within the limits as given in Table 20.5.6.

20.5.6 (See Table 20.5.6.)

Table 20.5.6 Maximum Length of Unvented Branch Waste

Size of Waste Pipe (in.)	Permissible Length (ft)
3	6
2	5
$1\frac{1}{2}$	$4\frac{1}{2}$
$1\frac{1}{4}$	$4\frac{1}{2}$

20.5.7 Fixture Branches. Fixture-branch connections at the stack shall be made by use of sanitary tees, and the branch drain shall be sloped not more than $\frac{1}{4}$ inch per foot.

▶   This piping arrangement is common to many trailers.

CHAPTER 21

Mobile-home Parts Standards

Introduction

In the preparation of the site for a trailer camp there are a number of basic requirements that should be analyzed before the actual design is made. Among the more important items the following are given as a guide:

(a) Space requirements and locations for water-supply source.

(b) Space requirements for the treatment plant in relation to water-supply source or location.

(c) Location of treatment plant in relation to size of property, neighborhood, and trailer-unit location, and particularly as it applies to the prevailing winds and the neighboring population.

(d) Water-supply source and its relation to sewage treatment.

(e) Prior to the preparation of the final trailer-park design, the tentative plans and specifications should be submitted to the state health department or the administrative authority having jurisdiction over this work.

(f) If the trailer park is located within the city jurisdiction the layout should likewise be submitted and approved by the local plumbing department.

The following standards have been prepared as a general guide for those who may wish to set up standards for trailer-park sanitary facilities.

21.1 Method of Disposal

21.1.2 Approval. It is recognized that the most satisfactory and desirable method of disposing of the sewage in a trailer camp is through a public sewer, and every effort shall be made to have these facilities extended within the camp, where possible. There is, however, the fact that this may be impracticable because a public sewer is not always available within a reasonable distance, in which case consideration should then be given to the construction of a community sewage-disposal system, the magnitude of which would depend upon the requirements of the state health department, the local authority having jurisdiction over this installation, and the trailer-park occupancy.

21.1.3 Plans and Specifications. In the preparation of the site plan it must be borne in mind that all the state health departments generally require the submission of complete specifications and plans showing in detail the entire sanitary facilities and water-supply distribution for the project.

▶ The modern type of trailer park is relatively new to general designers. The standard criteria for design are not readily applicable.

Today mobile homes utilizing the trailer park will not always be equipped with all sanitary facilities; many are equipped only with a small sink.

More accurate information can be gathered by visiting some of the more up-to-date installations.

Based on data available, the average occupancy per mobile home is $2\frac{1}{2}$ persons and the average water consumption is 30 gallons of water per day per coach.

To this, water requirements for park buildings, laundry, sprinkling, etc., must be added when figuring water-supply requirements for the park area.

21.2 Recommended Procedures

21.2.1 Detailed Information. Drawings and specifications should provide all necessary information, such as property boundary lines, orientation, grading, neighborhoods, usage of land within the adjoining neighborhood, name of ownership, architect's name, engineer's name, and all other pertinent data necessary for a thorough study of the project.

21.2.2 Preliminary discussions with the authority having jurisdiction over this project should include the following:

(a) Type of sewage-treatment plant.

(b) General design of the sewage-treatment plant.

(c) Minimum standards for sewer system.

(d) Discussion of type and size of trailer park.

(e) Prior to the preparation of the final trailer-park design the tentative plans and specifications should be submitted to the state health department or the administrative authority having jurisdiction over this work.

(f) If the trailer park is located within the city jurisdiction, the layout should likewise be submitted and approved by the local plumbing department.

▶ In estimating for plant design, Table A will provide approximate data in order to compute costs.

Table A. Data for Computing Trailer Camp Costs

No. of trailers	No. of persons	Water usage (gal/person/day)	Sewage flow (gal/day)	BOD (lb/day)	Solids (ppm)
25	75	35	2,600	8.20	3.80
50	150	35	5,000	16.25	3.70
75	212	30	6,750	24.70	4.40
100	275	30	8,500	32.00	4.30
150	415	25	11,250	49.00	5.40
200	540	25	14,000	65.00	5.30
300	810	25	18,000	99.00	6.60
400	1,140	20	23,000	130.00	6.50
500	1,350	20	27,000	150.00	6.50

21.3 Type of Disposal Plant

21.3.1 Type of System. The local administrative authority will determine the actual selection of the plant and system to be used.

21.3.2 Guide for Discussion. The following represents a guide for discussion with the administrative authority who is thoroughly familiar with the local conditions.

(a) Up to 75 trailers, the use of septic tank and either a tile absorption field or sand filter is recommended.

(b) From 75 to 150 trailer units, sand filters should be selected; if there is space available, trickling filters preceded by an Imhoff tank will be desirable.

(c) Above 150 trailer units, trickling filters and Imhoff tank is recommended, with the additional requirements of chlorination facilities to be included to reduce odors at such time as they may occur.

(d) Activated sludge with separate settling antidigestion is recommended only where available space is restricted, where the maximum treatment is required for the operation of the park, where the adjoining neighborhood to the park limits the scope of operation, and where 200 or more trailer units are to be served.

A discussion covering the general subject of sewage treatment is given here, owing to the fact that state boards of health recognize the importance of a proper and adequate method of sewage disposal in rural areas where public sewers are not available.

The main problem is to provide effective treatment of wastes from occupied trailers. This problem applies to motels as well.

Various types of waste, organic and inorganic, are those from the human body, from water used for bathing, laundry, and scrubbing, and from cooking, food preparation, and dishwashing.

Of the total liquid reaching the disposal plant, only about 0.2 per cent is solid material in suspension and solution which needs to be treated. Of this quantity of solids, only 25 per cent is removed by treatment, but this is the portion which is the source of pollution. The 0.2 per cent solids can be visualized as the equivalent of 3 tablespoons of vegetable and mineral matter placed in a barrel of water; nevertheless it would take only a fraction of the 3 tablespoons to contaminate the entire barrel of water.

The process used to remove solids to satisfy the oxygen demand of the organic matter, thereby stabilizing the nitrogen-containing material and reducing the bacteria, is what is known as sewage treatment.

The strength of the sewage to be treated is represented by the amount of oxygen needed to stabilize the oxidizable matter. This is called "biochemical oxygen demand" expressed by the letters BOD.

The primary process in sewage treatment consists of settling of the greater percentage of solids. This generally is effected by gravity. However, BOD removal at this stage is a small percentage, as BOD is mainly developed by colloidal or soluble material.

The secondary process of sewage treatment is oxidation; this is the breaking down of organic solids into stable organic minerals by the activity of the oxygen which has penetrated into the solid mass.

This secondary treatment depends on an adequate supply of free air in order to maintain the bacteriological life which continues the treatment.

The type of sewage-treatment plant to be established depends upon several local conditions:

(a) Proximity to neighbors.

(b) Point of discharge.

(c) Size of plant needed.

(d) If tile-fields are to be used, the ability of the ground to absorb pre-settled sewage is a determining factor.

(e) Possibility of contaminating nearby wells or cisterns.

When considering a discharge into a river or stream, an adequate amount of water for dilution, based on the lowest flow during dry seasons, is essential.

Generally a flow equal to sixty times the sewage flow is considered a minimum for septic-tank discharge.

In all cases the first factors are the standards and requirements established by the board of health having jurisdiction over the area.

21.4   Selection of Plant

21.4.1   Local Health Authority.   Because of some specific needs in certain localities, the system to be installed in a particular trailer park should be based on the recommendations of the local health authorities.

▶   See Chap. 16, Individual Sewage-disposal System, for recommendations as to septic tanks.

Where more than 75 living units are installed, it will be found that the Imhoff system will present many advantages which the individual septic tank does not have.

Figure 21-1 illustrates a cross section of an Imhoff tank, each section arranged to perform a function.   The center section is the flow chamber *a* through which the sewage flows.   The solids settle, dropping through the slot *b,* into the digestion chamber *c.*   In chamber *c* the sludge is digested; the gases which are generated rise to the surface and, because of the angle walls, are directed to the scum chambers *d,* one at each side of the tank.

The shape of the tank may be round or rectangular.   Generally, rectangular tanks are selected because of easier construction.

The settling chambers of an Imhoff tank are smaller than those in a septic tank because the retention period required for an Imhoff tank is only 2 to 3 hours.

The sloping sides *e* should be very smooth so that the settling solids will slide easily into the digesting chamber.

The sloping sides are overlapped *f* to form a trap so that the rising gases

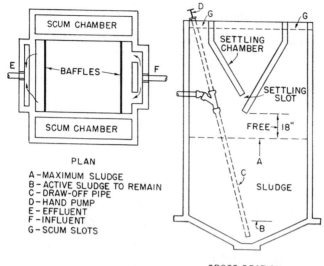

PLAN

A – MAXIMUM SLUDGE
B – ACTIVE SLUDGE TO REMAIN
C – DRAW-OFF PIPE
D – HAND PUMP
E – EFFLUENT
F – INFLUENT
G – SCUM SLOTS

CROSS SECTION

Fig. 21-1

are drawn to the scum chamber on each side of the tank and escape to the atmosphere *g*.

The drawoff pipe is open at the top so that sludge will be permitted to find its balance and be readily withdrawn. The open top also permits rodding of the drawoff pipe when it becomes clogged.

The gas-vent area is important, since the gases must have free escape. If the area is insufficient, the gas may lift the scum, causing foaming.

Temperature will have something to do with the speed of sludge digestion; cold climates will require longer periods of digestion than warmer climates.

Imhoff tanks properly operated generally produce 50 to 60 per cent reduction of solids and 30 per cent reduction of biological oxygen demand.

In the maintenance of an Imhoff tank the floor and slot must be cleaned regularly so that all solids readily drop to the digestion compartment. The scum chamber should be cleaned with a grease skimmer so that gases may escape readily.

Imhoff tanks are used ahead of sand filters. Or they are used with trickling filters for gravity operation, which will require about 7 feet of drop from the sewer inlet to the sand-filter outlet or 12 feet drop for a trickling filter; otherwise pumping will be required.

Larger treatment plants using Imhoff tanks will require the use of bar screens, sewage pumps, grease skimmers, trickling filters, and sludge-drying beds.

The design of a treatment plant is a matter for a well-trained engineer aware of the requirements and hazards and competent to fulfill the regulations of the public health officials having jurisdiction.

21.5   Sewer Installation

21.5.1   Separate Trenches. The sewer should be generally installed in a separate trench from the water-supply distribution.

21.5.2   Materials. The sewer shall be constructed of durable materials which are corrosion-resistant and shall be so installed as to remain watertight and be rootproof.

▶   The requirements for paragraphs 21.5.1 and 21.5.2 are similar to those for residential installations.

21.6   Materials

21.6.1   Cast-iron Pipe. Cast-iron soil pipe and fittings with hot-poured leaded joints.

21.6.2   Vitrified-clay Pipe. Vitrified-clay sewer pipe with hot-poured or precast bituminized joints.

21.6.3   Bituminized-fiber Pipe. Bituminized-fiber sewer pipe with tapered-type couplings and fittings of the same material as the pipe.

21.6.4   Asbestos-cement Pipe. Asbestos-cement pipe with rubber ring-type joints or concrete pipe with hot-poured joints.

21.6.5   Filled-in Ground. Sewers installed in filled or unstable ground shall be of cast-iron soil pipe, except that nonmetallic drains may be laid upon an approved pad or piers.

21.6.6   Calked Joints. Calked joints for cast-iron bell-and-spigot soil pipe shall be firmly packed with oakum or hemp and filled with molten lead not less than 1 inch deep. Lead shall be run in one pouring and calked tight. No paint, varnish, or other coatings shall be permitted on the jointing material until after the joint has been tested and approved.

21.6.7   Hot-poured Joints. Material for hot-poured joints for clay pipe shall not soften sufficiently to destroy the effectiveness of the joint when subjected to a temperature of 160°F nor be soluble in any of the wastes carried by the drainage system. The joint shall be first calked tight with jute, hemp, or other similar approved materials.

21.6.8   Tapered-type Joints. Joints in bituminized-fiber pipe shall be made with tapered-type couplings and of the same material as the pipe. All joints between bituminized-fiber pipe and metal shall be made by means of an adapter coupling calked as required in paragraph 21.6.6.

21.6.9   Asbestos-cement Joints. Joints in asbestos-cement pipe shall be made with sleeve couplings sealed with rubber rings and of the same composition as the pipe. All joints between asbestos-cement pipe and metal pipe shall be made by means of an adapter coupling calked as required in paragraph 21.6.6.

21.6.10   Cement Joints. Cement joints are permitted when sewers are installed in a separate trench from the water supply.

21.6.11   Sanitary Sewers. Sanitary sewers within the trailer-park area shall not receive storm or surface water.

21.7 Slope on Sewer Installations

21.7.1 Grade or Slope. Grade or slope for sewers shall be such as to maintain flow velocities within sewers at the rate of not less than 2 feet per second when flowing full.

21.7.2 Pipe Sizes. Table 21.7.3 is presented as a guide in computing pipe size in relation to slope.

21.7.3 (See Table 21.7.3.)

Table 21.7.3 Sewer-pipe Sizes

Sewer Size (in.)	Slope per Hundred Feet (in.)
4	15
6	8
8	5
10	$3\frac{1}{2}$
12	3

The objective is to provide a slope to permit a flow of 2 feet per second when one-half- or one-fourth-full.

21.8 Manholes

21.8.1 Manholes. Manholes shall be provided in sewer installation in the following manner:

(a) At the upper end of each main sewer line.

(b) At the outer end of the main sewer.

(c) At any point where the change of direction is 90 degrees or greater.

(d) At each junction of two or more branch sewers.

(e) At intervals of not more than 400 feet.

21.8.2 Laterals. Branch connections into main sewers or laterals shall be made by the use of 45-degree wyes. Short tees are prohibited.

21.8.3 Individual Trailer Units. Individual trailer units shall not be less than 3 inches in diameter.

When an individual branch to a trailer is installed at $\frac{1}{4}$- or $\frac{1}{2}$-in. slope, a 3-in.-diameter pipe will safely carry the discharge of two complete bathrooms.

21.9 Sewer Sizes

21.9.1 The sewer shall be sized in accordance with sizes given in Table 21.9.2.

21.9.2 (See Table 21.9.2.)

Table 21.9.2 Size of Sewer

Pipe Diameter (in.)	No. of Trailer Units Connected
4	50
6	100
8	400
10	10,000

21.10 Trailer Outlet

21.10.1 Traps. Each sewer lateral shall terminate with a P trap and then shall be extended to grade and terminate not less than 4 inches above grade.

21.10.2 Protection. Extension through ground shall be protected by metal casing or concrete mount.

▶   The metal casing or concrete mount is to prevent underground pipe breakage should the trailer wheels go over the outlet when it is being placed in position.

21.10.3 Connector. Each outlet for trailer unit shall be provided with a flexible connector furnished by the trailer-park operator.

21.10.4 Automatic Disconnection. Flexible connectors shall be so arranged as to readily clamp into the trailer-coach outlet and the connection so designed that in case of emergency, such as fire, trailer coach may be pulled out and the connection automatically disconnected without damage to piping or trailer coach.

▶   The automatic disconnection is provided so that, in the event of fire a truck can be quickly hitched to the burning coach and can pull it away from adjacent trailers.

21.10.5 Length of Connector. Sewer outlet for connecting each trailer shall be located centrally so that a flexible connector of sufficient length (provided by the trailer-park operator) may connect with the trailer sewer outlet located on the right side of the trailer and just behind the wheel housing.

21.11 Water-supply Distribution

21.11.1 Private Water Supply. Where connection to a municipal water supply or public water system is not possible, it is essential that certain precautions be taken in the development of individual supplies. Consideration must be given to the hydrological, geological, and bacteriological factors affecting the quantity and quality of available water. In many cases specific information on these matters may be obtained from the state or local health authorities. In any event, such authorities should be consulted prior to the development of any individual water supply.

▶   Chapter 18 on water-pipe sizing may be used in computing distribution piping for a trailer-park system. Use the fixture units assigned to trailer coaches and the curves for water-pipe sizing. A trailer coach usually uses slightly less water than fixtures in a private home.

21.11.2 Contamination. A ground-water supply should be properly located, constructed, and operated in order to be safeguarded against contamination.

21.11.3 Information. No matter what state or territory, the board of health has available data concerning public water systems and supplies. All can be obtained from these authorities merely by asking, and the specific regulations are available as well.

▶   See Chap. 15, Individual Water Supply, for detailed information and guidance.

21.11.4 Health Department. When it is desired to build a trailer park, the state will be glad to furnish data as to probable sources of water supply. They have records on nearby wells and can give some ideas on possible depths for potable water, as well as possible volumes available. They can offer recommended methods on the construction of the wells. This information is also available from any experienced drillers in the area.

21.11.5 Consultation. It is desirable that the state board of health be contacted regarding the possibility of obtaining water, before there is any commitment to purchase property for a trailer park, as lack of a proper water supply will nullify the use of the land for trailer-park purposes.

21.12   Materials

21.12.1 Materials. Material for water-distributing pipes and tubing shall be brass, copper, cast iron, wrought iron, open-hearth iron, or steel with appropriate approved fittings. All threaded ferrous pipe and fittings shall be galvanized (zinc coated) or cement lined. When used underground in corrosive soil, all ferrous pipe and fittings shall be coal-tar enamel coated and the threaded joints shall be coated and wrapped after installation.

21.12.2 Water Characteristics. When selecting the material and size for water-supply pipe, tubing, or fittings, due consideration shall be given to the action of the water on the interior and of the soil, fill, or other material on the exterior of the piping. No material that would produce toxic conditions in a potable-water system shall be used for water distribution.

21.13   Potable Water

21.13.1 Potable Water. The water shall contain no chemical or mineral substances capable of causing unfavorable physiological effects on those consuming the water.

21.13.2 The water shall be free from pathogenic bacteria and other disease-producing organisms.

21.13.3 Chlorination. The well should be chlorinated after construction or repair to remove any contamination which may have gained access to the supply. State or local health department should be contacted relative to bacteriological testing.)

21.14   Control Valves

21.14.1   Valves. In addition to the necessary valves on the distribution system each trailer-unit outlet shall be provided with a ¾-inch control valve.

21.14.2   Backflow. Each outlet valve shall be constructed so that backflow cannot occur from surface-contaminated water or any other source.

▶   See "cross connections" for guidance in the design of the water-supply piping.

21.14.3   Stop and Waste Valves. The use of ordinary stop and waste valves where aspiration or backflow can occur into the potable-water system is prohibited.

21.15   Trailer-outlet Connector

21.15.1   Distance. The trailer outlet shall have a distance of separation from the sewer outlet of not less than 5 feet.

21.15.2   Disconnection. The flexible connector between trailer-park outlet and trailer-coach outlet shall be of a type to readily permit quick attachment and in the event of emergency where a trailer coach may be pulled out it shall be so arranged to automatically disconnect without damaging the piping or trailer coach.

▶   Automatic disconnect on the water supply is for the same purpose as on the sewer connection. In the event of fire, the burning coach can be pulled out quickly without damaging the park's water-piping system.

21.15.3   Location. Trailer outlet shall be located at rear of lot.

21.16   Miscellaneous

21.16.1   Fire Protection. In the design of the water-distribution system in a trailer park, consideration for fire-outlet stations throughout the park should be considered as they apply to location and quantity of water necessary during an emergency period.

Part Three

TECHNICAL SECTION

CHAPTER 22

The Building Drainage System

22.1 Introduction

A general idea of the hydraulic and pneumatic phenomena that occur in the sanitary drainage system of a building is necessary before a detailed discussion of the various parts of the system is undertaken. The phenomena that occur in such drainage systems are very complicated and, for the most part, are not

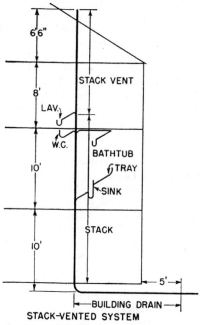

FIG. 22-1. Stack-vented system.

amenable to rational analysis because of this complexity. Essentially the problem is to design the system so as to use the smallest pipes that are consistent with rapidly carrying away the waste water from individual fixtures without clogging the pipes, without producing excessive pressure fluctuations at points where the fixture drains connect to the stack which might reduce the water seals

of the fixture traps sufficiently to permit positive-pressure fluctuations to force
sewer air back through the fixtures into the rooms, and without creating undue
noise.

In its simplest form, a building drainage system consists of a building sewer,
a building drain, a soil or waste stack, horizontal branches or fixture drains, and
vents.   The drainage system of a large building will consist of one or more building drains, each of which may have a number of primary and secondary branches,
and any number of soil or waste stacks, each of which in turn may have any
number of horizontal branches.   See Fig. 22-1 for the diagram of a simple stack-
vented system for a two-story single-family residence.   The general nature of
the hydraulic and pneumatic phenomena that occur in such a system will be
considered in what follows.

22.2   Nature of the Drainage Phenomena

1. Nonpressure Drainage Systems.   First of all it should be noted that
the drainage system of a building is, almost without exception, a nonpressure
system (pressure drainage in the building drain and sewer and in the lowest
part of the stack can be used to advantage in certain cases in large buildings).
By this we mean that the drainage pipes do not flow full, so that hydrostatic
pressures cannot exist in the system.   It is essential, for example, that the stack
should not flow more than one-fourth to one-third full if excessive pressure fluctuations and noises in the system are to be avoided (see Chap. 25.)   A fixture
drain may flow full during part of the time when the fixture to which it is
attached is discharging, the discharge from a fixture drain or horizontal branch
may occasionally fill the stack into which it empties at the level of the connection, and the occurrence of a hydraulic jump in the building drain or sewer may
fill the cross section of the drain or sewer when the flow is unusually heavy.
Nevertheless we can say in general that the system is a nonpressure system.

2. Demand and Drainage Loads.   A single-family dwelling will contain
certain plumbing fixtures—one or more bathroom groups, each consisting of a
water closet, a lavatory, and a bathtub or shower stall; a kitchen sink; and a
set of laundry trays.   It may also have an extra water closet and lavatory in
the basement.   Large buildings will also have other fixtures, for example, slop
sinks.   The important characteristic of these fixtures is the fact that they are
not used continuously.   Rather they are used with irregular frequencies that
vary greatly during the day.   This fact is brought out forcibly by a continuous
record of water demand in a residence (see Fig. 24-9).   In addition, the various
fixtures have quite different discharge characteristics, both as to the average
rate of flow per use and as to the duration of a single discharge.   The result is
that, while it is possible to specify what the maximum possible rate of flow in
the system might be—the flow produced by all the fixtures in the building
operating simultaneously—the probability of this occurring is negligible under
almost any circumstances of service use, and for large buildings with many
plumbing fixtures, this probability becomes vanishingly small.   Some idea of
this can be obtained by considering a hypothetical system consisting of 100 water
closets, each of which is discharged at random once in 5 min on the average

each use lasting for 9 sec. Under these conditions, the probability of finding none, one, two, three, four, etc., of the water closets in simultaneous operation at any arbitrarily chosen instant of observation is shown in Fig. 24-1. The figure shows that we are more likely to find three of the water closets in simultaneous operation than any other number. Furthermore, as we go to larger and larger numbers of water closets in simultaneous operation, we find that the probability of these occurrences falls off rapidly. For 10 water closets, for example, the probability is approximately 0.06 per cent. This shows that it would be absurd to design the system to carry the discharge of all 100 water closets operating simultaneously. How to select a reasonable number for design purposes will be shown in Chap. 24.

3. Traps and Trap Seals. The next thing to note is that, while waste water from the various fixtures must be able to flow freely through the drainage system to the street sewer, nevertheless some means must be provided for preventing sewer air from passing back through the fixtures to the rooms of the building. This is invariably achieved by the use of fixture traps, the commonest form of which is a U-shaped tube of the same or approximately the same diameter as the fixture drain, inserted between the drain and the fixture (see Fig. 27-1). The outlet of the U-shaped trap being at a higher level than the bottom of the U, there remains a water seal in the trap after the fixture has discharged. The existence and maintenance of this water seal impose on the drainage system the requirement that pressure fluctuations in the system due to the discharge of fixtures must not be sufficiently great at points where fixture drains and horizontal branches connect to the stack to suck so much water out of the trap seal that subsequent slight positive fluctuations will force sewer air through the seal into the room.

The discharge from an individual fixture takes place through the fixture trap and drain, the latter being laid to a slope that may range from, say $\frac{1}{8}$ to $\frac{1}{2}$ in. per ft, or even more under special circumstances. The discharge from the fixture may or may not fill the sloping drain completely. The discharge from most fixtures, such as lavatories, bathtubs, and sinks, starts off at a maximum rate and gradually tapers off, finally diminishing to a trickle which is called *trail flow*. This trail flow plays an important part in maintaining a safe trap seal in lavatories and some other fixtures.

4. Flow in Stacks. The flow in the drain empties into the vertical stack through a stack fitting, which may be a *long-turn tee-wye* or a *short-turn* or *sanitary tee*. Each of these fittings permits the flow from the drain to enter the stack with a component directed vertically downward, the first-named more than the second. Depending on the rate of flow out of the drain into the stack, the diameter of the stack, the type of stack fitting, and the flow down the stack from higher levels, if any, the discharge from the fixture drain may or may not fill the cross section of the stack at the level of entry. In any event, as soon as the water enters the stack, it is accelerated downward rapidly by the action of gravity, and before it has fallen very far, it has assumed the form of a sheet around the wall of the stack. This sheet of water continues to accelerate, its thickness being roughly in inverse proportion to its velocity, until the frictional force exerted by the wall of the stack on the falling sheet of water equals the force of gravity. From that point on—if the distance through which the water falls is great enough—the sheet will remain unchanged in thickness and velocity until it reaches the bottom of the stack, provided that no flows enter the stack at lower levels to interfere with the sheet. The ultimate vertical velocity that the sheet attains is called the "terminal velocity," and the distance through which the sheet must fall to attain this terminal velocity is called the *terminal length*. This distance is roughly of the order of a one-story height for a two-story residence.

Fig. 22-2. Interference of flows at junction of horizontal branch and stack. (*National Bureau of Standards.*)

At the center of the stack is a core of air which is dragged along with the water by friction and for which a source of supply must be provided, if excessive pressure reductions in the stack are to be avoided. The usual means of supplying this air is through the stack vent, as the portion of the stack above the highest fixture connection is called (see Fig. 22-1). The sucking of the air into the stack requires that a pressure reduction exist inside the stack at its upper end, and this pressure reduction is provided by the frictional effect of the falling sheet of water in dragging the core of air along with it.

If the falling sheet of water passes a stack fitting during its fall, some of the water may be thrown out into the core of air as a result of the sheet of water striking the lower edge of the side inlet of the stack fitting. Thus there will frequently be irregular masses of water falling through the central core of air. This water will ultimately return to the sheet flowing down the wall if the distance of fall is sufficiently great, say between one and two stories, at least.

If the sheet of water falling down the stack passes another stack fitting through which the discharge from a fixture is entering the stack, the water from the branch mixes with or deflects the rapidly moving sheet of water. Whichever way we picture the process, an excess pressure in the drain from which the water is entering the stack is required to deflect or mix with the sheet of water flowing downward, and the result is that a back pressure is set up in the branch, which increases with the rate and velocity of flow down the stack and with the rate of flow out of the drain. This problem will be discussed in more detail in Chap. 25.

This type of interference of flows is shown in Fig. 22-2. Here water is flowing down the stack from higher levels, and water is entering the stack from the drain on the right. The shadows in the picture give an idea of the interference of the two flows. This interference causes the water to boil into the entrance of the left-hand branch. Note the level of the meniscus in the manometer tube—near the top of the picture—showing the considerable back pressure developed.

5. Flow in the Building Drain. When the sheet of water reaches the bend at the bottom of the stack and is turned at approximately right angles into the building drain, if the thickness of the sheet of water is not too great, the sheet will make the turn without leaving the wall of the pipe, even at the top elements of the cross section. However, after it has traveled a distance equal to a few diameters in the drain, it will have left the upper part of the cross section and will flow at high velocity along the lower part of the cross section (see

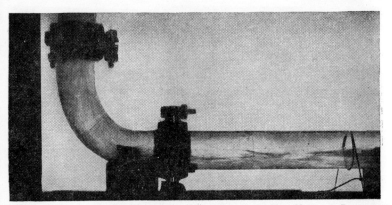

Fig. 22-3. Flow around glass bend at bottom of stack. (*National Bureau of Standards.*)

Fig. 22-3). Obviously the slope of the building drain will not be adequate to maintain the velocity that existed in the sheet when it reached the bottom of the stack. The result is that the velocity of the water flowing along the building drain and sewer decreases slowly with a corresponding increase in the wetted cross section, until a point is reached at which the depth of flow increases suddenly, often sufficiently to fill the cross section of the drain. This phenomenon is called a *hydraulic jump* (see Fig. 22-4). The drain may then tend to flow full in the downstream direction, large bubbles of air moving along with the

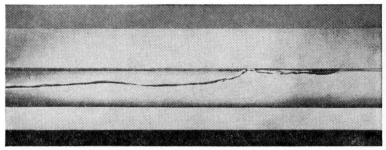

Fig. 22-4. Hydraulic jump in glass building drain. (*National Bureau of Standards.*)

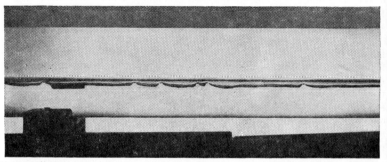

Fig. 22-5. Flow in building drain 108 drain diameters from stack. (*National Bureau of Standards.*)

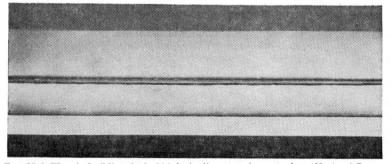

Fig. 22-6. Flow in building drain 324 drain diameters from stack. (*National Bureau of Standards.*)

water at the top of the section. Often, however, particularly if the drain is large enough to carry the flow adequately, the cross section will be filled at the point of the jump by what might be called the "rebound" of the water; but, if the drain will carry the discharge without filling the pipe, the water will fall away from the upper part of the cross section, and the drain will flow but partly full from that point on. Conditions at sections considerable distances downstream for the same flow conditions shown in Figs. 22-3 and 22-4 are shown in Figs. 22-5 and 22-6.

Any blocking of the cross section of the building drain or sewer will have an important effect on the pneumatic pressures in the lower part of the stack. A similar effect will be produced if the street sewer is flowing so full that the end of the building drain is flooded, so that air carried along with the water in the drain cannot pass freely into the street sewer.

6. Pneumatic Pressure Conditions in Stack and Building Drain. So far we have discussed mainly the flow of waste water in the drainage system from the individual fixtures to the street sewer. We now undertake a brief consideration of the pneumatic pressures in the stack and drain. We consider first the pressure conditions in a stack and in a building drain in which the water does not fill the cross section anywhere, so that the air can flow reasonably freely along with the water. We shall assume that waste water is entering the stack from a horizontal branch high up on the stack but that the flow from the drain does not fill the cross section of the stack at the level of entry. The water flowing down the wall of the stack drags air with it by friction and carries it through the building drain and sewer to the street sewer, which it enters freely if the building sewer is not submerged by the flow in the street sewer. When the air stream passes along the building drain and sewer, the conditions are somewhat different, for then the air is partly in contact with the moving stream of water under it and the stationary wall of the pipe above it, so that its movement will be somewhat retarded, and there will be a tendency for a positive pneumatic pressure to build up.

If air is to enter the top of the stack to replace that which is being carried along with the water, there must be a pressure reduction inside the stack. This pressure reduction is very small, however, amounting to only a small fraction of an inch head of water, considering the head loss necessary to accelerate the air and also to provide for the energy loss at the entrance. What causes appreciable pressure reductions is the partial or complete blocking of the stack by water flowing into the stack from a horizontal branch. The magnitude that these pressure reductions can attain is shown in Fig. 22-7 [22-1].* It can be seen from the figure that the pressure reduction reaches a maximum value a few feet below the level at which the water enters the stack and then decreases gradually. Under the conditions of Dawson and Kalinske's tests, the pressure reached atmospheric about halfway down the stack and then became increasingly a pressure increase toward the base of the stack. The pressure increase was due to some sort of blocking of the air flow in the building drain, and its effect extended for some distance back up the stack. The authors state: "Tests showed that if for any reason the house drain or sewer was submerged, or became entirely filled during flow of water down the stack, the pressures near the bottom of the stack rose to extremely high values. For instance, the pressure at the bottom of the 3-inch stack and in the house drain itself was about 45 inches of water for a rate of flow of 50 gallons per minute when the house sewer was submerged and without vents."

In view of the fact that pressures in the stack must be kept within about 1 in. of water above or below atmospheric pressure at the points where fixture drains

* Numbers in brackets refer to the bibliography at the end of the book.

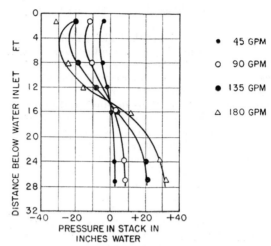

Fig. 22-7. Pneumatic pressures in stack below point of water entry.

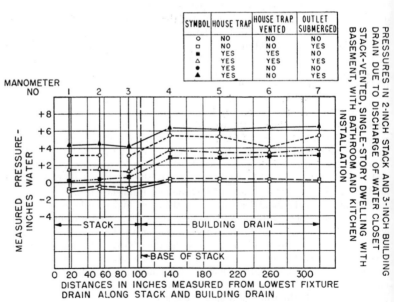

Fig. 22-8. Pneumatic pressures in 2-in. stack and 3-in. building drain due to discharge of a water closet.

enter the stack if the trap seals are to protect the interior of the building from the influx of sewer air, the significance of the foregoing figures is apparent. This consideration is extremely important in deciding upon the order in which the fixture drains from the water closet, bathtub, lavatory, and kitchen sink shall connect with the stack in a stack-vented system.

A small increase in pneumatic pressure will occur in the building drain or building sewer even if there is no complete blocking of the air flow by a hydraulic jump or by submergence of the outlet end of the building sewer. This is due to the decrease in the cross section available for air flow when the water flowing in the drain has adapted itself to the slope and diameter of the drain. This effect is shown in Fig. 22-8, taken from experimental work by Wyly at the National Bureau of Standards on a system consisting of two 2-in. stacks and a 3-in. building drain [22-2]. Unfortunately similar data on 3-in. stacks or larger are not available, but the principles involved will be shown just as clearly from the results on the 2-in. stack.

If there is a running trap in the building drain or if the street sewer submerges the outlet of the building sewer, a large positive pressure will be created in the building drain when a sudden discharge comes down the stack. This can be relieved to a considerable extent by a vent near the bottom of the stack. If a running trap is used, then this should be vented at its inlet end. Even then a considerable pressure is created in the drain when the discharge from a water closet strikes the inlet end of the running trap. Water from the discharge of a toilet on the second floor has been seen to jump up through the running trap vent to a height of at least six feet when the surge struck the inlet end of the trap.

7. Flow in Fixture Drains. The flow in a fixture drain requires special consideration. Here a single fixture discharges through a drain, with a trap between the fixture and the drain. In one sense the determination of the size of drain required is a relatively simple problem, since the fixture drain need be adequate to carry the discharge only from the fixture to which it is attached. However, because of the problem of self-siphonage (see Chap. 27), it is advisable to select the diameter of the drain so large that computations indicate that it should flow little more than half full under the maximum discharge that is likely to be imposed on it by the fixture.

Nevertheless, with a fixture drain we cannot, as we can with the building drain and sewer, simply compute the size of pipe that is required to carry the design load at not more than half depth. A lavatory drain, for example, that is capable of carrying the same steady rate of flow that we take as the load from a lavatory may still flow full over part or all of its length. There are several reasons for this. The vertical component of the flow out of the trap into the drain tends to make the water attach itself to the upper elements of the drain, and once attached there, the water is reluctant to release its hold. The result is that, if there is not sufficient air aspirated through the overflow, the pipe will flow full for part of its length, the average velocity of flow being less than the normal velocity for that rate of flow in the given drain at its given slope.

Furthermore, if the drain is connected to the stack with a long-turn tee-wye, the stream of water striking the fitting is apt to close off the entire cross section.

If the fixture considered is a water closet, the surge of water from the closet will continue almost without change even along a very long drain until it reaches the stack. Tests with a 3-in. transparent water-closet drain at the National Bureau of Standards showed this to be the case, even when the drain was 32 ft long and had a right-angled bend in it [22-3, page 27].

Thus it can be assumed for all practical purposes that the surge caused by the discharge of a water closet through a fixture drain reaches the stack or a horizontal branch with practically the same peak it had when it left the fixture. There is no appreciable flattening of this type of surge in this part of the drainage system (see Table 26-2), page 26–12.

8. Flattening of Surges in Stack and Building Drain. Considerable flattening of the surges takes place, however, in the stack and building drain. The late Dr. Roy B. Hunter at the National Bureau of Standards conducted experiments on this phenomenon [22-4]. His results are given in Table 26-3, page 26–13.

This flattening has an important effect on the capacities of the primary and secondary branches of the building drains in a large building covering a considerable ground area. This effect was taken into account in the loading tables of the Plumbing Manual, BMS66 [22-5].

CHAPTER 23

Demand and Discharge Rates of Plumbing Fixtures

23.1 Introduction

The average values of the volume of discharge, rate of discharge, and time of discharge for one operation of a plumbing fixture are fundamental to any attempt to establish design loads. Two investigations of this subject made by the National Bureau of Standards for the Housing and Home Finance Agency have been reported in recent years but have been published only in abbreviated form by the latter agency [23-1, 23-2, 23-3].*

There are so many variables that affect the demand and drainage loads imposed on a plumbing system by the various kinds of fixtures that the best that can be done is to determine average characteristic values for these quantities.

The only fixtures that are relatively free from the influence of these many variables are those which are wholly automatic in their action or which operate automatically once they have been put in operation by someone. Even these are dependent upon the line pressure and upon their adjustment.

23.2 Lavatories

The discharge pattern of a lavatory is dependent on the length, diameter, and slope of the fixture drain, on the type of stack fitting used, on the type and diameter of the trap, on the height of the overflow connection to the tail pipe or on the absence of such an opening if the lavatory has no overflow, on the diameter of the outlet orifice, on the type of plug used, on the size and shape of the lavatory, and on the volume of water in the lavatory.

It was concluded by Wyly and Hintz [23-2, page 45] from their tests at the National Bureau of Standards that good average values of the discharge rate of lavatories filled to the overflow is 10 gpm for $1\frac{3}{8}$-in. outlet orifices and 7.5 gpm for $1\frac{1}{8}$-in. outlet orifices. The rates for lavatories without overflows are much greater than these values, because the absence of an overflow connection results in there being a subatmospheric pressure in the tailpiece at the level where the overflow opening is ordinarily located, instead of atmospheric pressure, so that the head tending to produce flow out of the lavatory is greater than it would be if there were an overflow opening.

Tests show that the diameter of the outlet orifice almost entirely controls the rate of discharge of the lavatory. Wyly and Hintz showed that the exact form and size of the trap, drain, and tailpiece and the height of the orifice above the

---

* Numbers in brackets refer to the bibliography at the end of the book.

trap weir had only small effects on the average rate of discharge, the extreme values obtained in their tests on a given lavatory having a 1⅜-in. orifice being 9.96 and 10.18 gpm, when the lavatory was filled to the level of the overflow. In these tests numerous changes were made in the trap, drain, and length of tailpiece.

The volume of water contained in a lavatory filled to the overflow can be taken as about 1.5 gal, on the average. The time of emptying, then, will be 9 and 12 sec, respectively, for 1⅜- and 1⅛-in. orifices, respectively.

The lavatory is often used without the plug; that is, the water is allowed to run continuously at a low rate until the ablutions are finished. A rate of flow of 3 gpm appears to be about the maximum rate that is suitable for use in this way, if trouble from splashing is to be avoided. An average period of such use will be assumed as 15 sec. Then the average volume drawn at each such use would be ¾ gal.

Wyly and Hintz found that the average rate of flow from lavatories and bathtubs could be expressed fairly well by the formula

$$q = 4.33A \sqrt{h} \tag{23-1}$$

where q = rate of discharge, gpm
  A = effective area of the outlet orifice, sq in.
  h = vertical distance from water surface to level of overflow connection, in.

The tests showed that the presence of the crossbar strainers in lavatories had little effect on the rate of flow but that, with laundry trays and bathtubs, the projected area of the crossbars must be deducted from the cross-sectional area of the orifice.

23.3 Bathtubs

The tests made at the National Bureau of Standards to determine the effect of different factors on the discharge curve of a bathtub were made mainly on a 5-ft Master Pembroke enameled cast-iron recessed bathtub with a 1½-in. orifice outlet. A similar tub with a 2-in. orifice outlet was also used. Only P traps were used in the tests.

Owing to the location of the overflow opening into the drain, the vertical distance between the orifice outlet and the trap weir has practically no effect on the discharge curve for the tub. Neither does the exact form of trap used appear to have any appreciable effect. The discharge curve found for a round-bottomed tub, which was tested for comparison with the Master Pembroke, when the same volume of water was discharged, differed only slightly from that of the Master Pembroke.

Discharge curves for the Master Pembroke tubs with 1½-in. orifice and 2-in. orifice are shown in Fig. 23-1. The drain was 1½ in. in diameter (nominal) in the one case and 2 in. in diameter in the other. The drains were 4 ft long and were laid at a slope of ¼ in. per ft. In each test, 40 gal of water was discharged, the initial depth being 10 in.

The average rates of flow found for this type of bathtub are given in Table 23.1.

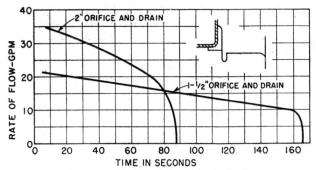

Fig. 23-1. Discharge curves for bathtub.

Table 23.1

Diameter of orifice and waste (in.)	Initial depth of water in tubs, measured from outlet orifice (in.)	Average rate of flow during discharge (gpm)
1½	10	14.0
1½	6	12.4
1½	4	11.1
2	10	25.2
2	6	22.3
2	4	19.9

Wyly and Hintz recommend the following characteristic values to be used for bathtubs when computing design loads [23-2]:

For orifice outlet 1½ in. in diameter:

Average discharge rate.......... 12 gpm
Volume discharged.............. 21 gal
Initial depth.................. 6 in.
Discharge period............... 1.7 min

For orifice outlet 2 in. in diameter:

Average discharge rate.............. 23 gpm
Discharge period.................... 0.9 min
Other quantities same as for.......... 1½ in.

23.4 Laundry Tubs

Typical data on laundry trays obtained from tests at the National Bureau of Standards follow [23-2]. Discharge tests on a 24- by 20-in. tray with 1½-in.-diameter outlet orifice and containing 16.2 gal of water (depth 12 in.) gave an average rate of discharge of 19.6 gpm, and the time of discharge was 49.8 sec when a 1½-in. drain 2 ft long and laid at a slope of ¼ in. per ft was used. A 1½-in. tailpiece and a cast-iron P trap were used. The stack fitting was a sanitary tee (see Fig. 23-2). When a 2-in. drain was substituted for the 1½-in.

drain, everything else remaining unchanged, the average rate of flow was 26.0 gpm, and the duration of the discharge was 26.0 sec. The use of a 1½-in. two-piece tubing trap in place of the cast-iron trap increased the rate of flow by about 10 per cent.

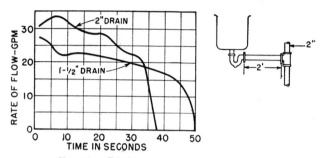

Fig. 23-2. Discharge curves for laundry tray.

Tests to determine the effect of increasing the vertical distance between the trap weir to the level of the outlet orifice from the 4.5 in. used in the tests reported above showed that the effect could be represented by the equation

$$q_1 = q_2 \sqrt{\frac{h_1}{h_2}} \tag{23-2}$$

where q_1 and q_2 are the average rates of flow corresponding to the heights h_1 and h_2, respectively, of the outlet orifice above the trap weir. Tests were run with these heights varying from 4.5 to 10.4 in.

As a result of their tests, Wyly and Hintz recommend the following characteristic values for laundry trays with 1½-in. orifice outlets:

$$
\begin{array}{ll}
\text{Average flow rate}\dots\dots\dots\dots & \text{16 gpm} \\
\text{Volume of discharge}\dots\dots\dots & \text{9.5 gal} \\
\text{Time of discharge}\dots\dots\dots\dots & \text{35 sec}
\end{array}
$$

23.5   Sinks

The usual type of sink has two construction features that make it possible for its rate of flow to be unusually high. The first is the fact that the sink has no overflow passage connecting into the tailpiece below the outlet orifice, as is customary with bathtubs and lavatories. As a result, the head tending to produce outflow from the sink is measured from the water surface in the sink to approximately the level of the trap weir, depending somewhat on the conditions of flow in the fixture drain. Thus, there is a relatively high head acting on the water in the sink.

The second factor, which is peculiar to sinks, is the removable basket strainer which can be used to change the effective diameter of the outlet orifice. If this strainer is removed when the sink is discharging, a very high rate of outflow is obtained. On the other hand, if the basket strainer is left in place, the rate of discharge is very much less, considerably less than when a flat strainer is used.

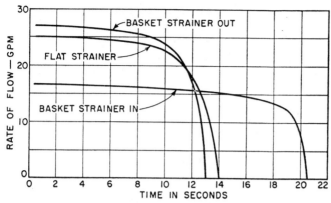

Fig. 23-3. Discharge curves for sink.

Discharge curves for three different conditions at the outflow orifice are shown in Fig. 23-3 for an American Standard P-7020 sink, 24 by 16 in., vertical distance from orifice outlet to level of trap weir 12 in., 1½-in. cast elbow trap, drain 1 ft long on slope of ¼ in. per ft, stack fitting a 2- by 1½-in. long-turn tee-wye. The average rates of flow and the times of flow for a discharge of this sink under the conditions represented in Fig. 23-3 are as given in Table 23-2.

Table 23.2

Condition	Avg rate of flow (gpm)	Time of discharge (sec)
Basket strainer out............	24.5	13.0
Basket strainer in.............	15.6	20.5
Flat strainer.................	22.8	14.0

The flat strainer used in one of the foregoing tests was American Standard B987 with a removable perforated grid for sinks with a 3½-in. outlet. The grid contained 43 holes, each ¼ in. in diameter. The outlet had a 1½-in. tailpiece. The basket strainer used is shown in Fig. 23-4.

Decreasing the vertical distance from the outlet orifice of the sink to the level of the trap weir from 12 to 6 in. decreased the average rate of flow with basket strainer out from 24.5 gpm to 18.9 gpm. The equation

$$q_1 = q_2 \sqrt{\frac{h_1}{h_2}} \tag{23-2}$$

can be used to predict approximately the effect of changing this vertical distance.

Tests made with different traps showed that the average rate of flow was affected less than 5 per cent by changing traps. This statement applies, of course, only to P traps 1½ in. in diameter. Changes in the slope of drains up

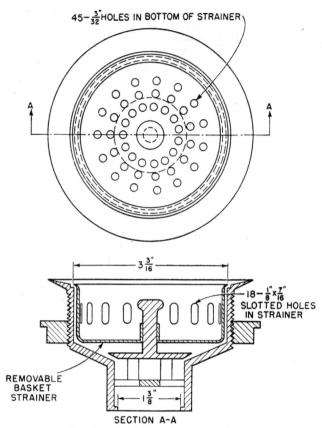

FIG. 23-4. Basket strainer used in tests.

to 8 ft long used with this sink also showed an effect of not over 5 per cent.   The range of slopes tested was $\frac{1}{32}$ to $\frac{1}{4}$ in. per ft.

As a result of these and other tests not reported here, Wyly and Hintz recommend the adoption of the following quantities for sinks for the purpose of computing design loads:

$$
\begin{aligned}
&\text{Average rate of flow}\ldots\ldots\ldots\ 22 \text{ gpm} \\
&\text{Volume of discharge}\ldots\ldots\ldots\ \ 5.5 \text{ gal} \\
&\text{Time of discharge}\ldots\ldots\ldots\ldots\ 15 \text{ sec}
\end{aligned}
$$

23.6   Combination Fixtures

In recent years there has been a marked tendency to use combination fixtures, such as double-compartment sinks and combination sink-and-laundry-tray fixtures.   With these fixtures it is customary to tie the waste from one compartment into the waste line of the other compartment just above the trap, so that the trap serves both compartments (see Fig. 23-5).

This arrangement has one result that does not occur with a single-compartment fixture. If one compartment of the combination fixture is discharged with the stopper of the other compartment out, this reduces the head acting to produce outflow to the vertical distance from the outflow orifice to the level of the opening of the waste from the compartment not discharging into the vertical leg of the waste from the compartment discharging. If the stopper is

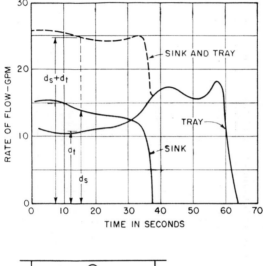

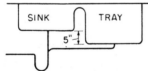

Fig. 23-5. Discharge curves for combination sink and tray.

in place, on the other hand, then the head is measured from the outflow orifice to approximately the level of the trap weir. This peculiarity of combination fixtures adds to the complexity of the flow conditions that are possible with such fixtures.

Wyly and Hintz at the National Bureau of Standards tested an American Standard cast-iron enameled 42- by 20-in. combination sink-and-tray fixture No. P-7415. The tray was 5 in. deeper than the sink compartment. The waste from the sink passed directly down into the trap, and the waste from the tray was brought into the vertical waste from the sink somewhat above the level of the outlet of the trap. The sloping fixture drain extended 2 ft beyond the trap, there being a 90° bend midway of the drain. The stack fitting was a long-turn tee-wye. Table 23-3 gives the results of some of the discharge tests conducted on this combination fixture:

Table 23.3   Discharge Rates for Combination Sink-and-Tray Fixtures.   American Standard P-7415

Compartment discharged	Total volume discharged (gal)	Vertical distance from orifice to trap weir (in.) sink	Basket strainer	Discharge period (sec)		Approximate peak rate of flow (gpm)			Average rate of flow (gpm)		
				Sink	Tray	Sink	Tray	Both	Sink	Tray	Both
Sink.............	8.4	19.7	In	56.8	....	12.2	....	....	8.9		
	8.4	19.7	In	56.4	....	12.2	....	....	8.9+		
	8.4	19.7	Removed	19.0	....	31.0	....	....	26.6		
	8.4	13.7	Removed	20.7	....	31.0	....	....	24.4		
Tray.............	13.5	19.7[1]	Removed	....	43.8	....	25.0	....	....	18.5	
	13.5	13.7[1]	Removed	....	48.8	....	25.0	....	....	16.7	
Sink and tray.......	21.9	19.7	Removed	31.7	56.0	17.6	20.8	30.4	15.9	14.5	29.5[2]
	21.9	13.7	Removed	37.5	63.8	15.2	18.0	26.4	13.4	12.7	24.8

[1] Outlet orifice of tray 5 in. lower than that of sink.
[2] Based on period of discharge from sink compartment.

If one compartment is discharged with the other compartment empty and its plug out, then the elevation of the drain has practically no effect on the rate of discharge.   However, if, instead, the stopper is left in, the orifice of the compartment not being discharged, then the elevation of the drain has a considerable effect.   Likewise, if both compartments are discharged simultaneously, the elevation of the drain has an appreciable effect on the rate of discharge.   The reason for this is, of course, that, when the stopper is out of the compartment not being discharged, an atmospheric pressure exists at the point where the drain from the compartment not discharging connects to the drain from the compartment that is discharging, and this controls the head tending to produce flow out of the compartment, regardless of the elevation of the drain beyond this point.

23.7   Water Closets

1. **Flushing Characteristics.**   The discharge of a water closet is a complicated hydraulic phenomenon.   Because the discharge of this fixture is produced by an inflow of water controlled by a flush tank or a flush valve, the nature of the discharge or flush is a function of the closet and the flushing device considered as a unit, not of either alone.   Consequently, in order to produce a flush that will be, on the one hand, adequate to remove the contents of the bowl completely, and on the other hand, economical in its use of water, the flushing device and the closet must be designed for use as a unit and, when a flush valve is used, must be adjusted to give the most effective results at the prevailing pressure in the supply line.

The water closet is the only commonly used plumbing fixture that depends on self-siphonage (see Fig. 23-6).   Initially the water in the bowl stands substantially at the weir crest.   When the flushing device is tripped, water enters the bowl through the rim passage and orifices, washing down the interior surface of the bowl, and also through the jet chamber and orifice in those bowls which utilize the jet.   The jet is directed into the upleg of the siphon and, by mixing with the water in the leg, imparts momentum to this water in the direction of discharge, thus tending to produce a quick priming of the siphon.

Successive stages in the flushing operation are shown in Figs. 23-6A, B, and C.   Figure 23-6A shows the situation just after the flush has started.   Water is entering the bowl through the rim orifices and through the jet orifice.   The water level has increased slightly above the initial level, and water is flowing over the weir at a slow but increasing rate.   This sheet of water carries air with it as a result of friction from the siphon, and the downleg of the siphon is so shaped that this sheet of water closes the entire cross section of the downleg, thereby preventing the backflow of air up this leg to replace the air that is carried out by the sheet of water.   As a result, the initial air space in the siphon is quickly filled with water, and the siphon begins to act, discharging water from the bowl at a much faster rate than it enters the bowl.   This condition is shown in Fig. 23-6B.

At this stage of the flush all the water initially in the bowl should have been removed, and the water remaining in the bottom of the bowl should have come from the flushing device during this operation.   The water level in the bowl has now fallen below the upper wall of the trap at the entrance, and air passes up the leg of the trap, as shown in Fig. 23-6C, breaking the siphon and reducing the rate of flow sharply. Then part of the water in the upleg of this siphon reverses its direction and flows back into the bottom of the bowl, partially refilling it, and still further refill comes from the slowly ceasing inflow from the flushing device.

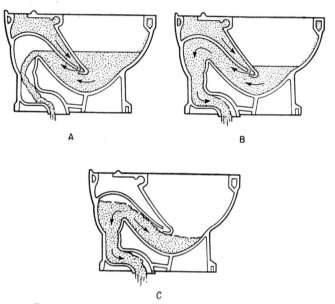

A   B

C

FIG. 23-6. Stages in the flushing of a water-closet bowl.

The entire operation occupies a time interval of, say, 9 to 15 sec, depending on the bowl and the flushing device used. If a flush valve is used, the time of its operation is practically the same as that of the bowl. If a flush tank is used instead, its time of emptying is practically the same as that of the operation of the bowl, but, after the flushing action has ceased, the tank requires 1 to 2 min to refill, because the rate of inflow to the tank is much less than the maximum rate of flow through the flush valve. As a consequence of this, the individual lines supplying flush valves must be considerably larger in diameter than those leading to flush tanks.

A great deal of consideration has been given as to what constitutes an adequate flush. For very low constant rates of flow into the bowl, the sheet of water falling through the downleg of the siphon is not able to close off the cross section of the downleg of the siphon, and the water simply spills steadily over the weir of the siphon, as shown in Fig. 23-6A. As the constant rate of inflow is increased, siphon action starts, as described above, but the rate of supply to the bowl is not at first sufficient to maintain the siphon action. As a result of this, intermittent siphon action occurs, the level of the water in the bowl rising and falling periodically. If the inflow is controlled by a flush valve or a flush tank, and if rate of flow during the first part of the flushing action is only sufficient to maintain this intermittent siphon action, this may result in a rate-of-flow curve having two peaks, the completion of the flushing action occurring before any further peaks can occur (see Fig. 23-7) [23-4]. This type of discharge curve does not yield a good flush.

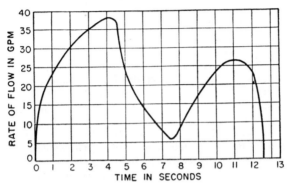

FIG. 23-7. Discharge curve for water-closet bowl.

If now the constant rate of inflow is increased still further, a point will be reached at which the inflow is sufficient to maintain steady siphon action, and the water level in the bowl falls until it is lower than the lip of the siphon. At this point air passes into the upleg of the siphon and halts its action. This condition gives the best flush.

Now, if the constant rate of inflow is raised above the value that produces the condition described in the preceding paragraph, the water level in the bowl builds up in order to provide an additional head to increase the rate of flow through the siphon, and effective cleansing action does not occur.

The following is quoted from "Recommended Minimum Requirements for Plumbing" [23-4, pages 79, 80]:

"The most certain and efficient cleansing of the water-closet bowl occurs when there is a strong siphon action in the first two or three seconds, followed by a period of weak or broken siphon action, during which the bowl is practically empty, and this in turn is followed by a second siphon action. These characteristics appear in the rate curves as a maximum point on from the second to the fourth second, followed by a minimum or decided tendency toward a minimum point, followed by a second point lower than the first. The curves showing these maxima and minima points as described are indicative of strong efficient flushes.

"If the rate of supply is too low, a complete break in the siphon action occurs, and in extreme cases the minimum point approaches zero while the bowl is refilling, following the first siphon action. The result is an uncertain and sluggish flush. If the rate of supply is too high, the siphon action becomes continuous with the bowl partially filled until the end of the flush. This may result in paper and fecal matter being floated in the bowl to settle at the bottom, or at best to be drawn into the trap at the end of the flush, and in an incomplete refill, due to the flush ending with a strong siphon action.   The curves showing a single maximum, with no tendency toward a minimum point are indicative of rates of supply that are too high for the best results.   The dividing line appears to be that which permits the discharge to drop from a maximum to an approximately constant rate of flow.   A rate lower than this permits the formation of a minimum.   A rate higher than this gives a continuous rate of discharge approximately equal to the maximum, which drops abruptly at the end of the discharge. The conclusion, therefore, is that a rate of supply that does not permit the formation of a minimum is unnecessarily high.''

As regards the quantity of water, the rate of flow, and the time of flow, Hunter has the following to say [23-4, page 81]:

"It is impossible to fix a definite value for either the rate of supply or the total quantity of water required which will give the best results for water-closets. These will vary with different bowls and conditions.   There are, however, pretty definite limits within which the serviceable rates for all water-closets employed in these tests, and we believe all water-closets that should be approved for general use, fall.   A study of the curves of discharge given will show that for washdown closets the curves indicating a strong efficient flush were obtained when the mean rate of discharge and approximately the mean rate of supply was between 27 and 30 gallons per minute.   For siphon-jet closets the range is between 24 and 36 gallons per minute.   This gives a mean value of approximately 30 gallons per minute as a rate of supply that, in general, will be satisfactory for either type of closet bowl.   The quantity of water depends on the duration of the flush.   The time varies from 6 to 10 seconds, the lower rate of supply requiring, in general, the longer time.   Considering this in connection with the curves of discharge indicates a range of from 3 to 5 gallons as a serviceable quantity.''

Thomas R. Camp, at the Massachusetts Institute of Technology, does not agree with the conclusions of Hunter as to the best form of rate curve for an efficient flush.   As a result of experiments that he conducted for the Massachusetts State Association of Master Plumbers [23-5], he writes the following:

" . . . much time was spent during the early part of the Institute program studying unsteady flow in an effort to produce an ideal rate curve for a flush. It was found desirable in these studies to use flush valves to furnish the supply. The supply was thus furnished at a variable rate during the flush, but not at a rate that could be made to vary in any desired manner.   Changes in the shape of the rate curve were made by adjustments of the flush valve, by changes in the static pressure, or by throttling the supply line by means of the flow regulating valve. . . .

"In these experiments with unsteady flow, no evidence was found to support the findings of Hunter and Snyder that a second peak in the rate curve is desirable.   Efforts to produce a second peak were uniformly unsuccessful with the bowls and flush valves experimented with, but adequate flushes were produced over a wide range of operating conditions with rate curves having a single peak.''

Much of Camp's experimental work was published in Progress in Plumbing Research at the Massachusetts Institute of Technology, Proceedings of the Fifth Conference of the Massachusetts State Association of Master Plumbers, 1931, and in a paper, Plumbing Research at the Massachusetts Institute of

Technology, Proceedings of the Sixth Master Plumbers Conference at the Massachusetts Institute of Technology, 1932.

Camp then proceeded to conduct further tests, using constant rates of supply to the bowl. Of the results of these tests, he writes the following:

"Adequate cleansing of all the bowls studied was accomplished with a constant rate of inflow just sufficient to maintain steady siphon action, provided this rate of flow was maintained for a sufficient time to permit the water surface to be drawn to the bottom of the bowl and to remain there long enough for the last of the original bowl contents to pass up the siphon leg. Paper upon the water surface was used as an index to cleansing, and cleansing was pronounced effective when the paper sheets were removed. A rate of flush just sufficient to maintain steady siphon action is accompanied by a water level at or near the bottom of the bowl with steady flow conditions. Hence with a reducing rate of flow, there is danger that the siphon may break before the water level reaches the bottom of the bowl, unless the rate is sufficiently high at the start of the flush, so that it will not be reduced below that required for steady siphon action until the flush is ended.

"The superiority of a constant rate of supply to a variable rate was demonstrated in comparing the rate curves obtained with a quick-opening valve with those obtained by means of a flush valve using the same bowl. The best flush that was obtained with a flush valve on this bowl required 3.19 gallons and a maximum rate of discharge from the bowl of 39.4 gallons per minute. With the quick-opening valve an adequate flush could be obtained with a constant rate of supply of 18 gpm for a period of 9 seconds, a total of 2.7 gallons. The rated "safe economic flush" for this bowl is 20 gallons per minute for 9 seconds, and trial flushes of this size produced a maximum rate of discharge *from* the bowl of about 30 gallons per minute and a total quantity of 3 gallons."

Table 23.4 presents characteristic data for seven water-closet bowls tested by

Table 23.4   Characteristics of Water-closet Bowls Tested by Camp

Type of bowl	Maximum diameter of passing trapway (in.)	Trap-seal depth (in.)	Safe economic time of supply (sec)	Quantity of flush (gal)	Rate of flow (supply) (gpm)	Peak discharge (gpm)
Washdown, siphon action with jet, rear inlet....	$1\frac{3}{4}$	$3\frac{1}{8}$	9.0	3.00	20.0	34.0
Washdown, siphon action with jet, rear inlet....	$1\frac{3}{4}$	$2\frac{7}{8}$	7.5	2.81	22.5	38.0
Reverse trap, siphon action with jet, inlet....	$1\frac{3}{4}$	$2\frac{3}{8}$	8.0	2.40	18.0	30.0
Washdown, siphon action with jet, spiral rim flow, rear inlet........	$1\frac{3}{4}$	$2\frac{5}{8}$	11.0	5.90	32.0	46.0
Siphon jet with two jet orifices, top inlet......	$2\frac{5}{8}$	$2\frac{3}{4}$	7.5	3.44	27.5	47.0
Siphon jet, top inlet.....	$2\frac{3}{8}$	$2\frac{7}{8}$	8.0	3.86	29.0	46.0
Siphon jet, top inlet.....	$2\frac{1}{8}$	$3\frac{3}{8}$	8.0	3.60	27.0	46.0

Camp, illustrating the characteristics of bowls commercially available at the time his tests were conducted (early thirties). The results show what can be done by the use of a constant rate of supply instead of the usual flushing devices with their variable rate of flow.

Wyly and Hintz at the National Bureau of Standards conducted a series of tests on water-closet bowls for the Housing and Home Finance Agency to determine what performance might be expected of present-day bowls when used with the usual flush tanks and flush valves [23-1, 23-2]. The purpose of the tests was to determine the relative effects of certain factors on the flow characteristics of the bowls. No measurements were made to determine efficiency of flushing.

2. Rate-of-discharge Curves Obtained with Two Different Bowls When Flush Tank Is Used. An American Standard Ejecto siphon vortex back-connected bowl was compared with a Crane Maurton reverse trap with jet bowl. The tank used in each case was an American Standard low-type tank with an American Standard B-1942 Water Control ball cock. The results of the comparison are shown in Fig. 23-8 and in Table 23.5. The data given are the averages of three successive tests.

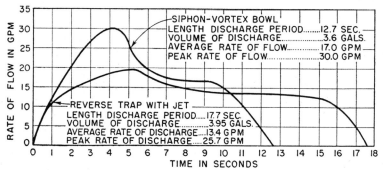

FIG. 23-8. Discharge curves for two different types of water-closet bowls with same low-hung back-connected flush tank.

Table 23.5

	Siphon vortex	Reverse trap
Average volume of discharge, gal.....	3.59	3.96
Average period of discharge, sec......	12.7	17.7
Average rate of flow, gpm............	16.95	13.42
Peak rate of flow, gpm..............	30	20

The two bowls exhibited rate curves of the same general shape, but the reverse-trap bowl gave a much lower peak and a longer period of discharge than did the siphon-jet bowl. The maxima given here are less than those cited in the source, since in the latter the value taken was that yielded by the highest of the three rate curves, these being averaged to provide a single curve here. In each group of three identical tests, the individual readings from which the rate curves were plotted agreed very well.

3. Effect of Supply-line Pressure on Quantity of Water Discharged through Flush Tank. When a flush tank is operated, some inflow from the supply line occurs while the tank is still discharging, so that the actual volume discharged is greater than the volume of water held by the tank. Because of this, there is a tendency for the volume discharged by a flush tank to be a little greater at high line pressures than at low pressures. To test this, the experimenters used a Crane Santonia close-coupled elongated siphon-jet type of bowl with a Crane low-type tank with a 2-in. outlet and an Indiana on-siphon ball cock. Line pressures of 30 and 70 psi (fixture not operating) were used. The comparative data obtained as a result of several identical tests are shown in Table 23.6.

Table 23.6

	Line pressure	
	30 psi	70 psi
Average volume of discharge, gal.............	4.32	4.53
Average discharge period, sec................	11.7	12.2
Average rate of discharge, gpm..............	22.2	22.3
Peak rate of discharge, gpm.................	40–45	40–45

4. Effect of Using Different Ball-cock Assemblies. A Crane Drexyl elongated siphon-jet bowl was used to study this matter. One of the ball cocks used was an elevated compound-lever type, similar to American Standard model B-1944. The other was an American Standard model B-1942 Water Control ball cock. The general pattern of the rate curves was found to be the same with these two ball cocks. The data obtained from several repeated tests with these two ball cocks are given in Table 23.7.

Table 23.7

	Elevated compound lever	American Standard Water Control
Average volume of discharge, gal...........	5.13	4.94
Average discharge period, sec..............	17.5	15.3
Average rate of discharge, gpm............	17.6	19.4
Peak rate of discharge, gpm...............	30	30

5. Relative Effect of Type of Supply. To investigate the relative effect on the rate curve of a water-closet bowl using a flush tank or a flush valve, an American Standard Madera siphon-jet bowl was used (1) with a low-type American Standard tank with 2-in. outlet and with an American Standard

B-1942 ball cock and (2) with a Coyne & Delany Presto No. 402 flush valve with 1-in. inlet and 1½ in. outlet. An attempt was made to adjust the flush valve to give the same volume of supply as the flush tank, but this effort was only partly successful, with the result that the flush valve delivered about 8 per cent less water than the flush tank at a line pressure of 30 psi (fixture not operating). The results of these tests (three identical runs with each type of supply) are shown in Fig. 23-9 and in Table 23.8.

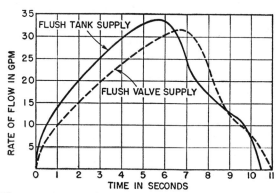

FIG. 23-9. Effect on rate curve for water-closet bowl if using two different types of supply.

Table 23.8

	Flush tank	Flush valve
Average volume of discharge, gal.........	3.65	3.34
Average discharge period, sec............	10.5	10.8
Average rate of flow, gpm................	20.85	17.12
Peak rate of flow, gpm...................	34	31.5

The data indicate that the rate curve for this water-closet bowl is only slightly affected by the type of supply used.

Wyly and Hintz conducted another investigation of water-closet bowls, in this case studying what Camp has called the "safe economic flush," in other words, the minimum flush that can be depended on to cleanse the bowl thoroughly [23-3]. The safe economic flush must be expressed as a rate of flow multiplied by a time, even though the product yields a volume.

In these tests they used a constant rate of flow, following Camp's suggestion as a result of his tests [23-5]. They controlled the rate of flow by installing both a gate valve and a quick-opening valve in the supply line, using the gate valve to give the desired rate of flow with the quick-opening valve wide open.

In these tests the trap of the bowl was filled with water, and a test load consisting of two simulated feces, each about 4 in. long and ¾ in. diameter, and 12 sheets of toilet paper was used. The material used to simulate the feces consisted of asbestos fiber and wood shavings moistened until it had the consistency of putty. The sheets of toilet paper were crumpled in groups of three sheets.

For any given rate of supply, the flush was considered adequate if the contents of the bowl were expelled as soon as, or slightly after, the water surface in the bowl had receded to the lip of the bowl. Tests were run with increasing rates of flow until this occurred, and the smallest flow for which this occurred and the period of flow were taken as the safe economic flush.

Fig. 23-10. Rate meter used in tests at National Bureau of Standards. (*National Bureau of Standards.*)

When an adequate flush had been obtained as described above, for a particular bowl, three consecutive runs were made, using the simulated test load. If all three flushes removed the contents of the bowl satisfactorily, a second series of three test runs was made without a test load, discharging into the rate meter shown in Fig. 23-10. From these runs, the discharge-rate curve for the bowl with constant rate of supply was obtained.

Finally a few of the bowls were tested with low-type flush tanks and with flush valves to determine whether the volume of flush that was found to be adequate when a constant rate of flow was used would also be adequate when the bowl was supplied through the usual flushing devices. The test load was used in these runs. Three consecutive runs were made with each bowl and with each of the two kinds of flushing devices.

In the tests using the tank supply, the tank was filled with the same volume of water that gave a safe economic flush with the bowl tested. When the flush valve was used, the valve was adjusted to give the minimum quantity of water that would flush the bowl adequately.

The results of the foregoing tests are given in Tables 23-9, 23-10, and 23-11. The outstanding fact that appears in Table 23-9 for the constant-rate supply is

Table 23.9   Comparison of Volumes of Water Required for Safe Economic Flushes with Different Methods of Supply

Type of bowl	Type of supply	Volume required (gal)		
		Constant rate	Flush tank	Flush valve
Siphon jet..........	Constant rate	2.55		
	Constant rate	3.30		
	Flush valve	....	....	2.68
Reverse trap........	Constant rate	2.83		
	Constant rate	4.21		
	Constant rate	2.39		
	Tank	....	2.82	
	Tank	....	2.22	
	Flush valve	....	....	3.88
	Flush valve	....	....	2.45
Washdown..........	Constant rate	3.04		
	Constant rate	3.13		
	Tank	....	3.08	
	Flush valve	....	....	4.71
Blowout............	Constant rate	1.86		
	Constant rate	1.94		
	Flush valve	....	....	3.56

the small amount of water required to give an adequate flush with the two blowout bowls tested. In each case the volume required was less than 2 gal. Unfortunately this type of bowl is not designed to operate with a flush tank, because line pressure is required to make the jet function properly. The single blowout bowl tested with a flush valve did not yield such favorable results, since it used 3.56 gal for an adequate flush. Table 23-9 compares the volumes of water required with the different types of bowls and supply devices to give a safe economic flush. Unfortunately the bowls are not all the same for the different supply methods; so the results cannot be taken too literally, since there was an appreciable difference in performance of different bowls of the same type.

The types of supply used in the tests were (1) American Standard low tank equipped with American Standard B-1942 ball-cock assembly and (2) Coyne & Delany Presto No. 402 type SC valve.

Table 23.10   Safe Economic Flushes of Water-closet Bowls with Constant Rate of Supply

Type of bowl	Supply time (sec)	Discharge time (sec)	Time to start siphon (sec)	Time to expel load (sec)	Volume required to flush bowl (gal)	Avg supply rate of flow (gpm)	Avg discharge rate of flow (gpm)	Peak discharge rate of flow (gpm)
Siphon jet..........	6.2	6.8	5.5	6.2	2.55	24.7	23.8	40.6
	8.9	9.7	8.3	8.9	3.30	22.2	21.4	46.7
Reverse trap.......	7.4	8.0	6.2	7.4	2.83	22.9	21.3	38.4
	11.3	11.7	11.2	11.3	4.21	22.3	22.1	33.6
	7.7	8.8	5.0	7.7	2.39	18.6	16.3	25.9
Washdown.........	10.3	11.3	7.0	10.3	3.04	17.7	16.6	30.6
	6.2	7.5	5.3	6.2	3.13	30.3	25.4	49.6
Siphon vortex......	10.9	13.13	12.7	10.9	4.11	22.6	20.2	39.9
Blowout...........	3.7	3.8	....	3.7	1.86	30.1	36.0	58.8
	3.9	4.2	....	3.9	1.94	29.8	30.6	57.5

Table 23.11   Safe Economic Flushes of Water-closet Bowls with Tank and Flushometer Valve Supply

Type of bowl	Type of supply	Time of discharge (sec)	Time to expel load (sec)	Supply required to flush bowl (gal)	Avg discharge rate of flow (gpm)	Peak discharge rate of flow (gpm)
Siphon jet........	Flush valve	6.0	5.4	2.38[1]	39.7	46.9
Reverse trap.....	Tank	9.0	...	2.82	19.4	39.6
	Tank	10.7	...	2.22	13.5	21.1
	Flush valve	7.0	...	3.39[2]	29.1	55.0
	Flush valve	6.0	5.4	2.21[3]	22.1	34.0
Washdown.......	Tank	8.3	...	3.08	23.0	48.4
	Flush valve	10.8	6.5	4.18[4]	23.2	49.5
Blowout.........	Flush valve	7.2	6.4	3.53[5]	29.4	75.5

[1] The flushometer actually delivered 2.68 gal; 0.30 gal was excess trail flow.
[2] The flushometer actually delivered 3.88 gal; 0.49 gal was excess trail flow.
[3] The flushometer actually delivered 2.45 gal; 0.24 gal was excess trail flow.
[4] The flushometer actually delivered 4.71 gal; 0.53 gal was excess trail flow.
[5] The flushometer actually delivered 3.56 gal; 0.03 gal was excess trail flow.

6. Quantity of Water Needed for Flushing—Summary.   It appears from the preceding data that a constant rate of flow during flushing is at least as economical in the use of water as is the variable rate furnished by the conventional supply devices, possibly better.   However, more tests should be made with a greater variety of water-closet bowls and supply devices before any definite conclusion can be ventured.

It seems to be a clear-cut fact, however, that it is possible to flush adequately most of the water-closet bowls in use today in the United States with considerably less water than is ordinarily used. Even though it must be recognized that the line-pressure conditions are never the same in two different installations, and that hence a factor of safety must be used, it is still believed that economies in the use of water with water-closet bowls can be achieved relatively easily. It is a known fact that in European countries water closets are designed to use considerably less water than do the American closets, and apparently they give satisfactory service. Typical volumes of a flush for the British water closets are 2 and 3 gal [23-6]. The best German water closets are even more sparing of water than this, using as little as 1.3 to 1.8 gal per flush [23-7].

As a result of their tests, Wyly and Hintz suggest the following average values for the characteristic performance quantities of American water-closet bowls and flushing devices as manufactured and used today, excluding the blowout type of bowl:

> Volume of discharge.............. 3.8 gal
> Period of discharge.............. 12.8 sec
> Average rate of flow............. 17.8 gpm
> Peak rate of discharge........... 33.4 gpm

23.8 Shower Heads

It is virtually impossible to set characteristic rates of flow or times of use of shower heads, since the rate of flow depends on the line pressure and the setting of the valve and the time of use per bath depends on the bathing characteristics of the user. Hence all that can be done is to set upper limits to these quantities. Tests on two shower heads of widely different capacities gave the results shown in Table 23-12.

Table 23.12

Degree of opening of control valve	Line pressure (psi)	Flow rate (gpm)	
		American Standard B-268	Kohler K-7325
One quarter........	30	9.5	1.6
One half...........	30	11.8	3.6
Wide open.........	30	12.0	4.7
One quarter........	70	15.0	1.8
One half...........	70	14.2	5.1
Wide open.........	70	17.0	5.2

Babbitt [23-8, page 388] recommends providing for a supply of 20 to 35 gpm to a shower head. He also states that a pressure greater than 5 to 10 psi will prove uncomfortable to the bather and that pressures less than 2 to 3 psi may prevent a proper supply of water to a large shower head.

CHAPTER 24

Design Loads for Plumbing Systems

24.1 Introduction

The problem of determining the pipe sizes required for the different parts of the water-distribution and drainage systems in a building resolves itself into two parts: (1) determining what the design load is (i.e., the rate of flow for which a pipe should be designed) and (2), with the design load established, determining what the diameter of the pipe to be used should be. Of course there is also the problem of what material to use for the pipe, but that problem is beyond the scope of this chapter.

The basic problem of determining the design load is the same for the water-distribution system in a building as it is for the drainage system, except that certain constants that specify the load-producing characteristics of the individual fixtures will be different in the two cases. Hence the following discussion is perfectly general, and the distinction will be made between the two systems only when the time comes to assign loading weights or "fixture-unit weights" to the fixtures.

24.2 Determining the Design Loads for the Various Parts of a Plumbing System

This problem is complicated owing to the fact that the plumbing fixtures, at least in a building which is intended primarily for human occupancy, are operated intermittently and at irregular frequencies. The different kinds of fixtures are not in uniform use during the day. Bathroom fixtures are commonly in most frequent use when the occupants arise in the morning and just before they retire at night and, more recently, during intermissions on television programs. Kitchen sinks are used intensively just before and after mealtime. Laundry trays are used most frequently during the latter part of the morning. And from midnight until about 6 A.M., there is relatively little use of the fixtures.

The fact that the operation of the fixtures is intermittent and that the total time they are in actual operation is quite small in comparison with the time they are not operating means that it is unnecessary—except for very small systems and for individual fixture drains and supply lines—to design for the maximum potential load, that is, the flow that would be caused by all the fixtures operating simultaneously. This is fortunate, for if it were necessary to design for this potential load, the sizes of the pipes would be much greater than is actually the case, and the cost of a plumbing system would be prohibitive.

Some idea of the smallness of the design load in comparison with the potential load can be had by considering for the moment a hypothetical system consisting of 100 water closets, each of which operates at random with an average frequency of once every 5 min, each operation lasting 9 sec. It will be shown further on in this chapter that, if we observe the system at any arbitrarily chosen instant, we are more likely to find three of the water closets in operation than any other number (see Fig. 24-1). Now, for reasons that will be discussed later, we would design this system to serve eight water closets in simultaneous operation instead of three, but, regardless of this, it is obvious that the number of fixtures for which we would design the system is very small in comparison with the number of fixtures on the system.

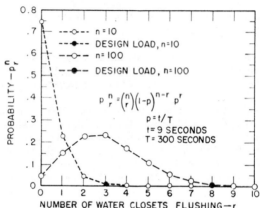

Fig. 24-1. Probability of finding r out of n water closets in operation at any arbitrary instant of observation.

Three distinct methods have been developed for determining the design loads for the different parts of the water-distribution system and the drainage system of a building.

1. The Empirical Method. In this method, for any given number of fixtures on the system, an arbitrary decision, based on experience and judgment, is made of the number of fixtures to be assumed in simultaneous operation. This is probably the best method to use for small numbers of fixtures.

a. The British Method. A group of persons who were experienced in the design of plumbing systems have established a table of "probable simultaneous demands" corresponding to different potential loads (see Table 24.1) [24-1].* A list of flow rates for the different fixtures heads the table. Then, considering the water-distribution system, we add the demands of all the fixtures that are served by a given pipe in the system, enter the table with the number of gallons per minute thus found, read the probable maximum simultaneous demand in gallons per minute, and design the pipe to carry this flow.†

* Numbers in brackets refer to the bibliography at the end of the book.

† A more recent method based on probability has been proposed at the Building Research Station in England. This method is described later in this chapter.

b. The Method of Dawson and Bowman. Analogous to this method is the one devised by Dawson and Bowman at the University of Wisconsin [24-2, 24-2A]. They prepared a table of the total number of plumbing fixtures of various kinds in single-family houses and in apartment houses containing up to six living units and specified the number and kinds of fixtures to be assumed in simultaneous use for determining design loads. Lewis H. Kessler has used this same method [24-3, 24-4].

Table 24.1

Discharge from Taps

Approximate Discharge Required from Hot- or Cold-water Points

Gpm

Bath (private).............	5
Bath (public).............	8
Sink....................	4
Basin...................	2
Shower spray.............	2
Shower, 4-in. rose.........	4
Shower, 6-in. rose.........	8

Simultaneous Demand for a Number of Draw-off Points

Discharge if all taps were run together (gpm)	Probable simultaneous demand (gpm)	Discharge if all taps were run together (gpm)	Probable simultaneous demand (gpm)
Up to 12	100% of the max possible	81	37
14	13	84	39
16	14.5	107	42
18	16	123	45
20	17.5	142	48
23	19	163	52
26	20.5	188	56
30	22.5	216	61
35	24	248	65
40	26	286	71
46	28	329	77
53	30	378	85
61	32	435	95
71	34	500	104
		Over 500	20% of the max possible

The simultaneous demand for a group of shower baths may exceed 90 per cent.

2. The German Square-root Method [24-5]. This method takes as a unit of flow the discharge of a ⅜-in. faucet under certain conditions, and a "load factor" of unity is assigned to this rate of flow. For any other fixture having a different rate of flow, a load factor is established by taking the ratio of the flow of this fixture to that of a ⅜-in. faucet and squaring the result. Then the load factor for each kind of fixture in the building is multiplied by the number of that kind of fixture in the building served by the line in question, the products are summed, and the square root is taken. The result is multiplied by the rate of flow for the ⅜-in. faucet to get the design load for the building drain or the main supply line to the building, whichever is in question. For pipes that serve only part of the fixtures in the building, only those fixtures which are served by the pipe in question are taken into account. The process of taking the square root allows in an arbitrary manner for the fact that the fixtures are not all in simultaneous use.

The algebraic details of the method follow:

1. Assume a unit of flow, which is taken as the "normal flow" of a $\frac{3}{8}$-in. faucet. This is assumed to be 0.25 liter per sec, which is closely equivalent to 4 gpm. This unit flow will be denoted by q_1, and the load factor f_1 for this faucet will be taken as unity.

2. Now assume that there are n_1 such faucets of this size supplied by the pipe for which the design load is to be determined. It is assumed that $\sqrt{n_1}$ of these faucets may be found in simultaneous operation at any instant of observation. The design load will be then

$$Q = q_1 \sqrt{f_1 n_1} \qquad (24\text{-}1)$$

or, inserting the values of q_1 and f_1,

$$Q = 4 \sqrt{n_1} \qquad \text{gpm} \qquad (24\text{-}2)$$

Now, by way of illustration, assume that there are also n_2 $\frac{3}{4}$-in. faucets served by this same supply pipe. It is assumed that a $\frac{3}{4}$-in. faucet imposes a demand of 12 gpm on the supply line when it is in operation. This is $1\frac{2}{4} = 3$ times as great a demand as that of the $\frac{3}{8}$-in. faucet. The load factor f_2 for the $\frac{3}{4}$-in. faucet is taken as $3^2 = 9$.

The design load for the two groups of faucets is given by

$$Q = 4 \sqrt{f_1 n_1 + f_2 n_2} \qquad \text{gpm} \qquad \text{or} \qquad 4\sqrt{n_1 + 9n_2} \qquad \text{gpm} \qquad (24\text{-}3)$$

Hence, in general, for any number of the several kinds of fixtures that are used intermittently on the system, we have the formula for the design load

$$Q = q \sqrt{f_1 n_1 + f_2 n_2 + \cdots + f_i n_i} \qquad \text{gpm} \qquad (24\text{-}4)$$

As has already been stated, this method of computing the design load ignores the frequency of use of each kind of fixture, also the time interval required for one use of the fixture, but it takes into account the average rate of demand of each kind of fixture. It ignores the difference between public and private use. Its virtue is that it is easy to understand, since the complicated concepts that are involved in this application of the theory of probability are replaced by the arbitrary assumption that the maximum load that need be taken into account is given by a simple square-root relation.

As with other methods, any continuous demands, such as supply to an air conditioner or a hose cock are taken into account by adding to the demand load, computed as described above, the loads imposed by these items. That is, if in addition to the loads imposed on the system by fixtures that operate intermittently for short intervals of time, we have n' outlets, each of which requires a continuous flow of q' gpm, then the total load for which the system should be designed is

$$Q = \sqrt{f_1 n_1 + f_2 n_2 + \cdots + f_i n_i} + n' q' \qquad (24\text{-}5)$$

Furthermore, in the application of this method, due consideration is given to special installations, such as batteries of lavatories or showers which may be subject to complete or nearly complete simultaneous use. Allowance is made for the demand of these groups of fixtures by multiplying the demand of each fixture by the number of fixtures, just as was done in the last term of Eq. (24-5).

3. The Method of Probability. The first application of the theory of probability to the determination of design loads in plumbing systems appears to have been made by the late Dr. Roy B. Hunter at the National Bureau of Standards. This is the most accurate and rational of any of the three methods mentioned, for it takes into account factors that affect the design load which are ignored by the other methods. The first exposition of this method appeared in Minimum Requirements for Plumbing in Dwellings and Similar Buildings, published in 1924 [24-6]. The same presentation of the subject was given in BH13, Minimum Requirements for Plumbing, 1932 [24-7]. The method as presented in these two reports was incomplete and not so direct as the treatment given in Hunter's later paper, Methods of Estimating Loads in Plumbing Systems [24-8]. In this paper there were given tables of load-producing characteristics (fixture-unit weights) of the commonly used plumbing fixtures and probability curves, which made it possible to apply the method easily to practical design problems. More recently there has appeared a brief and simple presentation of Hunter's method, Fixture Unit Ratings as Used in Plumbing System Design [24-9], published in an attempt to make available an elementary explanation of this method.

The French [24-10] and the Italians [24-11], possibly stimulated by Hunter's use of the theory of probability in connection with the problem, have applied the calculus of probabilities to it.

24.3 Application of the Theory of Probability to the Determination of Design Loads

1. Basis of the Method. In developing the application of the theory of probability to the problem of design loads, Hunter at the National Bureau of Standards first assumed that the operation of the principal fixtures making up the plumbing system could be considered as purely random events. While this is not entirely true, it nevertheless serves as a firm basis for the application of the theory to the problem, and approximate allowances can be made in some cases for deviation from complete randomness. He then determined the maximum frequencies of use of the principal fixtures that make up the load on the plumbing system in a residential building—flush valves, flush tanks, and bathtubs—basing his values of the frequencies on records obtained in hotels and apartment houses during the periods of maximum use. He also determined characteristic values of the average rates of use of water by the different fixtures and the time of a single operation of each.

The theoretical development that is about to be presented applies only to large groups of fixtures, such as may be found in apartment houses, hotels, office buildings, etc. A rather obvious reason for this is that, although the design load is a load that has a certain probability of not being exceeded, nevertheless it may be exceeded on rare occasions. With a system containing only a few fixtures, if it has been designed in accordance with the theory of probability, the additional load imposed on it by one fixture more than is given by the theory of probability might overload the system sufficiently to cause inconvenience or even interfere with the operation of the drainage system. On the other hand, if we are dealing with a large system, an overload of one or several fixtures would scarcely be noticeable, if at all.

Let us consider the water-distribution system of a large residential building, such as an apartment house or a hotel. In such a building the plumbing fixtures will be subjected to congested use at certain times of the day. The plumbing fixture will consist mainly of large numbers of water closets, bathtubs, lavatories, sinks, etc. Our problem is to determine what design loads should be assigned to the various pipes in the distribution system if satisfactory service is to be rendered by the system. "Satisfactory service" has been defined by Hunter [24-8, page 8] "as that in which interruption in service because of controllable factors, such as sizes and arrangement of pipes, is infrequent and is of sufficiently short duration to cause no inconvenience in the use of the fixtures or any unsanitary condition in the plumbing system."

It will be assumed that the system will give satisfactory service, or will be "adequately designed," if the pipes in the system are so proportioned that the system will supply satisfactorily the demand load for such a number m of the total of n fixtures in the building that not more than m fixtures will probably be found in simultaneous use more than 1 per cent of the time. Another way of expressing satisfactory service is "that in which interruption in service because of controllable factors, such as the sizes and arrangement of pipes, is infrequent and is of such short duration as to cause no inconvenience or any unsanitary condition in the plumbing system" [24-8, page 8].

The value of 1 per cent referred to above was chosen arbitrarily by Hunter in his pioneer application of the theory of probability to the problem of design loads in plumbing systems, and it has been used since 1940 by various construction organizations of the Federal government with success, in the sense that the use of this value has not led to the underdesign of systems. However, it may well be that the systems are still being overdesigned, and it is quite possible that the value of 2 per cent might still yield adequate designs. Only continuous records of water demands and drainage loads in buildings containing large number of fixtures will afford the evidence necessary to check this. Such information is just becoming available.

An additional consideration is the following: If the design load is exceeded, what will be the effect on the system? If the system comprises a large number of fixtures, and the value of m is established to meet the criterion stated in the preceding paragraph, then the probability of $m + 1$ fixtures being used simultaneously is quite remote; the probability of $m + 2$ fixtures being used simultaneously is still more remote; etc. Slight overloads will have no appreciable effect on the system if the total number of fixtures is reasonably large.

Kessler suggests the following principle* to assure that the flow of water to the fixtures shall be "adequate" or "ample." "The architect should never permit installation of piping adequate for the use of only one principal fixture

* Kessler is referring here to small buildings, i.e., those containing only a few plumbing fixtures.

at a time. He should, at the least, insist on piping adequate for average expected use, so that several fixtures can be used simultaneously. Piping adequate to supply *all* principal fixtures simultaneously, with some provision for planned future fixtures, should be encouraged; and when the budget permits, piping adequate for carrying all principal fixtures simultaneously, with *full* provision for added facilities and extra capacity as a safety factor, to permit adequate flow even though scale and corrosion deposits accumulate with age, is desirable" [24-4, page 89].

2. Application of the Theory of Probability to a Simple System. We define a "simple system" as one (obviously a hypothetical one) which consists of fixtures of a single kind—let us say of flush-valve-operated water closets only. Let there be a large number n of these water closets on the system. Let T be the time in seconds, on the average, between successive uses of each individual fixture. Let t be the duration in seconds of the demand on the supply system for each use of a fixture, i.e., the time occupied by a single flush. Then the probability p that *one particular fixture will be found flushing* at any arbitrarily chosen instant of observation of the system is

$$p = \frac{t}{T} \qquad (24\text{-}6)$$

Likewise the probability that *this particular fixture* (or any other particular fixture) *will not be found flushing* is

$$1 - p = 1 - \frac{t}{T} \qquad (24\text{-}7)$$

It will be shown later that suitable values for T and t are 5 min (500 sec) and 9 sec, respectively. Then

$$p = \frac{9}{300} = 0.03 \qquad \text{and} \qquad 1 - p = 1 - 0.03 = 0.97$$

for flush-valve operated water closets.

Note that what the other $n - 1$ closets may be doing at the instant when the system is observed has nothing to do with the probabilities given by Eqs. (24-6) and (24-7).

We next determine the probability that *two particular water closets will be found flushing* at any arbitrarily chosen instant of observation, disregarding what the other $n - 2$ closets may be doing at this instant. We have already seen that the probability of finding the first of these two selected closets in operation is p. Likewise the probability of finding the second of these two selected closets operating is p. Then the probability that both of these two particular closets will be found flushing is p^2, by the law of compound events. For the flush-valve-operated water closets, this is numerically

$$p^2 = (0.03)^2 = 0.0009$$

or approximately one part in a thousand. Similarly, the probability of finding *three particular water closets flushing* is $p^3 = (0.03)^3 = 0.000027$. And the probability of finding all the n water closets flushing is $(0.03)^n$.

We next consider the probability that *two particular water closets, but none of the other n − 2 closets, will be found flushing* at the arbitrarily chosen instant of observation.

Probability of finding the first closet flushing................ p
Probability of finding the second closet flushing.............. p
Probability of finding the third closet not flushing............ 1-p
Probability of finding the fourth closet not flushing........... 1-p
Probability of finding the fifth closet not flushing............ 1-p
. . . .
Probability of finding the nth closet not flushing............. 1-p

The probability of this compound event being observed at the chosen instant of observation is the product of the foregoing probabilities, or

$$P = (1 - p)^{n-2}p^2 \qquad (24\text{-}8)$$

For flush-valve-operated water closets, if $n = 5$, we have for this case

$$(1 - p)^{n-2}p^2 = (1 - 0.03)^3(0.03)^2 = 0.00082$$

We can now pass to the more general case in which *any two* of the n water closets, but none of the other $n − 2$ water closets, are found flushing at the arbitrarily chosen instant of observation. It has already been shown that the probability of finding *two particular* closets, but none of the other $n − 2$ closets, flushing is $(1 − p)^{n-2}p^2$. Now there are as many ways of selecting two closets out of n closets as there are combinations of n things taken two at a time. And in the general case, we are interested in determining how many ways of selecting r things from a total of n things there are. Any book on probability will give the expression for this, which is

$$\binom{n}{r} = \frac{n!}{r!(n - r)!} \qquad (24\text{-}9)$$

where $\binom{n}{r}$ is the symbol for n things taken r at a time and ! is the symbol for "factorial." To make this concrete; if $n = 5$ and $r = 2$,

$$\binom{n}{r} = \binom{5}{2} = \frac{5 \times 4 \times 3 \times 2 \times 1}{(2 \times 1)(3 \times 2 \times 1)} = 10$$

Thus, if $n = 5$ and $r = 2$, the probability that *any two of the five, but none of the other three, closets will be found flushing* at an arbitrarily chosen instant of observation is

$$10(0.97)^3(0.03)^2 = 0.0082$$

We can now write the perfectly general expression for the probability that *any r fixtures, and r only, out of a total of n fixtures will be found operating* at an arbitrarily selected instant of observation:

$$p_r^n = \binom{n}{r} (1 - p)^{n-r}p^r \qquad (24\text{-}10)$$

When we observe the system it is certain that we shall find some number r of n fixtures in operation, where r may have any integral value from 0 to n. In the theory of probability, certainty is represented by the number unity.   Hence if we sum all the probabilities represented by Eq. (24-10), which is the probability of one particular event out of those just mentioned, we get the relation

$$p_r^n = \sum_{r=0}^{r=n} \binom{n}{r} (1 - p)^{n-r} p^r = 1 \qquad (24\text{-}11)$$

We note also that Eq. (24-10) represents one term of and Eq. (24-11) represents the entire binomial expansion of $[p + (1 - p)]^n$, as can be found from any text on algebra.   Thus the distribution with which we have to do in this problem is of the binomial-expansion type.

We are now able to see how to determine the number m of fixtures out of a total of n fixtures we should assume to be in simultaneous operation for the purpose of determining the design load for the system.   Once we have established the value of m, the design load is found by multiplying m by the average rate of demand of one fixture

$$Q_d = mq \qquad (24\text{-}12)$$

The criterion that will be used for adequate design has already been stated as follows: *The system will be considered to operate satisfactorily if it is so proportioned that it will supply adequately the simultaneous demand load for such a number m of the n fixtures comprising the system that more than m will probably not be found in simultaneous operation more than 1 per cent of the time.*   This condition can be expressed as follows:

$$p_0^n + p_1^n + p_2^n + \cdots + p_{m-1}^n + p_m^n \geqq 0.99 \qquad (24\text{-}13)$$

m being the smallest integer for which this relation is true.   In this equation, p_0^n represents the probability of finding none of the n fixtures in operation, etc. The smallest value of m for which Eq. (24-13) is true gives the number of fixtures for which the system should be designed.

Equation (24-13) suffices to yield the desired value of m, but the computation is extremely laborious, and methods of reducing the labor to a minimum have been developed.   Tables are available giving the summation of the remainder of the series of Eq. (24-13), or

$$p_{m+1}^n + p_{m+2}^n + \cdots + p_{n-1}^n + p_n^n \leqq 0.01 \qquad (24\text{-}14)$$

which can also be written

$$\sum_{r=m+1}^{r=n} \binom{n}{r} (1 - p)^{n-r} p^r \leqq 0.01 \qquad (24\text{-}15)$$

which corresponds to the form given in the tables of the binomial probability distribution [24-12], except that here the expression $1 - p$ replaces the symbol q in the tables.   These tables give the summations for values of n up to 50. Another compilation of tables [24-13] gives the summations for n up to 150.

Before proceeding with the practical process of determining design loads, we shall compute a few values of the probabilities in the series given by Eq.

(24-13) for the hypothetical system of 100 flush-valve-operated water closets. It was assumed that each closet in this system flushes with the average frequency of once in 300 sec and that each flush lasts for 9 sec. This gives the elementary probability p of finding a particular water closet in operation at any arbitrarily chosen instant of observation of $\frac{9}{300}$, or 0.03.

Now the probability of finding none of the water closets in operation is

$$p_0^n = \binom{n}{0} (1 - p)^{n-0}p^0 = (1 - p)^n = (0.97)^{100} = 0.048$$

(see Fig. 24-1).

The probability of finding exactly one of the 100 closets flushing is

$$p_1^n = \binom{n}{1} (1 - p)^{n-1}p = \frac{n}{1!} (1 - p)^{n-1}p = 100(0.097)^{99}(0.03) = 0.1470$$

Proceeding in the same way, for computing the probability of finding exactly two water closets flushing

$$p_2^n = \binom{n}{2} (1 - p)^{n-2}p^2 = \frac{n(n - 1)}{2!} (1 - p)^{n-2}p^2 = \frac{100 \times 99}{2} (0.97)^{98}$$
$$(0.03)^2 = 0.2250$$

and for the probability of finding exactly three of the 100 closets flushing

$$p_3^n = \binom{n}{3} (1 - p)^{n-3}p^3 = \frac{n(n - 1)(n - 2)}{3!} (1 - p)^{n-3}p^3$$
$$= \frac{100 \times 99 \times 98}{3 \times 2} (0.97)^{97}(0.03)^3 = 0.2270$$

Proceeding in the same way, we compute the probabilities through p_{10}^n, and the results are given in Table 24.2 and Fig. 24-1.

Table 24.2   Values of the Probability of Finding 0, 1, 2, . . . , 10 Flush-valve-operated Water Closets out of 100 Water Closets in Simultaneous Operation

$p_0{}^{100}$	0.048	$p_6{}^{100}$	0.0496
$p_1{}^{100}$	0.1470	$p_7{}^{100}$	0.0206
$p_2{}^{100}$	0.2250	$p_8{}^{100}$	0.0074
$p_3{}^{100}$	0.2270	$p_9{}^{100}$	0.0023
$p_4{}^{100}$	0.1705	$p_{10}{}^{100}$	0.00065
$p_5{}^{100}$	0.1013		

If we sum these probabilities, commencing with p_0^n, we find that the smallest number of fixtures for which this sum exceeds 0.99 is 8. Hence we take 8 as the number of closets for the simultaneous flushing of which provision must be made in designing the system. The design load for the main supply pipe of this system is given by Eq. (24-12)

$$Q_d = mq = 8q \qquad \text{gpm}$$

where q is the average rate of flow in gallons per minute involved in the operation of one flush valve.

3. Application of the Method to a Mixed System. Before we can determine the curves giving values of m for various values of n for the three kinds of fixtures considered here—flush-valve-operated water closets, flush-tank-operated water closets, and bathtubs—we shall have to assume suitable values of t and T for these fixtures. This has already been done for the flush valves. Hunter considered that problem at some length in his original paper [24-8] and settled on the values shown in Table 24.3.

Table 24.3   Assumed Values of t and T for Fixtures

Fixture	t (sec)	T (sec)	t/T
Flush valve.........	9	300	0.03
Flush tank.........	60	300	0.02
Bathtub............	60	900	0.067
	120	1,800	0.067

These values are for congested use, for example, for the use of toilets in a public comfort station under rush conditions and for the use of bath-tubs in apartment house or hotel during the morning rising hours. These values of T are thus maximum values for all except very unusual conditions, such as an army barracks or in a school during recess. Such cases require special treatment.

We can now proceed to determine the relation between m and n for the foregoing three fixtures. The tables referred to earlier can be used for this purpose up to values of n of 150, but no higher. However, we wish to go to considerably higher values of n than this. For this purpose we resort to the Poisson exponential summation, which is an approximation to the series given by Eq. (24-14) and yields values that are quite accurate for small values of p, say, for p up to 0.10 or 0.15 [24-14].

The curves given in Fig. 5 of reference 24-14 have been utilized to prepare Table 24.4, which forms the basis for computing the probability curves for the plumbing fixtures that will be considered in what follows. *The values of np are those corresponding to the probability that more than m fixtures will not be found operating simultaneously more than 1 per cent of the time.* These values of np versus m should not be used for probabilities p much in excess of 0.15. For $p = 0.20$, this method gives results that are about 10 per cent too high.

To get the value of n corresponding to a given value of m, divide the value of a corresponding to the assumed value of m by the value of p for the type of fixture involved.

During the time that has elapsed since Hunter established values of the frequencies of use of the several fixtures, the time of one operation of each fixture, the average rate of flow of each fixture, and the total quantity of flow for one fixture for a single operation, the design of plumbing fixtures has changed sufficiently that these values should be reviewed. However, that will not

Table 24.4   Values of *np* Corresponding to Values of *m*
Poisson Probability Summation

m	*a = np*	*m*	*a = np*
1	0.25	18	10.30
2	.60	20	11.80
3	.95	25	16.25
4	1.35	30	19.50
5	1.85	35	23.45
6	2.35	40	27.50
7	2.90	45	31.55
8	3.50	50	35.65
9	4.10	60	44.15
10	4.75	70	52.85
12	6.00	80	61.55
14	7.42	90	70.3
16	8.85	100	79.0

be done here, but the values adopted by Hunter and the curves that he derived will be followed since they have formed the basis of the loading tables in many plumbing codes, and the difference between his curves and those which might be derived as representing more nearly present-day conditions would not differ too seriously.   The relations between *m* and *n* for flush valves, flush tanks, and bathtubs are given in Fig. 24-2.

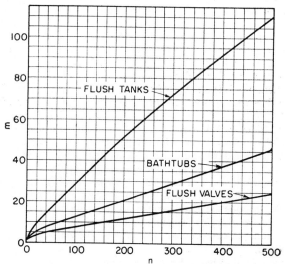

Fig. 24-2. Relation of design number of fixtures *m* to the total number of fixtures *n*, simple system.

The next step is to multiply the values of *m* corresponding to given values of *n* for flush valves by the average rate of flow that it is assumed each flush valve delivers during a flush. Following Hunter, we assume that this rate of flow is $q = 27$ gpm. Performing this multiplication we get the curve for flush valves in Fig. 24-3. We then carry out the same process for flush tanks and bathtubs, assuming that $q = 4$ gpm for flush tanks and $q = 8$ gpm for bathtubs, obtaining the curves for these fixtures in Fig. 24-3.

Thus, if we had a system composed entirely of n flush tanks operating at the average frequency assumed—i.e., once every 5 min—we would enter the curve for flush tanks in Fig. 24-3 and read off the design rate of flow from the scale of ordinates in this figure. The same procedure can be used for bathtubs and flush valves.

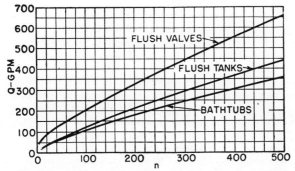

Fig. 24-3. Relation of design flow to total number of fixtures n, simple system.

However, in practice, systems do not consist of a single type of fixture exclusively, but rather of numbers of lavatories, sinks, toilets, bathtubs, and various special fixtures such as slop sinks, etc. Now it would not be correct to provide a curve for each fixture such as shown for three types of fixtures in Fig. 24-3, to sum the rates of flow for each kind of fixture, and to add them. If we did this we should overdesign the system, for the addition of the design loads for several groups of different kinds of fixtures making up a given system is not a matter of simple addition, because the probability function enters into the result. In other words, if we obtained a particular design load for n_1 flush valves, another design load for n_2 flush tanks, and still another design load for n_3 bathtubs on a given system, we cannot obtain the design load for the system as a whole by adding the three design loads thus found for the individual groups of different kinds of fixtures, since the true design load for the system will be somewhat less than this sum. The actual procedure of combining the loads contributed by the different kinds of fixtures can be carried out by the theory of probability, but the process is too complicated to be of practical use.

Hunter devised a very ingenious method of accomplishing this, however, by a simple process which gives results that are only approximate but which, in the few instances tested by comparison with the more accurate theory of probability, yielded results accurate within $\frac{1}{2}$ per cent. This accuracy is perfectly satisfactory for this problem in which we are dealing with uncertainties many times greater than this.

Hunter conceived the idea of assigning "fixture loading factors" or "fixture-unit weights" to the different kinds of fixtures to represent the degree to which they load a system when used at the maximum assumed frequency. It has been assumed by some that only the average rate of flow to or from a given fixture determines its loading effect on the system. It is easy to show the falsity of this assumption by considering a hypothetical system consisting of, say, 1,000 flush valves, each of which is operated once every 5 min on the average and discharges 4 gal of water at an average rate of 27 gpm in 9 sec. The demand of these 1,000 fixtures, or the drainage load, is the average rate of flow based on 4 gal used over a period of 5 min, or $1,000 \times \frac{4}{5} = 800$ gpm. Thus the rate of use of water by these 1,000 fixtures used as assumed above will fluctuate around a flow of 800 gpm.

Now assume the same system, but with the difference that the flush valves are now assumed to operate on an average of once in 60 min. The average flow in the system is then $1,000 \times 4/60 = 66.7$ gpm. This result shows clearly that the frequency of use cannot be ignored when we are dealing with systems consisting of large numbers of fixtures.

The loading factors or "fixture-unit ratings" of flush valves, flush tanks, and bathtubs as they relate to the supply system are determined as follows (see Table 24.5A, which has been prepared from Fig. 24-3). First a fixture-unit rating or weight of 10 is arbitrarily assigned to a flush valve. Now it can be seen from Fig. 24-3 that the numbers of flush valves, flush tanks, and bathtubs that correspond to a flow of 150 gpm are 57, 133, and 164, respectively. That is, the load on a system consisting of 57 water closets equipped with flush valves and used with the average frequency specified above would probably not exceed 150 gpm more than 1 per cent of the time. The same is true for a system consisting of 133 water closets equipped with flush tanks or for a system consisting of 164 bathtubs. Similar values of n are determined for the three fixtures, flush valves, flush tanks, and bathtubs, for rates of flow of 200, 250, and 300 gpm, which cover an adequate range of flows. These values are tabulated in Table 24.5A.

Referring now to Table 24.5A and a flow of 150 gpm, we multiply 10 fixture units by 57 and divide by 133 to obtain the corresponding fixture-unit rating of 4.29 fixture units for flush tanks at this rate of flow. The other individual fixture-unit ratings in the table are computed in this way.

It appears that the fixture-unit ratings of flush tanks and bathtubs increase relatively to the fixture-unit rating of flush valves as the rate of flow increases. However, the ratio appears to approach a limit for both flush tanks and bathtubs, instead of increasing indefinitely. Hence the fixture-unit ratings for flush tanks and bathtubs are averaged over the range of flows considered, with the results shown at the bottom of Table 24.5A. The uncertainties in the process of determining design loads are so great that there is no object in attempting to express fixture-unit ratings for these three fixtures closer than the nearest integer on the scale of 10 for flush valves. Hence the fixture-unit rating of a flush tank will be taken as the number 5 and that for a bathtub as the number 4. These are the same values adopted by Hunter [24-8, page 13].

It must be emphasized that these fixture-unit ratings are not rates of flow but rather are pure numbers that express the loading effect of the fixtures to which they apply on the plumbing system [24-8, page 13]. The sole purpose in introducing the concept is to make it possible to compute the design load directly for systems containing different kinds of fixtures, each having loading character- istics different from the others. The term "load factor" would probably be less misleading, but the terms fixture unit and fixture-unit rating have become so well established that no attempt will be made here to change them.

Table 24.5A Relative Demand Weights of Fixtures

Demand (gpm)	Flush valves		Flush tanks		Bathtubs	
	Number of fixtures n	Weight f	Number of fixtures n	Weight f	Number of fixtures n	Weight f
150	57	10	133	4.29	164	3.48
200	97	10	187	5.19	234	4.15
250	138	10	245	5.63	310	4.45
300	178	10	307	5.80	393	4.53
Average weight............		10		5.25		4.15
Value selected.............		10		5		4

Table 24.5B gives the number of fixture units fn for each of the three kinds of fixtures under consideration for the number of fixtures n listed. For each type of fixture, the value of fn is obtained by multiplying the value of n by the integral value of f in the bottom row of Table 24.5A. The results are plotted in Fig. 24-4.

Table 24.5B Relative Demand Weights of Fixtures

Demand (gpm)	Flush valves		Flush tanks		Bathtubs	
	n	fn	n	fn	n	fn
150	57	570	133	665	164	656
200	97	970	187	935	234	936
250	138	1,380	245	1,225	310	1,240
300	178	1,780	307	1,535	333	1,572

The general design-load curve can now be determined somewhat arbitrarily from Fig. 24-4. The portion of the curves in Fig. 24-4 from $fn = 0$ to $fn = 1,000$ (the approximate point at which the curves cross) is plotted in Fig. 24-5. The flush-valve curve is plotted as the upper branch in the figure, while the lower branch is an average of the curves for flush tanks and bathtubs in Fig. 24-4. Since water closets provide the heaviest part of the load in inhabited buildings, the upper (flush-valve) branch should be used when the building in question is provided with flush valves, and the lower branch should be used when the building is equipped with flush tanks.

For very large buildings, for which the range of fn in Fig. 24-5 is exceeded, the curves in Fig. 24-6 have been plotted, following the flush-valve curve in Fig. 24-4 (extrapolated by computation), to a value of $fn = 30,000$. For compactness, the curve has been plotted in two parts, the first from $fn = 1,000$ to $fn = 15,000$ (read to left and upward), and the second from $fn = 15,000$ to $fn = 30,000$ (read to the right and downward). This covers the higher range of values of fn that is likely to be encountered in practice.

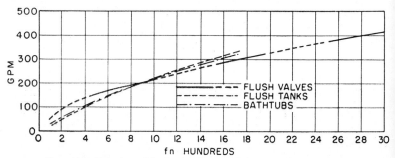

Fig. 24-4. Relation of design load to total fixture units on system.

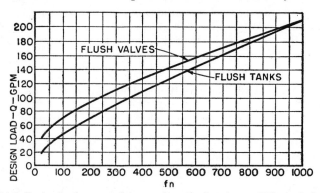

Fig. 24-5. Design loads versus fixture units, mixed system, middle part of curve.

For small buildings it is often convenient to be able to read design loads more accurately than can be done by the use of Fig. 24-5. To meet this need, a third design-load diagram is given in Fig. 24-7 for a range of fixture-unit values up to 200.

4. Wise and Croft Method. Another application of the method of probability has been made recently by Wise and Croft at the Building Research Station in England [24-15]. Their application is to the determination of design loads under conditions of noncongested use, such as may occur in individual dwellings and apartment houses. They first obtained data as to the frequencies of use of water closets, lavatories, baths, and kitchen sinks under con-

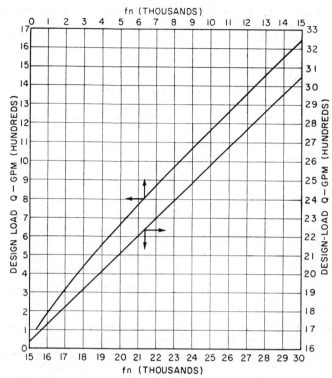

FIG. 24-6. Design load versus fixture units, mixed system, high part of curve.

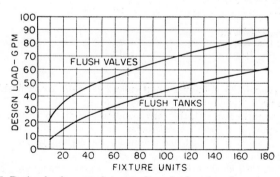

FIG. 24-7. Design load versus fixture units, mixed system, lowest part of range.

ditions of normal family use in the home. Records were kept between the hours of 5:30 A.M. and 10:30 A.M for each working day during a week by 108 families living in individual houses and in apartments. The results are summarized in Table 24.6, which is taken from the paper by the investigators.

Table 24.6   Frequency of Use of Fixtures in Flats during the Morning Peak

Fixture	Average for peak hour throughout the week		Average for worst hour in any day	
	No. of uses	Average time interval between uses (min)	No. of uses	Average time interval between uses (min)
Water closet.......	2.3	26	3.1	19
Lavatory..........	1.8	33	2.4	25
Sink.............	1.6	38	2.4	25

The average discharge rates and durations of discharge used by the investigators are given in Table 24.7.

Table 24.7   Flow Rates and Durations of Discharge of Fixtures

Fixture	Discharge rate (gpm)	Duration of discharge (sec)
Washdown water closet:		
2 gal........................	30	5
3 gal........................	30	7
Lavatory, $1\frac{1}{4}$-in. trap..........	8	10
Bath, $1\frac{1}{2}$-in. trap..............	14	75
Sink, $1\frac{1}{2}$-in. trap..............	12	25

Thus the probability of finding a particular 2-gal water closet flushing at any arbitrarily selected instant of observation is $5/(19 \times 60) = 0.0044$, at most. This may be contrasted with the corresponding probability of 0.03 chosen by Hunter to represent the same event under conditions of public congested use.

The investigators state that one reason for the seemingly small use of the lavatory was the fact that the observers were asked to record only those instances when they filled the lavatory and then removed the plug. There were numerous instances when the user ran the water without using the plug, but the small rates of flow and short periods of such use produced little load on the system.

The method used by these investigators is very similar to that used by Hunter, but there are several variations, the most important of which is the adoption of frequencies of use of the different household fixtures that are characteristic of normal household use, rather than of public, congested use.

Table 24.8   Probabilities of Simultaneous Discharge during the Morning Peak

Fixture	Duration of discharge t (sec)	Interval between discharges T (sec)	$p = \dfrac{t}{T}$	$1 - \dfrac{t}{T}$	Probability of finding r fixtures out of a total of 10 discharging		
					$r = 0$	$r = 1$	$r = 2$
Water closet:							
2 gal.........	5	1,140	0.0044	0.9956	0.956	0.0425	0.000841
3 gal.........	7	1,140	0.0061	0.9939	0.940	0.0576	0.00159
Lavatory.......	10	1,500	0.0067	0.9933	0.934	0.0630	0.0019
Sink..........	25	1,500	0.0167	0.9833	0.845	0.143	0.0110

Table 24.8 is taken from the investigators' paper [24-15, Table IV].

Wise and Croft next assumed that the test loading (or design load) will be given by the smallest load that has a probability of equaling or exceeding 0.01. They illustrate the method of considering the probabilities of the simultaneous discharge of sinks in Table 24.8 (see Table 24.9).

Table 24.9   Approximate Sums of Probabilities for the Simultaneous Discharge of r Fixtures out of a Total of 10 Fixtures[1]

$r = 0$ to 10	Probability = 1.000
$r = 1$ to 10	Probability = 0.1534
$r = 2$ to 10	Probability = 0.0124
$r = 3$ to 10	Probability = 0.00068
$r = 4$ to 10	Probability = 0.00002

[1] The values of the probabilities in this table are those obtained by the use of the Poisson approximation, rather than by the binomial expansion; hence they do not agree exactly with the values in Table 24.8.

Table 24.9 shows that two sinks is the largest number for which the probability of r to 10 sinks being found in simultaneous discharge is more than 0.01. Hence the design load, in terms of sinks, is two fixtures.   Applying the same procedure to the other fixtures, the authors obtain the values given in Table 24.10 [24-15, Table V].

The authors also considered a hypothetical evening peak based on the assumption that each bath is discharged once every 30 min and each water closet once every 19 min.   Their results for this peak are given in Table 24.11 [24-15, Table VI].

Referring to Table 24.10, if we have to do with seven apartments, for example, each with a water closet, lavatory, bath, and kitchen sink attached to the same stack, the design load, based on the morning peak, will be that due to the simultaneous discharges of one water closet, one lavatory, and one sink.   If, instead, there are, for example, 10 apartments, each with the same fixtures as just listed,

**Table 24.10   Numbers of Fixtures to Be Discharged Simultaneously
to Allow for the Morning Peak**

Number of fixtures	Water closets		Lavatories $p = 0.0067$	Sinks $p = 0.0167$
	2 gal $p = 0.0044$	3 gal $p = 0.0061$		
1– 8	1	1	1	1
9–20	1	1	1	2

**Table 24.11   Numbers of Fixtures to Be Discharged Simultaneously
to Allow for a Possible Evening Peak**

Number of fixtures n	Water closets $p = 0.0044$ or 0.0061	Bathtubs $p = 0.042$
1– 4	1	1
5–11	1	2
12–20	1	3

connected to the same stack, then the design load, based on the morning peak, is one water closet, one lavatory, and two sinks.

The design load, based on the evening peak, can be obtained similarly from Table 24.11 and compared with that obtained from the morning peak to see which is the greater.

Wise and Croft finally consider the possibility of the frequency of use being somewhat greater than the frequencies that they assume (for the worst hour in any day that was observed). They demonstrate by the theory of probability that the frequency of use can be increased to about double what they assumed without changing the design load.

The method of approach to the problem used by these investigators in considering design loads for plumbing systems containing relatively few fixtures is worthy of careful study. It should be compared in detail with the methods used by Dawson and Bowman [24-2] and by Kessler [24-3, 24-4].

5. Method of Dawson and Bowman. In 1933 Dawson and Bowman at the University of Wisconsin [24-2] proposed a table of values to be assumed for the design rates of flow in the water-distribution systems in small single-family houses, large single-family houses, and in apartment houses having up to and including six family units. The theory of probability is of dubious applicability when applied to such small numbers of fixtures, and, in addition, the frequencies of use adopted by Hunter for large buildings or the public use of fixtures are too high to apply to these buildings. Hence the adoption of empirical values by these two investigators on the basis of experience and judgment is justified. Table II in their paper is reproduced here as Table 24.12. Although other

Table 24.12 Recommended Flows for Use in Designing
Water-distribution Systems in Small
Residential Installations

Type of building	Fixtures	Total flow to all fixtures (gpm)	Flow for fixtures assumed in simultaneous use, design load (gpm)
Small single-family house	2 sill cocks	10.0	5.0
	2 laundry traps	16.0	8.0
	1 kitchen sink	7.5	
	1 lavatory	5.0	5.0
	1 water closet[1]	3.0	3.0
	1 bathtub	10.0	
		51.5	21.0
Large single-family house	2 sill cocks	10.0	5.0
	2 laundry trays	16.0	8.0
	1 kitchen sink	7.5	
	3 lavatories	15.0	5.0
	3 water closets	9.0	3.0
	2 bathtubs	20.0	10.0
		77.5	31.0
Two-family flat	2 sill cocks	10.0	5.0
	4 laundry trays	32.0	16.0
	2 kitchen sinks	15.0	7.5
	2 lavatories	10.0	5.0
	2 water closets	6.0	3.0
	2 bathtubs	20.0	
		93.0	36.5
Four-family apartment	2 sill cocks	10.0	5.0
	6 laundry trays	48.0	24.0
	4 kitchen sinks	30.0	15.0
	4 lavatories	20.0	5.0
	4 water closets	12.0	6.0
	4 bathtubs	40.0	
		160.0	55.0
Six-family apartment	2 sill cocks	10.0	5.0
	8 laundry trays	64.0	24.0
	6 kitchen sinks	45.0	21.5
	6 lavatories	20.0	10.0
	6 water closets	18.0	6.0
	6 bathtubs	60.0	10.0
		227.0	76.5

[1] All water closets are assumed to be of the tank type. If a flush valve is used, use the value
30 gpm in columns 3 and 4 for the water closet.

persons experienced in this field would undoubtedly have specified values differing somewhat from those in Table 24.12, the values selected are purely a matter of judgment, and the table can be recommended for general use in the design of pipe sizes for water distribution in small residential installations. Figure 24-8 is taken from the paper by Dawson and Bowman and is based on their Table II.

6. Method of Dawson and Kalinske. In another publication, Dawson and Kalinske [24-2A] presented the method just described and in addition gave two tables that can be used to determine design loads. The first of these, their Table II reproduced here as Table 24.13, is recommended by the authors of the

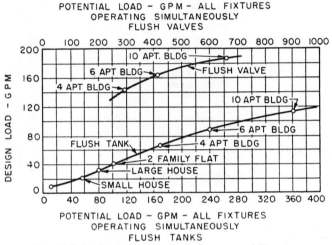

Fig. 24-8. Design-load curves from Dawson and Bowman.

paper for use in determining the probable maximum simultaneous use of closet-bowl fixtures. It will be noted that in this table, for 100 closet bowls, the number to assume in simultaneous operation for design purposes in sizing the distribution system is 16. Comparison with Fig. 24-2, based on Hunter's method, shows that the number of flush-valve-operated fixtures to be assumed in simultaneous operation in designing the supply system is 8, while for flush-tank-operated fixtures it is 24. The reason for the large difference in these last two values is the fact that the flush tank requires about six times as long to fill as the flush valve imposes a load on the supply system, and the rates of flow are in the inverse ratios of these figures. Dawson and Kalinske do not explain the basis of their table.

Their second table gives "simultaneous flow factors" by which the potential rate of demand on the system—i.e., all fixtures operating simultaneously—should be multiplied to give the design flow. Two kinds of use are recognized in the table: class A, which includes residences, apartment houses, and office buildings; and class B, which includes hotels, hospitals, schools, industrial buildings, restaurants, theaters, and public toilets. This table, Table II in the paper, is reproduced here as Table 24-14.

The use of Table 24.12 results in larger design loads than if the method of probability developed by Hunter is used. This is as it should be, since the probability method is applicable only to large numbers of fixtures and yields too low values of the design load for small dwellings. The reason for this is that,

Table 24.13

Total Number Similar Fixtures	Probable Number in Simultaneous Use
1	1
2	2
3	2
4	2
5	2
7	3
10	4
15	5
20	6
30	8
40	10
50	12
75	14
100	16

Table 24.14

| Total gpm | Simultaneous flow factor | |
	Class A	Class B
50	0.50	0.80
70	0.40	0.70
100	0.35	0.60
150	0.30	0.50
200	0.25	0.40
300	0.21	0.30
500	0.17	0.25
800	0.14	0.20
1,200	0.12	0.17
2,000	0.10	0.15
3,000	0.09	0.13
5,000	0.08	0.12

while it makes little difference in a system containing a large number of plumbing fixtures if one or two fixtures in excess of the design number m operate simultaneously in addition to the m fixtures, for a dwelling with only a few fixtures the simultaneous operation of even one fixture more than the number for which the system is designed may cause the system to perform inadequately.

7. Fixture-unit Ratings. For convenience in determining design loads for buildings containing large numbers of plumbing fixtures of different kinds, using the method of probability, tables of fixture-unit ratings for various kinds of fixtures that are in common use have been developed. Separate tables of these ratings are required for the demand on the water-distributing system of the building and for its drainage system. The reason for this is that, while it can be assumed in general that water supplied to a fixture must pass out through the drainage system, nevertheless the average rate of inflow may be quite different from that of the outflow, and consequently the time interval required to supply the fixture may be quite different from that required to drain it. Hence, even though the frequency of use is the same in the two cases, the fact that the time of filling is not the same as the time of emptying will have an effect on the computation of the design load by the method of probabilities. A good example of such a difference in filling and emptying time is afforded by the flush tank. While the tank will empty in about 9 or 10 sec when the closet is flushed, it takes about 60 sec to fill the tank.

a. Water-distribution Systems. It has already been shown how Hunter arrived at the relative values of fixture-unit weights for flush valves, flush tanks and bathtubs, considering the demand on the water-distributing system of the building. These values are 10, 5, and 4, respectively. We now have to consider how similar values can be assigned to other types of plumbing fixtures.

Although other fixtures, such as laundry trays, kitchen sinks, and lavatories are also installed in large numbers in buildings intended for human habitation, nevertheless the water closet and the bathtub have usually been assumed to impose the greater part of the peak demand. One difficulty encountered in dealing with any faucet-controlled fixture, such as a bathtub, laundry tray, sink, or lavatory, is the fact that the time of filling and the amount of water used in one operation depend on the personal characteristics of the persons using them. The situation is quite different with the water closet, for this fixture is completely automatic in its operation, the frequency of flushing being the only factor that is under the control of the individual using it. Hence water closets and urinals are much better adapted to treatment by the theory of probability than are the faucet-controlled fixtures. Nevertheless, in order to make this convenient and relatively accurate method of determining demand or drainage loads quite general, a way must be found to assign fixture-unit weights to these other fixtures, approximate though this procedure may be.

Considering first the lavatory, it will be noted that these are installed in approximately the same numbers as water closets and also that their load-producing characteristics are much less than that of a water closet, partly because the average rate of flow is much smaller than that of a flush valve and the time involved in a single use is much less than that required to fill a flush tank. Hunter proposed [24-8, page 15] that, in assigning fixture-unit ratings to fixtures that are used irregularly, the size of the supply outlet and the quantity of water used at each operation be used as a partial basis. From such considerations he arrived at the approximate value of two fixture units for a lavatory in congested service. This value is probably a little high, but a value of one fixture unit is probably a little low, and Hunter preferred to use the higher value as a matter of safety.

A method of demonstrating the reasonableness of this rating of two fixture units for a lavatory in congested use, for example, in a public toilet which is being used nearly to capacity, is as follows: For each use of a toilet or urinal, assumed to be once every 5 min, on the average, in congested use, there will be one use of a lavatory. Since we use as our basis of fixture-unit ratings the value of 10 for an individual flush-valve-operated water closet in congested use, this will serve as a base from which to assign a fixture-unit rating to a lavatory. It will be assumed that the water closet uses 4 gal of water at each flush. It will also be assumed that $\frac{1}{2}$ to $\frac{3}{4}$ gal of water is required for each use of the lavatory; $\frac{3}{4}$ gal will be assumed for safety. Since the frequencies of use of the lavatory and the water closet are the same, we can make the comparison simply on the basis of the amounts of water involved in a single use of each fixture. The water closet uses $4 \div \frac{3}{4} = 5.33$ times as much water as does the lavatory. Hence we can take as the fixture-unit rating of the lavatory the fixture-unit rating of the water closet (10) divided by 5.33, or 1.88. Since we are not justified in using fractions of a unit, we assume the value 2 for the fixture-unit rating of a lavatory in congested use. In a similar manner, fixture-unit ratings have been assigned to other commonly used fixtures that are in intermittent use.

Up to this point, we have been considering the fixture-unit ratings of four kinds of fixtures as related to the demand of the water-supply system—flush valves, flush tanks, bathtubs, and lavatories. This has been done under the following assumptions:

1. The ratings apply to individual fixtures, used separately.
2. The fixtures are used intermittently, at specified maximum frequencies of use, called "congested" or "public" use.

The following statements of Hunter [24-8, page 16] are of sufficient importance to quote here:

"(1) Fixtures that are relatively few in number and unlikely to be used when the predominant kinds are being used most frequently will add very little to the demand or to the peak sewage load and hence may be ignored, except in regard to branch-supply and branch-drain pipes of these fixtures. Slop or service sinks in office buildings, which are in use to any considerable extent only before or after office hours, add a negligible load to the peak loads of the day. Kitchen sinks and laundry trays in dwellings and residential apartments may also be placed in this category.

"(2) Fixtures so installed that they cannot in general be subject to congested conditions of service in the same sense as fixtures installed in public comfort stations, general toilet rooms in office buildings, and other buildings in which each fixture is open and accessible for use at all times should be given a rating in accordance with the possible extent or frequency of their use. Bathrooms in private dwellings, residential apartments, and private bathrooms in hotels may be considered in this class, and can be rated advantageously as a group.

"(3) Water services that demand a continuous flow, such as lawn sprinklers, air-conditioning equipment, gang showers in factories and athletic dressing rooms, present no element of chance in regard to overlapping and are not susceptible of a logical weighting in relation to water closets and other fixtures that use water at high rates for comparatively short periods of time. Hence the demand for this type of supply should be considered separately and estimated separately. If the use of these continuous water supplies is such that they overlap the rush period of the day for the weighted fixtures in the system, the separate estimates for the two classes of supply should be added to obtain the estimate for total demand on any supply pipe common to both services. If the two types of demand do not come at the same time of day, the greater demand of the two may be taken as the peak demand, or design estimate."

Hunter's assumption that the demands imposed by kitchen sinks (and possibly laundry trays) need not be taken into account in computing design loads might be questioned, in view of the large rates and volumes of flow. The

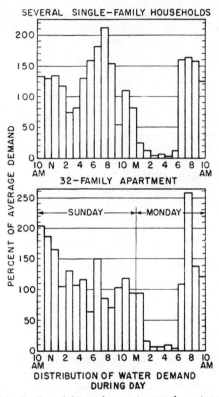

Fig. 24-9. Distribution of demand on water-supply system during day.

fact that tables of fixture-unit ratings in many plumbing codes include these fixtures shows that in common practice they are included in computing design loads.

Figure 24-9 offers some evidence on this score. This figure shows the distribution of water demand over the day for several single-family households and for a 32-family apartment house [24-16, page 69; 24-17]. Each of these diagrams shows the percentage of the average hourly volume of water used during the day for each hourly period. For example, Walasyk reports that, during the 24-hr period of measurement on the 32-family apartment house, a total of 5,221 gal of water was used. This gives an average hourly use of 217.5 ga

Thus from 6:00 to 7:00 P.M. on Sunday, when the percentage of use was 150, the quantity of water used was $1.5 \times 217.5 = 326$ gal.

The diagram for the single-family households represents averages for the different houses and for different days of the week. The diagram for the apartment house, it will be noted, is for a special 24-hr period, that is, from 10 A.M. on Sunday to 10 A.M. on Monday, a period during which the demand pattern would undoubtedly be different than at any other time during the week. Nevertheless we can draw certain inferences from these diagrams and from Walasyk's conclusion, of which the following seem to be pertinent:

"1. On weekdays there were two distinct peak hourly periods: 7–8 A.M. and 7–8 P.M. The ¼-minute maximum rate of flow always occurred during the morning peak hour. The evening peak showed a sustained, moderate rate of flow.

"2. On Saturday and Sunday only one peak was observed, usually before noon.

"Daily consumption of water remained approximately constant throughout the week."

Referring to the diagram in Fig. 24-9 for the single-family households, we note the prolonged peak during the late afternoon and early evening, this peak being higher than the morning peak, rather surprisingly. It seems clear that the afternoon-evening peak must be due mainly to the use of the kitchen sink in preparing the evening meal and washing the dishes resulting from this meal. This would indicate that the kitchen sink cannot be ignored in estimating design loads.

However there is no obvious pattern of use that facilitates assigning a fixture-unit rating to the sink. Hence we must estimate a suitable value for the fixture-unit rating of the sink from considerations of volume of water involved and rate of supply or discharge. It seems reasonable to take the rate of supply to a faucet-controlled sink as the same as that for a lavatory, or 3 to 5 gpm. The volume per use of the sink will be considerably greater than that of the lavatory (approximately 5 gal as against ¾ gal). However, the lavatory will be used more frequently than the sink. Since we have no reasonable method of evaluating these differences, the sink will be assumed to have the same load-producing value as the lavatory as far as demand load on the water-supply system is concerned.

Laundry trays ordinarily have larger faucets than lavatories and also discharge larger volumes of water at greater rates of flow. In small dwellings they will not add appreciably to the usual demand load, since they will usually be in use when the other fixtures that tend to load the system heavily are in lesser use. In apartments where the washing is done by the tenants themselves, there will ordinarily be a considerable load imposed by the laundry trays for a few hours on Monday morning. This seems to be reflected in the very high peak from 7:00 to 8:00 A.M. in the lower diagram in Fig. 24-9.

No attempt will be made here to justify the fixture-unit ratings assigned commonly to the other plumbing fixtures. The choice of these values is always a matter of judgment, and different persons would probably select somewhat different values for any given kind of fixture. There are so many safety factors introduced in applying the theory of probability to this problem, one of the most obvious being the assumption of the maximum frequencies of use, that these differences do not introduce any danger of overloading the system.

The fixture-unit ratings assigned to various plumbing fixtures, as regards their demand on the water-distribution system, are given in Table 18.3.5 of the National Plumbing Code.

b. Drainage System. Fixture-unit ratings for use in determining the sizes of soil and waste stacks and building drains and sewers are given in Table 11.4.2 of the National Plumbing Code.

Some confusion as to fixture-unit ratings has resulted from the fact that Hunter originally based the ratings on a value of 6 for a water closet [24-6]. Later he changed the basic value assumed for a flush-valve-operated water closet to 10 in order to obtain more flexibility in the assignment of integral numbers to the different fixtures. The result is that, in some plumbing codes which use this method of determining design loads, the fixture-unit ratings are based on Hunter's early value of 6 for a water closet, while others are based on the later value of 10. It is possible to tell which basic value is used in a code by looking for the value assigned to a flush-valve-operated water closet.

8. Illustrative Problem. The following problem illustrates the method of determining the design load for the water-service line for a building by the five methods treated in this chapter. The building used for this purpose is a six-family apartment house containing the fixtures listed in Table 24.15 [24-2A, page 10]. Column 3 in Table 24.15 gives the design loads by the Dawson method.

Table 24.15

Fixtures	Total potential flow (gpm)	Dawson's design flow (gpm)
6 lavatories at 5 gpm each..................	30	10.0
6 bathtubs at 10 gpm each..................	60	10.0
6 water closets at 3 gpm each..............	18	6.0
6 kitchen sinks at 7.5 gpm each.............	45	31.5
8 laundry trays at 8 gpm each..............	64	24.0
	217	71.5
2 sill cocks at 5 gpm each.................	10	5.0
	227	76.5

In applying the probability method developed at the National Bureau of Standards, we obtain the fixture-unit ratings of the fixtures from Table 11.4.2 as follows:

Fixtures	*Fixture Units*
6 bathroom groups (flush tank).....................	36
6 kitchen sinks....................................	12
8 laundry trays (3 fixture units for each pair).........	12
Total for fixtures used intermittently..............	60

From Fig. 24-7, we read from the flush-tank curve the design load of 32 gpm for the fixtures used intermittently. Adding now the 10 gpm for the two sill cocks, we obtain a final design load for the water-service line of 42 gpm.

In applying the German method, we use Eq. (24-4), determining the load factors as described,

Table 24.16

Fixture	Rate of flow (gpm)	Load factor f	Number of fixtures	fn
Lavatory..................	4 5	1 1.56	6	9.36
Bathtub..................	10	6.25	6	37.50
Water closet..............	3	0.56	6	3.36
Kitchen sink..............	7.5	3.52	6	21.12
Laundry trays.............	8	4.00	8	32.00
				103.34
Sill cocks................	5	1.56	2	3.12
				106.46

$$Q = q\sqrt{103.34} + 3.12 = 4(10.15 + 3.12) = 53 \text{ gpm}$$

which is the design load.

By the British method, we read 63 gpm as the design load corresponding to a potential load of 227 gpm from Table 24.1.

The following is a summary of the results by the five methods:

Method	Design Load (Gpm)
Probability, National Bureau of Standards...........	42
Dawson.......................................	76.6
German.......................................	53
British.......................................	63

The maximum design load computed here is nearly twice the minimum. The method of probability, which is intended for use only in connection with large numbers of fixtures, undoubtedly yields results that are too small, since we are dealing in this problem with only a six-family house. Presumably the safe design load lies nearer the highest value computed than to the lowest value.

24.4   Summary

The subject of design loads for plumbing systems needs reconsideration. The application of the theory of probability developed by Hunter is basically sound as applied to systems containing large numbers of fixtures, but two facts in regard to it should be remembered: (1) the frequencies of use of the household plumbing fixtures that he assumed are applicable only to congested public service, and they undoubtedly lead to overdesign when applied to ordinary living conditions; (2) fixture-discharge rates have increased appreciably since Hunter selected the values that he used.   Data from continuous records of the water demand or the sewage load in various types of buildings, over periods of at least several months, are urgently needed.   Some progress has been made in this direction, but the comparison of these data with the design loads as computed by Hunter's method still remains to be made. Zinkil reports such data [24-19] for apartment houses. Walasyk, at the Hackensack Water Company, has already published some data on the water demand of apartment houses [24-17], and he has a large number of records that have not been analyzed.

When we come to the problem of determining design loads for small residential buildings, the solution depends mainly on judgment resulting from experience. The methods that have been used so far range from the empirical method of Dawson and Bowman [24-2] to the use of the theory of probability, with greatly reduced frequencies, by Wise and Croft [24-15]. The empirical approach has also been considered by French, Eaton, and Wyly [24-20, page 13].

CHAPTER 25

Capacities of Plumbing Stacks in Buildings

25.1 Introduction

The general features of flow down a soil or waste stack have been discussed in Chap. 22, but they will be treated in more detail in what follows. A stack is a vertical drainage pipe which collects waste water and solids from fixture drains and horizontal branches from the different floors of a building, these wastes coming from water closets, urinals, lavatories, bathtubs, sinks, and other fixtures. A waste stack is one that collects these wastes from fixtures other than water closets and urinals. A soil stack is one that collects wastes from water closets and urinals.

In order to provide venting, that is, to make it possible for air to enter the top of the stack to replace air that is carried out of the stack into the building drain and sewer by the waste water, the stack is carried up through the roof, it being called a *stack vent* above the level of the highest fixture connection. The exposed portion of the stack vent above the level of the roof is called the *vent terminal*.

The horizontal branch connections to the stack are ordinarily made through a sanitary tee or a long-turn tee-wye. This fitting serves to bring the waste into the stack with an initial downward velocity, a condition which decreases the pneumatic pressure reductions which occur just below the point of entry into the stack, or which—looking at the matter from a different point of view—increases the rate of flow into the stack that can be tolerated at any given level. The long-turn tee-wye fitting gives the water a greater downward component at the point of entry than does the sanitary tee and hence is advantageous to use from the standpoint of stack capacities; but it is less favorable than the sanitary tee from the standpoint of self-siphonage of the fixture trap of the fixture which it drains (see Chap. 27).

The nature of the flow down a plumbing stack has been well described by Hunter in the following words [25-1]:*

"The character of the flow of water in partially filled vertical pipes varies with the extent to which the pipe is filled. . . . For small volumes of flow, amounting to little more than a trickle, the flow is entirely on the inner wall of the stack. With increase in volume, this adherence to the wall continues up to a point where the frictional resistance of the air causes it to diaphragm across the pipe temporarily, forming a short slug of water which descends as a slug filling the stack until the increased air pressure breaks through, the water forming the slug

---

* Numbers in brackets refer to the bibliography at the end of the book.

either being thrown against the wall or falling a short distance as separate streamlets in the center of the pipe. This diaphragming and forming slugs probably first appears in a 3-inch stack when the stack is from one-fourth to one-third full. As the volume of flow increases, the slugs thus formed become more frequent and persistent, and in a stack open at the lower end may not be broken through. This intermittent rate partially accounts for the rapid erratic oscillations of pressure in a plumbing system."

The falling sheet of water is acted on by the force of gravity and by the frictional effect of the wall of the stack, and it accelerates until it reaches the velocity at which these two forces balance, provided the distance through which the fall takes place is sufficiently great. An approximate formula can be derived to give the ultimate or "terminal" velocity which the sheet of water will attain if the distance through which it falls is sufficiently great. A derivation has been given by Dawson and Kalinske [25-2] and by Wyly and Eaton [25-3] treating the sheet of water as a solid hollow cylinder sliding down the inside wall of the pipe.

25.2   Terminal Velocities in Stacks

The approach to the problem presented by **Wyly and Eaton** is as follows: The mass of falling water is treated as a solid body falling under the influence of the force of gravity and retarded by the friction of the wall. This leads to the following differential equation:

$$m \frac{dv}{dt} = mg - \tau_0 \pi d_1 \Delta L \tag{25-1}$$

where ΔL = length of an elementary ring of water

d_1 = internal diameter of stack

τ_0 = wall shear per unit area

g = acceleration of gravity

v = average velocity of fall corresponding to any given distance of fall Δz

t = time

m = mass of water ρQ_1 passing a given cross section in time t

where ρ = mass density of water

Q_1 = volume rate of flow of water down stack

Making the substitution for m in Eq. (25-1) and defining τ_0 in terms of the dimensionless friction coefficient λ and the velocity v, we obtain

$$\frac{dv}{dt} = g - \frac{\pi \lambda}{2 Q_1} d_1 v^3 \tag{25-2}$$

We note that the terminal velocity v_t exists when $dv/dt = 0$; so substituting this relation in Eq. (25-2), we get

$$v_t = \frac{2}{\pi} \frac{g Q_1^{1/3}}{\lambda d_1} \tag{25-3}$$

It can be shown that the value of λ in Eq. (25-3) is equal to $f/4$, where f is the dimensionless friction coefficient in the Darcy-Weisbach formula

$$h = f \frac{l}{d} \frac{v^2}{2g} \tag{25-4}$$

for which values are given in any book treating the problem of flow through pipes.

The value of λ is also given by the expression [25-3, page 11]

$$\lambda = 0.0303 \left(\frac{k_s}{T}\right)^{1/3} \tag{25-5}$$

where k_s is the sand-roughness factor, which may be looked upon as representing the distances that grains of sand of a particular size would project from a surface having the same frictional resistance as the surface being considered, and T is the thickness of the sheet of water where its velocity is v.

The introduction of the sand-roughness factor k_s in Eq. (25-5) yields

$$v_t = \sqrt[3]{21g \frac{Q_1}{d_1} \left(\frac{T_t}{k_s}\right)^{1/3}} \tag{25-6}$$

or, eliminating the quantity T_t, the thickness of the sheet of water where terminal velocity exists, which would have to be computed separately, and also neglecting terms of the second order, leads to the equation

$$v_t = 2.22 \left(\frac{g^3}{k_s}\right)^{1/10} \left(\frac{Q_1}{d_1}\right)^{2/5} \tag{25-7}$$

where all the quantities are in foot-second units.

Now, if we introduce the value $k_s = 0.00083$ ft, which is a good value for new cast-iron pipe [25-3, page 12], we get the following working formulas:

$$v_t = 12.80 \left(\frac{Q_1}{d_1}\right)^{2/5} \tag{25-8}$$

where v_t is in feet per second
$\quad Q_1$ is in cubic feet per second
$\quad d_1$ is in feet

If we wish to express Q_1 in gallons per minute, d_1 in inches, and v_t in feet per second, we write

$$v_t = 3.0 \left(\frac{Q_1}{d_1}\right)^{2/5} \tag{25-9}$$

Equation (25-9) is plotted in Fig. 25-1. Values of the terminal velocity v_t measured by Dawson and Kalinske and by Hunter gave results about 40 per cent higher than those given by Eq. (25-9), but it was found upon investigating that the measurements had been made mainly in the outer layers of the falling sheet of water, where the velocities are considerably above the average value. Later measurements made by Wyly at the National Bureau of Standards, with this in mind, yielded values that averaged quite closely those given by Eq.

(25-9). Consequently it is believed that the relations given here for terminal velocities in vertical stacks of cast-iron pipe flowing partly full are sufficiently accurate for any computations that need be made on stacks.

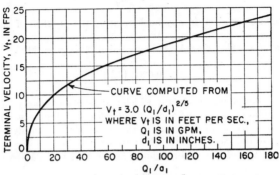

FIG. 25-1. Terminal velocities for partially filled stacks.

25.3 Terminal Lengths in Stacks

The next matter of interest is the distance that the sheet of water must flow down the stack before it attains the constant velocity v_t. To derive this equation, we first note that

$$\frac{dv}{dt} = v\,\frac{dv}{dz} \tag{25-10}$$

where z is the distance of fall measured downward from the point of entry. If this relation is substituted in Eq. (25-2) and the resulting equation is solved for dz, there results

$$dz = \frac{1}{g}\,\frac{v\,dv}{1 - \dfrac{\pi}{2}\dfrac{\lambda}{g}\dfrac{d_1}{Q_1}v^3} \tag{25-11}$$

Integrating this equation, we obtain an expression that gives an infinite value for the terminal length L_t. This is as it should be, for the velocity v approaches the limiting value v_t asymptotically and hence would require theoretically an infinite distance in which to do this. This difficulty is avoided by defining the effective terminal velocity as 0.99 times the true terminal velocity. The equation for terminal length then becomes

$$L_t = \frac{v_t^2}{3g}\,(\tfrac{1}{2}\log_e 29{,}700 - \tan^{-1} 2.98 - \tfrac{1}{2}\log_e 1 + \tan^{-1} 1)$$

or
$$L_t = 0.052v_t^2 = 0.156\left(\frac{Q_1}{d_1}\right)^{4/5} \tag{25-12}$$

where L_t is in feet and v_t is in feet per second. Equation (25-12) is plotted in Fig. 25-2.

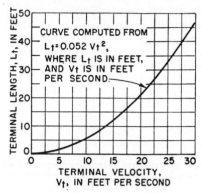

FIG. 25-2. Terminal lengths for partially filled stacks.

25.4 Permissible Rates of Flow in Stacks

To set upper limits to the permissible rates of flow in stacks of different diameters, we start with Eq. (25-8) and replace v_t with the rate of flow down the stack past the wetted cross section where terminal velocity has been attained. Thus:

$$v_t = \frac{Q_1}{a_t} \qquad (25\text{-}13)$$

where a_t is the wetted cross section of the stack where terminal velocity exists. There then results

$$Q_1 = 70.0 \frac{a_t^{5/3}}{d_1^{2/3}} = 471.8 \frac{T_t(d_1 - T_t)^{5/3}}{d_1^{2/3}} \qquad (25\text{-}14)$$

where Q_1, d_1, and T_t are all in foot-second units.

Table 25.1 has been computed from Eq. (25-14) for three different degrees of fullness of the stack where terminal velocity exists—$\frac{1}{4}$, $\frac{7}{24}$, and $\frac{1}{3}$ full. Whether or not Eq. (25-14) can be used safely to predict stack capacities remains to be investigated. However, it provides a definite law of variation of stack capacity with diameter, and if this law can be shown to hold for the lower part of the range of stack diameters, it should be valid for the larger diameters. It should be remembered that both Dawson and Hunter in entirely independent investigations came to the conclusion that slugs of water, with their concomitant violent pressure fluctuations, did not occur until the stack flowed $\frac{1}{4}$ to $\frac{1}{3}$ full.

The data in Table 25.1 are plotted in Fig. 25-3. Dawson's values evidently follow the law expressed by Eq. (25-14) for a stack flowing $\frac{1}{3}$ full. Actually Dawson and Kalinske assumed the stack to be flowing $\frac{1}{4}$ full, but their values for the terminal velocity were considerably higher than those recommended here, and this fact accounts for their data fitting the line in Fig. 25-3 for the stack $\frac{1}{3}$ full. Apparently their recommendation is that the curve for the stack flowing $\frac{1}{4}$ full be taken as the design curve.

Capacities in fixture units for stacks more than three stories high were read from Table 11.5.3 of the National Plumbing Code [25-4] and were converted into rates of flow in gallons per minute by the use of Figs. 24-5, 24-6, and 24-7. The plot of these values shows that the capacity of a 2-in. stack given by this table (40 gpm) apparently is abnormally high. This fact has been verified by tests made by Mayer at the National Bureau of Standards on a 2-in. stack in a trailer coach [25-5]. Mayer's tests checked reasonably well the value of 22.5 gpm computed from Eq. (25-14) for a 2-in. stack flowing $\frac{7}{24}$ full. The values taken from the National Plumbing Code check the formula quite well for diameters of

Table 25.1   Maximum Carrying Capacity of Stacks

Diameter of stack (in.)	Flow in stack in gpm for fullness ratios a_t/a_1 of			Carrying capacity of stock				Dawson and Kalinske [25-7] (gpm)
				National Plumbing Code, over three stories [25-4]		BMS66, Table 805(b)-III [25-6]		
	$\frac{1}{4}$	$\frac{7}{24}$	$\frac{1}{3}$	Fixture units	gpm	Fixture units	gpm	
2	. . . . . .	23.5	. . . . . .	24	38	24	38	
3	51.8	67.5	83.7	60	55	80	61	90
4	114.5	145	180	500	141	600	155	180
6	328	425	529	1,900	315	2,800	430	560
8	710	910	1,145	3,600	510	5,400	710	1,200
10	1,275	1,675	2,055	5,600	730	8,000	970	
12	2,080	2,680	3,365	8,400	1,020	14,000	1,550	

a_1 = cross-sectional area of stack.
a_t = cross-sectional area of sheet of water where terminal velocity exists.

3, 4, and 6 in. For diameters of 8, 10, and 12 in., however, the values given by the National Plumbing Code become progressively more conservative in the direction of smaller loadings.

The fact just pointed out—that the permissible stack loadings in the National Plumbing Code deviate more and more in the direction of smaller loadings as the diameter of stack increases from the curves plotted from Eq. (25-14) in Fig. 25-4—appears to be due to the use of the concept of "peak loads" by the Coordinating Committee that wrote the National Plumbing Code. This concept, originated by Hunter, is explained in Recommended Minimum Requirements for Plumbing [25-1, pages 191–193]. The following quotation is from this reference:

"It is evident that with only a few fixtures on the system the flow in the drains will be intermittent, but that as the number increases a point will be reached where with the same frequency of use the flow will be continuous but not regular. It is also evident that when the peak discharges do occur they will occur during periods of heaviest use, and the peak discharges will be added to the flow already in the drain and, therefore, the peak load may approach the sum of the continuous flow and peak discharge. Curve 3, which is proposed for estimating peak loads, is obtained by adding the ordinates of curve 1 to those of curve 2. Using this curve, the estimated peak load, up to about 12 fixture units, is the sum of the individual peak discharges from all fixtures on the system, or 100 per cent of the total possible discharge. As the number of fixtures on a system increases, the estimated peak load as a percentage of the total gradually decreases in accordance with the law of probability until for 5,400 fixture units it is less than 8 per cent of the total."

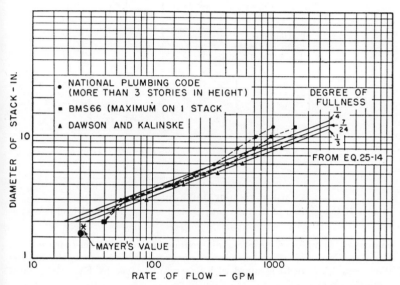

FIG. 25-3. Comparison of recommended permissible rates of flow in plumbing stacks.

The curves referred to in this quotation are plotted in Fig. 25-3.

There appears to be a fallacy in this reasoning. If we consider a building with a very large number of fixtures, each of which is being used at a definite average frequency, the flow in the building drain will fluctuate about a value given by the average flow curve in Fig. 25-4. The point that seems to have been overlooked in the quotation is that the average flow will be exceeded only as the frequency of use—which is a matter of probability, although the *average* frequency is fixed—exceeds intermittently the average frequency. Hence, if we add to the average flow the probability flow, we are adding in some of the individual discharges twice. The design load is given by curve 1 in Fig. 25-4, which is given in more detail in Figs. 24-5, 24-6, and 24-7 for actual design use.

Hence it would seem that the best way available at the present time to compute design loads for stacks is to use the law expressed by Eq. (25-14), assuming what appears to be a reasonable degree of fullness, such as $\frac{1}{4}$, $\frac{7}{24}$, or $\frac{1}{3}$. It has already been pointed out that this is what Dawson has recommended, using a fullness ratio of $\frac{1}{4}$. While only further laboratory tests and experience can determine what is the largest degree of fullness that should be used, attention has been called to the fact that the value of 23.5 gpm for a 2-in. stack (from the curve for a fullness ratio of $\frac{7}{24}$, Fig. 25-4) has been checked on trailer-coach stacks by Mayer [25-5] and has been found to be almost the same as the average

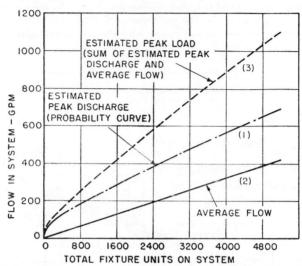

FIG. 25-4. Comparison of average flow, peak discharge, and peak-load curves as given by Hunter.

value that Mayer found for several different designs of the trailer-coach system. Hence, while this bit of evidence is far from conclusive, it is probable that the stack capacities can be assumed with safety to be given by Eq. (25-14) for a fullness ratio of $\frac{7}{24}$.

25.5 Permissible Rates of Entry into Stacks from Horizontal Branches

The foregoing discussion assumes that we are dealing with multistory structures, so that the total load on the stack will be made up of discharges from a number of different levels. If an attempt is made to introduce too large a flow into the stack at any one level, the inflow will fill the stack at that level and will even back up the water above the elevation of inflow, which will cause violent pressure fluctuations in the stack—resulting in the pulling of trap seals—and may also cause sluggish flow in the horizontal branch under consideration.

Hunter [25-1, page 101] conducted tests to determine what he called the "practical capacity of a stack," that is, the capacity of a stack of given diameter to accept the introduction of water through a stack fitting at a given level without the water filling the cross section of the stack at that level and backing up slightly above that level in the stack. He set up several stacks 2 and 3 in. in diameter, ranging in length from 30 to 45 ft, and mounted a double tee-wye fitting at the top of each. Water-storage tanks were connected to each of the branches, with sufficient capacity to produce a steady flow into the stack for periods of time between 15 and 30 sec.

These tanks were allowed to discharge into the top of the stack successively at greater and greater rates of flow until visual observation showed that the water was starting to back up in the fitting above the level of entry. The rate of flow at which this happened was taken as the "fitting capacity" or the "practical stack capacity." Table 25.2 gives the results of these tests and extrapolates the results up to 8-in. stacks.

Hunter found that the results that he obtained on 2- and 3-in. stacks could be represented by the equations

and

$$Q = 22.5d^2 \quad \text{for 45° double tee-wye stack fittings}$$
$$Q = 11.25d^2 \quad \text{for sanitary-tee double stack fittings} \tag{25-15}$$

where

$$Q = \text{rate of flow, gpm}$$
$$d = \text{nominal diameter of stack, in.} \tag{25-16}$$

Table 25.2   Capacity of Point of Entry of Stacks Constructed with Single or Double Fittings
(Water introduced at one level only)

Diameter of stack (in.)	Flow into stack through	
	Sanitary tee (gpm)	45° wye (gpm)
2 (experimental data)........	45	90
3 (experimental data).........	100	200
4 (extrapolated)..............	180	360
5 (extrapolated)..............	280	560
6 (extrapolated)..............	405	810
8 (extrapolated)..............	720	1,440

In one of the investigations of stacks conducted at the National Bureau of Standards a number of stack fittings were constructed to accurate dimensions, using a transparent plastic material, so that the flow phenomena occurring in them could be seen visually and photographed. One of these fittings with both inflow at the fitting level and flow down through it from a higher level is shown in Fig. 25-5. It is obvious that the flow shown exceeds the capacity of the fitting as just defined, although the case is not exactly comparable, owing to the fact that there is a flow down the stack from a higher level.

This brings us to the more complicated case in which we consider how great a rate of flow can be brought into a stack at a given intermediate level in a multi-story building when there is also a given flow coming down the stack from the higher floors. This problem was solved in a study of stack capacities made by Wyly and Eaton at the National Bureau of Standards for the Housing and Home Finance Agency in 1950 [25-3].

The physical conditions pertinent to this problem are illustrated in Fig. 25-6, which shows a diagram of a short section of stack, including a horizontal branch connection. Water is discharging down the stack from higher floors, and the horizontal branch is discharging a high enough rate of flow to fill the branch at its exit.

The water flowing out of the branch can enter the stack only by mixing with the stream flowing down the stack or by deflecting it, as indicated in the figure. Such a deflection of the high-velocity stream coming down the stack can be accomplished only if there is a large enough hydrostatic pressure in the branch,

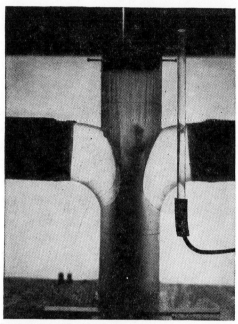

FIG. 25-5. Interference of flows seen in transparent plastic stack fitting. (*National Bureau of Standards.*)

since a force of some kind is required to deflect the downward flowing stream and therefore change its momentum. This hydrostatic pressure is built up by the backing up of the water in the branch until the head thus created suffices to change the momentum of the stream already in the stack enough to allow the flow from the branch to enter the stack.

The magnitude of the maximum hydrostatic pressure that should be permitted in the branch as a result of the backing up of the waste water was based on the consideration that this backing up should not be sufficiently great to cause the water to back up into a shower stall or to cause sluggish flow. It was taken as half the diameter of the horizontal branch at its connection to the stack. That is, it is the head measured at the axis of the pipe that will just cause the branch to flow full near the exit.

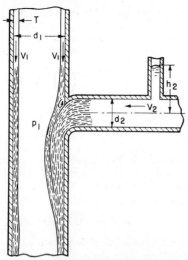

Fig. 25-6. Diagrammatic representation of interference of flows in stack fitting.

The theoretical analysis of the problem is so lengthy that it will not be presented here, but the reader is referred to the original paper for the details [25-3]. The final equation resulting from the analysis gives, for any rate of flow down the stack, within the limits of the capacity of the stack, the flow from a horizontal branch that will just cause the branch to flow full near its outlet. When a sanitary tee is used to connect the branch to the stack, the equation is

$$Y = 8.33 - 14.8 \left(\frac{T}{d_2}\right)^{5/8} \left(\frac{d_2}{d_1}\right)^{3/8} Y^{3/8} X^{5/8} \qquad (25\text{-}17)$$

where $X = \dfrac{v_1^2}{2g(h_2 - h_1)}$

$Y = \dfrac{v_2^2}{2g(h_2 - h_1)}$

h_2 = hydrostatic head in horizontal branch at a distance of 4 diameters back from the junction with stack, in feet head of water

h_1 = pneumatic pressure in stack at level of horizontal branch, in feet head of water, $= \rho/\rho g$

v_2 = mean velocity of flow out of branch, running full, in feet head of water

v_1 = mean velocity of sheet of water flowing down wall of stack, fps

T = thickness of sheet of water at level of horizontal branch (assumed to be terminal thickness), ft

d_1 = nominal diameter of stack, ft

d_2 = nominal diameter of drain, ft

When a long turn tee-wye is used to connect the branch to the stack, the water has a greater vertical component of velocity when it enters the stack than when a sanitary tee is used, and the back pressures should be smaller in this case for the same flows down the stack and in the branch. Tests by Wyly and Eaton at the National Bureau of Standards have shown this to be so, and the equation that they obtained, corresponding to Eq. (25-17), is [25-6]

$$Y = 6.0 - 9.4 \left(\frac{T}{d_2} \right)^{5/8} \left(\frac{d_2}{d_1} \right)^{3/8} Y^{3/8} X^{5/8} \qquad (25\text{-}18)$$

where the quantities are the same as those in Eq. (25-17).

The foregoing studies were continued by tests in a six-story 3-in. stack in which the branches were connected to the stack by sanitary tees. As might have been anticipated, the final relation obtained, corresponding to Eqs. (25-17) and (25-18), was simpler than these two equations, owing to the fact that the velocities of flow down the stack were not selected arbitrarily but were the terminal velocities resulting from flow down the stack from higher levels. The equation obtained for this case is [25-6]

$$Y = 8.33 - 2.48 Y^{0.3} X^{0.7} \qquad (25\text{-}19)$$

Equation (25-19) is not in convenient form to use. Replacing v_1 and v_2 in terms of Q_1, Q_2, d_1, and d_2 results in the equation

$$\frac{Q_2^2}{(h_2 - h_1)d_2^4} = 331 - 63.1 \left[\frac{d_1}{Q_1^{3/8}} \right]^{2.24} \left[\frac{Q_1^2}{(h_2 - h_1)d_1^4} \right]^{0.7} \left[\frac{Q_2^2}{(h_2 - h_1)d_2^4} \right]^{0.3} \qquad (25\text{-}20)$$

all quantities being expressed in foot-second units.

Unfortunately the investigation had to be terminated before it was possible to undertake the laborious task of rebuilding the stack with long-turn tee-wyes connecting the branches to the stack; so the formula for computing the back pressures in branches is available only for the case in which sanitary tees are used to connect the horizontal branches to the stacks.

25.6   Loading Tables for Stacks

The loading tables in most of the plumbing codes in this country are based fundamentally on the theory of probability of simultaneous operation of fixtures, and the method of determining design loads has been presented in Chap. 24. In order to use these loading tables, it is first necessary to add up the loading effects of all the fixtures discharging into the line under consideration. To facilitate this procedure each code includes a table of fixture-unit ratings for the different types of fixtures, and these values can be used to sum up the loading effect of the fixtures. Now if the loading tables, which give the maximum number of fixture units that it is permissible to connect to a given diameter of stack or drain, were not available, it would be necessary to use probability curves similar to those shown in Fig. 24-3 to obtain the maximum permissible rate of flow and then compute the pipe size required to carry this rate of flow by hydraulic formulas. This procedure is avoided by the use of the loading tables which allow for the maximum probable number of fixtures that may be considered to be in simultaneous operation and also determine the pipe size required.

The National Plumbing Code presents a table of fixture-unit ratings for various plumbing fixtures for use in computing the *drainage* systems. See Table 11.4.2, page 11-7.

This table is based on a fixture-unit rating of 10 for water closets in computing the probability curves. Some codes are based instead on the earlier practice of assigning a fixture-unit rating of 6 to water closets. This must be taken into account in comparing fixture-unit ratings in different codes.

The National Plumbing Code provides Table 11.5.3 for sizing stacks, based on the fixture-unit ratings in Table 11.4.2.

BMS66 [25-6] has the following to say about the fixture-unit values given in column 2 of Table 11.5.3, page 11-11:

"Sec. 805. Size of Soil and Waste Pipes. (a) Except as provided in (b) of this section, the total number of fixture units installed on a soil or waste stack or horizontal branch of given diameter shall be in accordance with table 805. No soil or waste stack shall be smaller than the largest horizontal branch connected thereto.

"(b) If the total fixture units are distributed on horizontal branches in three or more branch intervals of the stack, the total number of fixture units on a straight soil or waste stack of a given diameter may be increased from the values given in table 805 [column 2, Table 11.5.3] within the limits of table 805 (b)-III, part III, provided the maximum fixture units for one branch interval as computed in accordance with table 805 (b)-III is not exceeded in any branch interval of the system."

Table 805 (b)-III of BMS66 [25-6] is reproduced here as Table 25.4.

Table 25.4 Permissible Limits in Fixture Units on Soil and Waste Stacks

| Diameter (in.) | Limits in fixture units | | |
| | In any one branch interval for | | Maximum on 1 stack |
	One branch interval only N	Two or more branch intervals $N/2n + N/4$	
1¼	1	1	2
1½	3	2	8
2	6	6	24
3	32	$16/n + 8$	80
4	240	$120/n + 60$	600
5	540	$270/n + 135$	1,500
6	960	$480/n + 240$	2,800
8	1,800	$900/n + 450$	5,400
10	2,700	$1,350/n + 675$	8,000
12	4,200	$2,100/n + 1,050$	14,000

N is equal to the number of fixture units in column 2, and n is the number of branch intervals.

The following examples will illustrate the use of Table 25.4:

1. What is the maximum permissible number of fixture units that may be connected to a 4-in. stack in a four-story building, according to Table 25.4? In this case, $N = 240$ (see Table 25.4) and $n = 4$. Then

$$\frac{N}{2n} + \frac{N}{4} = \frac{240}{8} + \frac{240}{4} = 30 + 60 = 90 \text{ fixture units}$$

in one branch interval. For the entire stack, the total permissible number of fixture units will be $90 \times 4 = 360$ fixture units.

2. What is the permissible number of fixture units that may be connected to a 4-in. stack in an eight-story building, according to Table 25.4? In this case, $N = 240$, as before, and $n = 8$. Then

$$\frac{N}{2n} + \frac{N}{4} = \frac{240}{16} + \frac{240}{4} = 15 + 60 = 75 \text{ fixture units}$$

in one branch interval. For the entire stack, then, the number of fixture units that is permissible is $75 \times 8 = 600$ fixture units. This is the same as the maximum value set for a 4-in. stack by the table.

Table 25.5   Recommended Stack-loading Values

Diameter of stack (in.)	Stacks $\frac{7}{24}$ full		Stacks $\frac{1}{4}$ full	
	gpm	Fixture units	gpm	Fixture units
2	22.5	10	18.5	8
3	87.0	155	54.0	55
4	140	490	115	355
5	260	1,350	210	1,000
6	425	2,850	340	2,150
8	920	7,450	730	5,500
10	1,650	15,000	1,330	11,600
12	2,700	26,300	2,170	20,600

Table 25.5 is proposed for use as the stack-loading table in plumbing codes. It is based on the curves for stacks flowing $\frac{1}{4}$ full and $\frac{7}{24}$ full, as shown in Fig. 25-3. It is based on rational considerations; it agrees very well over all except the ends of the range with the loading tables in the National Plumbing Code, the Uniform Plumbing Code [25-8], and the Plumbing Manual, BMS66. It is a little more liberal (if the $\frac{7}{24}$ full curve is used) than the values recommended by Dawson and Kalinske, but this is merely because the curves based on stack fullness in Fig. 25-3 were determined for somewhat smaller values of the terminal velocity than those assumed by Dawson and Kalinske. It has already been explained why the terminal velocities adopted in the present work are believed to be more reliable than those measured by these two experimenters.

On the basis of the foregoing considerations, it is recommended that, in determining the maximum permissible loads on stacks, the curve for $\frac{1}{4}$ fullness in Fig. 25-3 be taken as the lower limit of these maximum stack loadings and the curve for $\frac{7}{24}$ fullness be taken as the upper limit of the maximum stack loadings permitted. This allows for the exercise of judgment by the code-writing authorities. It is believed that the $\frac{7}{24}$ fullness curve, giving the larger permissible loadings, is not unduly liberal. These two curves are the basis of the stack loadings, or design loads, expressed in fixture units, given in Table 25.5.

It is advisable to place the restrictions on the numbers of water closets that can be connected to 3-in. stacks that are given in the National Plumbing Code (see Table 11.5.3). That is, for 3-in. stacks, do not permit more than two water closets to connect to the stack in any one branch interval, and do not permit more than six water closets to connect to any stack of this diameter. And, obviously, do not permit water closets to be connected to stacks smaller in diameter than 3 in.

CHAPTER 26

Capacities of Sloping Drains

26.1 Introduction

The problem of the capacities of horizontal or sloping drains is a complicated one. While the underlying principle involved is to select the drain size so that the drain will flow approximately half full under the design load, it will not suffice to determine the size of a given drain by using one of the familiar hydraulic formulas for pipe flow. The reason for this is that these formulas assume a steady uniform flow to exist, whereas this is virtually never true in a partially filled sloping building drain, although it may be approximated temporarily toward the outlet end of a very long large-diameter drain serving a building containing a large number of plumbing fixtures. Actually the capacity of a drain may be greater under surging flow than under steady flow for the same peak rate of flow, as will be demonstrated.

The concept of flow on which the determination of drain sizes will be based is that of a highly fluctuating or surging condition in the horizontal branches which carry the discharges of fixtures to the soil or waste stack. After falling down the vertical stack, the water is assumed to enter the building drain with the peaks of the surges leveled off somewhat, but still in a surging condition.

In a large building covering considerable ground area there will probably be several primary branches* and certainly at least one secondary† branch. As the discharge travels down a primary branch, it continues to level off, becoming more and more nearly uniform, particularly after the hydraulic jump has occurred (see Fig. 22-4). If the secondary branch is long enough, and if the drain serves a large number of fixtures, the flow may become substantially uniform before it reaches the street sewer.

Looking at the problem of surging flow from the standpoint of duration of the surges instead of the flattening of the surges,‡ we conceive that the duration of a

---

* A primary branch of the building drain is the single sloping drain from the base of a soil or waste stack to its junction with the main building drain or with another branch thereof [26-1]. (Numbers in brackets refer to the bibliography at the end of the book.)

† A secondary branch of the building drain is any branch of the building drain other than a primary branch [26-1]. That is, a secondary branch may be a portion of the building drain that receives the discharge from two or more primary branches.

‡ The following discussion is based on the assumption that the entire load on the system is due to the discharge of water closets. There are several reasons for this assumption. The phenomenon of surging flow is accentuated by the discharge from water closets, since each discharge is at a high rate of flow and lasts for a very short period. In addition, some pertinent experimental data from tests of water closets are given.

surge is a minimum for the horizontal branches and that it gradually increases with increase in load and with distance from the point at which the closet discharges into the drainage system. For a system into which many water closets are discharging, the flow at points far distant from the points of entry will tend toward uniformity.

26.2 Rates of Flow for Steady Uniform Flow Conditions in Sloping Drains

Although the equations of steady uniform flow in sloping drains should not be used to determine the capacities of sloping drains in which surging flow exists, nevertheless flow computations based on these formulas afford a rough check on values obtained by the more complicated methods that are applicable to surging flow, particularly for large drains and relatively high slopes, as will be shown later. Hence several of the commonly used formulas for flow in pipes will be considered, and flow charts will be prepared for drains flowing half full, based on one of these—the Manning formula.

The three formulas that will be considered here are (1) the Hazen and Williams, (2) the Manning, and (3) the Darcy-Weisbach.

1. Hazen and Williams Formula. This formula is usually written

$$v = CR^{0.63}S^{0.54}(0.001)^{-0.04} = 1.318CR^{0.63}S^{0.54} \qquad \text{fps} \qquad (26\text{-}1)$$

where v = mean velocity of flow, fps

C = Hazen and Williams coefficient

R = hydraulic radius of pipe, ft*

S = slope of pressure gradient†

The exponents of R and S in Eq. (26-1) have been selected to make the coefficient C as nearly constant as possible for different pipe diameters and for different velocities of flow. Thus, C is approximately constant for a given pipe roughness.

This formula can be used to give the mean velocity of flow in the pipe when it is flowing full under no head by substituting the gradient of the pipe for the pressure gradient S. When this substitution is made, the desired form of the equation is obtained by multiplying both sides by the internal cross section A of the pipe:

$$Q = Av = 1.318 \left(\frac{\pi d^2}{4} \right) CR^{0.63}S^{0.54} \qquad \text{cfs} \qquad (26\text{-}2)$$

Or, if we want the rate of flow to be in gallons per minute, we multiply the right member by 449:

$$Q = 592 \left(\frac{\pi d^2}{4} \right) CR^{0.63}S^{0.54} \qquad \text{gpm} \qquad (26\text{-}3)$$

* The hydraulic radius R is defined as the wetted cross section of the flow divided by the wetted perimeter. For a circular pipe flowing either full or half full, the hydraulic radius is equal to $\pi d/4$, where d is the inside diameter of the pipe.

† For uniform flow in a sloping drain (constant depth at all cross sections) the slope of the water surface and the slope of the drain are both given by S.

To get the rate of flow for the pipe flowing half full, divide the right member of the last equation by 2:

$$Q = 296 \left(\frac{\pi d^2}{4}\right) CR^{0.63}S^{0.54} \quad \textbf{gpm} \quad (26\text{-}4)$$

Equation (26-4) can now be used to compute the rates of flow in pipes of different diameters, different roughnesses, and laid on different slopes, provided that the flow is steady and uniform.

2. Manning Formula. The Manning formula, which is similar to the Hazen and Williams formula, is usually written

$$v = \frac{1.486}{n} R^{2/3}S^{1/2} = \frac{1.486}{n} R^{0.67}S^{0.50} \quad \textbf{fps} \quad (26\text{-}5)$$

In this formula, n is the Manning coefficient, which is taken as constant for all diameters and rates of flow. It varies only with the roughness of the pipe. The rate of flow for the pipe flowing full or half full is obtained by multiplying both sides of the equation by the wetted cross section A.

$$Q = Av = \frac{\pi d^2}{4} \frac{1.486}{n} R^{0.67}S^{0.50} \quad \textbf{cfs} \quad (26\text{-}6a)$$

or

$$Q = 449 \frac{\pi d^2}{4} \frac{1.486}{n} R^{0.67}S^{0.50} \quad \textbf{gpm} \quad (26\text{-}6b)$$

for the pipe flowing full, and

$$Q = 224.5 \frac{\pi d^2}{4} \frac{1.486}{n} R^{0.67}S^{0.50} \quad \textbf{gpm} \quad (26\text{-}7)$$

for the pipe flowing half full.

3. Darcy-Weisbach Formula. In this formula the exponents of the physical quantities are integers, but the dimensionless friction coefficient f varies with the diameter of the pipe, the velocity of flow, the kinematic viscosity of the fluid flowing, and the roughness of the walls. It is usually written

$$h = f \frac{l}{d} \frac{v^2}{2g} \quad \text{or} \quad S = f \frac{1}{d} \frac{v^2}{2g} \quad (26\text{-}8)$$

where h = difference in level, in feet, of the menisci of water columns connected through static openings at the ends of the pipe of length l ft

g = acceleration of gravity, ft per sec^2

It follows that h/l is the slope of the hydraulic gradient S. Equation (26-8) can also be written

$$v = \sqrt{\frac{2gdS}{f}} = \sqrt{\frac{8gRS}{f}} \quad \textbf{fps} \quad (26\text{-}9)$$

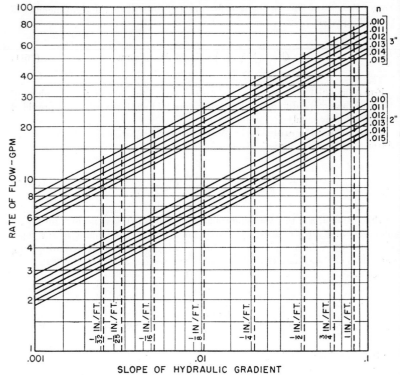

Fig. 26-1. Rates of flow in 2- and 3-in. drains flowing half full.

to put it in a form that is comparable with the Hazen and Williams and the Manning formulas. Then for the pipe flowing full under no head

$$Q = \frac{\pi d^2}{4} \sqrt{\frac{8gRS}{f}} \quad \text{cfs} \tag{26-10a}$$

or

$$Q = 449 \frac{\pi d^2}{4} \sqrt{\frac{8gRS}{f}} \quad \text{gpm} \tag{26-10b}$$

Similarly, to get the equation of the pipe flowing half full, we divide the right member by 2:

$$Q = 224.5 \frac{\pi d^2}{4} \sqrt{\frac{8gRS}{f}} \quad \text{gpm} \tag{26-11}$$

The Manning formula will be used to compute the rates of flow for building drains and sewers for cases in which the flow is steady and uniform. This formula is perhaps the best known of the three, the values of Manning's n are well established for different kinds of pipe, and it is convenient to use if any

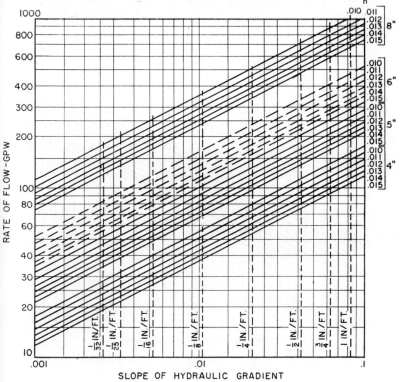

FIG. 26-2. Rates of flow in 4-, 5-, 6-, and 8-in. drains flowing half full.

mathematical manipulation is required, since the coefficient n is constant, except for variations in wall roughness. It should be remembered that this formula, as well as the other two discussed, is strictly applicable only to long pipes, so long that the entrance losses are negligible in comparison with the friction loss. Figures 26-1, 26-2, and 26-3 have been plotted from the Manning formula for pipes flowing half full [Eq. (26-7)]. Nominal diameters have been used in the computation.

4. Conversion from One Flow Formula to Another. Conversions from one formula to the other can be made through the following relations between C, n, and f, established by equating Eqs. (26-1) and (26-5), (26-1) and (26-9), and (26-5) and (26-9):

$$nC = 1.13 \left(\frac{R}{S}\right)^{0.04} \tag{26-12}$$

$$C\sqrt{f} = 12.2 \frac{1}{R^{0.13}S^{0.04}} \tag{26-13}$$

and

$$\frac{n}{\sqrt{f}} = 0.0925R^{0.17} \tag{26-14}$$

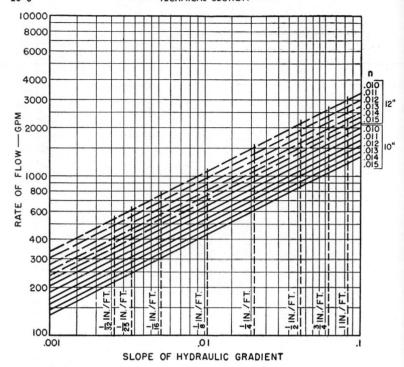

Fig. 26-3. Rates of flow in 10- and 12-in. drains flowing half full.

26.3   Computation of Rates of Flow in Drains for Any Degree of Fullness

For convenience in computing steady uniform rates of flow in sloping drains for different degrees of fullness from zero to half full, the necessary characteristics of circles are given in Table 26.1. This table can be used to obtain the area of wetted cross section A and the hydraulic radius R corresponding to the assumed degree of fullness, and these values can then be substituted in Eq. (26-6a).

The first column of Table 26.1 lists values of h/d, the ratio of the depth of flow in the pipe of diameter d. The second column gives corresponding values of the ratio of the wetted perimeter or arc to diameter. Column 3 gives values of the ratio of the wetted cross section to diameter squared. The fourth column gives values of the ratio of the hydraulic radius to diameter, obtained by dividing each value in column 3 by the corresponding value in column 2.

The values of A and R thus obtained are substituted in Eq. (26-6a)

$$Q = 449A \, \frac{1.486}{n} \, R^{2/3} S^{1/2} \qquad \text{gpm}$$

Table 26.1 Characteristics of Circles

$\dfrac{h}{d}$	$\dfrac{\text{Arc}}{d}$	$\dfrac{\text{Area}}{d^2}$	$\dfrac{R}{d}$	$\dfrac{h}{d}$	$\dfrac{\text{Arc}}{d}$	$\dfrac{\text{Area}}{d^2}$	$\dfrac{R}{d}$
0.00	0.000	0.0000	0.0000	0.25	1.045	0.1535	0.147
0.01	0.200	0.0013	0.0065	0.26	1.070	0.162	0.151
0.02	0.284	0.0037	0.0130	0.27	1.095	0.171	0.157
0.03	0.348	0.0069	0.0198	0.28	1.115	0.180	0.161
0.04	0.403	0.0105	0.0261	0.29	1.135	0.189	0.167
0.05	0.451	0.0147	0.0326	0.30	1.16	0.198	0.171
0.06	0.495	0.0192	0.0388	0.31	1.18	0.207	0.175
0.07	0.5355	0.0242	0.0452	0.32	1.20	0.217	0.181
0.08	0.5735	0.0294	0.0513	0.33	1.22	0.226	0.185
0.09	0.609	0.0350	0.0575	0.34	1.25	0.2355	0.189
0.10	0.6435	0.0409	0.0636	0.35	1.27	0.245	0.194
0.11	0.676	0.0470	0.0695	0.36	1.29	0.255	0.198
0.12	0.7075	0.0534	0.0755	0.37	1.31	0.264	0.202
0.13	0.738	0.0600	0.0813	0.38	1.33	0.274	0.206
0.14	0.767	0.0668	0.0871	0.39	1.35	0.284	0.211
0.15	0.795	0.0739	0.0930	0.40	1.37	0.293	0.214
0.16	0.823	0.0811	0.0985	0.41	1.39	0.303	0.218
0.17	0.850	0.0885	0.104	0.42	1.41	0.310	0.222
0.18	0.876	0.0961	0.110	0.43	1.43	0.323	0.226
0.19	0.902	0.104	0.115	0.44	1.45	0.333	0.229
0.20	0.927	0.112	0.121	0.45	1.47	0.343	0.233
0.21	0.952	0.120	0.126	0.46	1.49	0.353	0.237
0.22	0.976	0.128	0.131	0.47	1.51	0.363	0.240
0.23	1.000	0.1365	0.137	0.48	1.53	0.373	0.244
0.24	1.025	0.145	0.142	0.49	1.55	0.383	0.247
				0.50	1.57	0.393	0.2500

The nomenclature has the following significance in computing flow in sloping partially filled pipes:

h = depth of flow
d = inside diameter of pipe
Area = area of wetted cross section
Arc = length of arc in contact with water
R = hydraulic radius-wetted area divided by wetted perimeter (in this case the values in column 4 are obtained by dividing the values in column 3 by the corresponding values in column 2)

The following computation is made to illustrate this:
Assume that $d = 4$ in. $= 0.333$ ft and that $S = 1$ in. per ft.

$\dfrac{h}{d}$	$\dfrac{A}{d^2}$	$\dfrac{A}{\text{ft}^2}$	$\dfrac{\text{Arc}}{d}$	$R = \dfrac{A}{\text{Arc}}$ ft	$R^{2/3}$	S	$S^{1/2}$
0.3	0.198	0.0220	1.16	0.386	0.1495	0.0833	0.289

Then $\quad Q = 449 \times 0.0220 \times \dfrac{1.486}{0.011} \times 0.1495 \times 0.289 = 57.6$ gpm

A rough check on the computation can be had by comparing with the rate of flow when the pipe is flowing half full, by reading the latter value from Fig. 26-1, 26-2, or 26-3, whichever one is pertinent.

26.4   Capacities of Sloping Drains under Surging Flow

1. The General Concept of Surging Flow in Drains.   In what follows, it will be assumed that the system consists exclusively of water closets discharging into the drainage system.   It has already been pointed out that water closets, with their brief period of discharge and high rate of flow for each flush, afford an accentuated case of surging flow.   In an actual system containing a variety of plumbing fixtures, surging flow will still exist in drainage systems, but it will not be so marked as it would be if only water closets were involved.

In such a system the flow may be looked upon as a series of surges having maxima or peaks and different time durations imposed either (1) on an empty drain or (2) on a drain already flowing partly full.

It has already been pointed out that the surges passing through horizontal branches have minimum duration, this being governed almost entirely by the characteristics of the discharges from the plumbing fixtures discharging into the branch.   A little flattening of the surges occurs as they pass along the horizontal branch, a little more occurs as they fall down the stack, but they enter the primary branches of the building drain without much change.   As they pass along the primary branch and the secondary branches, if any, still further flattening occurs until, if the building drain and the building sewer are very long, the flow may approximate steady conditions as it nears the street sewer, for a building that has many plumbing fixtures in use (see Figs. 22-3 to 22-6).

Ignoring for the present the fact that the surges actually have their shortest duration in the horizontal branches, and confining our attention to the component parts of the building drain and to the building sewer, we can say that the surges imposed on 3- and 4-in. primary branches have minimum duration, and this duration increases with (1) increase in load, (2) diameter of drain, and (3) distance from stack.

If the duration of the surge is a minimum, it follows that the corresponding peak rate of flow will be a maximum.   Hence the peaks will decrease with increase of time of duration of the surge, that is, with increase in load and with increase in distance from the point of entry of the individual discharges.   Under this concept of flow in the drainage systems of buildings, we may look upon steady uniform flow as being the limiting case of surging flow as the ratio of peak flow to average flow approaches unity and the duration of the surge becomes infinite.*

Because of the leveling out of surges as they pass along the primary and

* This concept of surging flow is due to the late Dr. Roy B. Hunter of the National Bureau of Standards and is to be found in his papers, both published and unpublished [26-1].   Contributions to this concept have also been made by John L. French of the National Bureau of Standards [26-2].   The interpretation given by French has been drawn upon heavily in the preparation of this chapter.

secondary branches of building drains and through the building sewer, it is necessary to consider the following cases:

1. Primary branches
    a. Carrying capacity of empty drains when subjected to surging flow
    b. Carrying capacity of partially filled drains subjected to surging flow
2. Secondary branches and building sewers
3. Horizontal branches

2. Primary Branches. Primary branches may be looked upon as falling into two general groups. The first group consists of the smaller-diameter drains serving a relatively small number of fixtures, and these drains will be assumed to be substantially empty when a surge is imposed on the drain. The second group may be considered to comprise the larger-diameter drains serving a relatively large number of fixtures. Such drains will probably already be carrying an appreciable flow when a surge is imposed on them.

a. Carrying Capacity of Empty Drains When Subjected to Surging Flow. In 1939 Hunter conducted tests at the National Bureau of Standards on the capacities of horizontal (sloping) drains carrying fluctuating flows of water simulating the flow imposed on a drainage system by intermittent discharges of plumbing fixtures, in this case, water closets. Unfortunately, owing to his death, the results of these studies were never published. Following the war, however, his records and notes were salvaged by John L. French, who analyzed and summarized the data in the memorandum already referred to [26-2].

The tests under immediate consideration were made on a straight length of cast-iron soil-pipe drain approximately 70 ft long, with the water brought into the drain vertically downward through a long-sweep bend, thus simulating the flow from a stack into a building drain. Surges were produced by means of a quick-opening valve in the stack, the rate of flow being controlled by a gate valve. The duration of the surge was taken as the time that the quick-opening valve was open, and the capacity of the drain was taken as the minimum rate of flow at which the drain flowed full at some section.* The tops of the lengths of cast-iron pipe were slotted so that it could be determined visually when this was the case.

The results of these tests on a 3-in.-diameter system and on a 4-in.-diameter system are shown in Figs. 26-4 and 26-5. The data were obtained for drain slopes of $\frac{1}{16}$, $\frac{1}{8}$, and $\frac{1}{4}$ in. per ft and for surge durations from 5 to 30 sec.

The figures show clearly that the surge capacity of the drains becomes greater as the duration of the surge decreases. They also show that the effect of the slope of drain decreases as the surge duration decreases, also that the effect of the duration of surge on the surge capacity is smaller for the larger slopes than for the smaller slopes.

In order to put the data in Figs. 26-4 and 26-5 in a form convenient for use, they have been replotted in Fig. 26-6 with $Q/(\pi d^2/4)$ as ordinates and t as abscissas. Thus the ordinates represent the velocity of the surge when it just

---

* It should be noted that the term "drain capacity" as used here differs from that used elsewhere in this chapter. The capacity of a building drain is ordinarily taken as the rate of flow that will just make the pipe flow half full.

fills the cross section of the pipe.   As would be expected, a surge of short duration travels faster than a longer surge, and hence a drain of given size will carry
a larger rate of flow without being overloaded if the surges are relatively short
than if they are relatively long.

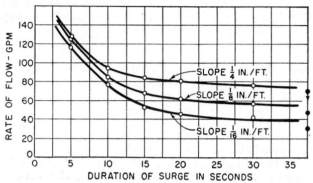

FIG. 26-4. Hunter's data—carrying capacity of 3-in. drains under surging flow.

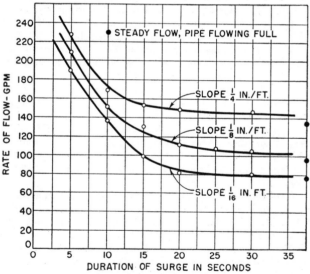

FIG. 26-5. Hunter's data—carrying capacity of 4-in. drains under surging flow.

It will be noted from the curves in Fig. 26-6 that the agreement between the
data from the two diameters of drain is surprisingly good, considering the rough
method used for determining when the drains just flowed full at some section.
The next question that arises is whether the data can be generalized to apply to
drain diameters greater than 4 in.   It would be expected that the velocity of
travel of a surge would increase with increase in diameter of the drain and with

the rate of flow. Yet there is no indication of this shown by the data for the 3- and 4-in. drains.

If we assume that the curves for the three different slopes apply to drain diameters up to and including 6 in., we are thereby establishing a factor of safety for the larger-diameter drains, since we are using lower velocities, and hence lower rates of flow, than would probably occur with these larger diameters of drain.

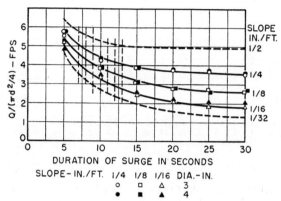

Fɪɢ. 26-6. Analysis of data on surging flow in 3- and 4-in. drains—drain empty.

In order that design loads may be determined for different slopes and diameters of drains, it is necessary to get at least a rough idea of the variation in duration of the surge from a water closet with the distance from the point at which the discharge enters the drain. In order to do this, unpublished data obtained by Hunter [26-2] on the flattening of surges from a water closet as they traveled along 3- and 4-in. drains will be considered. Figure 26-7 shows typical surges obtained by Hunter in the tests referred to.

While the surge from a water closet does not have the idealized rectangular form of the surges that supplied the data in Figs. 26-4, 26-5, and 26-6, the former can be put on a more nearly comparable basis with the latter by computing the time that the actual surge would last if it consisted of a constant rate of flow equal to the peak flow. For example, if we apply this procedure to the surge shown in Fig. 26-7, we have peak rates of flow of 36.5 gpm at the entrance, 34 gpm 11 ft downstream, 35 gpm 21 ft downstream, and 26 gpm 42 ft downstream. This gives for the surge durations 6.6, 7.1, 6.9, and 9.25 sec for distances of 0, 11, 21, and 42 ft, respectively, downstream from the entrance to the drain.

French [26-2] computed the durations given in Table 26.2 from other data obtained by Hunter on the discharge of water from a water closet passing along 3- and 4-in. drains laid on a slope of ¼ in. per ft.

The data in Table 26.2 show that the surge durations for the discharge of a single water closet increase gradually with the distance from the water closet and that the durations are the same for the 3-in. as for the 4-in. drain. This supports the evidence given by Fig. 26-6.

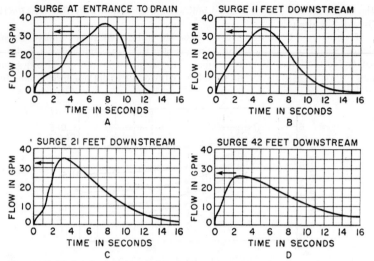

FIG. 26-7. Flattening of surges from water closet in passing along 4-in. drain.

The amount that the peak of each surge levels off as it travels along a horizontal branch and down the stack will vary with the length and slope of the branch and with the distance that it falls down the stack. Data on this are given in an unpublished manuscript by Hunter at the National Bureau of

Table 26.2   Surge Durations Produced in 3- and 4-in. Drains Sloping ¼ In. per Ft from the Discharge of a Water Closet

Distance from closet (ft)	Surge duration (sec)		Avg rate of flow (gpm)	
	3-in. drain	4-in. drain	3-in. drain	4-in. drain
0	6.5	6.5	37.0	37.0
6	6.9	7.1	34.8	33.8
11	7.1	7.1	33.8	33.8
21	6.8	6.9	35.4	34.8
41	9.5	9.6	25.3	25.0

Standards. He set up a single water closet on each of the fourth and tenth floors and discharged them into a 4-in. stack connecting to a 4-, a 5-, and a 6-in. building drain. The total volume of the flush was determined in each instance by catching the total discharge at the end of the building drain and measuring it. Then the outflow from the drain for each discharge was measured for the first 5 sec, the first 10 sec, and the first 15 sec of the outflow.

Hunter comments that 60 to 70 per cent of the discharge leaves the drain in the first 15 sec, after which the flow gradually decreases, reducing to a mere trickle at the end of about 45 sec for a 4-in. drain and in about 60 sec for a 6-in. drain.   The flush of the closets lasted 8 to 10 sec.

The data obtained in this investigation are given in Table 26.3.   Analysis of the rather scanty data in this table indicates that we can assume the peak flow in a surge from a water closet to be about 2 per cent for each 10 ft of fall, the stack

Table 26.3   Reduction in Peak Flow in the Surge from the Discharge of a Water Closet in a Stack and Building Drain

(Single water closet on fourth and tenth floors)

Length of fall in stack (ft)	Length of drain (ft)	Slope of drain (in./ft)	Reduction in peak flow (%)
4-in. stack and 4-in. building drain			
30	40	$\frac{1}{8}$	53
90	40	$\frac{1}{8}$	60
30	40	$\frac{1}{4}$	43
90	40	$\frac{1}{4}$	53
4-in. stack and 5-in. building drain			
30	40	$\frac{1}{8}$	44
90	40	$\frac{1}{8}$	56
30	40	$\frac{1}{4}$	35
90	40	$\frac{1}{4}$	45
30	40	$\frac{7}{16}$	33
90	40	$\frac{7}{16}$	45
4-in. stack and 6-in. building drain			
30	40	$\frac{1}{8}$	44
90	40	$\frac{1}{8}$	64
30	40	$\frac{1}{4}$	34
90	40	$\frac{1}{4}$	54

being 4 in. in diameter.   Probably the diameter of the stack has little effect on this figure.   We can also assume that the reduction in peak flow is about 1 per cent for each foot of travel along a building drain, at least for 4-, 5-, and 6-in. drains and for slopes ranging from $\frac{1}{8}$ to $\frac{7}{16}$ in. per ft.   These figures should be looked upon merely as approximate values that make it possible to get a rough idea of the flattening of surges of water closets as they pass down the stack and along the building drain.

There is one aspect of the curves in Fig. 26-6 that has not been pointed out. The curves are based on the assumption that the individual discharges making up the load on the drain or stack under consideration have the form of the surge as it leaves the fixture that creates it. That is, the average rate of flow and the duration of the flow are the same, regardless of the location of the surge in the drainage system. Or, putting the matter another way, no allowance was made for the leveling off of surges in preparing these curves.

The leveling off of a surge increases the duration of the surge and thus decreases the load that the drain can carry without becoming filled at some cross section (see Figs. 26-4 and 26-5). Furthermore, the discussion so far has concerned discharges from water closets, which yield a short surge with a relatively high rate of flow. Such fixtures as kitchen sinks, bathtubs, and laundry trays, yield relatively long flat surges lying to the right on the curves in Fig. 26-6.

On the basis of the foregoing considerations, French [26-2] chose the following surge durations for use in determining design loads for primary branches of the building drain for 6-in. and smaller diameters.*

Table 26.4 Surge Durations Assumed for 6-in. and Smaller Diameter Building Drains

Drain Diameter (in.)	Surge Duration (sec)
4	8
5	9
6	10

If the data shown in Figs. 26-4 and 26-5 are replotted as in Fig. 26-6 with values of $Q/(\pi d^2/4)$ as ordinates, the two curves for each slope but different diameters each coalesce into a single curve, there being a distinct curve for each slope. Note that the ordinates in Fig. 26-6 are velocities, specifically the velocities corresponding to the drain running full, as it is at the section where the flow fills the cross section.

Now these curves can be used to establish design loads for 3-, 4-, 5-, and 6-in. primary branches if it appears reasonable to assume that the fact that the curves for a given slope, but for 3-in and 4-in. diameters, coalesce when plotted as in this figure is an adequate basis for assuming that similar tests on 5-in and 6-in. drains would have yielded results that would also agree with Fig. 26-6. Obviously this cannot be known with certainty without actual test results. However, in the absence of such data, and since the curves do come together so markedly for the 3- and 4-in. diameters, it will be assumed for design purposes that the same would hold true for the two largest diameters.

The solid curves, for slopes of $\frac{1}{4}$, $\frac{1}{8}$, and $\frac{1}{16}$ in. per ft, were obtained from experimental data. The results have been extrapolated to furnish the corresponding curves for slopes of $\frac{1}{32}$ and $\frac{1}{2}$ in. per ft with the aid of the curve in Fig. 26-8. In determining this last-mentioned curve, it was assumed that the velocity depended on the slope of the drain in accordance with the following relation:

$$\frac{v_1}{v_2} = \left(\frac{S_1}{S_2}\right)^n \tag{26-15}$$

* In this report French was trying to explain the loading tables established by Hunter and used in the Plumbing Manual, BMS66 [26-1]. The results of this analysis by French agree well with the values established by Hunter, but Hunter's line of reasoning is not known, since his notes have been lost.

where the value of n can vary from zero up to 0.5, the latter being its value for steady flow. Taking the experimentally determined curves in pairs, corresponding values of v_1 and v_2 were read from the pair of curves under consideration, and the value of n was computed by using Eq. (26-15). The result is the curve in Fig. 26-8, giving n as a function of the duration of the surge. With these values of n determined, the dashed curves in Fig. 26-6 were computed for slopes of $\frac{1}{32}$ and $\frac{1}{2}$ in. per ft.

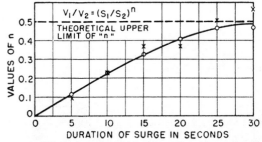

FIG. 26-8. Effect of slope on velocity of flow for surging flow.

b. *Carrying Capacity of Partially Filled Drains Subjected to Surging Flow. Primary Branches.* In the last section it was shown that the phenomenon of surging flow in sloping drains affords a logical basis for determining drain sizes for the smaller drains which may be assumed to be empty or nearly so, when a surge of waste water reaches them. It was assumed that drains up to and including 6-in. in diameter can be designed on this basis.

For drains larger than 6 in. in diameter, another approach must be used. It is assumed that such drains will in general be carrying an appreciable flow when a surge is imposed on them.

Hunter at the National Bureau of Standards conducted an investigation of this condition, and the results that he obtained are to be found in an unpublished manuscript. These data have been analyzed by French [26-2], and his analysis is used as the basis of the following discussion.

Hunter used a test system having a main line of 4-in. cast-iron soil pipe 40 ft long. A branch line also consisted of 4-in. cast-iron soil pipe connected into the main line through a wye-branch fitting. The pipe downstream from the junction of the two lines had longitudinal slots cut in it, so that visual observation of the filling of the cross section of the pipe at any point was possible. The lines were set at several different slopes for the tests. A 3-in. supply line discharged the constant rates of flow vertically downward through a 90° bend into the main line. A 2-in. supply pipe delivered the surging flow in the same way into the branch line.

Hunter's experimental results with this test installation are shown in Fig. 26-9. It is interesting to note that for certain conditions the capacity of the drain is less for the $\frac{1}{8}$-in.-per-ft slope than for the $\frac{1}{16}$-in.-per-ft slope. This can be attributed to the fact that the decrease in the peak of a surge is more for a $\frac{1}{16}$-in. slope than for a $\frac{1}{8}$-in. slope, so that this result is not contradictory.

Using the data just referred to, French carried out an analysis of drain capacities for the condition that surges are imposed on steady flow, as may be the case with the larger-diameter drains when used as primary branches. The procedure that he followed is rather complicated, and he found later that practically the same result could have been attained by assuming that the capacities of the larger drains are given by assuming surge durations of 10, 11, 12, and 13 sec for 6, 8, 10, and 12-in. drains, respectively. Consequently, because of the greater simplicity brought about in the analysis by this last assumption,

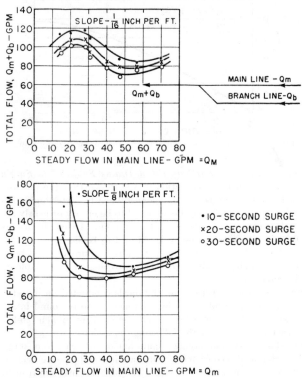

Fig. 26-9. Hunter's data on capacity of drains under surging flow—surge superimposed on steady flow in drain.

this procedure will be followed here. The computations are given in Table 26.5, along with the computations for the smaller drains. In this table a surge duration of 7 sec is assumed for a 3-in. drain, instead of 8 sec, as recommended by French.

26.5   Design Loads

1. Primary Branches of Building Drain. In the preparation of Table 26.5, values of v were read from the curves in Fig. 26-6. These values are listed in column 4 of the table. From these values and the cross-sectional areas of the different sizes of drain (the nominal diameters were used), values of the rate of flow, Q, are given in cubic feet per second and in gallons per minute (columns 5 and 6). These are the rates of flow that will just fill the pipe at some cross section. These values are next divided by 2 to give the rates

Table 26.5 Capacities of Sloping Drains under Surging Flow

Slope (in./ft)	Diameter (nominal) (in.)	Surge duration (sec)	$v = \dfrac{4Q}{\pi d^2}$ (fps)	Q		Q/2		
				cfs	gpm	Computed (gpm)	Manning formula $n = 0.015$ (gpm)	Design (gpm)
(1)	(2)	(3)	(4)	(5)	(6)	(7)	(8)	(9)
⅟₃₂	8	11	2.55	0.891	401	200.5	121	200
	10	12	2.38	1.310	589	294.5	215	300
	12	13	2.24	1.762	792	396.0	354	425
⅟₁₆	6	10	3.35	0.660	296	148.0	79.5	147
	8	11	3.10	1.085	487	243.5	170	245
	10	12	2.93	1.605	721	360.5	275	377
	12	13	2.77	2.175	976	488.0	505	555
⅟₈	3	7	4.75	0.234	105	52.5	17.5	51.5
	4	8	4.38	0.3825	171.5	85.8	38.0	84
	5	9	4.15	0.5685	255	127.5	69	125
	6	10	3.95	0.778	349.5	174.7	110	177
	8	11	3.76	1.315	591	295.5	242	300
	10	12	3.62	1.985	891	445.5	390	480
	12	13	3.48	2.73	1,226.5	613.3	710	740
¼	3	7	5.15	0.2535	113.8	56.9	24.5	58
	4	8	4.90	0.428	192	96.0	54	96
	5	9	4.65	0.637	286	143	98	146
	6	10	4.48	0.8825	396	198	146	208
	8	11	4.32	1.512	679	339.5	340	390
	10	12	4.20	2.302	1,033.5	516.8	555	660
	12	13	4.10	3.22	1,445	722.5	1,000	1,050
½	3	7	5.80	0.285	127	63.5	35	64
	4	8	5.60	0.486	218.5	109.3	76	112
	5	9	5.43	0.745	324.5	162.3	137	175
	6	10	5.28	1.04	467	233.5	225	265
	8	11	5.18	1.99	895	447.5	460	525
	10	12	5.10	2.80	1,258	629.0	780	910
	12	13	5.05	3.97	1,780	890	1,420	1,500

of flow that will just half fill the pipe. In column 8, values of the rates of flow that will just half fill the pipes, computed by the Manning formula (for steady flow) are given, computed for a Manning's n of 0.015, which represents fairly rough pipe. The rates of flow given were then plotted in Fig. 26-10. It will be noted that the curves obtained from the data on surging flow would cross the straight lines representing steady flow near the upper part of the figure (i.e., for the larger diameters) if plotted according to the data in column 8 in Table 26-5.

But we know that the velocities for surging flow can never be less than for steady flow; so these curves should not cross the Manning curves.

Consequently, the assumption is made that these curves for surging flow will approach the corresponding Manning formula curves asymptotically, and the curves are so drawn in the figure. Thus the left-hand family of curves in Fig. 26-10, representing surging flow, become the design curves for primary branches

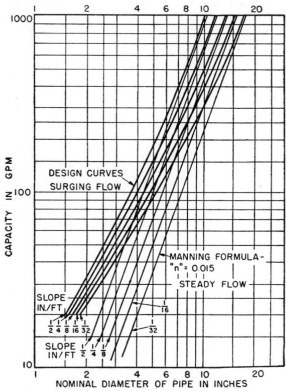

Fig. 26-10. Design loads for primary branches of building drains.

of the building drain, and the design-load values in column 9 of Table 26.5 were read from these curves.

The reason that the curves for surging flow do not agree with the Manning formula for large surge durations is that the variation of capacity with slope follows a different law for steady flow than it does for surging flow. Hunter's experimental results for surges imposed on an empty drain showed that the capacity varied with the square of the diameter (see Fig. 26-6), whereas the Manning formula makes the capacity vary with the $\frac{8}{3}$ power of the diameter.

The design loads in gallons per minute are next converted to fixture units by the use of Figs. 24-5, 24-6, and 24-7. These values are given in column 4 of

**Table 26.6   Comparison of Design Loads in Fixture Units
for Primary Branches of Building Drains**

Slope (in./ft.)	Diameter nominal (in.)	Design load computed (gpm)	Design loads (fixture units)			
			Computed	BMS66	NPC[1]	Manning formula
(1)	(2)	(3)	(4)	(5)	(6)	(7)
$\frac{1}{32}$	8	200.5	915	....	......	370
	10	294.5	1,700	....	......	1,000
	12	396.0	2,550	....	......	2,150
$\frac{1}{16}$	6	147	535	600	......	140
	8	245	1,250	1,400	1,400	700
	10	377	2,350	2,400	2,500	1,500
	12	555	4,000	3,600	3,900	3,500
$\frac{1}{8}$	3	51.5	51.5	36(24)[2]	20[3]	8
	4	84.0	169	180	180	24
	5	125	450	400	390	106
	6	177	735	660	700	305
	8	300	1,700	1,600	1,600	1,250
	10	480	3,350	2,700	2,900	2,500
	12	740	5,650	4,200	4,600	5,400
$\frac{1}{4}$	3	58	70	42(27)[2]	27[3]	11
	4	96	250	216	216	58
	5	146	535	480	480	235
	6	208	1,000	790	840	535
	8	390	2,500	1,920	1,920	2,100
	10	660	4,950	3,240	3,500	4,000
	12	1,050	8,700	5,000	5,600	8,200
$\frac{1}{2}$	3	64	87.5	50(36)[2]	36[3]	20
	4	112	315	250	250	134
	5	175	700	560	575	470
	6	265	1,400	940	1,000	1,000
	8	525	3,700	2,240	2,300	3,100
	10	910	7,300	3,780	6,700	6,100
	12	1,500	13,400	6,000	12,000	12,500

[1] National Plumbing Code [26-3].

[2] Soil.

[3] Not more than two water closets.

Table 26.6.   By way of comparison, the corresponding design loads specified by
the Plumbing Manual, BMS66 [26-1], and the National Plumbing Code [26-3]
are shown in columns 5 and 6, respectively, of Table 26.6.   Finally, design
loads computed from the Manning formula for steady flow are given in column 9
of the table.

This comparison demonstrates the usefulness of using a formula for steady
flow as a check on the results.   It would be expected that, as the diameter and

the slope of the drain increase, the design load should approach the capacity given by the formula for steady flow, yet should never be less than the latter. The design loads computed for surging flow satisfy this criterion. Thus it is believed that the seemingly high fixture-unit capacities for the 10- and 12-in. drains are justified.

The recommended design loads for primary branches of building drains are tabulated in Table 26.7.

Table 26.7   Design Loads for Primary Branches of Building Drains

Diameter of pipe (in.)	Maximum number of fixture units that may be connected to any primary branch of a building drain				
	Slope (in. per ft)				
	$\frac{1}{32}$	$\frac{1}{16}$	$\frac{1}{8}$	$\frac{1}{4}$	$\frac{1}{2}$
3 (soil)	. . . . .	. . . . .	20[1]	27[1]	36[1]
4	. . . . .	. . . . .	170	250	315
5	. . . . .	. . . . .	450	535	700
6	. . . . .	535	735	1,000	1,400
8	915	1,250	1,700	2,500	3,700
10	1,700	2,350	3,350	4,950	7,300
12	2,550	4,000	5,650	8,700	13,400

[1] Not more than two water closets.   Values taken from the National Plumbing Code, Table 11.5.2.

2. Building Sewer and Secondary Branches of Building Drain.   When we come to the consideration of the building sewer and the secondary branches of the building drain, we have to do with relatively steady flow. The larger the number of plumbing fixtures in a building (i.e., fixtures that are in use), and the longer the building drain and sewer, the more nearly will the flow in the portion of the line nearest the street sewer approach a steady condition. This means that a steady-flow formula, such as the Manning formula, will be approximately applicable. The larger the drain, the more nearly will this condition be approached.

The approach to the problem of design loads for primary branches of the building drain, based on Hunter's experiments, led to the conclusion that the capacity of a drain is greater for surging flow than for steady flow, the capacity gradually approaching that for steady flow as the surges flatten out. Thus we are led to the conclusion that the capacity of a secondary branch or building sewer of a given diameter is less than that of a primary branch of the same diameter. This might conceivably require that the building sewer be larger in diameter than the building drain in particular cases, even though it is carrying the same flow. It seems, however, that this will rarely be necessary, when it is considered that the design load is that load which will probably not make the drain flow more than half full more than 1 per cent of the time. It is obvious that a large factor of safety is involved here.

The method used to obtain the design loads in Table 26.8 is as follows: For each given slope, a plot was prepared of the capacity loads against drain diameter, using the values for surging flow given in Table 26.7 and the values for the Manning formula for steady flow given in column 7 of Table 26.6.   The results are plotted in Fig. 26-11 for three slopes of drain.   For each pair of curves thus

Table 26.8   Design Loads for Building Sewers and for Secondary Branches of Building Drains

Diameter of pipe	Maximum number of fixture units that may be connected to any secondary branch of a building drain or to the building sewer				
	Slope (in. per ft)				
	$\frac{1}{32}$	$\frac{1}{16}$	$\frac{1}{8}$	$\frac{1}{4}$	$\frac{1}{2}$
3	.....	.....	20[1]	27[1]	36[1]
4	.....	.....	170	240	300
5	.....	.....	380	400	670
6	.....	535	650	840	1,300
8	900	1,080	1,400	2,250	3,370
10	1,500	1,840	3,000	4,500	6,500
12	2,240	3,550	5,400	8,300	13,000

[1] Not more than two water closets.   Values taken from the National Plumbing Code.

drawn, representing one slope, a curve was then faired in, starting at or slightly above the design load for the 12-in. drain by the Manning formula and curving to meet the curve of capacities for surging flow at or near the smallest diameter for which a value was given.   The design loads were then read from the faired-in curve.

The design loads thus obtained represent surging flow for the smallest-diameter drains and approximately steady flow for the largest drains.   For drains of intermediate diameters, there is a gradual transition from one condition of flow to the other.

The design loads given in Table 26.8 for secondary branches of building drains and for building sewers may be compared with the values in Table 26.9, quoted from Table 807(c)-III of BMS66.   The fixture-unit values in this table are applicable, according to BMS66, to "secondary branches of the building drain, the main building drain, and building sewer of given diameter and slope . . . when the building drain has two or more primary branches of 3-inch or greater diameter and when the lowest horizontal branch or fixture drain is less than 3 feet above the grade line of the building drain."

Comparison of the fixture-unit values in Table 26.9 with those given for the Manning formula in the last column of Table 26.6 shows that the values in Table 807(c)-III in some instances greatly exceed those corresponding to the Manning formula.

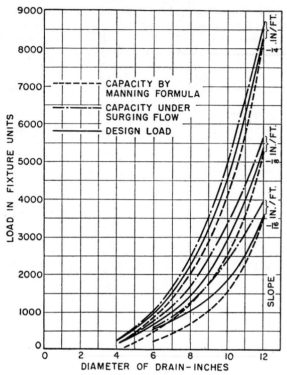

Fig. 26-11. Design loads for secondary branches of building drains.

Table 26.9   Limits in Fixture Units for Secondary Branch or Main

Diameter (in.)	$\frac{1}{16}$-in. fall	$\frac{1}{8}$-in. fall	$\frac{1}{4}$-in. fall	$\frac{1}{2}$-in. fall
3	. . . . .	90	125	180
4	. . . . .	450	630	900
5	600	850	1,200	1,700
6	950	1,350	1,900	2,700
8	1,950	2,800	3,900	5,600
10	3,400	4,900	6,800	9,800
12	5,600	8,000	11,200	16,000

A study of the values in Table 807(c)-III shows that, in preparing this table, Hunter used the concept of average flow in the system due to a large number of water closets as the basis for the table. He assumed the following values to be characteristic of water closets: average frequency of use, once in 5 min; volume of discharge per flush, 4 gal. Then the average flow in the system from one water closet is $\frac{4}{5}$ gpm, and the average flow from n water closets is $0.8n$ gpm.

The next step is to read from Fig. 26-1, 26-2, or 26-3 the rate of flow that will fill the selected diameter of drain half full at the slope chosen. Suppose, for example, that we make the computation for a 10-in. drain on a slope of $\frac{1}{4}$ in. per ft. From Fig. 26-3 we read, for a Manning's n of 0.015, the rate of flow, 550 gpm. Then

$$0.8n = 550$$

or

$$n = 668 \text{ water closets}$$

But a water closet has a fixture-unit rating of 10; so the number of fixture units corresponding to the flow of 550 gpm is $10n$, or 6,680. Examination of Table 807(c)-III gives the value 6,800 corresponding. Other values in Table 807(c)-III check equally well or better; hence it may be concluded that the average flow in the system due to water closets was the basis used by Hunter for establishing this table.

The values in Table 807(c)-III should be used only for drains that are at a considerable distance from the stacks and then only when two or more primary branches empty into them. Hunter used the logical procedure of making the permissible load on a secondary branch depend on the length of the branch, and his method is given on page 49 of BMS66. However, this procedure has been generally considered too complicated for adoption in plumbing codes; so it has not come into general use. The fact remains, however, that at least as far as loading tables are concerned BMS66 is the most logical code that has ever been written.

It seems appropriate to remark at this point that the basic principle that has been used to determine design loads for drains is unnecessarily conservative and leads to overdesign of the drains. The principle is that the design load shall be taken as that load which probably will not be exceeded more than 1 per cent of the time and that the drain shall not flow more than half full for this design load. Under these conditions, the flow probably will not fill the drain half full more than an extremely small part of the time, and the half-full condition will probably not be exceeded more than a vanishingly small part of the time, and then not very greatly. Thus there arises the question of whether the design of the building drains and sewers is not at present unduly conservative and unnecessarily expensive. The only factor that seems to operate in opposition to this view is the fouling of the drains, but it should be remembered that increasing the velocity of flow in a drain by a decrease in diameter tends to keep the drain scoured. No allowance has been made for these considerations in preparing Table 26.8 for secondary branches and building sewers.

3. Horizontal Branches. A study of Table 807-III of BMS66 makes it obvious that, in establishing the fixture-unit values given in it for horizontal branches, Hunter assigned the same values for diameters up to and including 6-in. branches as he assigned to primary branches for a slope of $\frac{1}{16}$ in. per ft. Also that, for 8, 10, and 12-in.-diameter branches, he selected values that correspond to a slope of $\frac{1}{32}$ in. per ft.

French has pointed out [26-2] that there are two reasons why allowance for the full effect of slope in prescribing design loads for horizontal branches need not be made. The first reason is that, since some flattening of the surges must occur between the horizontal branch and the primary branch that receives its load, the surges will be of shorter duration in the horizontal branch than in the primary branch. And Fig. 26-8 shows that the effect of slope becomes less and less as the duration of the surges decreases, becoming zero in the limit as the duration of the surge approaches zero.

The second point that French makes is this: He has shown from Hunter's data that flattening of surges takes place at a slower rate for high-drain slopes than for low slopes. Hence a horizontal drain laid at a high slope will deliver a severer load to a primary branch for the same fixture discharge than will the same drain laid at a low slope. But this has the same general effect on the selection of the drain sizes as does a lower slope; i.e., it tends to require a larger drain size than would otherwise be necessary. Hence it would seem that a

Table 26.10   Design Loads for Horizontal Branches

Diameter branch (in.)	Recommended design loads[1]			BMS66 design loads		
	Slope (in./ft)	Fixture units	Velocity[2] (fps)	Slope (in./ft)	Fixture units	Velocity[2] (fps)
(1)	(2)	(3)	(4)	(5)	(6)	(7)
3	$\frac{1}{4}$	70	2.25	$\frac{1}{16}$	20	1.10
4	$\frac{1}{4}$	250	2.60	$\frac{1}{16}$	160	1.35
4	$\frac{1}{8}$ [3]	170	1.90			
5	$\frac{1}{8}$	450	2.20	$\frac{1}{16}$	360	1.60
6	$\frac{1}{8}$	735	3.10	$\frac{1}{16}$	600	1.80
8	$\frac{1}{8}$	1,700	3.05	$\frac{1}{32}$	1,200	1.55
10	$\frac{1}{8}$	3,350	3.55	$\frac{1}{32}$	1,800	1.75
12	$\frac{1}{8}$	5,650	4.00	$\frac{1}{32}$	2,800	2.00

[1] From Table 26.6.

[2] Velocities from Manning formula with $n = 0.015$. Drain flowing half full.

[3] According to the National Plumbing Code, but not recommended because of low velocity.

simple and safe rule to apply to horizontal branches is to assign to them the same fixture-unit load as is assigned to primary branches of the same diameter *and* at the lowest slope that would be used for a horizontal branch of that diameter.

Computation shows that the minimum slopes permitted by the National Plumbing Code, if followed strictly in assigning fixture-unit values to horizontal branches,* with one exception, lead to velocities of flow (for the drain flowing at capacity, i.e., half full) that are greater than the minimum of 2 fps that is quite generally accepted† (see Table 26.10). The design loads recommended for horizontal branches, therefore, are those given in column 3 of Table 26.10 and are the same for any slope of drain equal to or greater than the minimum slopes given in column 2 of the table. The minimum recommended slope for a 4-in. branch is $\frac{1}{4}$ in. per ft, instead of the slope of $\frac{1}{8}$ in. per ft recommended by the National Plumbing Code.

* Not less than $\frac{1}{4}$ in. per ft for 3-in. diameters and smaller. Not less than $\frac{1}{8}$ in. per ft for diameters larger than 3-in.

† National Plumbing Code, Sec. 11.3.4.

4. Fixture Drains and Small Horizontal Branches. Since the methods of probability do not apply to the determination of design loads when small numbers of plumbing fixtures are involved, a different method must be used to determine drain sizes for these conditions. Adequate venting plays an important part in establishing the proper sizes for these small drains, and this subject will be treated in Chap. 27.

26.6   Minimum Velocities of Flow in Drains

The advent of the food-waste disposer in homes and commercial establishments has made it necessary to reconsider the matter of minimum permissible

Table 26.11   Minimum Flow Conditions Recommended to Move All Solid Materials through the Drainage System

Ref.	Diameter line (in.)	Velocity of flow (fps)	Slope of line (in. per ft)	Remarks
26-4	. . .	2.0		
26-5	8	1.0	. . .	Velocity used in sewer design
26-6	. . .	1.75	. . .	Sewers flowing full
26-7	4	1.5	$\frac{1}{4}$	Will not carry grease
26-8	4	1.4	$\frac{1}{8}$	Approximate values
26-8	6	1.0	$\frac{1}{16}$	Approximate values
26-8	8	0.7	$\frac{3}{64}$	Approximate values
26-9	8	1.5	$\frac{1}{36}$	Street sewer, half full
26-10	. . .	(2.5 gpm)		
26-11	. . .	(2.0 gpm)	. . .	Fixture drains

velocities of flow in the drainage systems of building and in the public sewer system. Numerous tests have been run and observations have been made on actual installations to determine what flow conditions will move all the solids discharged into the drainage system when food-waste disposers are added to the plumbing equipment. Table 26.11 summarizes some of the data and recommendations resulting from this work.

However a word of caution is necessary in regard to the discharge of large quantities of ground sea-food shells into the drainage system. It is reported [26-11] that trouble has been experienced with restaurants specializing in sea food and using food-waste disposers to get rid of the oyster and clam shells. It was found upon test that velocities of flow of even 5 fps were inadequate to dislodge the flat chips formed by grinding these shells.

CHAPTER 27

The Venting of Building Drainage Systems

27.1 Traps and Trap Seals

1. Purpose of Traps. An essential requisite of any building drainage system is that a means shall be provided to prevent sewer air from flowing from the building drain back through the plumbing fixtures into the rooms of the building. While the dangers inherent in breathing small quantities of sewer air have been greatly exaggerated [27-1],* nevertheless it would be inexcusable to

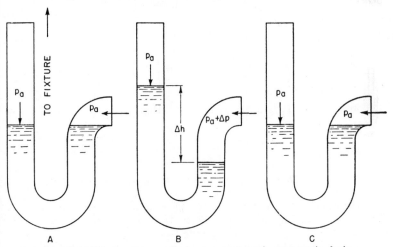

FIG. 27-1. Effect on trap seal of excess pneumatic pressure in drain.

allow the offensive odors of such air to penetrate the building. The means that has invariably been used to prevent this backflow of sewer air is the water-seal trap. See Fig. 27-1.

The water seal in the trap prevents the backflow of sewer air into the fixture and thence to the room unless the fluctuating pneumatic pressures in the drainage system exceed some value in excess of atmospheric pressure, so that air is forced through the water seal back into the room.

If anything happens to suck some of the water seal out of the trap (see Fig. 27-2A), then a much smaller excess of pneumatic pressure in the system may

* Numbers in brackets refer to the bibliography at the end of the book.

force sewer air back through the water seal. Hence the attempt is made to design the drainage system so that pressure reductions and excesses below and above atmospheric pressure *at the points where fixture drains enter the stack* shall not exceed some selected value which is usually taken as 1 in. of water in the United States.

There are two predominant ways in which trap seals are reduced, both of which are designated by the term *siphonage*. The first method is the one already discussed briefly, in which pneumatic-pressure fluctuations caused by the discharge of fixtures on the system other than the fixture to which the trap in question is attached may suck water out of the trap until the positive part of the fluctuation can force sewer air back through the trap seal. The second method is the reduction of a trap seal by the discharge of the fixture to which the

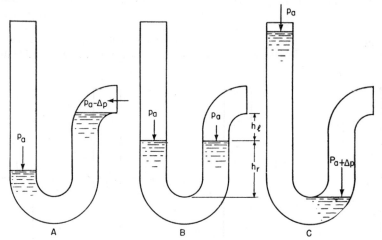

Fig. 27-2. Effect on trap seal of reduced pressure in building drain.

trap is attached. The first of these two phenomena has been quite generally called "siphonage" in the United States, but "induced siphonage" by the British. The latter term is considered to be more logical than the first mentioned, since the second phenomenon mentioned is also an example of siphonage. It is recommended, therefore, that the first phenomena described be called *induced siphonage*, following the British custom, while the second be called *self-siphonage*, as it has been in the past.

2. How Trap-seal Losses Occur. *a. Trap-seal Reduction through Induced Siphonage.* The phenomenon of induced siphonage will be considered first (see Figs. 27-1 and 27-2). Figure 27-1*A* shows a P trap, which is nothing more than a U tube with legs of unequal length filled with water to the level of the top of the shorter leg. This trap is inserted in the drainage line between the tail pipe attached to the fixture and the fixture drain. It is assumed that no discharge is taking place from the fixture to which the trap is attached and that atmospheric pressure p_a exists above the water levels in the two legs.

Now assume that a pressure fluctuation occurs in the stack at the level of entry of the fixture drain in question, so that the pneumatic pressure acting on the trap seal on the fixture-drain side is $p_a + \Delta p$, where

$$\Delta p = \rho g \Delta h \qquad (27\text{-}1)$$

where Δp = excess pneumatic pressure in drain
  ρ = density of the water in trap
  g = acceleration of gravity
  Δh = difference in level of the water surfaces in the two legs of the trap (see Fig. 27-1B)

Now if the excess pressure Δp becomes zero again, the water level in the two legs will return to the initial level, as shown in Fig. 27-1C, without any loss of trap seal, except possibly a very slight amount due to the overshooting of the water column when it returns to equilibrium.

Now assume that the pneumatic-pressure fluctuation in the stack and fixture drain causes a suction $p - \Delta p$ to be exerted on the water surface in the downstream leg of the trap, as shown in Fig. 27-2A. Obviously this condition will cause some of the water in the trap seal to flow out of the trap and down the fixture drain. Hence, when the negative-pressure fluctuation becomes zero and the water columns in the two legs of the trap stabilize, only part of the original trap seal will remain, as shown in Fig. 27-2B, and the trap-seal loss is measured by h_l and the remaining trap seal by h_r (see Fig. 27-2B).

Figure 27-2C shows the case in which a positive-pressure fluctuation has forced the water surface in the downstream leg of the trap down to the level of the dip of the trap. This is the maximum pressure difference for which the trap seal will resist the flow of sewer air back into the room. Note that this excess pressure—or head of water—is measured by twice the initial depth of trap seal as shown in Fig. 27-1A. Thus, when there is a depth of water h_r in the trap, the positive-pressure fluctuations on the downstream side of the trap will not force sewer air through the trap seal unless the excess pressure is greater than $2h_r$.

b. Trap-seal Reduction through Self-siphonage. The phenomenon of self-siphonage is very complicated and does not lend itself readily to analytical treatment. The phenomenon can be illustrated by considering the discharge of a lavatory shown diagrammatically in Fig. 27-3. A lavatory exhibits self-siphonage to a greater extent than any other commonly used plumbing fixture.

Lavatories are commonly built with rounded bottoms, and this shape produces a strong tendency to self-siphonage. The discharge of a lavatory is quite high at first, decreasing a little as the depth in the basin decreases, until suddenly the rate of discharge falls rapidly nearly to zero, with the coincidental formation of a vortex which allows air to be sucked down into the drain. With a flat-bottomed fixture, there is a prolonged "trail flow" at the end of the discharge, as the film of water on the surface of the fixture slowly drains off, tending to refill the trap, but this trail flow is very brief with a round-bottomed lavatory, so that there is very little tendency to refill the trap.

Lavatory drains and traps are usually $1\frac{1}{4}$ in. in diameter. While a drain of this diameter laid at a slope of $\frac{1}{4}$ in. per ft or greater has adequate capacity to carry the discharge from the lavatory without the cross section being filled, provided the water enters the drain smoothly approximately in the direction of the drain axis, actually the flow out of the trap is directed vertically, and as a result, for all except the smallest flow rates, the water clings to the upper element of the drain at the entrance, and a slug of water is formed filling the drain at that point. This slug often lengthens until it extends a considerable distance downstream, sometimes even to the outlet. Air that is drawn in through the overflow of the lavatory passes down the drain in the form of bubbles that are dragged along the highest element of the drain. If there is enough of this air traveling with the water, when the flow from the lavatory falls off, the bubbles enable the water to break loose from the upper element of the drain, so that the

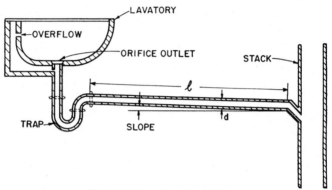

Fig. 27-3. Lavatory installation.

piston effect of the water that would otherwise occur is often prevented. If the slug of water continues to fill the cross section as the flow decreases, it moves downstream slowly, creating a reduced pressure behind it that sucks the water out of the trap just as happens when the reduced pressure is due to induced siphonage.

Again, the stream of water entering the stack fitting, if its velocity is sufficiently high, may shoot across the downwardly directed part of the sanitary tee or long-turn tee-wye, closing off the cross section at the outlet, and the slug thus formed may increase in length in the upstream direction, closing off the cross section. Then, if the discharge from the lavatory decreases, this slug acts like a piston, pulling the air in the drain behind it as it moves out of the drain, and again we have the conditions necessary to reduce the trap seal.

A typical case of flow in a drain resulting from the discharge of a lavatory is described in National Bureau of Standards BMS126, Self-siphonage of Fixture Traps [27-2].

"At first thought, it might seem that the flow taking place through a trap ordinarily consists of water only. However, this is not the case, as has already been pointed out. In most instances, air is carried out with the water also. We have observed this phenomenon in a transparent trap and fixture drain connected to a lavatory, and these observations indicated that air entered the trap in three ways. First, air was entrained by the water as it passed the overflow outlet just below the lavatory, and this air was carried through the trap in the form of bubbles.

"Second, as the water surface in the lavatory continued to recede, a vortex formed in the lavatory, and in this way additional air was carried through the trap into the drain with the water.

"Third, near the end of the discharge of the lavatory, with its attendant rapid decrease in the rate of flow through the lavatory outlet orifice, water was flowing out of the trap more rapidly than it entered, owing primarily to the inertia of the water in the trap and drain. Hence the water surface in the inlet leg of the trap receded to such an extent that in many instances air bubbled past the dip of the trap and entered the outlet leg of the trap. This latter manner in which air enters or passes through a trap is especially noticeable when a large pressure reduction occurs in the fixture drain near the end of the discharge period.

"Now if the rate of flow in the drain and the diameter of the drain are not sufficient to close off the passageway in the inlet branch of the stack fitting, this air can pass off to the vent or stack and exerts no particular effect on the nature of the flow in the drain.

"However, if the flow is sufficiently great to close off the passageway referred to, then the air in the drain becomes trapped between the solid mass of water in the vent fitting and the water in the trap and causes changes in the nature of the flow in the drain. This in turn affects the pressures in the drain and hence on the outlet end of the trap when the discharge from the fixture ceases.

"The following is typical of the phenomena that were observed when air entered the drain in the manner described above. The entrained air from the overflow outlet entered the drain in the form of bubbles, which rose to the top of the drain at some indefinite point along it. If the quantity of air that collected in this way was sufficiently large, the drain, which was flowing full from the trap weir to this point, flowed only part full from this point on to the vent fitting. As the volume of entrained air diminished near the end of the lavatory discharge, the water frequently rose to the top of the drain along one or more portions of its length, filling the entire cross-section of the drain. Thus one or more plugs of water formed in the drain near the end of the period of discharge from the lavatory.

"As the flow from the lavatory trailed off, the velocity of these plugs of water toward the vent fitting decreased, owing to the adverse head of water in the trap, which slowed them down; and at the same time the lengths of the plugs of water diminished, owing to the sloughing off of water at their upstream and downstream ends. If one of these plugs was sufficiently near the trap when this sloughing off occurred, some of the water that sloughed off from the upstream end of the plug flowed backward up the drain and partly or entirely refilled the trap. When the plug was further down the drain, this temporary backflow of water in the drain did not reach the trap, and hence no refill from this cause occurred."

It appears from the foregoing discussion that there are two ways in which refill of the trap can occur: (1) by trail flow from the fixture and (2) by backflow in the drain. In addition, it should be noted that when the drain can run full for all or part of its length, the presence of an abundant supply of air carried along with the water helps prevent trap-seal losses. Since much of this air comes from the overflow of the lavatory, it follows that a lavatory without an overflow is much more likely to suffer trap-seal losses due to self-siphonage than is a lavatory with an overflow. This has been investigated by Wyly at the National Bureau of Standards, but no report has ever been published by him.

3. Limiting Trap-seal Loss. Inasmuch as reductions in trap seals of fixture traps will be the basis for deciding limitations of drain lengths and slopes in what follows, a discussion of what trap-seal losses or remaining trap seals are to be considered permissible is necessary. The adequate protection of the building against the penetration of sewer air by passage through or past the trap seal depends on the depth of trap seal that can be maintained under all conditions and hence on the magnitude of the effects of induced siphonage and self-siphonage. Actually the important thing is the *remaining* trap seal, but in the United States current practice is to set a limit to *trap-seal losses,* it being agreed that traps shall not have less than some minimum depth of trap seal. The National Plumbing Code provides (paragraph 5.3.1) that "each fixture trap shall have a water seal of not less than 2 inches and not more than 4 inches, except where a deeper seal is required by the administrative authority." Only when the design of traps has been standardized can there be any definite general relation between the remaining trap seal and the trap-seal loss for a given trap.

The "limiting trap-seal loss" generally agreed on in this country is 1 in. of water, and this allows for some fouling of the fixture drain with time. The corresponding remaining trap seal for any given trap will then protect against the passage of sewer air back into the building past the trap seal as long as the excess pressure in the stack above atmospheric does not exceed twice the depth of water that is in the remaining trap seal.

27.2 Venting as a Means of Reducing Trap-seal Losses from Induced Siphonage

1. Introduction. The complete venting of a building drainage system is a very complicated matter, as can be seen from the great variety of vents that are involved (see Chap. 12). It will not be feasible to treat all these here. However, there is an extremely important problem involved that has never been treated in the literature to any great extent. This is the preparation of venting tables for stacks and for horizontal branches.

Owing to the fact that the conditions which tend to produce pneumatic pressures in the system that exceed or are below atmospheric pressure by considerable amounts vary so greatly from case to case, and also since the building drain may be wholly or partly submerged where it enters the street sewer, or it may not be submerged at all, it is not feasible to lay down rules for the venting of particular designs. Rather the scheme that will be followed here will be to assume the worst conditions that may reasonably be expected to exist and to prepare venting tables (i.e., the maximum lengths and minimum diameters of vents that may be used) for the worst conditions that may be anticipated.

The engineer who designs a particular system will then be expected to use his judgment as to how much he can relax the relatively severe requirements of the tables in his case.

When water flows down a stack or when it flows along a sloping drain, the cross section being only partly filled in both cases, it tends to drag air with it. If this flow of air is blocked toward the outlet in any way, for example, by a hydraulic jump in the building drain, or by a submerged building sewer exit, then a considerable positive pneumatic pressure may be built up in the building drain, and this pressure may extend up the stack for some distance, decreasing in the upward direction. If this excess pressure is to be prevented from occurring, adequate venting must be provided near the bottom of the stack, so that this air may be carried away without developing a pressure head of more than, say, 1 in. of water column in the stack where the vent is connected.

The outer layer in the sheet of water falling down a stack exerts a frictional drag on the core of air inside the sheet of water. If now the drain does not flow full at any section, the stream of air thus dragged along by the water is more or less free to flow out of the outlet end of the drain into the free atmosphere. Some retardation of the air stream will occur in the building drain and sewer owing to the facts that (1) the stream of water is slowed up somewhat in flowing along the drain, (2) the air is now in contact with the unwetted portion of the drain wall, and (3) a hydraulic jump may partially fill the cross section of the drain. This retardation will create a back pressure which will be felt at least part way up the stack. If the drain is completely filled at some section, the air flow is completely blocked, in the absence of vents, and the back pressure in the drain may become very high.

Considerable data are available on the pneumatic-pressure variations caused by sheet flow down vertical stacks, but the principal service rendered by these data is to demonstrate the magnitudes that these pressure variations can attain when the rate of flow greatly exceeds the recommended capacity of the stacks under test conditions that are not clearly defined. Consequently, the results are not of much practical value except as a means of demonstrating qualitatively certain general principles. A general understanding of the pressure phenomena that occur in stacks will be gained, however, by examining results reported by Dawson and Kalinske [27-3, 27-4], by Babbitt [27-5, 27-6], by Hunter [27-7], and by Wyly and Eaton [27-8].

The back pressure created by the partial blocking of the building drain is well illustrated in Fig. 22-7, which presents data obtained by Dawson and Kalinske [27-3]. A 3-in. stack about 30 ft high was connected to a 4-in. drain open at the outlet. Water was introduced at elevation 0 in the figure. The conditions at entry are not stated—the type of branch fitting used and the degree to which the cross section of the stack at entry was closed off by the water stream entering the stack for different rates of flow. If sanitary fittings were used, then, according to Eq. (25-16), the stack would have been completely filled at entry, and the water would have begun to back up above the level of entry when the rate of flow reached approximately 100 gpm. If, on the other hand, long-turn tee-wyes were used, this condition would have occurred when the rate of flow reached approximately 200 gpm, according to Eq. (25-15). Either rate of flow is greater than the recommended capacity of the stack (see Table 25.7). However, it seems likely that the cross section of the stack was completely filled at entry except possibly for the lowest rate of flow.

Whether or not a hydraulic jump occurred in the drain is not stated, but, if it did, it probably did not completely fill the drain. This opinion is supported by the statement of the authors [27-3]: "the pressure at the bottom of the 3-inch stack and in the house drain itself was about 45 inches of water, for a rate of flow of 50 gallons per minute when the house sewer was submerged and without vents. This means that an increase of approximately 35 inches of water was caused by the complete closure of the cross-section."

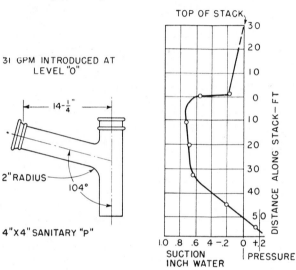

FIG. 27-4. Pneumatic pressure conditions in stack during flow of waste water.

Wyly and Eaton [27-8] report pressure measurements on a 3-in. stack for various rates of flow. Water was introduced into the stack through one side of a 3- by 3-in. sanitary cross at a height of 32 ft about the base. At the base of the stack the water passed through a long-sweep bend into 50 ft of 4-in. drain laid on a slope of $\frac{1}{4}$ in. per ft, discharging freely at the outlet. The data will not be presented here in detail since the original paper is in the process of publication. However, it can be said that for a rate of flow of 80 gpm (87 gpm is the recommended stack capacity) the maximum negative pressure just below the point of entry was about 6 in. of water below atmospheric pressure, while the maximum positive pressure near the base of the stack was slightly more than 1 in. of water above atmospheric pressure.

Figure 27-4 shows the results of pressure measurements in a 4-in. stack by Wise and Croft [27-14]. A flow of 31 gpm, considerably less than the capacity of the stack, was introduced through a 4-in. sanitary-P fitting, shown in the figure. Tests showed that this fitting introduced water into the stack with smaller pressure fluctuations than did several other fittings tested.

At the level of the fitting through which the water was introduced, a suction of 0.2 in. of water was observed. This was the pressure reduction necessary to suck air into the stack and to overcome wall friction in 30 ft of stack vent. At the level of water entry, the suction increased abruptly to a little more than 0.7 in. of water, and this decreased gradually down the stack to a level about 35 ft below the level of water entry. From this level on, the suction decreased rapidly, becoming a positive pressure about 10 ft above the level of the building drain.

Table 27.1   Pressures in Building Drain Produced by Discharging Various Fixtures on Test Setup

(Single-family dwelling, one story with basement 2-in. waste stack, 3-in. building drain)

Fixtures discharged	Combined discharge rate (gpm)	Pressure, in. of water. No house trap	Condition of submergence of house drain	Pressure, in. of water. Vented house trap
Sink....................	23.6	0.1	Submerged to a	
Water closet............	20.3	0.1	point 35 ft from	
Bathtub...............	12.6	0.1	point of measure-	
Laundry tray..........	25.4	0.8	ment of pressure	
Sink and laundry tray....	49.0	18.5		
Sink and water closet....	43.9	0.5		
Sink....................	23.6	1.5	Submerged to a	
Water closet............	20.3	0.3	point 12 ft down-	
Bathtub...............	12.6	0.1	stream from point	
Laundry tray...........	25.4	1.0	of measurement of	
Sink and laundry tray....	49.0	27.2	pressure	
Sink and water closet....	32.9	15.0		
Lavatory and bathtub....	22.5	Negligible	Not submerged	10.0
Water closet and bathtub	32.9	Negligible	Not submerged	17.0
Bathtub...............	12.6	⅛ in or	Not submerged	9.5
Sink and water closet....	43.9	less	Not submerged	50.9

Slope of building drain, ¼ in. per ft. Long-turn tee-wye fitting used for water closet, sanitary-tee fittings for all other fixtures. Pressures in drain were measured in an unvented floor drain 13 ft from the stack. The floor drain was capped, and a pressure connection was made to it.

From National Bureau of Standards Report 2521 [27-9].

This is a typical illustration of the variation in pneumatic pressure in a stack for a rate of flow that is considerably below the capacity of the stack, which would be 140 gpm for a 4-in. stack flowing $\frac{7}{24}$ full (see Table 25.6).

Wise and Croft measured the maximum pressure reduction (just below level 0) for different rates of flow down the stack, up to 50 gpm. At this flow, the maximum suction was about 1.2 in. of water. If the curve can be extrapolated to the design capacity of the stack, this would mean that the maximum suction for that flow would be about 4 in. of water.

In a study made for the Housing and Home Finance Agency, Wyly, at the National Bureau of Standards, measured pressure variations in a 2-in. stack and 3-in. building drain for many different conditions [27-9, 27-10]. The measurements in the stack do not have general applicability, since this diameter of stack is too small for a soil stack, but the data have some value as applied to waste stacks. Some of the data are given in Table 27.1. The data show that the limiting capacity of a 3-in. drain with a slight degree of submergence at exit is about 44 gpm. Also the data show the adverse pressure conditions caused by the insertion of a vented house trap in the building drain. An unvented house trap would be considerably worse.

2. The Purpose of Vents. The maximum trap-seal loss due to pressure fluctuations that is usually considered in the United States to be permissible is 1 in. of water. When a P trap is used, this means that a negative pressure of 2 in. of water is required to reduce the trap seal by approximately this amount for a single pressure fluctuation. It is found by experiment that still further trap-seal losses will occur if the same pressure reduction is applied to the trap without any refill occurring in the meantime. On the basis of these considerations, it is arbitrarily decided that the attempt should be made to keep pressure fluctuations in a building drainage system down to a maximum of ±1 in. of water.

It is not necessary that these fluctuations should not be exceeded anywhere in the system. The important thing is that they shall not be exceeded where fixture drains or horizontal branches connect to the stack of building drain.

27.3   Design of Vents to Control Induced Siphonage

1. Volume Rate of Flow of Air for Which Provision Should Be Made in Stacks. Considering first the flow of air down the stack, we can set an upper limit to the air flow, as has been pointed out by Dawson and Kalinske [27-3]. If we assume that the velocity of the core of air inside the sheet of water flowing down the wall of the stack is moving with the same velocity as the inner layer of the sheet of water, with which it is in contact, then we can write the equation

$$\frac{Q_w}{Q_a} = \frac{r}{1-r} = \frac{a_w/a}{1-a_w/a} \tag{27-2}$$

where Q_w = volume rate of flow of water down stack

Q_a = volume rate of flow of air down stack

a_w = cross-sectional area of sheet of water

a = cross-sectional area of stack

If Q_w and d, the diameter of the stack, are given, then the value of r can be computed from the formula

$$\frac{a_w}{a} = r = 0.100\frac{1}{d}\left(\frac{Q_w}{d}\right)^{3/5} \tag{27-3}$$

where d = diameter of vent pipe, in.

Q_w = rate of flow of water down stack, cfs

Equation (27-2) can be derived from Eq. (25-8).

Another convenient relation is the following equation connecting the thickness of the sheet of water flowing down the stack at terminal velocity Q_w and d:

$$4 \left(1 - \frac{T}{d} \right) \frac{T}{d} = r = 0.100 \frac{1}{d} \left(\frac{Q_w}{d} \right)^{3/5} \tag{27-4}$$

Equations (27-2) and (27-3) make it possible to compute Q_a when Q_w and d are given. With the maximum value of Q_a known for a given stack, it is then possible to compute the length of vent of a given diameter that will pass this rate of flow of air with a head loss of 1 in. of water.* This procedure will be presented in a later section.

Table 27.2   Maximum Volume Rates of Air Flow in Stacks for Which Provision Must Be Made by Venting, Based on the Design Load of the Stack

(Stacks flowing $7/24$ full)

Stack diameter (in.)	Design load Q_w (gpm)	$\dfrac{1 - r}{r}$ ($r = 7/24$)	Q_a (gpm)
3	87	2.43	212
4	140	2.43	340
5	260	2.43	630
6	425	2.43	1,030
8	920	2.43	2,230
10	1,650	2.43	4,000
12	2,700	2.43	6,550

The assumption that the core of air in the stack is traveling with the same velocity as the sheet of water flowing down the wall of the stack needs some consideration. This is, of course, only an approximation, since its velocity will depend not only on the velocity of the sheet of water but on the blocking effects that take place in the building drain and sewer. However, if we consider that the building sewer is submerged or that at some point of the building drain a hydraulic jump closes off the cross section of the drain and thus completely blocks the flow of air, then this flow must be maintained by the introduction of an adequate vent near the bottom of the stack if excessive pneumatic pressures are not to occur there.

Wyly [27-8] has made measurements radially of the velocity distribution in the falling sheet of water in a 3-in. stack in the region in which terminal velocity was known to exist. He found that the velocity near the outside of the sheet (the layer in contact with the air core) is approximately equal to the terminal velocity computed from Eq. (25-9). However, what he actually measured was the pitot pressures created by the moving water, and he has

---

* A remaining trap seal of 1 in. will just suffice to protect against a pneumatic pressure in the stack of 2 in. head of water in excess of atmospheric pressure. However, vents are usually designed to afford a factor of safety by keeping this excess pressure to 1 in. of water.

shown in another part of the same investigation [27-8] that the sheet of water flowing down the stack has an air content that varies from zero at the wall to about 50 per cent in the portion adjacent to the air core. Hence the actual velocity in this outer layer may have been about $\sqrt{2}$ times the computed terminal velocity.

Table 27.3   Computation of Rates of Air Flow in a 4-in. Stack

Q_w (gpm)	Q_w (cfs)	d (ft)	Q_w/d	$0.100(Q/d)^{3/5}$	r	$1-r$	$\dfrac{1-r}{r}$ $=Q_a/Q_w$	Q_a (gpm)
20	0.0446	0.336	0.1320	0.0300	0.0894	0.9106	10.2	204.0
40	0.0892	0.336	0.2650	0.0455	0.1355	0.8645	6.37	254.8
60	0.1335	0.336	0.397	0.0580	0.1725	0.8275	4.80	288.0
80	0.1780	0.336	0.530	0.0683	0.2035	0.7965	3.92	313.6
100	0.2225	0.336	0.663	0.0780	0.2320	0.7680	3.31	331.0
120	0.2670	0.336	0.795	0.0870	0.2590	0.7410	2.86	344.0
140	0.3120	0.336	0.928	0.0960	0.2860	0.7140	2.49	348.0
160	0.3560	0.336	1.060	0.1030	0.3070	0.6930	2.26	360.0

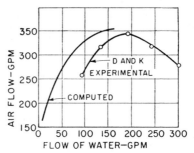

Fig. 27-5. Air flow in 4-in. stack for different rates of flow of waste water.

However, since the air stream is subject to an unknown retardation in the building drain and sewer, even when free outflow exists at the outlet and the hydraulic jump that occurs in the drain does not completely fill the cross section of the drain, refinement in the consideration of this velocity is not justified, and it will be assumed that the maximum velocity of the core of air in the stack is equal to the average terminal velocity given by Eq. (25-9).

The maximum volume rates of air flow for which provision must be made in stacks of different diameters, on this basis, can be computed from Eq. (27-2).

Dawson and Kalinske [27-3] give experimental data on air inflow for a 4-in. stack for flows of water up to 300 gpm. As would be expected, the volume rate of flow increases up to a maximum and then decreases, owing to the variation in the ratio $(1-r)/r$ and the product of this ratio with Q_w. Similar data have been computed from Eq. (27-2) and are superimposed on the data of Dawson and Kalinske [27-3] in Fig. 27-5. The then computed curve is carried only to approximately the design load, whereas Dawson and Kalinske carried their measurements considerably beyond this point.   Neither curve has reached its maximum by the time the design load has been reached.   The fact that the computed curve lies above the curve by Dawson and Kalinske indicates that in their tests the velocity of the air core was less than the terminal velocity of the water.

The computations for the computed curve in Fig. 27-5 are given in Table 27.3. The ratio r was computed from Eq. (27-4).

2. Volume Rate of Flow of Air for Which Provision Should Be Made in Horizontal Branches.   We assume the branch to be flowing half full at the design rate of flow and that the air in the upper half of the drain is flowing at the same velocity and hence volume rate as the water.   The rates of flow of air will then be equal to the design rates of flow of water, and these values can be taken from Table 26.5, column 9.

Table 27.4   Maximum Rates of Flow of Air for Which Provision Should Be Made in the Venting of Horizontal Branches

Diameter of branch (in.)	Slope (in. per ft)	Q_a (gpm)
1¼	½	4.5
1½	½	7.0
2	¼	8.8
2½	¼	15.5
3	¼	25.5
4	¼	54
5	⅛	69
6	⅛	112
8	⅛	240

This basis for determining the rates of flow of air for which provision should be made yields excessive values for small fixture drains, such af 1¼ and 1½-in. drains, since these drains are apt to flow full or nearly full during most of the discharge period.   For the largest horizontal branches considered here, it is possible that provision for more air flow than that specified above should be made for the case of the drain flowing less than half full.   However, the very considerable factor of safety involved in assuming that the air is flowing with the same mean velocity as the water would seem to provide amply for this; so the assumption is believed justified.

3. Permissible Lengths and Diameters of Vents for Stacks.   In order to establish the maximum permissible lengths of vents of a given diameter for a pressure drop of 1-in. head of water, it is necessary to compute pressure losses for different rates of air flow in vents of different diameters and for different ratios of l/d (length of vent to diameter of vent).

The Darcy-Weisbach equation will be used for this purpose in the form

$$h = \left(1.5 + f\frac{l}{d}\right)\frac{v^2}{2g} \tag{27-5}$$

where h = loss of head between ends of pipe in feet of air column of same
density as air flowing through vent
f = Darcy-Weisbach friction coefficient
l = length of vent, ft
d = diameter of vent, ft
v = mean velocity of flow of air through vent, fps
g = acceleration of gravity, ft per sec^2

The number 1.5 in the parenthesis represents the factor by which the velocity
head is multiplied to give the head loss necessary to accelerate the air to the
velocity $v[1.0(v^2/2g)]$ plus the entrance loss $[0.5(v^2/2g)]$.

Since we wish to measure the loss of head in terms of water column instead of
air column, we multiply h in Eq. (27-5) by the ratio of the density of air to the
density of water, and a suitable value of this ratio to assume is 0.0012. We also
multiply h by 12 in order that the result may be in inches of water column.
Consequently, Eq. (27-5) becomes

$$h = 0.0144 \left(1.5 + f \frac{l}{d} \right) \frac{v^2}{2g} \qquad (27\text{-}6)$$

where h is now measured in inches of water column.

The value of f cannot be assumed constant over the range of diameters from
$1\frac{1}{4}$ to 12 in. We assume a value of Manning's n (which does not vary with
diameter) of 0.012, a value somewhat less than that assumed for building
drains. The reason for this is that it seems reasonable to assume that the
vents will not foul up so much as do the drains. We compute the limiting
values of f (i.e., for fully developed turbulent flow) corresponding to $n = 0.012$
from

$$\frac{n}{\sqrt{f}} = 0.0925 R^{0.17} \qquad (26\text{-}14)$$

obtaining approximately 0.055 for the $1\frac{1}{4}$-in. vents and 0.032 for the 8-in.
vents. On the basis of these limiting values, the values of f given in Table
27.5 will be assigned to the vents of various diameters.

**Table 27.5   Values of Darcy-Weisbach f Assumed for Vents
of Different Diameters**

Diameter vent (in.)	Value of f	Diameter vent (in.)	Value of f
$1\frac{1}{4}$	0.055	4	0.045
$1\frac{1}{2}$	0.055	5	0.040
2	0.050	6	0.040
$2\frac{1}{2}$	0.050	8	0.035
3	0.045		

This method of computing values of the Darcy-Weisbach f takes into account
the diameter of the vent but not the velocity of the air flow through it. Actually, f depends on the diameter of the vent, the velocity of the flow of air, and
the kinematic viscosity of the air. However, the unavoidable indefiniteness of

any general approach to the problem of venting a plumbing stack is so great that the additional accuracy that would be achieved by taking velocity into account is not warranted. The values of f given in Table 27.5 correspond to fully developed turbulent flow.

An approach to the problem of assigning suitable values of f to vents of different diameters has been suggested by Wyly at the National Bureau of Standards. His proposed method would take into account the range of velocities of air flow in a vent of given diameter corresponding to the rates of air flow in stacks of diameters that can be vented suitably by a vent of the diameter under consideration. In other words, instead of assigning a single value of f to each diameter of vent, he would assign different values, depending on the diameter of the stack vented. This problem is being investigated further.

The procedure followed in computing the values in the venting Table 27.6 is as follows: First the rates of flow of air corresponding to rates of flow of water down the stack of a selected diameter were computed from Eqs. (27-2) and (27-3). These values are shown in Fig. 27-5 for a 4-in. stack. The relation between the rate of flow of air through a vent of given diameter for the value of l/d that would produce a pressure-head loss of 1 in. head of water was then computed from the following modification of Eq. (27-6):

$$Q_a = \frac{449 \times 52.6d^2}{\sqrt{1.5 + fl/d}} \quad \text{gpm} \ = \ \frac{1,550}{\sqrt{1.5 + fl/d}} \quad \text{gpm} \qquad (27\text{-}7)$$

d and l being measured in feet.

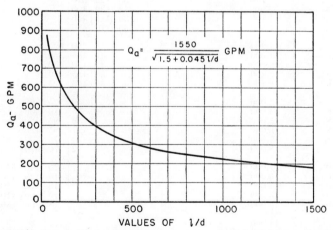

FIG. 27-6. Permissible lengths of 3-in. vent for a head loss of 1 in. of water.

The results for a 3-in. vent are shown in Fig. 27-6. Then, for any selected value of Q_w, the rate of flow of water down the 4-in. stack, for example, the value of Q_a can be read from Fig. 27-5. Next, entering Fig. 27-6 with this

Table 27.6   Sizes and Lengths of Vents for Stacks

Size of soil or waste stack (in.)	Fixture units connected	Diameter of vent (in.)										
		1¼	1½	2	2½	3	4	5	6	8	10	12
		Maximum permissible length of vent (ft)										
2	5	85	190	715								
2	7	70	145	550								
2	9	60	125	470								
2	11[1]	50	115	425								
2½	10	30	55	215	550							
2½	20	25	48	170	450							
2½	30	22	45	155	425							
2½	40	21	43	150	410							
2½	50[1]	20	42	145	400							
3	60	...	15	60	150	510						
3	90	...	15	55	140	490						
3	120	...	14	53	135	480						
3	150[1]	...	14	52	130	470						
4	100	...	...	...	45	150	560					
4	200	...	...	...	40	130	500					
4	300	...	...	...	36	120	475					
4	400	...	...	...	34	115	450					
4	500[1]	...	...	...	33	110	445					
5	500	...	...	...	...	40	130	525				
5	700	...	...	...	...	35	125	510				
5	900	...	...	...	...	32	120	490				
5	1,100	...	...	...	...	30	115	470				
5	1,300[1]	...	...	...	...	30	110	460				
6	1,200	...	...	...	...	...	55	220	620			
6	1,600	...	...	...	...	...	47	185	550			
6	2,000	...	...	...	...	...	42	170	500			
6	2,400	...	...	...	...	...	38	155	460			
6	2,800[1]	...	...	...	...	...	36	145	425			
8	3,000	...	...	...	...	...	...	40	125	560		
8	4,000	...	...	...	...	...	...	35	110	500		
8	5,000	...	...	...	...	...	...	30	95	460		
8	6,000	...	...	...	...	...	...	27	85	425		
8	7,000	...	...	...	...	...	...	24	75	390		
8	8,000[1]	...	...	...	...	...	...	22	70	370		
10	7,000	...	...	...	...	...	...	...	20	145	545	
10	9,000	...	...	...	...	...	...	...	16	125	490	
10	11,000	...	...	...	...	...	...	...	13	110	440	
10	13,000	...	...	...	...	...	...	...	10	100	410	
10	15,000[1]	...	...	...	...	...	...	...	8	90	380	
12	14,000	...	...	...	...	...	...	...	...	35	190	590
12	16,000	...	...	...	...	...	...	...	...	31	170	560
12	18,000	...	...	...	...	...	...	...	...	28	155	530
12	20,000	...	...	...	...	...	...	...	...	25	140	505
12	22,000	...	...	...	...	...	...	...	...	23	130	480
12	24,000	...	...	...	...	...	...	...	...	21	120	460
12	26,000[1]	...	...	...	...	...	...	...	...	19	110	450

[1] Approximately capacity of stack.

value of Q_a, we can read the value of the ratio l/d and compute the value of l. This value, rounded off, was then entered in the proper place in Table 27.6.

Comparison of the values in Table 27.6 with the corresponding values in Table 12.21.5 of the National Plumbing Code shows that many of the lengths given in the latter are considerably higher than those presented here. This does not mean necessarily that the values in Table 12.21.5 are too high, since it has already been explained that Table 27.6 is based on the maximum rates of flow of air that can conceivably be required. Particularly for the larger vents and stacks, such as will be involved in multistory buildings, there will be vents at intermediate floors connecting to the stack through the horizontal branches, and these will relieve the load on the main vent that is under consideration here. The result of this will be to increase the permissible lengths of main vent over the lengths given in Table 27.6. Hence the values in Table 27.6 should not be looked upon as rigid limits that must not be exceeded. When additional vents connect into the stack to relieve the pressure conditions, the lengths given in this table may even be doubled.

4. Permissible Lengths and Diameters of Vents for Horizontal Branches. It does not appear to have been generally recognized that the venting of horizontal branches does not require nearly so much provision for venting as is necessary for stacks. This is due to the fact that the velocity of flow of waste water in the branches is much less than in stacks. One code that does recognize this, however, is the Detroit code [27-11]. While the assumptions made in the preparation of that table were somewhat different than those used in the preparation of Table 27.7, the general method followed in the two cases was much the same.

The rates of flow of water in the horizontal branches as given in Table 27.4 were computed from Manning's formula, Eq. (26-7), and as explained earlier in this chapter, the rates of flow of air are assumed to be the same as the rates of flow of water. Maximum permissible lengths of vents for horizontal branches are given in Table 27.7. It will be of interest to compare these values with Table IVA of the Detroit code.

27.4 Restrictions on Drains Required to Control Self-siphonage

The most comprehensive studies made to determine the conditions under which fixture drains will be safe against excessive self-siphonage have been made at the National Bureau of Standards [27-2, 27-7] and at the Building Research Station in England [27-12, 27-17].

The earliest systematic investigation of the subject appears to have been carried out by Hunter at the National Bureau of Standards [27-7, page 122]. As a result of his tests with lavatories, kitchen sinks, laundry trays, and bathtubs, Hunter reached the following conclusions:

" . . . the following table summarizes the results of the experiments giving what are believed to be safe maximum lengths for nominally horizontal unvented wastes from fixtures connected to a stack or vented branch at points where they are free from detrimental aspirating or back-pressure effects.   It is understood that they refer to self-siphonage only.   Possible increase in self-siphonage due to fouling has been taken into account.

Lengths of Nominally Horizontal Unvented Waste Pipes Believed to Be Safe against Self-siphonage

Plain P traps nominal length, full seal (in.)	Safe length (ft) of waste pipes for		
	Wash basin with fall not greater than ½ in. to 1 ft or less than ¼ in. to 1 ft	Wide-bottomed fixtures with fall of	
		½ in. to 1 ft	¼ in. to 1 ft
2	4	4	8
3	6	6	12
4	8	8	16

"These lengths are from the center of the trap to the stack or larger vented branch waste and would permit one 90° elbow in the waste at a distance not greater than 18 inches from the inlet arm of the trap.   Elbows in other positions should be counted as equivalent lengths of pipe."

Hunter drew the correct inference that the rate of flow affected the self-siphonage of a trap but, unfortunately, did not leave a record of the rates of flow in his tests.   Consequently, since the discharge rates of fixtures have increased considerably since his work was done, his conclusions may not be sufficiently conservative for present-day conditions.   He also drew the conclusion that has been confirmed by later experimenters that increasing the depth of trap seal increases the loss of seal under given conditions, but also increases the remaining trap seal, so that deeper trap seals bring about greater safety against self-siphonage than do shallow seals.

The complexity of the self-siphonage process can be appreciated from the fact that French and Eaton [27-2] showed that loss of trap seal from this cause is affected by the rate of discharge from the fixture; the length, diameter, and slope of the fixture drain; the dimensions of the trap, particularly of the depth of the trap seal and the internal diameter of the trap; the type of stack fitting; and the amount and duration of the trail flow from the fixture.

The great majority of the tests made by these two experimenters were carried out on lavatories, since a round-bottomed lavatory is more highly subject to self-siphonage than is any other commonly used fixture.   Kitchen sinks also exhibit self-siphonage, but bathtubs are practically free from it because of their large flat bottom area, and they will certainly be safe against it if the same criteria are used for them that are recommended for sinks.

French found that the results of his self-siphonage tests on lavatories with drains laid at different slopes could be simplified in certain instances if he plotted trap-seal losses against the dimensionless variable Sl/d and in the other cases by plotting trap-seal loss against $S^{1/2}l/d$, where S is the slope of the drain in feet per foot, l is the length of the drain, and d is the inside diameter of the drain in the same units as those in which is expressed.

Table 27.7 Maximum Permissible Lengths of Vents for Horizontal Branches

Diameter of horizontal drainage branch (in.)	Slope of drainage branch (in./ft)	Maximum length of vent (ft) Diameter of vent (in.)									
		1¼	1½	2	2½	3	4	5	6	8	10
1¼	½	*									
1½	½	*	*								
2	⅛	*	*	*							
2	¼	*	*	*							
2	½	*	*	*							
2½	⅛	*	*	*	*						
2½	¼	805	*	*	*						
2½	½	460	905	*	*						
3	⅛	660	*	*	*	*					
3	¼	335	710	*	*	*					
3	½	150	390	*	*	*					
4	⅛	132	364	*	*	*	*				
4	¼	69	147	600	*	*	*				
4	½	39	74	272	*	*	*				
5	⅛	...	94	355	845	*	*	*			
5	¼	...	47	160	412	*	*	*			
5	½	...	21	81	206	715	*	*			
6	⅛	...	35	124	320	*	*	*	*		
6	¼	...	...	60	155	555	*	*	*		
6	½	...	...	21	72	256	957	*	*		
8	⅛	...	...	...	62	230	840	*	*	*	
8	¼	...	...	...	29	115	455	*	*	*	
8	½	...	...	...	...	51	218	780	*	*	
10	⅛	...	...	...	...	90	319	*	*	*	*
10	¼	...	...	...	...	26	168	590	*	*	*
10	½	...	...	...	...	...	75	253	760	*	*

* More than 1,000 ft.

The ratio l/d is, of course, nothing but the length of the drain expressed in pipe diameters. Then the variable Sl/d represents the distance through which the drain falls between the inlet and outlet expressed in pipe diameters.

Figure 27-7 shows the results that French obtained for a lavatory installation with a 1¼-in. trap and with the drain connected to the stack through a sanitary tee or short-turn stack fitting. It will be seen that no self-siphonage occurs until $S^{1/2}l/d$ reaches a value of about 6, and then self-siphonage starts and increases rapidly as $S^{1/2}l/d$ increases, gradually leveling off to approach a trap-seal loss equal to the normal depth of the trap seal. Each plotted point represents the average result of 10 consecutive tests under as nearly identical conditions as could be attained.

The results of two different slopes of drain are brought together by the use of the variable $S^{1/2}l/d$, but there is considerable scatter of the data. This scatter is characteristic of self-siphonage tests, for the phenomenon is highly sensitive to the slightest differences in the test conditions. Only approximate agreement can be expected in such tests, even when the utmost care is taken to reproduce the conditions of test on consecutive runs.

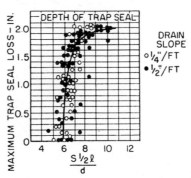

FIG. 27-7. Self-siphonage experimental data.

French found that, when a $1\frac{1}{4}$-in. trap and drain were used in the lavatory tests, the use of the variable $S^{1/2}l/d$ brought better order out of the data than did the use of the variable Sl/d. However, when a $1\frac{1}{2}$-in. trap and drain were used, the opposite was true. No explanation has been found for this fact. Also he found that the limiting value of the variable (i.e., the value that corresponded to a trap-seal loss of 1 in. of water) was different for the sanitary tee than for the long-turn tee-wye. A lavatory drainage system that connects to the stack through a sanitary tee is less subject to self-siphonage than is one that connects to the stack through a long-turn tee-wye (see Table 27.8).

In an unpublished report, Wyly, at the National Bureau of Standards, has summarized the permissible unvented lengths of lavatory drain resulting from the investigation just discussed [27-13]. These lengths are given for a *remaining trap seal* of 1 in. and $\frac{1}{2}$ in. The data were obtained with an 18- by 20-in. lavatory and with several conventional P traps that gave the worst self-siphonage losses of any of the traps tested. The data are based on the *maximum* trap-seal losses obtained in either 5 or 10 consecutive runs as nearly identical as they could be made, with the lavatory filled to the overflow. Wyly showed also the maximum permissible unvented lengths of drain corresponding to a remaining trap seal of $\frac{1}{2}$ in. Since a remaining trap seal of $\frac{1}{2}$ in. will protect fixture traps against excess pneumatic pressures in the system of up to 1 in. of water (which is the limit set in designing the venting system), it would seem that this remaining trap seal would suffice in many simple systems.

**Table 27.8 Permissible Unvented Lengths of Lavatory Drains
for Remaining Trap Seals of 1 In. and ½ In.**

Remaining trap seal of 1 in.

Trap and drain diameter (in.) nominal	Average flow (gpm)	Vent fitting	Criterion	Maximum permissible length of drain (in.)		
				¼ in./ft	½ in./ft	¾ in./ft
1¼	10.9	Long turn	$S^{1/2}ld = 2.6$	22	16	13
1¼	10.9	Sanitary tee	$S^{1/2}ld = 6.2$	54	38	31
1½	13.2	Long turn	$Sl/d = 1.0$	72	36	24
1½	13.2	Sanitary tee	$Sl/d = 1.2$	86	43	29

Remaining trap seal of ½ in.

1¼	10.9	Long turn	$S^{1/2}l/d = 3.0$	26	18	15
1¼	10.9	Sanitary tee	$S^{1/2}l/d = 6.6$	57	40	33
1½	13.2	Long turn	$Sl/d = 1.18$	85	42	28
1½	13.2	Sanitary tee	$Sl/d = 1.58$	114	57	38

*

The results of tests made by French on kitchen sinks may be summarized by saying that

$$\frac{Sl}{d} = 1.0$$

may be used as the criterion for the self-siphonage of kitchen sinks when the drain is connected to the stack through a long-turn fitting and

$$\frac{Sl}{d} = 1.4$$

when a sanitary-tee or short-turn fitting is used.

Tests made on a conventional bathtub 5 ft long connected to a 1¼-in.-diameter trap and drain yielded no trap-seal loss in any instance. Drains 17 and 25 ft long were used, and they were laid at slopes of ¼, ½, and ¾ in. per ft.

While self-siphonage is ordinarily an undesirable phenomenon, water closets depend on self-siphonage for satisfactory operation. With the water closet, the fixture trap is designed to make self-siphonage occur when the fixture is flushed in order that the contents of the bowl may be removed properly. The trail discharge from the tank or flush valve is designed to refill the bowl properly without loss of trap seal.

Tests conducted by French on water closets having drains up to 25 ft in length and laid at slopes of ¼ and ½ in. per ft showed only minor trap-seal losses. Hence it is concluded that there is apparently no need to limit the length of a water-closet drain because of self-siphonage.

The results given in Table 27.8 were considered by the Coordinating Committee for a National Plumbing Code but were thought to be too complicated to be used in their entirety in a code. The values adopted by the Committee and given in Table 12.9.3 taken from the National Plumbing Code are based on these results, however.

It has been pointed out that a remaining trap seal of $\frac{1}{2}$ in. will be satisfactory in many instances (see conclusion 10 following). For that reason Wyly included in his table of permissible unvented lengths of drain the values based on a $\frac{1}{2}$-in. remaining trap seal.

Among the conclusions drawn by French and Eaton as a result of their investigation of the self-siphonage of fixture traps are the following [27-2]:

"1. Increasing the diameter of the outlet orifice of a lavatory from $1\frac{1}{8}$ to $1\frac{1}{4}$ inches increases the trap seal loss greatly, frequently more than 100 per cent, owing to the increased discharge rate.

"2. Flat-bottomed fixtures cause smaller trap-seal losses than do round-bottomed fixtures, owing to the greater trail discharge from the former.

"3. With a $1\frac{1}{2}$-inch fixture trap and drain, an 18- by 20-inch lavatory gave greater trap-seal losses than did a 20- by 24-inch lavatory, presumably owing to the greater trail discharge of the latter. When a $1\frac{1}{4}$-inch trap and drain were used, no particular difference was noted in the trap-seal losses caused by the two lavatories.

"4. The elimination of the overflow in lavatories will increase the trap-seal losses substantially.

"5. The effect on trap-seal losses of varying the vertical distance from the fixture to the trap from 6 to 12 inches appears to be negligible.

"6. For a given rate of discharge from a lavatory, decreasing the diameter of the drain will increase trap-seal losses.

"7. An increase in slope or a decrease in diameter of the fixture drain will tend to cause increased losses due to self-siphonage, and these two dimensions are fully as important as the length of fixture drain in causing self-siphonage.

"8. Trap-seal losses are usually much greater when a long-turn vent fitting is used than when a short-turn or a straight-tee fitting is used. No significant difference between the behavior of short-turn and straight-tee fittings in this respect was observed. Thus, since it is known that a long-turn fitting is more effective in introducing water from a horizontal branch into the stack than is either the short-turn or straight-tee fitting, the characteristics of these fittings are contradictory in these respects. The fitting that is most advantageous from the standpoint of introducing the water into the stack is the least advantageous from the standpoint of self-siphonage.

"9. The permissible values of $S^{\frac{1}{2}}l/d_2$ and Sl/d_2, given in table . . . ,* which are based on a remaining trap seal of 1 inch, are adequate for lavatory installations throughout the plumbing system.

"10. The permissible values of $S^{\frac{1}{2}}l/d_2$ and Sl/d_2 given in table . . . ,* based on a remaining trap seal of $\frac{1}{2}$ inch, are adequate for lavatory installations on the top floor or at other locations in the drainage system where the venting system is sufficiently underloaded or otherwise designed so that negative pressures either do not occur or are negligible in magnitude.

"11. The permissible values of $S^{\frac{1}{2}}l/d_2$ and Sl/d_2 in tables . . . can be increased appreciably by proper choice of the lavatory and trap.

* Table 27.8 of this chapter.

"12. With short-turn vent fittings and with long-turn vent fittings when used with drains on a slope of $\frac{1}{4}$ inch per foot and less, a trap-seal loss of more than half the depth of the trap seal will not be obtained if the drain is so designed that the value of

$$\frac{Q}{d_2^2} \sqrt{gd_2}$$

is less than about 0.5.

"13. Trap-seal losses are increased if the internal diameter of a P-trap is less than that of the fixture drain. Thus, if we are to prevent excessive trap-seal losses for a P-trap due to self-siphonage, we should use a trap having a fairly large internal diameter. Furthermore, siphonage of the trap due to pressure reductions caused by the discharge of other fixtures on the system can be rendered less harmful by using a trap with a large depth of seal. While increasing the depth of seal may lead to greater trap-seal losses, it also results in a greater remaining trap-seal than if a trap with a shallow seal were used.

"14. If a remaining trap seal of 1 inch is adopted as the dividing line between satisfactory and unsatisfactory operation, the relation

$$\frac{Sl}{d_2} = 1.0$$

when a long-turn vent fitting is used, and the relation

$$\frac{Sl}{d_2} = 1.4$$

when a short-turn vent fitting is used, will give satisfactory maximum permissible unvented lengths of fixture drains for ordinary types of sinks and combination fixtures for $1\frac{1}{2}$ and 2-inch-diameter traps and drains. . . .

"15. From limited data on bathtubs, it is concluded that the permissible values of Sl/d_2 for sinks can be applied with at least equal safety to bathtubs. It is believed that more extensive data on the self-siphonage characteristics of bathtub traps will indicate that self-siphonage of this fixture is not serious under any commonly used method of installation, and that the permissible values of Sl/d_2 suggested here can be increased with ample safety.

"16. The test results on the self-siphonage of water closets have indicated that the unvented length of drain for these fixtures need not be limited because of self-siphonage.

"17. Permissible unvented lengths of drains for fixtures for which specific data are lacking can be obtained from figures 17 to 19, inclusive.* The permissible unvented lengths of drain obtained in this manner will be safe, but, for most fixtures, and especially for those with appreciable trail discharge, the data in figures 17 to 19 will yield drain lengths considerably shorter than those that might be used with complete safety.

"18. Standardization of the dimensions of fixture traps, and especially of lavatory traps, with regard to internal diameter and depth of trap seal is highly desirable. Minor restrictions on these dimensions can lead to substantially increased lengths of fixture drains.

* These figures are not reproduced here.

"19. Standardization of the hydraulic characteristics of fixtures is desirable, at least for lavatories, sinks, and combination fixtures. Substantially increased permissible unvented lengths of fixture drains can be obtained for a moderate decrease in the discharge rates of the fixtures.

"20. Increase in depth of trap seal above the 2-inch minimum commonly permitted by codes will make it possible to increase appreciably the maximum permissible unvented lengths of fixture drains."

The foregoing conclusions point out emphatically the fact that longer unvented lengths of drains could be used and the construction of plumbing drainage systems made less expensive in many instances if proper design of fixtures and fixture-drain lines are used to accomplish this and if the maximum discharge rate of faucet-controlled fixtures is limited to a reasonable value. Standardization could accomplish a great deal in this regard.

Research on self-siphonage at the Building Research Station in England [27-12, 27-17] has brought about a better understanding of the phenomenon and means of combatting it. The study showed, in agreement with work in this country, that self-siphonage need not be serious if proper precautions are taken and that lavatories, because of their shape, are more subject to self-siphonage than other fixtures. The investigation also included a study of two types of flow that occur in fixture drains—plug flow and the formation of a hydraulic jump—and their effect on self-siphonage was determined. In particular, analytical methods were applied successfully to a study of the plug motion, which is a very complicated phenomenon.

27.5   Stack Venting

1. **Advantage of and Restrictions on Stack Venting.**   In stack venting the fixtures are connected *independently* through their fixture drains to the stack without any venting other than what is afforded through the stack and stack vent (see Fig. 27-8D). Since no back venting is used when the fixtures are stack-vented, economy of installation is achieved.

However, with this type of venting, certain precautions must be observed if the trap seals of the stack-vented fixtures are not to be depleted excessively by the pneumatic-pressure variations within the stack. One precaution that must be observed is to connect the fixtures on the floor in question to the stack in the proper order vertically upward. They should be connected in order of decreasing rate of discharge in the upward direction. Thus the lavatory drain should be the drain that is highest on the stack. The reason for this is that the discharge of a fixture drain into the stack causes pressure reductions for some distance below the point of entry, and this pressure reduction is greater, the greater the rate of discharge.

Another precaution that is observed in the United States is to permit stack venting only in single-story structures or on the top floor of multistory buildings (see Sec. 12.13.1 of the National Plumbing Code). The reason for this is that flows of waste water from higher floors of a building may cause sufficiently large pressure reductions in the stack at the levels where the fixture drains from the stack-vented fixtures connect to cause excessive losses of trap seal.

It should be noted, however, that the British have installed some systems with stack venting on every floor of multistory buildings and report that it is working satisfactorily. Wise and Croft report [27-14] that a single-stack* system in a five-story flat is operating with negligible trap-seal losses. They go on to cite the following:

"A four-story single-stack system in a block of flats in Harlow has given satisfactory service for over two years; results of tests on this installation made available to the authors by the council surveyor of Epping agree reasonably

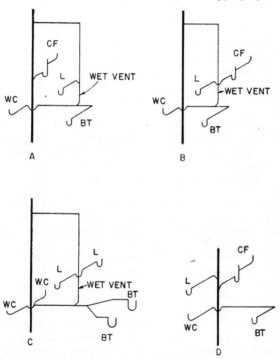

Fig. 27-8. Diagram of wet-vented systems.

well with the results obtained by the laboratory. Systems installed by Willeden Borough Council in eight-story maisonettes occupied in 1953 are giving satisfactory service. F. C. Cook [27-15] has reported that a single-stack system in five-story flats built in 1936 is still working efficiently with only negligible seal losses. Besides these, a number of one-pipe installations with w.c.'s only ventilated are in use in various parts of the country. . . . " They go on to add:

"Many objections have been raised to it [i.e., the single-stack system] on the grounds that the slightest seal reduction is likely to cause unhygienic conditions in buildings. However, it is so simple a method and saves so much money and material that it has been tried on several occasions recently. These trials have

* By "single-stack" the authors mean a stack-vented system. See Fig. 4a of the reference cited.

met with complete success, and one experimenter [27-16] has claimed that, with careful design, vent pipes can be omitted with '. . . . no danger to health, no loss of efficiency, and a saving in costs . . . in the neighborhood of 25 per cent.' . . . Results of an investigation of simple installations have already been published" [27-17, 27-18].

One reason why the British have been able to use stack venting successfully on more than the highest floor of multistory buildings is probably the fact that the rates of discharge from their plumbing fixtures are apparently smaller in general than is the case in the United States—for example, 2- and 3-gal flushes for water closets [27-14]. However, they show a willingness to effect economies by resorting to careful design by competent engineers to a greater extent than is the case here. The tendency in this country is to simplify procedures in the design of plumbing systems so that persons without technical training can apply them. The result is an unnecessary increase in cost.

The possibility of the house sewer being submerged at the outlet also needs consideration. French has pointed out [27-19] that " . . . if the house or building sewer is sufficiently submerged by the water flowing in the street sewer, it is possible, under certain conditions, to obtain a momentary positive pressure in the stack at the point where the stack-vented water closet and bathtub connect to the stack. It is obvious that, if these positive pressures are sufficiently great, sewer gas or air will be forced out of the system through the water-closet and bathtub traps and into the dwelling."

He goes on to show that there are three cases to be considered in this connection: (1) a stack-vented group of bathroom and kitchen fixtures on the top floor of a multistory building in which vented fixtures connect to the stack at lower levels; (2) a single-story dwelling in which only a single bathroom group of fixtures is stack-vented; and (3) a single-story dwelling in which a kitchen sink or combination fixture and a bathroom group of fixtures are stack-vented.

In a multistory building, with the stack-vented fixtures on the top floor, there is no need to be concerned, since the positive pressure caused by a submerged building sewer will not reach so far up the stack.

With regard to the second class listed above, French made tests on such a system (see Fig. 27-1) with the street sewer flowing full. He showed that "the discharge of the lavatory, tub, and water closet, in coincidence or in any combination, will not cause positive pressures sufficiently large to break the seal of any trap. Hence it is apparent that the performance of a stack-vented single group of bathroom fixtures on a single-story stack will not be adversely affected by submergence of the house sewer."

However, when the sink or combination fixture is stack-vented, in addition to the bathroom group, then submergence of the house sewer led to the bubbling of sewer air back through the water-closet trap when either the sink or tray compartments of the combination fixture were discharged. While the amount of air that bubbled back could by no stretch of the imagination be considered a health hazard, nevertheless on esthetic grounds alone, such a condition should be prevented.

The conclusions reached by French [27-19] are as follows:

"1. A group of stack-vented bathroom fixtures consisting of a water closet, lavatory, and a shower stall or bathtub, with or without shower head, will operate satisfactorily under the pressure conditions occurring in a plumbing drainage system, provided that:

(a) The water closet and tub or shower drains connect to the stack at the same level,

(b) The stack is 3 or more inches in diameter,

(c) No other fixtures connect to the stack at a higher level,

(d) The lengths and slopes of the fixture drains are such that self-siphonage of the fixture traps does not occur.

"2. A stack-vented group of fixtures consisting of the fixtures of a single bathroom and a kitchen sink or combination fixture located on the top floor of a multi-story system will operate satisfactorily under the pressure conditions occurring in a plumbing drainage system, provided the conditions of conclusion are observed and vented fixtures connect to the stack below the top floor or that the stack or building drain is otherwise vented below that point.

"3. A stack-vented group of fixtures, consisting of the fixtures of a single bathroom and a kitchen sink or combination fixture located on the top floor of a system in which no vented fixtures connect to the stack below the top floor, or the building drain is not otherwise vented, will operate satisfactorily under all normal vacuums and positive pressures occurring in the stack, but will be subject to objectionable bubbling of air from the drainage system through the water-closet and bathroom traps when the street sewer is sufficiently overloaded to cause frequent and severe submergence of the outlet end of the house or building sewer."

A few remarks may be in order about the application of the foregoing rules or, rather, the misapplication of them. There have been cases in which stack venting has been rejected on the basis of tests in which the bathtub drain connected into the water-closet elbow. Successive flushes of the water closet reduced the trap seal of the bathtub to the danger point. This, however, is not stack venting. The individual fixture drains must run *independently* to the stack according to the definition of stack venting given earlier.

Again, cases have occurred in which stack venting has been disapproved because trap seals of the stack-vented fixtures were depleted excessively when *all* the fixtures on the system were operated simultaneously. The probability of such a condition occurring was ignored. The question of the probability of simultaneous operation of fixtures has been treated in Chap. 24, but the treatment there dealt with large numbers of fixtures. The problem will be reconsidered here in order to reach conclusions as to what might be considered a reasonable design load for the case under consideration, i.e., a group of stack-vented fixtures.

French has treated this problem in some detail [27-19]. He points out that his tests showed that the discharge of the tub or the water closet had no effect on trap-seal losses. Hence attention can be confined to the discharges of the lavatory and the sink or tray compartments of the combination fixture. Now we have little reliable data on which to base assumptions as to the maximum frequency of use of these fixtures, but we can make assumptions that are obviously too severe and see what probabilities result. French assumed that the sink compartment of the combination fixture is filled and emptied at random every 5 min, the tray compartment once every 10 min, and the lavatory once every 3 min. It can hardly be argued that these frequencies of use are less than would occur in service. The duration of discharge was assumed to be 15 sec for the sink, 40 sec for the tray, and 9 sec for the lavatory.

Then it is easy to compute that the probability of finding all three fixtures discharging at any arbitrarily chosen instant of observation is

$$P = {}^{15}\!\!/_{300} \times {}^{40}\!\!/_{600} \times {}^{9}\!\!/_{180} = 0.000167$$

or about 1 in 6,000. It would seem that an occurrence that would probably happen much less frequently than 1 in 6,000 need not be considered as a design load. This is particularly true when it is considered that the occurrence of the simultaneous discharge of all three fixtures, with the consequent excessive reduction of trap seals, will have no serious results, but is rather merely objectionable esthetically.

In a similar manner the probability of finding either the sink and tray, the sink and lavatory, or the tray and lavatory discharging simultaneously with the third fixture not discharging can be computed:

$$P = {}^{15}\!\!/_{300} \times {}^{9}\!\!/_{180} \times {}^{560}\!\!/_{600} + {}^{15}\!\!/_{300} \times {}^{40}\!\!/_{600} \times {}^{171}\!\!/_{180} + {}^{40}\!\!/_{600} \times {}^{9}\!\!/_{180}$$
$$\times {}^{285}\!\!/_{300} = 0.00868$$

or about 1 part in 115.

The probability of the simultaneous discharge of any pair of the fixtures—sink, tray, and lavatory—would seem to be sufficiently great to warrant selecting the pair that gives the worst results as providing the test load for the system.

Wise and Croft at the Building Research Station in England have also considered this problem, although they were considering design loads, rather than test loads, when small numbers of different kinds of fixtures are involved [27-14]. They concluded that the test load for stacks should be based on a probability of occurrence of 0.01 and that combinations of discharges that are less probable than this should be ignored [27-1]. This value is in good agreement with the value of 0.00868 given above.

27.6   Wet Venting

1. Introduction. A *wet vent* is a vent that vents a particular fixture and at the same time receives the discharge from other fixtures (see Fig. 27-8). In practice, such a vent receives the discharge only from low-rated fixtures, such as lavatories, sinks, etc., never from a water closet or from a number of fixtures.

The principal object of using wet vents is to reduce the vent piping required for a given installation by making individual pipes serve two purposes. Because the use of wet venting simplifies the drainage system and thereby decreases the cost of installation, there is an increasing tendency among code-writing authorities to permit its use under suitable restrictions that are necessary to prevent excessive trap-seal losses.

Hunter, at the National Bureau of Standards, conducted tests on wet venting and reported the results in Recommended Minimum Requirements for Plumbing in Dwellings and Similar Buildings (BH2, 1924, out of print), and later in BH13 [27-7]. He showed that, under certain conditions, wet venting could be used without danger of reducing trap seals excessively. In a later publication

[27-20] he indicated that bathroom fixtures back to back can be wet-vented satisfactorily, provided the bathtub drains between the wet vent and the bathtub trap are laid on a uniform slope and otherwise comply with the conditions necessary to prevent excessive self-siphonage.

Extensive tests on the wet venting of fixtures were carried out at the National Bureau of Standards for the Housing and Home Finance Agency by French, Eaton, and Wyly, and the results are reported in BMS119 [27-21].

2. Nature of Wet-venting Phenomena. The nature of the phenomena involved in wet venting can be visualized readily from the description given in BMS119 (page 4):

"In the tests made with transparent tubing on the test installation shown in figure 2, B [Fig. 27-8B], it was observed that, if the flow through the wet vent was started before or at the end of the period of tub discharge the tub drain remained substantially filled with water, and small quantities of air bubbled from the wet vent through the tub waste and formed a pocket in the drain at the trap, with the water-air interface forming, of course, a horizontal plane.

"As discharge continued through the wet vent and air bubbles continued to move up the tub drain to the air pocket over the trap, a gradual lowering of the water surface occurred. At the end of the period of flow from the wet vent, a group of large air bubbles moved rapidly upstream toward the trap, immediately relieving the vacuum over the trap weir and allowing the water seal in the trap to return to equilibrium.

"If, prior to the flow through the wet vent, sufficient air had been admitted to the tub drain to reduce the depth of water over the trap weir to a small value or zero, a larger trap-seal loss was obtained than if only a small pocket of air formed, and the depth of water over the trap weir was relatively large. This was due to the fact that, if the depth of water over the trap weir was relatively large at the time when the flow through the wet vent ceased, the trap was refilled, at least in part, by flow from the tub drain into the tub trap, and only a small, if any, trap-seal reduction resulted. On the other hand, if the pocket of air was large enough so that the water level in the tub drain was at or below the level of the tub-trap weir, there was not in general any flow of water from the drain into the trap, and large trap-seal losses would result under certain conditions.

"In these tests, in which the tub was discharged while flow from the wet vent was occurring, the amount of tub trap-seal loss thus depended upon the size of the air pocket in the tub drain and more specifically upon the height of the water surface in the tub drain with respect to the trap weir. The depth of water over the trap weir was observed to depend on a number of factors, some of them being relatively indefinite.

"First, and as would be expected, the water surface in the tub drain could be made to remain above the trap weir with small or no resulting trap-seal losses by making the tub drain sufficiently short or by laying it on a sufficiently low slope. In addition, the amount of air that bubbled back into the tub drain was observed to be highly variable, depending on a number of factors, such as the rate and duration of the discharge through the wet vent, and the diameters of the wet vent and the horizontal branch . . . .

"The physical phenomena occurring when flow through the wet vent is taking place at the end of the period of discharge from the tub are further complicated by the fact that under certain circumstances air is drawn into the tub drain through the tub trap. This may occur either at the end of the period of flow from the tub or at the end of the flow from the wet vent. The flow of air through the tub trap at the end of the period of discharge of the tub appears to be principally due to the entrainment of air by the flowing water during the formation of the vortex which occurs in the tub when the depth of water over the outlet orifice has become sufficiently small, but it is also undoubtedly due partly at least to the inertia forces in the tub drain operating at the end of the period of tub flow and causing the water surface in the down leg of the trap to recede below the dip of the trap, with consequent flow of air through the tub

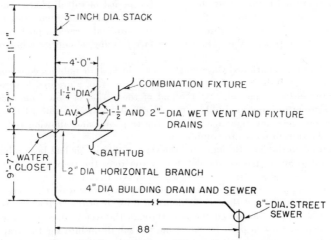

FIG. 27-9. Installation used for wet-venting tests.

trap and into the drain. The air drawn through the tub trap in this manner has the effect, of course, of increasing the size of the air pocket over the trap and hence of decreasing the depth of water over the trap weir. In this way it may cause increased trap-seal losses."

3. Trap-seal Losses for Different Discharges through a Wet Vent.
The test installation used for this purpose at the National Bureau of Standards is shown in Fig. 27-9. Here the lavatory and combination fixture are back-vented, while the tub is wet-vented. The common waste for the lavatory and the combination fixture serves as the wet vent for the bathtub.

In these tests the flow in the wet vent was obtained in two ways: (1) by filling the fixtures discharging through the wet vent and then pulling the plugs and (2) by allowing water to flow continuously from the faucets of the fixtures. The first type of flow will be termed "plug flow" here. The lavatory was filled to the overflow level, the sink and tray compartments of the combination fixture were filled to a level approximately 1 in. below the rim, and the tub was filled to a depth of 6 in.

Table 27.9 gives the results of one series of tests in which the tub drain, $1\frac{1}{2}$ in. in diameter, sloped $\frac{1}{2}$ in. per ft and was varied in length from 4 to 6 ft. Two diameters of wet vent were used—$1\frac{1}{2}$ and 2 in. The table shows clearly the adequacy of the 2-in.-diameter vent even for discharges through the wet vent as high as 45.6 gpm from the sink, tray, and lavatory. There were no losses of seal in the tub trap observed when the 2-in.-diameter wet vent was

Table 27.9   Tub Trap-seal Losses—Tub Drain on $\frac{1}{2}$ In. per Ft Slope—Tub Not Discharged—Plug Discharge of Fixtures

(Each value based on 10 consecutive runs)

Fixtures discharged	Type of fitting connecting lavatory and combination fixture to wet vent	Rate of flow through wet vent (gpm)	Diameter of wet vent (in.)	Tub trap-seal loss (in.)			
				Tub drain 4 ft long		Tub drain 6 ft long	
				Max	Avg	Max	Avg
Sink (basket strainer in)	Long-turn	18.0	$1\frac{1}{2}$	....	....	0.50	0.35
	Short-turn	18.0	$1\frac{1}{2}$	....	....	0.12	0.12
Sink (basket strainer out)	Long-turn	32.0	$1\frac{1}{2}$	....	....	0.38	0.23
	Short-turn	32.0	$1\frac{1}{2}$	....	....	0.50	1.33
Sink, lavatory (basket strainer in)	Long-turn	28.6	$1\frac{1}{2}$	0.38	0.33	0.38	0.28
	Short-turn	28.6	$1\frac{1}{2}$	0.25	0.22	0.25	0.17
Sink, lavatory (basket strainer out)	Long-turn	42.6	$1\frac{1}{2}$	1.00	0.80	0.88	0.57
	Short-turn	42.6	$1\frac{1}{2}$	0.88	0.65	1.12	0.85
Sink, tray, lavatory (basket strainer in)	Long-turn	41.7	$1\frac{1}{2}$	0.62	0.46	0.75	0.57
	Short-turn	41.7	$1\frac{1}{2}$	....	....	1.00	0.75
Sink, tray, lavatory (basket strainer out)	Long-turn	45.6	$1\frac{1}{2}$	1.00	0.85	1.00	0.78
	Short-turn	45.6	$1\frac{1}{2}$	....	....	1.12	1.00
Sink (basket strainer in)	Long-turn	18.0	2	....	....	0	0
	Short-turn	18.0	2	....	....	0	0
Sink (basket strainer out)	Long-turn	32.0	2	....	....	0	0
	Short-turn	32.0	2	....	....	0	0
Sink, lavatory (basket strainer in)	Long-turn	28.6	2	....	....	0	0
	Short-turn	28.6	2	0	0	0	0
Sink, lavatory (basket strainer out)	Long-turn	42.6	2	....	....	0	0
	Short-turn	42.6	2	0	0	0	0
Sink, tray, lavatory (basket strainer in)	Long-turn	41.7	2	....	....	0	0
	Short-turn	41.7	2	....	....	0	0
Sink, tray, lavatory (basket strainer out)	Long-turn	45.6	2	....	....	0	0
	Short-turn	45.6	2	....	....	0	0

used. On the other hand, appreciable losses occurred when a $1\frac{1}{2}$-in. wet vent was used.

Tests in which the slope of the tub drain was reduced to $\frac{1}{4}$ in. per ft showed no increase in trap-seal loss over the losses for the $\frac{1}{2}$-in. per ft slope.

Two series of tests were carried out on the same test system under extremely severe conditions—tests in which the tub was discharged also and tests in which the water closet was discharged in addition to the fixtures discharging through the wet vent. The results of the first-mentioned series of tests are given in Table 27.10.

The effect of adding the water-closet discharge to that of the fixtures connected to the wet vent is shown in Table 27.11 for wet vents 1½ and 2 in. in diameter.

Table 27.10   Tub Trap-seal Losses—Tub Drain on Slope of ½ In.
per Ft—Tub Discharged—Maximum Losses
Observed in 10 Runs
(Each value based on 10 consecutive runs)

Fixtures discharged	Type of fitting connecting lavatory and combination fixture to wet vent	Diameter of wet vent (in.)	Rate of flow through wet vent (gpm)	Tub trap-seal losses (in.)	
				Tub drain 4 ft long	Tub drain 6 ft long
Sink (basket strainer in)	Long-turn	1½	18.0	....	0.75
	Short-turn	1½	18.0	....	0.25
Sink (basket strainer out)	Long-turn	1½	32.0	....	0.62
	Short-turn	1½	32.0	....	0.50
Sink, lavatory (basket strainer in)	Long-turn	1½	28.6	0.38	0.75
	Short-turn	1½	28.6	....	0.50
Sink, lavatory (basket strainer out)	Long-turn	1½	42.6	0.25	0.50
	Short-turn	1½	42.6	....	1.00
Sink, tray, lavatory (basket strainer in)	Long-turn	1½	41.7	0.50	1.00
	Short-turn	1½	41.7	0.50	0.75
Sink, tray, lavatory (basket strainer out)	Long-turn	1½	45.6	0.25	0.88
	Short-turn	1½	45.6	0.25	1.00
Sink (basket strainer in)	Long-turn	2	18.0	....	0.25
	Short-turn	2	18.0	0	0.25
Sink (basket strainer out)	Long-turn	2	32.0	....	0.25
	Short-turn	2	32.0	0	0.25
Sink, lavatory (basket strainer in)	Long-turn	2	28.6	....	0.25
	Short-turn	2	28.6	0	0.50
Sink, lavatory (basket strainer out)	Long-turn	2	42.6	....	0.25
	Short-turn	2	42.6	0	0.50
Sink, tray, lavatory (basket strainer in)	Long-turn	2	41.7	....	0.38
	Short-turn	2	41.7	0	0.50
Sink, tray, lavatory (basket strainer out)	Long-turn	2	45.6	....	0.38
	Short-turn	2	45.6	0	0.50

The trap-seal losses listed in Tables 27.9, 27.10, and 27.11 should be considered in the light of the probability of occurrence of the combinations of discharge for which the trap-seal losses are given. This problem is discussed at some length by French, Eaton, and Wyly [27-21], and on the basis of very high assumed frequencies of use of the fixtures, the approximate probabilities shown in Table 27.12 are given.

4. Conclusions Regarding the Use of Wet Venting. In view of the probabilities given in Table 27.12 the conclusion reached by French, Eaton, and Wyly, that "a loading consisting of the simultaneous discharge of the two fixtures on the system which cause the largest trap-seal losses has been adopted as the design or test loading of the system," appears to be reasonable. Table 27.13 is a summary of the maximum trap-seal losses for different combinations of discharge in Tables 27.9 and 27.10.

Further tests by the same experimenters showed that, when only a lavatory

Table 27.11   Effect of Adding Water-closet Discharge to Test Loading
(Tub not discharged and tub discharged)

| Fixtures discharged | Tub trap-seal reduction (in.) | | | |
| | 1½-in.-diameter wet vent | | 2-in.-diameter wet vent | |
	Max of 5 runs	Avg of 5 runs	Max of 5 runs	Avg of 5 runs
Sink, lavatory...................	1.12	0.85	0.50	0.35
Sink, tray, lavatory.............	1.12	1.00	0.62	0.60
Sink, tray, water closet...........	0.75	0.60		
Sink, tray, lavatory, water closet..	1.38	1.20	0.62	0.55
Sink, lavatory, tub..............	1.00	0.63	0.62	0.37
Sink, tray, lavatory, tub..........	1.00	0.70	0.75	0.45
Sink, tray, lavatory, water closet, tub............................	1.50	1.20	0.75	0.30

Table 27.12   Approximate Probabilities of Finding the Listed Fixtures Operating at Any Arbitrarily Chosen Instant of Observation

Fixtures	Probability
Bathtub or laundry tray.................	1/18
Sink or lavatory........................	1/25
Water closet...........................	1/42
Laundry tray and bath..................	1/260
Sink and bath.........................	1/350
Lavatory and bath.....................	1/350
Sink and lavatory......................	1/500
Sink, lavatory, tray....................	1/6600
Sink, lavatory, bath....................	1/6600
Sink, lavatory, water closet.............	1/11,000
Sink, tray, water closet.................	1/15,000
Sink, tray, bath, water closet.............	1/160,000
Sink, tray, lavatory, water closet..........	1/210,000

is connected to the wet vent, a 1½-in. vent is adequate to keep trap-seal losses of the tub trap down to low values. Tests on a two-story duplex wet-vented system with two lavatories connected to a 1½-in. and 2-in. wet vent showed that such a system would operate satisfactorily. Little difference was observed in these last tests between the trap-seal losses when the 1½-in. wet vent was used and when the 2-in. vent was used.

The conclusions drawn by French, Eaton, and Wyly as a result of their investigation of wet venting are as follows:

"From test data presented it is concluded that the wet venting of one or two bathtubs on the highest branch interval of systems such as those shown in figures 6, 21, and 22 [figure 6 shows a single lavatory and a combination fixture connected to the wet vent for a single bathtub; figure 21 shows a single lavatory connected to a wet vent for a single bathtub; figure 22 shows two lavatories

**Table 27.13　Maximum Trap-seal Loss Observed for Discharge
of Any Two, Three, or Four Fixtures**

Number of fixtures	Trap-seal loss (in.)	
	1½-in. wet vent	2-in. wet vent
Two...................................	1.12[1]	0
Three...............................	1.12[1]	0.50
Four (three through wet vent)...........	1.00	0.50

[1] These figures were obtained with a 6-ft bathtub drain laid at a ½-in.-per-ft slope.　These conditions are not permissible according to the criterion given in the conclusions.

connected to a wet vent for two bathtubs] is an adequate and satisfactory method of venting, provided:

"1. The slope and length of the tub drains and the diameter of the wet vent are such that the value of the quantity, Sl/d, does not exceed unity;*

"2. The diameter of the horizontal branch is not less than 1½ inches when one lavatory connects to the vent and not less than 2 inches when two lavatories or a lavatory and a kitchen sink, or a lavatory and a combination fixture connect to the wet vent; and

"3. The fixtures on the wet vent connect to this vent at the same level. It should be remembered that, in computing values of Sl/d, the slope should be computed in terms of inches per inch or feet per foot, so that it will be dimensionless."

27.7　Dimensions of Fixture Drains

The National Plumbing Code gives provisions for the sizes of fixture drains in Table 11.4.3.　Illustrations of typical drain sizes are given in Table 27.14.

Table 27.14

Drain size (in.)	Fixture units	Fixtures
1¼	1	Lavatory, small-orifice outlet Floor drain
1½	2	Lavatory, large-orifice outlet Domestic dishwasher Bathtub Kitchen sink, domestic Shower stall, domestic
2	3	Combination sink and tray Kitchen sink, domestic, with food-waste disposer
2½	4	Combination sink and tray, with food-waste disposer

* S and l are the slope and length, respectively, of the tub drain, and d is the diameter of the wet vent.

27.8 Frost Closure of Roof Vents

1. Nature of the Phenomenon. In prolonged spells of very cold weather, roof vents may become partially or wholly blocked by frost on the inside of the exposed portion or on top of the vent. In such a case, the free inflow of air to replace air carried down the stack by the discharge or waste water from fixtures will be hindered or entirely prevented. This leads to reductions in pneumatic pressure in the upper part of the stack, with consequent reductions in seals in fixture traps connected to the stack. The result of this is that positive-pressure fluctuations may then force sewer air through these reduced trap seals.

The phenomenon is well known in the northern part of the United States and is common in Canada. However, particularly in Canada, because it has been so troublesome there, several expedients to prevent or minimize it have been devised. These will be considered later.

The source of the ice or frost that forms in a roof vent is as follows: In cold weather a current of warm moist air commonly rises through the plumbing stack of a building at times when there is little or no flow of waste water down the stack. This upward flow of air is caused by the temperature difference between the air outside the building and that of the air inside the drainage system. Since the air in the system is warmer than the free atmosphere outside, the inside air is lighter than that outside the building, and hence a pressure difference exists, tending to produce a flow of air up through the stack and out at the roof vent. The condition is analogous to that of a chimney through which hot gases are rising.

A drainage system without a house trap is shown in Fig. 27-10*A*. The sewer air has free passage from the street sewer through the building sewer and drain and up through the stack and roof vent. A similar system, but one containing a house trap and fresh-air vent, is shown in Fig. 27-10*B*. In this system the water seal in the house trap prevents the air from the street sewer from entering the building. Since cold air would enter through the fresh-air vent, there is little circulation of air inward through the fresh-air vent and up the stack. Hence little trouble should be experienced from frost closure of the roof vent if this system is used.

When there is no house trap in the building drain, the relatively warm and moist air from the sewer furnishes the supply of air that passes up through the stack. When this warm moist air reaches the chilled surface of the roof vent, some of the moisture condenses out in the form of water droplets, some of which pass up and out of the vent in the air stream. Others strike the cold wall of the vent and freeze there. If this process continues for a considerable time, a continually thickening layer of frost forms on the inside wall of the vent. And, if the cold weather persists for a sufficiently long time, this layer of frost may fill the cross section of the exposed portion of the vent completely or it may reach equilibrium at some definite thickness that depends on the diameter of the vent, the air temperatures, and the wind velocity.

An alternative effect or one that may happen in conjunction with the formation of this annular ring of frost on the inside of the vent is the formation of a frost cap on top of the vent, this cap having a hole in it through which the warm air flows. This latter form is more familiar than the first, since it can be observed from a distance without the necessity of getting on the roof and looking directly down the vent.

2. Investigation of Frost Closure. The problem of frost closure, that is, the extent to which exposed roof vents of various diameters can freeze up in cold weather under different conditions of air temperature and wind velocity, has been investigated both experimentally and theoretically by Eaton and Wyly at the National Bureau of Standards [27-22]. They simulated actual conditions

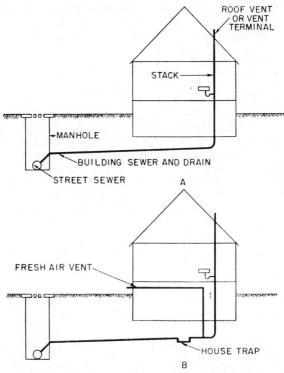

Fig. 27-10. Building drainage systems with and without house traps.

by constructing a 3-in. stack-vented single-story-with-basement building drainage system and mounted a low-temperature chamber around the roof vent. In this way the roof vent could be kept at temperatures below −30°F.

Since the low outside air temperatures could not be simulated in the test as far as producing the pressure differential necessary to produce an air current up the stack, air was blown up through the system at velocities that were computed for different conditions of outside air temperatures. The necessary moisture was provided by allowing a small stream of hot water to flow down the stack at all times during the tests. This was adequate practically to saturate the current of air flowing through the stack and vent.

In tests conducted with the temperature of the vent at −30°F., it was demonstrated that a 3-in.-diameter vent would freeze up solidly given sufficient time. Tests were also made with a 4-in. vent, but it was not feasible to continue the test long enough to demonstrate whether complete closure would result.

A theoretical analysis of the problem was made by Eaton and Wyly based on the laws of heat transfer (1) from the air stream in the vent to the ice surface on the wall of the vent, (2) through the layer of ice and the wall of the pipe, and (3) from the outside wall of the pipe to the wind.

The derivation of the equation resulting from an analysis of the heat transfer is beyond the scope of this text, and the reader is referred to the original paper for a discussion of it. The equation yields a series of values of the temperature of the ice-air surface in the vent, the significance of which will be explained next.

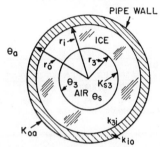

FIG. 27-11. Cross section through partially frosted roof vent.

A given temperature difference $\theta_s - \theta_a$ is available to bring about the transfer of heat from the air stream in the vent to the wind outside (see Fig. 27-11). As the ice layer increases in thickness, a greater and greater portion of this temperature difference is used to transmit the heat through the layer of ice. But, since the conditions outside the ice layer are assumed to remain constant, this means that the temperature of the ice-air surface in the vent must rise as the layer of ice increases in thickness. This rise in temperature cannot go on indefinitely, however. If the temperature of the ice-air surface increases to +32°F., the droplets of water will no longer freeze on that surface but will run down the inside of the vent in the form of water.

Also, if the roof vent is relatively small in diameter (see Fig. 27-12) and if the conditions are sufficiently severe, the temperature of the ice-air surface may not increase to +32°F, and the vent will keep on freezing up to closure, provided the severe conditions persist long enough. Then, ultimately, the temperature throughout the ice layer will become the same as the outside air temperature when the vent is frozen solid.

These conditions are illustrated in Figs. 27-12, 27-13, and 27-14, for a 3-in., a 6-in., and an 8-in.-diameter vent, respectively. In Fig. 27-12, for example, the curve for an outside air temperature of +20°F intersects the +32°F line when the diameter of the opening in the ice is about 0.85 times the inside diameter of the pipe. The ice layer will not increase in thickness beyond this point as long as the conditions remain constant. However, it can be seen that, if the outside

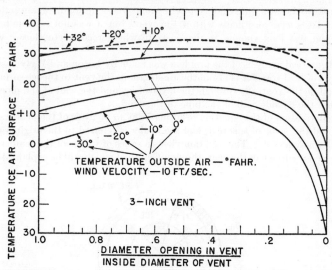

Fig. 27-12. Temperature of ice-air surface in a 3-in. roof vent for different outside air temperatures and for a wind velocity of 10 fps.

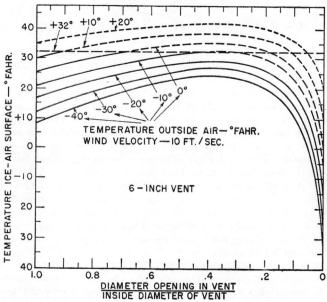

Fig. 27-13. Temperature of ice-air surface in a 6-in. roof vent for different outside air temperatures and for a wind velocity of 10 fps.

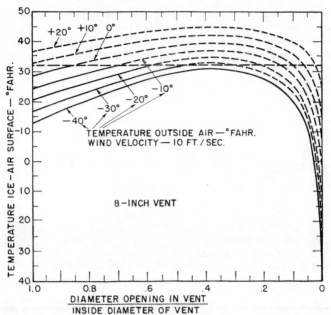

Fɪɢ. 27-14. Temperature of ice-air surface in an 8-in. roof vent for different outside air temperatures and for a wind velocity of 10 fps.

air temperature is lower than about $+13°F$, the ice will continue to thicken until complete closure results.

The equation giving the temperature of the ice-air surface in the vent is

$$\frac{\theta_3 - \theta_a}{\theta_s - \theta_3} = \frac{r_3}{r_i} r_i K_{s3} \left[\frac{1}{k_{3i}} \ln \frac{r_i}{r_3} = \frac{1}{k_{i0}} \ln \frac{r_0}{r_i} + \frac{1}{r_0 K_{0a}} \right] \quad (27\text{-}8)$$

where θ_3 = temperature of the ice-air surface, °F

θ_s = temperature of air stream entering roof vent, °F

θ_a = temperature of free atmosphere outside building, °F

r_0, r_i, and r_3 = radii, ft, defined in Fig. 27-11

K_{s3} = coefficient of heat transfer from air stream to wall, Btu/(hr)(ft²)(°F)

k_{3i} = coefficient of thermal conductivity of ice, Btu/(hr)(ft)(°F)

k_{i0} = coefficient of thermal conductivity of material of pipe wall, Btu/(hr)(ft)(°F)

K_{0a} = coefficient of heat transfer from outer wall of vent to wind stream, Btu/(hr)(ft²)(°F)

The values of K_{3i} and K_{0a} were determined from relations given in "Heat Transmission" by W. H. McAdams.* The value of k_{3i} was taken as 1.0 Btu/(hr)(ft)(°F) for the ice and 30 Btu/(hr)(ft)(°F) for the steel pipe wall.

* William H. McAdams, "Heat Transmission," 3d ed., McGraw-Hill Book Company, Inc., New York, 1954.

In order to evaluate the coefficient K_{s3}, it was necessary to compute the velocity of air flow through the vent for different degrees of frost closure, i.e., for different values of r_3/r_i (see Fig. 27-11). This made it necessary to assume the dimensions of the system—the lengths and diameters of the house sewer, house drain, stack, and vent. For simplicity, the diameters of the various components of each system computed were assumed to be the same. The head of water h available to produce flow up the stack was then computed for each set of conditions assumed.

The velocity of flow v_1 in the stack was next computed for different assumed conditions of frost closure (values of d_3) from the equation

$$\Delta h = \left[r_2 \left\{ \frac{1}{2} + f\frac{L_2}{d_1} + C_b \right\} + r_1 \left\{ f\frac{L_1}{d_1} + \left(f\frac{L_3}{d_3} + C_c + 1 \right) \left(\frac{d_1}{d_3} \right)^4 \right\} \right] \frac{v_1^2}{2g} \quad (27\text{-}9)$$

where Δh = head of water tending to produce air flow up stack, in feet of water column

$\quad\quad r_2$ = ratio of density of air in building sewer and building drain to density of water (temperature of air assumed to be 50°F)

$\quad\quad r_1$ = ratio of density of air in stack to density of water (temperature of air assumed to be 60°F)

$\quad\quad f$ = dimensionless Darcy-Weisbach friction coefficient

$\quad L_1, L_2$, and L_3 = lengths of stack, building sewer plus building drain, and roof vent, respectively, ft

$\quad\quad d_1$ = diameter of stack, building drain, and building sewer, assumed equal, ft

$\quad\quad d_3$ = diameter of opening in vent, ft

$\quad\quad v_1$ = velocity of air flow in stack, fps

$\quad\quad C_b$ = bend-loss coefficient for bend from stack to building drain

$\quad\quad C_c$ = coefficient of contraction at junction of stack and exposed part of vent

$\quad\quad g$ = acceleration of gravity, ft per sec²

When the value of v_1 has been found, the value of v_3 can be computed from

$$v_3 = v_1 \left(\frac{d_1}{d_3} \right)^4 \quad (27\text{-}10)$$

3. Practical Expedients for Preventing or Minimizing the Occurrence of Frost Closure.

Two expedients for preventing or minimizing frost closure have been developed in Canada. One is to allow the vent terminal to project only an inch or two above the roof (see Fig. 27-15). In this way there is virtually no exposed terminal. According to advice from Canada, the occasional blocking of the vent by snow during a storm causes no trouble due to depletion of trap seals, since the snow is so porous that air can pass through it quite freely. Furthermore, the snow melts fairly promptly.

A second expedient that has been used with considerable success is to enlarge the stack vent just below the roof. This has two effects—the increased diameter reduces the chance of the complete closure of the terminal (see Figs. 27-12, 27-13, and 27-14), and the stream of air issuing from the smaller-diameter portion of the vent tends to pass up through the enlarged portion without touching the wall and hence without any great amount of chilling.

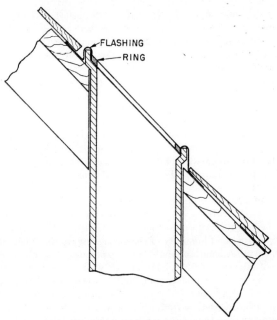

FLASHING

RING

FIG. 27-15. Installation for preventing frost closure.

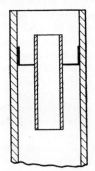

FIG. 27-16. Installation reported to prevent frost closure.

Another method of construction is to enclose the vent terminal with flashing, leaving an air space between the terminal and the flashing that is closed except at the bottom where it connects with the heated space below the roof.

Still another expedient that is said to have worked successfully in preventing frost closure where it had occurred is shown in principle in Fig. 27-16.* This also eliminated trouble that had been experienced from gusts of wind striking the top of the stack and affecting the trap seals of fixtures in the building. The

* Reported by Thomas P. McDermott, Copper and Brass Research Association, retired.

reduction in diameter of the stack vent by the insertion of the inner short length of pipe has the effect of reducing the pressure changes within the system due to the gusts, while, at the same time, the reduction is not enough to interfere appreciably with the inflow of air into the stack to replace air carried down by the flow of waste water.

In Niagara Falls a curious cause of the closure of roof terminals by ice exists. Spray from the falls is sometimes carried over the city by a south or southeast wind, and in very cold weather it causes some of the vent terminals on buildings to ice up. In most cases the situation can be taken care of by 4- or 6-in. vents, but in some extreme cases it has been necessary to jacket the roof terminal with a spiral of copper tubing and to pass hot water or steam through the tubing.

4. Conclusions Regarding Frost Closure. As a result of their investigation of the subject, Eaton and Wyly drew the following conclusion in regard to frost closure:

"1. The roof vents of building drainage systems may become partially or completely closed by frost in very cold weather under certain conditions. Among the factors that affect frost closure are: (*a*) temperature of the outside air, (*b*) temperature and humidity of the air passing up the stack and the vent, (*c*) wind velocity, (*d*) length of vent that is exposed to the outside atmosphere, (*e*) diameter of the vent, (*f*) thermal insulation, if any, of the exposed part of the vent, or the use of a vent pipe of some material that is highly resistant to the transmission of heat, (*g*) whether or not a house trap is inserted in the building drain, either with or without a fresh-air vent, (*h*) whether or not the diameter of the vent is greater than that of the stack, and the distance to which such expansion extends below the roof, (*i*) the temperature conditions in the air space below the roof, (*j*) the exposure, whether northern, southern, etc., and (*k*) the velocity of air flow upward through the vent.

"2. Frost closure has been observed in two general forms: (1) as a concentric layer that builds up on the inner wall of the vent, and (2) as a cap that builds up from the rim of the vent at its outlet. The latter form is the one that has been the more frequently observed, possibly because it is the more easily observed of the two. Sometimes the two forms occur simultaneously.

"3. In general, it appears that there is little likelihood of trouble from frost closure unless the outside air temperature falls below about 10°F and remains there for at least several days.

"4. Reducing the length of the exposed portion of the vent as much as possible appears to be the most certain way of reducing or preventing frost closure.

"5. Uninsulated small-diameter vents in heated attics may freeze solid unless protected by insulation.

"6. The discharge of hot water into the stack, particularly at night, when the upward convective air current is most pronounced, tends to increase the humidity of the air passing up the stack and thus increases the tendency to frost closure.

"7. The larger the diameter of the vent, the less likely it is to close completely because: (1) a longer period of cold weather is required to create the necessary thickness of ice, and (2) because, with the larger diameter vents, the temperature of the ice-air surface in the vents is generally higher for a given thickness of ice layer than with the smaller diameter vents . . . . Freezing stops when a temperature of 32°F is attained at the ice-air surface.

"8. As the air from the street sewer is relatively moist and warm, the use of a house trap to prevent this moist air from passing up the stack should reduce the tendency to frost closure. Even if a fresh-air inlet is provided on the house side of the trap, this provides a source of relatively cold dry air that carries with it less moisture to condense out and freeze in the vent.

"9. Snow storms may close the vent temporarily, but the snow is porous, and evidence seems to be available that this does not cause any serious difficulty.

"10. Reconnecting the vent pipes to the stack before it passes up through the roof has been found to reduce or prevent siphonage of trap seals when the vent was completely closed by frost.

"11. Increasing the diameter of the vent above that of the stack may help in two ways: (1) It affords the advantage of a larger diameter of vent, so that it requires a longer time for the vent to freeze up completely, and (2) it would seem that if the expanded portion of the vent is relatively short, the stream of air passing up through the vent may not expand soon enough to reach the chilled wall of the vent, and hence less moisture reaches the wall than would otherwise be the case, so that the tendency to freeze is decreased.

"12. The greater the wind velocity, the greater the tendency to closure. In general, however, the lower the temperature, the smaller is the wind velocity. Less trouble seems to be experienced when a vent has a southern exposure (in the northern hemisphere) than when it is exposed on the shady side of the roof.

"13. The use of a material for the vent pipe that has a higher resistance to the flow of heat than does steel has a favorable effect.

"14. As a rough estimate of the rate at which the thickness of the ice layer in a vent may increase in cold weather, we may take a value of 0.07 in./hr, or roughly 1½ in./day, assuming that the convective current of air persists during the greater part of the day. This value was obtained in laboratory experiments on 3-inch vents for an outdoor air temperature of −30°F and with the air passing up through the vent saturated with moisture at a temperature of about 70°F. Values of about 0.08 and 0.06 in./hr were obtained for 1½-in. and 4-in. vents, respectively."

CHAPTER 28

Strength of Buried Conduits under Earth Loads

28.1 Introduction

Buried pipes are subjected to backfill loads and to loads due to concentrated surface loads, such as truck-wheel and roller loads. These loads set up bending moments in the walls of the pipe and, consequently, tensile and compressive stresses in the pipe wall. Should these stresses become too great, the pipe will break, and while sewer pipes have been known to suffer fracture without collapsing [28-1],* nevertheless the breaks in sewer pipes offer an opportunity for sewage to leak out into the surrounding soil, on the one hand, and, on the other hand, for infiltration to occur, adding to the load that the sewer must carry and that the treatment plant must handle. Furthermore, there is the danger that, should the broken pipe be subjected to internal pressure due to an unusually large flow, the pipe may collapse.

Until about 1913, no theory of earth loads on buried pipes was available, and engineering judgment was the only basis for determining whether or not a particular pipe would be strong enough to stand, without damage, the unknown load that was to be imposed on it by a given depth of backfill and a given fill material. Neither had tests to determine the crushing strength of pipe been devised and the strength thus determined been related to the strength of the pipe under backfill loads.

Because of these deficiencies in engineering knowledge and because of the great economic importance of the problem, Prof. Anson Marston at the Iowa State College commenced a long series of theoretical and experimental investigations of the loads that are imposed on buried pipes under various conditions; and this work was continued by M. G. Spangler, W. J. Schlick, and others. Their achievements are presented in a long series of bulletins of the Iowa State College Engineering Experiment Station and in several engineering journals, also in a book written by Spangler [28-2].

Today, as a result of this careful work, a sound basis for computing loads on buried pipes is available. Computing the load is only part of the problem, however, since we must also determine the strength of the pipe under an earth load before we can predict whether its crushing strength is adequate to resist the loads that will come upon it. Therefore standard laboratory crushing tests of the pipe are involved and the relating of the strength thus determined to the strength of the same pipe under conditions of earth loading.

In the past, for the most part, engineers who have had to face these problems

---

* Numbers in brackets refer to the bibliography at the end of the book.

have been concerned mainly with street sewers, intercepting sewers, and water mains, in other words, with relatively large pipes. This has been due partly to the large costs of such lines; partly to the fact that, because of the large diameters and considerable depths of trench often involved, the loads on the pipe were much greater than they are on house-connection pipes; and partly because the factors of safety involved were probably less than they are usually with the small-diameter house-connection lines.

Today the smaller-diameter pipes (say, up to and including 8-in. nominal diameters) are being used under conditions of backfill and concentrated surface loads that often make it essential to utilize available engineering knowledge of such loads in selecting pipe and determining the conditions of backfill. It is also necessary to have some knowledge of the relative strengths of flexible, semirigid, and rigid pipe under the several types of crushing tests used in the laboratory and the strength of these same pipes under earth loads.

A somewhat different approach to the computation of the loads due to backfill from that used generally with large-diameter pipes will be used for the small-diameter pipes, and it will be necessary to extend the coefficient curves over a wider range of values than is given in the earlier literature in order to make them useful for computing loads on small-diameter pipes.

The following discussion will be primarily concerned with water and gas service lines, house-connection lines, septic-tank distribution lines, and subsurface drainage lines, i.e., to pipes of small diameters. The diameters considered will be up to and including 8-in. nominal diameters.

28.2   The Theory of Backfill Loads on Buried Pipes

Buried pipes fall into two principal classes as regards earth loading: (1) ditch conduits and (2) projecting conduits. A *ditch* conduit is one that is placed at

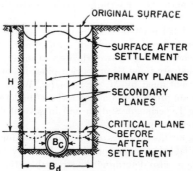

FIG. 28-1. Diagram showing ditch conditions.

the bottom of a ditch dug in undisturbed soil and then covered with backfill (see Fig. 28-1). A *positive projecting* conduit is one which rests on the undisturbed surface of the ground and is then covered with an embankment (see Fig. 28-2). As might be anticipated, the width of the ditch enters in the equation applying to the case of the ditch conduit, whereas there is no width of ditch involved in the case of the positive projecting conduit, and the outside diameter of the pipe enters the equation instead.   There is also a case termed the *negative projecting conduit*, but this will not concern us here, although it may be involved when a small-diameter pipe is installed in a narrow shallow ditch at the bottom of a trench that is wider than the transition width.

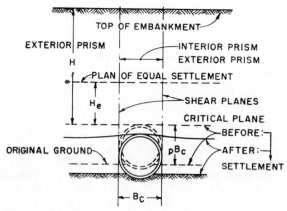

FIG. 28-2. Diagram showing positive projection conditions.

1. Ditch Conduits.   A typical case of a ditch conduit is shown in Fig. 28-1, in which a *rigid* pipe is shown at the bottom of a trench that has been backfilled level with the surface of the undisturbed ground.   After some time has elapsed, the surface of the ground at the top of the trench will have settled, assuming a form somewhat as shown in exaggerated fashion in the figure.   Since there is a greater depth of fill beside the pipe than there is directly over it, there will be more settlement over the portions of the trench between the sides of the pipe and the trench walls than there is directly over the pipe, since the pipe is assumed to be rigid.

We consider a hypothetical "critical plane" to exist in the fill, as shown in Fig. 28-1, at the time when the backfill has just been completed.   This is a horizontal plane tangent to the top element of the pipe.   Points in this plane are considered to move with the particles of fill as the latter settles, so that, when the backfill has settled to form the curved surface shown at the top of the trench, the critical plane has assumed a similar form, but one that is not so pronounced as the first mentioned.

In considering the problem of backfill loads on the pipe, it is convenient to assume the vertical primary and secondary planes shown in Fig. 28-1.   The primary planes are tangent to the ends of the horizontal diameters of the pipe, while the secondary planes are located at the lowest points of the troughs formed by the surface curve and the curve of the secondary plane.   Since these two curves are horizontal at the points where they are cut by the secondary planes, no vertical shear in the soil can be transmitted through them.   In other words, the weight of the fill between the two secondary planes is all transmitted to the pipe and to that portion of the trench bottom lying between the pipe and the secondary planes. The weight of the fill outside the secondary planes is all carried by the bottom of the trench and the walls of the trench. When the pipe is rigid and the fill on each side of it is relatively compressible, it is assumed that the weight of all the backfill above the top of the pipe and between the two secondary planes is carried by the pipe. This assumption is involved in Eq. (28-1).

For a pipe of given diameter and for a given fill material, the secondary planes shown in Fig. 28-1 move outward as the trench increases in width, and hence the load on the pipe tends to increase as the trench is widened. There is a limit to this increase, however; and beyond a certain width of trench, called the *transition width*, which varies with the diameter of the pipe, its flexibility, and the characteristics of the backfill, the load on the pipe for conditions that are otherwise the same will remain constant as the trench is widened further. This constant load is equal to the load that would be exerted on the pipe if it were placed on the undisturbed subgrade and an embankment built up over it equal in height to the depth of the trench [28-3]. This condition, called the *positive-projection* condition, will be considered later (see Fig. 28-2).

If, instead of being quite rigid, the pipe is flexible, and if the fills at the side of the pipe are well tamped, the stiffness of the side fills may be as great as that of the conduit, or even greater, and then the load on the pipe will usually be equal to or less than the weight of the fill between the two primary planes, depending on the relative stiffnesses of the pipe and the fill. When the pipe is rigid, the load on it is greater than that of the fill lying between the primary planes. Thus it is apparent that the load on a given pipe is greater if the pipe is rigid than if the pipe is flexible, other conditions being the same.

The equation for computing the backfill load on a *rigid* pipe buried under the ditch condition with relatively compressible fills is

$$W = C_d w B_d{}^2 \qquad (28\text{-}1)$$

where
$$C_d = \frac{1 - e^{-K\mu' \, H/Bd}}{2K\mu'} \qquad (28\text{-}2)$$

In the above equations,

W = load on pipe, lb per ft of length

C_d = load coefficient for ditch conduits

w = weight of backfill material, lb per cu ft

B_d = width of trench at level of top of conduit, ft

e = base of natural logarithms

H = depth of trench to top of conduit, ft

K = ratio of active unit lateral pressure to unit vertical pressure

μ' = coefficient of friction between fill material and sides of trench

Values of the coefficient C_d are plotted in Fig. 28-3 for several values of $K\mu'$ corresponding to different fill material characteristics.

Values of K can be computed from the formula

$$K = \frac{1 - \sin \phi}{1 + \sin \phi} \qquad (28\text{-}3)$$

or they can be taken from Table 28.1.

A glance at the equation giving the value of C_d shows that it is not the value of K alone or either μ^* or μ' alone that determines these coefficients, but rather the products $K\mu$ or $K\mu'$. Now the coefficient μ' may be equal to or less than μ, but it cannot be greater.

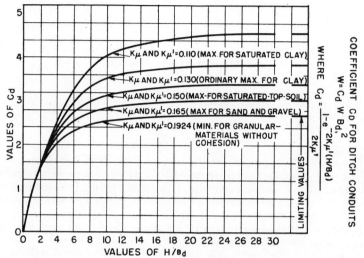

FIG. 28-3. Values of coefficient C_d for ditch conditions.

Table 28.1 Values of ϕ and K for Different Fill Materials

Backfill material	ϕ, deg	ϕ, deg	K
Soft plastic clay	5	0	1.000
Wet fine silty sand	20	5	0.840
Dry sand	30	10	0.704
Gravel	35	15	0.589
Loose loam	35	20	0.490
Compact loam	35	25	0.406
Compact clay	35	30	0.333
Cinders	35	35	0.271
Compact sand-clay	45	40	0.217
		50	0.133

The values of $K\mu = K\mu'$ recommended by Spangler are shown on the curves in Fig. 28-3 and are listed in Table 28.2.

It should be noted carefully that Eq. (28-1) applies to the case of a rigid pipe under ditch conditions and to a relatively compressible fill. The equation assumes tacitly that all the weight of material lying between the secondary planes is carried by the pipe. If, however, the pipe is flexible and if the side fill is well tamped, so that the two possess approximately the same degree of stiff-

* μ is the coefficient of internal friction of the fill material, see Eq. (28-9).

ness, then, according to Spangler [28-1, page 413], Eq. (28-4) represents approximately the condition of loading:

$$W = C_d w B_c B_d \tag{28-4}$$

where B_c is the outside diameter of the pipe in feet, and the other quantities have already been defined. Values of C_d can be obtained from Fig. 28-3.

Table 28.2   Recommended Values of $K\mu = K\mu'$ to Use for Different Types of Backfill

Minimum for granular materials without cohesion........... 0.1924
Minimum for sand and gravel............................. 0.165
Maximum for saturated topsoil.......................... 0.150
Ordinary maximum for clay.............................. 0.130
Maximum for saturated clay............................. 0.110

The foregoing equations are designed to yield the maximum load that can be imposed on the pipe for the assumed conditions. However, the maximum load on the conduit may not occur for some time, and the load varies appreciably with the moisture content. Spangler states that this lag in developing the maximum load may last for several years and that the increase may amount to as much as 20 to 25 per cent of the total load.

2. Positive Projecting Conduits. A positive projecting conduit is one that rests on the undisturbed surface of the ground and is buried under an embankment (see Fig. 28-2). The backfill load on such a conduit is the upper limit of the loads that are imposed on a ditch conduit as the width of the ditch is increased, all other conditions remaining constant. This fact has been demonstrated experimentally [28-3]. The width of trench for which the load on the pipe computed from the ditch formula [Eq. (28-1)] is equal to the load computed from the positive projection formula [Eq. (28-6)] is called the *transition width*.

In order that the conditions affecting the load exerted on a positive projecting conduit may be understood clearly, certain concepts must be explained. Figure 28-2 shows the fill over and adjacent to the pipe divided into an interior prism and two exterior prisms. The height of the interior prism is less than that of the exterior prisms, and hence the settlement of the fill directly over the pipe will be less than that of the exterior prisms unless the pipe is very flexible. Thus there will be vertical shearing forces along the *shear planes* shown in Fig. 28-2, the direction of this shear depending on the relative settlements of the interior and the exterior prisms and, hence, on the relative compressibilities of the fill and the pipe. The direction of these shearing forces has a marked effect on the load exerted on the pipe by the backfill. If the vertical shearing forces on the shear planes enclosing the interior prism act upward on the prism, then the load on the pipe is less than the weight of the backfill comprising the interior prism. If they act downward on the shear planes enclosing the vertical prism, the load on the pipe is greater than the weight of the backfill comprising the interior prism.

It can be shown [28-2, page 417; 28-7, pages 861ff.] that, if the embankment is quite high, there will be a horizontal plane within the embankment, called *the plane of equal settlement* (see Fig. 28-2), above which the settlement of successive layers of the fill will be equal and above which the vertical shearing forces on the shear planes are zero everywhere. If the embankment is quite low, however, these shearing forces may extend all the way to the top of the embankment. The load coefficients are quite different for these two cases, as will appear later.

Another quantity that must be defined is the *projection ratio*. If the natural surface of the ground is shaped to fit the bottom of the pipe, then the pipe will project above the natural ground surface by an amount less than its outside diameter B_c. The distance that the pipe projects above the natural surface of the ground is expressed as pB_c, where p is defined as the projection ratio (see Figs. 28-2 and 28-4).

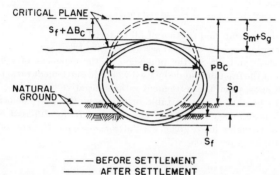

FIG. 28-4. Settlements affecting loads on positive projecting conduits.

A quantity that is fundamental in determining the backfill load that will be exerted on a positive projecting conduit is the "settlement ratio" (see Fig. 28-4). This ratio takes into account the relative settlements of the interior and exterior prisms of fill. Spangler [28-2, page 421] defines this ratio as

$$r_{sd} = \frac{(s_m + s_g) - (s_f + \Delta B_c)}{s_m} \tag{28-5}$$

where s_m = compression of fill material adjacent to pipe in height, pB_c

s_g = amount by which natural ground surface adjacent to pipe settles

s_f = amount by which invert of pipe settles relatively to natural ground surface

ΔB_c = shortening of vertical diameter of pipe under load

All these quantities should be expressed in the same units of length—feet, inches, etc.

For a rigid pipe the settlement ratio is normally positive, and the backfill load on the pipe is greater than the weight of the backfill between the primary planes. For a flexible pipe the settlement ratio may be negative, in which case the backfill load on the pipe is less than the weight of the backfill between the primary planes.

The formula for the backfill load on a positive projecting conduit given by Marston and Spangler is

$$W = C_c w B_c^2 \tag{28-6}$$

In this equation,

$$C_c = \frac{e^{\pm 2K\mu H/B_c} - 1}{\pm 2K\mu} \tag{28-7}$$

for the case in which the plane of equal settlement lies outside the embankment and

$$C_c = \frac{e^{\pm 2K\mu H_e/B_c} - 1}{\pm 2K\mu} + \left(\frac{H}{B_c} - \frac{H_e}{B_c}\right) e^{\pm 2K\mu H_e/B_c} \tag{28-8}$$

for the case in which the plane of equal settlement lies within the embankment.

In the foregoing equations, μ is the coefficient of internal friction of the fill material defined by

$$\mu = \tan \phi \tag{28-9}$$

where ϕ = angle of internal friction of fill material

H_e = height of plane of equal settlement (see Fig. 28-2)

In Eqs. (28-7) and (28-8), the plus signs in the exponent of e and in the denominator of the fraction should be used when the settlement ratio is positive; the negative signs, when the settlement ratio is negative.

In order to prepare a plot or table of values of the load coefficient C_c in Eq. (28.8), it is necessary to compute the values of H_e for different conditions. Marston and Spangler have given several formulas for H_e, one of which is [28-4, page 10; 28-7, page 865]

$$e^{\pm 2K\mu H_e/B_c} \pm \frac{2K\mu H_e}{B_c} = \pm 2K\mu r_{sd}p + 1 \tag{28-10}$$

In Eq. (28-10), use the $+$, $-$, $+$ signs when the settlement ratio is positive and the $-$, $+$, $-$ signs when it is negative.

This equation has been solved for suitable values of $r_{sd}p$, and the resulting values of C_c are plotted in Fig. 28-5. We may commence a consideration of this plot with the line corresponding to $r_{sd}p = 0$. This case represents the situation when the pipe compresses exactly as much under the backfill load as the fill beside it does, and it will be seen from the plot that when this is true $C_c = H/B_c$. For this particular case then, Eq. (28-6) becomes

$$W = wHB_c \tag{28-11}$$

according to which the load on the pipe is equal to the weight of the fill directly over it, i.e., the weight of the fill lying between the two primary planes.

Now if the pipe is more compressible than the fill beside it, the coefficient lines to the right of the line just considered apply, and we have involved two subdivisions of the class of positive projecting conduits—the *incomplete ditch condition* and the *complete ditch condition*. The complete ditch condition is represented by the coefficient curve at the extreme right. For this condition the pipe is more flexible than the fill beside it, and the plane of equal settlement lies outside the embankment, or is imaginary. The incomplete ditch condition is represented by the lines lying between the line $C_c = H/B_c(r_{sd}p = 0.0)$ and the extreme right-hand curve. This condition applies to the case in which the pipe is more flexible than the fill beside it, and the plane of equal settlement lies

within the embankment.   Thus the incomplete ditch condition applies to high
embankments and the complete ditch condition to low embankments.

Passing now to the case in which the pipe is stiffer than the fill beside it, we
have the curves to the left of the curve $C_c = H/B_c$.   Correspondingly there are
two subdivisions of the main classification here.   The *complete projection condition* is represented by the curve at the extreme left of the plot, and this corresponds to the case of a low embankment for which the plane of equal settlement lies outside the embankment.   The intermediate lines represent the case

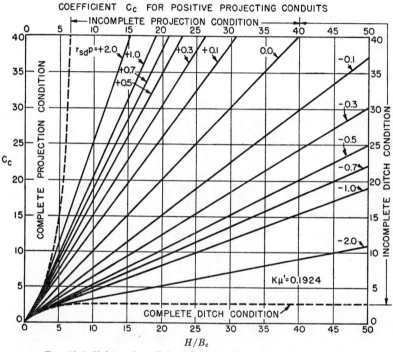

FIG. 28-5. Values of coefficient C_c for positive projecting conduits.

called the *incomplete projection condition* and correspond to high embankments
for which the plane of equal settlement lies within the embankment.

It is obvious from Fig. 28-5 that a rigid pipe of a given outside diameter will
have a larger backfill load on it than a flexible pipe of the same diameter for
conditions that are the same, since in general, the coefficient lines to the right of
the middle line represent the case of flexible pipes, while those to the left of the
middle line represent the conditions that exist when the buried pipes are rigid.

Computation shows that for practically all the cases of buried pipes not
greater than 8 in. in diameter practical considerations require the trench to be
wider than the transition width.   This is the range of diameters in which we
are interested.   In the few cases that may involve large diameters and deep

trenches, the load on the pipe will be only a little less than the load computed on the assumption that the width of trench is the transition width; hence the following tables and plots of backfill loads will be based on the transition width of trench.

Curves giving transition width ratios for $K = 0.165$ are given in Fig. 28-6. It will be noted that these are given only for positive values of the settlement ratio $r_{sd}p$, since the transition width has no significance for negative values of $r_{sd}p$, and the critical plane (see Fig. 28-2) after settlement has occurred is concave upward in this case. These curves were computed by applying the

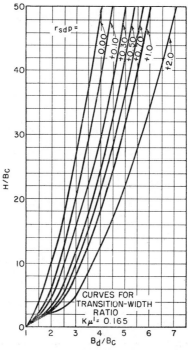

Fig. 28-6. Curves of transition-width ratios.

principle that, for the transition width, the load computed by Eqs. (28-1) and (28-2) is equal to that computed from Eqs. (28-6), (28-7) and (28-8).

Transition widths for rigid and flexible pipe having nominal diameters of 4, 6, and 8 in. are shown in Fig. 28-7. It is assumed arbitrarily that the outside diameters of these pipes are 5, 7, and 9 in., respectively. The values were obtained by computing values of H/B_c, reading the corresponding values of B_d/B_c from the proper curve in Fig. 28-6 (B_d is here the transition width), and then computing B_d. For the rigid pipe, the value of $r_{sd}p$ was taken as $+0.50$, and for the flexible pipe it was taken as 0.00 (see Table 28.3). It would seem clear from Fig. 28-7 that in only a few cases might the trench that would have to be excavated for these diameters of pipe be less than the transition width.

In order to compute the loads on any given pipe and for any given conditions of backfill, we proceed as follows: Spangler [28-2, page 422] recommends that the following values of the settlement ratio r_{sd} be used in the absence of any further information.   When house-connection pipes are involved or, in fact, any of the

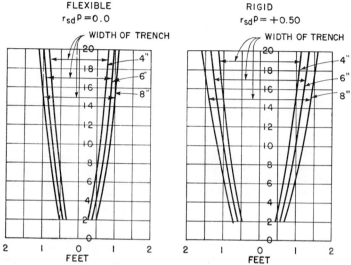

FIG. 28-7. Transitions widths for small rigid and flexible pipes.

small-diameter pipes considered in this discussion, the pipes will ordinarily rest on the undisturbed ground, so that the projection ratio will be equal to unity. For this case,

$$r_{sd} = r_{sd}p$$

Table 28.3   Recommended Values of the Settlement Ratio

Condition	Settlement Ratio
Rigid culvert on foundation of rock or unyielding soil............	+1.0
Rigid culvert on foundation of ordinary soil.....................	+0.5 to +0.8
Rigid culvert on foundation of material that yields with respect to adjacent natural ground....................................	0 to +0.5
Flexible culvert with poorly compacted side fills................	−0.4 to 0
Flexible culvert with well-compacted side fills..................	−0.2 to +0.8

On the basis of Table 28.3, it will be assumed for purposes of computation in what follows that for rigid pipe $r_{sd} = +0.50$ and for flexible pipe $r_{sd} = 0.00$. It is assumed that these values represent average conditions for the several types of pipe.   Considerable variation from these values may occur in individual cases, and the person making the computation will have the responsibility for deciding what value to use.

Marston has given the terms *rigid*, *semirigid*, and *flexible* significance in their application to earth loads on buried conduits [28-4, page 5]:

"Rigid conduits [are those] whose cross-sectional shapes cannot be distorted more than 0.1 per cent without causing materially injurious cracks; including all rectangular conduits, and all cylindrical conduits made of plain or reinforced concrete masonry or burnt clay pipes.

"Semi-rigid conduits [are those] whose cross-sectional shapes can be distorted sufficiently to change their vertical or horizontal dimensions more than 0.1 per cent, but not more than 3.0 per cent, without causing materially injurious cracks; including segmental block conduits, and those made of cast iron pipe, together with some stone masonry cylindrical conduits.

"Flexible conduits [are those] whose cross-sectional shapes can be distorted sufficiently to change their vertical or horizontal dimensions more than 3.0 per cent before causing materially injurious cracks; including those made of corrugated pipe, thin steel or wrought iron pipe, and probably some conduits made of brick or stone block masonry."

It is doubtful whether these definitions are workable when applied to small-diameter pipes. For example, Marston classified cast-iron pipe as semirigid. It would hardly seem that cast-iron soil pipe in diameters of 8 in. and less should be so classified but that it should rather be considered to be rigid.

At the other extreme is a very flexible pipe such as polyethylene, which is coming into quite common use for water-service lines. This pipe has no true crushing strength in the usual sense of the word. Its resistance to excessive flattening under backfill loads is due almost entirely to the active and passive side thrusts exerted on it by the backfill. The first of these—the active side thrust—is due to the internal friction of the backfill material and is exerted equally on rigid and flexible pipe. The second-named—the passive side thrust—is due to forces that come into play because of the compression of the side fill as a result of the outward movement of the sides of the pipe wall as the pipe flattens under the vertical backfill load. This passive thrust is approximately proportional to the distance moved by the side walls, and hence it is much larger for a flexible pipe than for a rigid pipe. Hence, even though the pipe may have little elastic resistance to the vertical backfill load, the cross section ultimately stabilizes in somewhat flattened form under the earth pressures applied around its circumference.

Bituminized-fiber pipe, because it is subject to cold flow under sustained loads, also possesses this same characteristic, but the deformation takes place at a much slower rate than it does for flexible plastic pipe. Because of this characteristic, bituminized-fiber pipe and flexible plastic pipes will sustain surprisingly high backfill loads with relatively little flattening of the cross section.

It does not seem feasible to make any clear-cut classification of small-diameter pipes (up to and including 8 in. diameters) from the standpoint of earth loads. Certain kinds of pipe, such as cast-iron, concrete, vitrified-clay, and thick-walled steel and copper, should be classed as rigid. Thin-walled steel and copper, much plastic pipe, and bituminized-fiber may be classed as flexible. Most other pipe will lie between these two extremes.

Another uncertainty in computing backfill loads on buried pipes is the fact that we can usually only estimate the characteristics of the backfill that affect the load on the particular buried pipe, and hence we must assume average conditions for these characteristics.   Thus the backfill loads given in Figs. 28-8 to 28-11 should not be considered exact by any means, but only approximate.

Figures 28-8 and 28-9 give backfill loads on small-diameter flexible and rigid pipes, respectively.   Since it is not feasible to prepare individual plots to take account of each kind of pipe involved, because of differences in outside diameters for the same nominal diameter, the lines are computed for the actual diameters with which they are labeled, and it is necessary to interpolate for the actual outside diameter of the pipe in question.   The lines are for a weight of

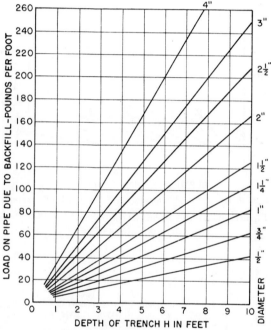

FIG. 28-8. Backfill loads on flexible pipes up to 4-in. diameters.

backfill of 100 lb per cu ft, and corresponding loads for other weights of backfill can be obtained by direct proportion.

The lines in Fig. 28-8 for flexible pipe were computed by use of the formula

$$W = wHB_c \qquad (28\text{-}11)$$

The lines in Fig. 28-9 for rigid pipe were computed by using the formula

$$W = C_c w B_c^2 \qquad (28\text{-}6)$$

Values of C_c were read from the curve for $r_{sd}p = +0.50$ in Fig. 28-5.   When the computed values of H/B_c lay outside the limits of the figure, the value of C_c was computed from the equation of the line representing $r_{sd}p = +0.5$ (see Table 28.4).

Strictly the lines in Fig. 28-9 should not be quite straight, but the deviation from linearity is negligible in comparison with other factors; so they are shown as straight in the figure.

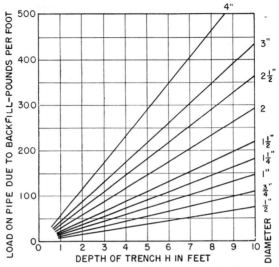

Fig. 28-9. Backfill loads on rigid pipes up to 4-in. diameters.

Table 28.4   Equations of the Straight Lines in Fig. 28-5 Representing the Various Values of $r_{sd}p$

$r_{sd}p$	Equation of Line
+2.0	$C_c = -2.74 + 2.77H/B_c$
+1.0	$C_c = -1.32 + 2.16H/B_c$
+0.7	$C_c = -0.810 + 1.92H/B_c$
+0.5	$C_c = -0.63 + 1.77H/B_c$
+0.3	$C_c = -0.31 + 1.55H/B_c$
+0.1	$C_c = -0.105 + 1.23H/B_c$
0.0	$C_c = 0 + H/B_c$
−0.1	$C_c = +0.098 + 0.74H/B_c$
−0.3	$C_c = +0.25 + 0.595H/B_c$
−0.5	$C_c = +0.41 + 0.50H/B_c$
−0.7	$C_c = +0.55 + 0.43H/B_c$
−1.0	$C_c = +0.675 + 0.37H/B_c$
−2.0	$C_c = +1.025 + 0.21H/B_c$

Backfill loads are given for flexible and rigid pipes, respectively, in Figs. 28-10 and 28-11, for diameters ranging from 4 to 9 in., by half inches. The range of depths is extended to 20 ft, since house-connection lines are often laid at depths in excess of 10 ft, the range of depths used for smaller diameter pipes in Figs. 28-8 and 28-9. Furthermore, since again the outside diameters of pipes of different materials may differ considerably for the same nominal diameter, the lines in Figs. 28-10 and 28-11 are computed for each half inch from 4 to 9 in. The loads corresponding to the actual outside diameters can be obtained by interpolation.

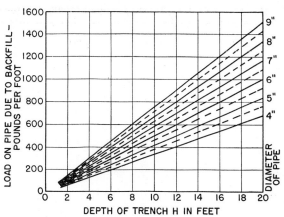

Fig. 28-10. Backfill loads on flexible pipes up to 9-in. diameters. $r_{sd}p = 0.00$; $w = 100$ lb/ft³.

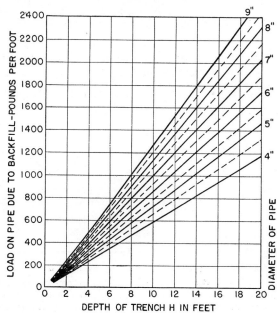

Fig. 28-11. Backfill loads on rigid pipes up to 9-in. diameters. $r_{sd}p = +0.50$; $w = 100$ lb/ft³.

Table 28.5 gives unit weights of various kinds of backfill under different degrees of compaction and moisture content. These values were determined by Dean Marston by direct measurement [28-1, Table 2].

Outside diameters of house-connection pipes are given in Table 28.6.

Table 28.5 Typical Weights of Backfill Materials

Material	Condition	Weight (lb per ft)
Black topsoil........................	Loose, wet, 20% water	60
Black topsoil........................	Loose, damp, from 2 ft depth	75
Mixture, black topsoil and yellow clay.	Loose, wet, 19.4% water	80
Yellow clay, slightly sandy...........	Loose, damp, from 4 ft depth	75
Yellow clay, very sandy.............	Loose, damp, from 6 ft depth	85
Blue clay..........................	Loose, dry, from 15 ft depth	83
Sand..............................	Dry	99
Black topsoil........................	Saturated	100
Black topsoil........................	25% water	108
Yellow clay........................	Saturated, 17% water	127
Yellow clay........................	Saturated, 26% water	145
Yellow clay........................	Dropped 3 ft into ditch	84
Yellow clay........................	Dropped 7.8 ft into ditch	88
Mixture, yellow and blue clay........	Cold weather, dropped 14.7 ft into ditch	96–101
Yellow clay weighing 87 lb per cu ft..	Immediately after thoroughly wetting	97
Yellow clay weighing 87 lb per cu ft...	After standing 6 days	101

Table 28.6 Outside Diameters of House-connection Pipes of Various Materials

Material	Nominal diameter (in.)					
	2	3	4	5	6	8
Asbestos cement..............	....	....	4.78	5.83	6.82	
Bituminized fiber.............	2.46	3.56	4.68	5.82	6.92	9.14
Cast iron, service weight.......	2.25	3.25	4.25	5.25	6.25	8.38
Cast iron, extra heavy.........	2.38	3.50	4.50	5.50	6.50	8.63
Concrete, nonreinforced........	....	....	5	....	7¼	9½
Vitrified clay, standard........	....	....	5	....	7¼	9½
Vitrified clay, extra...........	....	....	....	....	7¼	9½

3. Illustrative Examples. *Problem 1.* A 1¼-in. type WS polyethylene water-service line is installed in a trench with 4 ft of cover. Backfill is yellow clay weighing 110 lb per cu ft, when wet. What is the backfill load on the pipe? The trench is 2 ft wide, and the fill is tamped to the top of the pipe. The outside diameter of the pipe is 1.85 in.

Since the width of the trench is greater than the transition width, the load will be read from Fig. 28-8, which is based on Eq. (28-11) for a positive projecting conduit for conditions such that $r_{sd}p = 0.0$. Interpolating for the diameter 1.85 in., the load is read as about 64 lb per ft from Fig. 28-8. This is for backfill weighing 100 lb per ft. To get the corresponding value for $w = 110$ lb per ft, multiply 64 by 110/100, which gives $W = 70.5$ lb per ft.   Computing the load by Eq. (28-11), we have

$$W = 110 \times 4 \times \frac{1.85}{12} = 68 \text{ lb per ft}$$

Problem 2.   A 6-in. bituminized-fiber house-connection pipe is installed in a 30-in. wide trench with a cover of 11 ft of sandy yellow clay, weighing 85 lb per cu ft.   The fill is tamped to the level of the top of the pipe.   The outside diameter of the pipe is 6.92 in. (Table 28.6).   What is the backfill load on the pipe?

Examination of Fig. 28-7 shows that the actual width of trench is greater than the transition width.   Hence the positive projection formula, Eq. (28-6), is valid.   Since the fill is tamped to the top of the pipe, this will tend to impose more load on the pipe than if the fill were not tamped.   Hence, instead of assuming $r_{sd}p = 0.00$, which is a good value to use when it is merely known that the pipe is flexible, we assume (see Table 28.3) that $r_{sd}p = +0.3$.   Then the value of C_c can be read from the proper coefficient curve in Fig. 28-5 ($r_{sd}p = +0.03$) for $H/B_c = 11 \times 12/6.92 = 19.1$ or 28.7.   Then, using Eq. (28-6)

$$W = 28.7 \times 85 \times \left(\frac{6.92}{12}\right)^2 = 811 \text{ lb per ft}$$

While the use of the settlement ratio $r_{sd}p = +0.3$ increases the computed load on the pipe over that which would result if $r_{sd}p$ is assumed equal to 0.00 (the value on which the load curves in Fig. 28-10 were based), the strength of the pipe will also be increased under this load as the settlement ratio increases.

Problem 3.   An 8-in. vitrified-clay (standard-weight) house-connection line is to be installed in a trench 2 ft wide and with 9 ft of yellow clay backfill cover. The clay weighs 87 lb per cu ft.

From Fig. 28-7 we see that the transition width for this case is about $2\frac{1}{2}$ ft. Since the trench is narrower than this, use

$$W = C_d w B_d^2 \tag{28-1}$$

$H/B_d = \frac{9}{2} = 4.5$.   We obtain the value of C_d from Fig. 28-3, using the curve for $K\mu' = 0.130$.   Then $C_d = 2.37$, and

$$W = 2.37 \times 87 \times 2^2 = 825 \text{ lb per ft}$$

28.3   Superloads on Surface of the Ground

In addition to backfill loads, a buried pipe may be called upon to resist loads imposed by concentrated or distributed loads on the surface of the ground.   A typical concentrated load might be a wheel load from a truck, the load due to a roller used to compact the backfill, that due to a bulldozer, an airplane, etc.

The problem of determining the loads on a buried pipe due to surface loads of the types just mentioned was first attacked successfully as the result of a suggestion of J. H. Griffith [28-5] that the solution by Boussinesq [28-6] for the stress distribution in a semi-infinite elastic solid be applied to the distribution of stress in soils due to superposed surface loads.   In this case, the surface of the ground constitutes the plane boundary of the semi-infinite solid, which extends to infinity in all directions horizontally and downward.

1. Concentrated Static Load Directly over the Pipe. The first problem that will be considered is that of the vertical pressure on a finite area caused by a concentrated load on the fill directly over the center of a symmetrical figure

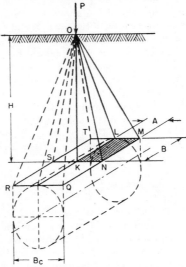

FIG. 28-12. Diagram for computing load on pipe due to concentrated surface load directly over pipe.

lying in a horizontal plane at a distance H directly below the concentrated load at the depth involved (see Fig. 28-12). Table 28.7 gives values of the influence coefficient C to be used in the formula

$$W = CP \tag{28-12}$$

where W is the load in pounds on the rectangular area $KLMN$ having the sides A and B, this being one of the four equal rectangles arranged about the point K directly under the origin O at the surface of the fill, at which point the concentrated load P lb is applied.

In Fig. 28-12, the rectangle $MQRT$ represents the horizontal projection of a section of the buried pipe of length $2B$ and of diameter $B_c = 2A$. The coefficients in Table 28.7 are given for values of $m = A/H$ and $n = B/H$. Since Eq. (28-12) gives the vertical load on the rectangle $LMNK$, this result must be multiplied by 4 to give the entire vertical load on the length $2B$ of the pipe (the length of pipe is commonly taken as 1 ft).

2. Eccentric Concentrated Static Load. The next problem to be considered is that in which the concentrated surface load is not directly over the pipe (see Fig. 28-13). Here the surface load P is concentrated at the point O. The horizontal projection of the length of pipe considered is represented by the rectangle $MQRT$, and the center of this rectangle point K is centered under the point I so that the eccentricity of the load is $OI = JK$. In this figure, the rectangle $MNJV$ corresponds to the rectangle $KLMN$ in Fig. 28-13. Now if we compute the load due to P on rectangle $MNJV$ and subtract from this the load due to P on $JVTS$, we obtain the load on one-half of the projected area of the length of pipe under consideration.

In the computation of the load on rectangle $MNJV$, $m = 2A'/H$ and $n = B/H$. The corresponding value of the coefficient C in Eq. (28-12) is found in Table 28.7, and the load on area $MNJV$ is computed from Eq. (28-12). Call this load L_1.

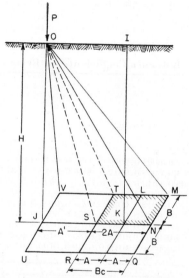

Fig. 28-13. Diagram for computing load on pipe due to concentrated surface load eccentric to pipe.

In the computation of the load on area $JVTS$, $m = A'/H$ and $n = B/H$. The coefficient C for this area is found as before, and the load L_2 on area $JVTS$ is found by Eq. (28-12). Then the load on area $MNST$ is found by taking the difference of L_1 and L_2, and the load on the length $2B$ of the pipe is obtained by multiplying $L_1 - L_2$ by 2.

The problems just discussed are treated at greater length by Spangler [28-2, Chap. 17; 28-7] and by Marston [28-4]. A still further problem, that of computing the pressure at a point below the surface of the fill due to a distributed load over it resting on the surface of the fill, will be mentioned but not treated here. For this problem, see Spangler [28-2, Chap. 17] and Newmark [28-9].

3. Concentrated Live Loads. The effect of impact due to concentrated live loads at the surface of the ground on the load to which a buried pipe is subjected has been studied by Spangler, Winfrey, and Mason at the State College of Iowa [28-8].

As a result of this study, Marston proposed the following formula for the static and impact loads imposed on a buried pipe [28-2, page 432]:

$$W = \frac{1}{L} ICP \qquad (28\text{-}13)$$

or, for a 1-ft length of pipe,

$$W = ICP \qquad (28\text{-}14)$$

where W = average load per foot of conduit, lb per ft

L = length of conduit in feet for which the load is computed

I = impact factor, ranging from 1.5 to 2.0 for trucks driving on an unpaved roadway

C = load coefficient, to be obtained from Table 28.7

P = concentrated surface load, lb

Table 28.7   Influence Coefficients for Rectangular Area

m	n								
	0.02	0.04	0.06	0.08	0.10	0.2	0.3	0.4	0.5
0.02	0.0002	0.0004	0.0006	0.0008	0.0010	0.0019	0.0027	0.0034	0.0040
0.04	0.0004	0.0008	0.0012	0.0016	0.0019	0.0037	0.0054	0.0068	0.0080
0.06	0.0006	0.0012	0.0018	0.0024	0.0029	0.0056	0.0081	0.0101	0.0120
0.08	0.0008	0.0016	0.0024	0.0030	0.0038	0.0074	0.0107	0.0135	0.0159
0.10	0.0010	0.0019	0.0029	0.0038	0.0047	0.0092	0.0132	0.0168	0.0198
0.2	0.0019	0.0037	0.0056	0.0074	0.0092	0.0179	0.0258	0.0328	0.0387
0.3	0.0027	0.0054	0.0081	0.0107	0.0132	0.0258	0.0373	0.0474	0.0559
0.4	0.0034	0.0068	0.0101	0.0135	0.0168	0.0328	0.0474	0.0602	0.0711
0.5	0.0040	0.0080	0.0120	0.0159	0.0198	0.0387	0.0559	0.0711	0.0840

m	n								
	0.6	0.7	0.8	0.9	1.0	1.2	1.4	1.6	1.8	2.0
0.02	0.0044	0.0048	0.0051	0.0054	0.0056	0.0058	0.0060	0.0061	0.0062	0.0063
0.04	0.0089	0.0097	0.0103	0.0108	0.0111	0.0117	0.0120	0.0122	0.0124	0.0125
0.06	0.0133	0.0145	0.0155	0.0162	0.0167	0.0176	0.0181	0.0184	0.0186	0.0187
0.08	0.0177	0.0193	0.0206	0.0216	0.0223	0.0234	0.0240	0.0244	0.0247	0.0249
0.10	0.0222	0.0242	0.0258	0.0270	0.0279	0.0293	0.0301	0.0306	0.0309	0.0311
0.2	0.0435	0.0474	0.0504	0.0528	0.0547	0.0573	0.0589	0.0599	0.0606	0.0610
0.3	0.0629	0.0686	0.0731	0.0766	0.0794	0.0832	0.0856	0.0871	0.0880	0.0887
0.4	0.0801	0.0837	0.0931	0.0977	0.1013	0.1063	0.1094	0.1114	0.1126	0.1134
0.5	0.0947	0.1034	0.1104	0.1158	0.1202	0.1263	0.1300	0.1324	0.1340	0.1350

This table is based on Table 1 of Ref. 28-9.   Values are those of the coefficient C in Eq. (28-12).

When the load is static, the value of I is unity.   When the load is moving, the value of I depends on the speed and vibration of the vehicle and on the roughness of the roadway.

4. Illustrative Examples. *Problem 1.* A 6-in. plastic drain line passes under an unpaved highway with a depth of cover of 3 ft.   There is a slight depression in the roadway directly over the pipe.   A heavily loaded truck with 8,000 lb on each rear wheel, moving at moderate speed, passes over the pipe. What is the load on the pipe directly under one of the wheels due to both wheel loads?   Assume that the distance between the center lines of the wheels is 4.5 ft.   There is then a concentrated load of 8,000 lb directly over the portion of the pipe under consideration and a concentrated eccentric load of 8,000 lb at a distance of 4.5 ft from the point on the pipe that is under consideration.

Compute first the static load on the pipe due to the wheel load that is directly over it.   The outside diameter of the pipe will be assumed to be 6.5 in. or 0.542 ft.   A 1-ft length of pipe will be considered.

Referring to Fig. 28-12, $B = 0.5$ ft and $A = 0.271$ ft.   Then

$$m = \frac{A}{H} = \frac{0.271}{3} = 0.090$$

$n = B/H = 0.5/3 = 0.167$.   From Table 28.7 we obtain by interpolation the value $C = 0.0076$.   Now if we assume an impact factor of 1.75,

$$W = 4ICP = 4 \times 1.75 \times 0.0076 \times 8,000 = 425 \text{ lb per ft}$$

The factor 4 is due to the fact that the coefficient C gives the load on one-quarter of the projected area of the pipe.

Compute next the load on the pipe due to the wheel load of 8,000 lb that is 4.5 ft off center.   Referring to Fig. 28-13: $OI = JK = 4.5$ ft and

$$JN = 4.5 + 0.5 = 5.0 \text{ ft}$$

(Since for this case the axis of the pipe is projected into the line JN and the outside diameter of the pipe is MQ.)

The coefficient for area $JVMN$ will be computed first.

$$m = \frac{B}{H} = \frac{0.27}{3} = 0.090$$

and $m = (45 + 0.5)/H = \frac{5}{3} = 1.67$.   From Table 28.7, $C' = 0.0276$.

The coefficient C'' for area $JVTS$ will be computed next.

$$m = \frac{B}{H} = \frac{0.271}{3} = 0.090$$

$n = A/H = (4.5 - 0.5)/3 = 1.33$.   Then $C'' = 0.0269$.   Then

$$W = 2I(C' - C'')P = 2 \times 1.75 \times 0.0007 \times 8,000 = 20 \text{ lb per ft}$$

The total load on the pipe at the designated point due to the two wheel loads is $425 + 20 = 445$ lb per ft.

5. General Remarks. Thoroughly tamping the backfill beside the pipe is an advantage, regardless of whether the pipe is rigid or flexible. If the soil beside a rigid pipe is thus compacted, more of the load from the backfill is carried by the bottom of the trench than if the fill beside the pipe is unconsolidated. If the pipe is flexible, consolidation of the fill beside it increases the horizontal passive thrust on the sides of the pipe, and this effect overbalances the increased vertical load, so that the pipe actually flattens less under a given backfill condition when the fill beside it is compacted than when it is not compacted.

Allowing the pipe to rest on the flat bottom of the trench without shaping the bed to the curve of the pipe is a very unsatisfactory method of bedding, but because the installation of a house-connection line involves relatively little expense, proper inspection is usually lacking, to say nothing of adequate specifications for the installation. Fortunately, the strength of the pipe in crushing is usually more than adequate to meet the conditions of burial; however, carelessness in the installation is often the rule and not infrequently leads to trouble. In extreme cases, when the owner is willing to spend the necessary money to have the installation made and inspected properly, improved methods of bedding, described by Spangler [28-2] and others, can be used.

Conditions of bedding even worse than that in which the pipe has line contact with the bottom of the trench are not uncommon with house-connection pipe. Conditions do occur in which the bottom of the trench is not in contact with the lowest element of the pipe and in which the backfill is not forced under the pipe to support it. In such a case bending stresses are added to the crushing stresses, and the effect on the strength of the pipe can only be guessed, but the pipe is certainly less capable of carrying backfill loads when this condition occurs.

With flexible pipes, the ordinary concepts of crushing strength as a requisite to enable the pipe to resist backfill loads without failure do not apply. Thousands of polyethylene water-service lines and at least one experimental polyethylene sewer have been installed without trouble from backfill or wheel loads. Yet polyethylene pipe has no crushing strength in the usual sense of the word, since it resembles rubber hose in this respect. The form of cross section of such a pipe stabilizes under the earth pressures, vertical and horizontal, and it may well be said that such a pipe is little more than a lining for a hole in the ground.

Bituminized-fiber pipe behaves elastically under suddenly applied transient loads, but it is subject to plastic flow under loads that persist over a long period of time. This is an advantage as far as backfill loads are concerned. When the backfill is first placed over a line of bituminized-fiber pipe, the pipe undergoes a slight flattening, amounting in most cases to a few hundredths of an inch, this being accompanied by the creation of elastic stresses in the wall. As time goes on, the tensile stresses are slowly relieved through the plastic flow of the material, and the pipe flattens still further. As this happens, the side walls move outward, the horizontal diameter shortening by approximately the same amount that the vertical diameter shortens, and this movement develops a horizontally directed passive thrust that replaces the elastic stresses in resisting flattening. Ultimately, therefore, the form of the cross section stabilizes under the system of vertical and horizontal external forces exerted by the earth around the pipe, with only small tensile stresses remaining in the wall. However, if the pipe, when in this condition, is suddenly subjected to a transient concentrated load at the surface of the fill over it, it responds to this load elastically. Consequently, after a line of bituminized-fiber pipe has been in the ground for some time, it is only slightly stressed in tension by the backfill load, and hence it can carry greater concentrated surface loads than if the backfill were stressing it.

28.4 Relation of Crushing Strength of Pipe in Standard Laboratory Tests to Its Strength under Backfill and Wheel Loads

1. Discussion of Laboratory Crushing Tests.   There are three commonly used methods of testing pipe that is to be buried in the ground for crushing strength (see Fig. 28-14). These are (1) the three-edge bearing test, (2) the two-edge bearing or flat-plate test, and (3) the sand-bearing test.

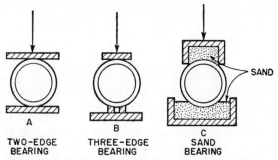

Fɪɢ. 28-14. Standard laboratory crushing tests of pipes.

The three-edge bearing test has been quite commonly used in the past because it offers stable condition of support, particularly for the larger diameters of pipe. The following is the ASTM specification for this test:

"16. When the three-edge-bearing method is used, the ends of each specimen of pipe shall be accurately marked in halves of the circumference prior to the test. The lower bearings shall consist of two wooden strips with vertical sides having their interior top corners rounded to a radius of approximately ½ inch. The strips shall be straight and shall be securely fastened to a rigid block at least 6 by 6 in. in cross-section. The interior vertical sides of the strips shall be parallel and spaced a distance apart of 1 in. per foot of pipe diameter, but in no case less than 1 in. Before the pipe is placed, a fillet of plaster of Paris or other equalizing material, such as sand and sulfur, thick enough to compensate for the inequalities of the pipe barrel shall be cast on and between the lower bearings. The pipe shall be placed on the fillet while the plaster of Paris is still somewhat plastic; the use of the plaster of Paris fillet may be dispensed with when agreeable to the manufacturer and the purchaser. The upper bearing shall be a rigid wooden block at least 6 by 6 inches in cross-section, straight and true from end to end. A fillet of plaster of Paris thick enough to compensate for the inequalities of the pipe barrel shall also be cast along the length of the crown. The upper bearing shall be brought in contact while the plaster of Paris is still somewhat plastic. The upper and lower bearings shall extend the full length of the socket."

When small-diameter pipes are involved, under 12 in. in diameter, the three-edge bearing method does not give comparable bending moments in the pipe wall for different diameters, since the lower bearing blocks are spaced the same distance apart for these diameters. Furthermore, no difficulty is experienced with the stability of these small-diameter pipes under the two-edge bearing test. Consequently, the latter method of testing would seem to be preferable for such pipes as house-connection pipes, because of its greater simplicity and because there is no deviation from geometrical similarity when pipes of different diameters are tested. The specifications for vitrified-clay pipe (Federal Specifications SS-P-361a), concrete sewer pipe (Federal Specification SS-P-371), and asbestos-cement sewer pipe (Johns-Manville Standard Specifications, October, 1949) require the three-edge bearing test to be used, while Commercial Standard CS116-54 and Federal Specification SS-P-356 for bituminized-fiber house-connection pipe specify the two-edge bearing test.

The requirement in Federal Specification SS-P-356 concerning the crushing test of bituminized-fiber pipe reads as follows:

"*4.3.2.2 Dry crushing strength.* A 12-inch length (6-inch optional) cleanly sawed from each sample shall be kept in air at a temperature of not more than 75°F. for 24 hours. The specimen shall be laid horizontally between two flat plates in a testing machine having a head speed of 0.5 inch per minute. The specimen shall be checked for conformance with 6.3.2 with the load at rupture reported in pounds per linear foot."

For rigid pipe the sand-bearing test gives a strength that is frequently assumed to approximate the strength of properly bedded pipe under backfill loads. This is not true for flexible pipe, since much of the strength of the flexible pipe is derived from the horizontal passive thrust of the earth against the sides of the pipe, and this thrust is lacking in the three laboratory tests mentioned above. As a result, it should be recognized that a flexible pipe will stand without failure greater backfill loads than would be determined from crushing tests by the sand-bearing method.

The sand-bearing test is sometimes substituted for the three-edge test where rigid pipe is involved. The ASTM specification for this test reads:

"Sand-Bearing Method

"17. (a) When the sand-bearing method is used, the ends of each of the specimens of pipe shall be accurately marked in quarters of the circumference prior to the test. Specimens shall be carefully bedded in sand, above and below, for one-fourth the circumference of the pipe measured on the middle line of the barrel. The depth of bedding above and below the pipe at the thinnest points shall be one half the radius of the middle line of the barrel.

"(b) The sand used shall be clean and moist and shall be such as will pass a 4760 micron (No. 4) sieve conforming to the requirements of the Standard Specifications for Sieves for Testing Purposes (A.S.T.M. Designation: Ell). The sand in the lower bearing shall be loose when the pipe is placed.

"(c) The top bearing frame shall not be allowed to come in contact with the pipe nor with the top bearing plate. The upper surface of the sand in the top bearing shall be struck off level with a rigid top bearing plate, the lower surface of which is a true plane, made of heavy timbers or other rigid material, capable of distributing the test load uniformly without appreciable bending. The test load shall be applied at the exact center of this top bearing plate in such a manner as to permit free motion of the plate in all directions. For this purpose a spherical bearing is preferred, but two rollers at right angles may be used."

Since the same kind of crushing test is not used for all kinds of water and sewer pipe and since the results of these laboratory crushing tests do not afford direct information as to the strength of the pipe under backfill loads, further consideration of these tests will be given here.

2. Maximum Bending Moments in the Pipe Wall for Various Conditions of Loading. *a. Two-edge Bearing Test* (see Fig. 28-14A). The maximum bending moment for this condition is at the top (and bottom) of the pipe and is given by [28-10, page 8]

$$M_2 = 0.159WD \qquad (28\text{-}15)$$

where M_2 = bending moment, in.-lb
W = vertical load, lb per in. of length
D = mean diameter of pipe, in.

b. Three-edge Bearing Test (see Fig. 28-14B). A general expression for the maximum bending moment in the wall of a pipe subjected to the three-edge bearing test (without the plaster-of-paris fillets) has been developed by G. H. Keulegan at the National Bureau of Standards [28-11]. The maximum bending moment occurs at the crown of the pipe and is given by the following expression:

$$M_3 = \frac{1}{4\pi}\left(\frac{\cos\alpha + 1 - \alpha\sin\alpha}{\cos\alpha}\right)WD = \frac{1}{4\pi}KWD \qquad (28\text{-}16)$$

where M = bending moment at crown
α = angle made by each reaction with the vertical (see Fig. 28-15).
Strictly this equation can be considered valid only for rigid pipes.

The angle α becomes zero for the two-edge bearing test, and Eq. (28-16) then becomes

$$M_2 = \frac{1}{2\pi}WD = 0.159WD \qquad (28\text{-}17)$$

which agrees with Eq. (28-15).

Then the ratio of the maximum bending moments M_3/M_2 for the three-edge bearing test and the two-edge bearing test for the same applied load W is

$$\frac{M_3}{M_2} = \frac{K}{2} \qquad (28\text{-}18)$$

where the value of K is to be obtained from Eq. (28-16). Hence the relative strengths of the pipe under these two tests are given by

$$\frac{S_3}{S_2} = \frac{2}{K} \qquad (28\text{-}19)$$

Values of the ratio S_3/S_2 are plotted in Fig. 28-16, giving a means of relating the crushing strength of a pipe by the three-edge bearing method to its strength by the two-edge method, for diameters up to 8 in.

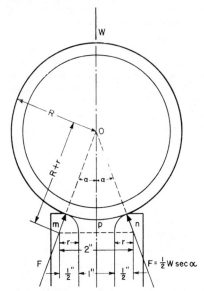

FIG. 28-15. Forces on ring in three-edge bearing test.

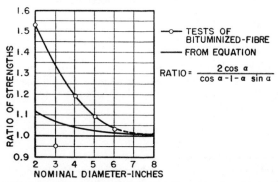

FIG. 28-16. Ratio of crushing strengths of pipe: three-edge bearing test to two-edge bearing test.

Wyly and Fishburn at the National Bureau of Standards made comparative tests on bituminized-fiber sewer pipe by these two methods [28-12]. They used 2-, 3-, 4-, 5-, and 6-in. nominal diameter samples of this flexible pipe and obtained values of the ratio considerably higher than those yielded by Eq. (28-19) (see Fig. 28-16).

The reason that the values of the ratio obtained in these tests were higher than those yielded by the moment formulas has not been explained, but it is probably due to the fact that Eq. (28-16) applies to rigid pipe, while the pipe that was tested was flexible.

One other point in regard to the three-edge bearing test requires comment. The use of plaster-of-paris fillets changes the bending moment appreciably from the relation given by Eq. (28-16), at least for the small diameters that are considered here. The use of the fillets increases the crushing strength. However, this does not explain the high values of the ratio of crushing strengths obtained in the tests at the National Bureau of Standards, since no fillets were used in these tests (see Fig. 28-16).

c. Sand-bearing Test. See Fig. 28-14C. The maximum bending moment in the wall of a pipe subjected to the sand-bearing test is

$$M_s = 0.0845WD \tag{28-20}$$

28-1, 28-12]. Then, if we take the ratio of crushing strengths, based on the ratio of the moments M_2/M_s, we obtain

$$\frac{S_s}{S_2} = \frac{0.159}{0.0845} = 1.88 \tag{28-21}$$

3. Crushing Strengths under Condition of Installation. In comparing the crushing strength of house-connection pipes under backfill conditions with their strengths under the several laboratory tests discussed, we shall utilize the *load factor*, which is defined as the "ratio of the field supporting strength to the three-edge bearing laboratory strength of similar pipe" [28-14, page 13]. Furthermore the following discussion is restricted to rigid pipes. The supporting strength of buried pipe is affected by the distribution of the vertical loads, upon the types of bedding used, and upon the distribution and magnitude of active lateral pressure on the sides of the pipe. This latter consideration requires that we distinguish between the ditch condition and the positive-projection condition, since it is only under the latter of these conditions that the active lateral pressure can develop fully. It may be remarked here that Marston's assumption that the vertical load is distributed uniformly over the breadth of the pipe has been confirmed by measurements as well as the assumption that active lateral pressures are about equal to those computed by Rankine's formula [28-2, page 317].

Spangler classifies bedding conditions *for ditch conduits* as follows [28-2, page 434]:

Impermissible bedding is that method of bedding a ditch conduit in which there is line contact between the pipe and the bottom of the ditch and no care is taken to pack the spaces under the pipe with at least partly compacted granular material (see Fig. 28-17A).

Ordinary bedding is that method of bedding a ditch conduit in which the foundation is shaped with "ordinary care" to fit the bottom of the pipe with reasonable closeness for at least 50 per cent of the width of the pipe and in which the backfill is hand placed and tamped thoroughly to a height of at least 6 in. above the top of the pipe. All spaces under the pipe must be completely filled with granular material thoroughly packed (see Fig. 28-17B).

First-class bedding is that method of bedding a ditch conduit in which the foundation is shaped to fit the bottom of the pipe for at least 60 per cent of the breadth of the latter, in which the pipe is then placed in a layer of fine granular material in the shaped foundation, and in which the pipe is completely surrounded to a height of at least 12 in. above its top by fine granular material that is carefully packed into all spaces under and adjacent to the pipe and is thoroughly tamped in layers not exceeding 6 in. in thickness (see Fig. 28-17C).

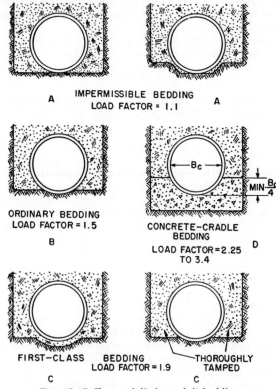

A   IMPERMISSIBLE BEDDING   A
LOAD FACTOR = 1.1

ORDINARY BEDDING
LOAD FACTOR = 1.5
B

CONCRETE-CRADLE
BEDDING
LOAD FACTOR = 2.25
TO 3.4   D

FIRST—CLASS   BEDDING   THOROUGHLY
LOAD FACTOR = 1.9   TAMPED
C   C

FIG. 28-17. Types of ditch-conduit bedding.

Concrete-cradle bedding is that method of bedding a ditch conduit in which the lower part of the pipe is bedded in concrete of adequate thickness under the invert of the pipe and extending upward on each side of the conduit for a greater or less proportion of its height (see Fig. 28-17D).

Spangler recommends the following load factors for these several kinds of bedding [28.2, page 436]:

Considering the usual lack of care in installing house drains and house sewers, it would seem advisable to assume that the impermissible method of bedding is used and to adopt the load factor of 1.1 for house-connection lines when they are installed as ditch conduits. If the pipe is laid under an embankment (or,

Table 28.8   Load Factors for Several Methods
of Bedding Ditch Conduits

Impermissible bedding............ 1.1
Ordinary bedding................ 1.5
First-class bedding.............. 1.9
Concrete-cradle bedding.......... 2.2 to 3.4

presumably, if the trench in which it is laid is considerably wider than the transition width), the load factor may be appreciably greater than the value of 1.1, and the value can be computed by a formula [28.2, page 436; 28-14, page 38] that takes into account the projection ratio, the existence of the active lateral pressure, the internal friction of the backfill, etc.   Spangler gives several tables of calculated values of the load factor, using this formula [28.14, pages 48–50]. For the method of impermissible bedding, these values of the load factor range approximately from 1.5 for very small depths of fill to about 1.3 for fills that are ten times the outside diameter of the pipe in depth.   These values decrease very slightly as the projection ratio decreases.   For the purposes of this book, the load factors *for rigid pipe and for impermissible bedding* will be assumed to range from 1.1 to 1.3.

Fɪɢ. 28-18. Typical form of trench bottom formed by ditching machine.

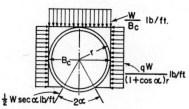

Fɪɢ. 28-19. Load distribution on pipe resting in ditch such as shown in Fig. 28-18.

Another aspect of the problem of the load factor is presented by Schilfgaarde, Frevert, and Schlick [28-15] in a paper in which they investigate the values of the load factor that result from laying the pipe directly on the bottom of a trench cut by a trenching machine.   These machines have been found to leave an irregular bottom, a typical case of which is shown in Fig. 28-18.   The investigators made plaster casts of the shapes of a number of forms of ditch bottoms left by trenching machines and then ran crushing tests on 5- and 10-in. tile when supported on surfaces shaped like these casts.

This form of trench bottom leads to the loading shown in Fig. 28-19.

It is assumed that the backfill load, acting vertically downward on the top of the pipe, is distributed uniformly over the full diameter of the pipe. This load W produces two reactions acting radially at the points of contact of the pipe with the bottom of the trench (see Fig. 28-19). In addition there is the active pressure thrust qW, where q is the ratio of the active thrust to the vertical load, acting horizontally and distributed uniformly over part of the diameter of the pipe, given by the proportion $2/(1 + \cos \alpha)$.

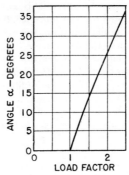

Fig. 28-20. Load factor as a function of α for pipe resting in ditch as shown in Fig. 28-18.

The authors of the paper computed values of the *load factor* for different values of α and for the two selected diameters using the distribution of loading shown in Fig. 28-19, and the relation that they find is shown in Fig. 28-20. When α is zero, the crushing strength under backfill conditions according to Fig. 28-20 is equal to the strength by the three-edge test. As α increases in value, the strength under backfill conditions increases, as would be expected, reaching a value of about 2.25 for α equal to 35°.

Bibliography

General

Published by American Society of Mechanical Engineers,
   29 West 39th St., New York 18, N.Y.:
   Plumbing Code, ASA-440.
American Standards Association, Inc.:
   Air Gaps in Plumbing Systems, A40.4-1942.   25 cents.
   Back-flow Preventers in Plumbing Systems, A40.6-1943.
   Brass Fittings for Flared Copper Tube, A40.2-1936.   45 cents.
   Cast-brass Soldered Joint Fittings, B16-1940.
   Copper Water Tube (K, L, M), H23-1-1949.
   National Plumbing Code, ASA A40.8-1955. $3.50.
   Soldered Joint Fittings for Copper Tube, A40.3-1941.   55 cents.
   Threaded Cast Iron Pipe for Drainage Systems, A40.5-1943.   30 cents.
   Wrought-iron Pipe, B16.2-1939.   60 cents.
Housing and Home Finance Agency:
   Report of the Coordinating Committee for a National Plumbing Code (with the
      U.S. Department of Commerce), 1951.   50 cents.
   Fixture Unit Ratings as Used in Plumbing System Design, H. N. Eaton and
      J. L. French, Housing Research Paper No. 15, 1951.   15 cents.
U.S. Public Health Service:
   Drinking Water Standards, U.S. Public Health Reprint No. 2679.
U.S. Department of Commerce:
   Recommended Minimum Requirements for Plumbing, Report of the Sub-
      committee on Plumbing of the Building Code Committee, U.S. Department
      of Commerce, Bureau of Standards, Elimination of Waste Series, BH13,
      1932 ("Hoover Code"). $1.25.
National Bureau of Standards Building Materials and Structures Series:
   Backflow Prevention in Over-rim Water Supplies, G. E. Golden and Roy B.
      Hunter, BMS28, 1939.   Out of print.
   Strength of Soft-soldered Joints in Copper Tubing, A. R. Maupin and W. H.
      Swanger, BMS58.   15 cents.
   Methods of Estimating Loads in Plumbing Systems, R. B. Hunter, BMS65,
      1940.   Out of print.
   Plumbing Manual, Report of the Subcommittee on Plumbing, Central Housing
      Committee on Research, Design, and Construction, U.S. Department of
      Commerce, National Bureau of Standards, 1940, BMS66.   40 cents.
   Water Distributing Systems for Buildings, R. B. Hunter, BMS79, 1941.   20
      cents.
   Stack Venting of Plumbing Fixtures, J. L. French, BMS118, 1950.   25 cents.
   Wet Venting of Plumbing Fixtures, J. L. French, H. N. Eaton, and R. S. Wyly,
      BMS119, 1950.   25 cents.
   Self-siphonage of Fixture Traps, J. L. French and H. N. Eaton, BMS126, 1951.
      20 cents.
   Capacities of Plumbing Stacks in Buildings, R. S. Wyly and H. N. Eaton,
      BMS132, 1952.   25 cents.
   Frost Closure of Roof Vents in Plumbing Systems, H. N. Eaton and R. S. Wyly,
      BMS142, 1954.   25 cents.
Building Research Institute, National Academy of Sciences:
   Pressure Drainage Systems for Buildings, H. N. Eaton, Technical Reprint
      No. 8, 1956. $1.00.

National Bureau of Standards Commercial Standards Series:
  Bituminized-fibre Drain and Sewer Pipe, CS116-54. 10 cents.
  Calking Lead, CS94.41. 5 cents.
  Earthenware (Vitreous Glazed) Plumbing Fixtures, CS77-48. 10 cents.
  Enameled Cast-iron Plumbing Fixtures, CS77-48. 10 cents.
  Formed Metal Porcelain-enameled Sanitary Ware, CS114-47. 10 cents.
  Lead Pipe, CS95-41. 5 cents.
  Lead Traps and Bends, CS96-41. 5 cents.
  Pipe Nipples: Brass, Copper, Steel and Wrought Iron, CS5-46. 5 cents.
  Porcelain-enameled Tanks for Domestic Use, CS115-44. 5 cents.
  Staple Porcelain (all clay) Plumbing Fixtures," CS4-29. 15 cents.
  Staple Vitreous China Plumbing Fixtures, CS20-47. 10 cents.
  Underground Corrosion, R. H. Logan. C450.
Published by National Association of Plumbing Contractors,
  1016 20th St., NW, Washington 6, D.C.:
  How the Public Protects Itself with Plumbing Codes. Editorial Staff of
    Plumbing and Heating Business magazine.
  Report on Hydraulic and Pneumatics of the Plumbing and Drainage System,
    F. M. Dawson and A. A. Kalinske, Bulletin No. 2. 50 cents.
  Report on Plumbing Cross-connections and Back-siphonage Research, F. M.
    Dawson and A. A. Kalinske, Bulletin No. 1. $1.00.
  Water Supply Piping for the Plumbing System, F. M. Dawson and A. A.
    Kalinske, Bulletin No. 3. $1.00.
  Report on Loop and Circuit Venting Research, F. M. Dawson and D. E. Metzler.
    50 cents.
Published by American Gas Association Laboratories, Cleveland, Ohio:
  A Study and Observation of the Effectiveness of Temperature and Pressure
    Relief Devices and Emergency Gas Shut-offs for Gas Water Heaters.
Published by Copper and Brass Research Association,
  420 Lexington Ave., New York 17, N.Y.:
  Brass Pipe Handbook for Plumbing Installations, 29-B-4.
  Copper Tube; A Handbook on Plumbing and Heating, 29-B-41.
  Pipe and Tube Bending Handbook.

References for Chapter 22

22-1. Dawson, F. M., and A. A. Kalinske: Report on Hydraulics and Pneumatics
      of the Plumbing Drainage System, *Technical Bulletin* 2, National Association of
      Master Plumbers of the United States, Inc., 1939.
22-2. Wyly, Robert S.: Hydraulics and Pneumatics of 2-inch Building Drainage
      Stacks, National Bureau of Standards Report 2521, 1953 (unpublished).
22-3. French, John L., and Herbert N. Eaton: Self-siphonage of Fixture Traps,
      National Bureau of Standards Building Materials and Structures Report
      BMS126, Oct. 15, 1951.
22-4. Hunter, Roy B.: Surging Flow in Sloping Pipes, National Bureau of Standards,
      unpublished manuscript.
22-5. Plumbing Manual, Report of the Subcommittee on Plumbing, Central Housing
      Committee on Research, Design, and Construction, U.S. Department of
      Commerce, National Bureau of Standards Building Materials and Structures
      Report BMS66, 1940.

References for Chapter 23

23-1. Performance of Plumbing Fixtures and Drainage Stacks, Housing and Home
      Finance Agency, Housing Research Paper 31, March, 1954.
23-2. Wyly, Robert S., and Otto Hintz: Report on the Discharge Characteristics of
      Household Plumbing Fixtures, National Bureau of Standards Report 1131
      (unpublished), Aug. 27, 1951.

23-3. Wyly, Robert S., and Otto Hintz: Report on Safe Economic Flushes of Water Closets, National Bureau of Standards Report 1633 (unpublished), May 1, 1952.

23-4. Recommended Minimum Requirements for Plumbing, Report of the Subcommittee on Plumbing of the Building Code Committee, U.S. Department of Commerce, Bureau of Standards BH13, 1932.

23-5. Camp, Thomas R.: Report of Research on the Hydraulics of Water Closet Bowls and Flushing Devices, Massachusetts State Association of Master Plumbers, 1936.

23-6. Wise, A. F. E., and J. Croft: Investigation of Single-stack Drainage for Multistory Flats, reprint of paper for Royal Sanitary Institute, April, 1954.

23-7. Mengeringhausen, Max: Untersuchungen an Klosetteinrichtungen (Investigation of Water Closet Equipment), *Gesundheits-Ingenieur*, vol. 59:44, Nov. 4, 1936, p. 642; also vol. 59:45, Nov. 11, 1936, p. 659.

23-8. Babbitt, Harold E.: "Plumbing," 2d ed., McGraw-Hill Book Company, Inc., New York, 1950.

References for Chapter 24

24-1. Pipe-sizing Data and Tables for Ducts, The Institution of Heating and Ventilating Engineers, 75 Eaton Place, London S.W.1, 1946 edition.

24-2. Dawson, F. M., and J. S. Bowman: Interior Water Supply Piping for Residential Buildings, University of Wisconsin Engineering Experiment Station Series, *Bulletin 77*, 1933.

24-2A. Dawson, F. M., and A. A. Kalinske: Water-supply Piping for the Plumbing System, *Technical Bulletin 3*, National Association of Master Plumbers of the United States, Inc., 1932.

24-3. Kessler, Lewis H.: Hydraulics in Small House Plumbing, Report of Proceedings, American Society of Sanitary Engineering, 1933, 1934, p. 215.

24-4. Kessler, Lewis H.: Residential Water-supply Piping Design, *Materials and Methods*, November, 1946, p. 89.

24-5. Richtlinien für die Berechnung der Kaltwasserleitungen in Hausanlagen (Rules for the Computation of Cold-water Distribution Lines in Buildings), *Gas- und Wasserfach*, vol. 83:29, 1940, p. 345.

24-6. Recommended Minimum Requirements for Plumbing in Dwellings and Similar Buildings, Final Report of the Subcommittee on Plumbing of the Building Code Committee, U.S. Department of Commerce, Bureau of Standards, BH2, 1924 (out of print).

24-7. Recommended Minimum Requirements for Plumbing, Report of the Subcommittee on Plumbing of the Building Code Committee, U.S. Department of Commerce, Bureau of Standards BH13, 1932.

24-8. Hunter, Roy B.: Methods of Estimating Loads in Plumbing Systems, National Bureau of Standards Building Materials and Structures Report BMS65, 1940.

24-9. Eaton, H. N., and J. L. French: Fixture Unit Ratings As Used in Plumbing System Design, Housing and Home Finance Arency Housing Research Paper 15, March, 1951.

24-10. Bolant, R.: Recherche des débits admissibiles dans les canalisations per le calcul des probabilités (Research on the Permissible Fows in Networks of Pipes by the Calculus of Probabilities), *La Houille blanche*, May–June, 1949, p. 315.

24-11. Marchetti, Mario: Impianti interni di distribuzione d'acqua—una applicazione del calcolo della probabilita (Domestic Installations of Water Distribution—An Application of the Calculus of Probabilities), Memorie e Studi, Instituto di Idraulica e Costruzioni Idraulica del Politecnico di Milano, No. 69, 1948.

24-12. Tables of Binomial Probability Distribution, National Bureau of Standards, Applied Mathematics Series 6, 1950.

24-13. Tables of Cumulative Probability, ORDP 20-1, Office of Technical Services, U.S. Department of Commerce.

24-14. Thorndike, Francis: Applications of Poisson's Probability Summation, *Bell System Telephone Journal*, vol. 5, p. 604, 1926.

24-15. Wise, A. F. E., and J. Croft: Investigation of Single-stack Drainage for Multi-storey Flats, The Royal Sanitary Institute, preprint of paper to be represented to the Conference of Engineers and Surveyors, Scarborough Health Congress, Apr. 23, 1954.

24-16. Weibel, S. R., C. P. Straub, and J. R. Thoman: Studies on Household Sewage Disposal Systems, Part I, Federal Security Agency, Public Health Service, Environmental Health Center, Cincinnati, Ohio, 1949.

24-17. Walasyk, Edward: Recording Customer Use of Water—Apartment Building Use, *Journal American Water Works Association*, October, 1950, p. 921.

24-18. American Standard National Plumbing Code, ASA A40.8, 1955, American Standards Association.

24-19. Zinkil, R. H.: Peak Loads on Water-supply Systems of Apartment Houses, *Plumbing and Heating Business*, September, 1950, p. 165.

24-20. French, J. L., H. N. Eaton, and R. S. Wyly: Wet Venting of Plumbing Fixtures, National Bureau of Standards Building Materials and Structures Report BMS119, 1950.

References for Chapter 25

25-1. Recommended Minimum Requirements for Plumbing, Report of the Subcommittee on Plumbing of the Building Code Committee, U.S. Department of Commerce, Bureau of Standards, BH13, 1932.

25-2. Dawson, F. M., and A. A. Kalinske: Report on Hydraulics and Pneumatics of Plumbing Drainage System, State University of Iowa Studies in Engineering, *Bulletin* 10, 1937.

25-3. Wyly, R. S., and H. N. Eaton: Capacities of Plumbing Stacks in Buildings, National Bureau of Standards Building Materials and Structures Report BMS132, 1952.

25-4. American Standard National Plumbing Code, ASA A40.8, 1955, American Standards Association.

25-5. Mayer, Ronald G.: Fifth and Sixth Progress Reports to the McPherson Foundation for Sanitary Research, Sept. 26, 1952, National Bureau of Standards (not available for distribution).

25-6. Plumbing Manual, Report of the Subcommittee on Plumbing, Central Housing Committee on Research, Design, and Construction, U.S. Department of Commerce, National Bureau of Standards Building Materials and Structures Report BMS66, 1940.

25-7. Dawson, F. M., and A. A. Kalinske: Report on Hydraulics and Pneumatics of the Plumbing Drainage System, *Technical Bulletin* 2, National Association of Master Plumbers of the United States, Inc., 1939.

25-8. Report of the Uniform Plumbing Code Committee, issued jointly by the U.S. Department of Commerce and the Housing and Home Finance Agency, July, 1949.

References for Chapter 26

26-1. Plumbing Manual, Report of the Subcommittee on Plumbing, Central Housing Committee on Research, Design, and Construction, U.S. Department of Commerce, National Bureau of Standards Building Materials and Structures Report BMS66, 1940.

26-2. French, John L.: Proposed A.S.A. Plumbing Code, unpublished memorandum, National Bureau of Standards, July 29, 1946.

26-3. American Standard National Plumbing Code, ASA A40.8, 1955, American Standards Association.

26-4. Tholin, A. L.: An Evaluation of Household Food-waste Disposers, American Public Works Association, Public Works Engineers' Special Report 13, May, 1951.

26-5. Cosens, Kenneth W., and Eric J. Hannemann: *American City*, January, 1949.

26-6. Poole, B. A., and G. K. Erganian: Recent Developments in Dual Disposal—A Discussion, *Sewage and Industrial Wastes*, vol. 23:3, March, 1951.

26-7. Burnson, B. I.: Oakland Expects No Trouble, *American City*, vol. 63:8, August, 1948.

26-8. Cosens, Kenneth W.: Household Garbage Grinders—How They Affect Sewers, *American City*, vol. 64:9, September, 1949.

26-9. Rawn, A. M.: Some Effects of Home Garbage Grinding upon Domestic Sewage, *American City*, vol. 66:3, March, 1951.

26-10. Zimmer, E. J.: An Evaluation of Household Food Waste Disposers, American Public Works Association, Public Works Engineers' Special Report 13, May, 1951.

26-11. Cohn, Morris M.: The Combined Collection and Disposal of Sewage and Food Wastes, Report of Proceedings, 1935 Annual Meeting of the American Society of Sanitary Engineering, p. 677.

References for Chapter 27

27-1. Wise, A. F. E.: Design Factors for One-pipe Drainage, *Journal of the Royal Sanitary Institute*, vol. 74-4, April, 1954.

27-2. French, John L., and Herbert N. Eaton: Self-siphonage of Fixture Traps, National Bureau of Standards Building Materials and Structures Report BMS126, 1951.

27-3. Dawson, F. M., and A. A. Kalinske: Report on Hydraulics and Pneumatics of Plumbing Drainage System, *Technical Bulletin* 2, National Association of Master Plumbers of the United States, Inc., 1939.

27-4. Dawson, F. M., and A. A. Kalinske: Report on Hydraulics and Pneumatics of Plumbing Drainage Systems, Part I, University of Iowa Studies in Engineering, *Bulletin* 10, 1937.

27-5. Babbitt, H. E.: Tests on the Hydraulics and Pneumatics of House Plumbing Systems, University of Illinois Engineering Experiment Station, *Bulletin* 143, 1924.

27-6. Babbitt, H. E.: Tests on the Hydraulics and Pneumatics of House Plumbing Systems, University of Illinois Engineering Experiment Station, *Bulletin* 178, 1928.

27-7. Recommended Minimum Requirements for Plumbing, Report of the Subcommittee on Plumbing of the Building Code Committee, U.S. Department of Commerce, Bureau of Standards BH13, 1932.

27-8. Wyly, R. S., and H. N. Eaton: Capacities of Plumbing Stacks in Building, unpublished manuscript of the National Bureau of Standards, 1954.

27-9. Wyly, Robert S.: Hydraulics and Pneumatics of 2-inch Building Drainage Stacks, National Bureau of Standards Report 2521, May 27, 1953 (not available for distribution).

27-10. Performance of Plumbing Fixtures and Drainage Stacks, Housing and Home Finance Agency, Housing Research Paper 31, March, 1954.

27-11. Official Plumbing Code of the City of Detroit, 1954.

27-12. Wise, A. F. E.: Self-siphonage in Plumbing Drainage Systems, Proceedings of the Institution of Civil Engineers, December, 1954.

27-13. Wyly, Robert S.: Special Report on Maximum Permissible Unvented Lengths of Fixture Drains, National Bureau of Standards unpublished report, June 1, 1950.

27-14. Wise, A. F. E., and J. Croft: Investigation of Single-stack Drainage for Multi-storey Flats, Royal Sanitary Institute, preprint of paper presented to Conference 2—Engineers and Surveyors, Scarborough Health Congress, Apr. 29, 1954.

27-15. Cook, F. C.: *The Plumber*, vol. 75, p. 889, 1953.

27-16. Walsh, F. W.: Some Experiences on the Use of the Simplified One-pipe System, *Bulletin of the Sanitary Inspectors Association*, London, April, 1953.

27-17. Wise, A. F. E.: One-pipe Plumbing—Some Recent Experimental Hydraulics at the Building Research Station, *Journal of the Institute of Sanitary Engineers*, vol. 51, parts 1 and 2, pp. 20–50, and 113–132, 1952.

27-18. One-pipe (Single-stack) Plumbing for Housing, Building Research Station Digests 48 and 49, 1952 (London).

27-19. French, John L.: Stack Venting of Plumbing Fixtures, National Bureau of Standards Building Materials and Structures Report BMS118, 1950.

27-20. Plumbing Manual, Report of the Subcommittee on Plumbing of the Central Housing Committee on Research, Design, and Construction, U.S. Department of Commerce, National Bureau of Standards Building Materials and Structures Report BMS66, 1940.

27-21. French, John L., Herbert N. Eaton, and Robert S. Wyly: Wet Venting of Plumbing Fixtures, National Bureau of Standards Building Materials and Structures Report BMS119, 1950.

27-22. Eaton, Herbert N., and Robert S. Wyly: Frost Closure of Roof Vents in Plumbing Systems, National Bureau of Standards Building Materials and Structures Report BMS142, 1954.

References for Chapter 28

28-1. Marston, A., and A. O. Anderson: The Theory of Loads on Pipes in Ditches and Tests of Cement and Clay Drain Tile and Sewer Pipe, Iowa State College Engineering Experiment Station, *Bulletin* 31, 1913.

28-2. Spangler, M. G.: "Soil Engineering," International Textbook Company, Scranton, Pa., 1951.

28-3. Schlick, W. J.: Loads on Pipe in Wide Ditches, Iowa State College Engineering Experiment Station, *Bulletin* 108, 1926.

28-4. Marston, A.: The Theory of External Loads on Closed Conduits in the Light of the Latest Experiments, Iowa State College Engineering Experiment Station, *Bulletin* 96, 1930.

28-5. Revised Report of the Subcommittee on Soils, U.S. Bureau of Standards, Proceedings of the American Society of Civil Engineers, Appendix A, vol. 46, No. 6, August, 1920, pp. 916–941; also May, 1933, pp. 798–808.

28-6. Boussinesq, J.: "Application des potentials," pp. 65, 66, Paris, 1885.

28-7. Spangler, M. G.: Underground Conduits—An Appraisal of Modern Research, American Society of Civil Engineers, Papers and Discussions, vol. 73, p. 855, 1947.

28-8. Spangler, M. G., Robley Winfrey, and Clyde Mason: Experimental Determination of Static and Impact Loads Transmitted to Culverts, Iowa State College Engineering Experiment Station, *Bulletin* 76, 1926.

28-9. Newmark, Nathan M., Simplified Computations of Vertical Pressures in Elastic Foundations, University of Illinois Engineering Experiment Station, *Circular* 24, vol. 33, No. 4, 1935.

28-10. Talbot, Arthur N.: Tests of Cast-iron and Reinforced-concrete Culvert Pipe, University of Illinois Engineering Experiment Station, *Bulletin* 22, 1908.

28-11. Keulegan, Garbis H.: unpublished manuscript, National Bureau of Standards, 1954.

28-12. Everhart, J. O.: Behavior of Fired-clay Ring Sections under Load, *Journal of the Ceramic Society*, vol. 32:2, 1949, p. 53.

28-13. Wyly, Robert S., and Herbert N. Eaton: Final Report of Performance Requirements for Domestic House Sewer Connections and Septic-tank-to-field Connections, National Bureau of Standards Report 1434, 1952 (not available for distribution).

28-14. Spangler, M. G.: The Supporting Strength of Rigid Pipe Culverts, Iowa State College Engineering Experiment Station, *Bulletin* 112, 1933.

28-15. Schilfgaarde, Jan van, R. K. Frevert, and W. J. Schlick: Effect of Present Installation Practices on Drain Tile Loading, *Agricultural Engineering*, vol. 37-7, July, 1951, pp. 371–374, 378.